ab   JANE KIRK.   12   EK.

Dawn Kyzial 12

alleana Sayler.   12   98/99.

K Yaremchuk   12   99/00

Jolene Kitt   12   2000/2001

Conrad Semenitlt   12   2001/2002

Jennifer Metronec   12   02/03

E Krywiak

Amanda Roach 12 05/06

STORY AND STRUCTURE

LAURENCE PERRINE

Southern Methodist University

Story and Structure

CANADIAN EDITION

Theresa M. Ford, Editorial Consultant, Canadian Edition
Supervisor of Secondary Language Arts
Edmonton Catholic School System

HARCOURT
BRACE
CANADA

Harcourt Brace & Company, Canada
Toronto • Orlando • San Diego • London • Sydney

Material from earlier editions: copyright © 1959, 1966, by Harcourt Brace & World, Inc.

Printed and bound in Canada
ISBN 0-7747-1195-7

14 15 16   96 95 94

Canadian Cataloguing in Publication Data
Perrine, Laurence.
   Story and structure

ISBN 0-7747-1195-7

1. Short stories. 2. Short story. I. Ford,
Theresa M. II. Title.

PN6014.P47 1981   808.83'1   C81-094560-6

   Every effort has been made to obtain permission for copyright material used in this book, and to acknowledge all such indebtedness accurately. All errors and omissions called to our attention will be corrected in future printings. In particular, we would be grateful for any information regarding the following:
   "The First Born Son" by Ernest Buckler; and "E Equals MC Squared" by Hugh Garner.

CONTENTS

Preface

Story and Structure is written for the student who is beginning a serious study of fiction. Its initial assumption is that some stories repay more richly than others the time and effort of reading them, and its objective is to help the reader identify, understand, enjoy, and prefer such stories. To this end it examines the major elements of fiction and suggests some criteria for critical judgment.

A short story is "a short fiction." Attempts to define it more narrowly prove unsuccessful, for exceptions always exist which escape the definer's net. No such attempt is made here. Our interest is in the art of fiction, in understanding and enjoying it and making judgments about it. Though short stories are used for illustration, the elements discussed are elements in all fiction.

The second edition differs from the first in three ways: twenty-five of the forty stories are new, the chapters have been reordered so that point of view is presented earlier, and illustrative examples discussed in the text are changed to fit the new selection and ordering of stories.

For help with the original edition I wish to thank Professor Maynard Mack, Yale University; Professor Mark Schorer, the University of California; Margaret Morton Blum and Marshall Terry, Southern Methodist University; and all those who by their writings have labored to make the art of fiction more clear. For help with the second edition, I am grateful to those users of the first edition who have favored me with suggestions and criticisms.

L.P.

Southern Methodist University
Dallas, Texas

December, 1965

A NOTE ON THE CANADIAN EDITION

In this edition, sixteen of the forty-one stories are new, twelve of which are by Canadian writers. As with the second edition, illustrative examples discussed in the text reflect, in part, the new selections. The bold face number in parentheses after each title in Part Two of the Table of Contents indicates the unit in Part One with which the story in question can best be taught.

Part One

THE ELEMENTS OF THE SHORT STORY

1

Escape and Interpretation

The first question to ask about fiction is: Why bother to read it? With life as short as it is, with so many pressing demands on our time, with books of information, instruction, and discussion waiting to be read, why should we spend precious time on works of imagination? The eternal answers to this question are two: enjoyment and understanding.

Since the invention of language, people have taken pleasure in following and participating in the imaginary adventures and imaginary experiences of imaginary people. Whatever—without causing harm—serves to make life less tedious, to make the hours pass more quickly and pleasurably, surely needs nothing else to recommend it. Enjoyment—and ever more enjoyment—is the first aim and justification of reading fiction.

But unless fiction gives something more than pleasure, it hardly justifies itself as a subject of study. Unless it expands or refines our minds or quickens our sense of life, its value is not appreciably greater than that of miniature golf, bridge, or ping-pong. To have a compelling claim on our attention, it must yield not only enjoyment, but understanding.

The experience of people through the ages is that literature may furnish such understanding, and do so effectively—that the depiction of imagined experiences can provide authentic insights. "The truest history," said Diderot of the novels of Samuel Richardson, "is full of falsehoods, and your romance is full of truths." But the bulk of fiction does not present such insights. Only some does. Initially, therefore, fiction may be classified into two broad categories: literature of escape and literature of interpretation.

ESCAPE LITERATURE is that written purely for entertainment—to help us pass the time agreeably. INTERPRETIVE LITERATURE is written to broaden and deepen and sharpen our awareness of life. Escape literature takes us *away* from the real world: it enables us temporarily to forget our troubles. Interpretive literature takes us, through the imagination, deeper *into* the real world: it enables us to understand our troubles. Escape literature has as its only object pleasure. Interpretive literature has as its object pleasure *plus* understanding.

Having established a distinction, however, we must not exaggerate or oversimplify it. Escape and interpretation are not two great bins, into one or the other of which we can toss any given story. Rather, they are opposite ends of a scale, the two poles between which the world of fiction spins. The difference between them does not lie in the absence or presence of a "moral." The story which in all of its incidents and characters is shallow may have an unimpeachable moral, while the interpretive story may have no moral at all in any conventional sense. The difference does not lie in the absence or presence of "facts." The historical romance may be full of historical information and yet be pure escape in its depiction of human behavior. The difference does not lie in the presence or absence of an element of fantasy. The escape story may have a surface appearance of everyday reality, while the tale of seeming wildest fancy may press home on us some sudden truth. The difference between the two kinds of literature is deeper and more subtle than any of these distinctions. A story becomes interpretive as it illuminates some aspect of human life or behavior. An interpretive story presents us with an insight—large or small—into the nature and conditions of our existence. It gives us a keener awareness of what it is to be a human being in a universe sometimes friendly, sometimes hostile. It helps us to understand our neighbors and ourselves.

Perhaps we can clarify the difference by suggestion. The escape writer is like an inventor who devises a contrivance for our diversion. When we push the button, lights flash, bells ring, and cardboard figures move jerkily across a painted horizon. The interpretive writer is a discoverer: he takes us out into the midst of life and says, "Look, here is the world!" The escape writer is full of tricks and surprises: he pulls rabbits out of hats, saws a beautiful woman in two, and snatches brightly colored balls out of the air. The interpretive writer takes us behind the scenes, where he shows us the props and mirrors and seeks to make clear the illusions. This is not to say that the interpretive writer is merely a reporter. More surely than the escape writer he shapes and gives form to his materials. But he shapes and forms them always with the intent that we may see and feel and understand them better, not for the primary purpose of furnishing entertainment.

Now just as there are two kinds of fiction, there are also two kinds of reader. The immature or inexperienced reader seeks only escape. Even when he thinks he is reading for interpretation or some useful moral, he insists that what he reads return him always some pleasant or exciting image of the world or some flattering image of himself. We all begin with fairy tales. Our early reading experiences are likely to be with stories such as that of Cinderella, whose fairy godmother transforms a pumpkin and mice into a coach-and-four, whose slim foot is the only one that fits the crystal slipper, who rises superior to her cruel stepmother and taunting sisters to marry and "live happily ever after" with the charming prince, and who, never for a moment anything but sweet and virtuous, forgives her former tormentors who tried to keep her a cinder girl.

Though most people move on from fairy tales into a seemingly more adult kind of reading, they may well be mistaken in thinking that they have progressed. The element of unreality does not lie primarily in magic wands and fairy godmothers but in a superficial treatment of life. The story of a shopgirl who is lifted from the painful conditions of her work and home life by a handsome young suitor from the upper classes may be as truly a Cinderella story as the one we read in childhood, though its setting is Mississauga rather than a kingdom by the sea. Unfortunately many readers—indeed most—never grow beyond the fairy tale except in the most elementary of senses. In some ways, perhaps, their movement is backward, for it involves a loss of that sense of wonder which marks the child's vision.

There are many signs of the inexperienced reader. He makes fixed demands of every story he reads, and he feels frustrated and disappointed unless these demands are satisfied. Often he sticks to one type of subject matter. Instead of being receptive to any story which puts human beings in human situations, he reads only sports stories, Western stories, love stories, or crime stories. If he is willing to accept a wider range of experience, he still wishes every story to conform at bottom to several strict though perhaps unconsciously formulated expectations. Among the most common of these expectations are: (1) a sympathetic hero (or heroine)—one with whom the reader can in imagination identify himself as he reads and whose adventures and triumphs he can share; (2) a plot in which something exciting is always happening, and in which there is a strong element of suspense; (3) a happy outcome, which sends the reader away undisturbed and optimistic about the world in which he lives; (4) a theme—if the story has a theme—which confirms his already-held opinions of the world.

There is nothing wrong with any of these characteristics as story elements. Significant fiction has been written with them all. The error lies in elevating these characteristics into a set of rigid requirements which a story must meet to be enjoyed. Such limitations restrict drastically one's opportunity for expanding his experience or broadening his insights. They reduce one's demands on literature to a formula.[1]

The inexperienced reader wants the essentially familiar combined with superficial novelty. Each story must have a slightly new setting or twist or "gimmick," though the fundamental features of the characters and situations remain the same. He evaluates a story not by its truth but by its twists and turns and surprises, by its suspense or its love interest. He wants his stories to be mainly pleasant. Evil, danger, and misery may appear in them, but not in such a way that they need be taken really seriously—are felt to be oppressive or permanent. He wants reading which slips easily and smoothly through the mind, requiring

[1]The magazines which appear on our newsracks may be roughly divided into three classes: pulp, slick, and quality. The PULP magazines are so called because they are printed on cheap pulp paper for low cost and quick turnover. They generally specialize in one sort of fiction: crime stories, adventure stories, sports stories, Western stories, supernatural stories, or science fiction. These stories are basically escape fiction and usually conform to formula. They are generally characterized by a good deal of physical conflict and by crude contrasts between good and evil. The SLICK magazines are printed on a more expensive, glazed paper, and they have large circulations. They print nonfiction as well as fiction, and the fiction is not confined to one subject matter. The stories, however, still comply mostly with certain basic formulas and conventions and are essentially escape fiction, though of a more sophisticated kind, having less obvious contrasts between good and evil and putting less emphasis on physical conflict. The most general formula is: A sympathetic hero is faced with obstacles which he finally overcomes to achieve his goal. The most frequent goal of the hero is to win the hand of the heroine; therefore the commonest sub-type of the formula is: boy-meets-girl, boy-loses-girl, boy-wins-girl. Needless to say, the hero is usually handsome and the heroine beautiful. Even when the hero's primary object is something else, a beautiful girl is usually tossed in to supply "love interest." Possibly three-quarters of all fiction published uses this "young-love" type of plot. Slick fiction is also often concerned with marital problems which find a happy solution, and with sentimental treatments of children or old people in which the "innocent wisdom" of childhood or the "mellow wisdom" of old age is shown to be greater than the practical wisdom of the years between. The QUALITY magazines are often printed, like the pulps, on unglazed paper; they are more expensive, however, than the pulps and slicks and have lower circulations. Like the slicks they publish both fiction and nonfiction, but their fiction does not rely upon tested formulas. It is more original, sometimes experimental, and seeks to be interpretive.

The quality magazines appeal to a more highly educated audience than the slicks, and the slicks to a more educated audience than the pulps. Fiction written for popular consumption, whether for the pulps or the slicks, is known as COMMERCIAL fiction. Fiction written with a more serious artistic intention is known as QUALITY fiction. It is published in the quality magazines, occasionally in the slicks, and sometimes for the first time in book form. Over nine-tenths of published fiction is commercial fiction. The above classifications are meant to be broadly suggestive rather than rigid. We cannot, of course, judge any work of fiction by the kind of paper it is printed on or the magazine it is published in, nor can we make hard-and-fast distinctions between commercial and quality fiction, escape and interpretation, or inexperienced and experienced readers.

little mental effort. Most of all he wants something which helps sustain his fantasy life, providing ready-made daydreams in which he overcomes his limitations, thwarts his enemies, and wins success or fame or the girl.

The discriminating reader, in contrast, takes deeper pleasure in fiction that deals with life significantly than in fiction based on the formulations of escape. He does not reject escape literature, for escape literature need not be cheap or trite. It may be original, witty, absorbing, beautifully written, and artistically constructed. Some of literature's most enduring masterpieces are essentially escape—Barrie's *Peter Pan* and Stevenson's *Treasure Island*, for instance. Such reading may be a refreshment for the mind and spirit. For a steady diet, however, he prefers interpretive literature. He knows, moreover, that an exclusive diet of escape, especially of the cruder sorts, has two dangers: (1) it may leave us with merely superficial attitudes toward life; (2) it may actually distort our view of reality and give us false concepts and false expectations.

Fiction, like food, is of different nutritive values. Some is rich in protein and vitamins; it builds bone and sinew. Some is highly agreeable to the taste but not permanently sustaining. Some may be adulterated and actually harmful to our health. Escape fiction is of the latter two sorts. The harmless kind bears frankly on the face of it what it is. It pretends to be nothing else than pleasant diversion and never asks to be taken seriously. The second kind masquerades under the appearance of interpretation. It pretends to give a faithful treatment of life as it is, perhaps even thinks that it does so, but through its shallowness it subtly falsifies life in every line. Such fiction, taken seriously and without corrective, may give us false notions of reality and lead us to expect from experience what experience does not provide.

It is important to realize as well that literary analysis and interpretation are accompanied by, and often dependent upon, personal response. The individual reader's preferences and emotions exert a powerful influence on how he reads and what he reads. Personal response often precedes thoughtful analysis, sometimes accompanies it and, on occasion, supplants it. One reader may be amused while another is annoyed, even angered, by a writer's tone. A perceptive reader should be able to discuss a story's strengths as well as, even in spite of, his personal reactions to it. Previous experience, both direct and vicarious, is important to an individual's response in addition to his ability to grasp the author's meaning. The depth of the reader's literary experience also affects his response to allusions, structure, form, technique, and style. Maturity of response includes awareness and examination of any personal response to what is read. Readers should be able to recognize the effectiveness and literary worth of a work they do not like.

When we enter a library and glance at the books on the shelves, we are at first likely to be bewildered by their variety and profusion. Thousands of books sit there, each making its claim on our attention, each seeming to cry out "Read me! Read me! Read me!" or "No, read *me!*" We have time to read only a fraction of them. If we are wise, we shall read as many as we can without neglecting the other claims of life. Our problem is how to get the most out of what time we have. To make the richest use of our portion, we need to know two things: (1) how to get the most out of any book we read; (2) how to choose the books that will best repay the time and attention we devote to them. The assumption of *Story and Structure* is that a proper selection will include both fiction and nonfiction—nonfiction as an indispensable fund of information and idea, of one kind of knowledge of the world; fiction as an equally indispensable source of a different kind of knowledge—a knowledge of experience, felt in the emotions as well as apprehended by the mind. The aim of *Story and Structure* is to aid in the growth of understanding and of judgment.

Margaret Laurence

HORSES OF THE NIGHT

I never knew I had distant cousins who lived up north, until Chris came down to Manawaka to go to high school. My mother said he belonged to a large family, relatives of ours, who lived at Shallow Creek, up north. I was six, and Shallow Creek seemed immeasurably far, part of a legendary winter country where no leaves grew and where the breath of seals and polar bears snuffled out steamily and turned to ice.

"Could plain people live there?" I asked my mother, meaning people who were not Eskimos. "Could there be a farm?"

"How do you mean?" she said, puzzled. "I told you. That's where they live: On the farm. Uncle Wilf—that was Chris's father, who died a few years back—he got the place as a homestead, donkey's years ago."

"But how could they grow anything? I thought you said it was up north."

"Mercy," my mother said, laughing, "it's not *that* far north, Vanessa."

HORSES OF THE NIGHT From *A Bird in the House* by Margaret Laurence reprinted by permission of The Canadian Publishers, McClelland and Stewart Limited, Toronto.

It's about a hundred miles beyond Galloping Mountain. You be nice to Chris, now, won't you? And don't go asking him a whole lot of questions the minute he steps inside the door."

How little my mother knew of me, I thought. Chris had been fifteen. He could be expected to feel only scorn towards me. I detested the fact that I was so young. I did not think I would be able to say anything at all to him.

"What if I don't like him?"

"What if you don't?" my mother responded sharply. "You're to watch your manners, and no acting up, understand? It's going to be quite difficult enough without that."

"Why does he have to come here, anyway?" I demanded crossly. "Why can't he go to school where he lives?"

"Because there isn't any high school up there," my mother said. "I hope he gets on well here, and isn't too homesick. Three years is a long time. It's very good of your grandfather to let him stay at the Brick House."

She said this last accusingly, as though she suspected I might be thinking differently. But I had not thought of it one way or another. We were all having dinner at the Brick House because of Chris's arrival. It was the end of August, and sweltering. My grandfather's house looked huge and cool from the outside, the high low-sweeping spruce trees shutting out the sun with their dusky out-fanned branches. But inside it wasn't cool at all. The woodstove in the kitchen was going full blast, and the whole place smelled of roasting meat.

Grandmother Connor was wearing a large mauve apron. I thought it was a nicer colour than the dark bottle-green of her dress, but she believed in wearing sombre shades lest the spirit give way to vanity, which in her case was certainly not much of a risk. The apron came up over her shapeless bosom and obscured part of her cameo brooch, the only jewellery she ever wore, with its portrait of a fiercely bearded man whom I imagined to be either Moses or God.

"Isn't it nearly time for them to be getting here, Beth?" Grandmother Connor asked.

"Train's not due until six," my mother said. "It's barely five-thirty, now. Has Father gone to the station already?"

"He went an hour ago," my grandmother said.

"He would," my mother commented.

"Now, now, Beth," my grandmother cautioned and soothed.

At last the front screen door was hurled open and Grandfather Connor strode into the house, followed by a tall lanky boy. Chris was wearing a white shirt, a tie, grey trousers. I thought, unwillingly, that he looked handsome. His face was angular, the bones showing through the brown skin. His grey eyes were slightly slanted, and his hair was the colour of couchgrass at the end of summer when it has been bleached to a light yellow by the sun. I had not planned to like him, not even a little, but somehow I wanted to defend him when I heard what my mother whispered to my grandmother before they went into the front hall.

"Heavens, look at the shirt and trousers—must've been his father's, the poor kid."

I shot out into the hall ahead of my mother, and then stopped and stood there.

"Hi, Vanessa," Chris said.

"How come you knew who I was?" I asked.

"Well. I knew your mother and dad only had one of a family, so I figured you must be her," he replied grinning.

The way he spoke did not make me feel I had blundered. My mother greeted him warmly but shyly. Not knowing if she were expected to kiss him or to shake hands, she finally did neither. Grandmother Connor, however, had no doubts. She kissed him on both cheeks and then held him at arm's length to have a proper look at him.

"Bless the child," she said.

Coming from anyone else, this remark would have sounded ridiculous, especially as Chris was at least a head taller. My grandmother was the only person I have ever known who could say such things without appearing false.

"I'll show you your room, Chris," my mother offered.

Grandfather Connor, who had been standing in the living room doorway in absolute silence, looking as granite as a statue in the cemetery, now followed Grandmother out to the kitchen.

"Train was forty minutes late," he said weightily.

"What a shame," my grandmother said. "But I thought it wasn't due until six, Timothy."

"Six!" my grandfather cried. "That's the mainline train. The local's due at five-twenty."

This was not correct, as both my grandmother and I knew. But neither of us contradicted him.

"What on earth are you cooking a roast for, on a night like this?" my grandfather went on. "A person could fry an egg on the sidewalk, it's that hot. Potato salad would've gone down well."

Privately I agreed with this opinion, but I could never permit myself to acknowledge agreement with him on anything. I automatically and emotionally sided with Grandmother in all issues, not because she was inevitably right but because I loved her.

"It's not a roast," my grandmother said mildly. "It's mock-duck. The stove's only been going for an hour. I thought the boy would be hungry after the trip."

My mother and Chris had come downstairs and were now in the living room. I could hear them there, talking awkwardly, with pauses.

"Potato salad," my grandfather declaimed, "would've been plenty good enough. He'd have been lucky to get it, if you ask me anything. Wilf's family hasn't got two cents to rub together. It's me that's paying for the boy's keep."

The thought of Chris in the living room, and my mother unable to explain, was too much for me. I sidled over to the kitchen door, intending to close it. But my grandmother stopped me.

"No," she said, with unexpected firmness. "Leave it open, Vanessa."

I could hardly believe it. Surely she couldn't want Chris to hear? She herself was always able to move with equanimity through a hurricane because she believed that a mighty fortress was her God. But the rest of us were not like that, and usually she did her best to protect us. At the time I felt only bewilderment. I think now that she must have realised Chris would have to learn the Brick House sooner or later, and he might as well start right away.

I had to go into the living room. I had to know how Chris would take my grandfather. Would he, as I hoped, be angry and perhaps even speak out? Or would he, meekly, only be embarrassed?

"Wilf wasn't much good, even as a young man," Grandfather Connor was trumpeting. "Nobody but a simpleton would've taken up a homestead in a place like that. Anybody could've told him that land's no use for a thing except hay."

Was he going to remind us again how well he had done in the hardware business? Nobody had ever given him a hand, he used to tell me. I am sure he believed that this was true. Perhaps it even was true.

"If the boy takes after his father, it's a poor lookout for him," my grandfather continued.

I felt the old rage of helplessness. But as for Chris—he gave no sign of feeling anything. He was sitting on the big wing-backed sofa that curled into the bay window like a black and giant seashell. He began to talk to me, quite easily, just as though he had not heard a word my grandfather was saying.

This method proved to be the one Chris always used in any dealings with my grandfather. When the bludgeoning words came, which was often, Chris never seemed, like myself, to be holding back with a terrible strained force for fear of letting go and speaking out and having the known world unimaginably fall to pieces. He would not argue or defend himself, but he did not apologise, either. He simply appeared to be absent, elsewhere. Fortunately there was very little need for response, for when Grandfather Connor pointed out your shortcomings, you were not expected to reply.

But this aspect of Chris was one which I noticed only vaguely at the time. What won me was that he would talk to me and wisecrack as though I were his same age. He was—although I didn't know the phrase then—a respecter of persons.

On the rare evenings when my parents went out, Chris would come over to mind me. These were the best times, for often when he was supposed to be doing his homework, he would make fantastic objects for my amusement, or his own—pipecleaners twisted into the shape of wildly prancing midget men, or an old set of Christmas-tree lights fixed onto a puppet theatre with a red velvet curtain that really pulled. He had skill in making miniature things of all kinds. Once for my birthday he gave me a leather saddle no bigger than a matchbox, which he had sewn himself, complete in every detail, stirrups and horn, with the criss-cross lines that were the brand name of his ranch, he said, explaining it was a reference to his own name.

"Can I go to Shallow Creek sometime?" I asked one evening.

"Sure. Some summer holidays, maybe. I've got a sister about your age. The others are all grownup."

I did not want to hear. His sisters—for Chris was the only boy—did not exist for me, not even as photographs, because I did not want them to exist. I wanted him to belong only here. Shallow Creek existed, though, no longer filled with ice mountains in my mind but as some beckoning country beyond all ordinary considerations.

"Tell me what it's like there, Chris."

"My gosh, Vanessa, I've told you before, about a thousand times."

"You never told me what your house is like."

"Didn't I? Oh well—it's made out of trees grown right there beside the lake."

"Made out of trees? Gee. Really?"

I could see it. The trees were still growing, and the leaves were firmly and greenly on them. The branches had been coaxed into formations of towers and high-up nests where you could look out and see for a hundred miles or more.

"That lake, you know," Chris said. "It's more like an inland sea. It goes on for ever and ever amen, that's how it looks. And you know what? Millions of years ago, before there were any human beings at all, that lake was full of water monsters. All different kinds of dinosaurs. Then they all died off. Nobody knows for sure why. Imagine them—all those huge creatures, with necks like snakes and some of them had hackles on their heads, like a rooster's comb only very tough, like hard leather. Some guys from Winnipeg came up a few years back, there, and dug up dinosaur bones, and they found footprints in the rocks."

"Footprints in the *rocks?*"

"The rocks were mud, see, when the dinosaurs went trampling

through, but after trillions of years the mud turned into stone and there were these mighty footprints with the claws still showing. Amazing, eh?"

I could only nod, fascinated and horrified. Imagine going swimming in those waters. What if one of the creatures had lived on?

"Tell me about the horses," I said.

"Oh, them. Well, we've got these two riding horses. Duchess and Firefly. I raised them, and you should see them. Really sleek, know what I mean? I bet I could make racers out of them."

He missed the horses, I thought with selfish satisfaction, more than he missed his family. I could visualise the pair, one sorrel and one black, swifting through all the meadows of summer.

"When can I go, Chris?"

"Well, we'll have to see. After I get through high school, I won't be at Shallow Creek much."

"Why not?"

"Because," Chris said, "what I am going to be is an engineer, civil engineer. You ever seen a really big bridge, Vanessa? Well, I haven't either, but I've seen pictures. You take the Golden Gate Bridge in San Francisco, now. Terrifically high—all those thin ribs of steel, joined together to go across this very wide stretch of water. It doesn't seem possible, but it's there. That's what engineers do. Imagine doing something like that, eh?"

I could not imagine it. It was beyond me.

"Where will you go?" I asked. I did not want to think of his going anywhere.

"Winnipeg, to college," he said with assurance.

The Depression did not get better, as everyone had been saying it would. It got worse, and so did the drought. That part of the prairies where we lived was never dustbowl country. The farms around Manawaka never had a total crop failure, and afterwards, when the drought was over, people used to remark on this fact proudly, as though it had been due to some virtue or special status, like the Children of Israel being afflicted by Jehovah but never in real danger of annihilation. But although Manawaka never knew the worst, what it knew was bad enough. Or so I learned later. At the time I saw none of it. For me, the Depression and drought were external and abstract, malevolent gods whose names I secretly learned although they were concealed from me, and whose evil I sensed only superstitiously, knowing they threatened us but not how or why. What I really saw was only what went on in our family.

"He's done quite well all through, despite everything," my mother said. She sighed, and I knew she was talking about Chris.

"I know," my father said. "We've been over all this before, Beth. But quite good just isn't good enough. Even supposing he managed to get a scholarship, which isn't likely, it's only tuition and books. What about room and board? Who's going to pay for that? Your father?"

"I see I shouldn't have brought up the subject at all," my mother said in an aloof voice.

"I'm sorry," my father said impatiently. "But you know, yourself, he's the only one who might possibly—"

"I can't bring myself to ask Father about it, Ewen. I simply cannot do it."

"There wouldn't be much point in asking," my father said, "when the answer is a foregone conclusion. He feels he's done his share, and actually, you know, Beth, he has, too. Three years, after all. He may not have done it gracefully, but he's done it."

We were sitting in the living room, and it was evening. My father was slouched in the grey armchair that was always his. My mother was slenderly straight-backed in the blue chair in which nobody else ever sat. I was sitting on the footstool, beige needlepoint with mathematical roses, to which I had staked my own claim. This seating arrangement was obscurely satisfactory to me, perhaps because predictable, like the three bears. I was pretending to be colouring into a scribbler on my knee, and from time to time my lethargic purple crayon added a feather to an outlandish swan. To speak would be to invite dismissal. But their words forced questions in my head.

"Chris isn't going away, is he?"

My mother swooped, shocked at her own neglect.

"My heavens—are you still up, Vanessa? What am I thinking of?"

"Where is Chris going?"

"We're not sure yet," my mother evaded, chivvying me up the stairs. "We'll see."

He would not go, I thought. Something would happen, miraculously, to prevent him. He would remain, with his long loping walk and his half-slanted grey eyes and his talk that never excluded me. He would stay right here. And soon, because I desperately wanted to, and because every day mercifully made me older, quite soon I would be able to reply with such a lightning burst of knowingness that it would astound him, when he spoke of the space or was it some black sky that never ended anywhere beyond this earth. Then I would not be innerly belittled for being unable to figure out what he would best like to hear. At that good and imagined time, I would not any longer be limited. I would not any longer be young.

I was nine when Chris left Manawaka. The day before he was due to go, I knocked on the door of his room in the Brick House.

"Come in," Chris said. "I'm packing. Do you know how to fold socks, Vanessa?"

"Sure. Of course."

"Well, get folding on that bunch there, then."

I had come to say goodbye, but I did not want to say it yet. I got to work on the socks. I did not intend to speak about the matter of college, but the knowledge that I must not speak about it made me uneasy. I was afraid I would blurt out a reference to it in my anxiety not to. My mother had said, "He's taken it amazingly well—he doesn't even mention it, so we mustn't either."

"Tomorrow night you'll be in Shallow Creek," I ventured.

"Yeh." He did not look up. He went on stuffing clothes and books into his suitcase.

"I bet you'll be glad to see the horses, eh?" I wanted him to say he didn't care about the horses any more and that he would rather stay here.

"It'll be good to see them again," Chris said. "Mind handing over those socks now, Vanessa? I think I can just squash them in at the side here. Thanks. Hey, look at that, will you? Everything's in. Am I an expert packer or am I an expert packer?"

I sat on his suitcase for him so it would close, and then he tied a piece of rope around it because the lock wouldn't lock.

"Ever thought what it would be like to be a traveller, Vanessa?" he asked.

I thought of Richard Halliburton, taking an elephant over the Alps and swimming illicitly in the Taj Mahal lily pool by moonlight.

"It would be keen," I said, because this was the word Chris used to describe the best possible. "That's what I'm going to do someday."

He did not say, as for a moment I feared he might, that girls could not be travellers.

"Why not?" he said. "Sure you will, if you really want to. I got this theory, see, that anybody can do anything at all, anything, if they really set their minds to it. But you have to have this total concentration. You have to focus on it with your whole mental powers, and not let it slip away by forgetting to hold it in your mind. If you hold it in your mind, like, then it's real, see? You take most people, now. They can't concentrate worth a darn."

"Do you think I can?" I enquired eagerly, believing that this was what he was talking about.

"What?" he said. "Oh—sure. Sure I think you can. Naturally."

Chris did not write after he left Manawaka. About a month later we had a letter from his mother. He was not at Shallow Creek. He had not gone back. He had got off the northbound train at the first stop after

Manawaka, cashed in his ticket, and thumbed a lift with a truck to Winnipeg. He had written to his mother from there, but had given no address. She had not heard from him since. My mother read Aunt Tess's letter aloud to my father. She was too upset to care whether I was listening or not.

"I can't think what possessed him, Ewen. He never seemed irresponsible. What if something should happen to him? What if he's broke? What do you think we should do?"

"What can we do? He's nearly eighteen. What he does is his business. Simmer down, Beth, and let's decide what we're going to tell your father."

"Oh Lord," my mother said. "There's that to consider, of course."

I went out without either of them noticing. I walked to the hill at the edge of the town, and down into the valley where the scrub oak and poplar grew almost to the banks of the Wachakwa River. I found the oak where we had gone last autumn, in a gang, to smoke cigarettes made of dried leaves and pieces of newspaper. I climbed to the lowest branch and stayed there for a while.

I was not consciously thinking about Chris. I was not thinking of anything. But when at last I cried, I felt relieved afterwards and could go home again.

Chris departed from my mind, after that, with a quickness that was due to the other things that happened. My Aunt Edna, who was a secretary in Winnipeg, returned to Manawaka to live because the insurance company cut down on staff and she could not find another job. I was intensely excited and jubilant about her return, and could not see why my mother seemed the opposite, even though she was as fond of Aunt Edna as I was. Then my brother Roderick was born, and that same year Grandmother Connor died. The strangeness, the unbelievability, of both these events took up all of me.

When I was eleven, almost two years after Chris had left, he came back without warning. I came home from school and found him sitting in our living room. I could not accept that I had nearly forgotten him until this instant. Now that he was present, and real again, I felt I had betrayed him by not thinking of him more.

He was wearing a navy-blue serge suit. I was old enough now to notice that it was a cheap one and had been worn a considerable time. Otherwise, he looked the same, the same smile, the same knife-boned face with no flesh to speak of, the same unresting eyes.

"How come you're here?" I cried. "Where have you been, Chris?"

"I'm a traveller," he said. "Remember?"

He was a traveller all right. One meaning of the word *traveller* in our part of the world, was a travelling salesman. Chris was selling vacuum cleaners. That evening he brought out his line and showed us. He went through his spiel for our benefit, so we could hear how it sounded.

"Now look, Beth," he said, turning the appliance on and speaking loudly above its moaning roar, "see how it brightens up this old rug of yours? Keen, eh?"

"Wonderful," my mother laughed. "Only we can't afford one."

"Oh well—" Chris said quickly, "I'm not trying to sell one to you. I'm only showing you. Listen, I've only been in this job a month, but I figure this is really a going thing. I mean, it's obvious, isn't it? You take all those old wire carpet-beaters of yours, Beth. You could kill yourself over them and your carpet isn't going to look one-tenth as good as it does with this."

"Look, I don't want to seem—" my father put in, "but, hell, they're not exactly a new invention, and we're not the only ones who can't afford—"

"This is a pretty big outfit, you know?" Chris insisted. "Listen, I don't plan to stay, Ewen. But a guy could work at it for a year or so, and save—right? Lots of guys work their way through university like that."

I needed to say something really penetrating, something that would show him I knew the passionate truth of his conviction.

"I bet—" I said, "I bet you'll sell a thousand, Chris."

Two years ago, this statement would have seemed self-evident, unquestionable. Yet now, when I had spoken, I knew that I did not believe it.

The next time Chris visited Manawaka, he was selling magazines. He had the statistics worked out. If every sixth person in town would get a subscription to *Country Guide*, he could make a hundred dollars in a month. We didn't learn how he got on. He didn't stay in Manawaka a full month. When he turned up again, it was winter. Aunt Edna phoned.

"Nessa? Listen, kiddo, tell your mother she's to come down if it's humanly possible. Chris is here, and Father's having fits."

So in five minutes we were scurrying through the snow, my mother and I, with our overshoes not even properly done up and our feet getting wet. We need not have worried. By the time we reached the Brick House, Grandfather Connor had retired to the basement, where he sat in the rocking chair beside the furnace, making occasional black pronouncements like a subterranean oracle. These loud utterances made my mother and aunt wince, but Chris didn't seem to notice any more than he ever had. He was engrossed in telling us about the mechanism he was holding. It had a cranker handle like an old-fashioned sewing machine.

"You attach the ball of wool here, see? Then you set this little switch here, and adjust this lever, and you're away to the races. Neat, eh?"

It was a knitting machine. Chris showed us the finished products. The men's socks he had made were coarse wool, one pair in grey heather and another in maroon. I was impressed.

"Gee—can I do it, Chris?"

"Sure. Look, you just grab hold of the handle right here."

"Where did you get it?" my mother asked.

"I've rented it. The way I figure it, Beth, I can sell these things at about half the price you'd pay in a store, and they're better quality."

"Who are you going to sell them to?" Aunt Edna enquired.

"You take all these guys who do outside work—they need heavy socks all year round, not just in winter. I think this thing could be quite a gold mine."

"Before I forget," my mother said, "how's your mother and the family keeping?"

"They're okay," Chris said in a restrained voice. "They're not short of hands, if that's what you mean, Beth. My sisters have their husbands there."

Then he grinned, casting away the previous moment, and dug into his suitcase.

"Hey, I haven't shown you—these are for you, Vanessa, and this pair is for Roddie."

My socks were cherry-coloured. The very small ones for my brother were turquoise.

Chris only stayed until after dinner, and then he went away again.

After my father died, the whole order of life was torn. Nothing was known or predictable any longer. For months I lived almost entirely within myself, so when my mother told me one day that Chris couldn't find any work at all because there were no jobs and so he had gone back to Shallow Creek to stay, it made scarcely any impression on me. But that summer, my mother decided I ought to go away for a holiday. She hoped it might take my mind off my father's death. What, if anything, was going to take her mind off his death, she did not say.

"Would you like to go to Shallow Creek for a week or so?" she asked me. "I could write to Chris's mother."

Then I remembered, all in a torrent, the way I had imagined it once, when he used to tell me about it—the house fashioned of living trees, the lake like a sea where monsters had dwelt, the grass that shone like green wavering light while the horses flew in the splendour of their pride.

"Yes," I said. "Write to her."

The railway did not go through Shallow Creek, but Chris met me at Challoner's Crossing. He looked different, not only thinner, but—what was it? Then I saw that it was the fact that his face and neck were tanned red-brown, and he was wearing denims, farm pants, and a blue plaid shirt open at the neck. I liked him like this. Perhaps the change was not so much in him as in myself, now that I was thirteen. He looked masculine in a way I had not been aware of, before.

"C'mon, kid," he said. "The limousine's over here."

It was a wagon and two horses, which was what I had expected, but the nature of each was not what I had expected. The wagon was a long and clumsy one, made of heavy planking, and the horses were both plough horses, thick in the legs, and badly matched as a team. The mare was short and stout, matronly. The gelding was very tall and gaunt, and he limped.

"Allow me to introduce you," Chris said. "Floss—Trooper—this is Vanessa."

He did not mention the other horses, Duchess and Firefly, and neither did I, not all the fortnight I was there. I guess I had known for some years now, without realising it, that the pair had only ever existed in some other dimension.

Shallow Creek wasn't a town. It was merely a name on a map. There was a grade school a few miles away, but that was all. They had to go to Challoner's Crossing for their groceries. We reached the farm, and Chris steered me through the crowd of aimless cows and wolfish dogs in the yard, while I flinched with panic.

It was perfectly true that the house was made out of trees. It was a fair-sized but elderly shack, made out of poplar poles and chinked with mud. There was an upstairs, which was not so usual around here, with three bedrooms, one of which I was to share with Chris's sister, Jeannie, who was slightly younger than I, a pallid-eyed girl who was either too shy to talk or who had nothing to say. I never discovered which, because I was so reticent with her myself, wanting to push her away, not to recognise her, and at the same time experiencing a shocked remorse at my own unacceptable feelings.

Aunt Tess, Chris's mother, was severe in manner and yet wanting to be kind, worrying over it, making tentative overtures which were either ignored or repelled by her older daughters and their monosyllabic husbands. Youngsters swam in and out of the house like shoals of nameless fishes. I could not see how so many people could live here, under one roof, but then I learned they didn't. The married daughters had their own dwelling places, nearby, but some kind of communal life was maintained. They wrangled endlessly but they never left one another alone, not even for a day.

Chris took no part at all, none. When he spoke, it was usually to the children, and they would often follow him around the yard or to the barn, not pestering but just trailing along in clusters of three or four. He never told them to go away. I liked him for this, but it bothered me, too. I wished he would return his sisters' bickering for once, or tell them to clear out, or even yell at one of the kids. But he never did. He closed himself off from squabbling voices just as he used to do with Grandfather Connor's spearing words.

The house had no screens on the doors or windows, and at meal times the flies were so numerous you could hardly see the food for the iridescent-winged blue-black bodies squirming all over it. Nobody noticed my squeamishness except Chris, and he was the only one from whom I really wanted to conceal it.

"Fan with your hand," he murmured.

"It's okay," I said quickly.

For the first time in all the years we had known each other, we could not look the other in the eye. Around the table, the children stabbed and snivelled, until Chris's oldest sister, driven frantic, shrieked, *Shut up shut up shut up*. Chris began asking me about Manawaka then, as though nothing were going on around him.

They were due to begin haying, and Chris announced that he was going to camp out in the bluff near the hayfields. To save himself the long drive in the wagon each morning, he explained, but I felt this wasn't the real reason.

"Can I go, too?" I begged. I could not bear the thought of living in the house with all the others who were not known to me, and Chris not here.

"Well, I don't know—"

"Please. Please, Chris. I won't be any trouble. I promise."

Finally he agreed. We drove out in the big hayrack, its slatted sides rattling, its old wheels jolting metallically. The road was narrow and dirt, and around it the low bushes grew, wild rose and blueberry and wolf willow with silver leaves. Sometimes we would come to a bluff of pale-leaved poplar trees, and once a red-winged blackbird flew up out of the branches and into the hot dusty blue of the sky.

Then we were there. The hayfields lay beside the lake. It was my first view of the water which had spawned saurian giants so long ago. Chris drove the hayrack through the fields of high coarse grass and on down almost to the lake's edge, where there was no shore but only the green rushes like floating meadows in which the water birds nested. Beyond the undulating reeds the open lake stretched, deep, green-grey, out and out, beyond sight.

No human word could be applied. The lake was not lonely or untamed. These words relate to people, and there was nothing of people here. There was no feeling about the place. It existed in some world in which man was not yet born. I looked at the grey reaches of it and felt threatened. It was like the view of God which I had held since my father's death. Distant, indestructible, totally indifferent.

Chris had jumped down off the hayrack.

"We're not going to camp *here*, are we?" I asked and pleaded.

"No. I just want to let the horses drink. We'll camp up there in the bluff."

I looked. "It's still pretty close to the lake, isn't it?"

"Don't worry," Chris said, laughing. "You won't get your feet wet."

"I didn't mean that."

Chris looked at me.

"I know you didn't," he said. "But let's learn to be a little tougher, and not let on, eh? It's necessary."

Chris worked through the hours of sun, while I lay on the half-formed stack of hay and looked up at the sky. The blue air trembled and spun with the heat haze, and the hay on which I was lying held the scents of grass and dust and wild mint.

In the evening, Chris took the horses to the lake again, and then he drove the hayrack to the edge of the bluff and we spread out our blankets underneath it. He made a fire and we had coffee and a tin of stew, and then we went to bed. We did not wash, and we slept in our clothes. It was only when I was curled up uncomfortably with the itching blanket around me that I felt a sense of unfamiliarity at being here, with Chris only three feet away, a self-consciousness I would not have felt even the year before. I do not think he felt this sexual strangeness. If he wanted me not to be a child and he did—it was not with the wish that I would be a woman. It was something else.

"Are you asleep, Vanessa?" he asked.

"No. I think I'm lying on a tree root."

"Well, shift yourself, then," he said. "Listen, kid, I never said anything before, because I didn't really know what to say, but—you know how I felt about your dad dying, and that, don't you?"

"Yes," I said chokingly. "It's okay. I know."

"I used to talk with Ewen sometimes. He didn't see what I was driving at, mostly, but he'd always listen, you know? You don't find many guys like that."

We were both silent for a while.

"Look," Chris said finally. "Ever noticed how much brighter the stars are when you're completely away from any houses? Even the lamps up at the farm, there, make enough of a glow to keep you from seeing properly like you can out here. What do they make you think about, Vanessa?"

"Well—"

"I guess most people don't give them much thought at all, except maybe to say—*very pretty*— or like that. But the point is, they aren't like that. The stars and planets, in themselves, are just not like that, not *pretty*, for heaven's sake. They're gigantic—some of them burning—imagine those worlds tearing through space and made of pure fire. Or the ones that are absolutely dead—just rock or ice and no warmth in them. There must be some, though, that have living creatures. You wonder what *they* could look like, and what they feel. We won't ever get to know. But somebody will know, someday. I really believe that. Do you ever think about this kind of thing at all?"

He was twenty-one. The distance between us was still too great. For years I had wanted to be older so I might talk with him, but now I felt unready.

"Sometimes," I said, hesitantly, making it sound like *Never*.

"People usually say there must be a God," Chris went on, "because otherwise how did the universe get here? But that's ridiculous. If the stars and planets go on to infinity, they could have existed forever, for no reason at all. Maybe they weren't ever created. Look—what's the alternative? To believe in a God who is brutal. What else could He be? You've only got to look anywhere around you. It would be an insult to Him to believe in a God like that. Most people don't like talking about this kind of thing—it embarrasses them, you know? Or else they're not interested. I don't mind. I can always think about things myself. You don't actually need anyone to talk to. But about God, though—if there's a war, like it looks there will be, would people claim that was planned? What kind of a God would pull a trick like that? And yet, you know, plenty of guys would think it was a godsend, and who's to say they're wrong? It would be a job, and you'd get around and see places."

He paused, as though waiting for me to say something. When I did not, he resumed.

"Ewen told me about the last war, once. He hardly ever talked about it, but this once he told me about seeing the horses in the mud, actually going under, you know? And the way their eyes looked when they realised they weren't going to get out. Ever seen horses' eyes when they're afraid, I mean really berserk with fear, like in a bush-fire? Ewen said a guy tended to concentrate on the horses because he didn't dare think what was happening to the men. Including himself. Do you ever listen to the news at all, Vanessa?"

"I—"

I could only feel how foolish I must sound, still unable to reply as I would have wanted, comprehendingly. I felt I had failed myself utterly. I could not speak even the things I knew. As for the other things, the things I did not know, I resented Chris's facing me with them. I took refuge in pretending to be asleep, and after a while Chris stopped talking.

Chris left Shallow Creek some months after the war began, and joined the Army. After his basic training he was sent to England. We did not hear from him until about a year later, when a letter arrived for me.

"Vanessa—what's wrong?" my mother asked.

"Nothing."

"Don't fib," she said firmly. "What did Chris say in his letter, honey?"

"Oh—not much."

She gave me a curious look and then she went away. She would never have demanded to see the letter. I did not show it to her and she did not ask about it again.

Six months later my mother heard from Aunt Tess. Chris had been sent home from England and discharged from the Army because of a mental breakdown. He was now in the provincial mental hospital and they did not know how long he would have to remain there. He had been violent, before, but now he was not violent. He was, the doctors had told his mother, passive.

Violent. I could not associate the word with Chris, who had been so much the reverse. I could not bear to consider what anguish must have catapulted him into that even greater anguish. But the way he was now seemed almost worse. How might he be? Sitting quite still, wearing the hospital's grey dressing-gown, the animation gone from his face?

My mother cared about him a great deal, but her immediate thought was not for him.

"When I think of you, going up to Shallow Creek that time," she said, "and going out camping with him, and what might have happened—"

I, also, was thinking of what might have happened. But we were not thinking of the same thing. For the first time I recognised, at least a little, the dimensions of his need to talk that night. He must have understood perfectly well how impossible it would be, with a thirteen-year-old. But there was no one else. All his life's choices had grown narrower and narrower. He had been forced to return to the alien lake of home, and when finally he saw a means of getting away, it could only be into a turmoil which appalled him and which he dreaded even more than he knew. I had listened to his words, but I had not really heard them, not until now. It would not have made much difference to what happened, but I wished it were not too late to let him know.

Once when I was on holiday from college, my mother got me to help her clean out the attic. We sifted through boxes full of junk, old clothes, schoolbooks, bric-a-brac that once had been treasures. In one of the boxes I found the miniature saddle that Chris had made for me a long time ago.

"Have you heard anything recently?" I asked, ashamed that I had not asked sooner.

She glanced up at me. "Just the same. It's always the same. They don't think there will be much improvement."

Then she turned away.

"He always used to seem so—hopeful. Even when there was really nothing to be hopeful about. That's what I find so strange. He *seemed* hopeful, didn't you think?"

"Maybe it wasn't hope," I said.

"How do you mean?"

I wasn't certain myself, I was thinking of all the schemes he'd had, the ones that couldn't possibly have worked, the unreal solutions to which he'd clung because there were no others, the brave and useless strokes of fantasy against a depression that was both the world's and his own.

"I don't know," I said. "I just think things were always more difficult for him than he let on, that's all. Remember that letter?"

"Yes."

"Well—what it said was that they could force his body to march and even to kill, but what they didn't know was that he'd fooled them. He didn't live inside it any more."

"Oh Vanessa—" my mother said. "You must have suspected right then."

"Yes, but—"

I could not go on, could not say that the letter seemed only the final heartbreaking extension of that way he'd always had of distancing himself from the absolute unbearability of battle.

I picked up the tiny saddle and turned it over in my hand.

"Look. His brand, the name of his ranch. The Criss-Cross."

"What ranch?" my mother said, bewildered.

"The one where he kept his racing horses. Duchess and Firefly."

Some words came into my head, a single line from a poem I had once heard. I knew it referred to a lover who did not want the morning to come, but to me it had another meaning, a different relevance.

Slowly, slowly, horses of the night—

The night must move like this for him, slowly, all through the days and nights. I could not know whether the land he journeyed through was inhabited by terrors, the old monster-kings of the lake, or whether he had discovered at last a way for himself to make the necessary dream perpetual.

I put the saddle away once more, gently and ruthlessly, back into the cardboard box.

QUESTIONS

1. Describe the steps Chris takes throughout his life to escape the "absolute unbearability of battle." At what point in the story is the reader first aware that Chris is living in a world of delusions? Is this world of fantasy Chris's only refuge from potential insanity? Explain.
2. Vanessa often worries that she is incapable of saying the right thing. Find examples of this. Do the other characters have the same difficulty? Examine how this theme of communication helps you in your understanding of "Horses of the Night."
3. Trace the horse motif in this story. Does this motif imply a generalization about everyone's life or does it apply only to Chris?
4. Keeping in mind your answer to question 3, interpret the line of poetry, "Slowly, slowly, horses of the night."
5. Compare the views of God held by Vanessa and Chris. What circumstances in their lives have led them to their beliefs?
6. Find examples in the story which explain why Vanessa finds it impossible to associate the word "violent" with Chris. Do you agree with Vanessa's assessment of Chris? Why or why not?
7. Compare the first and the final impressions of Chris held by Vanessa; by Vanessa's parents; by the Connors. What is your final impression of Chris?
8. The letter Chris writes is very revealing. How do you interpret the lines that Vanessa repeats to her mother?
9. What do we learn about Vanessa from her thoughts concerning Chris's letter? Look at your answer to question 2. Do you now have a new understanding of Vanessa?
10. This story depends a great deal on descriptive writing. In the following sentence, for example, Laurence uses verbs very effectively. "The blue air trembled and spun with the heat haze, and the hay on which I was lying held the scents of grass and dust and wild mint." Find other such passages and examine how Laurence achieves her effect.

Katherine Anne Porter

THE JILTING OF GRANNY WEATHERALL

She flicked her wrist neatly out of Doctor Harry's pudgy careful fingers and pulled the sheet up to her chin. The brat ought to be in knee breeches. Doctoring around the country with spectacles on his nose! "Get along now, take your schoolbooks and go. There's nothing wrong with me."

Doctor Harry spread a warm paw like a cushion on her forehead where the forked green vein danced and made her eyelids twitch. "Now, now, be a good girl, and we'll have you up in no time."

"That's no way to speak to a woman nearly eighty years old just because she's down. I'd have you respect your elders, young man."

"Well, Missy, excuse me." Doctor Harry patted her cheek. "But I've got to warn you, haven't I? You're a marvel, but you must be careful or you're going to be good and sorry."

"Don't tell me what I'm going to be. I'm on my feet now, morally speaking. It's Cornelia. I had to go to bed to get rid of her."

Her bones felt loose, and floated around in her skin, and Doctor Harry floated like a balloon around the foot of the bed. He floated and pulled down his waistcoat and swung his glasses on a cord. "Well, stay where you are, it certainly can't hurt you."

"Get along and doctor your sick," said Granny Weatherall. "Leave a well woman alone. I'll call for you when I want you . . . Where were you forty years ago when I pulled through milk-leg and double pneumonia? You weren't even born. Don't let Cornelia lead you on," she shouted, because Doctor Harry appeared to float up to the ceiling and out. "I pay my own bills, and I don't throw my money away on nonsense!"

She meant to wave good-by, but it was too much trouble. Her eyes closed of themselves, it was like a dark curtain drawn around the bed. The pillow rose and floated under her, pleasant as a hammock in a light wind. She listened to the leaves rustling outside the window. No, somebody was swishing newspapers: no, Cornelia and Doctor Harry were whispering together. She leaped broad awake, thinking they whispered in her ear.

"She was never like this, *never* like this!" "Well, what can we expect?" "Yes, eighty years old. . . ."

Well, and what if she was? She still had ears. It was like Cornelia to whisper around doors. She always kept things secret in such a public way. She was always being tactful and kind. Cornelia was dutiful; that was the trouble with her. Dutiful and good: "So good and dutiful," said Granny, "that I'd like to spank her." She saw herself spanking Cornelia and making a fine job of it.

"What'd you say, Mother?"

Granny felt her face tying up in hard knots.

"Can't a body think, I'd like to know?"

"I thought you might want something."

"I do. I want a lot of things. First off, go away and don't whisper."

She lay and drowsed, hoping in her sleep that the children would keep out and let her rest a minute. It had been a long day. Not that she was tired. It was always pleasant to snatch a minute now and then. There was always so much to be done, let me see: tomorrow.

Tomorrow was far away and there was nothing to trouble about. Things were finished somehow when the time came; thank God there was always a little margin over for peace: then a person could spread out the plan of life and tuck in the edges orderly. It was good to have everything clean and folded away, with the hair brushes and tonic bottles sitting straight on the white embroidered linen: the day started without fuss and the pantry shelves laid out with rows of jelly glasses and brown jugs and white stone-china jars with blue whirligigs and words painted on them: coffee, tea, sugar, ginger, cinnamon, allspice and the bronze clock with the lion on top nicely dusted off. The dust that lion could collect in twenty-four hours! The box in the attic with all those letters tied up, well, she'd have to go through that tomorrow. All those letters—George's letters and John's letters and her letters to them both—lying around for the children to find afterwards made her uneasy. Yes, that would be tomorrow's business. No use to let them know how silly she had been once.

While she was rummaging around she found death in her mind and it felt clammy and unfamiliar. She had spent so much time preparing for death there was no need for bringing it up again. Let it take care of itself now. When she was sixty she had felt very old, finished, and went around making farewell trips to see her children and grandchildren, with a secret in her mind: This is the very last of your mother, children! Then she made her will and came down with a long fever. That was all just a notion like a lot of other things, but it was lucky too, for she had once for all got over the idea of dying for a long time. Now she couldn't be worried. She hoped she had better sense now. Her father had lived to be one hundred and two years old and had drunk a noggin of strong hot toddy on his last birthday. He told the reporters it was his daily habit, and he owed his long life to that. He had made quite a scandal and was very pleased about it. She believed she'd just plague Cornelia a little.

"Cornelia! Cornelia!" No footsteps, but a sudden hand on her cheek. "Bless you, where have you been?"

"Here, Mother."

"Well, Cornelia, I want a noggin of hot toddy."

"Are you cold, darling?"

"I'm chilly, Cornelia. Lying in bed stops the circulation. I must have told you that a thousand times."

Well, she could just hear Cornelia telling her husband that Mother was getting a little childish and they'd have to humor her. The thing that most annoyed her was that Cornelia thought she was deaf, dumb, and blind. Little hasty glances and tiny gestures tossed around her and over her head saying, "Don't cross her, let her have her way, she's eighty years old," and she sitting there as if she lived in a thin glass cage. Sometimes Granny almost made up her mind to pack up and move back to her own house where nobody could remind her every minute that she was old. Wait, wait, Cornelia, till your own children whisper behind your back!

In her day she had kept a better house and had got more work done. She wasn't too old yet for Lydia to be driving eighty miles for advice when one of the children jumped the track, and Jimmy still dropped in and talked things over: "Now, Mammy, you've a good business head, I want to know what you think of this? ..." Old. Cornelia couldn't change the furniture around without asking. Little things, little things! They had been so sweet when they were little. Granny wished the old days were back again with the children young and everything to be done over. It had been a hard pull, but not too much for her. When she thought of all the food she had cooked, and all the clothes she had cut and sewed, and all the gardens she had made—well, the children showed it. There they were, made out of her, and they couldn't get away from that. Sometimes she wanted to see John again and point to them and say, Well, I didn't do so badly, did I? But that would have to wait. That was for tomorrow. She used to think of him as a man, but now all the children were older than their father, and he would be a child beside her if she saw him now. It seemed strange and there was something wrong in the idea. Why, he couldn't possibly recognize her. She had fenced in a hundred acres once, digging the post holes herself and clamping the wires with just a negro boy to help. That changed a woman. John would be looking for a young woman with the peaked Spanish comb in her hair and the painted fan. Digging post holes changed a woman. Riding country roads in the winter when women had their babies was another thing: sitting up nights with sick horses and sick negroes and sick children and hardly ever losing one. John, I hardly ever lost one of them! John would see that in a minute, that would be something he could understand, she wouldn't have to explain anything!

It made her feel like rolling up her sleeves and putting the whole place to rights again. No matter if Cornelia was determined to be everywhere at once, there were a great many things left undone on this place. She would start tomorrow and do them. It was good to be strong enough for everything, even if all you made melted and changed and slipped under your hands, so that by the time you finished you almost forgot what you were working for. What was it I set out to do? she asked herself intently, but she could not remember. A fog rose over the valley, she saw it marching across the creek swallowing the trees and moving up the hill like an army of ghosts. Soon it would be at the near edge of the orchard, and then it was time to go in and light the lamps. Come in, children, don't stay out in the night air.

Lighting the lamps had been beautiful. The children huddled up to her and breathed like little calves waiting at the bars in the twilight. Their eyes followed the match and watched the flame rise and settle in a blue curve, then they moved away from her. The lamp was lit, they didn't have to be scared and hang on to mother any more. Never, never, never more. God, for all my life I thank Thee. Without Thee, my God, I could never have done it. Hail, Mary, full of grace.

I want you to pick all the fruit this year and see that nothing is wasted. There's always someone who can use it. Don't let good things rot for want of using. You waste life when you waste good food. Don't let things get lost. It's bitter to lose things. Now, don't let me get to thinking, not when I am tired and taking a little nap before supper. . . .

The pillow rose about her shoulders and pressed against her heart and the memory was being squeezed out of it: oh, push down the pillow, somebody: it would smother her if she tried to hold it. Such a fresh breeze blowing and such a green day with no threats in it. But he had not come, just the same. What does a woman do when she has put on the white veil and set out the white cake for a man and he doesn't come? She tried to remember. No, I swear he never harmed me but in that. He never harmed me but in that . . . and what if he did? There was the day, the day, but a whirl of dark smoke rose and covered it, crept up and over into the bright field where everything was planted so carefully in orderly rows. That was hell, she knew hell when she saw it. For sixty years she had prayed against remembering him and against losing her soul in the deep pit of hell, and now the two things were mingled in one and the thought of him was a smoky cloud from hell that moved and crept in her head when she had just got rid of Doctor Harry and was trying to rest a minute. Wounded vanity, Ellen, said a sharp voice in the top of her mind. Don't let your wounded vanity get the upper hand of you. Plenty of girls get jilted. You were jilted, weren't you? Then stand up to it. Her eyelids wavered and let in streamers of blue-gray light like tissue paper over her eyes. She must get up and pull the shades down or she'd never sleep. She was in bed again and the shades were not down. How could that happen? Better turn over, hide from the light, sleeping in the light gave you nightmares. "Mother, how do you feel now?" and a stinging wetness on her forehead. But I don't like having my face washed in cold water!

Hapsy? George? Lydia? Jimmy? No, Cornelia, and her features were swollen and full of little puddles. "They're coming, darling, they'll all be here soon." Go wash your face, child, you look funny.

Instead of obeying, Cornelia knelt down and put her head on the pillow. She seemed to be talking but there was no sound. "Well, are you tongue-tied? Whose birthday is it? Are you going to give a party?"

Cornelia's mouth moved urgently in strange shapes. "Don't do that, you bother me, daughter."

"Oh, no, Mother. Oh, no. . . ."

Nonsense. It was strange about children. They disputed your every word. "No what, Cornelia?"

"Here's Doctor Harry."

"I won't see that boy again. He just left five minutes ago."

"That was this morning, Mother. It's night now. Here's the nurse."

"This is Doctor Harry, Mrs. Weatherall. I never saw you look so young and happy!"

"Ah, I'll never be young again—but I'd be happy if they'd let me lie in peace and get rested."

She thought she spoke up loudly, but no one answered. A warm weight on her forehead, a warm bracelet on her wrist, and a breeze went on whispering, trying to tell her something. A shuffle of leaves in the everlasting hand of God, He blew on them and they danced and rattled. "Mother, don't mind, we're going to give you a little hypodermic." "Look here, daughter, how do ants get in this bed? I saw sugar ants yesterday." Did you send for Hapsy too?

It was Hapsy she really wanted. She had to go a long way back through a great many rooms to find Hapsy standing with a baby on her arm. She seemed to herself to be Hapsy also, and the baby on Hapsy's arm was Hapsy and himself and herself, all at once, and there was no surprise in the meeting. Then Hapsy melted from within and turned flimsy as gray gauze and the baby was a gauzy shadow, and Hapsy came up close and said, "I thought you'd never come," and looked at her very searchingly and said, "You haven't changed a bit!" They leaned forward to kiss, when Cornelia began whispering from a long way off, "Oh, is there anything you want to tell me? Is there anything I can do for you?"

Yes, she had changed her mind after sixty years and she would like to see George. I want you to find George. Find him and be sure to tell him I forgot him. I want him to know I had my husband just the same and my children and my house like any other woman. A good house too and a good husband that I loved and fine children out of him. Better than I hoped for even. Tell him I was given back everything he took away and more. Oh, no, oh, God, no, there was something else besides the house and the man and the children. Oh, surely they were not all? What was it? Something not given back. . . . Her breath crowded down under her ribs and grew into a monstrous frightening shape with cutting edges; it bored up into her head, and the agony was unbelievable: Yes, John, get the Doctor now, no more talk, my time has come.

When this one was born it should be the last. The last. It should have been born first, for it was the one she had truly wanted. Everything came in good time. Nothing left out, left over. She was strong, in three days she would be as well as ever. Better. A woman needed milk in her to have her full health.

"Mother, do you hear me?"

"I've been telling you—"

"Mother, Father Connolly's here."

"I went to Holy Communion only last week. Tell him I'm not so sinful as all that."

"Father just wants to speak to you."

He could speak as much as he pleased. It was like him to drop in and inquire about her soul as if it were a teething baby, and then stay on for a cup of tea and a round of cards and gossip. He always had a funny story of some sort, usually about an Irishman who made his little mistakes and confessed them, and the point lay in some absurd thing he would blurt out in the confessional showing his struggles between native piety and original sin. Granny felt easy about her soul. Cornelia, where are your manners? Give Father Connolly a chair. She had her secret comfortable understanding with a few favorite saints who cleared a straight road to God for her. All as surely signed and sealed as the papers for the new Forty Acres. Forever . . . heirs and assigns forever. Since the day the wedding cake was not cut, but thrown out and wasted. The whole bottom dropped out of the world, and there she was blind and sweating with nothing under her feet and the walls falling away. His hand had caught her under the breast, she had not fallen, there was the freshly polished floor with the green rug on it, just as before. He had cursed like a sailor's parrot and said, "I'll kill him for you." Don't lay a hand on him, for my sake leave something to God. "Now, Ellen, you must believe what I tell you. . . ."

So there was nothing, nothing to worry about any more, except sometimes in the night one of the children screamed in a nightmare, and they both hustled out shaking and hunting for the matches and calling, "There, wait a minute, here we are!" John, get the doctor now, Hapsy's time has come. But there was Hapsy standing by the bed in a white cap. "Cornelia, tell Hapsy to take off her cap. I can't see her plain."

Her eyes opened very wide and the room stood out like a picture she had seen somewhere. Dark colors with the shadows rising towards the ceiling in long angles. The tall black dresser gleamed with nothing on it but John's picture, enlarged from a little one, with John's eyes very black when they should have been blue. You never saw him, so how do you know how he looked? But the man insisted the copy was perfect, it was very rich and handsome. For a picture, yes, but it's not my husband. The table by the bed had a linen cover and a candle and a crucifix. The light was blue from Cornelia's silk lampshades. No sort of light at all, just frippery. You had to live forty years with kerosene lamps to appreciate honest electricity. She felt very strong and she saw Doctor Harry with a rosy nimbus around him.

"You look like a saint, Doctor Harry, and I vow that's as near as you'll ever come to it."

"She's saying something."

"I heard you, Cornelia. What's all this carrying-on?"

"Father Connolly's saying—"

Cornelia's voice staggered and bumped like a cart in a bad road. It rounded corners and turned back again and arrived nowhere. Granny stepped up in the cart very lightly and reached for the reins, but a man sat beside her and she knew him by his hands, driving the cart. She did not look in his face, for she knew without seeing, but looked instead down the road where the trees leaned over and bowed to each other and a thousand birds were singing a Mass. She felt like singing too, but she put her hand in the bosom of her dress and pulled out a rosary, and Father Connolly murmured Latin in a very solemn voice and tickled her feet. My God, will you stop that nonsense? I'm a married woman. What if he did run away and leave me to face the priest by myself? I found another a whole world better. I wouldn't have exchanged my husband for anybody except St. Michael himself, and you may tell him that for me with a thank you in the bargain.

Light flashed on her closed eyelids, and a deep roaring shook her. Cornelia, is that lightning? I hear thunder. There's going to be a storm. Close all the windows. Call the children in. . . . "Mother, here we are, all of us." "Is that you, Hapsy?" "Oh, no, I'm Lydia. We drove as fast as we could." Their faces drifted above her, drifted away. The rosary fell out of her hands and Lydia put it back. Jimmy tried to help, their hands fumbled together, and Granny closed two fingers around Jimmy's thumb. Beads wouldn't do, it must be something alive. She was so amazed her thoughts ran round and round. So, my dear Lord, this is my death and I wasn't even thinking about it. My children have come to see me die. But I can't, it's not time. Oh, I always hated surprises. I wanted to give Cornelia the amethyst set—Cornelia, you're to have the amethyst set, but Hapsy's to wear it when she wants, and, Doctor Harry, do shut up. Nobody sent for you. Oh, my dear Lord, do wait a minute. I meant to do something about the Forty Acres. Jimmy doesn't need it and Lydia will later on, with that worthless husband of hers. I meant to finish the altar cloth and send six bottles of wine to Sister Borgia for her dyspepsia. I want to send six bottles of wine to Sister Borgia, Father Connolly, now don't let me forget.

Cornelia's voice made short turns and tilted over and crashed. "Oh, Mother, oh, Mother, oh, Mother. . . ."

"I'm not going, Cornelia. I'm taken by surprise. I can't go."

You'll see Hapsy again. What about her? "I thought you'd never come." Granny made a long journey outward, looking for Hapsy. What if I don't find her? What then? Her heart sank down and down, there was no bottom to death, she couldn't come to the end of it. The blue light from Cornelia's lampshade drew into a tiny point in the center of her brain, it flickered and winked like an eye, quietly it fluttered and dwindled. Granny lay curled down within herself, amazed and watchful, staring at the point of light that was herself; her body was now only a deeper mass of shadow in an endless darkness and this darkness would curl around the light and swallow it up. God, give a sign!

For the second time there was no sign. Again no bridegroom and the priest in the house. She could not remember any other sorrow because this grief wiped them all away. Oh, no, there's nothing more cruel than this—I'll never forgive it. She stretched herself with a deep breath and blew out the light.

QUESTIONS

1. What is the significance of the name "Weatherall"? Why would Porter assign such an obvious name to the woman? Compare Granny Weatherall to Grandmother Connor in "Horses of the Night." How have their life experiences contributed to the development of their personalities?

2. Why does Granny feel that she is treated as though she "lived in a thin glass cage"? Do you accept Granny's assessment of Cornelia? How do you think Cornelia will react to her mother's death? Compare your ideas with Vanessa's reaction to her father's death in "Horses of the Night."

3. List the references to the man who jilted Granny and describe her emotions each time she remembers him.

4. "No use to let them know how silly she had been once." Why does Granny feel she must keep this distance from her children?

5. Porter gives us several examples of how she thinks Granny Weatherall feels, in mind and in body, as she approaches death. Find some examples and comment on their effectiveness.

6. It is often difficult to follow Granny's thought processes. Porter writes this way deliberately because she is matching her writing style to the content of the story. When we as readers feel confused, we are more nearly approaching the actual state of Granny's mind. Discuss this idea.

7. Interpret the images of the fog rising over the valley and of the lighting of the lamps. Trace the image of the lamp throughout the story.

8. In "Horses of the Night," Chris moves towards insanity. In "The Jilting of Granny Weatherall," Granny moves towards death. Compare and contrast Chris and Granny.

9. "I never saw you look so young and happy!" Why does the doctor say this to a dying, 80-year-old woman? Is Granny looking forward to death?

10. With reference to question 9, does a change occur in Granny during her last moments of life? Explain her thought, "Again no bridegroom and the priest in the house."

11. How do you feel when Granny Weatherall dies? Has Porter prepared you for this feeling?

12. Re-read the introductory essay to this chapter, "Escape and Interpretation." How would you classify "Horses of the Night" and "The Jilting of Granny Weatherall"? Do they take us "away from the real world" or "deeper into the real world"? Explain how these stories "sharpen our awareness of life."

Morley Callaghan

THE LITTLE BUSINESS MAN

That summer when twelve-year-old Luke Baldwin came to live with his Uncle Henry in the house on the stream by the sawmill, he did not forget that he had promised his dying father he would try to learn things from his uncle; so he used to watch him very carefully.

Uncle Henry, who was the manager of the sawmill, was a big, burly man weighing more than two hundred and thirty pounds, and he had a rough-skinned, brick-coloured face. He looked like a powerful man, but his health was not good. He had aches and pains in his back and shoulders which puzzled the doctor. The first thing Luke learned about Uncle Henry was that everybody had great respect for him. The four men he employed in the sawmill were always polite and attentive when he spoke to them. His wife, Luke's Aunt Helen, a kindly, plump, straightforward woman, never argued with him. "You should try and be like your Uncle Henry," she would say to Luke. "He's so wonderfully practical. He takes care of everything in a sensible, easy way."

Luke used to trail around the sawmill after Uncle Henry not only because he liked the fresh clean smell of the newly cut wood and the big piles of sawdust, but because he was impressed by his uncle's precise, firm tone when he spoke to the men.

Sometimes Uncle Henry would stop and explain to Luke something

THE LITTLE BUSINESS MAN From *Morley Callaghan's Stories* © Morley Callaghan 1959. Reprinted by permission of Macmillan of Canada. A Division of Gage Publishing Limited.

about a piece of timber. "Always try and learn the essential facts, son," he would say. "If you've got the facts, you know what's useful and what isn't useful, and no one can fool you."

He showed Luke that nothing of value was ever wasted around the mill. Luke used to listen, and wonder if there was another man in the world who knew so well what was needed and what ought to be thrown away. Uncle Henry had known at once that Luke needed a bicycle to ride to his school, which was two miles away in town, and he bought him a good one. He knew that Luke needed good, serviceable clothes. He also knew exactly how much Aunt Helen needed to run the house, the price of everything, and how much a woman should be paid for doing the family washing. In the evenings Luke used to sit in the living-room watching his uncle making notations in a black notebook which he always carried in his vest pocket, and he knew that he was assessing the value of the smallest transaction that had taken place during the day.

Luke promised himself that when he grew up he, too, would be admired for his good, sound judgement. But, of course, he couldn't always be watching and learning from his Uncle Henry, for too often when he watched him he thought of his own father; then he was lonely. So he began to build up another secret life for himself around the sawmill, and his companion was the eleven-year-old collie, Dan, a dog blind in one eye and with a slight limp in his left hind leg. Dan was a fat, slow-moving old dog. He was very affectionate and his eye was the colour of amber. His fur was amber too. When Luke left for school in the morning, the old dog followed him for half a mile down the road, and when he returned in the afternoon, there was Dan waiting at the gate.

Sometimes they would play around the millpond or by the dam, or go down the stream to the lake. Luke was never lonely when the dog was with him. There was an old rowboat that they used as a pirate ship in the stream, and they would be pirates together, with Luke shouting instructions to Captain Dan and with the dog seeming to understand and wagging his tail enthusiastically. His amber eye was alert, intelligent, and approving. Then they would plunge into the brush on the other side of the stream, pretending they were hunting tigers. Of course, the old dog was no longer much good for hunting; he was too slow and too lazy. Uncle Henry no longer used him for hunting rabbits or anything else.

When they came out of the brush, they would lie together on the cool, grassy bank being affectionate with each other, with Luke talking earnestly, while the collie, as Luke believed, smiled with the good eye. Lying in the grass, Luke would say things to Dan he could not say to his uncle or his aunt. Not that what he said was important; it was just stuff about himself that he might have told to his own father or mother if they had been alive. Then they would go back to the house for dinner, and after dinner Dan would follow him down the road to Mr. Kemp's house, where they would ask old Mr. Kemp if they could go with him to round up his four cows. The old man was always glad to see them. He seemed to like watching Luke and the collie running around the cows, pretending they were riding on a vast range in the foothills of the Rockies.

Uncle Henry no longer paid much attention to the collie, though once when he tripped over him on the veranda, he shook his head and said thoughtfully, "Poor fellow, he's through. Can't use him for anything. He just eats and sleeps and gets in the way."

One Sunday during Luke's summer holidays, when they had returned from church and had had their lunch, they all moved out to the veranda where the collie was sleeping. Luke sat down on the steps, his back against the veranda post, Uncle Henry took the rocking-chair, and Aunt Helen stretched herself out in the hammock, sighing contentedly. Then Luke, eyeing the collie, tapped the step with the palm of his hand, giving three little taps like a signal, and the collie, lifting his head, got up stiffly with a slow wagging of the tail as an acknowledgement that the signal had been heard, and began to cross the veranda to Luke. But the dog was sleepy; his bad eye was turned to the rocking-chair; in passing, his left front paw went under the rocker. With a frantic yelp, the dog went bounding down the steps and hobbled around the corner of the house, where he stopped, hearing Luke coming after him. All he needed was the touch of Luke's hand. Then he began to lick the hand methodically, as if apologizing.

"Luke," Uncle Henry called sharply, "bring that dog here."

When Luke led the collie back to the veranda, Uncle Henry nodded and said, "Thanks, Luke." Then he took out a cigar, lit it, put his big hands on his knees, and began to rock in the chair, while he frowned and eyed the dog steadily. Obviously he was making some kind of an important decision about the collie.

"What's the matter, Uncle Henry?" Luke asked nervously.

"That dog can't see any more," Uncle Henry said.

"Oh, yes, he can," Luke said quickly. "His bad eye got turned to the chair, that's all, Uncle Henry."

"And his teeth are gone, too," Uncle Henry went on, paying no attention to what Luke said. Turning to the hammock, he called, "Helen, sit up a minute, will you?"

When she got up and stood beside him, he went on, "I was thinking about this old dog the other day, Helen. It's not only that he's just about blind, but did you notice that when we drove up after church he didn't even bark?"

"It's a fact, he didn't, Henry."

"No, not much good even as a watch-dog now."

"Poor old fellow. It's a pity, isn't it?"

"And no good for hunting either. And he eats a lot, I suppose."

"About as much as he ever did, Henry."

"The plain fact is the old dog isn't worth his keep any more. It's time we got rid of him."

"It's always so hard to know how to get rid of a dog, Henry."

"I was thinking about it the other day. Some people think it's best to shoot a dog. I haven't had any shells for that shot-gun for over a year. Poisoning is a hard death for a dog. Maybe drowning is the easiest and quickest way. Well, I'll speak to one of the mill hands and have him look after it."

Crouching on the ground, his arms around the old collie's neck, Luke cried out, "Uncle Henry, Dan's a wonderful dog! You don't know how wonderful he is!"

"He's just a very old dog, son," Uncle Henry said calmly. "The time comes when you have to get rid of any old dog. We've got to be practical about it. I'll get you a pup, son. A smart little dog that'll be worth its keep. A pup that will grow up with you."

"I don't want a pup!" Luke cried, turning his face away. Circling around him, the dog began to bark, then flick his long pink tongue at the back of Luke's neck.

Aunt Helen, catching her husband's eye, put her finger on her lips, warning him not to go on talking in front of the boy. "An old dog like that often wanders off into the brush and sort of picks a place to die when the time comes. Isn't that so, Henry?"

"Oh, sure," he agreed quickly. "In fact, when Dan didn't show up yesterday, I was sure that was what had happened." Then he yawned and seemed to forget about the dog.

But Luke was frightened, for he knew what his uncle was like. He knew that if his uncle had decided that the dog was useless and that it was sane and sensible to get rid of it, he would be ashamed of himself if he were diverted by any sentimental considerations. Luke knew in his heart that he couldn't move his uncle. All he could do, he thought, was keep the dog away from his uncle, keep him out of the house, feed him when Uncle Henry wasn't around.

Next day at noontime Luke saw his uncle walking from the mill toward the house with old Sam Carter, a mill hand. Sam Carter was a dull, stooped, slow-witted man of sixty with an iron-gray beard, who was wearing blue overalls and a blue shirt. Watching from the veranda, Luke noticed that his uncle suddenly gave Sam Carter a cigar, which Sam put in his pocket. Luke had never seen his uncle give Sam a cigar or pay much attention to him.

Then, after lunch, Uncle Henry said lazily that he would like Luke to take his bicycle and go into town and get him some cigars.

"I'll take Dan," Luke said.

"Better not, son," Uncle Henry said. "It'll take you all afternoon. I want those cigars. Get going, Luke."

His uncle's tone was so casual that Luke tried to believe they were not merely getting rid of him. Of course he had to do what he was told. He had never dared to refuse to obey an order from his uncle. But when he had taken his bicycle and had ridden down the path that followed the stream to the town road and had got about a quarter of a mile along the road, he found that all he could think of was his uncle handing old Sam Carter the cigar.

Slowing down, sick with worry now, he got off the bike and stood uncertainly on the sunlit road. Sam Carter was a gruff, aloof old man who would have no feeling for a dog. Then suddenly Luke could go no farther without getting some assurance that the collie would not be harmed while he was away. Across the fields he could see the house.

Leaving the bike in the ditch, he started to cross the field, intending to get close enough to the house so Dan could hear him if he whistled softly. He got about fifty yards away from the house and whistled and waited, but there was no sign of the dog, which might be asleep at the front of the house, he knew, or over at the sawmill. With the saws whining, the dog couldn't hear the soft whistle. For a few minutes Luke couldn't make up his mind what to do, then he decided to go back to the road, get on his bike, and go back the way he had come until he got to the place where the river path joined the road. There he could leave his bike, go up the path, then into the tall grass and get close to the front of the house and the sawmill without being seen.

He had followed the river path for about a hundred yards, and when he came to the place where the river began to bend sharply toward the house his heart fluttered and his legs felt paralysed, for he saw the old rowboat in the one place where the river was deep, and in the rowboat was Sam Carter with the collie.

The bearded man in the blue overalls was smoking his cigar; the dog, with a rope around its neck, sat contentedly beside him, its tongue going out in a friendly lick at the hand holding the rope. It was all like a crazy dream picture to Luke; all wrong because it looked so lazy and friendly, even the curling smoke from Sam Carter's cigar. But as Luke cried out, "Dan, Dan! Come on, boy!" and the dog jumped at the water, he saw that Sam Carter's left hand was hanging deep in the water, holding a foot of rope with a heavy stone at the end. As Luke cried out wildly, "Don't! Please don't!" Carter dropped the stone, for the cry came too late; it was blurred by the screech of the big saws at the mill.

But Carter was startled, and he stared stupidly at the river bank, then he ducked his head and began to row quickly to the bank.

But Luke was watching the collie take what looked like a long, shallow dive, except that the hind legs suddenly kicked up above the surface, then shot down, and while he watched, Luke sobbed and trembled, for it was as if the happy secret part of his life around the sawmill was being torn away from him. But even while he watched, he seemed to be following a plan without knowing it, for he was already fumbling in his pocket for his jack-knife, jerking the blade open, pulling off his pants, kicking his shoes off, while he muttered fiercely and prayed that Sam Carter would get out of sight.

It hardly took the mill hand a minute to reach the bank and go slinking furtively around the bend as if he felt that the boy was following him. But Luke hadn't taken his eyes off the exact spot in the water where Dan had disappeared. As soon as the mill hand was out of sight, Luke slid down the bank and took a leap at the water, the sun glistening on his slender body, his eyes wild with eagerness as he ran out to the deep place, then arched his back and dived, swimming under water, his open eyes getting used to the greenish-gray haze of the water, the sandy bottom, and the imbedded rocks.

His lungs began to ache, then he saw the shadow of the collie, floating at the end of the taut rope, rock-held in the sand. He slashed at the rope with his knife. He couldn't get much strength in his arm because of the resistance of the water. He grabbed the rope with his left hand, hacking with his knife. The collie suddenly drifted up slowly, like a water-soaked log. Then his own head shot above the surface, and, while he was sucking in the air, he was drawing in the rope, pulling the collie toward him and treading water. In a few strokes he was away from the deep place and his feet touched the bottom.

Hoisting the collie out of the water, he scrambled toward the bank, lurching and stumbling in fright because the collie felt like a dead weight.

He went on up the bank and across the path to the tall grass, where he fell flat, hugging the dog and trying to warm him with his own body. But the collie didn't stir, the good amber eye remained closed. Then suddenly Luke wanted to act like a resourceful, competent man. Getting up on his knees, he stretched the dog out on its belly, drew him between his knees, felt with trembling hands for the soft places on the flanks just above the hip-bones, and rocked back and forth, pressing with all his weight, then relaxing the pressure as he straightened up. He hoped that he was working the dog's lungs like a bellows. He had read that men who had been thought drowned had been saved in this way.

"Come on, Dan. Come on, old boy," he pleaded softly. As a little water came from the collie's mouth, Luke's heart jumped, and he muttered over and over, "You can't be dead, Dan! You can't, you can't! I won't let you die, Dan!" He rocked back and forth tirelessly, applying the pressure to the flanks. More water dribbled from the mouth. In the collie's body he felt a faint tremor. "Oh, gee, Dan, you're alive," he whispered. "Come on, boy. Keep it up."

With a cough the collie suddenly jerked his head back, the amber eye opened, and there they were looking at each other. Then the collie, thrusting his legs out stiffly, tried to hoist himself up, staggered, tried again, then stood there in a stupor. Then he shook himself like any other wet dog, turned his head, eyed Luke, and the red tongue came out in a weak flick at Luke's cheek.

"Lie down, Dan," Luke said. As the dog lay down beside him, Luke closed his eyes, buried his head in the wet fur, and wondered why all the muscles of his arms and legs began to jerk in a nervous reaction, now that it was all over. "Stay there, Dan," he said softly, and he went back to the path, got his clothes, and came back beside Dan and put them on. "I think we'd better get away from this spot, Dan," he said. "Keep down, boy. Come on." And he crawled on through the tall grass till they were about seventy-five yards from the place where he had undressed. There they lay down together.

In a little while he heard his aunt's voice calling, "Luke. Oh, Luke! Come here, Luke!"

"Quiet, Dan," Luke whispered. A few minutes passed, and then Uncle Henry called, "Luke, Luke!" and he began to come down the path. They could see him standing there, massive and imposing, his hands on his hips as he looked down the path, then he turned and went back to the house.

As he watched the sunlight shine on the back of his uncle's neck, the exultation Luke had felt at knowing the collie was safe beside him turned to bewildered despair, for he knew that even if he should be forgiven for saving the dog when he saw it drowning, the fact was that his uncle had been thwarted. His mind was made up to get rid of Dan, and in a few days' time, in another way, he would get rid of him, as he got rid of anything around the mill that he believed to be useless or a waste of money.

As he lay back and looked up at the hardly moving clouds, he began to grow frightened. He couldn't go back to the house, nor could he take the collie into the woods and hide him and feed him there unless he tied him up. If he didn't tie him up, Dan would wander back to the house.

"I guess there's just no place to go, Dan," he whispered sadly. "Even if we start off along the road, somebody is sure to see us."

But Dan was watching a butterfly that was circling crazily above them. Raising himself a little, Luke looked through the grass at the corner of the house, then he turned and looked the other way to the wide blue lake. With a sigh he lay down again, and for hours they lay there together, until there was no sound from the saws in the mill and the sun moved low in the western sky.

"Well, we can't stay here any longer, Dan," he said at last. "We'll just have to get as far away as we can. Keep down, old boy," and he began to crawl through the grass, going farther away from the house. When he could no longer be seen, he got up and began to trot across the field toward the gravel road leading to town.

On the road, the collie would turn from time to time as if wondering why Luke shuffled along, dragging his feet wearily, head down. "I'm stumped, that's all, Dan," Luke explained. "I can't seem to think of a place to take you."

When they were passing the Kemp place, they saw the old man sitting on the veranda, and Luke stopped. All he could think of was that Mr. Kemp had liked them both and it had been a pleasure to help him get the cows in the evening. Dan had always been with them. Staring at the figure of the old man on the veranda, he said in a worried tone, "I wish I could be sure of him, Dan. I wish he was a dumb, stupid man who wouldn't know or care whether you were worth anything . . . Well, come on." He opened the gate bravely, but he felt shy and unimportant.

"Hello, son. What's on your mind?" Mr. Kemp called from the veranda. He was a thin, wiry man in a tan-coloured shirt. He had a gray, untidy moustache, his skin was wrinkled and leathery, but his eyes were always friendly and amused.

"Could I speak to you, Mr. Kemp?" Luke asked when they were close to the veranda.

"Sure. Go ahead."

"It's about Dan. He's a great dog, but I guess you know that as well as I do. I was wondering if you could keep him here for me."

"Why should I keep Dan here, son?"

"Well, it's like this," Luke said, fumbling the words awkwardly: "My uncle won't let me keep him any more . . . says he's too old." His mouth began to tremble, then he blurted out the story.

"I see, I see," Mr. Kemp said slowly, and he got up and came over to the steps and sat down and began to stroke the collie's head. "Of course, Dan's an old dog, son," he said quietly. "And sooner or later you've got to get rid of an old dog. Your uncle knows that. Maybe it's true that Dan isn't worth his keep."

"He doesn't eat much, Mr. Kemp. Just one meal a day."

"I wouldn't want you to think your uncle was cruel and unfeeling, Luke," Mr. Kemp went on. "He's a fine man . . . maybe just a little bit too practical and straightforward."

"I guess that's right," Luke agreed, but he was really waiting and trusting the expression in the old man's eyes.

"Maybe you should make him a practical proposition."

"I—I don't know what you mean."

"Well, I sort of like the way you get the cows for me in the evenings," Mr. Kemp said, smiling to himself. "In fact, I don't think you need me to go along with you at all. Now, supposing I gave you seventy-five cents a week. Would you get the cows for me every night?"

"Sure I would, Mr. Kemp. I like doing it, anyway."

"All right, son. It's a deal. Now I'll tell you what to do. You go back to your uncle, and before he has a chance to open up on you, you say right out that you've come to him with a business proposition. Say it like a man, just like that. Offer to pay him the seventy-five cents a week for the dog's keep."

"But my uncle doesn't need seventy-five cents, Mr. Kemp," Luke said uneasily.

"Of course not," Mr. Kemp agreed. "It's the principle of the thing. Be confident. Remember that he's got nothing against the dog. Go to it, son. Let me know how you do," he added, with an amused smile. "If you know your uncle at all, I think it'll work."

"I'll try it, Mr. Kemp," Luke said. "Thanks very much." But he didn't have any confidence, for even though he knew that Mr. Kemp was a wise old man who would not deceive him, he couldn't believe that seventy-five cents a week would stop his uncle, who was an important man. "Come on, Dan," he called, and he went slowly and apprehensively back to the house.

When they were going up the path, his aunt cried from the open window, "Henry, Henry, in heaven's name, it's Luke with the dog!"

Ten paces from the veranda, Luke stopped and waited nervously for his uncle to come out. Uncle Henry came out in a rush, but when he saw the collie and Luke standing there, he stopped stiffly, turned pale, and his mouth hung open loosely.

"Luke," he whispered, "that dog had a stone around his neck."

"I fished him out of the stream," Luke said uneasily.

"Oh. Oh, I see," Uncle Henry said, and gradually the colour came back to his face. "You fished him out, eh?" he asked, still looking at the dog uneasily. "Well, you shouldn't have done that. I told Sam Carter to get rid of the dog, you know."

"Just a minute, Uncle Henry," Luke said, trying not to falter. He gained confidence as Aunt Helen came out and stood beside her husband, for her eyes seemed to be gentle, and he went on bravely, "I want to make you a practical proposition, Uncle Henry."

"A what?" Uncle Henry asked, still feeling insecure, and wishing the boy and the dog weren't confronting him.

"A practical proposition," Luke blurted out quickly. "I know Dan isn't worth his keep to you. I guess he isn't worth anything to anybody but me. So I'll pay you seventy-five cents a week for his keep."

"What's this?" Uncle Henry asked, looking bewildered. "Where would you get seventy-five cents a week, Luke?"

"I'm going to get the cows every night for Mr. Kemp."

"Oh, for heaven's sake, Henry," Aunt Helen pleaded, looking distressed, "let him keep the dog!" and she fled into the house.

"None of that kind of talk!" Uncle Henry called after her. "We've got to be sensible about this!" But he was shaken himself, and overwhelmed with a distress that destroyed all his confidence. As he sat down slowly in the rocking-chair and stroked the side of his big face, he wanted to say weakly, "All right, keep the dog," but he was ashamed of being so weak and sentimental. He stubbornly refused to yield to this emotion; he was trying desperately to turn his emotion into a bit of good, useful common sense, so he could justify his distress. So he rocked and pondered. At last he smiled, "You're a smart little shaver, Luke," he said slowly. "Imagine you working it out like this. I'm tempted to accept your proposition."

"Gee, thanks, Uncle Henry."

"I'm accepting it because I think you'll learn something out of this," he went on ponderously.

"Yes, Uncle Henry."

"You'll learn that useless luxuries cost the smartest of men hard-earned money."

"I don't mind."

"Well, it's a thing you'll have to learn some time. I think you'll learn, too, because you certainly seem to have a practical streak in you. It's a streak I like to see in a boy. O.K., son," he said, and he smiled with relief and went into the house.

Turning to Dan, Luke whispered softly, "Well, what do you know about that?"

As he sat down on the step with the collie beside him and listened to Uncle Henry talking to his wife, he began to glow with exultation. Then gradually his exultation began to change to a vast wonder that Mr. Kemp should have had such a perfect understanding of Uncle Henry. He began to dream of some day being as wise as old Mr. Kemp and knowing exactly how to handle people. It was possible, too, that he had already learned some of the things about his uncle that his father had wanted him to learn.

Putting his head down on the dog's neck, he vowed to himself fervently that he would always have some money on hand, no matter what became of him, so that he would be able to protect all that was truly valuable from the practical people in the world.

QUESTIONS

1. Suspense is a very important element in the escape story. How does Callaghan create and maintain suspense in this story?

2. Perrine states that escape and interpretation "are opposite ends of a scale," and not "two great bins, into one or the other of which we can toss any given story." The three stories in this section all fall at different places along this scale. Consider the selections carefully. Explain where you think each belongs, giving as many reasons as possible.

3. Conflict, or tension, occurs twice in this story. Find these two episodes and explain how they differ. Which episode is more important? Which one is the climax of the story?

4. If Dan had drowned, the story would have had a very different ending. Plan out a possible conclusion for this new version, choosing a new title as well. Do you think the story would then fit more readily under the heading "interpretive fiction"?

5. Do you find Luke a realistic character? Find evidence in the story to support your point of view. Luke is often afraid of his Uncle Henry. Has Callaghan portrayed childhood fear accurately?

6. Re-read the last paragraph of this story. What has Luke discovered about people? Why does he say "practical people" rather than "bad people"? What does this tell you about Luke? about Uncle Henry? Compare the lesson Luke learns about "practical people" to the knowledge Vanessa has gained at the end of "Horses of the Night."

2

Plot

PLOT is the sequence of incidents or events of which a story is composed. When recounted by itself, it bears about the same relationship to a story as a map does to a journey. Just as a map may be drawn on a finer or grosser scale, so a plot may be recounted with lesser or greater detail. It may include what a character says or thinks, as well as what he does. But it leaves out description and analysis, concentrating ordinarily on major happenings.

Because plot is the easiest element in fiction to comprehend and put into words, the beginning reader tends to equate it with the content of the work. When asked what a story is about, he will say that it is about a person to whom particular events happen, not that it is about a certain kind of person or that it presents a particular insight into life. The immature reader reads chiefly for plot; the mature reader reads for whatever revelations of character or life may be presented by means of plot. Because he reads chiefly for plot, the beginning reader may put a high valuation on intricacy of plot or on violent physical action. On the one hand, he may want schemes and intrigues, mixed identities, disguises, secret letters, hidden passages, and similar paraphernalia. On the other, he may demand fights by land and sea, dangerous missions, hazardous journeys, hairbreadth escapes. There is nothing improper in liking such things, of course, and sometimes the greatest fiction provides them. But if a reader can be satisfied *only* with stories having these elements, he is like a person who can enjoy only highly spiced food. Physical action by itself, after all, is meaningless. In a good story a minimum of physical action may be used to yield a maximum of insight. Every story must have some action, but for a worthwhile story it must be *significant* action. For a discerning reader there may be as much significant action in the way a man greets a friend as in how he handles a sword.

Conceivably a plot might consist merely of a sequence of related actions. Ordinarily, however, both the excitement craved by the beginning reader and the meaningfulness demanded by the mature reader arise out of some sort of CONFLICT—a clash of actions, ideas, desires, or wills. The main character may be pitted against some other person or groups of persons (*man-against-man*); he may be in conflict with some external force—physical nature, society, or "fate" (*man-against-environment*); or he may be in conflict with some element in his own nature (*man-against-himself*). The conflict may be physical, mental, emotional, or moral. There is conflict in a chess game, where the competitors sit quite still for hours, as surely as in a wrestling match; emotional conflict may be raging within a person sitting quietly in an empty room. The central character in the conflict, whether he be a sympathetic or an unsympathetic person, is referred to as the PROTAGONIST;[1] the forces arrayed against him, whether persons, things, conventions of society, or traits of his own character, are the ANTAGONISTS. In some stories the conflict is single, clear-cut, and easily identifiable. In others it is multiple, various, and subtle. A person may be in conflict with other persons, with society or nature, and with himself all at the same time, and sometimes he may be involved in conflict without being aware of it.

"Horses of the Night" illustrates many of these kinds of conflict. Chris is in conflict with his environment because of the dire poverty of his family and his consequent lack of opportunities. Further environmental conflict exists because of the depressed economic situation at that time. This, in part, is responsible for Chris's failure as a salesman. Personal conflicts are indicated both in Grandfather Connor's vocal reactions to the boy's plight, foreshadowing tension between them, and in the alienation and lack of communication between Chris and the adult members of his immediate family. Finally, there is intense internal conflict throughout the story as Chris is torn between the inner sensitivity of his soul and his failure to come to grips with the realities of his life: poverty and personal failure. Ultimately, his most agonizing inner conflict is expressed in the letter which he writes to Vanessa while serving in the army. Vanessa, in turn, reports to her mother: ". . . what it said was that they could force his body to march and even to kill, but what they didn't know was that he'd fooled them. He didn't live inside it anymore." Chris's antagonists, therefore, are environmental, human, and internal.

[1]The technical term *protagonist* is preferable to the popular term "hero" because it is less ambiguous. The protagonist is simply the central character, the one whose struggles we follow with interest, whether he or she be good or bad, sympathetic or repulsive. A "hero" or "heroine" may be *either* a person of heroic qualities *or* simply the main character, heroic or unheroic.

Excellent interpretive fiction has been made from all three of the major kinds of conflict. The varieties of commercial fiction on which the pulp magazines rely usually emphasize conflict between man and man and depend for their main excitement on physical conflict. It is hard to conceive of a Western story without a fist fight or a gun fight. Even in the crudest kinds of fiction, however, something more will be found than mere physical combat. Good men will be arrayed against bad men, and thus the conflict will also be between moral values. In cheap fiction this conflict is usually clearly defined in terms of white *vs.* black, hero *vs.* villain. In interpretive fiction the contrasts are likely to be less marked. Good may be opposed to good, or half-truth against half-truth. There may be difficulty in determining what *is* the good, and internal conflict tends therefore to be more frequent than physical conflict. In the world in which we live, significant moral issues are seldom sharply defined, judgments are difficult, and choices are complex rather than simple. The interpretive writer is aware of this complexity and is more concerned with catching its endless shadings of gray than with presenting glaring contrasts of black and white.

SUSPENSE is that quality in a story which makes the reader ask, "What is going to happen next?" or "How will this turn out?" and impels him to read on to find the answers to these questions. Suspense is greatest when the reader's curiosity is combined with anxiety about the fate of some sympathetic character. Thus in the old serial movies— often appropriately called "cliffhangers"—a strong element of suspense was created at the end of each episode by leaving the hero hanging from the edge of a cliff or the heroine tied to the railroad tracks with the express train rapidly approaching. In murder mysteries— often called "who-dun-its"—suspense is created by the question of who committed the murder. In love stories it is created by the question, "Will the boy win the girl?" or "Will the lovers be re-united, and how?" In more sophisticated forms of fiction the suspense often involves not so much the question *what* as the question *why*—not "What will happen next?" but "How is the protagonist's behavior to be explained in terms of human personality and character?" The forms of suspense range from crude to subtle and may concern not only actions but psychological considerations and moral issues. Two common devices for achieving suspense are to introduce an element of MYSTERY—an unusual set of circumstances for which the reader craves an explanation, or to place the hero or heroine in a DILEMMA—a position in which he must choose between two courses of action, both undesirable. But suspense can be readily created for most readers by placing *anybody* on a seventeenth-story window ledge, or simply by bringing together a physically attractive young woman and a man.

In some stories, however, the build-up of suspense is more subtle.

This is evident in "Horses of the Night" which emphasizes character rather than plot. The reader sees Chris primarily through Vanessa's eyes, yet also through the eyes of Vanessa's parents and grandparents. As the reader begins to suspect that Chris is living in a fantasy world, a delicate suspense begins to build. Will Chris tell Vanessa the truth about his home, the lake, the horses? Will Grandfather Connor finance Chris's university education or will the boy be forced to forsake his dreams? Will Vanessa's admiration for Chris be diminished after she learns the truth about his illusions? Will Chris be killed while serving in the army or will he return a changed man? Only at the end of the story are all these questions answered.

Suspense is usually the first quality mentioned by a young reader when asked what makes a good story—and, indeed, unless a story makes us eager to keep on reading it, it can have little merit at all. Nevertheless, the importance of suspense is often over-rated. After all, we don't listen to a Beethoven symphony to discover how it will turn out. A good story, like a good dinner, should furnish its pleasure as it goes, because it is amusing or well-written or morally penetrating or because the characters are interesting to live with. One test of a story is whether it creates a desire to read it again. Like the Beethoven symphony, a good story should be as good or better on a second or third encounter—when we already know what is going to happen—as on the first. The discriminating reader, therefore, while he does not disvalue suspense, may be suspicious of stories in which suspense is artificially created—by the simple withholding of vital information, for instance—or in which suspense is all there is. He will ask whether the author's purpose has been merely to keep him guessing what will happen next or whether it has been to reveal something about experience. He will be less interested in whether the man on the seventeenth-story window ledge will jump than in the reasons that impel him to jump. When a reader's primary interest is shifted from "What happens next?" to "*Why* do things happen as they do?" or "What is the significance of this series of events?" he has taken his most important step forward.

Closely connected with the element of suspense in a short story is the element of SURPRISE. If we know ahead of time exactly what is going to happen in a story, and why, there can be no suspense; as long as we don't know, whatever happens comes with an element of surprise. The surprise is proportional to the unexpectedness of what happens; it becomes pronounced when the story departs radically from our expectation. In the short story such radical departure is most often found in a surprise ending: one which reveals a sudden new turn or twist.

As with physical action and suspense, the inexperienced reader makes a heavier demand for surprise than does the experienced reader. The escape story more frequently supplies a surprise ending than does the interpretive. There are two ways by which the legitimacy and value of a surprise ending may be judged: (1) by the fairness with which it is achieved; (2) by the purpose which it serves. If the surprise is brought about as the result of an improbable coincidence or an unlikely series of small coincidences, or by the planting of false clues—details whose only purpose is to mislead the reader, or through the withholding of information which the reader ought to have been given earlier in the story, or by manipulation of the point of view (see Chapter 5), then we may well dismiss it as a cheap trick. If, on the other hand, the ending which comes at first as a surprise seems perfectly logical and natural as we look back over the story, we may grant it as fairly achieved. Again, a surprise ending may be judged as trivial if it exists simply for its own sake—to shock or to titillate the reader. We may judge it as a fraud if it serves, as it does in much routine commercial fiction, to conceal earlier weaknesses in the story by giving the reader a shiny bauble at the end to absorb and concentrate his attention. Its justification comes when it serves to open up or to reinforce the meaning of the story. The worthwhile surprise is one which furnishes illumination, not just a reversal of expectation.

Whether or not a story has a surprise ending, the beginning reader usually demands that it have a HAPPY ENDING: the protagonist must solve his problems, defeat the villain, win the girl, "live happily ever after." A common obstacle confronting the reader who is making his first attempts to enjoy interpretive stories is that they often—though by no means always—end unhappily. He is likely to label such stories as "depressing" and to complain that "real life has troubles enough of its own" or, conversely, that "real life is seldom as unhappy as all that."

Two justifications may be made for the UNHAPPY ENDING. First, many situations in real life have unhappy endings; therefore, if fiction is to illuminate life, it must present defeat as well as triumph. The commercial sports-story writer usually writes of how an individual or a team achieves victory against odds. Yet if one team wins the pennant, nine others must lose it, and if a golfer wins a tournament, fifty or a hundred others must fail to win it. In situations like these, at least, success is much less frequent than failure. Sometimes the sports writer, for a variant, will tell how an individual lost the game but learned some important moral lesson—good sportsmanship, perhaps, or the importance of fair play. But here again, in real life, such compensations are only occasionally gained. Defeat, in fact, sometimes embitters a person and makes him less able to cope with life than before. Thus we need to understand and perhaps expect defeat as well as victory.

Secondly, the unhappy ending has a peculiar value for the writer who wishes us to ponder life. The story with a happy ending has been "wrapped up" for us: the reader is sent away feeling pleasantly if vaguely satisfied with the world, and ceases to think about the story searchingly. The unhappy ending, on the other hand, may cause him to brood over the results, to go over the story in his mind, and thus by searching out its implications to get more from it. Just as we can judge men better when we see how they behave in trouble, so we can see deeper into life when it is pried open for inspection. The unhappy endings are more likely to raise significant issues. Shakespeare's tragedies reverberate longer and more resonantly than his comedies.

The discriminating reader evaluates an ending, not by whether it is happy or unhappy, but by whether it is logical in terms of what precedes it[2] and by the fullness of revelation it affords. He has learned that an ending which meets these tests can be profoundly satisfying, whether happy or unhappy. He has learned also that a story, to be artistically satisfying, need have no ending at all in the sense that its central conflict is resolved in favor of protagonist or antagonist. In real life some problems are never solved and some contests never permanently won. A story, therefore, may have an INDETERMINATE ENDING, one in which no definitive conclusion is arrived at. Conclusion of some kind there must of course be: the story, if it is to be an artistic unit, cannot simply stop. But the conclusion need not be in terms of a resolved conflict. We never learn in Faulkner's "That Evening Sun" (page 269) the outcome of the conflict between Nancy and Jesus. But the story is more effective without a resolution, for this individual conflict merely symptomizes a larger social conflict that has no easy solution.

ARTISTIC UNITY is essential to a good plot. There must be nothing in the story which is irrelevant, which does not contribute to the total meaning, nothing which is there only for its own sake or its own excitement. A good writer exercises a rigorous selection: he includes nothing that does not advance the central intention of the story. But he must not only select; he must also arrange. The incidents and episodes should be placed in the most effective order, which is not necessarily the chronological order, and, when rearranged in chronological order, should make a logical progression. In a highly unified story each event grows out of the preceding one in time and leads logically to the next. The various stages of the story are linked together in a chain of cause-and-effect. With such a story one seldom feels that events might as easily have taken one turn as another. One does not feel that the author is managing the plot, but rather that the plot has a quality of inevitability, given a certain set of characters and an initial situation.

---

[2]The movies frequently make a book with an unhappy ending into a film with a happy ending. Such an operation, if the book was artistically successful, sets aside the laws of logic and the expectations we naturally build on them.

When an author gives his story a turn unjustified by the situation or the characters involved, he is guilty of PLOT MANIPULATION. Any unmotivated action furnishes an instance of plot manipulation. We suspect the author of plot manipulation also if he relies too heavily upon chance or upon coincidence to bring about a solution to his story.[3]

Chance cannot be barred from fiction, of course, any more than it can be barred from life. But if an author uses an improbable chance to effect a resolution to his story, the story loses its sense of conviction and inevitability. The objections to such a use of coincidence[4] are even more forcible, for coincidence is chance compounded. Coincidence may be justifiably used to initiate a story, and occasionally to complicate it, but not to resolve it. It is objectionable in proportion to its improbability, its importance to the story, and its nearness to the end. If two characters in a story both start talking of the same topic at once, it may be a coincidence but hardly an objectionable one. If they both decide suddenly to kill their mothers at the same time, we may find the coincidence less acceptable. But the use of even a highly improbable coincidence may be perfectly appropriate at the start of a story. Just as a chemist may wonder what will happen if certain chemical elements are placed together in a test tube, an author may wonder what will happen if two former lovers accidently meet long after they have married and in Majorca where they longed as young lovers to go. The improbable initial situation is justified because it offers a chance to observe human nature in conditions that may be particularly revealing, and the good reader demands only that the author develop his story logically from that initial situation. But if the writer uses a similar coincidence to resolve his story, then we feel that he has been avoiding the logic of life rather than revealing it. It is often said that fact is stranger than fiction: it *should* be stranger than fiction. In life almost any concatenation of events is possible; in a story the sequence of events should be probable.

There are various approaches to the analysis of plot. We may, if we wish, draw diagrams of different kinds of plots or trace the development

[3]This kind of coincidental resolution is sometimes referred to as DEUS EX MACHINA ("god from the machine") after the practice of some ancient Greek dramatists in having a god descend from heaven (in the theater by means of a stage-machine) to rescue their protagonist at the last minute from some impossible situation.

[4]CHANCE is the occurrence of an event which has no apparent cause in antecedent events or in predisposition of character. In an automobile accident in which a drunk, coming home from a party, crashes into a sober driver from behind, we say that the accident was a chance event in the life of the sober driver but that it was a logical consequence in the life of the drunk. COINCIDENCE is the chance concurrence of *two* events which have a peculiar correspondence. If the two drivers involved in the above accident had been brothers, and were coming from different places, it would be coincidence.

of rising action, climax, and falling action. Such procedures, however, if they are concerned with the examination of plot *per se*, are not likely to take us far into the story. Better questions will concern themselves with the *function* of plot—with the relationship of each incident to the total meaning of the story. Plot is important, in interpretive fiction, for what it reveals. The analysis of a story through its central conflict is likely to be especially fruitful, for it rapidly takes us to what is truly at issue in the story. In testing a story for quality, it is useful to examine how the incidents and episodes are connected, for such an examination is a test of the story's probability and unity. We can never get very far, however, by analysis of plot alone. In any good story plot is inextricable from character and total meaning. Plot by itself gives little more indication of the total story than a map gives of the quality of a journey.

Graham Greene

THE DESTRUCTORS

I

It was on the eve of August Bank Holiday that the latest recruit became the leader of the Wormsley Common Gang. No one was surprised except Mike, but Mike at the age of nine was surprised by everything. "If you don't shut your mouth," somebody once said to him, "you'll get a frog down it." After that Mike had kept his teeth tightly clamped except when the surprise was too great.

The new recruit had been with the gang since the beginning of the summer holidays, and there were possibilities about his brooding silence that all recognised. He never wasted a word even to tell his name until that was required of him by the rules. When he said "Trevor" it was a statement of fact, not as it would have been with the others a statement of shame or defiance.. Nor did anyone laugh except Mike, who finding himself without support and meeting the dark gaze of the newcomer opened his mouth and was quiet again. There was every reason why T., as he was afterwards referred to, should have been an object of mockery—there was his name (and they substituted the initial because otherwise they had no excuse not to laugh at it), the fact that his father, a former architect and present clerk, had "come down in the world" and that his mother considered herself better than the neighbours. What but an odd quality of danger, of the unpredictable,

THE DESTRUCTORS "The Destructors" by Graham Greene from *Collected Stories*, published by The Bodley Head and William Heinemann. Reprinted by permission of Laurence Pollinger Limited.

established him in the gang without any ignoble ceremony of initiation?

The gang met every morning in an impromptu car-park, the site of the last bomb of the first blitz. The leader, who was known as Blackie, claimed to have heard it fall, and no one was precise enough in his dates to point out that he would have been one year old and fast asleep on the down platform of Wormsley Common Underground Station. On one side of the car-park leant the first occupied house, No. 3, of the shattered Northwood Terrace—literally leant, for it had suffered from the blast of the bomb and the side walls were supported on wooden struts. A smaller bomb and some incendiaries had fallen beyond, so that the house stuck up like a jagged tooth and carried on the further wall relics of its neighbour, a dado, the remains of a fireplace. T., whose words were almost confined to voting "Yes" or "No" to the plan of operations proposed each day by Blackie, once startled the whole gang by saying broodingly, "Wren built that house, father says."

"Who's Wren?"

"The man who built St. Paul's."

"Who cares?" Blackie said. "It's only Old Misery's."

Old Misery—whose real name was Thomas—had once been a builder and decorator. He lived alone in the crippled house, doing for himself: once a week you could see him coming back across the common with bread and vegetables, and once as the boys played in the car-park he put his head over the smashed wall of his garden and looked at them.

"Been to the loo," one of the boys said, for it was common knowledge that since the bombs fell something had gone wrong with the pipes of the house and Old Misery was too mean to spend money on the property. He could do the redecorating himself at cost price, but he had never learnt plumbing. The loo was a wooden shed at the bottom of the narrow garden with a star-shaped hole in the door: it had escaped the blast which had smashed the house next door and sucked out the window-frames of No. 3.

The next time the gang became aware of Mr. Thomas was more surprising. Blackie, Mike and a thin yellow boy, who for some reason was called by his surname Summers, met him on the common coming back from the market. Mr. Thomas stopped them. He said glumly, "You belong to the lot that play in the car-park?"

Mike was about to answer when Blackie stopped him. As the leader he had responsibilities. "Suppose we are?" he said ambiguously.

"I got some chocolates," Mr. Thomas said. "Don't like 'em myself. Here you are. Not enough to go round, I don't suppose. There never is," he added with sombre conviction. He handed over three packets of Smarties.

The gang were puzzled and perturbed by this action and tried to explain it away. "Bet someone dropped them and he picked 'em up," somebody suggested.

"Pinched 'em and then got in a bleeding funk," another thought aloud.

"It's a bribe," Summers said. "He wants us to stop bouncing balls on his wall."

"We'll show him we don't take bribes," Blackie said, and they sacrificed the whole morning to the game of bouncing that only Mike was young enough to enjoy. There was no sign from Mr. Thomas.

Next day T. astonished them all. He was late at the rendezvous, and the voting for that day's exploit took place without him. At Blackie's suggestion the gang was to disperse in pairs, take buses at random and see how many free rides could be snatched from unwary conductors (the operation was to be carried out in pairs to avoid cheating). They were drawing lots for their companions when T. arrived.

"Where you been, T.?" Blackie asked. "You can't vote now. You know the rules."

"I've been *there*," T. said. He looked at the ground, as though he had thoughts to hide.

"Where?"

"At Old Misery's." Mike's mouth opened and then hurriedly closed again with a click. He had remembered the frog.

"At Old Misery's?" Blackie said. There was nothing in the rules against it, but he had a sensation that T. was treading on dangerous ground. He asked hopefully, "Did you break in?"

"No. I rang the bell."

"And what did you say?"

"I said I wanted to see his house."

"What did he do?"

"He showed it me."

"Pinch anything?"

"No."

"What did you do it for then?"

The gang had gathered round: it was as though an impromptu court were about to form and to try some case of deviation. T. said, "It's a beautiful house," and still watching the ground, meeting no one's eyes, he licked his lips first one way, then the other.

"What do you mean, a beautiful house?" Blackie asked with scorn.

"It's got a staircase two hundred years old like a corkscrew. Nothing holds it up."

"What do you mean, nothing holds it up. Does it float?"

"It's to do with opposite forces, Old Misery said."

"What else?"

"There's panelling."

"Like in the Blue Boar?"

"Two hundred years old."

"Is Old Misery two hundred years old?"

Mike laughed suddenly and then was quiet again. The meeting was in a serious mood. For the first time since T. had strolled into the car-park on the first day of the holidays his position was in danger. It only needed a single use of his real name and the gang would be at his heels.

"What did you do it for?" Blackie asked. He was just, he had no jealousy, he was anxious to retain T. in the gang if he could. It was the word "beautiful" that worried him—that belonged to a class world that you could still see parodied at the Wormsley Common Empire by a man wearing a top hat and a monocle, with a haw-haw accent. He was tempted to say, "My dear Trevor, old chap," and unleash his hell hounds. "If you'd broken in," he said sadly—that indeed would have been an exploit worthy of the gang.

"This was better," T. said. "I found out things." He continued to stare at his feet, not meeting anybody's eye, as though he were absorbed in some dream he was unwilling—or ashamed—to share.

"What things?"

"Old Misery's going to be away all tomorrow and Bank Holiday."

Blackie said with relief, "You mean we could break in?"

"And pinch things?" somebody asked.

Blackie said, "Nobody's going to pinch things. Breaking in—that's good enough, isn't it? We don't want any court stuff."

"I don't want to pinch anything," T. said. "I've got a better idea."

"What is it?"

T. raised eyes, as grey and disturbed as the drab August day. "We'll pull it down," he said. "We'll destroy it."

Blackie gave a single hoot of laughter and then, like Mike, fell quiet, daunted by the serious implacable gaze. "What'd the police be doing all the time?" he said.

"They'd never know. We'd do it from inside. I've found a way in." He said with a sort of intensity, "We'd be like worms, don't you see, in an apple. When we came out again there'd be nothing there, no staircase, no panels, nothing but just walls, and then we'd make the walls fall down—somehow."

"We'd go to jug," Blackie said.

"Who's to prove? and anyway we wouldn't have pinched anything." He added without the smallest flicker of glee, "There wouldn't be anything to pinch after we'd finished."

"I've never heard of going to prison for breaking things," Summers said.

"There wouldn't be time," Blackie said. "I've seen housebreakers at work."

"There are twelve of us," T. said. "We'd organise."

"None of us know how . . ."

"I know," T. said. He looked across at Blackie, "Have you got a better plan?"

"Today," Mike said tactlessly, "we're pinching free rides . . ."

"Free rides," T. said. "You can stand down, Blackie, if you'd rather. . . ."

"The gang's got to vote."

"Put it up then."

Blackie said uneasily, "It's proposed that tomorrow and Monday we destroy Old Misery's house."

"Here, here," said a fat boy called Joe.

"Who's in favour?"

T. said, "It's carried."

"How do we start?" Summers asked.

"He'll tell you," Blackie said. It was the end of his leadership. He went away to the back of the car-park and began to kick a stone, dribbling it this way and that. There was only one old Morris in the park, for few cars were left there except lorries: without an attendant there was no safety. He took a flying kick at the car and scraped a little paint off the rear mudguard. Beyond, paying no more attention to him than to a stranger, the gang had gathered round T.; Blackie was dimly aware of the fickleness of favour. He thought of going home, of never returning, of letting them all discover the hollowness of T.'s leadership, but suppose after all what T. proposed was possible—nothing like it had ever been done before. The fame of the Wormsley Common car-park gang would surely reach around London. There would be headlines in the papers. Even the grown-up gangs who ran the betting at the all-in wrestling and the barrow-boys would hear with respect of how Old Misery's house had been destroyed. Driven by the pure, simple and altruistic ambition of fame for the gang, Blackie came back to where T. stood in the shadow of Misery's wall.

T. was giving his orders with decision: it was as though this plan had been with him all his life, pondered through the seasons, now in his fifteenth year crystallised with the pain of puberty. "You," he said to Mike, "bring some big nails, the biggest you can find, and a hammer. Anyone else who can better bring a hammer and a screwdriver. We'll need plenty of them. Chisels too. We can't have too many chisels. Can anybody bring a saw?"

"I can," Mike said.

"Not a child's saw," T. said. "A real saw."

Blackie realised he had raised his hand like any ordinary member of the gang.

"Right, you bring one, Blackie. But now there's a difficulty. We want a hacksaw."

"What's a hacksaw?" someone asked.

"You can get 'em at Woolworth's," Summers said.

The fat boy called Joe said gloomily, "I knew it would end in a collection."

"I'll get one myself," T. said. "I don't want your money. But I can't buy a sledge-hammer."

Blackie said, "They are working on No. 15. I know where they'll leave their stuff for Bank Holiday."

"Then that's all," T. said. "We meet here at nine sharp."

"I've got to go to church," Mike said.

"Come over the wall and whistle. We'll let you in."

2

On Sunday morning all were punctual except Blackie, even Mike. Mike had had a stroke of luck. His mother felt ill, his father was tired after Saturday night, and he was told to go to church alone with many warnings of what would happen if he strayed. Blackie had had difficulty in smuggling out the saw, and then in finding the sledge-hammer at the back of No. 15. He approached the house from a lane at the rear of the garden, for fear of the policeman's beat along the main road. The tired evergreens kept off a stormy sun: another wet Bank Holiday was being prepared over the Atlantic, beginning in swirls of dust under the trees. Blackie climbed the wall into Misery's garden.

There was no sign of anybody anywhere. The loo stood like a tomb in a neglected graveyard. The curtains were drawn. The house slept. Blackie lumbered nearer with the saw and the sledge-hammer. Perhaps after all nobody had turned up: the plan had been a wild invention: they had woken wiser. But when he came close to the back door he could hear a confusion of sound, hardly louder than a hive in swarm: a clickety-clack, a bang bang bang, a scraping, a creaking, a sudden painful crack. He thought: it's true, and whistled.

They opened the back door to him and he came in. He had at once the impression of organisation, very different from the old happy-go-lucky ways under his leadership. For a while he wandered up and down stairs looking for T. Nobody addressed him: he had a sense of great urgency, and already he could begin to see the plan. The interior of the house was being carefully demolished without touching the outer walls. Summers with hammer and chisel was ripping out the skirting-boards in the ground floor dining-room: he had already smashed the panels of the door. In the same room Joe was heaving up the parquet blocks, exposing the soft wood floor-boards over the cellar. Coils of wire came out of the damaged skirting and Mike sat happily on the floor, clipping the wires.

On the curved stairs two of the gang were working hard with an inadequate child's saw on the banisters—when they saw Blackie's big saw they signalled for it wordlessly. When he next saw them a quarter of the banisters had been dropped into the hall. He found T. at last in the bathroom—he sat moodily in the least cared-for room in the house, listening to the sounds coming up from below.

"You've really done it," Blackie said with awe. "What's going to happen?"

"We've only just begun," T. said. He looked at the sledge-hammer and gave his instructions. "You stay here and break the bath and the wash-basin. Don't bother about the pipes. They come later."

Mike appeared at the door. "I've finished the wire, T.," he said.

"Good. You've just got to go wandering round now. The kitchen's in the basement. Smash all the china and glass and bottles you can lay hold of. Don't turn on the taps—we don't want a flood—yet. Then go into all the rooms and turn out drawers. If they are locked get one of the others to break them open. Tear up any papers you find and smash all the ornaments. Better take a carving-knife with you from the kitchen. The bedroom's opposite here. Open the pillows and tear up the sheets. That's enough for the moment. And you, Blackie, when you've finished in here crack the plaster in the passage up with your sledge-hammer."

"What are you going to do?" Blackie asked.

"I'm looking for something special," T. said.

It was nearly lunch-time before Blackie had finished and went in search of T. Chaos had advanced. The kitchen was a shambles of broken glass and china. The dining-room was stripped of parquet, the skirting was up, the door had been taken off its hinges, and the destroyers had moved up a floor. Streaks of light came in through the closed shutters where they worked with the seriousness of creators—and destruction after all is a form of creation. A kind of imagination had seen this house as it had now become.

Mike said, "I've got to go home for dinner."

"Who else?" T. asked, but all the others on one excuse or another had brought provisions with them.

They squatted in the ruins of the room and swapped unwanted sandwiches. Half an hour for lunch and they were at work again. By the time Mike returned, they were on the top floor, and by six the superficial damage was completed. The doors were all off, all the skirtings raised, the furniture pillaged and ripped and smashed—no one could have slept in the house except on a bed of broken plaster. T. gave his orders—eight o'clock next morning, and to escape notice they climbed singly over the garden wall, into the car-park. Only Blackie and T. were left: the light had nearly gone, and when they touched a switch; nothing worked—Mike had done his job thoroughly.

"Did you find anything special?" Blackie asked.

T. nodded. "Come over here," he said, "and look." Out of both pockets he drew bundles of pound notes. "Old Misery's savings," he said. "Mike ripped out the mattress, but he missed them."

"What are you going to do? Share them?"

"We aren't thieves," T. said. "Nobody's going to steal anything from this house. I kept these for you and me—a celebration." He knelt down on the floor and counted them out—there were seventy in all. "We'll burn them," he said, "one by one," and taking it in turns they held a note upwards and lit the top corner, so that the flame burnt slowly toward their fingers. The grey ash floated above them and fell on their heads like age. "I'd like to see Old Misery's face when we are through," T. said.

"You hate him a lot?" Blackie asked.

"Of course I don't hate him," T. said. "There'd be no fun if I hated him." The last burning note illuminated his brooding face. "All this hate and love," he said, "it's soft, it's hooey. There's only things, Blackie," and he looked round the room crowded with the unfamiliar shadows of half things, broken things, former things. "I'll race you home, Blackie," he said.

3

Next morning the serious destruction started. Two were missing—Mike and another boy whose parents were off to Southend and Brighton in spite of the slow warm drops that had begun to fall and the rumble of thunder in the estuary like the first guns of the old blitz. "We've got to hurry," T. said.

Summers was restive. "Haven't we done enough?" he said. "I've been given a bob for slot machines. This is like work."

"We've hardly started," T. said. "Why, there's all the floors left, and the stairs. We haven't taken out a single window. You voted like the others. We are going to *destroy* this house. There won't be anything left when we've finished."

They began again on the first floor picking up the top floor-boards next the outer wall, leaving the joists exposed. Then they sawed through the joists and retreated into the hall, as what was left of the floor heeled and sank. They had learnt with practise, and the second floor collapsed more easily. By the evening an odd exhilaration seized them as they looked down the great hollow of the house. They ran risks and made mistakes: when they thought of the windows it was too late to reach them. "Cor," Joe said, and dropped a penny down into the dry rubble-filled well. It cracked and span among the broken glass.

"Why did we start this?" Summers asked with astonishment; T. was already on the ground, digging at the rubble, clearing a space along the outer wall. "Turn on the taps," he said. "It's too dark for anyone to see now, and in the morning it won't matter." The water overtook them on the stairs and fell through the floorless rooms.

It was then they heard Mike's whistle at the back. "Something's wrong," Blackie said. They could hear his urgent breathing as they unlocked the door.

"The bogies?" Summers asked.

"Old Misery," Mike said. "He's on his way." He put his head between his knees and retched. "Ran all the way," he said with pride.

"But why?" T. said. "He told me . . ." He protested with the fury of the child he had never been, "It isn't fair."

"He was down at Southend," Mike said, "and he was on the train coming back. Said it was too cold and wet." He paused and gazed at the water. "My, you've had a storm here. Is the roof leaking?"

"How long will he be?"

"Five minutes. I gave Ma the slip and ran."

"We better clear," Summers said. "We've done enough, anyway."

"Oh no, we haven't. Anybody could do this—" "this" was the shattered hollowed house with nothing left but the walls. Yet walls could be preserved. Façades were valuable. They could build inside again more beautifully than before. This could again be a home. He said angrily, "We've got to finish. Don't move. Let me think."

"There's no time," a boy said.

"There's got to be a way," T. said. "We couldn't have got thus far . . ."

"We've done a lot," Blackie said.

"No. No, we haven't. Somebody watch the front."

"We can't do any more."

"He may come in at the back."

"Watch the back too." T. began to plead. "Just give me a minute and I'll fix it. I swear I'll fix it." But his authority had gone with his ambiguity. He was only one of the gang. "Please," he said.

"Please," Summers mimicked him, and then suddenly struck home with the fatal name. "Run along home, Trevor."

T. stood with his back to the rubble like a boxer knocked groggy against the ropes. He had no words as his dreams shook and slid. Then Blackie acted before the gang had time to laugh, pushing Summers backward. "I'll watch the front, T.," he said, and cautiously he opened the shutters of the hall. The grey wet common stretched ahead, and the lamps gleamed in the puddles. "Someone's coming, T. No, it's not him. What's your plan, T.?"

"Tell Mike to go out to the loo and hide close beside it. When he hears me whistle he's got to count ten and start to shout."

"Shout what?"

"Oh, 'Help', anything."

"You hear, Mike," Blackie said. He was the leader again. He took a quick look between the shutters. "He's coming, T."

"Quick, Mike. The loo. Stay here, Blackie, all of you till I yell."

"Where are you going, T.?"

"Don't worry. I'll see to this. I said I would, didn't I?"

Old Misery came limping off the common. He had mud on his shoes and he stopped to scrape them on the pavement's edge. He didn't want to soil his house, which stood jagged and dark between the bomb-sites, saved so narrowly, as he believed, from destruction. Even the fanlight had been left unbroken by the bomb's blast. Somewhere somebody whistled. Old Misery looked sharply round. He didn't trust whistles. A child was shouting: it seemed to come from his own garden. Then a boy ran into the road from the car-park. "Mr. Thomas," he called, "Mr. Thomas."

"What is it?"

"I'm terribly sorry, Mr. Thomas. One of us got taken short, and we thought you wouldn't mind, and now he can't get out."

"What do you mean, boy?"

"He's got stuck in your loo."

"He'd no business . . . Haven't I seen you before?"

"You showed me your house."

"So I did. So I did. That doesn't give you the right to . . ."

"Do hurry, Mr. Thomas. He'll suffocate."

"Nonsense. He can't suffocate. Wait till I put my bag in."

"I'll carry your bag."

"Oh no, you don't. I carry my own."

"This way, Mr. Thomas."

"I can't get in the garden that way. I've got to go through the house."

"But you *can* get in the garden this way, Mr. Thomas. We often do."

"You often do?" He followed the boy with a scandalised fascination. "When? What right? . . ."

"Do you see . . . ? the wall's low."

"I'm not going to climb walls into my own garden. It's absurd."

"This is how we do it. One foot here, one foot there, and over." The boy's face peered down, an arm shot out, and Mr. Thomas found his bag taken and deposited on the other side of the wall.

"Give me back my bag," Mr. Thomas said. From the loo a boy yelled and yelled. "I'll call the police."

"Your bag's all right, Mr. Thomas. Look. One foot there. On your right. Now just above. To your left." Mr. Thomas climbed over his own garden wall. "Here's your bag, Mr. Thomas."

"I'll have the wall built up," Mr. Thomas said, "I'll not have you boys coming over here, using my loo." He stumbled on the path, but the boy caught his elbow and supported him. "Thank you, thank you, my boy," he murmured automatically. Somebody shouted again through the dark. "I'm coming, I'm coming," Mr. Thomas called. He said to the boy beside him, "I'm not unreasonable. Been a boy myself. As long as things are done regular. I don't mind you playing round the place Saturday mornings. Sometimes I like company. Only it's got to be regular. One of you asks leave and I say Yes. Sometimes I'll say No. Won't feel like it. And you come in at the front door and out at the back. No garden walls."

"Do get him out, Mr. Thomas."

"He won't come to any harm in my loo," Mr. Thomas said, stumbling slowly down the garden. "Oh, my rheumatics," he said. "Always get 'em on Bank Holiday. I've got to go careful. There's loose stones here. Give me your hand. Do you know what my horoscope said yesterday? 'Abstain from any dealings in first half of week. Danger of serious crash.' That might be on this path," Mr. Thomas said. "They speak in parables and double meanings." He paused at the door of the loo. "What's the matter in there?" he called. There was no reply.

"Perhaps he's fainted," the boy said.

"Not in my loo. Here, you, come out," Mr. Thomas said, and giving a great jerk at the door he nearly fell on his back when it swung easily open. A hand first supported him and then pushed him hard. His head hit the opposite wall and he sat heavily down. His bag hit his feet. A hand whipped the key out of the lock and the door slammed. "Let me out," he called, and heard the key turn in the lock. "A serious crash," he thought, and felt dithery and confused and old.

A voice spoke to him softly through the star-shaped hole in the door. "Don't worry, Mr. Thomas," it said, "we won't hurt you, not if you stay quiet."

Mr. Thomas put his head between his hands and pondered. He had noticed that there was only one lorry in the car-park, and he felt certain that the driver would not come for it before the morning. Nobody could hear him from the road in front, and the lane at the back was seldom used. Anyone who passed there would be hurrying home and would not pause for what they would certainly take to be drunken cries. And if he did call "Help," who, on a lonely Bank Holiday evening, would have the courage to investigate? Mr. Thomas sat on the loo and pondered with the wisdom of age.

After a while it seemed to him that there were sounds in the silence—they were faint and came from the direction of his house. He stood up and peered through the ventilation-hole—between the cracks in one of the shutters he saw a light, not the light of a lamp, but the wavering light that a candle might give. Then he thought he heard the sound of hammering and scraping and chipping. He thought of burglars—perhaps they had employed the boy as a scout, but why should burglars engage in what sounded more and more like a stealthy form of carpentry? Mr. Thomas let out an experimental yell, but nobody answered. The noise could not even have reached his enemies.

4

Mike had gone home to bed, but the rest stayed. The question of leadership no longer concerned the gang. With nails, chisels, screw-drivers, anything that was sharp and penetrating they moved around the inner walls worrying at the mortar between the bricks. They started too high, and it was Blackie who hit on the damp course and realised the work could be halved if they weakened the joints immediately above. It was a long, tiring, unamusing job, but at last it was finished. The gutted house stood there balanced on a few inches of mortar between the damp course and the bricks.

There remained the most dangerous task of all, out in the open at the edge of the bomb-site. Summers was sent to watch the road for passers-by, and Mr. Thomas, sitting on the loo, heard clearly now the sound of sawing. It no longer came from his house, and that a little reassured him. He felt less concerned. Perhaps the other noises too had no significance.

A voice spoke to him through the hole. "Mr. Thomas."

"Let me out," Mr. Thomas said sternly.

"Here's a blanket," the voice said, and a long grey sausage was worked through the hole and fell in swathes over Mr. Thomas's head.

"There's nothing personal," the voice said. "We want you to be comfortable to-night."

"To-night," Mr. Thomas repeated incredulously.

"Catch," the voice said. "Penny buns—we've buttered them, and sausage-rolls. We don't want you to starve, Mr. Thomas."

Mr. Thomas pleaded desperately. "A joke's a joke, boy. Let me out and I won't say a thing. I've got rheumatics. I got to sleep comfortable."

"You wouldn't be comfortable, not in your house, you wouldn't. Not now."

"What do you mean, boy?" but the footsteps receded. There was only the silence of night: no sound of sawing. Mr. Thomas tried one more yell, but he was daunted and rebuked by the silence—a long way off an owl hooted and made away again on its muffled flight through the soundless world.

At seven next morning the driver came to fetch his lorry. He climbed into the seat and tried to start the engine. He was vaguely aware of a voice shouting, but it didn't concern him. At last the engine responded and he backed the lorry until it touched the great wooden shore that supported Mr. Thomas's house. That way he could drive right out and down the street without reversing. The lorry moved forward, was momentarily checked as though something were pulling it from behind, and then went on to the sound of a long rumbling crash. The driver was astonished to see bricks bouncing ahead of him, while stones hit the roof of his cab. He put on his brakes. When he climbed out the whole landscape had suddenly altered. There was no house beside the car-park, only a hill of rubble. He went round and examined the back of his car for damage, and found a rope tied there that was still twisted at the other end round part of a wooden strut.

The driver again became aware of somebody shouting. It came from the wooden erection which was the nearest thing to a house in that desolation of broken brick. The driver climbed the smashed wall and unlocked the door. Mr. Thomas came out of the loo. He was wearing a grey blanket to which flakes of pastry adhered. He gave a sobbing cry. "My house," he said. "Where's my house?"

"Search me," the driver said. His eye lit on the remains of a bath and what had once been a dresser and he began to laugh. There wasn't anything left anywhere.

"How dare you laugh," Mr. Thomas said. "It was my house. My house."

"I'm sorry," the driver said, making heroic efforts, but when he remembered the sudden check to his lorry, the crash of bricks falling, he became convulsed again. One moment the house had stood there with such dignity between the bomb-sites like a man in a top hat, and then, bang, crash, there wasn't anything left—not anything. He said, "I'm sorry. I can't help it, Mr. Thomas. There's nothing personal, but you got to admit it's funny."

QUESTIONS

1. Who is the protagonist in this story—Trevor, Blackie, or the gang? Who or what is the antagonist? Identify the conflicts of the story.
2. How is suspense created?
3. This story uses the most common basic formula of commercial fiction: protagonist aims at a goal, is confronted with various obstacles between himself and his goal, overcomes the obstacles and achieves his goal. Comment on the differences. Does this story have a happy ending?
4. Discuss the gang's motivations, taking into account (a) the age and beauty of the house, (b) Blackie's reasons for not going home after losing his position of leadership, (c) the seriousness with which the gang work at their task, and their loss of concern over their leadership, (d) the burning of the banknotes, (e) their consideration for Old Misery, (f) the lorry driver's reaction. What characteristics do the gang's two named exploits—pinching free rides, and destroying the house—have in common?
5. Of what significance, if any, is the setting of this story in blitzed London? Does the story have anything to say about the consequences of war? about the causes of war?

6. Explain as fully as you can the causes of the gang's delinquency, taking into account (a) their reaction to the name Trevor, (b) their reaction to Old Misery's gift of chocolates, (c) Blackie's reaction to the word "beautiful," (d) Trevor's comments on "hate and love," (e) Summers' reaction to the word "Please," (f) the setting.

7. What good qualities do the delinquents in this story have? Do they differ as a group from other delinquent gangs you have read or know about? If so, account for these differences.

8. On the surface this is a story of action, suspense, and adventure. At a deeper level it is about delinquency, war, and human nature. Try to sum up what the story says about human nature in general.

9. What point of view is story written in?

10.) Define irony. What is ironical about Old Misery's horoscope

11.) What are 2 reasons Trevor wants to destroy the house?

Hugh Garner

E EQUALS MC SQUARED

There were two guys standing at the inspection bench when I came back from the water fountain. A short Bulgarian we called Joe had an angle bracket with holes at each end. I picked it up, glanced at the layout on the greasy blueprint, and measured the diameters and positions of the holes with my scale. Most of the operators liked to bring their work to the counter, especially the first ones off the press, for it gave them a short break away from their machines.

"Is good?" Joe asked.

"Sure. You've got a tolerance a mile wide on this," I told him.

I filled out a "first off" tag and attached it to the inspected part.

In those days, just after the war, Malloy-Harrison was swamped with orders for self-propelled combines, and the plant was humming three shifts a day, six days a week. Every shift another trainload of the big red reaper-threshers came off the assembly lines and began their journey to West Germany, Ireland, Turkey, South Africa, and a dozen other countries you'd hardly even heard of. We had a good union and a closed shop, and you could make fifty bucks a week without overtime. Changing shifts every week was murder, though, and nobody really liked working for Malloy-Harrison, but the money was better than most places, and the whole world needed farm machinery.

Matt Colby, one of the gang-press operators, placed a long piece of T-stock on the metal counter top.

"Give me a first off on this, Eric," he said.

"What do you think of the heat, Matt?"

He shook his head wearily. "It's hotter'n the hubs a'hell in here," he answered. "I don't know how those guys on the forges can stand it."

"I hear two of them collapsed on the four-to-twelve shift," I told him. "The forge foreman can't get some of them to take the salt tablets."

Matt gave a cynical laugh. "I guess they think anything Malloy-Harrison gives for free has a catch in it," he said.

His length of T-stock was punched with a complicated series of holes, not counting the ones drilled in the machine-shop. The part would become a movable component of the combine when it was finished, and it was pretty tricky. There could be no guesswork on it—all the holes had to be scaled, and calipered too.

Matt was stripped to the waist, as most of the operators were during this July heatwave. Except for some oil streaks on his chest and back his skin was a dead white beneath the dim naked lights hung high in the vault-like chamber the punch press shared with the forges. He wore a faded tattoo on his upper arm: a small warship with the name H.M.C.S. *Burnaby* beneath it.

"This heat hasn't let up since last Thursday," he said as I inspected the piece. "One of my kids has got pneumonia, and this heat is hard on him. The heat's worse than cold when you've got pneumonia."

When I looked up I saw that his thoughts were a thousand miles from the farm implement plant. I felt sorry for all the guys whose marriages kept them stuck in a crummy job like this. Alex Bellamy, the chief inspector, used to say that our part of the factory had been built to change the swords of 1812 into ploughshares, and I think he was right. Most of the other departments were housed in modern buildings, but management seemed to think that this rickety old hole was good enough for unskilled forge and press operators.

The pressmen were looked down on by the machinists, moulders, pattern-makers—and even by the jerks on sub-assembly. In the cafeteria, a quarter of a mile from our little corner of hell, some of the smart-alecs greeted us by folding a couple of fingers into a fist, as if they'd been amputated. We didn't have to joke about such things; there were enough guys in our department minus fingers and hands to turn the joke sour.

Matt said, "Connolly, the guy that was working my press on the four-to-twelve, quit the job tonight. The time-study people have raised production on this part to three hundred and forty a shift, and he couldn't punch more than two-eighty-five. If I didn't have a family and a mortgage I'd quit this lousy job myself."

I didn't answer him but concentrated on the inspection. The tolerances were pretty fine, and McKillup, the punch-press foreman, was sure to check the piece himself.

"That stinking gang press slips too," Matt went on. "I shoulda told the superintendent when I come off shift yesterday mornin'. I told McKillup about it, but that rat-faced clown is too worried about his production figures. He told me I'm not workin' the foot-pedal right." I looked up, and his mouth had tightened nervously. "It's dangerous. I think that's the real reason Connolly quit."

I attached a tag to his piece of stock. "This piece is good, Matt," I said. "Take it easy, and don't worry about production—or McKillup either."

He picked up the piece from the counter, and I watched him as he threaded his way down the aisle towards the room across the alley where the three gang presses were housed.

It was nearly one-thirty before Larry Stepanich, the other inspector, came down the aisle, dodging a speeding forklift being driven by a young truck-jockey from final assembly. The echoing noise joined with the heat to frazzle your nerve ends—the clump-thud-swish of half a hundred presses, the fiery roar of the forges, and the bell-like clang of steel parts boxes as they were moved from beside the machines. From overhead the ancient shafts and belts moaned and rattled, and threatened to bring down the roof.

"All the presses running, Step?" I asked my partner as he came around the counter.

"The die-setters are working on eighteen, nineteen, and thirty-seven," he said. "Only one of the gang presses is operating."

"I know. I gave a first off to Matt Colby."

Step pulled a bottle of Coke from the lukewarm water in the washbowl, and knocked off its top against the steel edge of the inspection bench. He was wearing a once-white undershirt and army fatigue pants. A paperback book peeked from a pocket of his oily fatigues. He tilted his head back and drained the bottle at a gulp.

I picked up my gloves, and shoved my scale and calipers into the back pocket of my dungarees. As I reached for my clipboard, Step said, "Did you hear about McKillup?"

"No."

"You know about the new specifications for those lengths of one-eighth spring stock?"

I nodded, and pointed to the note clipped to my board.

"The drawing calls for a length of twelve and three-sixteenths, but engineering asked for a change in length during the day shift, and old Ernie is shearing them to eleven and three-sixteenths."

Ernie Colby was Matt's father, a union stewart who had operated a shearing press for thirty years.

"What happened?" I asked, smiling in anticipation.

"Everybody knew about the change in length but McKillup. You know how he'd like a chance to hurt old Ernie." Step began to laugh. "That dopey foreman. He didn't bother to check with me, but just picked up a handful of the shortened stock, and the blueprint, and stormed off to his office."

"Go on," I said.

"He called up the chief inspector first, but Alex hung up on him. Then McKillup, hotter'n a two-dollar pistol by now, called up the department superintendent."

"Old Walters himself? In the middle of the night!"

"Sure." We both laughed. "Walters chewed him out for not knowing that the specifications had been changed, and for waking him up at a quarter to one in the morning."

"I'd sure like to have seen his face."

"The timekeeper told me he just kept opening and shutting his mouth but nothing came out."

After we stopped laughing, Step pulled his book from his pocket and sat down on our only stool. Step was pretty bright. He had graduated from technical high, and was going to university in the fall to take an engineering course. I liked him, but his choice of reading material used to bug me.

"What's the name of the book?" I asked him.

He held it up. It was something called "Breakthroughs in Scientific Thought."

"You really like that kind of stuff, Step?"

"This is very good," he said, slapping the book against his knee. "Imagine a guy like Albert Einstein sitting down and just thinking that E equalled MC squared. It baffles the mind."

"It baffles mine how you can read stuff like that," I said as I headed around the counter.

"Watch out for McKillup, he's really on the warpath now," Step shouted after me.

I gave a fleeting thought or two to E equalling MC squared, but I forgot about it by the time I reached my first press. Bobby Earle pulled a bar strut from his machine and handed it to me.

"You tryin' out for the bowling team, Eric?" he asked.

"Sure thing. You?"

"May as well. Run-offs are on Thursday night," he said.

I distributed tags to all the machines but those that were being set up, marking the press and part numbers, and the time, on my inspection sheet. I finished in the big room before I looked at my watch. It was almost three o'clock.

"Hi, Eric!" shouted Pete Adams, one of the forge operators, from where he was standing at the drinking fountain.

I crossed the grime-slippery floor and watched him gargle a mouthful of water before spitting it into the floor drain. He was soaking wet, and the drops of sweat were quicksilver against his black skin as they gathered to run down his body in rivulets. He was wearing shoes and socks, and a pair of jockey shorts.

I told him about McKillup, but he disliked the foreman as much as the rest of us, and he didn't laugh.

He sluiced some water down his glistening chest. "The guy who said Negroes could stand the heat sure never worked a forge press this weather," he remarked.

"You taking your salt pills, Pete?" I asked him.

"Man, I'm eatin' them like popcorn," he answered laughing.

"I'll see you, Pete," I said as I hurried away from the terrible heat from the forges.

When I reached the yard between the big press room and the smaller one holding the gang presses, I paused in the unbelievable quiet and coolness and lit a cigarette. There was a breeze blowing across the railroad yards, and a switch engine was moving a string of flat-cars from a company siding. Each car carried three big red-painted combines, all wedged and strapped securely for their trip to a seaport or out west. Seeing the finished product, like this, was the only time that the punch-press department seemed to make any sense.

"Is that what you're being paid for?" a familiar voice snarled in my ear.

Without looking around I knew it was McKillup. I wiped the sweat from my throat with the backs of my cotton gloves. The foreman had no jurisdiction over the inspectors, even if he could make trouble by reporting you.

"I see you guys haven't put no hold tags on the parts coming from the gang press."

I turned to him then. "I gave Colby a first off at the beginning of the shift," I said. "I'm just on my way to the gang press now."

He leaned his mean unsweated face into mine and said, "Colby spoiled the last twenty pieces. You ever heard of torn and cracked walls in a punched hole?"

"Sure."

"Then take a look at this." He shoved a length of T-stock into my hands.

I carried it over to the lighted doorway of the shop and glanced down at it. It was a mess, the only good holes along its entire length being those drilled in the machine-shop. Those made by the gang press were uneven and oblique, their edges ringed with sunbursts of tiny cracks.

"You think they can countersink them holes?" McKillup asked.

I shook my head.

"Colby's lucky I didn't fire him on the spot," the foreman said.

There was something phony about his generosity towards Ernie Colby's son, and I thought I knew what it was.

"You having the bull-gang fix that press?" I asked him. "I know Colby reported to you that it was slipping."

"That's no business of the inspectors. If you and that bohunk partner of yours had checked the gang press as you're supposed to, Colby mightn't have spoiled so many pieces."

He was a real nice guy. I threw the long piece of T-stock back to him, and he had to grab it fast to keep it from dropping on his toes.

When I reached the gang-press room I couldn't see Colby's press, which was hidden from the doorway by the other giant machines. Except for a dim sound of hammering the room was unnaturally quiet. The big hydraulic presses stood silent, their terrible punch-toothed maws waiting for a foot on their treadles to make them close with a room-shaking bite. The mere sight of their size and power made me hate to enter the place, and I was always happy to leave the room again when my job was finished.

A long hoarse hoot of the factory whistle announced the lunch break, and I dropped my clipboard and gloves onto the table of the nearest machine and scooted up the passageway towards the cafeteria. This time I'd be lucky and beat the mob to the cafeteria queue.

I ate a lunch of meat pie, mashed and gravy with Larry Stepanich, Pete Adams, and another forge operator called Morgan. We all got quite a bang over the story about McKillup calling up Walters, the super. Step asked Pete Adams how his other job was coming, and Pete smiled and shrugged. Adams was a jazz pianist who hadn't got it made yet, and he played piano in a downtown restaurant at the dinner hour. He didn't swing his shifts, but worked a steady graveyard.

Morgan nodded his head in the direction of a table across the room. We looked over to where old Ernie Colby was eating his homemade sandwiches. He was with a couple of his cronies from the machine-shop.

"Those three old geezers have worked here since they invented the gang plough," Morgan said.

"Even before that," added Step.

"Man, what a horrible way to die!" Pete exclaimed, his black face splitting with a burst of laughter.

Both Pete and Step were working for Malloy-Harrison with an end in view. I guess I was too, but right then I didn't know what it was. The idea of working all my life at the plant, like Ernie Colby had done, scared me. The deadly sameness of the work, and conditions that even the union hadn't been able to change, made me despise people like Ernie. Running a shearing press for thirty years had made him an unthinking part of his machine.

I wondered why he had ever got his son a job in the place. In a few years Matt Colby would be just like his father, held to his press not by love or loyalty but by a lethargy that wouldn't let him quit. I realized I had to get away myself, before a steady pay envelope conned me out of whatever ambitions were in the back of my mind.

"Why didn't Matt come up here tonight?" Step asked.

I told him about meeting McKillup, and about the spoiled pieces from the gang press.

"I knew that machine was slipping. When are they going to fix it?"

"It's being fixed right now. I could hear the bull-gang hammering in there just as the lunch whistle blew."

The tables were clearing, and a noisy gang from sub-assembly were shoving and skylarking their way through the door, when the alarm bell began to ring. The three short rings showed it was an accident, and the two longs and a short which followed gave the location.

"It's the paint shop," Pete said. "One of those monkeys musta sprayed the foreman."

My laugh died on my lips as Morgan said, "It's the press room. The gang-press room."

The meat pie turned a flip in my stomach as I thought of the men of the bull-gang—any accident in the gang press was sure to be a bad one.

We all left our paper cups and sandwich papers and hurried out of the cafeteria.

There was a small crowd clustered in the gang-press doorway, and somebody mentioned that the doctor and the safety director had been called on the phone. I shouldered my way in and picked up my clipboard and gloves from where I'd thrown them when the lunch whistle went. There were whispered voices at the back end of the room, and I made my way between the presses and the wall.

The body was hanging out from the clenched lips of the press, its feet suspended in the air. It looked like a messy doll hanging over the edge of a shelf. The machine was clamped across it near the shoulders, leaving one limp and lifeless arm hanging down beside the body. Through the seeping blood that dripped inexorably to the floor I saw a tattooed ship on the hanging arm. Three or four men stood in a white-faced group apart from the machine, keeping their eyes on me so they wouldn't have to look at the other. I turned away sickened, and got out of the place fast.

Back at the inspection bench Step said, "It's a breach of company and union regulations for an operator to fix his own machine."

"I know it is."

"McKillup will deny that he ordered Colby to fix it himself. You can bet he's already filled out a breakdown report to the millwrights."

"Sure."

Step said, "When they told old Ernie that Matt was dead, he didn't say anything . . . or want to go see him . . . or anything. He just shut off his press, took off his apron, and walked to the time clocks. He seemed incapable of any feelings at all, as if the last thirty years had crushed them completely. You'd have thought . . . happening to his own son . . ." He picked up his clipboard and hurried from the inspection bench.

As Step had said he would, the foreman denied having ordered Matt Colby to make the repairs on the machine, and he had a time-stamped breakdown report to the millwrights to back up his lie. The verdict of the coroner's jury was accidental death, and all that happened was a rash of safety posters for a while. Matt's widow was given a compensation pension, and neither the union nor the company pressed for a further investigation.

The terrible accident to McKillup happened near the end of the summer, on the four-to-twelve shift. The usual absenteeism at that time of year, and some breakdown in the decrepit machinery, had put the department behind. The foreman was worried about his production figures, and he was all over the floor cursing and ranting at the operators. Sub-assembly was running short of parts, the most important being some quarter-inch strapping, a reaper cutter-bar we called the BF-204. The piece had to be sheared and punched before going to the forge to be extruded, and only old Ernie Colby's press was set up to do the job. The day-shift assembly had caught up, and even with a lift truck hurrying the parts to the forge we were falling behind.

Larry Stepanich, who was doing the floor inspection, told me that McKillup had ordered old Ernie to feed two pieces at a time into his machine.

The old man had stared at him for a minute. "It'll ruin the dies," he told the foreman. "She's on'y set up to take one piece at a punch."

"I know that, but we can't shut down the sub-assembly," McKillup said, anger and panic fighting for his voice.

The old man shrugged. "I ain't goin' to take the responsibility though," he said.

McKillup called Step over as a witness, and ordered the old man to feed the pieces two at a time. Ernie did as he was ordered, with only a shake of his head to show his disapproval.

Step said that the machine nearly tore itself from its bed, but it sheared the pieces all right. By seven-thirty we had caught up with the sub-assembly. Then the press jammed.

Ernie wasted several minutes fooling around with it, but finally found the foreman and got him to call the bull-gang. McKillup ranted and raged, for he found that the millwrights were busy in the machine-shop and it would be another hour before they could come down to fix the shearing press. When the lunch whistle blew, old Ernie followed the rest of us to the cafeteria, leaving the foreman staring angrily at the shut-down press.

We had only just begun our lunch when the alarm bell rang, so the only ones who got up were the first-aid men. By the time I got back to the punch-press department McKillup had been rushed to the hospital and the mess had all been cleared up. The die-setters were setting up two other machines to punch and shear the BF-204 parts. By half-past ten we had caught up once more with sub-assembly.

There was an investigation about McKillup's accident, and some talk about a missing cam from the gear box of the shearing press. Ernie Colby was questioned but he told the safety committee that he knew nothing about a cam, and that he'd reported the breakdown to the foreman as soon as he'd been able to find him. The board decided that McKillup had been negligent, and the walls broke out once more in a display of safety slogans.

On his final shift before he left the job to go to university, I asked Larry Stepanich, "What will McKillup do, now that he has no arms and gets no compensation?"

"The company will give him a watchman's job or something, I guess."

"It's funny how that cam came to be missing from the gear box. The head of the machine was sure to fall if anybody reached inside and moved the gears."

He nodded.

"Do you think the cam was taken out on purpose, Step?"

"The board didn't seem to think so. Anyhow, McKillup wasn't supposed to try to clear the machine himself."

"I guess nobody'll ever know how it happened."

Step gave me a long look. "It works for more things than relativity," he said. And, seeing my bewilderment, added, "Remember, Eric? The night Matt was killed, E equals MC squared?"

I didn't know what he was talking about. "What do those letters stand for anyway?"

"Well, in this case MC could stand for Matt Colby, if you wanted them to."

It was long after I too had left the plant that I found what the letters really stood for. Einstein's equation might mean one thing to science, but to me it will always mean Matt Colby's death, and the awful retribution to the foreman. It ties them both together neatly, squaring off one with the other, and pointing to the relative factor E, which could mean Ernie. I don't know whether I really believe that or not—it's a theory, that's all.

A short time ago I was driving past the main gate of the Malloy-Harrison plant, and I noticed McKillup tending the gates. One uniform sleeve was empty, and the other ended above one of those steel mechanical hands. The sight of him brought it all back to me, but I'd just as soon forget it if I could.

QUESTIONS

1. From your point of view, is it necessary that you be familiar with the factory and machinery in "E Equals MC Squared" in order to understand the story?

2. The phrase "our little corner of hell" sums up the attitude of the men towards the factory. Outline the complaints of the workers. List the reasons why the men continue to work at the factory.

3. Contrast the character of Eric, the inspector, and that of McKillup, the foreman. If Step were the narrator instead of Eric, how might Eric be depicted? Would the story be told differently if Step were the narrator?

4. The reader is aware in this story that something gruesome is going to happen. Find examples of foreshadowing.

5. Do you believe in the reality of this story? Why or why not? Point out devices and details by which the author has tried to keep this story factual. Would you agree that Garner has exercised a "rigorous selection" in his inclusion of these details?

6. "There was something phony about his (McKillup's) generosity towards Ernie Colby's son, and I thought I knew what it was." What did Eric think was the motive behind McKillup's apparent generosity?

7. Why does Ernie "seem incapable of any feelings at all" when he is told of his son's death? Do any of the narrator's comments throughout the story help you to understand Ernie's reaction? Will a comparison of Ernie and Eric give you an insight into this story?

8. Describe the conflict in "E Equals MC Squared." Is this conflict resolved? How would you apply the terms protagonist and antagonist in this particular story?

3

Character

In the last chapter plot was considered apart from character, as if the two were separable. Actually, like the ends of a seesaw, the two are one substance; there can be no movement at one end without movement at the other. The two ends of the seesaw may be talked about separately, however, and we can determine which element in any story is being emphasized—which end is up and which is down. As fiction passes from escape to interpretive, the character end is likely to go up. The good reader is less interested in actions done by characters than in characters doing actions.

Reading for character is more difficult than reading for plot, for character is much more complex, variable, and ambiguous. Anyone can repeat what a person has done in a story, but considerable skill may be needed to describe what a person *is*. Even the puzzles posed by the detective story are less complex and put less strain on comprehension than does human nature. Hence, escape fiction tends to emphasize plot and to present characters that are relatively simple and easy to understand. The limited reader demands that the characters be easily identifiable and clearly labeled as good or bad; they must not be so complex as to tax his understanding.

The limited reader also demands that the main character always be an attractive one. Though he need not be perfect, he must ordinarily be fundamentally decent—honest, good-hearted, and preferably good-looking. If he is not virtuous, he must have strong compensatory qualities—he must be daring, dashing, or gallant. He may defy law and order only if he has a tender heart, a great love, or a gentleman's code. The reader who makes these demands does so because for him the story is not a vehicle for understanding but material for a daydream. Identifying himself as he reads with the main character, he vicariously shares that character's adventures and escapes and triumphs. The main character must therefore return him a pleasing image of self. He must be someone such as the reader imagines himself to be or such as he would like to be. In this way the story subtly flatters the reader, who forgets his own inadequacies and satisfies his ego. If the hero has vices, they must be such as the reader himself would not mind or would enjoy having. Some escape fiction has been about the man or woman who is appealing but sexually casual. The reader has thus been able to indulge imaginatively in forbidden pleasures without losing a flattering self-image.

Interpretive fiction does not renounce the attractive central character. It simply furnishes a greater variety of central characters, characters that are less easily labeled and pigeonholed, characters that are sometimes unsympathetic. Human nature is not often either black or white, and interpretive fiction deals usually with characters that are neither.

Once we get past the need of a mechanical opposition between hero and villain we discover that fiction offers an unparalleled opportunity to observe human nature in all its complexity and multiplicity. It enables us to know people, to understand them, and to learn compassion for them, as we might not otherwise do. In some respects we can know fictional characters even better than we know real people. For one thing, we are enabled to observe them in situations that are always significant and which serve to bring forth their character as the ordinary situations of life only occasionally do. For another, we can view their inner life in a way that is impossible to us in ordinary life. An author can tell us, if he wishes, exactly what is going on in a character's mind and exactly what the character feels. In real life we can only guess at these inner thoughts and feelings from a person's external behavior, which may be designed to conceal what is going on inside. In limited ways, therefore, we can know people in fiction more thoroughly than we can know them in real life, and by knowing fictional characters we can also understand people in real life better than we otherwise could do.

An author may present his characters either directly or indirectly. In DIRECT PRESENTATION he tells us straight out, by exposition or analysis, what a character is like, or has someone else in the story tell us what he is like. In INDIRECT PRESENTATION the author *shows* us the character in action; we infer what he is like from what he thinks or says or does. Callaghan uses direct presentation when he describes Uncle Henry's thoughts about keeping the dog. "As he sat down slowly in the rocking-chair and stroked the side of his big face, he wanted to say weakly, 'All right, keep the dog,' but he was ashamed of being so weak and sentimental. He stubbornly refused to yield to this emotion; he was trying desperately to turn his emotion into a bit of good, useful common sense, so he could justify his distress." The author uses indirect presentation when he shows Uncle Henry talking to his wife and to Luke about getting rid of the dog. We realize what a practical man Uncle Henry is because of his own words.

The method of direct presentation has the advantages of being clear and economical, but it can never be used alone. The characters must act, if there is to be a story; when they do not act, the story approaches the condition of an essay. The direct method, moreover, unless supported by the indirect, will not be emotionally convincing. It will give us not a character but an explanation. The reader must be shown as well as told. He needs to see and hear and overhear. A story will be successful only when the characters are DRAMATIZED—shown speaking and acting, as in a drama. If we are really to believe in the selfishness of a character, we must see him acting selfishly. The successful writer must therefore rely mainly upon indirect presentation, and may use it entirely.

To be convincing, characterization must also observe three other principles. First, the characters must be CONSISTENT in their behavior: they must not behave one way on one occasion and a different way on another unless there is a clearly sufficient reason for the change. Second, the characters must be clearly MOTIVATED in whatever they do, especially when there is any change in their behavior: we must be able to understand the reasons for what they do, if not immediately, at least by the end of the story. Third, the characters must be PLAUSIBLE or lifelike. They must be neither paragons of virtue nor monsters of evil nor an impossible combination of contradictory traits. Whether we have observed anyone like them in our own experience or not, we must feel that they have come from the author's experience—that they could appear somewhere in the normal course of events.

In proportion to the fullness of their development, the characters in a story are relatively flat or round.[1] The FLAT CHARACTER is characterized by one or two traits; he can be summed up in a sentence. The ROUND CHARACTER is complex and many-sided; he might require an essay for full analysis. Both types of character may be given the vitality that good fiction demands. Round characters live by their very roundness, by the many points at which they touch life. Huck Finn, in all respects an individual, lives vigorously in the imagination of the reader, while scholars and critics debate his moral development. Flat characters, though they touch life at only one or two points, may be made memorable in the hands of an expert author through some individualizing detail of appearance, gesture, or speech. Ebenezer Scrooge, in Dickens' "Christmas Carol," can be summed up and fully

[1]These terms were originated by the novelist E.M. Forster, who discusses them in *Aspects of the Novel* (New York: Harcourt, Brace, & World, 1927), pp. 103-18.

expressed in the two words "miserly misanthropy," but his "Bah! Humbug!" makes him live vividly in every reader's memory.

The requirement of good fiction is that each character be fully enough characterized to justify his role in the story and make it convincing. Most short stories will hardly have room for more than one or two very fully developed characters. Minor characters must necessarily remain flat. If the primary intention of a story is something other than the exhibition of character, none of the characters need be fully developed. Inferior fiction, however, is often developed with characters who are insufficiently characterized to justify their roles. The essential nature and motivations of the protagonist may be so vaguely indicated that we are neither shocked nor convinced by any unusual action he performs or change of nature he undergoes. If a thief suddenly reforms and becomes an honest man, we must obviously know a great deal about him if the change is to be truly convincing. It is easier, however, for the writer to leave the characterization shadowy and hope that this weakness will slip by his readers unnoticed—as with uncritical readers it well may do.

A special kind of flat character is the STOCK CHARACTER—the stereotyped figure who has occurred so often in fiction that his nature is immediately known: the strong silent sheriff, the brilliant detective of eccentric habits, the mad scientist who performs fiendish experiments on living human beings, the beautiful international spy of mysterious background, the comic Englishman with a monocle and an exaggerated Oxford accent, the handsome brave hero, the beautiful modest heroine, the cruel stepmother, the sinister villain with waxed black mustaches. Such stock characters are found very often in inferior fiction because they require neither imagination nor observation on the part of the writer and are instantly recognizable to the reader. Like interchangeable parts, they might be transferred from one story to another with little loss of efficiency. The really good writer, however, may take a conventional type and by individualizing touches create a new and memorable figure. Conan Doyle's Sherlock Holmes is constructed on a pattern often imitated since, but he outlives the imitations and remains in our imaginations long after we have forgotten the details of his adventures. In proportion as an author gives his characters such individualizing touches, they become less flat and accordingly less stock.

All fictional characters may be classified as static or developing. The STATIC CHARACTER is the same sort of person at the end of the story as he was at the beginning. The DEVELOPING (or dynamic) CHARACTER undergoes a permanent change in some aspect of his character, personality, or outlook. The change may be a large or a small one; it may be for better or for worse; but it is something important and basic: it is more than a change in condition or a minor change in opinion. Cinderella is a static character, though she rises from cinder girl to princess. The boy Frederick in "Tears, Idle Tears" (page 101) is a dynamic character, for at the end he is cured of his fits of irrational crying. Paul in "Paul's Case" (page 170) is likewise dynamic, for his need to escape from everyday reality grows progressively worse.

Obviously, we must not expect many developing characters in *any* piece of fiction: in a short story there is not usually room for more than one. A not infrequent basic plan of short stories, however, is to show change in the protagonist as the result of a crucial situation in his life. When this is done in an interpretive story, the change is likely to be the surest clue to the story's meaning. To state and explain the change will be the best way to get at the point of the story. In escape fiction changes in character are likely to be more superficial, intended merely to ensure a happy ending. Such changes will necessarily be less believable. To be convincing, a change must meet three conditions: (1) it must be within the possibilities of the character who makes it; (2) it must be sufficiently motivated by the circumstances in which the character finds himself; and (3) it must be allowed sufficient time for a change of its magnitude believably to take place. Basic changes in human character seldom occur suddenly. The interpretive writer does not present bad men who suddenly reform at the end of the story and become good, or drunkards who jump on the wagon at a moment's notice. He is satisfied with smaller changes that are carefully prepared for.

Human life began, we are told, when God breathed life into a handful of dust and created Adam. Fictional life begins when an author breathes life into his characters and convinces us of their reality. Though fullness of characterization need not be his aim, soundness of characterization is a test by which he stands or falls. The reader of good fiction lives in a world where the initial act of creation is repeated again and again by the miracle of imagination.

James Joyce

A LITTLE CLOUD

Eight years before he had seen his friend off at the North Wall and wished him godspeed. Gallaher had got on. You could tell that at once by his travelled air, his well-cut tweed suit, and fearless accent. Few

A LITTLE CLOUD   From *Dubliners* by James Joyce. Copyright © 1967 by the Estate of James Joyce. Reprinted by permission of Viking Penguin Inc.

fellows had talents like his and fewer still could remain unspoiled by such success. Gallaher's heart was in the right place and he had deserved to win. It was something to have a friend like that.

Little Chandler's thoughts ever since lunch-time had been of his meeting with Gallaher, of Gallaher's invitation and of the great city London where Gallaher lived. He was called Little Chandler because, though he was but slightly under the average stature, he gave one the idea of being a little man. His hands were white and small, his frame was fragile, his voice was quiet and his manners were refined. He took the greatest care of his fair silken hair and moustache and used perfume discreetly on his handkerchief. The half-moons of his nails were perfect and when he smiled you caught a glimpse of a row of childish white teeth.

As he sat at his desk in the King's Inns he thought what changes those eight years had brought. The friend whom he had known under a shabby and necessitous guise had become a brilliant figure on the London Press. He turned often from his tiresome writing to gaze out of the office window. The glow of a late autumn sunset covered the grass plots and walks. It cast a shadow of kindly golden dust on the untidy nurses and decrepit old men who drowsed on the benches; it flickered upon all the moving figures—on the children who ran screaming along the gravel paths and on everyone who passed through the gardens. He watched the scene and thought of life; and (as always happened when he thought of life) he became sad. A gentle melancholy took possession of him. He felt how useless it was to struggle against fortune, this being the burden of wisdom which the ages had bequeathed to him.

He remembered the books of poetry upon his shelves at home. He had bought them in his bachelor days and many an evening, as he sat in the little room off the hall, he had been tempted to take one down from the bookshelf and read out something to his wife. But shyness had always held him back; and so the books had remained on their shelves. At times he repeated lines to himself and this consoled him.

When his hour had struck he stood up and took leave of his desk and of his fellow-clerks punctiliously. He emerged from under the feudal arch of the King's Inns, a neat modest figure, and walked swiftly down Henrietta Street. The golden sunset was waning and the air had grown sharp. A horde of grimy children populated the street. They stood or ran in the roadway or crawled up the steps before the gaping doors or squatted like mice upon the thresholds. Little Chandler gave them no thought. He picked his way deftly through all that minute vermin-like life and under the shadow of the gaunt spectral mansions in which the old nobility of Dublin had roystered. No memory of the past touched him, for his mind was full of a present joy.

He had never been in Corless's but he knew the value of the name. He knew that people went there after the theatre to eat oysters and drink liqueurs; and he had heard that the waiters there spoke French and German. Walking swiftly by at night he had seen cabs drawn up before the door and richly dressed ladies, escorted by cavaliers, alight and enter quickly. They wore noisy dresses and many wraps. Their faces were powdered and they caught up their dresses, when they touched earth, like alarmed Atalantas. He had always passed without turning his head to look. It was his habit to walk swiftly in the street even by day and whenever he found himself in the city late at night he hurried on his way apprehensively and excitedly. Sometimes, however, he courted the causes of his fear. He chose the darkest and narrowest streets and, as he walked boldly forward, the silence that was spread about his footsteps troubled him, the wandering, silent figures troubled him; and at times a sound of low fugitive laughter made him tremble like a leaf.

He turned to the right towards Capel Street. Ignatius Gallaher on the London Press! Who would have thought it possible eight years before? Still, now that he reviewed the past, Little Chandler could remember many signs of future greatness in his friend. People used to say that Ignatius Gallaher was wild. Of course, he did mix with a rakish set of fellows at that time, drank freely and borrowed money on all sides. In the end he had got mixed up in some shady affair, some money transaction: at least, that was one version of his flight. But nobody denied him talent. There was always a certain ... something in Ignatius Gallaher that impressed you in spite of yourself. Even when he was out at elbows and at his wits' end for money he kept up a bold face. Little Chandler remembered (and the remembrance brought a slight flush of pride to his cheek) one of Ignatius Gallaher's sayings when he was in a tight corner:

"Half time now, boys," he used to say light-heartedly. "Where's my considering cap?"

That was Ignatius Gallaher all out; and, damn it, you couldn't but admire him for it.

Little Chandler quickened his pace. For the first time in his life he felt himself superior to the people he passed. For the first time his soul revolted against the dull inelegance of Capel Street. There was no doubt about it: if you wanted to succeed you had to go away. You could do nothing in Dublin. As he crossed Grattan Bridge he looked down the river towards the lower quays and pitied the poor stunted houses. They seemed to him a band of tramps, huddled together along the river-banks, their old coats covered with dust and soot, stupefied by the panorama of sunset and waiting for the first chill of night to bid them arise, shake themselves and begone. He wondered whether he could write a poem to express his idea. Perhaps Gallaher might be able to get it into some London paper for him. Could he write something original? He was not sure what idea he wished to express but the thought that a poetic moment had touched him took life within him like an infant hope. He stepped onward bravely.

Every step brought him nearer to London, farther from his own sober inartistic life. A light began to tremble on the horizon of his mind. He was not so old—thirty-two. His temperament might be said to be just at the point of maturity. There were so many different moods and impressions that he wished to express in verse. He felt them within him. He tried to weigh his soul to see if it was a poet's soul. Melancholy was the dominant note of his temperament, he thought, but it was a melancholy tempered by recurrences of faith and resignation and simple joy. If he could give expression to it in a book of poems perhaps men would listen. He would never be popular: he saw that. He could not sway the crowd but he might appeal to a little circle of kindred minds. The English critics, perhaps, would recognise him as one of the Celtic school by reason of the melancholy tone of his poems; besides that, he would put in allusions. He began to invent sentences and phrases from the notice which his book would get. *"Mr. Chandler has the gift of easy and graceful verse."* . . . *"A wistful sadness pervades these poems."* . . . *"The Celtic note."* It was a pity his name was not more Irish-looking. Perhaps it would be better to insert his mother's name before the surname: Thomas Malone Chandler, or better still: T. Malone Chandler. He would speak to Gallaher about it.

He pursued his revery so ardently that he passed his street and had to turn back. As he came near Corless's his former agitation began to overmaster him and he halted before the door in indecision. Finally he opened the door and entered.

The light and noise of the bar held him at the doorways for a few moments. He looked about him, but his sight was confused by the shining of many red and green wine-glasses. The bar seemed to him to be full of people and he felt that the people were observing him curiously. He glanced quickly to right and left (frowning slightly to make his errand appear serious), but when his sight cleared a little he saw that nobody had turned to look at him: and there, sure enough, was Ignatius Gallaher leaning with his back against the counter and his feet planted far apart.

"Hallo, Tommy, old hero, here you are! What is it to be? What will you have? I'm taking whisky: better stuff than we get across the water. Soda? Lithia? No mineral? I'm the same. Spoils the flavour. . . . Here, *garçon*, bring us two halves of malt whisky, like a good fellow. . . . Well, and how have you been pulling along since I saw you last? Dear God, how old we're getting! Do you see any signs of aging in me—eh, what? A little grey and thin on the top—what?"

Ignatius Gallaher took off his hat and displayed a large closely cropped head. His face was heavy, pale and clean-shaven. His eyes, which were of bluish slate-colour, relieved his unhealthy pallor and shone out plainly above the vivid orange tie he wore. Between these rival features the lips appeared very long and shapeless and colourless. He bent his head and felt with two sympathetic fingers the thin hair at the crown. Little Chandler shook his head as a denial. Ignatius Gallaher put on his hat again.

"It pulls you down," he said, "Press life. Always hurry and scurry, looking for copy and sometimes not finding it: and then, always to have something new in your stuff. Damn proofs and printers, I say, for a few days. I'm deuced glad, I can tell you, to get back to the old country. Does a fellow good, a bit of a holiday. I feel a ton better since I landed again in dear dirty Dublin. . . . Here you are, Tommy. Water? Say when."

Little Chandler allowed his whisky to be very much diluted.

"You don't know what's good for you, my boy," said Ignatius Gallaher. "I drink mine neat."

"I drink very little as a rule," said Little Chandler modestly. "An odd half-one or so when I meet any of the old crowd: that's all."

"Ah, well," said Ignatius Gallaher, cheerfully, "here's to us and to old times and old acquaintance."

They clinked glasses and drank the toast.

"I met some of the old gang to-day," said Ignatius Gallaher. "O'Hara seems to be in a bad way. What's he doing?"

"Nothing," said Little Chandler. "He's gone to the dogs."

"But Hogan has a good sit, hasn't he?"

"Yes; he's in the Land Commission."

"I met him one night in London and he seemed to be very flush. . . . Poor O'Hara! Boose, I suppose?"

"Other things, too," said Little Chandler shortly.

Ignatius Gallaher laughed.

"Tommy," he said, "I see you haven't changed an atom. You're the very same serious person that used to lecture me on Sunday mornings when I had a sore head and a fur on my tongue. You'd want to knock about a bit in the world. Have you never been anywhere even for a trip?"

"I've been to the Isle of Man," said Little Chandler.

Ignatius Gallaher laughed.

"The Isle of Man!" he said. "Go to London or Paris: Paris, for choice. That'd do you good."

"Have you seen Paris?"

"I should think I have! I've knocked about there a little."

"And is it really so beautiful as they say?" asked Little Chandler.

He sipped a little of his drink while Ignatius Gallaher finished his boldly.

"Beautiful?" said Ignatius Gallaher, pausing on the word and on the flavour of his drink. "It's not so beautiful, you know. Of course, it is beautiful.... But it's the life of Paris; that's the thing. Ah, there's no city like Paris for gaiety, movement, excitement...."

Little Chandler finished his whisky and, after some trouble, succeeded in catching the barman's eye. He ordered the same again.

"I've been to the Moulin Rouge," Ignatius Gallaher continued when the barman had removed their glasses, "and I've been to all the Bohemian cafés. Hot stuff! Not for a pious chap like you, Tommy."

Little Chandler said nothing until the barman returned with two glasses: then he touched his friend's glass lightly and reciprocated the former toast. He was beginning to feel somewhat disillusioned. Gallaher's accent and way of expressing himself did not please him. There was something vulgar in his friend which he had not observed before. But perhaps it was only the result of living in London amid the bustle and competition of the Press. The old personal charm was still there under this new gaudy manner. And, after all, Gallaher had lived, he had seen the world. Little Chandler looked at his friend enviously.

"Everything in Paris is gay," said Ignatius Gallaher. "They believe in enjoying life—and don't you think they're right? If you want to enjoy yourself properly you must go to Paris. And, mind you, they've a great feeling for the Irish there. When they heard I was from Ireland they were ready to eat me, man."

Little Chandler took four or five sips from his glass.

"Tell me," he said, "is it true that Paris is so... immoral as they say?"

Ignatius Gallaher made a catholic gesture with his right arm.

"Every place is immoral," he said. "Of course you do find spicy bits in Paris. Go to one of the students' balls, for instance. That's lively, if you like, when the *cocottes* begin to let themselves loose. You know what they are, I suppose?"

"I've heard of them," said Little Chandler.

Ignatius Gallaher drank off his whisky and shook his head.

"Ah," he said, "you may say what you like. There's no woman like the Parisienne—for style, for go."

"Then it is an immoral city," said Little Chandler, with timid insistence—"I mean, compared with London or Dublin?"

"London!" said Ignatius Gallaher. "It's six of one and half-a-dozen of the other. You ask Hogan, my boy. I showed him a bit about London when he was over there. He'd open your eye.... I say, Tommy, don't make punch of that whisky: liquor up."

"No, really...."

"O, come on, another one won't do you any harm. What is it? The same again, I suppose?"

"Well... all right."

"*François*, the same again. . . . Will you smoke, Tommy?"

Ignatius Gallaher produced his cigar-case. The two friends lit their cigars and puffed at them in silence until their drinks were served.

"I'll tell you my opinion," said Ignatius Gallaher, emerging after some time from the clouds of smoke in which he had taken refuge, "it's a rum world. Talk of immorality! I've heard of cases—what am I saying?—I've known them: cases of . . . immorality. . . ."

Ignatius Gallaher puffed thoughtfully at his cigar and then, in a calm historian's tone, he proceeded to sketch for his friend some pictures of the corruption which was rife abroad. He summarised the vices of many capitals and seemed inclined to award the palm to Berlin. Some things he could not vouch for (his friends had told him), but of others he had had personal experience. He spared neither rank nor caste. He revealed many of the secrets of religious houses on the Continent and described some of the practices which were fashionable in high society and ended by telling, with details, a story about an English duchess—a story which he knew to be true. Little Chandler was astonished.

"Ah, well," said Ignatius Gallaher, "here we are in old jog-along Dublin where nothing is known of such things."

"How dull you must find it," said Little Chandler, "after all the other places you've seen!"

"Well," said Ignatius Gallaher, "it's a relaxation to come over here, you know. And, after all, it's the old country, as they say, isn't it? You can't help having a certain feeling for it. That's human nature. . . . But tell me something about yourself. Hogan told me you had . . . tasted the joys of connubial bliss. Two years ago, wasn't it?"

Little Chandler blushed and smiled.

"Yes," he said. "I was married last May twelve months."

"I hope it's not too late in the day to offer my best wishes," said Ignatius Gallaher. "I didn't know your address or I'd have done so at the time."

He extended his hand, which Little Chandler took.

"Well, Tommy," he said, "I wish you and yours every joy in life, old chap, and tons of money, and may you never die till I shoot you. And that's the wish of a sincere friend, an old friend. You know that?"

"I know that," said Little Chandler.

"Any youngsters?" said Ignatius Gallaher.

Little Chandler blushed again.

"We have one child," he said.

"Son or daughter?"

"A little boy."

Ignatius Gallaher slapped his friend sonorously on the back.

"Bravo," he said, "I wouldn't doubt you, Tommy."

Little Chandler smiled, looked confusedly at his glass and bit his lower lip with three childishly white front teeth.

"I hope you'll spend an evening with us," he said, "before you go back. My wife will be delighted to meet you. We can have a little music and——"

"Thanks awfully, old chap," said Ignatius Gallaher, "I'm sorry we didn't meet earlier. But I must leave to-morrow night."

"To-night perhaps . . . ?"

"I'm awfully sorry, old man. You see I'm over here with another fellow, clever young chap he is too, and we arranged to go to a little card party. Only for that . . ."

"O, in that case. . . ."

"But who knows?" said Ignatius Gallaher considerately. "Next year I may take a little skip over here now that I've broken the ice. It's only a pleasure deferred."

"Very well," said Little Chandler, "the next time you come we must have an evening together. That's agreed now, isn't it?"

"Yes, that's agreed," said Ignatius Gallaher. "Next year if I come, *parole d'honneur.*"

"And to clinch the bargain," said Little Chandler, "we'll just have one more now."

Ignatius Gallaher took out a large gold watch and looked at it.

"Is it to be the last?" he said. "Because you know, I have an a.p."

"O, yes, positively," said Little Chandler.

"Very well, then," said Ignatius Gallaher "let us have another one as a *deoc an doruis*—that's good vernacular for a small whisky, I believe."

Little Chandler ordered the drinks. The blush which had risen to his face a few moments before was establishing itself. A trifle made him blush at any time: and now he felt warm and excited. Three small whiskies had gone to his head and Gallaher's strong cigar had confused his mind, for he was a delicate and abstinent person. The adventure of meeting Gallaher after eight years, of finding himself with Gallaher in Corless's surrounded by lights and noise, of listening to Gallaher's stories and of sharing for a brief space Gallaher's vagrant and triumphant life, upset the equipoise of his sensitive nature. He felt acutely the contrast between his own life and his friend's, and it seemed to him unjust. Gallaher was his inferior in birth and education. He was sure that he could do something better than his friend had ever done, or could ever do, something higher than mere tawdry journalism if he only got the chance. What was it that stood in his way? His unfortunate timidity! He wished to vindicate himself in some way, to assert his

deoc an doruis: a stirrup cup (Gaelic)

manhood. He saw behind Gallaher's refusal of his invitation. Gallaher was only patronising him by his friendliness just as he was patronising Ireland by his visit.

The barman brought their drinks. Little Chandler pushed one glass towards his friend and took up the other boldly.

"Who knows?" he said, as they lifted their glasses. "When you come next year I may have the pleasure of wishing long life and happiness to Mr. and Mrs. Ignatius Gallaher."

Ignatius Gallaher in the act of drinking closed one eye expressively over the rim of his glass. When he had drunk he smacked his lips decisively, set down his glass and said:

"No blooming fear of that, my boy. I'm going to have my fling first and see a bit of life and the world before I put my head in the sack—if I ever do."

"Some day you will," said Little Chandler calmly.

Ignatius Gallaher turned his orange tie and slate-blue eyes full upon his friend.

"You think so?" he said.

"You'll put your head in the sack," repeated Little Chandler stoutly, "like everyone else if you can find the girl."

He had slightly emphasised his tone and he was aware that he had betrayed himself; but, though the colour had heightened in his cheek, he did not flinch from his friend's gaze. Ignatius Gallaher watched him for a few moments and then said:

"If ever it occurs, you may bet your bottom dollar there'll be no mooning and spooning about it. I mean to marry money. She'll have a good fat account at the bank or she won't do for me."

Little Chandler shook his head.

"Why, man alive," said Ignatius Gallaher, vehemently, "do you know what it is? I've only to say the word and to-morrow I can have the woman and the cash. You don't believe it? Well, I know it. There are hundreds—what am I saying?—thousands of rich Germans and Jews, rotten with money, that'd only be too glad. . . . You wait a while, my boy. See if I don't play my cards properly. When I go about a thing I mean business, I tell you. You just wait."

He tossed his glass to his mouth, finished his drink and laughed loudly. Then he looked thoughtfully before him and said in a calmer tone:

"But I'm in no hurry. They can wait. I don't fancy tying myself up to one woman, you know."

He imitated with his mouth the act of tasting and made a wry face.

"Must get a bit stale, I should think," he said.

.   .   .

Little Chandler sat in the room off the hall, holding a child in his arms. To save money they kept no servant but Annie's young sister Monica came for an hour or so in the morning and an hour or so in the evening to help. But Monica had gone home long ago. It was a quarter to nine. Little Chandler had come home late for tea and, moreover, he had forgotten to bring Annie home the parcel of coffee from Bewley's. Of course she was in a bad humour and gave him short answers. She said she would do without any tea but when it came near the time at which the shop at the corner closed she decided to go out herself for a quarter of a pound of tea and two pounds of sugar. She put the sleeping child deftly in his arms and said:

"Here. Don't waken him."

A little lamp with a white china shade stood upon the table and its light fell over a photograph which was enclosed in a frame of crumpled horn. It was Annie's photograph. Little Chandler looked at it, pausing at the thin tight lips. She wore the pale blue summer blouse which he had brought her home as a present one Saturday. It had cost him ten and elevenpence; but what an agony of nervousness it had cost him! How he had suffered that day, waiting at the shop door until the shop was empty, standing at the counter and trying to appear at his ease while the girl piled ladies' blouses before him, paying at the desk and forgetting to take up the odd penny of his change, being called back by the cashier, and finally, striving to hide his blushes as he left the shop by examining the parcel to see if it was securely tied. When he brought the blouse home Annie kissed him and said it was very pretty and stylish; but when she heard the price she threw the blouse on the table and said it was a regular swindle to charge ten and elevenpence for it. At first she wanted to take it back but when she tried it on she was delighted with it, especially with the make of the sleeves, and kissed him and said he was very good to think of her.

Hm! . . .

He looked coldly into the eyes of the photograph and they answered coldly. Certainly they were pretty and the face itself was pretty. But he found something mean in it. Why was it so unconscious and ladylike? The composure of the eyes irritated him. They repelled him and defied him: there was no passion in them, no rapture. He thought of what Gallaher had said about rich Jewesses. Those dark Oriental eyes, he thought, how full they are of passion, of voluptuous longing! . . . Why had he married the eyes in the photograph?

He caught himself up at the question and glanced nervously round the room. He found something mean in the pretty furniture which he had bought for his house on the hire system. Annie had chosen it herself and it reminded him of her. It too was prim and pretty. A dull resentment against his life awoke within him. Could he not escape from his little house? Was it too late for him to try to live bravely like Gallaher? Could he go to London? There was the furniture still to be paid for. If he could only write a book and get it published, that might open the way for him.

A volume of Byron's poems lay before him on the table. He opened it cautiously with his left hand lest he should waken the child and began to read the first poem in the book:

> "Hushed are the winds and still the evening gloom,
> Not e'en a Zephyr wanders through the grove,
> Whilst I return to view my Margaret's tomb
> And scatter flowers on the dust I love."

He paused. He felt the rhythm of the verse about him in the room. How melancholy it was! Could he, too, write like that, express the melancholy of his soul in verse? There were so many things he wanted to describe: his sensation of a few hours before on Grattan Bridge, for example. If he could get back again into that mood. . . .

The child awoke and began to cry. He turned from the page and tried to hush it: but it would not be hushed. He began to rock it to and fro in his arms but its wailing cry grew keener. He rocked it faster while his eyes began to read the second stanza:

> "Within this narrow cell reclines her clay,
> That clay where once . . ."

It was useless. He couldn't read. He couldn't do anything. The wailing of the child pierced the drum of his ear. It was useless, useless! He was a prisoner for life. His arms trembled with anger and suddenly bending to the child's face he shouted:

"Stop!"

The child stopped for an instant, had a spasm of fright and began to scream. He jumped up from his chair and walked hastily up and down the room with the child in his arms. It began to sob piteously, losing its breath for four or five seconds, and then bursting out anew. The thin walls of the room echoed the sound. He tried to soothe it but it sobbed more convulsively. He looked at the contracted and quivering face of the child and began to be alarmed. He counted seven sobs without a break between them and caught the child to his breast in fright. If it died! . . .

The door was burst open and a young woman ran in, panting.

"What is it? What is it?" she cried.

The child, hearing its mother's voice, broke out into a paroxysm of sobbing.

"It's nothing, Annie . . . it's nothing. . . . He began to cry . . ."

She flung her parcels on the floor and snatched the child from him. "What have you done to him?" she cried, glaring into his face.

Little Chandler sustained for one moment the gaze of her eyes and his heart closed together as he met the hatred in them. He began to stammer:

"It's nothing. . . . He . . . he began to cry. . . . I couldn't . . . I didn't do anything. . . . What?"

Giving no need to him she began to walk up and down the room, clasping the child tightly in her arms and murmuring:

"My little man! My little mannie! Was 'ou frightened, love? . . . There now, love! There now! . . . Lambabaun! Mamma's little lamb of the world! . . . There now!"

Little Chandler felt his cheeks suffused with shame and he stood back out of the lamplight. He listened while the paroxysm of the child's sobbing grew less and less; and tears of remorse started to his eyes.

QUESTIONS

1. What is suggested about Little Chandler by the use of such phrases as "a little man," "childish white teeth," "an infant hope," and "a little cloud"? What are the implications of the title?
2. What do we learn about Chandler's character from his attitude toward Corless's? his sometimes walking "boldly" through dark narrow streets at night? his questions about the immorality of Paris? his blushing at questions about his marriage and his children? his wish "to assert his manhood" (page 86)? his feelings while buying a blouse for his wife? his thoughts about his wife's photograph?
3. What trait of Little Chandler's is suggested by his reactions to thoughts about "life" (page 80) and by his taste in poetry?
4. Does Chandler have genuine poetic ability? Explain your answer.
5. "There was no doubt about it: if you wanted to succeed you had to go away. You could do nothing in Dublin." Evaluate this idea of Little Chandler's in the light of his character.
6. What do we learn about Gallaher from his remarks about Paris and London? his insistence that Little Chandler "liquor up"? his attitude toward marriage? Is Chandler's admiration of him merited?
7. Characters who contrast strongly, so that the traits of each are emphasized by contrast with those of the other, are called CHARACTER FOILS. In what ways are Chandler and Gallaher character foils?—In which way are they alike?
8. Why does Chandler shout at his child? How does this action sum up the story?

Sherwood Anderson

I'M A FOOL

It was a hard jolt for me, one of the most bitterest I ever had to face. And it all came about through my own foolishness, too. Even yet sometimes, when I think of it, I want to cry or swear or kick myself. Perhaps, even now, after all this time, there will be a kind of satisfaction in making myself look cheap by telling of it.

It began at three o-clock one October afternoon as I sat in the grand stand at the fall trotting and pacing meet at Sandusky, Ohio.

To tell the truth, I felt a little foolish that I should be sitting in the grand stand at all. During the summer before I had left my home town with Harry Whitehead and, with a nigger named Burt, had taken a job as swipe with one of the two horses Harry was campaigning through the fall race meets that year. Mother cried and my sister Mildred, who wanted to get a job as a schoolteacher in our town that fall, stormed and scolded about the house all during the week before I left. They both thought it something disgraceful that one of our family should take a place as a swipe with race horses. I've an idea Mildred thought my taking the place would stand in the way of her getting the job she'd been working so long for.

But after all I had to work, and there was no other work to be got. A big lumbering fellow of nineteen couldn't just hang around the house and I had got too big to mow people's lawns and sell newspapers. Little chaps who could get next to people's sympathies by their sizes were always getting jobs away from me. There was one fellow who kept saying to everyone who wanted a lawn mowed or a cistern cleaned that he was saving money to work his way through college, and I used to lay awake nights thinking up ways to injure him without being found out. I kept thinking of wagons running over him and bricks falling on his head as he walked along the street. But never mind him.

I got the place with Harry and I liked Burt fine. We got along splendid together. He was a big nigger with a lazy sprawling body and soft, kind eyes, and when it came to a fight he could hit like Jack Johnson. He had Bucephalus, a big black pacing stallion that could do 2.09 or 2.10 if he had to, and I had a little gelding named Doctor Fritz that never lost a race all fall when Harry wanted him to win.

We set out from home late in July, in a box car with the two horses and after that, until late November, we kept moving along to the race

I'M A FOOL "I'm a Fool" by Sherwood Anderson from the February 1922 issue of *The Dial*. Copyright © 1922 by the Dial Publishing Company, Inc. Renewed 1949 by Eleanor Copenhaver Anderson. Reprinted by permission of Harold Ober Associates Incorporated.

meets and the fairs. It was a peachy time for me, I'll say that. Sometimes now I think that boys who are raised regular in houses, and never have a fine nigger like Burt for best friend, and go to high schools and college, and never steal anything, or get drunk a little, or learn to swear from fellows who know how, or come walking up in front of a grand stand in their shirt sleeves and with dirty horsy pants on when the races are going on and the grand stand is full of people all dressed up—What's the use of talking about it? Such fellows don't know nothing at all. They've never had no opportunity.

But I did. Burt taught me how to rub down a horse and put the bandages on after a race and steam a horse out and a lot of valuable things for any man to know. He could wrap a bandage on a horse's leg so smooth that if it had been the same color you would think it was his skin, and I guess he'd have been a big driver, too, and got to the top like Murphy and Walter Cox and the others if he hadn't been black.

Gee whizz! it was fun. You got to a county-seat town, maybe say on a Saturday or Sunday, and the fair began the next Tuesday and lasted until Friday afternoon. Doctor Fritz would be, say, in the 2.25 trot on Tuesday afternoon and on Thursday afternoon Bucephalus would knock 'em cold in the "free-for-all" pace. It left you a lot of time to hang around and listen to horse talk, and see Burt knock some yap cold that got too gay, and you'd find out about horses and men and pick up a lot of stuff you could use all the rest of your life, if you had some sense and salted down what you heard and felt and saw.

And then at the end of the week when the race meet was over, and Harry had run home to tend up to his livery-stable business, you and Burt hitched the two horses to carts and drove slow and steady across country, to the place for the next meeting, so as to not overheat the horses, etc., etc., you know.

Gee whizz! Gosh amighty! the nice hickory-nut and beechnut and oaks and other kinds of trees along the roads, all brown and red, and the good smells, and Burt singing a song called "Deep River," and the country girls at the windows of houses and everything. You can stick your colleges up your nose for all me. I guess I know where I got my education.

Why, one of those little burgs of towns you came to on the way, say now on a Saturday afternoon, and Burt says, "Let's lay up here." And you did.

And you took the horses to a livery stable and fed them, and you got your good clothes out of a box and put them on.

And the town was full of farmers gaping, because they could see you were racehorse people, and the kids maybe never see a nigger before and was afraid and run away when the two of us walked down their main street.

And that was before prohibition and all that foolishness, and so you went into a saloon, the two of you, and all the yaps come and stood around, and there was always some one pretended he was horsy and knew things and spoke up and began asking questions, and all you did was to lie and lie all you could about what horses you had, and I said I owned them, and then some fellow said, "Will you have a drink of whisky?" and Burt knocked his eye out the way he could say, offhand like, "Oh, well, all right, I'm agreeable to a little nip. I'll split a quart with you." Gee whizz!

But that isn't what I want to tell my story about. We got home late in November and I promised mother I'd quit the race horses for good. There's a lot of things you've got to promise a mother because she don't know any better.

And so, there not being any work in our town any more than when I left there to go to the races, I went off to Sandusky and got a pretty good place taking care of horses for a man who owned a teaming and delivery and storage and coal and real-estate business there. It was a pretty good place with good eats, and a day off each week, and sleeping on a cot in a big barn, and mostly just shoveling in hay and oats to a lot of big good-enough skates of horses that couldn't have trotted a race with a toad. I wasn't dissatisfied and I could send money home.

And then, as I started to tell you, the fall races come to Sandusky and I got the day off and I went. I left the job at noon and had on my good clothes and my new brown derby hat I'd bought the Saturday before, and a stand-up collar.

First of all I went downtown and walked about with the dudes. I've always thought to myself, "Put up a good front," and so I did it. I had forty dollars in my pockets and so I went into the West House, a big hotel, and walked up to the cigar stand. "Give me three twenty-five-cent cigars," I said. There was a lot of horsemen and strangers and dressed-up people from other towns standing around in the lobby and in the bar, and I mingled amongst them. In the bar there was a fellow with a cane and a Windsor tie on, that it made me sick to look at him. I like a man to be a man and dressed up, but not to go put on that kind of airs. So I pushed him aside, kind of rough, and had me a drink of whisky. And then he looked at me, as though he thought maybe he'd get gay, but he changed his mind and didn't say anything. And then I had another drink of whisky, just to show him something, and went out and had a hack out to the races, all to myself, and when I got there I bought myself the best seat I could get up in the grand stand, but didn't go in for any of these boxes. That's putting on too many airs.

And so there I was, sitting up in the grand stand as gay as you please and looking down on the swipes coming out with their horses, and with their dirty horsy pants on and the horseblankets swung over their shoulders, same as I had been doing all the year before. I liked one thing about the same as the other, sitting up there and feeling grand and being down there and looking up at the yaps and feeling grander and more important, too.

One thing's about as good as another, if you take it just right. I've often said that.

Well, right in front of me, in the grand stand that day, there was a fellow with a couple of girls and they was about my age. The young fellow was a nice guy, all right. He was the kind maybe that goes to college and then comes to be a lawyer or maybe a newspaper editor or something like that, but he wasn't stuck on himself. There are some of that kind are all right and he was one of the ones.

He had his sister with him and another girl and the sister looked around over his shoulder, accidental at first, not intending to start anything—she wasn't that kind—and her eyes and mine happened to meet.

You know how it is. Gee, she was a peach! She had on a soft dress, kind of a blue stuff and it looked carelessly made, but was well sewed and made and everything. I knew that much. I blushed when she looked right at me and so did she. She was the nicest girl I've ever seen in my life. She wasn't stuck on herself and she could talk proper grammar without being like a schoolteacher or something like that. What I mean is, she was O.K. I think maybe her father was well-to-do, but not rich to make her chesty because she was his daughter, as some are. Maybe he owned a drug store or a dry-goods store in their home town, or something like that. She never told me and I never asked.

My own people are all O.K. too, when you come to that. My grandfather was Welsh and over in the old country, in Wales he was—But never mind that.

The first heat of the first race come off and the young fellow setting there with the two girls left them and went down to make a bet. I knew what he was up to, but he didn't talk big and noisy and let everyone around know he was a sport, as some do. He wasn't that kind. Well, he come back and I heard him tell the two girls what horse he'd bet on, and when the heat trotted they all half got to their feet and acted in the excited, sweaty way people do when they've got money down on a race, and the horse they bet on is up there pretty close at the end, and they think maybe he'll come on with a rush, but he never does because he hasn't got the old juice in him, come right down to it.

And then, pretty soon, the horses came out for the 2.18 pace and there was a horse in it I knew. He was a horse Bob French had in his string but Bob didn't own him. He was a horse owned by a Mr. Mathers down at Marietta, Ohio.

This Mr. Mathers had a lot of money and owned some coal mines or something and he had a swell place out in the country, and he was stuck on race horses, but was a Presbyterian or something, and I think more than likely his wife was one, too, maybe a stiffer one than himself. So he never raced his horses hisself, and the story around the Ohio race tracks was that when one of his horses got ready to go to the races he turned him over to Bob French and pretended to his wife he was sold.

So Bob had the horses and he did pretty much as he pleased and you can't blame Bob, at least, I never did. Sometimes he was out to win and sometimes he wasn't. I never cared much about that when I was swiping a horse. What I did want to know was that my horse had the speed and could go out in front, if you wanted him to.

And, as I'm telling you, there was Bob in this race with one of Mr. Mathers' horses, was named "About Ben Ahem" or something like that, and was fast as a streak. He was a gelding and had a mark of 2.21, but could step in .08 or .09.

Because when Burt and I were out, as I've told you, the year before, there was a nigger Burt knew, worked for Mr. Mathers and we went out there one day when we didn't have no race on at the Marietta Fair and our boss Harry was gone home.

And so everyone was gone to the fair but just this one nigger and he took us all through Mr. Mathers' swell house and he and Burt tapped a bottle of wine Mr. Mathers had hid in his bedroom, back in a closet, without his wife knowing, and he showed us this Ahem horse. Burt was always stuck on being a driver but didn't have much chance to get to the top, being a nigger, and he and the other nigger gulped the whole bottle of wine and Burt got a little lit up.

So the nigger let Burt take this About Ben Ahem and step him a mile in a track Mr. Mathers had all to himself, right there on the farm. And Mr. Mathers had one child, a daughter, kinda sick and not very good looking, and she came home and we had to hustle and get About Ben Ahem stuck back in the barn.

I'm only telling you to get everything straight. At Sandusky, that afternoon I was at the fair, this young fellow with the two girls was fussed, being with the girls and losing his bet. You know how a fellow is that way. One of them was his girl and the other his sister. I had figured that out.

"Gee whizz," I says to myself, "I'm going to give him the dope."

He was mighty nice when I touched him on the shoulder. He and the girls were nice to me right from the start and clear to the end. I'm not blaming them.

And so he leaned back and I give him the dope on About Ben Ahem. "Don't bet a cent on this first heat because he'll go like an oxen hitched to a plow, but when the first heat is over go right down and lay on your pile." That's what I told him.

Well, I never saw a fellow treat any one sweller. There was a fat man sitting beside the little girl, that had looked at me twice by this time, and I at her, and both blushing, and what did he do but have the nerve to turn and ask the fat man to get up and change places with me so I could set with his crowd.

Gee whizz, craps amighty. There I was. What a chump I was to go and get gay up there in the West House bar, and just because that dude was standing there with a cane and that kind of a necktie on, to go and get all balled up and drink that whisky, just to show off.

Of course she would know, me setting right beside her and letting her smell of my breath. I could have kicked myself right down out of that grand stand and all around that race track and made a faster record than most of the skates of horses they had there that year.

Because that girl wasn't any mutt of a girl. What wouldn't I have give right then for a stick of chewing gum to chew, or a lozenger, or some licorice, or most anything. I was glad I had those twenty-five-cent cigars in my pocket and right away I give that fellow one and lit one myself. Then that fat man got up and we changed places and there I was, plunked right down beside her.

They introduced themselves and the fellow's best girl, he had with him, was named Miss Elinor Woodbury, and her father was a manufacturer of barrels from a place called Tiffin, Ohio. And the fellow himself was named Wilbur Wessen and his sister was Miss Lucy Wessen.

I suppose it was their having such swell names that got me off my trolley. A fellow, just because he has been a swipe with a race horse, and works taking care of horses for a man in the teaming, delivery, and storage business isn't any better or worse than any one else. I've often thought that, and said it too.

But you know how a fellow is. There's something in that kind of nice clothes, and the kind of nice eyes she had, and the way she had looked at me, awhile before, over her brother's shoulder, and me looking back at her, and both of us blushing.

I couldn't show her up for a boob, could I?

I made a fool of myself, that's what I did. I said my name was Walter Mathers from Marietta, Ohio, and then I told all three of them the smashingest lie you ever heard. What I said was that my father owned the horse About Ben Ahem and that he had let him out to this Bob French for racing purposes, because our family was proud and had never gone into racing that way, in our own name, I mean, and Miss Lucy Wessen's eyes were shining, and I went the whole hog.

I told about our place down at Marietta, and about the big stables and the grand brick house we had on a hill, up above the Ohio River, but I knew enough not to do it in no bragging way. What I did was to start things and then let them drag the rest out of me. I acted just as reluctant to tell as I could. Our family hasn't got any barrel factory, and since I've known us, we've always been pretty poor, but not asking anything of any one at that, and my grandfather, over in Wales—but never mind that.

We set there talking like we had known each other for years and years, and I went and told them that my father had been expecting maybe this Bob French wasn't on the square, and had sent me up to Sandusky on the sly to find out what I could.

And I bluffed it through I had found out all about the 2.18 pace, in which About Ben Ahem was to start.

I said he would lose the first heat by pacing like a lame cow and then he would come back and skin 'em alive after that. And to back up what I said I took thirty dollars out of my pocket and handed it to Mr. Wilbur Wessen and asked him, would he mind, after the first heat, to go down and place it on About Ben Ahem for whatever odds he could get. What I said was that I didn't want Bob French to see me and none of the swipes.

Sure enough the first heat came off and About Ben Ahem went off his stride, up the back stretch, and looked like a wooden horse or a sick one, and come in to be last. Then this Wilbur Wessen went down to the betting place under the grand stand and there I was with the two girls, and when that Miss Woodbury was looking the other way once, Lucy Wessen kinda, with her shoulder you know, kinda touched me. Not just tucking down, I don't mean. You know how a woman can do. They get close, but not getting gay either. You know what they do. Gee whizz.

And then they give me a jolt. What they had done, when I didn't know, was to get together, and they had decided Wilbur Wessen would bet fifty dollars, and the two girls had gone and put in ten dollars each, of their own money, too. I was sick then, but I was sicker later.

About the gelding, About Ben Ahem, and their winning their money, I wasn't worried a lot about that. It come out O.K. Ahem stepped the next three heats like a bushel of spoiled eggs going to market before they could be found out, and Wilbur Wessen had got nine to two for the money. There was something else eating at me.

Because Wilbur come back, after he had bet the money, and after that he spent most of his time talking to that Miss Woodbury, and Lucy Wessen and I was left alone together like on a desert island. Gee, if I'd only been on the square or if there had been any way of getting myself on the square. There ain't any Walter Mathers, like I said to her and them, and there hasn't ever been one, but if there was, I bet I'd go to Marietta, Ohio, and shoot him tomorrow.

There I was, big boob that I am. Pretty soon the race was over, and

Wilbur had gone down and collected our money, and we had a hack downtown, and he stood us a swell supper at the West House, and a bottle of champagne beside.

And I was with that girl and she wasn't saying much, and I wasn't saying much either. One thing I know. She wasn't stuck on me because of the lie about my father being rich and all that. There's a way you know. . . . Craps amighty. There's a kind of girl you see just once in your life, and if you don't get busy and make hay, then you're gone for good and all, and might as well go jump off a bridge. They give you a look from inside of them somewhere, and it ain't no vamping, and what it means is—you want that girl to be your wife, and you want nice things around her like flowers and swell clothes, and you want her to have the kids you're going to have, and you want good music played and no ragtime. Gee whizz.

There's a place over near Sandusky, across a kind of bay, and it's called Cedar Point. And after we had supper we went over to it in a launch, all by ourselves. Wilbur and Miss Lucy and that Miss Woodbury had to catch a ten o'clock train back to Tiffin, Ohio, because, when you're out with girls like that you can't get careless and miss any trains and stay out all night, like you can with some kinds of Janes.

And Wilbur blowed himself to the launch and it cost him fifteen cold plunks, but I wouldn't never have knew if I hadn't listened. He wasn't no tin horn kind of a sport.

Over at the Cedar Point place, we didn't stay around where there was a gang of common kind of cattle at all.

There was big dance halls and dining places for yaps, and there was a beach you could walk along and get where it was dark, and we went there.

She didn't talk hardly at all and neither did I, and I was thinking how glad I was my mother was all right, and always made us kids learn to eat with a fork at table, and not swill soup, and not be noisy and rough like a gang you see around a race track that way.

Then Wilbur and his girl went away up the beach and Lucy and I sat down in a dark place, where there was some roots of old trees the water had washed up, and after that the time, till we had to go back in the launch and they had to catch their trains, wasn't nothing at all. It went like winking your eye.

Here's how it was. The place we were setting in was dark, like I said, and there was the roots from that old stump sticking up like arms, and there was a watery smell, and the night was like—as if you could put your hand out and feel it—so warm and soft and dark and sweet like an orange.

I most cried and I most swore and I most jumped up and danced, I was so mad and happy and sad.

When Wilbur come back from being alone with his girl, and she saw him coming, Lucy she says, "We got to go to the train now," and she was most crying too, but she never knew nothing I knew, and she couldn't be so all busted up. And then, before Wilbur and Miss Woodbury got up to where we was, she put her face up and kissed me quick and put her head up against me and she was all quivering and— Gee whizz.

Sometimes I hope I have cancer and die. I guess you know what I mean. We went in the launch across the bay to the train like that, and it was dark, too. She whispered and said it was like she and I could get out of the boat and walk on the water, and it sounded foolish, but I knew what she meant.

And then quick we were right at the depot, and there was a big gang of yaps, the kind that goes to the fairs, and crowded and milling around like cattle, and how could I tell her? "It won't be long because you'll write and I'll write to you." That's all she said.

I got a chance like a hay barn afire. A swell chance I got.

And maybe she would write me, down at Marietta that way, and the letter would come back, and stamped on the front of it by the U.S.A. "there ain't any such guy," or something like that, whatever they stamp on a letter that way.

And me trying to pass myself off for a big-bug and a swell—to her, as decent a little body as God ever made. Craps amighty—a swell chance I got!

And then the train come in, and she got on it, and Wilbur Wessen, he come and shook hands with me, and that Miss Woodbury was nice too and bowed to me, and I at her, and the train went and I busted out and cried like a kid.

Gee, I could have run after that train and made Dan Patch look like a freight train after a wreck but, socks amighty, what was the use? Did you ever see such a fool?

I'll bet you what—if I had an arm broke right now or a train had run over my foot—I wouldn't go to no doctor at all. I'd go set down and let her hurt and hurt—that's what I'd do.

I'll bet you what—if I hadn't a drunk that booze I'd a never been such a boob as to go tell such a lie—that couldn't never be made straight to a lady like her.

I wish I had that fellow right here that had on a Windsor tie and carried a cane. I'd smash him for fair. Gosh darn his eyes. He's a big fool—that's what he is.

And if I'm not another you just go find me one and I'll quit working and be a bum and give him my job. I don't care nothing for working, and earning money, and saving it for no such boob as myself.

QUESTIONS

1. This story is told by an uneducated boy who is handicapped in the telling by bad grammar, an inadequate vocabulary, ignorance, and a digressive story-telling method. Find a good exemplification of each. Why do these handicaps advance rather than hinder the story? What is the story's main purpose?
2. What kind of moral standards does the swipe have? Is he mean? Where does he get his moral standards?
3. What is the swipe's attitude toward education? Can you reconcile "You can stick your colleges up your nose for all me" with "The young fellow was a nice guy, all right. He was the kind maybe that goes to college and then comes to be a lawyer ..."? What is an *ambivalent* attitude? What is *rationalization*? Explain the swipe's attitude.
4. The main tenet of the swipe's rather rudimentary philosophy of life is "Put up a good front." On what occasions in the story does the swipe put up a good front? Is this the philosophy of a mature individual? What is the difference between "putting up a good front" and "putting on airs"?
5. Another tenet of the swipe's philosophy is that "A fellow, just because he has been a swipe with a race horse, and works taking care of horses for a man in the teaming, delivery, and storage business, isn't any better or worse than any one else." Why has the swipe "often thought that, and said it too"? Why is he so impressed by the "swell names" and good clothes of the Wessens and Miss Woodbury? What is his attitude toward being a swipe? What does he like about being a swipe?
6. Why does the swipe resent the man in the Windsor tie? Why does he like Burt and the Wessens and Miss Woodbury? Why does he refer to most people as "yaps"?
7. Evaluate the swipe's emotional maturity in the light of his reactions to the little chap who got jobs away from him, what he'd do to the real Walter Mathers if there were one, his behavior toward the man in the Windsor tie, what he'd like to happen to himself at the end of the story.
8. What psychological term might be used to explain the swipe? Account for his behavior in terms of his size, his social and economic background, his success in school, his earning ability.
9. The swipe blames his whopper at the race track on the whisky, and he blames the whisky on the man in the Windsor tie. What is the real reason for his behavior?
10. How is your attitude toward the swipe affected by the fact that you hear his story from himself? How would it be different if you had heard it from, say, a high school principal?

Elizabeth Bowen

TEARS, IDLE TEARS

Frederick burst into tears in the middle of Regent's Park. His mother, seeing what was about to happen, had cried: "Frederick, you *can't*—in the middle of Regent's Park!" Really, this was a corner, one of those lively corners just inside a big gate, where two walks meet and a bridge starts across the pretty winding lake. People were passing quickly; the bridge rang with feet. Poplars stood up like delicate green brooms; diaphanous willows whose weeping was not shocking quivered over the lake. May sun spattered gold through the breezy trees; the tulips though falling open were still gay; three girls in a long boat shot under the bridge. Frederick, knees trembling, butted towards his mother a crimson convulsed face, as though he had the idea of burying himself in her. She whipped out a handkerchief and dabbed at him with it under his grey felt hat, exclaiming meanwhile in fearful mortification: "You really haven't got to be such a *baby!*" Her tone attracted the notice of several people, who might otherwise have thought he was having something taken out of his eye.

He was too big to cry: the whole scene was disgraceful. He wore a grey flannel knickerbocker suit and looked like a schoolboy; though in fact he was seven, still doing lessons at home. His mother said to him almost every week: "I don't know what they will think when you go to school!" His tears were a shame of which she could speak to no one; no offensive weakness of body could have upset her more. Once she had got so far as taking her pen up to write to the Mother's Advice Column of a helpful woman's weekly about them. She began: "I am a widow; young, good tempered, and my friends all tell me that I have great control. But my little boy—" She intended to sign herself "Mrs. D., Surrey." But then she had stopped and thought no, no: after all, he is Toppy's son. . . . She was a gallant-looking, correct woman, wearing to-day in London a coat and skirt, a silver fox, white gloves and a dark-blue toque put on exactly right—not the sort of woman you ought to see in a Park with a great blubbering boy belonging to her. She looked a mother of sons, but not of a son of this kind, and should more properly, really, have been walking a dog. "Come on!" she said, as though the bridge, the poplars, the people staring were to be borne no longer. She began to walk on quickly, along the edge of the lake, parallel with the park's girdle of trees and the dark, haughty windows of Cornwall Terrace looking at her over the red may. They had meant to go to the Zoo, but now she had changed her mind: Frederick did not deserve the Zoo.

Frederick stumbled along beside her, too miserable to notice. His mother seldom openly punished him, but often revenged herself on him in small ways. He could feel how just this was. His own incontinence in the matter of tears was as shocking to him, as bowing-down, as annulling, as it could be to her. He never knew what happened—a cold black pit with no bottom opened inside himself; a red-hot bellwire jagged up through him from the pit of his frozen belly to the caves of his eyes. Then the hot gummy rush of tears, the convulsion of his features, the terrible square grin he felt his mouth take all made him his own shameful and squalid enemy. Despair howled round his inside like a wind, and through his streaming eyes he saw everything quake. Anyone's being there—and most of all his mother—drove this catastrophe on him. He never cried like this when he was alone.

Crying made him so abject, so outcast from other people that he went on crying out of despair. His crying was not just reflex, like a baby's; it dragged up all unseemliness into view. No wonder everyone was repelled. There is something about an abject person that rouses cruelty in the kindest breast. The plate-glass windows of the lordly houses looked at him through the may-trees with judges' eyes. Girls with their knees crossed, reading on the park benches, looked up with unkind smiles. His apathetic stumbling, his not seeing or caring that they had given up their trip to the Zoo, became more than Mrs. Dickinson, his mother, could bear. She pointed out, in a voice tense with dislike: "I'm not taking you to the Zoo."

"Mmmph-mmph-mmph," sobbed Frederick.

"You know, I so often wonder what your father would think."

"Mmmph-mmph-mmph."

"He used to be so proud of you. He and I used to look forward to what you'd be like when you were a big boy. One of the last things he ever said was: 'Frederick will take care of you.' You almost make me glad he's not here now."

"Oough-oough."

"What do you say?"

"I'm t-t-trying to stop."

"Everybody's looking at you, you know."

She was one of those women who have an unfailing sense of what not to say, and say it: despair, perversity or stubborn virtue must actuate them. She had a horror, also, of the abnormal and had to hit out at it before it could hit at her. Her husband, an R.A.F. pilot who had died two days after a ghastly crash, after two or three harrowing spaces of consciousness, had never made her ashamed or puzzled her. Their intimacies, then even his death, had had a bold naturalness.

"Listen, I shall walk on ahead," said Frederick's mother, lifting her chin with that noble, decided movement so many people liked. "You stay here and look at that duck till you've stopped that noise. Don't catch me up till you have. No, I'm really ashamed of you."

She walked on. He had *not* been making, really, so very much noise. Drawing choppy breaths, he stood still and looked at the duck that sat folded into a sleek white cypher on the green grassy margin of the lake. When it rolled one eye open over a curve, something unseeing in its expression calmed him. His mother walked away under the gay tree-shadows; her step quickened lightly, the tip of her fox fur swung. She thought of the lunch she had had with Major and Mrs. Williams, the party she would be going to at five. First, she must leave Frederick at Aunt Mary's, and what would Aunt Mary say to his bloated face? She walked fast; the gap between her and Frederick widened: she was a charming woman walking by herself.

Everybody had noticed how much courage she had; they said: "How plucky Mrs. Dickinson is." It was five years since her tragedy and she had not remarried, so that her gallantness kept on coming into play. She helped a friend with a little hat shop called *Isobel* near where they lived in Surrey, bred puppies for sale and gave the rest of her time to making a man of Frederick. She smiled nicely and carried her head high. Those two days while Toppy had lain dying she had hardly turned a hair, for his sake: no one knew when he might come conscious again. When she was not by his bed she was waiting about the hospital. The chaplain hanging about her and the doctor had given thanks that there were women like this; another officer's wife who had been her friend had said she was braver than could be good for anyone. When Toppy finally died the other woman had put the unflinching widow into a taxi and driven back with her to the Dickinsons' bungalow. She kept saying: "Cry, dear, cry: you'd feel better." She made tea and clattered about, repeating: "Don't mind me, darling: just have a big cry." The strain became so great that tears streamed down her own face. Mrs. Dickinson looked past her palely, with a polite smile. The empty-feeling bungalow with its rustling curtains still smelt of Toppy's pipe; his slippers were under a chair. Then Mrs. Dickinson's friend, almost tittering with despair, thought of a poem of Tennyson's she had learnt as a child. She said: "Where's Frederick? He's quiet. Do you think he's asleep?" The widow, rising, perfectly automatic, led her into the room where Frederick lay in his cot. A nursemaid rose from beside him, gave them one morbid look and scurried away. The two-year-old baby, flushed, and drawing up his upper lip in his sleep as his father used to do, lay curved under his blue blanket, clenching one fist on nothing. Something suddenly seemed to strike his mother, who, slumping down by the cot, ground her face and forehead into the fluffy blanket, then began winding the blanket round her two fists. Her convulsions, though proper, were fearful: the cot shook. The friend crept away into the kitchen, where she stayed an half-hour, muttering to the maid. They made more tea and waited for Mrs. Dickinson to give full birth to her grief. Then extreme silence drew them back to the cot. Mrs. Dickinson knelt asleep, her profile pressed to the blanket, one arm crooked over the baby's form. Under his mother's arm, as still as an image, Frederick lay wide awake, not making a sound. In conjunction with a certain look in his eyes, the baby's silence gave the two women the horrors. The servant said to the friend: "You would think he knew."

Mrs. Dickinson's making so few demands on pity soon rather alienated her women friends, but men liked her better for it: several of them found in her straight look an involuntary appeal to themselves alone, more exciting than coquetry, deeply, nobly exciting: several wanted to marry her. But courage had given her a new intractable kind of virgin pride: she loved it too much; she could never surrender it. "No, don't ask me that," she would say, lifting her chin and with that calm, gallant smile. "Don't spoil things. You've been splendid to me: such a support. But you see, there's Frederick. He's the man in my life now. I'm bound to put him first. That wouldn't be fair, would it?" After that, she would simply go on shaking her head. She became the perfect friend for men who wished to wish to marry but were just as glad not to, and for married men who liked just a little pathos without being upset.

Frederick had stopped crying. This left him perfectly blank, so that he stared at the duck with abstract intensity, perceiving its moulded feathers and porcelain-smooth neck. The burning, swirling film had cleared away from his eyes, and his diaphragm felt relief, as when retching has stopped. He forgot his focus of grief and forgot his mother, but saw with joy a quivering bough of willow that, drooping into his gaze under his swollen eyelids, looked as pure and strong as something after the Flood. His thought clutched at the willow, weak and wrecked but happy. He knew he was now qualified to walk after his mother, but without feeling either guilty or recalcitrant did not wish to do so. He stepped over the rail—no park keeper being at hand to stop him—and, tenderly and respectfully, attempted to touch the white duck's tail. Without a blink, with automatic uncoyness, the duck slid away from Frederick into the lake. Its lovely white china body balanced on the green glass water as it propelled itself gently round the curve of the bank. Frederick saw with a passion of observation its shadowy webbed feet lazily striking out.

"The keeper'll eat you," said a voice behind him.

Frederick looked cautiously round with his bunged-up eyes. The *individual* who had spoken sat on a park bench; it was a girl with a despatch case beside her. Her big bony knee-joints stuck out through her thin crepe-de-chine dress; she was hatless and her hair made a frizzy, pretty outline, but she wore spectacles, her skin had burnt dull red: her smile and the cock of her head had about them something pungent and energetic, not like a girl's at all. "Whatcher mean, eat me?"

"You're on his grass. And putting salt on his duck's tail."

Frederick stepped back carefully over the low rail. "I haven't got any salt." He looked up and down the walk: his mother was out of sight but from the direction of the bridge a keeper was approaching, still distant but with an awesome gait. "My goodness," the girl said, "what's been biting *you*?" Frederick was at a loss. "Here," she said, "have an apple." She opened her case, which was full of folded grease-paper that must have held sandwiches, and rummaged out an apple with a waxy, bright skin. Frederick came up, tentative as a pony, and finally took the apple. His breath was still hitching and catching; he did not wish to speak.

"Go on," she said, "swallow: it'll settle your chest. Where's your mother gone off to? What's all the noise about?" Frederick only opened his jaws as wide as they would go, then bit slowly, deeply into the apple. The girl re-crossed her legs and tucked her thin crepe-de-chine skirt round the other knee. "What had you done—cheeked her?"

Frederick swept the mouthful of apple into one cheek. "No," he said shortly. "Cried."

"I should say you did. Bellowed. I watched you all down the path." There was something ruminative in the girl's tone that made her remark really not at all offensive; in fact, she looked at Frederick as though she were meeting an artist who had just done a turn. He had been standing about, licking and biting the apple, but now he came and sat down at the other end of the bench. "How do you do it?" she said.

Frederick only turned away: his ears began burning again.

"What gets at you?" she said.

"Don't know."

"Someone coming it over you? I know another boy who cries like you, but he's older. He knots himself up and bellows."

"What's his name?"

"George."

"Does he go to school?"

"Oh, lord, no; he's a boy at the place where I used to work." She raised one arm, leaned back, and watched four celluloid bangles, each of a different colour, slide down it to her elbow joint, where they stuck. "He doesn't know why he does it," she said, "but he's got to. It's as though he saw something. You can't ask him. Some people take him that way: girls do. I never did. It's as if he knew about something he'd better not. I said once, well, what just *is* it, and he said if he *could* tell me he wouldn't do it. I said, well, what's the *reason*, and he said, well, what's the reason not to? I knew him well at one time."

Frederick spat out two pips, looked round cautiously for the keeper, then dropped the apple-core down the back of the seat. "Where'd's George live?"

"I don't know now," she said, "I often wonder. I got sacked from that place where I used to work, and he went right off and I never saw him again. You snap out of that, if you can, before you are George's age. It does you no good. It's all in the way you see things. Look, there's your mother back. Better move, or there'll be *more* trouble." She held out her hand to Frederick, and when he put his in it shook hands so cheerfully, with such tough decision, that the four celluloid bangles danced on her wrist. "You and George," she said. "Funny to meet two of you. Well, good-bye, Henry: cheer up."

"I'm Frederick."

"Well, cheer up, Freddie."

As Frederick walked away, she smoothed down the sandwich papers inside her despatch case and snapped the case shut again. Then she put a finger under her hair at each side, to tuck her spectacles firmly down on her ears. Her mouth, an unreddened line across her harshly-burnt face, still wore the same truculent, homely smile. She crossed her arms under the flat chest, across her stomach, and sat there holding her elbows idly, wagging one foot in its fawn sandal, looking fixedly at the lake through her spectacles wondering about George. She had the afternoon, as she had no work. She saw George's face lifted abjectly from his arms on a table, blotchy over his clerk's collar. The eyes of George and Frederick seemed to her to be wounds in the world's surface, through which its inner, terrible, unassuageable, necessary sorrow constantly bled away and as constantly welled up.

Mrs. Dickinson came down the walk under the band of trees, carefully unanxious, looking lightly at objects to see if Frederick were near them: he had been a long time. Then she saw Frederick shaking hands with a sort of girl on a bench and started to come her way. So she quickly turned her frank, friendly glance on the lake, down which, as though to greet her, a swan came swimming. She touched her fox fur lightly, sliding it up her shoulder. What a lovely mother to have. "Well, Frederick," she said, as he came into earshot, "coming?" Wind sent a puff of red mayflowers through the air. She stood still and waited for Frederick to come up. She could not think what to do now: they had an hour to put in before they were due at Aunt Mary's. But this only made her manner calmer and more decisive.

Frederick gave a great skip, opened his mouth wide, shouted: "Oo, I say, mother, I nearly caught a duck!"

"Frederick, dear, how silly you are: you couldn't."

"Oo, yes, I could, I could. If I'd had salt for its tail!" Years later, Frederick could still remember, with ease, pleasure and with a sense of lonely shame being gone, that calm white duck swimming off round the bank. But George's friend with the bangles, and George's trouble, fell through a cleft in his memory and were forgotten soon.

QUESTIONS

1. By what means is Mrs. Dickinson characterized? What kind of person is she? What are her chief motivations? Does she love her son?
2. Explain Mrs. Dickinson's behavior after her husband's death. Why has she not remarried?
3. In what respect are Frederick and his mother character foils? In what ways are Frederick's mother and the girl on the park bench character foils?
4. Why cannot Frederick cure himself of his habit of crying? In what way does his mother attempt to cure him? How does he feel toward his mother?
5. Is there any suggestion as to the origin of Frederick's crying?
6. Is Frederick a static or a dynamic character? What effect does his conversation with the girl have on him? Why? Why does he remember the duck years later?
7. The title is a literary allusion. If you are unable to explain it, look up in an anthology the famous poem that begins with those words. Literary allusions are a kind of literary shorthand: what does knowledge of this poem add to the meaning of the title and of the story?

4

Theme

"Daddy, the man next door kisses his wife every morning when he leaves for work. Why don't you do that?"

"Gracious, little one, I don't even know the woman."

"Daughter, your young man stays until a very late hour. Hasn't your mother said anything to you about this habit of his?"

"Yes, father. Mother says men haven't altered a bit."

For the reader who contemplates the two jokes above, a significant difference emerges between them. The first joke depends only upon a reversal of expectation. We expect the man to explain why he doesn't kiss his wife; instead he explains why he doesn't kiss his neighbor's wife. The second joke, though it contains a reversal of expectation, depends as much or more for its effectiveness on a truth about human life; namely, that *Men tend to grow more conservative as they grow older,* or that *Fathers often scold their children for doing exactly what they did themselves when young.* This truth, which might be stated in different ways, is the *theme* of the joke.

The THEME of a piece of fiction is its controlling idea or its central insight. It is the unifying generalization about life stated or implied by the story. To derive the theme of a story, we must ask what its central *purpose* is: what view of life it supports or what insight into life it reveals.

Not all stories have theme. The purpose of a horror story may be simply to scare the reader and give him gooseflesh. The purpose of an adventure story may be simply to carry the reader through a series of exciting escapades. The purpose of a murder mystery may be simply to pose a problem for the reader to try to solve (and to prevent him from solving it, if possible, until the last paragraph). The purpose of some stories may be simply to provide suspense or to make the reader laugh or to surprise him with a sudden twist at the end. Theme exists only (1) when an author has seriously attempted to record life accurately or to reveal some truth about it, or (2) when he has mechanically introduced some concept or theory of life into it which he uses as a unifying element and which his story is meant to illustrate. Theme exists in all interpretive fiction but only in some escape fiction. In interpretive fiction it is the purpose of the story; in escape fiction it is merely an excuse, a peg to hang the story from.

In many stories the theme may be equivalent to the revelation of human character. If a story has as its central purpose to exhibit a certain kind of human being, our statement of theme may be no more than a concentrated description of the person revealed, with the addition, "Some people are like this." Frequently, however, a story through its portrayal of specific persons in specific situations will have something to say about the nature of all men or about the relationship of human beings to each other or to the universe. Whatever central generalization about life arises from the specifics of the story constitutes theme.

The theme of a story, like its plot, may be stated very briefly or at greater length. With a simple or very brief story, we may be satisfied to sum up the theme in a single sentence. With a more complex story, if successfully unified, we can still state the theme in a single sentence, but we may feel that a paragraph—or occasionally even an essay—is needed to state it adequately. A rich story will give us many and complex insights into life. In stating the theme in a sentence we must pick the *central* insight, the one which explains the greatest number of elements in the story and relates them to each other. For theme is what gives a good story its unity. In any story at all complex, however, we are likely to feel that a one-sentence statement of theme leaves out a great part of the story's meaning. Though the theme of *Othello* may be expressed as "Jealousy exacts a terrible cost," such a statement does not begin to suggest the range and depth of Shakespeare's play. Any successful story is a good deal more and means a good deal more than any one-sentence statement of theme that we may extract from it, for the story will modify and expand this statement in various and subtle ways.

We must never think, once we have stated the theme of a story, that the whole purpose of the story has been to yield up this abstract statement. If this were so, there would be no reason for the story: we could start with the abstract statement. The function of the interpretive writer is not to state a theme but to vivify it. He wishes to deliver it not simply to our intellects, but to our emotions, our senses, and our imaginations. The theme of a story may be little or nothing except as it is embodied and vitalized by the story. Unembodied, it is a dry backbone, without flesh or life.

Sometimes the theme of a story is explicitly stated somewhere in the story, either by the author or by one of the characters. In "Youth" the narrator Marlow makes several statements which, with slight editorial changes, would serve admirably as statements of theme. More often, however, the theme is implied. The story writer, after all, is a story writer, not an essayist or a philosopher. His first business is to reveal life, not to comment on it. He may well feel that unless the story somehow expresses its own meaning, without his having to point it out, he has not told the story well. Or he may feel that if the story is to have its maximum emotional effect, he must refrain from interrupting it or making remarks about it. He is also wary of spoiling a story for the perceptive reader by "explaining" it as some people ruin jokes by explaining them. For these reasons theme is more often left implicit than stated explicitly. The good writer does not ordinarily write a story to "illustrate" a theme, as does the writer of parables or fables. He writes the story to bring alive some segment of human existence. When he does so searchingly and coherently, theme arises naturally out of what he has written. The good reader may state the generalizations for himself.

Some readers—especially student readers—look for a "moral" in everything they read—some rule of conduct which they regard as applicable to their lives. They consider the words "theme" and "moral" to be interchangeable. Sometimes the words are interchangeable. Occasionally the theme of a story may be expressed as a moral principle without doing violence to the story. More frequently, however, the word "moral" is too narrow to fit the kind of illumination provided by a first-rate story. It is hardly suitable, for instance, for the kind of story which simply displays human character. It would be entirely inappropriate for a story like "A Little Cloud." Such terms as "moral" and "lesson" are therefore best avoided in the discussion of fiction. The critical term *theme* is preferable for several reasons. First, it is less likely to obscure the fact that a story is not a preachment or a sermon: a story's *first* object is enjoyment. Second, it should keep us from trying to wring from every story a didactic pronouncement about life. The person who seeks a moral in every story is likely to oversimplify and conventionalize it—to reduce it to some dusty platitude like "Be kind to animals" or "Look before you leap" or "Crime does not pay." The purpose of the interpretive story writer is to give us a greater awareness and a greater understanding of life, not to inculcate a code of moral rules for regulating daily conduct. In getting at the theme of the story it is better to ask not *What does this story teach?* but *What does this story reveal?*

The reader who interprets Anderson's "I'm a Fool" as being merely a warning against lying has missed nine-tenths of the story. It is really a marvelously penetrating exploration of a complex personality. The theme is *not* "Honesty is the best policy" but something more like this: "A young man of respectable background who fails in various enterprises may develop ambivalent or contradictory values as well as feelings of inferiority. Consciously or unconsciously he will adopt various stratagems to compensate for these feelings by magnifying his importance both in his own eyes and in the eyes of others. If these stratagems backfire, he may recognize his folly but not the underlying reasons for it." Obviously, this dry statement is a poor thing beside the living reality of the story. But it is a more faithful abstracting of the content of the story than any "moral."

The revelation offered by a good story may be something fresh or something old. The story may bring us some insight into life that we had not had before, and thus expand our horizons, or it may make us *feel* or *feel again* some truth of which we have long been merely intellectually aware. We may know in our minds, for instance, that "War is horrible" or that "Old age is often pathetic and in need of understanding," but these are insights that need to be periodically renewed. *Emotionally* we may forget them, and, if we do, we are less alive and complete as human beings. The story writer performs a service for us—interprets life for us—whether he gives us new insights or refreshes and extends old ones.

The themes of commercial and quality stories may be identical, but frequently they are different. Commercial stories, for the most part, confirm their readers' prejudices, endorse their opinions, ratify their feelings, and satisfy their wishes. Usually, therefore, the themes of such stories are widely accepted platitudes of experience which may or may not be supported by the life around us. They represent life as we would like it to be, not always as it is. We should certainly like to believe, for instance, that "Motherhood is sacred," that "True love always wins through," that "Virtue and hard work are rewarded in the end," that "Cheaters never win," that "Old age brings a mellow wisdom which compensates for its infirmity," and that "Every human being has a soft spot in him somewhere." The interpretive writer, however, being a thoughtful observer of life, is likely to question these beliefs and often to challenge them. His ideas about life are not simply taken over ready-made from what he was taught in Sunday school or from the books he read as a child; they are the formulation of a sensitive and independent observer who has collated all that he has read and been taught with life itself. The themes of his stories therefore do not often correspond to the pretty little sentiments we find inscribed on candy valentines. They may sometimes represent rather somber truths. Much of the process of maturing as a reader lies in the discovery that there may be more nourishment and deeper enjoyment in assimilating these somber truths than in licking the sugar off of candy valentines.

We do not, however, have to accept the theme of an interpretive story any more than we do that of a commercial story. Though we should never summarily dismiss it without reflection, we may find that the theme of a story represents a judgment on life with which, on examination, we cannot agree. If it is the reasoned view of a seasoned and serious artist, nevertheless, it cannot be without value to us. There is value in knowing what the world looks like to other men, and we can thus use a judgment to expand our knowledge of human experience even though we cannot ourselves accept it. A genuine artist and thoughtful observer, moreover, can hardly fail to present us with partial insights along the way although we disagree with his total view. A good reader, therefore, will not reject a story because he rejects its theme. He can enjoy any story which arises from sufficient depth of observation and reflection and is artistically composed, though he disagrees with its theme; and he will prefer it to a shallower, less thoughtful, or less successfully integrated story which presents a theme which he endorses.

Discovering and stating the theme of a story is often a delicate task. Sometimes we will *feel* what the story is about strongly enough, and yet find it difficult to put this feeling into words. If we are skilled readers, it is perhaps unnecessary that we do so. The bare statement of the theme, so lifeless and impoverished when abstracted from the story, may seem to diminish the story to something less than it is. Often, however, the attempt to state theme will reveal to us aspects of a story which we should otherwise not have noticed, and will thereby lead to more thorough understanding. The ability to state theme, moreover, is a test of our understanding of a story. Beginning readers often think they understand a story when in actuality they have misunderstood it. They understand the events but not what the events add up to. Or, in adding up the events, they arrive at an erroneous total. People sometimes miss the point of a joke. It is not surprising that they should frequently miss the point of a good piece of fiction, which is many times more complex than a joke.

There is no prescribed method for discovering theme. Sometimes we can best get at it by asking in what way the main character has changed in the course of the story and what, if anything, he has learned before its end. Sometimes the best approach is to explore the nature of the central conflict and its outcome. Sometimes the title will provide an important clue. At all times we should keep in mind the following principles:

1. Theme must be expressible in the form of a statement with a

subject and predicate. It is insufficient to say that the theme of a story is motherhood or loyalty to country. Motherhood and loyalty are simply subjects. Theme must be a statement *about* the subject. For instance, "Motherhood sometimes has more frustrations than rewards," or "Loyalty to country often inspires heroic self-sacrifice." If we express the theme in the form of a phrase, the phrase must be convertible to sentence form. A phrase such as "the futility of envy," for instance, may be converted to the statement "Envy is futile": it may therefore serve as a statement of theme.

2. The theme must be stated as a *generalization* about life. In stating theme we do not use the names of the characters in the story, for to do so is to make a specific rather than a general statement. The theme of "The Little Business Man" is not that "Luke learns how to deal with his uncle, a man with a very practical approach to life." Rather, it is something like this: "A young, lonely boy learns that practical people, through their precise and exact attitude toward life, are capable of destroying things of great value."

3. We must be careful not to make the generalization larger than is justified by the terms of the story. Terms like *every, all, always,* should be used very cautiously; terms like *some, sometimes, may,* are often more accurate. The theme of "E Equals MC Squared" is not that "Evil actions will always be punished," for we are presented with only the one instance of retribution in the story. Furthermore, there are no evil qualities in Matt Colby that warrant his grisly death, and *his* death, therefore, would undermine such a theme. The theme of this story might be expressed thus: "Even an apparently passive and harmless individual may sometimes react with calculated and irreversible revenge." Notice that we have said *may sometimes,* not *will always.* Only occasionally will the theme of a story be expressible as a universal generalization. In "Youth," (page 456), we may well accept the theme of this story as having, if not universal, at least widespread application.

4. Theme is the *central* and *unifying* concept of the story. Therefore, (a) it must account for all the major details of the story. If we cannot explain the bearing of an important incident or character on the theme, either in exemplifying it or modifying it in some way, it is probable that our interpretation is partial and incomplete, that at best we have got hold only of a sub-theme. Another alternative, though it must be used with caution, is that the story itself is imperfectly constructed and lacks entire unity. (b) The theme must not be contradicted by any detail of the story. If we have to overlook or blink at or "force" the meaning of some significant detail in order to frame our statement, we may be sure that our statement is defective. (c) The theme must not rely upon supposed facts—facts not actually stated or clearly implied by the story. The theme must exist *inside,* not *outside* the story. It must be based on the

data of the story itself, not on assumptions supplied from our own experience.

5. There is no *one* way of stating the theme of a story. The story is not a guessing game or an acrostic which is supposed to yield some magic verbal formula which won't work if a syllable is changed. It merely presents a view of life, and, as long as the above conditions are fulfilled, that view may surely be stated in more than one way. Here, for instance, are three possible ways of stating the theme of "Horses of the Night." (a) "Sensitivity and creativity are often not appreciated by those whose main goal in life is to make a living or win a war." (b) "Those who are sensitive and creative may lose their sanity as a result of the pressures of society." (c) "A sensitive, creative individual frequently finds it difficult, often impossible, to cope with the realities of a mundane, pragmatic, sometimes cruel society; as a result, complete withdrawal may be the only solution." The third of these statements is fuller and therefore more precise than the first two, but each is a valid formulation.

6. We should avoid any statement which reduces the theme to some familiar saying that we have heard all our lives, such as "You can't judge a book by its cover" or "A stitch in time saves nine." Although such a statement *may* express the theme accurately, too often it is simply the lazy man's short cut which impoverishes the essential meaning of the story in order to save mental effort. When a reader forces every new experience into an old formula, he loses the chance for a fresh perception. Instead of letting the story expand his knowledge and awareness of the world, he falls back dully on a cliché. To come out with "Honesty is the best policy" as the theme of "I'm a Fool" is almost to lose the whole value of the story. If the impulse arises to express the meaning of a story in a ready-made phrase, it should be suppressed.

Alice Munro

BOYS AND GIRLS

My father was a fox farmer. That is, he raised silver foxes, in pens; and in the fall and early winter, when their fur was prime, he killed them and skinned them and sold their pelts to the Hudson's Bay Company or the Montreal Fur Traders. These companies supplied us with heroic calendars to hang, one on each side of the kitchen door. Against a background of cold blue sky and black pine forests and treacherous northern rivers, plumed adventurers planted the flags of England or of France; magnificent savages bent their backs to the portage.

For several weeks before Christmas, my father worked after supper in the cellar of our house. The cellar was white-washed, and lit by a hundred-watt bulb over the worktable. My brother Laird and I sat on the top step and watched. My father removed the pelt inside-out from the body of the fox, which looked surprisingly small, mean and rat-like, deprived of its arrogant weight of fur. The naked, slippery bodies were collected in a sack and buried at the dump. One time the hired man, Henry Bailey, had taken a swipe at me with this sack, saying, "Christmas present!" My mother thought that was not funny. In fact she disliked the whole pelting operation—that was what the killing, skinning, and preparation of the furs was called—and wished it did not have to take place in the house. There was the smell. After the pelt had been stretched inside-out on a long board my father scraped away delicately, removing the little clotted webs of blood vessels, the bubbles of fat; the smell of blood and animal fat, with the strong primitive odour of the fox itself, penetrated all parts of the house. I found it reassuringly seasonal, like the smell of oranges and pine needles.

Henry Bailey suffered from bronchial troubles. He would cough and cough until his narrow face turned scarlet, and his light blue, derisive eyes filled up with tears; then he took the lid off the stove, and, standing well back, shot out a great clot of phlegm—hsss—straight into the heart of the flames. We admired him for this performance and for his ability to make his stomach growl at will, and for his laughter, which was full of high whistlings and gurglings and involved the whole faulty machinery of his chest. It was sometimes hard to tell what he was laughing at, and always possible that it might be us.

After we had been sent to bed we could still smell fox and still hear Henry's laugh, but these things, reminders of the warm, safe, brightly lit downstairs world, seemed lost and diminished, floating on the stale cold air upstairs. We were afraid at night in the winter. We were not afraid of *outside* though this was the time of year when snowdrifts curled around our house like sleeping whales and the wind harassed us all night, coming up from the buried fields, the frozen swamp, with its old bugbear chorus of threats and misery. We were afraid of *inside*, the room where we slept. At this time the upstairs of our house was not finished. A brick chimney went up one wall. In the middle of the floor was a square hole, with a wooden railing around it; that was where the stairs came up. On the other side of the stairwell were the things that nobody had any use for any more—a soldiery roll of linoleum, standing on end, a wicker baby carriage, a fern basket, china jugs and basins with cracks in them, a picture of the Battle of Balaclava, very sad to look at. I had told Laird, as soon as he was old enough to understand such things, that bats and skeletons lived over there; whenever a man escaped from the county jail, twenty miles away, I imagined that he had somehow let himself in the window and was hiding behind the linoleum. But we had rules to keep us safe. When the light was on, we were safe as long as we did not step off the square of worn carpet which defined our bedroom-space; when the light was off no place was safe but the beds themselves. I had to turn out the light kneeling on the end of my bed, and stretching as far as I could to reach the cord.

In the dark we lay on our beds, our narrow life rafts, and fixed our eyes on the faint light coming up the stairwell, and sang songs. Laird sang "Jingle Bells," which he would sing any time, whether it was Christmas or not, and I sang "Danny Boy." I loved the sound of my own voice, frail and supplicating, rising in the dark. We could make out the tall frosted shapes of the windows now, gloomy and white. When I came to the part, *When I am dead, as dead I well may be*—a fit of shivering caused not by the cold sheets but by pleasurable emotion almost silenced me. *You'll kneel and say, an Ave there above me*—What was an Ave? Every day I forgot to find out.

Laird went straight from singing to sleep. I could hear his long, satisfied, bubbly breaths. Now for the time that remained to me, the most perfectly private and perhaps the best time of the whole day, I arranged myself tightly under the covers and went on with one of the stories I was telling myself from night to night. These stories were about myself, when I had grown a little older; they took place in a world that was recognizably mine, yet one that presented opportunities for courage, boldness and self-sacrifice, as mine never did. I rescued people from a bombed building (it discouraged me that the real war had gone on so far away from Jubilee). I shot two rabid wolves who were menacing the schoolyard (the teachers cowered terrified at my back). I rode a fine horse spiritedly down the main street of Jubilee, acknowl- edging the towns-people's gratitude for some yet-to-be-worked-out piece of heroism (nobody ever rode a horse there, except King Billy in the Orangeman's Day parade). There was always riding and shooting in these stories, though I had only been on a horse twice—bareback because we did not own a saddle—and the second time I had slid right around and dropped under the horse's feet; it had stepped placidly over me. I really was learning to shoot, but I could not hit anything yet, not even tin cans on fence posts.

Alive, the foxes inhabited a world my father made for them. It was surrounded by a high guard fence, like a medieval town, with a gate that was padlocked at night. Along the streets of this town were ranged large, sturdy pens. Each of them had a real door that a man could go through, a wooden ramp along the wire, for the foxes to run up and down on, and a kennel—something like a clothes chest with airholes—where they slept and stayed in winter and had their young. There were feeding and watering dishes attached to the wire in such a way that they could be emptied and cleaned from the outside. The dishes were made of old tin cans, and the ramps and kennels of odds and ends of old lumber. Everything was tidy and ingenious; my father was tirelessly inventive and his favourite book in the world was Robinson Crusoe. He had fitted a tin drum on a wheelbarrow, for bringing water down to the pens. This was my job in summer, when the foxes had to have water twice a day. Between nine and ten o'clock in the morning, and again after supper, I filled the drum at the pump and trundled it down through the barnyard to the pens, where I parked it, and filled my watering can and went along the streets. Laird came too, with his little cream and green gardening can, filled too full and knocking against his legs and slopping water on his canvas shoes. I had the real watering can, my father's, though I could only carry it three-quarters full.

The foxes all had names, which were printed on a tin plate and hung beside their doors. They were not named when they were born, but when they survived the first year's pelting and were added to the breeding stock. Those my father had named were called names like Prince, Bob, Wally and Betty. Those I had named were called Star or Turk, or Maureen or Diana. Laird named one Maud after a hired girl we had when he was little, one Harold after a boy at school, and one Mexico, he did not say why.

Naming them did not make pets out of them, or anything like it. Nobody but my father ever went into the pens, and he had twice had blood-poisoning from bites. When I was bringing them their water they prowled up and down on the paths they had made inside their pens, barking seldom—they saved that for nighttime, when they might get up a chorus of community frenzy—but always watching me, their eyes burning, clear gold, in their pointed, malevolent faces. They were beautiful for their delicate legs and heavy, aristocratic tails and the bright fur sprinkled on dark down their backs—which gave them their name—but especially for their faces, drawn exquisitely sharp in pure hostility, and their golden eyes.

Besides carrying water I helped my father when he cut the long grass, and the lamb's quarter and flowering money-musk, that grew between the pens. He cut with the scythe and I raked into piles. Then he took a pitchfork and threw fresh-cut grass all over the top of the pens, to keep the foxes cooler and shade their coats, which were browned by too much sun. My father did not talk to me unless it was about the job we were doing. In this he was quite different from my mother, who, if she was feeling cheerful, would tell me all sorts of things—the name of a dog she had had when she was a little girl, the names of boys she had gone out with later on when she was grown up, and what certain dresses of hers had looked like—she could not imagine now what had become of them. Whatever thoughts and stories my father had were private, and I was shy of him and would never ask him questions. Nevertheless I worked willingly under his eyes, and with a feeling of pride. One time a feed salesman came down into the pens to talk to him and my father said, "Like to have you meet my new hired man." I turned away and raked furiously, red in the face with pleasure.

"Could of fooled me," said the salesman. "I thought it was only a girl."

After the grass was cut, it seemed suddenly much later in the year. I walked on stubble in the earlier evening, aware of the reddening skies, the entering silences, of fall. When I wheeled the tank out of the gate and put the padlock on, it was almost dark. One night at this time I saw my mother and father standing talking on the little rise of ground we called the gangway, in front of the barn. My father had just come from the meathouse; he had his stiff bloody apron on, and a pail of cut-up meat in his hand.

It was an odd thing to see my mother down at the barn. She did not often come out of the house unless it was to do something—hang out the wash or dig potatoes in the garden. She looked out of place, with her bare lumpy legs, not touched by the sun, her apron still on and damp across the stomach from the supper dishes. Her hair was tied up in a kerchief, wisps of it falling out. She would tie her hair up like this in the morning, saying she did not have time to do it properly, and it would stay tied up all day. It was true, too; she really did not have time. These days our back porch was piled with baskets of peaches and grapes and pears, bought in town, and onions and tomatoes and cucumbers grown at home, all waiting to be made into jelly and jam and preserves, pickles and chili sauce. In the kitchen there was a fire in the stove all day, jars clinked in boiling water, sometimes a cheesecloth bag was strung on a pole between two chairs, straining blue-black grape pulp for jelly. I was given jobs to do and I would sit at the table peeling peaches that had been soaked in the hot water, or cutting up onions, my eyes smarting and streaming. As soon as I was done I ran out of the house, trying to get out of earshot before my mother thought of what she wanted me to do next. I hated the hot dark kitchen in summer, the green blinds and the flypapers, the same old oilcloth table and wavy mirror and bumpy linoleum. My mother was too tired and preoccupied to talk to me, she had no heart to tell about the Normal School Graduation Dance; sweat trickled over her face and she was always counting under her breath, pointing at jars, dumping cups of sugar. It seemed to me that work in the house was endless, dreary and peculiarly depressing; work done out of doors, and in my father's service, was ritualistically important.

I wheeled the tank up to the barn, where it was kept, and I heard my mother saying, "Wait till Laird gets a little bigger, then you'll have a real help."

What my father said I did not hear. I was pleased by the way he stood listening, politely as he would to a salesman or a stranger, but with an air of wanting to get on with his real work. I felt my mother had no business down here and I wanted him to feel the same way. What did she mean about Laird? He was no help to anybody. Where was he now? Swinging himself sick on the swing, going around in circles, or trying to catch caterpillars. He never once stayed with me till I was finished.

"And then I can use her more in the house," I heard my mother say. She had a dead-quiet, regretful way of talking about me that always made me uneasy. "I just get my back turned and she runs off. It's not like I had a girl in the family at all."

I went and sat on a feed bag in the corner of the barn, not wanting to appear when this conversation was going on. My mother, I felt, was not to be trusted. She was kinder than my father and more easily fooled, but you could not depend on her, and the real reasons for the things she said and did were not to be known. She loved me, and she sat up late at night making a dress of the difficult style I wanted, for me to wear when school started, but she was also my enemy. She was always plotting. She was plotting now to get me to stay in the house more, although she knew I hated it (because she knew I hated it) and keep me from working for my father. It seemed to me she would do this simply out of perversity, and to try her power. It did not occur to me that she could be lonely, or jealous. No grown-up could be; they were too fortunate. I sat and kicked my heels monotonously against a feedbag, raising dust, and did not come out till she was gone.

At any rate, I did not expect my father to pay any attention to what she said. Who could imagine Laird doing my work—Laird remembering the padlock and cleaning out the watering-dishes with a leaf on the end of a stick, or even wheeling the tank without it tumbling over? It showed how little my mother knew about the way things really were.

I have forgotten to say what the foxes were fed. My father's bloody apron reminded me. They were fed horsemeat. At this time most farmers still kept horses, and when a horse got too old to work, or broke a leg or got down and would not get up, as they sometimes did, the owner would call my father, and he and Henry went out to the farm in the truck. Usually they shot and butchered the horse there, paying the farmer from five to twelve dollars. If they had already too much meat on hand, they would bring the horse back alive, and keep it for a few days or weeks in our stable, until the meat was needed. After the war the farmers were buying tractors and gradually getting rid of horses altogether, so it sometimes happened that we got a good healthy horse, that there was just no use for any more. If this happened in the winter we might keep the horse in our stable till spring, for we had plenty of hay and if there was a lot of snow—and the plow did not always get our road cleared—it was convenient to be able to go to town with a horse and cutter.

The winter I was eleven years old we had two horses in the stable. We did not know what names they had had before, so we called them Mack and Flora. Mack was an old black workhorse, sooty and indifferent. Flora was a sorrel mare, a driver. We took them both out in the cutter. Mack was slow and easy to handle. Flora was given to fits of violent alarm, veering at cars and even at other horses, but we loved her speed and high-stepping, her general air of gallantry and abandon. On Saturdays we went down to the stable and as soon as we opened the door on its cosy, animal-smelling darkness Flora threw up her head, rolled her eyes, whinnied despairingly and pulled herself through a crisis of nerves on the spot. It was not safe to go into her stall; she would kick.

This winter also I began to hear a great deal more on the theme my mother had sounded when she had been talking in front of the barn. I no longer felt safe. It seemed that in the minds of the people around me there was a steady under-current of thought, not to be deflected, on this one subject. The word *girl* had formerly seemed to me innocent and unburdened, like the word *child;* now it appeared that it was no such thing. A girl was not, as I had supposed, simply what I was; it was what I had to become. It was a definition, always touched with emphasis, with reproach and disappointment. Also it was a joke on me. Once Laird and I were fighting, and for the first time ever I had to use all my strength against him; even so, he caught and pinned my arm for a moment, really hurting me. Henry saw this, and laughed, saying, "Oh, that there Laird's gonna show you, one of these days!" Laird was getting a lot bigger. But I was getting bigger too.

My grandmother came to stay with us for a few weeks and I heard other things. "Girls don't slam doors like that." "Girls keep their knees together when they sit down." And worse still, when I asked some questions, "That's none of girls' business." I continued to slam the doors and sit as awkwardly as possible, thinking that by such measures I kept myself free.

When spring came, the horses were let out in the barnyard. Mack stood against the barn wall trying to scratch his neck and haunches, but Flora trotted up and down and reared at the fences, clattering her hooves against the rails. Snow drifts dwindled quickly, revealing the hard grey and brown earth, the familiar rise and fall of the ground, plain and bare after the fantastic landscape of winter. There was a great feeling of opening-out, of release. We just wore rubbers now, over our shoes; our feet felt ridiculously light. One Saturday we went out to the stable and found all the doors open, letting in the unaccustomed sunlight and fresh air. Henry was there, just idling around looking at his collection of calendars which were tacked up behind the stalls in a part of the stable my mother had probably never seen.

"Come to say goodbye to your old friend Mack?" Henry said. "Here, you give him a taste of oats." He poured some oats into Laird's cupped hands and Laird went to feed Mack. Mack's teeth were in bad shape. He ate very slowly, patiently shifting the oats around in his mouth, trying to find a stump of a molar to grind it on. "Poor old Mack," said Henry mournfully. "When a horse's teeth's gone, he's gone. That's about the way."

"Are you going to shoot him today?" I said. Mack and Flora had been in the stable so long I had almost forgotten they were going to be shot.

Henry didn't answer me. Instead he started to sing in a high, trembly, mocking-sorrowful voice, *Oh, there's no more work, for poor Uncle Ned, he's gone where the good darkies go.* Mack's thick, blackish tongue worked diligently at Laird's hand. I went out before the song was ended and sat down on the gangway.

I had never seen them shoot a horse, but I knew where it was done. Last summer Laird and I had come upon a horse's entrails before they were buried. We had thought it was a big black snake, coiled up in the sun. That was around in the field that ran up beside the barn. I thought that if we went inside the barn, and found a wide crack or a knothole to look through, we would be able to see them do it. It was not something I wanted to see; just the same, if a thing really happened, it was better to see it, and know.

My father came down from the house, carrying the gun.

"What are you doing here?" he said.

"Nothing."

"Go on up and play around the house."

He sent Laird out of the stable. I said to Laird, "Do you want to see them shoot Mack?" and without waiting for an answer led him around to the front door of the barn, opened it carefully, and went in. "Be quiet or they'll hear us," I said. We could hear Henry and my father talking in the stable, then the heavy, shuffling steps of Mack being backed out of his stall.

In the loft it was cold and dark. Thin, crisscrossed beams of sunlight fell through the cracks. The hay was low. It was a rolling country, hills and hollows, slipping under our feet. About four feet up was a beam going around the walls. We piled hay up in one corner and I boosted

Laird up and hoisted myself. The beam was not very wide; we crept along it with our hands flat on the barn walls. There were plenty of knotholes, and I found one that gave me the view I wanted—a corner of the barnyard, the gate, part of the field. Laird did not have a knothole and began to complain.

I showed him a widened crack between two boards. "Be quiet and wait. If they hear you you'll get us in trouble."

My father came in sight carrying the gun. Henry was leading Mack by the halter. He dropped it and took out his cigarette papers and tobacco; he rolled cigarettes for my father and himself. While this was going on Mack nosed around in the old, dead grass along the fence. Then my father opened the gate and they took Mack through. Henry led Mack away from the path to a patch of ground and they talked together, not loud enough for us to hear. Mack again began searching for a mouthful of fresh grass, which was not to be found. My father walked away in a straight line, and stopped short at a distance which seemed to suit him. Henry was walking away from Mack too, but sideways, still negligently holding on to the halter. My father raised the gun and Mack looked up as if he had noticed something and my father shot him.

Mack did not collapse at once but swayed, lurched sideways and fell, first on his side; then he rolled over on his back and, amazingly, kicked his legs for a few seconds in the air. At this Henry laughed, as if Mack had done a trick for him. Laird, who had drawn a long, groaning breath of surprise when the shot was fired, said out loud, "He's not dead." And it seemed to me it might be true. But his legs stopped, he rolled on his side again, his muscles quivered and sank. The two men walked over and looked at him in a businesslike way; they bent down and examined his forehead where the bullet had gone in, and now I saw his blood on the brown grass.

"Now they just skin him and cut him up," I said. "Let's go." My legs were a little shaky and I jumped gratefully down into the hay. "Now you've seen how they shoot a horse," I said in a congratulatory way, as if I had seen it many times before. "Let's see if any barn cat's had kittens in the hay." Laird jumped. He seemed young and obedient again. Suddenly I remembered how, when he was little, I had brought him into the barn and told him to climb the ladder to the top beam. That was in the spring, too, when the hay was low. I had done it out of a need for excitement, a desire for something to happen so that I could tell about it. He was wearing a little bulky brown and white checked coat, made down from one of mine. He went all the way up, just as I told him, and sat down on the top beam with the hay far below him on one side, and the barn floor and some old machinery on the other. Then I ran screaming to my father, "Laird's up on the top beam!" My father came, my mother came, my father went up the ladder talking very quietly and brought Laird down under his arm, at which my mother leaned against the ladder and began to cry. They said to me, "Why weren't you watching him?" but nobody ever knew the truth. Laird did not know enough to tell. But whenever I saw the brown and white checked coat hanging in the closet, or at the bottom of the rag bag, which was where it ended up, I felt a weight in my stomach, the sadness of unexorcized guilt.

I looked at Laird who did not even remember this, and I did not like the look on this thin, winter-pale face. His expression was not frightened or upset, but remote, concentrating. "Listen," I said, in an unusually bright and friendly voice, "you aren't going to tell, are you?"

"No," he said absently.

"Promise."

"Promise," he said. I grabbed the hand behind his back to make sure he was not crossing his fingers. Even so, he might have a nightmare; it might come out that way. I decided I had better work hard to get all thoughts of what he had seen out of his mind—which, it seemed to me, could not hold very many things at a time. I got some money I had saved and that afternoon we went into Jubilee and saw a show, with Judy Canova, at which we both laughed a great deal. After that I thought it would be all right.

Two weeks later I knew they were going to shoot Flora. I knew from the night before, when I heard my mother ask if the hay was holding out all right, and my father said, "Well, after to-morrow there'll just be the cow, and we should be able to put her out to grass in another week." So I knew it was Flora's turn in the morning.

This time I didn't think of watching it. That was something to see just one time. I had not thought about it very often since, but sometimes when I was busy, working at school, or standing in front of the mirror combing my hair and wondering if I would be pretty when I grew up, the whole scene would flash into my mind: I would see the easy, practised way my father raised the gun, and hear Henry laughing when Mack kicked his legs in the air. I did not have any great feeling of horror and opposition, such as a city child might have had; I was too used to seeing the death of animals as a necessity by which we lived. Yet I felt a little ashamed, and there was a new wariness, a sense of holding-off, in my attitude to my father and his work.

It was a fine day, and we were going around the yard picking up tree branches that had been torn off in winter storms. This was something we had been told to do, and also we wanted to use them to make a teepee. We heard Flora whinny, and then my father's voice and Henry's shouting, and we ran down to the barnyard to see what was going on.

The stable door was open. Henry had just brought Flora out, and she had broken away from him. She was running free in the barnyard, from one end to the other. We climbed up on the fence. It was exciting to see her running, whinnying, going up on her hind legs, prancing and threatening like a horse in a Western movie, an unbroken ranch horse, though she was just an old driver, an old sorrel mare. My father and Henry ran after her and tried to grab the dangling halter. They tried to work her into a corner, and they had almost succeeded when she made a run between them, wild-eyed, and disappeared around the corner of the barn. We heard the rails clatter down as she got over the fence, and Henry yelled, "She's into the field now!"

That meant she was in the long L-shaped field that ran up by the house. If she got around the centre, heading towards the lane, the gate was open; the truck had been driven into the field this morning. My father shouted to me, because I was on the other side of the fence, nearest the lane, "Go shut the gate!"

I could run very fast. I ran across the garden, past the tree where our swing was hung, and jumped across a ditch into the lane. There was the open gate. She had not got out, I could not see her up on the road; she must have run to the other end of the field. The gate was heavy. I lifted it out of the gravel and carried it across the roadway. I had it half-way across when she came in sight, galloping straight towards me. There was just time to get the chain on. Laird came scrambling through the ditch to help me.

Instead of shutting the gate, I opened it as wide as I could. I did not make any decision to do this, it was just what I did. Flora never slowed down; she galloped straight past me, and Laird jumped up and down, yelling, "Shut it, shut it!" even after it was too late. My father and Henry appeared in the field a moment too late to see what I had done. They only saw Flora heading for the township road. They would think I had not got there in time.

They did not waste any time asking about it. They went back to the barn and got the gun and the knives they used, and put these in the truck; then they turned the truck around and came bouncing up the field toward us. Laird called to them, "Let me go too, let me go too!" and Henry stopped the truck and they took him in. I shut the gate after they were all gone.

I supposed Laird would tell. I wondered what would happen to me. I had never disobeyed my father before, and I could not understand why I had done it. Flora would not really get away. They would catch up with her in the truck. Or if they did not catch her this morning somebody would see her and telephone us this afternoon or tomorrow. There was no wild country here for her to run to, only farms. What was more, my father had paid for her, we needed the meat to feed the foxes, we needed the foxes to make our living. All I had done was make more work for my father who worked hard enough already. And when my father found out about it he was not going to trust me any more; he would know that I was not entirely on his side. I was on Flora's side, and that made me no use to anybody, not even to her. Just the same, I did not regret it; when she came running at me and I held the gate open, that was the only thing I could do.

I went back to the house, and my mother said, "What's all the commotion?" I told her that Flora had kicked down the fence and got away. "Your poor father," she said, "now he'll have to go chasing over the countryside. Well, there isn't any use planning dinner before one." She put up the ironing board. I wanted to tell her, but thought better of it and went upstairs and sat on my bed.

Lately I had been trying to make my part of the room fancy, spreading the bed with old lace curtains, and fixing myself a dressing-table with some leftovers of cretonne for a skirt. I planned to put up some kind of barricade between my bed and Laird's, to keep my section separate from his. In the sunlight, the lace curtains were just dusty rags. We did not sing at night any more. One night when I was singing Laird said, "You sound silly," and I went right on but the next night I did not start. There was not so much need to anyway, we were no longer afraid. We knew it was just old furniture over there, old jumble and confusion. We did not keep to the rules. I still stayed awake after Laird was asleep and told myself stories, but even in these stories something different was happening, mysterious alterations took place. A story might start off in the old way, with a spectacular danger, a fire or wild animals, and for a while I might rescue people; then things would change around, and instead, somebody would be rescuing me. It might be a boy from our class at school, or even Mr. Campbell, our teacher, who tickled girls under the arms. And at this point the story concerned itself at great length with what I looked like—how long my hair was, and what kind of dress I had on; by the time I had these details worked out the real excitement of the story was lost.

It was later than one o'clock when the truck came back. The tarpaulin was over the back, which meant there was meat in it. My mother had to heat dinner up all over again. Henry and my father had changed from their bloody overalls into ordinary working overalls in the barn, and they washed their arms and necks and faces at the sink, and splashed water on their hair and combed it. Laird lifted his arm to show off a streak of blood. "We shot old Flora," he said, "and cut her up in fifty pieces."

"Well I don't want to hear about it," my mother said. "And don't come to my table like that."

My father made him go and wash the blood off.

We sat down and my father said grace and Henry pasted his chewing-gum on the end of his fork, the way he always did; when he took it off he would have us admire the pattern. We began to pass the bowls of steaming, overcooked vegetables. Laird looked across the table at me and said proudly, distinctly, "Anyway it was her fault Flora got away."

"What?" my father said.

"She could of shut the gate and she didn't. She just open' it up and Flora run out."

"Is that right?" my father said.

Everybody at the table was looking at me. I nodded, swallowing food with great difficulty. To my shame, tears flooded my eyes.

My father made a curt sound of disgust. "What did you do that for?"

I did not answer. I put down my fork and waited to be sent from the table, still not looking up.

But this did not happen. For some time nobody said anything, then Laird said matter-of-factly, "She's crying."

"Never mind," my father said. He spoke with resignation, even good humour, the words which absolved and dismissed me for good. "She's only a girl," he said.

I didn't protest that, even in my heart. Maybe it was true.

QUESTIONS

1. In what ways do the mother and father carry out the traditional, stereotyped, male-female roles? Would either one wish to change? Explain.
2. "A girl was not, as I had supposed, simply what I was: it was what I had to become. It was a definition, always touched with emphasis, with reproach and disappointment. Also it was a joke on me." First explain, then paraphrase these remarks. Write a statement beginning, "A boy . . . ."
3. The narrator remains nameless throughout the story, but we are told that her younger brother's name is Laird. What does his name mean? What is the significance of these two facts?
4. List instances of the love-hate relationship between the mother and daughter. What has precipitated this feeling?
5. Describe the girl's attitude toward the foxes, which is typified in such lines as ". . . pointed, malevolent faces . . . drawn exquisitely sharp in pure hostility." Find other examples of her attitude. How significant are the foxes in this story?
6. The foxes are what we shall later refer to as a *symbol* (see Chapter 6). What qualities or abstractions do the foxes seem to represent to you?
7. Trace the changes that take place in the girl. How does she manifest them outwardly?
8. The author uses exceptionally visual images: "its arrogant weight of fur"; snowdrifts . . . like sleeping whales." List other examples and explain their effectiveness.

9. What is the central conflict of the story? Is it external or internal? Is it a dilemma?
10. What is the central theme? Is it explicit or implicit?
11. At the end of the story, the girl appears to have capitulated and is prepared to accept her stereotyped role as "only a girl." Would this classify as a "happy ending"? Justify your position.

Roch Carrier

A SECRET LOST IN THE WATER

After I started going to school my father scarcely talked any more. I was very intoxicated by the new game of spelling; my father had little skill for it (it was my mother who wrote our letters) and was convinced I was no longer interested in hearing him tell of his adventures during the long weeks when he was far away from the house.

One day, however, he said to me:

"The time's come to show you something."

He asked me to follow him. I walked behind him, not talking, as we had got in the habit of doing. He stopped in the field before a clump of leafy bushes.

"Those are called alders," he said.

"I know."

"You have to learn how to choose," my father pointed out.

I didn't understand. He touched each branch of the bush, one at a time, with religious care.

"You have to choose one that's very fine, a perfect one, like this."

I looked; it seemed exactly like the others.

My father opened his pocket knife and cut the branch he'd selected with pious care. He stripped off the leaves and showed me the branch, which formed a perfect Y.

"You see," he said, "the branch has two arms. Now take one in each hand. And squeeze them."

I did as he asked and took in each hand one fork of the Y, which was thinner than a pencil.

"Close your eyes," my father ordered, "and squeeze a little harder . . . Don't open your eyes! Do you feel anything?"

"The branch is moving!" I exclaimed, astonished.

A SECRET LOST IN THE WATER By Roch Carrier, translated by Sheila Fischman, from *The Hockey Sweater and Other Stories*, (Toronto: House of Anansi Press, 1979). Reprinted by permission of the publisher.

Beneath my clenched fingers the alder was wriggling like a small, frightened snake. My father saw that I was about to drop it.

"Hang on to it!"

"The branch is squirming," I repeated. "And I hear something that sounds like a river!"

"Open your eyes," my father ordered.

I was stunned, as though he'd awakened me while I was dreaming.

"What does it mean?" I asked my father.

"It means that underneath us, right here, there's a little freshwater spring. If we dig, we could drink from it. I've just taught you how to find a spring. It's something my own father taught me. It isn't something you learn in school. And it isn't useless: a man can get along without writing and arithmetic, but he can never get along without water."

Much later, I discovered that my father was famous in the region because of what the people called his 'gift': before digging a well they always consulted him; they would watch him prospecting the fields or the hills, eyes closed, hands clenched on the fork of an alder bough. Wherever my father stopped, they marked the ground; there they would dig; and from there water would gush forth.

Years passed; I went to other schools, saw other countries, I had children, I wrote some books and my poor father is lying in the earth where so many times he had found fresh water.

One day someone began to make a film about my village and its inhabitants, from whom I've stolen so many of the stories that I tell. With the film crew we went to see a farmer to capture the image of a sad man: his children didn't want to receive the inheritance he'd spent his whole life preparing for them—the finest farm in the area. While the technicians were getting cameras and microphones ready the farmer put his arm around my shoulders, saying:

"I knew your father well."

"Ah! I know. Everybody in the village knows each other . . . No one feels like an outsider."

"You know what's under your feet?"

"Hell?" I asked, laughing.

"Under your feet there's a well. Before I dug I called in specialists from the Department of Agriculture; they did research, they analyzed shovelfuls of dirt; and they made a report where they said there wasn't any water on my land. With the family, the animals, the crops, I need water. When I saw that those specialists hadn't found any I thought of your father and I asked him to come over. He didn't want to; I think he was pretty fed up with me because I'd asked those specialists instead of him. But finally he came; he went and cut off a little branch, then he walked around for a while with his eyes shut; he stopped, he listened to something we couldn't hear and then he said to me: 'Dig right here, there's enough water to get your whole flock drunk and drown your specialists besides.' We dug and found water. Fine water that's never heard of pollution."

The film people were ready; they called to me to take my place.

"I'm gonna show you something," said the farmer, keeping me back. "You wait right here."

He disappeared into a shack which he must have used to store things, then came back with a branch which he held out to me.

"I never throw nothing away; I kept the alder branch your father cut to find my water. I don't understand, it hasn't dried out."

Moved as I touched the branch, kept out of I don't know what sense of piety—and which really wasn't dry—I had the feeling that my father was watching me over my shoulder; I closed my eyes and, standing above the spring my father had discovered, I waited for the branch to writhe. I hoped the sound of gushing water would rise to my ears.

The alder stayed motionless in my hands and the water beneath the earth refused to sing.

Somewhere along the roads I'd taken since the village of my childhood I had forgotten my father's knowledge.

"Don't feel sorry," said the man, thinking no doubt of his farm and his childhood; "nowadays fathers can't pass on anything to the next generation."

And he took the alder branch from my hands.

QUESTIONS

1. The forked stick which the father uses to locate water is called a divining rod. Why did the father feel compelled to teach his son the art of divining? The son obviously inherited his father's gift: is there any evidence in the story that he ever used this gift? What explanation can you give for this fact?
2. A religious atmosphere pervades the beginning and end of the story. Find some examples. Why is this atmosphere appropriate? What other moods does the narrator experience?
3. Authors frequently spend a long time determining titles. What is the significance of this title?
4. This story demonstrates how a very slight plot may be used to provide a considerable illumination of life. How would you describe, in a sentence, the purpose of the story?
5. Although this story contains little action, it dramatizes a significant conflict. Is the conflict external or internal? Is it resolved?
6. What is the theme of this story? Is it a true expression of some relationships today? Explain.
7. How do you feel at the end of this story? Does your mood help you understand the theme?

Philip Roth

DEFENDER OF THE FAITH

In May of 1945, only a few weeks after the fighting had ended in Europe, I was rotated back to the States, where I spent the remainder of the war with a training company at Camp Crowder, Missouri. Along with the rest of the Ninth Army, I had been racing across Germany so swiftly during the late winter and spring that when I boarded the plane, I couldn't believe its destination lay to the west. My mind might inform me otherwise, but there was an inertia of the spirit that told me we were flying to a new front, where we would disembark and continue our push eastward—eastward until we'd circled the globe, marching through villages along whose twisting, cobbled streets crowds of the enemy would watch us take possession of what, up till then, they'd considered their own. I had changed enough in two years not to mind the trembling of the old people, the crying of the very young, the uncertainty and fear in the eyes of the once arrogant. I had been fortunate enough to develop an infantryman's heart, which, like his feet, at first aches and swells but finally grows horny enough for him to travel the weirdest paths without feeling a thing.

Captain Paul Barrett was my C.O. in Camp Crowder. The day I reported for duty, he came out of his office to shake my hand. He was short, gruff, and fiery, and—indoors or out—he wore his polished helmet liner pulled down to his little eyes. In Europe, he had received a battlefield commission and a serious chest wound, and he'd been returned to the States only a few months before. He spoke easily to me, and at the evening formation he introduced me to the troops. "Gentlemen," he said, "Sergeant Thurston, as you know, is no longer with this company. Your new first sergeant is Sergeant Nathan Marx, here. He is a veteran of the European theater, and consequently will expect to find a company of soldiers here, and not a company of *boys*."

I sat up late in the orderly room that evening, trying half-heartedly to solve the riddle of duty rosters, personnel forms, and morning reports. The Charge of Quarters slept with his mouth open on a mattress on the floor. A trainee stood reading the next day's duty roster, which was posted on the bulletin board just inside the screen door. It was a warm evening, and I could hear radios playing dance music over in the barracks. The trainee, who had been staring at me whenever he thought I wouldn't notice, finally took a step in my direction.

DEFENDER OF THE FAITH From *Goodbye, Columbus* by Philip Roth. Copyright © 1959 by Philip Roth. Reprinted by permission of Houghton Mifflin Company.

"Hey, Sarge—we having a G.I. party tomorrow night?" he asked. A G.I. party is a barracks cleaning.

"You usually have them on Friday nights?" I asked him.

"Yes," he said, and then he added, mysteriously, "that's the whole thing."

"Then you'll have a G.I. party."

He turned away, and I heard him mumbling. His shoulders were moving, and I wondered if he was crying.

"What's your name, soldier?" I asked.

He turned, not crying at all. Instead, his green-speckled eyes, long and narrow, flashed like fish in the sun. He walked over to me and sat on the edge of my desk. He reached out a hand. "Sheldon," he said.

"Stand on your feet, Sheldon."

Getting off the desk, he said, "Sheldon Grossbart." He smiled at the familiarity into which he'd led me.

"You against cleaning the barracks Friday night, Grossbart?" I said. "Maybe we shouldn't have G.I. parties. Maybe we should get a maid." My tone startled me. I felt I sounded like every top sergeant I had ever known.

"No, Sergeant." He grew serious, but with a seriousness that seemed to be only the stifling of a smile. "It's just—G.I. parties on Friday night, of all nights."

He slipped up onto the corner of the desk again—not quite sitting, but not quite standing, either. He looked at me with those speckled eyes flashing, and then made a gesture with his hand. It was very slight—no more than a movement back and forth of the wrist—and yet it managed to exclude from our affairs everything else in the orderly room, to make the two of us the center of the world. It seemed, in fact, to exclude everything even about the two of us except our hearts.

"Sergeant Thurston was one thing," he whispered, glancing at the sleeping C.Q., "but we thought that with you here things might be a little different."

"We?"

"The Jewish personnel."

"Why?" I asked, harshly. "What's on your mind?" Whether I was still angry at the "Sheldon" business, or now at something else, I hadn't time to tell, but clearly I was angry.

"We thought you—Marx, you know, like Karl Marx. The Marx Brothers. Those guys are all—M-a-r-x. Isn't that how *you* spell it, Sergeant?"

"M-a-r-x."

"Fishbein said—" He stopped. "What I mean to say, Sergeant—" His face and neck were red, and his mouth moved but no words came out. In a moment, he raised himself to attention, gazing down at me. It was as though he had suddenly decided he could expect no more sympathy from me than from Thurston, the reason being that I was of Thurston's faith, and not his. The young man had managed to confuse himself as to what my faith really was, but I felt no desire to straighten him out. Very simply, I didn't like him.

When I did nothing but return his gaze, he spoke, in an altered tone. "You see, Sergeant," he explained to me, "Friday nights, Jews are supposed to go to services."

"Did Sergeant Thurston tell you you couldn't go to them when there was a G.I. party?"

"No."

"Did he say you had to stay and scrub the floors?"

"No, Sergeant."

"Did the Captain say you had to stay and scrub the floors?"

"That isn't it, Sergeant. It's the other guys in the barracks." He leaned toward me. "They think we're goofing off. But we're not. That's when Jews go to services, Friday night. We have to."

"Then go."

"But the other guys make accusations. They have no right."

"That's not the Army's problem, Grossbart. It's a personal problem you'll have to work out yourself."

"But it's un*fair*."

I got up to leave. "There's nothing I can do about it," I said.

Grossbart stiffened and stood in front of me. "But this is a matter of *religion*, sir."

"Sergeant," I said.

"I mean 'Sergeant,'" he said, almost snarling.

"Look, go see the chaplain. You want to see Captain Barrett, I'll arrange an appointment."

"No, no. I don't want to make trouble, Sergeant. That's the first thing they throw up to you. I just want my rights!"

"Damn it, Grossbart, stop whining. You have your rights. You can stay and scrub floors or you can go to shul—"

The smile swam in again. Spittle gleamed at the corners of his mouth. "You mean church, Sergeant."

"I mean shul, Grossbart!"

I walked past him and went outside. Near me, I heard the scrunching of a guard's boots on gravel. Beyond the lighted windows of the barracks, young men in T shirts and fatigue pants were sitting on their bunks, polishing their rifles. Suddenly there was a light rustling behind me. I turned and saw Grossbart's dark frame fleeing back to the

shul: synagogue

barracks, racing to tell his Jewish friends that they were right—that, like Karl and Harpo, I was one of them.

The next morning, while chatting with Captain Barrett, I recounted the incident of the previous evening. Somehow, in the telling, it must have seemed to the Captain that I was not so much explaining Grossbart's position as defending it. "Marx, I'd fight side by side with a nigger if the fella proved to me he was a man. I pride myself," he said, looking out the window, "that I've got an open mind. Consequently, Sergeant, nobody gets special treatment here, for the good *or* the bad. All a man's got to do is prove himself. A man fires well on the range, I give him a weekend pass. He scores high in P.T., he gets a weekend pass. He *earns* it." He turned from the window and pointed a finger at me. "You're a Jewish fella, am I right, Marx?"

"Yes, sir."

"And I admire you. I admire you because of the ribbons on your chest. I judge a man by what he shows me on the field of battle, Sergeant. It's what he's got *here*," he said, and then, though I expected he would point to his chest, he jerked a thumb toward the buttons straining to hold his blouse across his belly. "Guts," he said.

"O.K., sir. I only wanted to pass on to you how the men felt."

"Mr. Marx, you're going to be old before your time if you worry about how the men feel. Leave that stuff to the chaplain—that's his business, not yours. Let's us train these fellas to shoot straight. If the Jewish personnel feels the other men are accusing them of gold-bricking—well, I just don't know. Seems awful funny that suddenly the Lord is calling so loud in Private Grossman's ear he's just got to run to church."

"Synagogue," I said.

"Synagogue is right, Sergeant. I'll write that down for handy reference. Thank you for stopping by."

That evening, a few minutes before the company gathered outside the orderly room for the chow formation, I called the C.Q., Corporal Robert LaHill, in to see me. LaHill was a dark, burly fellow whose hair curled out of his clothes wherever it could. He had a glaze in his eyes that made one think of caves and dinosaurs. "LaHill," I said, "when you take the formation, remind the men that they're free to attend church services *whenever* they are held, provided they report to the orderly room before they leave the area."

LaHill scratched his wrist, but gave no indication that he'd heard or understood.

"LaHill," I said, "*church*. You remember? Church, priest, Mass, confession."

He curled one lip into a kind of smile; I took it for a signal that for a second he had flickered back up into the human race.

"Jewish personnel who want to attend services this evening are to fall out in front of the orderly room at 1900," I said. Then, as an afterthought, I added, "By order of Captain Barrett."

A little while later, as the day's last light—softer than any I had seen that year—began to drop over Camp Crowder, I heard LaHill's thick, inflectionless voice outside my window: "Give me your ears, troopers. Toppie says for me to tell you that at 1900 hours all Jewish personnel is to fall out in front, here, if they want to attend the Jewish Mass."

At seven o'clock, I looked out the orderly-room window and saw three soldiers in starched khakis standing on the dusty quadrangle. They looked at their watches and fidgeted while they whispered back and forth. It was getting dimmer, and, alone on the otherwise deserted field, they looked tiny. When I opened the door, I heard the noises of the G.I. party coming from the surrounding barracks—bunks being pushed to the walls, faucets pounding water into buckets, brooms whisking at the wooden floors, cleaning the dirt away for Saturday's inspection. Big puffs of cloth moved round and round on the window-panes. I walked outside, and the moment my foot hit the ground I thought I heard Grossbart call to the others, " 'Ten-*hut*!" Or maybe, when they all three jumped to attention, I imagined I heard the command.

Grossbart stepped forward, "Thank you, sir," he said.

" 'Sergeant,' Grossbart," I reminded him. "You call officers 'sir'. I'm not an officer. You've been in the Army three weeks—you know that."

He turned his palms out at his sides to indicate that, in truth, he and I lived beyond convention. "Thank you, anyway," he said.

"Yes," a tall boy behind him said. "Thanks a lot."

And the third boy whispered, "Thank you," but his mouth barely fluttered, so that he did not alter by more than a lip's movement his posture of attention.

"For what?" I asked.

Grossbart snorted happily. "For the announcement. The Corporal's announcement. It helped. It made it—"

"Fancier." The tall boy finished Grossbart's sentence.

Grossbart smiled. "He means formal, sir. Public," he said to me. "Now it won't seem as though we're just taking off—goldbricking because the work has begun."

"It was by order of Captain Barrett," I said.

"Aaah, but you pull a little weight," Grossbart said. "So we thank you." Then he turned to his companions. "Sergeant Marx, I want you to meet Larry Fishbein."

The tall boy stepped forward and extended his hand. I shook it. "You from New York?" he asked.

"Yes."

"Me, too." He had a cadaverous face that collapsed inward from his cheekbone to his jaw, and when he smiled—as he did at the news of our communal attachment—revealed a mouthful of bad teeth. He was blinking his eyes a good deal, as though he were fighting back tears. "What borough?" he asked.

I turned to Grossbart. "It's five after seven. What time are services?"

"Shul," he said, smiling, "is in ten minutes. I want you to meet Mickey Halpern. This is Nathan Marx, our sergeant."

The third boy hopped forward. "Private Michael Halpern." He saluted.

"Salute officers, Halpern," I said. The boy dropped his hand, and, on its way down, in his nervousness, checked to see if his shirt pockets were buttoned.

"Shall I march them over, sir?" Grossbart asked. "Or are you coming along?"

From behind Grossbart, Fishbein piped up. "Afterward, they're having refreshments. A ladies' auxiliary from St. Louis, the rabbi told us last week."

"The chaplain," Halpern whispered.

"You're welcome to come along," Grossbart said.

To avoid his plea, I looked away, and saw, in the windows of the barracks, a cloud of faces staring out at the four of us. "Hurry along, Grossbart," I said.

"O.K., then," he said. He turned to the others. "Double time, *march!*"

They started off, but ten feet away Grossbart spun around and, running backward, called to me, "Good *shabbus*, sir!" And then the three of them were swallowed into the alien Missouri dusk.

Even after they had disappeared over the parade ground, whose green was now a deep blue, I could hear Grossbart singing the double-time cadence, and as it grew dimmer and dimmer, it suddenly touched a deep memory—as did the slant of the light—and I was remembering the shrill sounds of a Bronx playground where, years ago, beside the Grand Concourse, I had played on long spring evenings such as this. It was a pleasant memory for a young man so far from peace and home, and it brought so many recollections with it that I began to grow exceedingly tender about myself. In fact, I indulged myself in a reverie so strong that I felt as though a hand were reaching down inside me. It had to reach so very far to touch me! It had to reach past those days in the forests of

shabbus: Sabbath

Belgium, and past the dying I'd refused to weep over; past the nights in German farmhouses whose books we'd burned to warm us; past endless stretches when I had shut off all softness I might feel for my fellows, and had managed even to deny myself the posture of a conqueror—the swagger that I, as a Jew, might well have worn as my boots whacked against the rubble of Wesel, Münster, and Braunschweig.

But now one night noise, one rumor of home and time past, and memory plunged down through all I had anesthetized, and came to what I suddenly remembered was myself. So it was not altogether curious that, in search of more of me, I found myself following Grossbart's tracks to Chapel No. 3, where the Jewish services were being held.

I took a seat in the last row, which was empty. Two rows in front of me sat Grossbart, Fishbein, and Halpern, holding little white Dixie cups. Each row of seats was raised higher than the one in front of it, and I could see clearly what was going on. Fishbein was pouring the contents of his cup into Grossbart's, and Grossbart looked mirthful as the liquid made a purple arc between Fishbein's hand and his. In the glaring yellow light, I saw the chaplain standing on the platform at the front; he was chanting the first line of the responsive reading. Grossbart's prayer book remained closed on his lap; he was swishing the cup around. Only Halpern responded to the chant by praying. The fingers of his right hand were spread wide across the cover of his open book. His cap was pulled down low onto his brow, which made it round, like a yarmulke. From time to time, Grossbart wet his lips at the cup's edge; Fishbein, his long yellow face a dying light bulb, looked from here to there, craning forward to catch sight of the faces down the row, then of those in front of him, then behind. He saw me, and his eyelids beat a tattoo. His elbow slid into Grossbart's side, his neck inclined toward his friend, he whispered something, and then, when the congregation next responded to the chant, Grossbart's voice was among the others. Fishbein looked into his book now, too; his lips, however, didn't move.

Finally, it was time to drink the wine. The chaplain smiled down at them as Grossbart swigged his in one long gulp, Halpern sipped, meditating, and Fishbein faked devotion with an empty cup. "As I look down amongst the congregation"—the chaplain grinned at the word— "this night, I see many new faces, and I want to welcome you to Friday-night services here at Camp Crowder. I am Major Leo Ben Ezra, your chaplain." Though an American, the chaplain spoke deliberately— syllable by syllable, almost—as though to communicate, above all, with the lip readers in his audience. "I have only a few words to say

yarmulke: skull cap

before we adjourn to the refreshment room, where the kind ladies of the Temple Sinai, St. Louis, Missouri, have a nice setting for you."

Applause and whistling broke out. After another momentary grin, the chaplain raised his hands, palms out, his eyes flicking upward a moment, as if to remind the troops where they were and Who Else might be in attendance. In the sudden silence that followed, I thought I heard Grossbart cackle, "Let the goyim clean the floors!" Were those the words? I wasn't sure, but Fishbein, grinning, nudged Halpern. Halpern looked dumbly at him, then went back to his prayer book, which had been occupying him all through the rabbi's talk. One hand tugged at the black kinky hair that stuck out under his cap. His lips moved.

The rabbi continued. "It is about the food that I want to speak to you for a moment. I know, I know, I know," he intoned, wearily, "how in the mouths of most of you the *trafe* food tastes like ashes. I know how you gag, some of you, and how your parents suffer to think of their children eating foods unclean and offensive to the palate. What can I tell you? I can only say, close your eyes and swallow as best you can. Eat what you must to live, and throw away the rest. I wish I could help more. For those of you who find this impossible, may I ask that you try and try, but then come to see me in private. If your revulsion is so great, we will have to seek aid from those higher up."

A round of chatter rose and subsided. Then everyone sang "Ain Kelohainu"; after all those years, I discovered I still knew the words. Then, suddenly, the service over, Grossbart was upon me. "Higher up? He means the General?"

"Hey, Shelly," Fishbein said, "he means God." He smacked his face and looked at Halpern. "How high can you go!"

"Sh-h-h!" Grossbart said. "What do you think, Sergeant?"

"I don't know," I said. "You better ask the chaplain."

"I'm going to. I'm making an appointment to see him in private. So is Mickey."

Halpern shook his head. "No, no, Sheldon—"

"You have rights, Mickey," Grossbart said. "They can't push us around."

"It's O.K.," said Halpern. "It bothers my mother, not me."

Grossbart looked at me. "Yesterday he threw up. From the hash. It was all ham and God knows what else."

"I have a cold—that was why," Halpern said. He pushed his yarmulke back into a cap.

"What about you, Fishbein?" I asked. "You kosher, too?"

goyim: gentiles   trafe: non-kosher food

"Ain Kelohanoh": There's no God like our God"

He flushed. "A little. But I'll let it ride. I have a very strong stomach, and I don't eat a lot anyway." I continued to look at him, and he held up his wrist to reinforce what he'd just said; his watch strap was tightened to the last hole, and he pointed that out to me.

"But services are important to you?" I asked him.

He looked at Grossbart. "Sure, sir."

" 'Sergeant.' "

"Not so much at home," said Grossbart, stepping between us, "but away from home it gives one a sense of his Jewishness."

"We have to stick together," Fishbein said.

I started to walk toward the door; Halpern stepped back to make way for me.

"That's what happened in Germany," Grossbart was saying, loud enough for me to hear. "They didn't stick together. They let themselves get pushed around."

I turned. "Look, Grossbart. This is the Army, not summer camp."

He smiled. "So?"

Halpern tried to sneak off, but Grossbart held his arm.

"Grossbart, how old are you?" I asked.

"Nineteen."

"And you?" I said to Fishbein.

"The same. The same month, even."

"And what about him?" I pointed to Halpern, who had by now made it safely to the door.

"Eighteen," Grossbart whispered. "But like he can't tie his shoes or brush his teeth himself. I feel sorry for him."

"I feel sorry for all of us, Grossbart," I said, "but just act like a man. Just don't overdo it."

"Overdo what, sir?"

"The 'sir' business, for one thing. Don't overdo that," I said.

I left him standing there. I passed by Halpern, but he did not look at me. Then I was outside, but, behind, I heard Grossbart call, "Hey, Mickey, my *liebchen*, come on back. Refreshments!"

"*Liebchen!*" My grandmother's word for me!

One morning a week later, while I was working at my desk, Captain Barrett shouted for me to come into his office. When I entered, he had his helmet liner squashed down so far on his head that I couldn't even see his eyes. He was on the phone, and when he spoke to me, he cupped one hand over the mouthpiece. "Who the hell is Grossbart?"

"Third platoon, Captain," I said. "A trainee."

"What's all this stink about food? His mother called a goddam

liebchen: darling

congressman about the food." He uncovered the mouthpiece and slid his helmet up until I could see his bottom eyelashes. "Yes, sir," he said into the phone. "Yes, sir. I'm still here, sir. I'm asking Marx, here, right now—"

He covered the mouthpiece again and turned his head back toward me. "Lightfoot Harry's on the phone," he said, between his teeth. "This congressman calls General Lyman, who calls Colonel Sousa, who calls the Major, who calls me. They're just dying to stick this thing on me. Whatsa matter?" He shook the phone at me. "I don't feed the troops? What is this?"

"Sir, Grossbart is strange—" Barrett greeted that with a mockingly indulgent smile. I altered my approach. "Captain, he's a very orthodox Jew, and so he's only allowed to eat certain foods."

"He throws up, the congressman said. Every time he eats something, his mother says, he throws up!"

"He's accustomed to observing the dietary laws, Captain."

"So why's his old lady have to call the White House?"

"Jewish parents, sir—they're apt to be more protective than you expect. I mean, Jews have a very close family life. A boy goes away from home, sometimes the mother is liable to get very upset. Probably the boy mentioned something in a letter, and his mother misinterpreted."

"I'd like to punch him one right in the mouth," the Captain said. "There's a war on, and he wants a silver platter!"

"I don't think the boy's to blame, sir. I'm sure we can straighten it out by just asking him. Jewish parents worry—"

"*All* parents worry, for Christ's sake. But they don't get on their high horse and start pulling strings—"

I interrupted, my voice higher, tighter than before. "The home life, Captain, is very important—but you're right, it may sometimes get out of hand. It's a very wonderful thing, Captain, but because it's so close, this kind of thing . . ."

He didn't listen any longer to my attempt to present both myself and Lightfoot Harry with an explanation for the letter. He turned back to the phone. "Sir?" he said. "Sir—Marx, here, tells me Jews have a tendency to be pushy. He says he thinks we can settle it right here in the company. . . . Yes, sir. . . . I *will* call back, sir, soon as I can." He hung up. "Where are the men, Sergeant?"

"On the range."

With a whack on the top of his helmet, he crushed it down over his eyes again, and charged out of his chair. "We're going for a ride," he said.

The Captain drove, and I sat beside him. It was a hot spring day, and under my newly starched fatigues I felt as though my armpits were melting down onto my sides and chest. The roads were dry, and by the time we reached the firing range, my teeth felt gritty with dust, though my mouth had been shut the whole trip. The Captain slammed the brakes on and told me to get the hell out and find Grossbart.

I found him on his belly, firing wildly at the five-hundred-feet target. Waiting their turns behind him were Halpern and Fishbein. Fishbein, wearing a pair of steel-rimmed G.I. glasses I hadn't seen on him before, had the appearance of an old peddler who would gladly have sold you his rifle and the cartridges that were slung all over him. I stood back by the ammo boxes, waiting for Grossbart to finish spraying the distant targets. Fishbein straggled back to stand near me.

"Hello, Sergeant Marx," he said.

"How are you?" I mumbled.

"Fine, thank you. Sheldon's really a good shot."

"I didn't notice."

"I'm not so good, but I think I'm getting the hang of it now. Sergeant, I don't mean to, you know, ask what I shouldn't—" The boy stopped. He was trying to speak intimately, but the noise of the shooting forced him to shout at me.

"What is it?" I asked. Down the range, I saw Captain Barrett standing up in the jeep, scanning the line for me and Grossbart.

"My parents keep asking and asking where we're going," Fishbein said. "Everybody says the Pacific. I don't care, but my parents—If I could relieve their minds, I think I could concentrate more on my shooting."

"I don't know where, Fishbein. Try to concentrate anyway."

"Sheldon says you might be able to find out."

"I don't know a thing, Fishbein. You just take it easy, and don't let Sheldon—"

"*I'm* taking it easy, Sergeant. It's at home—"

Grossbart had finished on the line, and was dusting his fatigues with one hand. I called to him. "Grossbart, the Captain wants to see you."

He came toward us. His eyes blazed and twinkled. "Hi!"

"Don't point that rifle!" I said.

"I wouldn't shoot you, Sarge." He gave me a smile as wide as a pumpkin, and turned the barrel aside.

"Damn you, Grossbart, this is no joke! Follow me."

I walked ahead of him, and had the awful suspicion that, behind me, Grossbart was *marching*, his rifle on his shoulder, as though he were a one-man detachment. At the jeep, he gave the Captain a rifle salute. "Private Sheldon Grossbart, sir."

"At ease, Grossman." The Captain sat down, slid over into the empty seat, and, crooking a finger, invited Grossbart closer.

"Bart, sir. Sheldon Gross*bart*. It's a common error." Grossbart nodded at me; *I* understood, he indicated. I looked away just as the mess truck pulled up to the range, disgorging a half-dozen K.P.s with rolled-up sleeves. The mess sergeant screamed at them while they set up the chowline equipment.

"Grossbart, your mama wrote some congressman that we don't feed you right. Do you know that?" the Captain said.

"It was my father, sir. He wrote to Representative Franconi that my religion forbids me to eat certain foods."

"What religion is that, Grossbart?"

"Jewish."

"'Jewish, *sir*,'" I said to Grossbart.

"Excuse me, sir, Jewish, sir."

"What have you been living on?" the Captain asked. "You've been in the Army a month already. You don't look to me like you're falling to pieces."

"I eat because I have to, sir. But Sergeant Marx will testify to the fact that I don't eat one mouthful more than I need to in order to survive."

"Is that so, Marx?" Barrett asked.

"I've never seen Grossbart eat, sir," I said.

"But you heard the rabbi," Grossbart said. "He told us what to do, and I listened."

The Captain looked at me. "Well, Marx?"

"I still don't know what he eats and doesn't eat, sir."

Grossbart raised his arms to plead with me, and it looked for a moment as though he were going to hand me his weapon to hold. "But, Sergeant—"

"Look, Grossbart, just answer the Captain's questions," I said sharply.

Barrett smiled at me, and I resented it. "All right, Grossbart," he said. "What is it you want? The little piece of paper? You want out?"

"No, sir. Only to be allowed to live as a Jew. And for the others, too."

"What others?"

"Fishbein, sir, and Halpern."

"They don't like the way we serve, either?"

"Halpern throws up, sir. I've seen it."

"I thought *you* throw up."

"Just once, sir. I didn't know the sausage was sausage."

"We'll give menus, Grossbart. We'll show training films about the food, so you can identify when we're trying to poison you."

Grossbart did not answer. The men had been organized into two long chow lines. At the tail end of one, I spotted Fishbein—or, rather, his glasses spotted me. They winked sunlight back at me. Halpern stood next to him, patting the inside of his collar with a khaki handkerchief. They moved with the line as it began to edge up toward the food. The mess sergeant was still screaming at the K.P.s. For a moment, I was actually terrified by the thought that somehow the mess sergeant was going to become involved in Grossbart's problem.

"Marx," the Captain said, "you're a Jewish fella—am I right?"

I played straight man. "Yes, sir."

"How long you been in the Army? Tell this boy."

"Three years and two months."

"A year in combat, Grossbart. Twelve goddam months in combat all through Europe. I admire this man." The Captain snapped a wrist against my chest. "Do you hear him peeping about the food? Do you? I want an answer, Grossbart. Yes or no."

"No, sir."

"And why not? He's a Jewish fella."

"Some things are more important to some Jews than other things to other Jews."

Barrett blew up. "Look, Grossbart. Marx, here, is a good man—a goddam hero. When you were in high school, Sergeant Marx was killing Germans. Who does more for the Jews—you, by throwing up over a lousy piece of sausage, a piece of first-cut meat, or Marx, by killing those Nazi bastards? If I was a Jew, Grossbart, I'd kiss this man's feet. He's a goddam hero, and *he* eats what we give him. Why do you have to cause trouble is what I want to know! What is it you're buckin' for—a discharge?"

"No, sir."

"I'm talking to a wall! Sergeant, get him out of my way." Barrett swung himself back into the driver's seat. "I'm going to see the chaplain." The engine roared, the jeep spun around in a whirl of dust, and the Captain was headed back to camp.

For a moment, Grossbart and I stood side by side, watching the jeep. Then he looked at me and said, "I don't want to start trouble. That's the first thing they toss up to us."

When he spoke, I saw that his teeth were white and straight, and the sight of them suddenly made me understand that Grossbart actually did have parents—that once upon a time someone had taken little Sheldon to the dentist. He was their son. Despite all the talk about his parents, it was hard to believe in Grossbart as a child, an heir—as related by blood to anyone, mother, father, or, above all, to me. This realization led me to another.

"What does your father do, Grossbart?" I asked as we started to walk back toward the chow line.

"He's a tailor."

"An American?"

"Now, yes. A son in the Army," he said, jokingly.

"And your mother?" I asked.

He winked. "A *ballabusta*. She practically sleeps with a dustcloth in her hand."

"She's also an immigrant?"

"All she talks is Yiddish, still."

"And your father, too?"

"A little English. 'Clean,' 'Press,' 'Take the pants in.' That's the extent of it. But they're good to me."

"Then, Grossbart—" I reached out and stopped him. He turned toward me, and when our eyes met, his seemed to jump back, to shiver in their sockets. "Grossbart—you were the one who wrote that letter, weren't you?"

It took only a second or two for his eyes to flash happy again. "Yes." He walked on, and I kept pace. "It's what my father *would* have written if he had known how. It was his name, though. *He* signed it. He even mailed it. I sent it home. For the New York postmark."

I was astonished, and he saw it. With complete seriousness, he thrust his right arm in front of me. "Blood is blood, Sergeant," he said, pinching the blue vein in his wrist.

"What the hell *are* you trying to do, Grossbart?" I asked. "I've seen you eat. Do you know that? I told the Captain I don't know what you eat, but I've seen you eat like a hound at chow."

"We work hard, Sergeant. We're in training. For a furnace to work, you've got to feed it coal."

"Why did you say in the letter that you threw up all the time?"

"I was really talking about Mickey there. I was talking *for* him. He would never write, Sergeant, though I pleaded with him. He'll waste away to nothing if I don't help. Sergeant, I used my name—my father's name—but it's Mickey, and Fishbein, too, I'm watching out for."

"You're a regular Messiah, aren't you?"

We were at the chow line now.

"That's a good one, Sergeant," he said, smiling. "But who knows? Who can tell? Maybe you're the Messiah—a little bit. What Mickey says is the Messiah is a collective idea. He went to Yeshiva, Mickey, for a while. He says *together* we're the Messiah. Me a little bit, you a little bit. You should hear that kid talk, Sergeant, when he gets going."

"Me a little bit, you a little bit," I said. "You'd like to believe that, wouldn't you, Grossbart? That would make everything so clean for you."

"It doesn't seem too bad a thing to believe, Sergeant. It only means we should all *give* a little, is all."

ballabusta: housewife   *Yeshiva:* seminary

I walked off to eat my rations with the other noncoms.

Two days later, a letter addressed to Captain Barrett passed over my desk. It had come through the chain of command—from the office of Congressman Franconi, where it had been received, to General Lyman, to Colonel Sousa, to Major Lamont, now to Captain Barrett. I read it over twice. It was dated May 14, the day Barrett had spoken with Grossbart on the rifle range.

Dear Congressman:

First let me thank you for your interest in behalf of my son, Private Sheldon Grossbart. Fortunately, I was able to speak with Sheldon on the phone the other night, and I think I've been able to solve our problem. He is, as I mentioned in my last letter, a very religious boy, and it was only with the greatest difficulty that I could persuade him that the religious thing to do—what God Himself would want Sheldon to do—would be to suffer the pangs of religious remorse for the good of his country and all mankind. It took some doing, Congressman, but finally he saw the light. In fact, what he said (and I wrote down the words on a scratch pad so as never to forget), what he said was "I guess you're right, Dad. So many millions of my fellow-Jews gave up their lives to the enemy, the least I can do is live for a while minus a bit of my heritage so as to help end this struggle and regain for all the children of God dignity and humanity." That, Congressman, would make any father proud.

By the way, Sheldon wanted me to know—and to pass on to you—the name of a soldier who helped him reach this decision: SERGEANT NATHAN MARX. Sergeant Marx is a combat veteran who is Sheldon's first sergeant. This man has helped Sheldon over some of the first hurdles he's had to face in the Army, and is in part responsible for Sheldon's changing his mind about the dietary laws. I know Sheldon would appreciate any recognition Marx could receive.

Thank you and good luck. I look forward to seeing your name on the next election ballot.

Respectfully,
Samuel E. Grossbart

Attached to the Grossbart communiqué was another, addressed to General Marshall Lyman, the post commander, and signed by Representative Charles E. Franconi, of the House of Representatives. The communiqué informed General Lyman that Sergeant Nathan Marx was a credit to the U.S. Army and the Jewish people.

What was Grossbart's motive in recanting? Did he feel he'd gone too far? Was the letter a strategic retreat—a crafty attempt to strengthen what he considered our alliance? Or had he actually changed his mind, via an imaginary dialogue between Grossbart *père* and Grossbart *fils*? I was puzzled, but only for a few days—that is, only until I realized that, whatever his reasons, he had actually decided to disappear from my life; he was going to allow himself to become just another trainee. I saw him at inspection, but he never winked; at chow formations, but he never flashed me a sign. On Sundays, with the other trainees, he would sit around watching the noncoms' softball team, for which I pitched, but not once did he speak an unnecessary word to me. Fishbein and Halpern retreated, too—at Grossbart's command, I was sure. Apparently he had seen that wisdom lay in turning back before he plunged over into the ugliness of privilege undeserved. Our separation allowed me to forgive him our past encounters, and, finally, to admire him for his good sense.

Meanwhile, free of Grossbart, I grew used to my job and my administrative tasks. I stepped on a scale one day, and discovered I had truly become a noncombatant; I had gained seven pounds. I found patience to get past the first three pages of a book. I thought about the future more and more, and wrote letters to girls I'd known before the war. I even got a few answers. I sent away to Columbia for a Law School catalogue. I continued to follow the war in the Pacific, but it was not my war. I thought I could see the end, and sometimes, at night, I dreamed that I was walking on the streets of Manhattan—Broadway, Third Avenue, 116th Street, where I had lived the three years I attended Columbia. I curled myself around these dreams and I began to be happy.

And then, one Sunday, when everybody was away and I was alone in the orderly room reading a month-old copy of the *Sporting News*, Grossbart reappeared.

"You're a baseball fan, Sergeant?"

I looked up. "How are you?"

"Fine," Grossbart said. "They're making a soldier out of me."

"How are Fishbein and Halpern?"

"Coming along," he said. "We've got no training this afternoon. They're at the movies."

"How come you're not with them?"

"I wanted to come over and say hello."

He smiled—a shy, regular-guy smile, as though he and I well knew that our friendship drew its sustenance from unexpected visits, remembered birthdays, and borrowed lawnmowers. At first it offended me, and then the feeling was swallowed by the general uneasiness I felt at the thought that everyone on the post was locked away in a dark movie theater and I was here alone with Grossbart. I folded up my paper.

"Sergeant," he said, "I'd like to ask a favor. It is a favor, and I'm making no bones about it."

He stopped, allowing me to refuse him a hearing—which, of course, forced me into a courtesy I did not intend. "Go ahead."

"Well, actually it's two favors."

I said nothing.

"The first one's about these rumors. Everybody says we're going to the Pacific."

"As I told your friend Fishbein, I don't know," I said. "You'll just have to wait to find out. Like everybody else."

"You think there's a chance of any of us going East?"

"Germany?" I said. "Maybe."

"I meant New York."

"I don't think so, Grossbart. Offhand."

"Thanks for the information, Sergeant," he said.

"It's not information, Grossbart. Just what I surmise."

"It certainly would be good to be near home. My parents—you know." He took a step toward the door and then turned back. "Oh, the other thing. May I ask the other?"

"What is it?"

"The other thing is—I've got relatives in St. Louis, and they say they'll give me a whole Passover dinner if I can get down there. God, Sergeant, that'd mean an awful lot to me."

I stood up. "No passes during basic, Grossbart."

"But we're off from now till Monday morning, Sergeant. I could leave the post and no one would even know."

"I'd know. You'd know."

"But that's all. Just the two of us. Last night, I called my aunt, and you should have heard her. 'Come—come,' she said. 'I got gefilte fish, *chrain*—the works!' Just a day, Sergeant. I'd take the blame if anything happened."

"The Captain isn't here to sign a pass."

"You could sign."

"Look, Grossbart—"

"Sergeant, for two months, practically, I've been eating *trafe* till I want to die."

"I thought you'd made up your mind to live with it. To be minus a little bit of heritage."

gefilte fish: stuffed fish   *chrain:* horseradish

He pointed a finger at me. "You!" he said. "That wasn't for you to read."

"I read it. So what?"

"That letter was addressed to a congressman."

"Grossbart, don't feed me any baloney. You *wanted* me to read it."

"Why are you persecuting me, Sergeant?"

"Are you kidding!"

"I've run into this before," he said, "but never from my own!"

"Get out of here, Grossbart! Get the hell out of my sight!"

He did not move. "Ashamed, that's what you are," he said. "So you take it out on the rest of us. They say Hitler himself was half a Jew. Hearing you, I wouldn't doubt it."

"What are you trying to do with me, Grossbart?" I asked him. "What are you after? You want me to give you special privileges, to change the food, to find out about your orders, to give you weekend passes."

"You even talk like a goy!" Grossbart shook his fist. "Is this just a weekend pass I'm asking for? Is a Seder sacred, or not?"

Seder! It suddenly occurred to me that Passover had been celebrated weeks before. I said so.

"That's right," he replied. "Who says no? A month ago—and I was in the field eating hash! And now all I ask is a simple favor. A Jewish boy I thought would understand. My aunt's willing to go out of her way—to make a Seder a month later. . . ." He turned to go, mumbling.

"Come back here!" I called. He stopped and looked at me. "Grossbart, why can't you be like the rest? Why do you have to stick out like a sore thumb?"

"Because I'm a Jew, Sergeant. I *am* different. Better, maybe not. But different."

"This is a war, Grossbart. For the time being *be* the same."

"I refuse."

"What?"

"I refuse. I can't stop being me, that's all there is to it." Tears came to his eyes. "It's a hard thing to be a Jew. But now I understand what Mickey says—it's a harder thing to stay one." He raised a hand sadly toward me. "Look at *you*."

"Stop crying!"

"Stop this, stop that, stop the other thing! *You* stop, Sergeant. Stop closing your heart to your own!" And, wiping his face with his sleeve, he ran out the door. "The least we can do for one another—the least . . ."

An hour later, looking out of the window, I saw Grossbart headed across the field. He wore a pair of starched khakis and carried a little

---

goy: gentile   *Seder:* ceremonial dinner on first day of Passover leather ditty bag. I went out into the heat of the day. It was quiet; not a soul was in sight except, over by the mess hall, four K.P.s sitting around a pan, sloped forward from their waists, gabbing and peeling potatoes in the sun.

"Grossbart!" I called.

He looked toward me and continued walking.

"Grossbart, get over here!"

He turned and came across the field. Finally, he stood before me.

"Where are you going?" I asked.

"St. Louis. I don't care."

"You'll get caught without a pass."

"So I'll get caught without a pass."

"You'll go to the stockade."

"I'm *in* the stockade." He made an about-face and headed off.

I let him go only a step or two. "Come back here," I said, and he followed me into the office, where I typed out a pass and signed the Captain's name, and my own initials after it.

He took the pass and then, a moment later, reached out and grabbed my hand. "Sergeant, you don't know how much this means to me."

"O.K.," I said. "Don't get in any trouble."

"I wish I could show you how much this means to me."

"Don't do me any favors. Don't write any more congressmen for citations."

He smiled. "You're right. I won't. But let me do something."

"Bring me a piece of that gefilte fish. Just get out of here."

"I will!" he said. "With a slice of carrot and a little horseradish. I won't forget."

"All right. Just show your pass at the gate. And don't tell *anybody*."

"I won't. It's a month late, but a good Yom Tov to you."

"Good Yom Tov, Grossbart," I said.

"You're a good Jew, Sergeant. You like to think you have a hard heart, but underneath you're a fine, decent man. I mean that."

Those last three words touched me more than any words from Grossbart's mouth had the right to. "All right, Grossbart," I said. "Now call me 'sir,' and get the hell out of here."

He ran out the door and was gone. I felt very pleased with myself; it was a great relief to stop fighting Grossbart, and it had cost me nothing. Barrett would never find out, and if he did, I could manage to invent some excuse. For a while, I sat at my desk, comfortable in my decision. Then the screen door flew back and Grossbart burst in again. "Sergeant!" he said. Behind him I saw Fishbein and Halpern, both in starched khakis, both carrying ditty bags like Grossbart's.

Yom Tov: holiday (literally, good day)

"Sergeant, I caught Mickey and Larry coming out of the movies. I almost missed them."

"Grossbart—did I say tell no one?" I said.

"But my aunt said I could bring friends. That I should, in fact."

"*I'm* the Sergeant, Grossbart—not your aunt!"

Grossbart looked at me in disbelief. He pulled Halpern up by his sleeve. "Mickey, tell the Sergeant what this would mean to you."

Halpern looked at me and, shrugging, said, "A lot."

Fishbein stepped forward without prompting. "This would mean a great deal to me and my parents, Sergeant Marx."

"No!" I shouted.

Grossbart was shaking his head. "Sergeant, I could see you denying me, but how you can deny Mickey, a Yeshiva boy—that's beyond me."

"I'm not denying Mickey anything," I said. "You just pushed a little too hard, Grossbart. *You* denied him."

"I'll give him my pass, then," Grossbart said. "I'll give him my aunt's address and a little note. At least let him go."

In a second, he had crammed the pass into Halpern's pants pocket. Halpern looked at me, and so did Fishbein. Grossbart was at the door, pushing it open. "Mickey, bring me a piece of gefilte fish, at least," he said, and then he was outside again.

The three of us looked at one another, and then I said, "Halpern, hand that pass over."

He took it from his pocket and gave it to me. Fishbein had now moved to the doorway, where he lingered. He stood there for a moment with his mouth slightly open, and then he pointed to himself. "And me?" he asked.

His utter ridiculousness exhausted me. I slumped down in my seat and felt pulses knocking at the back of my eyes. "Fishbein," I said, "you understand I'm not trying to deny you anything, don't you? If it was my Army, I'd serve gefilte fish in the mess hall. I'd sell *kugel* in the PX, honest to God."

Halpern smiled.

"You understand, don't you, Halpern?"

"Yes, Sergeant."

"And you, Fishbein? I don't want enemies. I'm just like you—I want to serve my time and go home. I miss the same things you miss."

"Then, Sergeant," Fishbein said, "why don't you come, too?"

"Where?"

"To St. Louis. To Shelly's aunt. We'll have a regular Seder. Play hide-the-matzah." He gave me a broad, black-toothed smile.

I saw Grossbart again, on the other side of the screen.

kugel: suet pudding   *matzah:* unleavened bread eaten at Passover

"Pst!" He waved a piece of paper. "Mickey, here's the address. Tell her I couldn't get away."

Halpern did not move. He looked at me, and I saw the shrug moving up his arms into his shoulders again. I took the cover off my typewriter and made out passes for him and Fishbein. "Go," I said. "The three of you."

I thought Halpern was going to kiss my hand.

That afternoon, in a bar in Joplin, I drank beer and listened with half an ear to the Cardinal game. I tried to look squarely at what I'd become involved in, and began to wonder if perhaps the struggle with Grossbart wasn't as much my fault as his. What was I that I had to *muster* generous feelings? Who was I to have been feeling so grudging, so tight-hearted? After all, I wasn't being asked to move the world. Had I a right, then, or a reason, to clamp down on Grossbart, when that meant clamping down on Halpern, too? And Fishbein—that ugly, agreeable soul? Out of the many recollections of my childhood that had tumbled over me these past few days I heard my grandmother's voice: "What are you making a *tsimas*?" It was what she would ask my mother when, say, I had cut myself while doing something I shouldn't have done, and her daughter was busy bawling me out. I needed a hug and a kiss, and my mother would moralize. But my grandmother knew— mercy overrides justice. I should have known it, too. Who was Nathan Marx to be such a penny pincher with kindness? Surely, I thought, the Messiah himself—if He should ever come—won't niggle over nickles and dimes. God willing, he'll hug and kiss.

The next day, while I was playing softball over on the parade ground, I decided to ask Bob Wright, who was noncom in charge of Classification and Assignment, where he thought our trainees would be sent when their cycle ended, in two weeks. I asked casually, between innings, and he said, "They're pushing them all into the Pacific. Shulman cut the orders on your boys the other day."

The news shocked me, as though I were the father of Halpern, Fishbein, and Grossbart.

That night, I was just sliding into sleep when someone tapped on my door. "Who is it?" I asked.

"Sheldon."

He opened the door and came in. For a moment, I felt his presence without being able to see him. "How was it?" I asked.

He popped into sight in the near-darkness before me. "Great, Sergeant." Then he was sitting on the edge of the bed. I sat up.

tsimas: a to-do

)

"How about you?" he asked. "Have a nice weekend?"

"Yes."

"The others went to sleep." He took a deep, paternal breath. We sat silent for a while, and a homey feeling invaded my ugly little cubicle; the door was locked, the cat was out, the children were safely in bed.

"Sergeant, can I tell you something? Personal?"

I did not answer, and he seemed to know why. "Not about me. About Mickey. Sergeant, I never felt for anybody like I feel for him. Last night I heard Mickey in the bed next to me. He was crying so, it could have broken your heart. Real sobs."

"I'm sorry to hear that."

"I had to talk to him to stop him. He held my hand, Sergeant—he wouldn't let it go. He was almost hysterical. He kept saying if he only knew where we were going. Even if he knew it *was* the Pacific, that would be better than nothing. Just to know."

Long ago, someone had taught Grossbart the sad rule that only lies can get the truth. Not that I couldn't believe in the fact of Halpern's crying; his eyes *always* seemed red-rimmed. But, fact or not, it became a lie when Grossbart uttered it. He was entirely strategic. But then—it came with the force of indictment—so was I! There are strategies of aggression, but there are strategies of retreat as well. And so, recognizing that I myself had not been without craft and guile, I told him what I knew. "It is the Pacific."

He let out a small gasp, which was not a lie. "I'll tell him. I wish it was otherwise."

"So do I."

He jumped on my words. "You mean you think you could do something? A change, maybe?"

"No, I couldn't do a thing."

"Don't you know anybody over at C. and A.?"

"Grossbart, there's nothing I can do," I said. "If your orders are for the Pacific, then it's the Pacific."

"But Mickey—"

"Mickey, you, me—everybody, Grossbart. There's nothing to be done. Maybe the war'll end before you go. Pray for a miracle."

"But—"

"Good night, Grossbart." I settled back, and was relieved to feel the springs unbend as Grossbart rose to leave. I could see him clearly now; his jaw had dropped, and he looked like a dazed prizefighter. I noticed for the first time a little paper bag in his hand.

"Grossbart." I smiled. "My gift?"

"Oh, yes, Sergeant. Here—from all of us." He handed me the bag. "It's egg roll."

"Egg roll?" I accepted the bag and felt a damp grease spot on the bottom. I opened it, sure that Grossbart was joking.

"We thought you'd probably like it. You know—Chinese egg roll. We thought you'd probably have a taste for—"

"Your aunt served egg roll?"

"She wasn't home."

"Grossbart, she invited you. You told me she invited you and your friends."

"I know," he said. "I just reread the letter. *Next* week."

I got out of bed and walked to the window. "Grossbart," I said. But I was not calling to him.

"What?"

"What are you, Grossbart? Honest to God, what are you?"

I think it was the first time I'd asked him a question for which he didn't have an immediate answer.

"How can you do this to people?" I went on.

"Sergeant, the day away did us all a world of good. Fishbein, you should see him, he *loves* Chinese food."

"But the Seder," I said.

"We took second best, Sergeant."

Rage came charging at me. I didn't sidestep. "Grossbart, you're a liar!" I said. "You're a schemer and a crook. You've got no respect for anything. Nothing at all. Not for me, for the truth—not even for poor Halpern! You use us all—"

"Sergeant, Sergeant, I feel for Mickey. Honest to God, I do. I *love* Mickey. I try—"

"You try! You feel!" I lurched toward him and grabbed his shirt front. I shook him furiously. "Grossbart, get out! Get out and stay the hell away from me. Because if I see you, I'll make your life miserable. *You understand that?*"

"Yes."

I let him free, and when he walked from the room, I wanted to spit on the floor where he had stood. I couldn't stop the fury. It engulfed me, owned me, till it seemed I could only rid myself of it with tears or an act of violence. I snatched from the bed the bag Grossbart had given me and, with all my strength, threw it out the window. And the next morning, as the men policed the area around the barracks, I heard a great cry go up from one of the trainees, who had been anticipating only his morning handful of cigarette butts and candy wrappers. "Egg roll!" he shouted. "Holy Christ, Chinese goddam egg roll!"

A week later, when I read the orders that had come down from C. and A., I couldn't believe my eyes. Every single trainee was to be shipped to Camp Stoneman, California, and from there to the Pacific—every trainee but one. Private Sheldon Grossbart. He was to be sent to Fort Monmouth, New Jersey. I read the mimeographed sheet several times. Dee, Farrell, Fishbein, Fuselli, Fylypowycz, Glinicki, Gromke, Gucwa, Halpern, Hardy, Helebrandt, right down to Anton Zygadlo—all were to be headed West before the month was out. All except Grossbart. He had pulled a string, and I wasn't it.

I lifted the phone and called C. and A.

The voice on the other end said smartly, "Corporal Shulman, sir."

"Let me speak to Sergeant Wright."

"Who is this calling, sir?"

"Sergeant Marx."

And, to my surprise, the voice said. *"Oh!"* Then, "Just a minute, Sergeant."

Shulman's *"Oh!"* stayed with me while I waited for Wright to come to the phone. Why *"Oh!"*? Who was Shulman? And then, so simply, I knew I'd discovered the string that Grossbart had pulled. In fact, I could hear Grossbart the day he'd discovered Shulman in the PX, or in the bowling alley, or maybe even at services. "Glad to meet you. Where you from? Bronx? Me, too. Do you know So-and-So? And So-and-So? Me, too! You work at C. and A.? Really? Hey, how's chances of getting East? Could you do something? Change something? Swindle, cheat, lie? We gotta help each other, you know. If the Jews in Germany . . ."

Bob Wright answered the phone. "How are you, Nate? How's the pitching arm?"

"Good. Bob, I wonder if you could do me a favor." I heard clearly my own words, and they so reminded me of Grossbart that I dropped more easily than I could have imagined into what I had planned. "This may sound crazy, Bob, but I got a kid here on orders to Monmouth who wants them changed. He had a brother killed in Europe, and he's hot to go to the Pacific. Says he'd feel like a coward if he wound up Stateside. I don't know, Bob—can anything be done? Put somebody else in the Monmouth slot?"

"Who?" he asked cagily.

"Anybody. First guy in the alphabet. I don't care. The kid just asked if something could be done."

"What's his name?"

"Grossbart, Sheldon."

Wright didn't answer.

"Yeah," I said. "He's a Jewish kid, so he thought I could help him out. You know."

"I guess I can do something," he finally said. "The Major hasn't been around here for weeks. Temporary duty to the golf course. I'll try, Nate, that's all I can say."

"I'd appreciate it, Bob. See you Sunday." And I hung up, perspiring.

The following day, the corrected orders appeared: Fishbein, Fuselli, Fylypowycz, Glinicki, Gromke, Grossbart, Gucwa, Halpern, Hardy . . . Lucky Private Harley Alton was to go to Fort Monmouth, New Jersey, where, for some reason or other, they wanted an enlisted man with infantry training.

After chow that night, I stopped back at the orderly room to straighten out the guard-duty roster. Grossbart was waiting for me. He spoke first.

"You son of a bitch!"

I sat down at my desk, and while he glared at me, I began to make the necessary alterations in the duty roster.

"What do you have against me?" he cried. "Against my family? Would it kill you for me to be near my father, God knows how many months he has left to him?"

"Why so?"

"His heart," Grossbart said. "He hasn't had enough troubles in a lifetime, you've got to add to them. I curse the day I ever met you, Marx! Shulman told me what happened over there. There's no limit to your anti-Semitism, is there? The damage you've done here isn't enough. You have to make a special phone call! You really want me dead!"

I made the last few notations in the duty roster and got up to leave. "Good night, Grossbart."

"You owe me an explanation!" He stood in my path.

"Sheldon, you're the one who owes explanations."

He scowled. "To *you*?"

"To me, I think so—yes. Mostly to Fishbein and Halpern."

"That's right, twist things around. I owe nobody nothing, I've done all I could do for them. Now I think I've got the right to watch out for myself."

"For each other we have to learn to watch out, Sheldon. You told me yourself."

"You call this watching out for me—what you did?"

"No. For all of us."

I pushed him aside and started for the door. I heard his furious breathing behind me, and it sounded like steam rushing from an engine of terrible strength.

"*You'll* be all right," I said from the door. And, I thought, so would Fishbein and Halpern be all right, even in the Pacific, if only Grossbart continued to see—in the obsequiousness of the one, the soft spirituality of the other—some profit for himself.

I stood outside the orderly room, and I heard Grossbart weeping behind me. Over in the barracks, in the lighted windows, I could see the boys in their T shirts sitting on their bunks talking about their orders, as they'd been doing for the past two days. With a kind of quiet nervousness, they polished shoes, shined belt buckles, squared away underwear, trying as best they could to accept their fate. Behind me, Grossbart swallowed hard, accepting his. And then, resisting with all my will an impulse to turn and seek pardon for my vindictiveness, I accepted my own.

QUESTIONS

1. More use of dilemma is made in this story than in any other in this text. Identify some of the dilemmas the protagonist finds himself in. Are they used primarily to create suspense, to reveal character, or to illuminate theme? Might all of these dilemmas be classified as specific applications of one general dilemma? If so, how might this general dilemma be described? (One suggestion for an answer is contained in the terms used by Nathan Marx's grandmother on page 150).

2. Sergeant Marx finds himself in so many dilemmas because he is trying to reconcile three roles—those of top sergeant, Jew, and human being. To what extent do these roles conflict? Point out places where Marx is thinking or acting primarily as a sergeant, as a Jew, as a human being.

3. The plot has four major episodes, centering in conflicts over (a) attendance at Friday night services, (b) company food, (c) pass to St. Louis, (d) shipping orders. In so far as these involve external conflict between Sergeant Marx and Grossbart, which is the victor in each?

4. "What are you, Grossbart? Honest to God, what are you?" asks Sergeant Marx (page 152). Answer this question as precisely as possible. What is Grossbart's philosophy? Catalogue the various methods he uses to achieve his goals.

5. Even more important to Sergeant Marx is the question, Who is Sergeant Marx? What does the fact that he asks this question (cf page 150) tell us about him? By what principles does he try to govern his conduct? On page 151 Marx speaks of "strategies of aggression" and "strategies of retreat"; on what occasions does *he* use strategies similar to Grossbart's?

6. What are Sergeant Marx's motivations in his final decision? In which of his roles—sergeant, Jew, human being—is he acting at this point? Is his decision right?

7. What is meant by Sergeant Marx's final statement that he accepted his fate? What *is* his fate?

8. Describe as precisely as possible Captain Barrett's attitude toward Jews.

9. Differentiate Grossbart, Fishbein, and Halpern. How would you rank these three, Captain Barrett, and Sergeant Marx on a scale of human worth?

10. To what character (or characters) does the title refer? Is it used straightforwardly or ironically?

11. This story—by a Jewish author about Jewish characters—has a complex theme. Does the theme at its most general level necessarily involve the idea of Jewishness? Is it more crucial to the story that Nathan Marx is a Jew or a top sergeant? Try stating the theme without mentioning the idea of Jewishness. Now expand it to include the idea of Jewishness. Can it be stated without mentioning the idea of responsibility for command and judgment?

5

Point of View

The primitive storyteller, unbothered by considerations of form, simply spun a tale. "Once upon a time," he began, and proceeded to narrate the story to his listeners, describing the characters when necessary, telling what they thought and felt as well as what they did, and interjecting comments and ideas of his own. The modern fiction writer is artistically more self-conscious. He realizes that there are many ways of telling a story; he decides upon a method before he begins, and may even set up rules for himself. Instead of telling the story himself, he may let one of his characters tell it for him; he may tell it by means of letters or diaries; he may confine himself to recording the thoughts of one of his characters. With the growth of artistic consciousness, the question of POINT OF VIEW, of who tells the story, and, therefore, of how it gets told, has assumed special importance.

To determine the point of view of a story we ask, "Who tells the story?" and "How much is he allowed to know?" and, especially, "To what extent does the author look inside his characters and report their thoughts and feelings?"

Though many variations and combinations are possible, the basic points of view are four, as follows:

1. Omniscient

2. Limited omniscient { (a) Major character
                        (b) Minor character

3. First person { (a) Major character
                  (b) Minor character

4. Objective

1. In the OMNISCIENT POINT OF VIEW the story is told by the author, using the third person, and his knowledge and prerogatives are unlimited. He is free to go wherever he wishes, to peer inside the minds and hearts of his characters at will and tell us what they are thinking or feeling. He can interpret their behavior; and he can comment, if he wishes, on the significance of the story he is telling. He knows all. He can tell us as much or as little as he pleases.

The following version of Aesop's fable "The Ant and the Grasshopper" is told from the omniscient point of view. Notice that in it we are told not only what both characters do and say, but also what they think and feel; also, that the author comments at the end on the significance of his story. (The phrases in which the author enters into the thoughts or feelings of the ant and the grasshopper have been italicized; the comment by the author is printed in small capitals.)

> *Weary in every limb*, the ant tugged over the snow a piece of corn he had stored up last summer. *It would taste mighty good at dinner tonight.*
>
> A grasshopper, *cold and hungry*, looked on. *Finally he could bear it no longer.* "Please, friend ant, may I have a bite of corn?"
>
> "What were you doing all last summer?" asked the ant. He looked the grasshopper up and down. *He knew its kind.*
>
> "I sang from dawn till dark," replied the grasshopper, *happily unaware of what was coming next.*
>
> "Well," said the ant, *hardly bothering to conceal his contempt*, "since you sang all summer, you can dance all winter."
>
> HE WHO IDLES WHEN HE'S YOUNG
> WILL HAVE NOTHING WHEN HE'S OLD.

Stories told from the omniscient point of view may differ widely in the amount of omniscience the author allows himself. In "Tears, Idle Tears" we share the thoughts and perceptions of Frederick, Frederick's mother, the girl on the park bench, and, fleetingly, the mother's women and men friends, a chaplain, and a doctor—almost everyone, indeed, except the duck. In "The Destructors," though we are taken into the minds of Blackie, Mike, the gang as a group, Old Misery, and the lorry-driver, we are not taken into the mind of Trevor, who is the most important character.

The omniscient is the most flexible point of view, and permits the widest scope. It is also the most subject to abuse. It offers constant danger that the author may come between the reader and the story, or that the continual shifting of viewpoint from character to character may cause a breakdown in coherence or unity. Used skillfully it enables the author to achieve simultaneous breadth and depth. Unskillfully used, it can destroy the illusion of reality which the story attempts to create.

2. In the LIMITED OMNISCIENT POINT OF VIEW the author tells the story in the third person, but he tells it from the viewpoint of one character in the story. The author places himself at the elbow of this character, so to speak, and looks at the events of the story through his eyes and through his mind. He moves both inside and outside this character, but never leaves his side. He tells us what this character sees and hears, and what he thinks and feels; he possibly interprets the character's thoughts and behavior. He knows everything about this character—more than the character knows about himself; but he shows no knowledge of what *other* characters are thinking or feeling or doing—except for what his chosen character knows or can infer. The chosen character may be either a major or minor character, a participant or an observer, and this choice also will be a very important one for the story. "A Little Cloud" is told from the limited omniscient point of view, from the viewpoint of the main character. The use of this viewpoint with a minor character is rare. Here is "The Ant and the Grasshopper" told, in the third person, from the point of view of the ant. Notice that this time we are told nothing of what the grasshopper thinks or feels. We see and hear and know of him only what the ant sees and hears and knows.

> *Weary in every limb,* the ant tugged over the snow a piece of corn he had stored up last summer. *It would taste mighty good at dinner tonight. It was then that he noticed the grasshopper, looking cold and pinched.*
> "Please, friend ant, may I have a bite of your corn?" asked the grasshopper.
> He looked the grasshopper up and down. "What were you doing all last summer?" he asked. *He knew its kind.*
> "I sang from dawn till dark," replied the grasshopper.
> "Well," said the ant, *hardly bothering to conceal his contempt,* "since you sang all summer, you can dance all winter."

The limited omniscient point of view, since it acquaints us with the world through the mind and senses of only one person, approximates more closely than the omniscient the conditions of real life; it also offers a ready-made unifying element, since all details of the story are the experience of one person. At the same time it offers a limited field of observation, for the reader can go nowhere except where the chosen character goes, and there may be difficulty in having him naturally cognizant of all important events. A clumsy writer will constantly have his focal character listening at keyholes, accidently overhearing important conversations, or coincidentally being present when important events occur.

3. In the FIRST PERSON POINT OF VIEW the author disappears into one of the characters, who tells the story in the first person. This

character, again, may be either a major or minor character, protagonist or observer, and it will make considerable difference whether the protagonist tells his own story or someone else tells it. In "I'm a Fool," "Defender of the Faith," "E Equals MC Squared," and in "Horses of the Night," the protagonist tells the story in the first person. In "That Evening Sun," (page 269), and, technically, in "Youth," (page 456), the story is told by an observer. The story below is told in the first person from the point of view of the grasshopper. (The whole story is italicized, because it all comes out of the grasshopper's mind.)

> *Cold and hungry, I watched the ant tugging over the snow a piece of corn he had stored up last summer. My feelers twitched, and I was conscious of a tic in my left hind leg. Finally I could bear it no longer. "Please, friend ant," I asked, "may I have a bite of your corn?"*
>
> *He looked me up and down. "What were you doing all last summer?" he asked, rather too smugly it seemed to me.*
>
> *"I sang from dawn till dark," I said innocently, remembering the happy times.*
>
> *"Well," he said, with a priggish sneer, "since you sang all summer, you can dance all winter."*

The first person point of view shares the virtues and limitations of the limited omniscient. It offers, sometimes, a gain in immediacy and reality, since we get the story directly from a participant, the author as middleman being eliminated. It offers no opportunity, however, for *direct* interpretation by the author, and there is constant danger that the narrator may be made to transcend his sensitivity, his knowledge, or his powers of language in telling the story. "Youth" avoids this danger, for the narrator is a highly literate, educated man who reads books like Carlyle's *Sartor Resartus* during his off-hours; but "I'm a Fool" may not altogether escape it. A good author, however, can make tremendous literary capital out of the very limitations of his narrator. The first person point of view offers excellent opportunities for dramatic irony and for studies in limited or blunted human perceptivity. Often, as in "I'm a Fool" and "Horses of the Night," the very heart of the story may lie in the difference between what the narrator perceives and what the reader perceives. In such stories the author offers an interpretation of his materials *indirectly*, through the use of irony. He may also indicate his own judgment, more straightforwardly though still indirectly, by expressing it through the lips of a discerning and sympathetic narrator. In "Defender of the Faith" the reader is disposed to accept Sergeant Marx's interpretation of characters and events as being largely the author's own. Such identifications of a narrator's attitude with the author's, however, must always be undertaken with extreme caution; they are justified only if the total material of the story supports them. In

"Defender of the Faith" the moral sensitivity and intelligence of the narrator reflects the author's own; nevertheless, much of the interest of the story arises from Marx's own uncertainty about his judgments—the nagging apprehension that he may be mistaken.

4. In the OBJECTIVE POINT OF VIEW the author disappears into a kind of roving sound camera. This camera can go anywhere, but can record only what is seen and heard. It cannot comment, interpret, or enter a character's mind. With this point of view (sometimes called also the DRAMATIC POINT OF VIEW) the reader is placed in the position of a spectator at a movie or play. He sees what the characters do and hears what they say, but can only infer what they think or feel and what they are like. The author is not there to explain. The purest example of a story told from the objective point of view would be one written entirely in dialogue, for as soon as the author adds words of his own, he begins to interpret through his very choice of words. Actually, few stories using this point of view are antiseptically pure, for the limitations it imposes on the author are severe. However, "Millstone for the Sun's Day," (page 203), "April 2000—The Third Expedition," (page 287), "Thus I Refute Beelzy," (page 301), and Lord Dunsany's "The Guest" (page 326) are essentially objective in their narration, as is the following version of "The Grasshopper and the Ant." (Since we are nowhere taken into the thoughts or feelings of the characters, none of this version is printed in italics.)

> The ant tugged over the snow a piece of corn he had stored up last summer, perspiring in spite of the cold.
>
> A grasshopper, its feelers twitching and with a tic in its left hind leg, looked on for some time. Finally he asked, "Please, friend ant, may I have a bite of your corn?"
>
> The ant looked the grasshopper up and down. "What were you doing all last summer?" he snapped.
>
> "I sang from dawn till dark," replied the grasshopper, not changing his tone.
>
> "Well," said the ant, and a faint smile crept into his face, "since you sang all summer, you can dance all winter."

The objective point of view has the most speed and the most action; also, it forces the reader to make his own interpretations. On the other hand, it must rely heavily on external action and dialogue, and it offers no opportunities for interpretation by the author.

Each of the points of view has its advantages, its limitations, and its peculiar uses. Ideally the choice of the author will depend on his story materials and his purpose. He should choose the point of view which enables him to present his particular materials most effectively in terms of his purpose. If he is writing a murder mystery, he will ordinarily avoid using the point of view of the murderer or the brilliant detective: otherwise he would have to reveal at the beginning the secrets which he wishes to conceal till the end. On the other hand, if he is interested in exploring criminal psychology, the murderer's point of view might be by far the most effective. In the Sherlock Holmes stories, A. Conan Doyle effectively uses the somewhat imperceptive Dr. Watson as his narrator, so that the reader may be kept in the dark as long as possible and then be as amazed as Watson is by Holmes's deductive powers. In Dostoevsky's *Crime and Punishment*, however, the author is interested, not in mystifying and surprising, but in illuminating the moral and psychological operations of the human soul in the act of taking life; he therefore tells the story from the viewpoint of a sensitive and intelligent murderer.

For the reader the examination of point of view may be important both for understanding and for evaluating the story. First, he should know whether the events of the story are being interpreted by the author or by one of the characters. If the latter, he must ask how this character's mind and personality affect his interpretation, whether the character is perceptive or imperceptive, and whether his interpretation can be accepted at face value or must be discounted because of ignorance, stupidity, or self-deception. Often, as in "I'm a Fool," and "That Evening Sun," an author achieves striking and significant effects by using a narrator not aware of the full import of the events he is reporting.

Next, the reader should ask whether the writer has chosen his point of view for maximum revelation of his material or for another reason. The author may choose his point of view mainly to conceal certain information till the end of the story and thus maintain suspense and create surprise. He may even deliberately mislead the reader by presenting the events through a character who puts a false interpretation on them. Such a false interpretation may be justified if it leads eventually to more effective revelation of character and theme. If it is there merely to trick the reader, it is obviously less justifiable.

Finally, the reader should ask whether the author has used his selected point of view fairly and consistently. Even with the escape story, we have a right to demand fair treatment. If the person to whose thoughts and feelings we are admitted has pertinent information which he does not reveal, we legitimately feel cheated. To have a chance to solve a murder mystery, we must know what the detective knows. A writer also should be consistent in his point of view; or, if he shifts it, he should do so for a just artistic reason. The serious interpretive writer chooses and uses point of view so as to yield ultimately the greatest possible insight, either in fullness or in intensity.

Ernest Buckler

FIRST BORN SON

The pale cast of fatigue smudged Martin's skin and little grooves of it emptied into the corners of his mouth. But this land was his own, and a son of his own flesh was holding the plow that broke it. His thoughts were tired half-thoughts but they did not ache.

He felt the wine of the fall day and for a minute his feet wandered, inattentive, from the furrow. The dogged, slow-eyed oxen followed him, straining nose-down at his heels. The plow ran out wide in the sod. David tried to flip over the furrow with a sudden wrench of the handles, but the chocolate-curling lip of earth broke and the share came clear.

"Whoa!" David yelled.

"Whoa!" Martin roared at the oxen.

"For God's sake, Dad, can't you watch where you're going? It's hard enough to hold this damn thing when you keep 'em straight."

"Now don't get high," Martin said. But there was no echo of David's temper in his voice. He knew David was tired. And David could not learn to handle his weariness. He fought it. It was no use to do that. If you let it come and go, quietly, after supper it made a lazy song in your muscles and was good to think about. Martin remembered the night David was born. They had thought Ellen would die. It was Christmas Eve. There was not a breath of wind in the moonlit, Christmas-kindled air. Snow lay in kind folds on the ground, shadowed in the dead-still moonlight like the wrinkles of a white cloak. On the brook Martin could watch the gay, meaningless movements of the children skating. And sometimes a fragment of their heartless laughter would break away and fall inside the room. Ellen's pain-tight face stared at her pale hands outside the quilt. The kind-smelling Christmas tree was a cruel mockery. Now and then Martin would go outside and listen, bare-headed, for the doctor's sleighbells, trying to separate their faint, far-off tinkle from the frost-crackle of the spruces. He would think he heard them. Then there would be nothing. Runner tracks shone like ising-glass in the moonlight. He heard nothing but the heartless laughter of the children.

It seemed hours later, when he was not listening at all, that he looked out and all at once the dark body of the horse turned in the gate, by the corner of the house. His heart gave a great leap. The helplessness left him. This man could hold Ellen back from death. The moonlight seemed to turn warm. After the doctor went in with Ellen the laughing of the children did not seem so far-off and strange.

The quick white grip of fear came again when he heard the doctor's hand on the door again . . . but Martin looked up and the doctor was *smiling*. Suddenly the whole night was a great, neighbourly, tear-starting friend. He had a son now. He knew it would be a son.

Martin felt shy to kiss Ellen in front of the doctor, but there was a new peace and a strange swagger in his soul. When he got the doctor's horse for him, it seemed like the best horse in all the world; and half-ashamed and half-afraid not to, but somehow wanting desperately to thank *someone*, he knelt down for a minute on the hay and prayed. Outside the barn, the voices of the children laughing were a glad song in his ears, now. In the bedroom, Ellen murmured "My own little Jesus" . . . and the thick spruce-cosy smell of the Christmas tree and the shining moonlight outside and the soft peace after danger past clothed the minutes in a sweet armour . . . A son . . . A son . . . And Ellen well . . . Martin couldn't believe how good it was. He would never die now. He had a son, now . . . when he was too old to break up the land he loved, any more, this son would come in at night and they would plan together, just the same. This son's sons . . . .

"Well, maybe you think it's *easy* to hold this damn thing," David said. It *must* be that he's tired, Martin thought. He can't mean that . . . this same David . . . my own son cannot find it hard to plow this land of our own. I never found it so, when I was young. Plowed land was always the prettiest sight in the world to me. It was always good at the end of the day, to stand and look over the brown waves of earth and know that I had opened my land to the sun and the air and the rain. I don't like to hear this son of mine talk that way. He says too many things like that. I don't like to hear my son talk that way. The plowed land was here before us and it will last after us and our hands should be proud to work in it.

"Haw," Martin called, and the lip of the earth curled back and buried the grass again.

In the city, David thought, their bodies are not dead-tired now. They have not walked all day in their own tracks . . . back and forth, back and forth, in their own damn tracks. There is movement and lights and laughing. Every day there is something *new* . . . something to keep alive for. The same people here . . . the same talk . . . the same eternal drudgery . . . your nose in the ground all day long, from morning till night, like a damned ox . . . cooped up in that damned circle of trees.

The last brown beech leaves on the hardwood hill drifted down to the ground, dreamily, a little sad to die. A flock of partridges made their heavy headlong flight into an apple tree and began to bud. In the fields, the potato stalks lay in blackened heaps. The earth was grey and brown. All the colour was in the sky or hung in the thin air. Only the stray pumpkins, left to ripen on the withered vines, gave back any of it. They were like bubbles of the sad October sunshine. Martin loved these quick chill dusks, and then later the kind eye of lamplight in the window, and the friendly, wood-warmed, table-set kitchen.

They came to the end of the furrow. Martin split the rest of the acre with his eye.

"Will we finish her before supper, son?" he asked.

"Do you want to work all night too!"

Martin stopped the oxen.

"What's wrong with you today, Dave?" he said. "If you planned to go after the partridges . . . ."

"Partridges, hell!"

"Well then, what's . . . ."

David hesitated.

"I'm so damn sick of this place I . . . ."

"Is *that* so!" Martin said slowly. "What's wrong with this place?" He kicked over a sod with the toe of his shabby boot. An old man looked out of his face for the first time. It was true, then . . . It had never been because David was tired or lonely or weak or young . . . It was because David had always *hated* this land . . . the land that would be his own some day. A sick little cloud settled on his heart. He *had* no son, then.

"What's *wrong* with it?" David said. "The same damn thing over and over from morning till night . . . every day and every day . . . what future is there for anyone here?" David kept his back bent to the plow handles. He felt a little mean and ashamed when he heard the sound of his own words.

"What future is there here?" The question sounded meaningless to Martin. He had the truth, to contradict it. There is the first day in April when the fields stir again and it is good all day just to feel your breathing . . . There is the sky-blue August day when the whole green wind is full of leaves and growing, and Sunday morning you walk in the waving growth-full garden rows and wish you could keep this day forever, hold it back from going . . . It is good, too, when the snow whistles cold and mournful because it can never get inside the pane to warm itself . . . It is *all* good, all of it . . . Men live here as long as their sons live, to see the clearings their axes have made and the living grass that sprang from their tracks in the first furrow and the green things their hands gave life to . . . "The same thing over and over . . ." Martin did not speak. Only his sick thoughts pleaded, patiently, silently, incredulously. We did not plough yesterday, David. We took the day off and last night this time we sat at the edge of the woods and waited for the shy-eyed deer to come out into the old back field.

I thought it was good to sit there and smoke with my son after we boiled the supper kettle, not talking much but not feeling the silence either, and watch the dead leaves drifting down past the rocks in the cool-talking brook. The fire itself felt good, in spite of the sun, and it was good to hear the nervous twitter of the partridges in the apple trees just before it got too dark to pick out their heads along the sights of the gun . . . Or is this like the day last spring we nodded at each other across the pool with the foam on it each time we held a broken-neck trout throbbing in the tight of our palms? Or the day we cursed the heat in the alder-circled meadow and our shirts stuck to our backs like broken blisters? The hay smelt good that night, just the same, and it was good to hear the wagon wheels groan on the sill just before the dark thunder-frown of the sky burst and the barn roof beat back the rain. I remember the night we ate our first supper in the house I had built with my own hands. That night the neighbours came in, and we danced half the night to the fiddles. It was easy with everyone, like with brothers, and we loved them all . . . and it was good that night to lie in bed and let sleep's drowsy wind blow out the candles of thought. The day they brought your brother Peter home loose in their arms before it was dinner time, his dead body so broken your mother could not hold it, that day was different . . . And the next day . . . And the next day . . . .

"Well what kind of a place suits *you*?" Martin said at last. David straightened.

"The city, of course! Who'd want to live in this God-forsaken hole when you can get a job in the city?"

"Did you say the *city*?"

"Yeah. The city," he said laconically.

Martin listened with sick wonder to this stranger who had been his son. The city . . . It's *there* the days are the same. I thought it was very lonely in the city, the time I was there. The stone things move, but they do not change. My feet were always on stone. I could not walk on the ground and look over it and know it was my own. They never looked at the sky there, or listened for the rain.

When I looked at the sky there, the sun I saw was a strange one . . . it did not make friends with the stone. The stone houses were alike, and the days were alike, and never till they died could the people lie in bed at night and listen to rain on the corn after a long heat. They had nothing to breathe but their own tired breaths. I remember their faces. There was stone in them, too. They were all alike. They looked as if they never awoke from their tired dreams of the night. Their minds kept turning in their own tracks, like the weary wheels that could find no rest on the pavements. The soft-fingered women-faced men lived in houses, and the house-smell clung to everything they said or did when they went outside. When they talked, it was empty, because their eyes saw nothing but the stone things that their hands had not built . . . and none of them had anything to say that could not be said with words. It was very lonely there. They laughed too much. But not even love or death could melt their aloneness. Even when they laughed, their eyes did not change.

And when they died, no one remembered, and there was nothing left of them.

I liked it in the city, now, this time, David thought. The street lights began to come on, a little before it was dark, and excitement seemed to stir in the busy pavements. The wind was not strong enough to lift itself above the street, but the women's skirts clung to their bodies as they passed. So many different women's bodies! What if they *didn't* speak? The bright, metallic faces of always-rich women seemed to shine in the shop-window light, and you knew you would feel clumsy and ashamed with them, but it was good to think of having their soft flesh alone somewhere in the dark. There was so much light there, then . . . and life. Like when you took off your work-clothes and shaved and felt smoother and brighter and ready for things. There was life, not death, at the end of the day. Here, my God . . . the same old bare maples weaving back and forth against a sky that made your lips blue just to look at it, and never the sound of a strange voice, and later the snow sifting lonely through the spokes of the wagon wheels . . . What a God-forsaken place to be *young* in. Maybe his father didn't mind, they didn't seem to mind *missing* things when they got old. Old people didn't seem to dread being quiet and letting things slip like this. They thought it was because they were wise . . . it was because they were half-dead already. If he thought he'd ever get like that about things when he got old . . . He'd never get old. He swore a desperate promise to himself that he'd never, never, never get that awful patience like his father . . . standing there now, with that stupid look on his face, like one of the oxen . . . .

"But Dave," Martin said slowly, "this place will be *yours* some day, you know that."

"What do *I* want of this old *place*?"

A whiteness came into Martin's face that was different from the whiteness of the cold or the weariness. He remembered the day his father had said the same thing to him. They had both felt shy and awkward, and he could say nothing, but as soon as he was alone, he had looked over this land, the tight tears of pride came warm into his eyes. He had kept this place, the best thing he had, till he could give it to his own son, and now when he offered it to David he saw it meant nothing. That he despised it. He had known through and through how his own father felt.

"It was always good enough here for *me*," Martin said.

"All right, but what did you ever *amount* to?"

Martin was stung into a sudden anger. "As much as *you* ever will, you . . . ."

Then he looked over the fields, slowly, and a break came into his anger. Why today, only a few hours ago, starting to plow, it had been, without a thought, so sweet, so safe, so sure . . . he and his son plowing and him trying to show David how to turn the furrow better and David trying his best. Things just didn't come handy for David, it must be that. He had half felt Ellen working quiet and happy in the house and the smoke went straight from the chimney into the clear, sun-filled air and there had been no hurry or fret in the fields or the slow oxen or his thoughts. Now . . . it could never be the same again between him and David, now. Every time they said a sharp word to each other now, these sick things would all come back . . . What if David was right? What *had* he ever amounted to? Well, he had been young here, and youth was very fresh and full here in the fields and the sun and very long, some of it never died, it grew green again with each April sun. He had had a wife of his own kind, and everything they had, they had got with their own hands, his hands and hers. There had been a lot of tiredness but there was always the quiet night afterwards and the slow kindly talk. There had never been an end of work, but you could always stop to talk across the fields to your neighbour, and you got along just the same. There had not been much money, but there had always been the sweet smell of bread in the kitchen and the soft song of wood in the kitchen stove. There had been no strangers among them, and when you died these men you had lived your whole life with would not work that day, even if there was clover to be hauled in and rain in the wind . . . and you would lie in the land that your hands and your feet knew best, and the same breezes you had breathed would always blow over you. Surely that was enough for a man. If your son . . . If David . . . It was hard to believe that your own son stayed on . . . It was hard to believe that your own son was not like you wanted him to be. But, Martin thought sadly, you couldn't make him see, if he didn't feel that way. You wished . . . but if he felt that way, there was no way to make him see.

"Well Dave," Martin said slowly, "if you're *bound* to go away, I suppose . . . ."

"Oh," David said impatiently, "let it go, let it go . . . I'll stay," he added sullenly.

He is almost afraid of me, Martin thought. He won't even talk it over with me. He has no use for my talk. He wants to keep me away from him. He don't think I can understand him at all. I try . . . .

He walked around to the oxen's heads and picked up the whip.

"Haw," he said quietly. "Just cut her light here, son."

David put his hands back on the handles but he didn't speak. He threw the plow around when they turned the furrows, so the chain jerked taut in the yoke. "Easy now, boys," Martin cajoled the oxen.

A bare little wind started in the bare maples. The sun burned cold and lonesome in the blind windows of the church across the road and the long withered grass bent over the cold grey sand in the middle of the built-up graves. Peter's grave . . . Peter would coax to hold the whip. He could hardly make his small voice loud enough to stir the oxen, but they obeyed him. Martin could see the crazy nostrils of the running horses and then Peter's small crumpled body on the rock heap where the wheel had struck . . . .

The cows came up from the pasture, calling hollowly to be let in. The sky looked away from its own darkening face in the mud-bottomed puddles of the road. The blood in Martin's face came blue to the skin, and his blue eyes, a little faded with weariness, looked like frozen spots holding up the weight of his face. He walked back-to, guiding the oxen by the horns to help David keep the furrow straight, but David did not straighten his back, even when Martin stopped for a rock. Martin would come around and kick out the rock himself.

Martin blew on his hands and tried to start a smile in the corners of his tired, cold-thin lips.

"Time for mittens, I guess. *Your* hands cold?"

"No," David said.

A shaft of the sun broke for a minute through the blue, wind-cold clouds. Long bands of it searchlit the grey rocks, without warming them.

"Snow comin'," Martin said.

The sun went down, and the sky made a few cold-pink patterns at the horizon. It would not be as sad again until April.

Martin turned the oxen for one more furrow. He could not stop, until he was *sure* how David . . . Maybe if he kept on, David would say something himself about stopping, and he could show him then how ready he was to listen to him and take the oxen off the tongue.

"*I'll* never ask him to stop if he plows all night . . ." David was so tired the muscles in his legs felt like a frayed rope and a tight cord drew his temples together. The blood seemed to drain from his face and throb heavy in his neck. The ashes of weariness sifted through the bright surface of his thoughts. The oxen lifted their heavy feet and deposited them carefully on the ground. The plow dug its slow way through the earth.

"I guess we're just gettin' her done in time," Martin said.

David said nothing.

"I guess this clears things up, about, for winter. You'll have a little more time to hunt, now, Dave."

Ellen came to the corner of the house, holding down her apron with one hand against the tug of the wind, and called supper.

"All right," Martin called back.

"Hungry, Dave?" he said.

"No."

David glanced at his father's face. For the first time he noticed how tired it looked. He felt sorry for his father, for a minute, and a little ashamed. He'd *have* to stay as long as his father was alive, he supposed.

They came to the end of the furrow. Martin hesitated.

"Well, I guess we'll let her go at that for tonight," he said. "We can wind her up in the morning, easy." He hesitated again.

"Dave," he said, "if you really *want* to go away. . . ."

David's impatience flared again. He forgot his father's face.

"Oh, for God's sake," he said, "can't you let that *drop*? I said I'd stay, didn't I? What more do you want? I'll stay here as long as *you're* here, anyway. So you need not worry."

So it is that way. A small coal touched suddenly against Martin's heart. He will wait, but he will be glad . . . so he can go away. If he was waiting for it, so the place would be all his own then, it would be . . . but he will be waiting, so he can go away. There will be a stranger here, and nothing will be done the same. There will be a strange name in my house, and maybe they will let the alders creep back over the acre field because they did not clear it for the first time and plow it with their own hands . . . and the grass will grow tall and strange over the graves.

He pulled the bolt from the tongue. It was true. It was true, then. He *had* no son. David took his hands from the plow. Martin waited for a minute to see if he would line the plow up for the next furrow in the morning. David did not move. Martin walked around to the plow. David went to the oxen's head, took up the whip and started with them to the barn. Martin pulled the plow around and lay the chain straight out along the next furrow. Ellen came to the corner of the house and called supper again, but Martin did not answer. He watched David take the oxen past the house. He saw Ellen say something to him, but David did not reply.

He bent down and dug the mud from the plowshare. It shone underneath, where the earth had polished it, like a sword. The earth smelled cold and silent. He moved a few stones, absently, with his foot and stood for a minute with his eyes on the ground. Like the night they buried Peter. He felt lost in the long, dead day.

In the porch, he listened to see if David might be talking to the oxen. There was no sound but the bells, as David jerked the yoke-straps. Martin caught his breath quickly. He *had* no son. Peter was dead. He *had* no son, now. He scraped the dirt from his heels with a stick from the chipyard and went inside the house.

"Well, what in the *world* have you two been doing?" Ellen said, moving across the scrubbed soft-wood floor from the stove to the table. The warm breath of food rose sweet in the oil-lamplight. She held the dipper of water for Martin's hands over the basin in the sink. "Are you goin' to do a coupla more acres after supper?" she joked.

"Yeah, I was kinda thinkin' we might," Martin laughed.
But his laughter was heavy and grey, like a hawk rising.

QUESTIONS

1. The reader of this story is presented with an alternating point of view. Why has Buckler done this? With which character do you empathize more? How has the author led you to this feeling?
2. " 'What future is there here?' The question sounded meaningless to Martin. He had the truth, to contradict it." In his thoughts, Martin contradicts David's question. Outline David's thoughts if he were asked to answer his father's "truth."
3. Martin and David have many differences of opinion. What are their views of the city and the farm?
4. In the second paragraph the author writes, "He felt the wine of the fall day ...." Give other examples of the author's metaphorical language. How many of your examples are based on the senses? How many examples are hyphenated words?
5. The author makes frequent use of the flashback technique. Find some examples and explain their effectiveness.
6. This story is similar in many ways to "A Secret Lost in the Water." Make as many comparisons as possible.
7. Formulate the theme of this story. (Your answer to question 6 should be helpful.) In what way is the theme of "First Born Son" relevant to your own life? Can you bring your own personal understanding to this story?

Willa Cather

PAUL'S CASE

It was Paul's afternoon to appear before the faculty of the Pittsburgh High School to account for his various misdemeanors. He had been suspended a week ago, and his father had called at the Principal's office and confessed his perplexity about his son. Paul entered the faculty room suave and smiling. His clothes were a trifle outgrown, and the tan velvet on the collar of his open overcoat was frayed and worn; but for all that there was something of the dandy about him, and he wore an opal pin in his neatly knotted black four-in-hand, and a red carnation in his buttonhole. This latter adornment the faculty somehow felt was not properly significant of the contrite spirit befitting a boy under the ban of suspension.

PAUL'S CASE   Copyright 1905, 1920, 1933 by Willa Cather. From *Youth and the Bright Medusa*, by Willa Cather, by permission of Alfred A. Knopf, Inc.

Paul was tall for his age and very thin, with high, cramped shoulders and a narrow chest. His eyes were remarkable for a certain hysterical brilliancy, and he continually used them in a conscious, theatrical sort of way, peculiarly offensive in a boy. The pupils were abnormally large, as though he were addicted to belladonna, but there was a glassy glitter about them which that drug does not produce.

When questioned by the Principal as to why he was there, Paul stated, politely enough, that he wanted to come back to school. This was a lie, but Paul was quite accustomed to lying; found it, indeed, indispensable for overcoming friction. His teachers were asked to state their respective charges against him, which they did with such a rancour and aggrievedness as evinced that this was not a usual case. Disorder and impertinence were among the offences named, yet each of his instructors felt that it was scarcely possible to put into words the real cause of the trouble, which lay in a sort of hysterically defiant manner of the boy's; in the contempt which they all knew he felt for them, and which he seemingly made not the least effort to conceal. Once, when he had been making a synopsis of a paragraph at the blackboard, his English teacher had stepped to his side and attempted to guide his hand. Paul had started back with a shudder and thrust his hands violently behind him. The astonished woman could scarcely have been more hurt and embarrassed had he struck at her. The insult was so involuntary and definitely personal as to be unforgettable. In one way and another, he had made all his teachers, men and women alike, conscious of the same feeling of physical aversion. In one class he habitually sat with his hand shading his eyes; in another he always looked out of the window during the recitation; in another he made a running commentary on the lecture, with humorous intent.

His teachers felt this afternoon that his whole attitude was symbolized by his shrug and his flippantly red carnation flower, and they fell upon him without mercy, his English teacher leading the pack. He stood through it smiling, his pale lips parted over his white teeth. (His lips were continually twitching, and he had a habit of raising his eyebrows that was contemptuous and irritating to the last degree.) Older boys than Paul had broken down and shed tears under that ordeal, but his set smile did not once desert him, and his only sign of discomfort was the nervous trembling of the fingers that toyed with the buttons of his overcoat, and an occasional jerking of the other hand which held his hat. Paul was always smiling, always glancing about him, seeming to feel that people might be watching him and trying to detect something. This conscious expression, since it was as far as possible from boyish mirthfulness, was usually attributed to insolence or "smartness."

As the inquisition proceeded, one of his instructors repeated an impertinent remark of the boy's, and the Principal asked him whether he thought that a courteous speech to make to a woman. Paul shrugged his shoulders slightly and his eyebrows twitched.

"I don't know," he replied. "I didn't mean to be polite or impolite, either. I guess it's a sort of way I have, of saying things regardless."

The Principal asked him whether he didn't think that a way it would be well to get rid of. Paul grinned and said he guessed so. When he was told that he could go, he bowed gracefully and went out. His bow was like a repetition of the scandalous red carnation.

His teachers were in despair, and his drawing-master voiced the feeling of them all when he declared there was something about the boy which none of them understood. He added: "I don't really believe that smile of his comes altogether from insolence; there's something sort of haunted about it. The boy is not strong, for one thing. There is something wrong about the fellow."

The drawing-master had come to realize that, in looking at Paul, one saw only his white teeth and the forced animation of his eyes. One warm afternoon the boy had gone to sleep at his drawing-board, and his master had noted with amazement what a white, blue-veined face it was; drawn and wrinkled like an old man's about the eyes, the lips twitching even in his sleep.

His teachers left the building dissatisfied and unhappy; humiliated to have felt so vindictive toward a mere boy, to have uttered this feeling in cutting terms, and to have set each other on, as it were, in the gruesome game of intemperate reproach. One of them remembered having seen a miserable street cat set at bay by a ring of tormentors.

As for Paul, he ran down the hill whistling the Soldiers' Chorus from "Faust," looking behind him now and then to see whether some of his teachers were not there to witness his light-heartedness. As it was now late in the afternoon and Paul was on duty that evening as usher at Carnegie Hall, he decided that he would not go home to supper.

When he reached the concert hall, the doors were not yet open. It was chilly outside, and he decided to go up into the picture gallery—always deserted at this hour—where there were some of Raffelli's gay studies of Paris streets and an airy blue Venetian scene or two that always exhilarated him. He was delighted to find no one in the gallery but the old guard, who sat in the corner, a newspaper on his knee, a black patch over one eye and the other closed. Paul possessed himself of the place and walked confidently up and down, whistling under his breath. After a while he sat down before a blue Rico and lost himself. When he bethought him to look at his watch, it was after seven o'clock, and he rose with a start and ran downstairs, making a face at Augustus Caesar, peering out from the cast-room, and an evil gesture at the Venus of Milo as he passed her on the stairway.

When Paul reached the ushers' dressing-room, half a dozen boys were there already, and he began excitedly to tumble into his uniform. It was one of the few that at all approached fitting, and Paul thought it very becoming—though he knew the tight, straight coat accentuated his narrow chest, about which he was exceedingly sensitive. He was always excited while he dressed, twanging all over to the tuning of the strings and the preliminary flourishes of the horns in the music-room; but tonight he seemed quite beside himself, and he teased and plagued the boys until, telling him that he was crazy, they put him down on the floor and sat on him.

Somewhat calmed by his suppression, Paul dashed out to the front of the house to seat the early comers. He was a model usher. Gracious and smiling he ran up and down the aisles. Nothing was too much trouble for him; he carried messages and brought programmes as though it were his greatest pleasure in life, and all the people in his section thought him a charming boy, feeling that he remembered and admired them. As the house filled, he grew more and more vivacious and animated, and the colour came to his cheeks and lips. It was very much as though this were a great reception and Paul were the host. Just as the musicians came out to take their places, his English teacher arrived with cheques for the seats which a prominent manufacturer had taken for the season. She betrayed some embarrassment when she handed Paul the tickets, and a hauteur which subsequently made her feel very foolish. Paul was startled for a moment, and had the feeling of wanting to put her out; what business had she here among all these fine people and gay colours? He looked her over and decided that she was not appropriately dressed and must be a fool to sit downstairs in such togs. The tickets had probably been sent her out of kindness, he reflected, as he put down a seat for her, and she had about as much right to sit there as he had.

When the symphony began, Paul sank into one of the rear seats with a long sigh of relief, and lost himself as he had done before the Rico. It was not that symphonies, as such, meant anything in particular to Paul, but the first sigh of the instruments seemed to free some hilarious spirit within him; something that struggled there like the Genius in the bottle found by the Arab fisherman. He felt a sudden zest of life; the lights danced before his eyes and the concert hall blazed into unimaginable splendour. When the soprano soloist came on, Paul forgot even the nastiness of his teacher's being there, and gave himself up to the peculiar intoxication such personages always had for him. The soloist chanced to be a German woman, by no means in her first youth, and the mother of many children; but she wore a satin gown and a tiara, and she had that indefinable air of achievement, that world-shine upon her, which always blinded Paul to any possible defects.

After a concert was over, Paul was often irritable and wretched until he got to sleep—and to-night he was even more than usually restless. He had the feeling of not being able to let down; of its being impossible to give up this delicious excitement which was the only thing that could be called living at all. During the last number he withdrew and, after hastily changing his clothes in the dressing-room, slipped out to the side door where the singer's carriage stood. Here he began pacing rapidly up and down the walk, waiting to see her come out.

Over yonder the Schenley, in its vacant stretch, loomed big and square through the fine rain, the windows of its twelve stories glowing like those of a lighted cardboard house under a Christmas tree. All the actors and singers of any importance stayed there when they were in Pittsburgh, and a number of the big manufacturers of the place lived there in the winter. Paul had often hung about the hotel, watching the people go in and out, longing to enter and leave schoolmasters and dull care behind him forever.

At last the singer came out, accompanied by the conductor, who helped her into her carriage and closed the door with a cordial *auf wiedersehen*—which set Paul to wondering whether she were not an old sweetheart of his. Paul followed the carriage over to the hotel, walking so rapidly as not to be far from the entrance when the singer alighted and disappeared behind the swinging glass doors which were opened by a Negro in a tall hat and a long coat. In the moment that the door was ajar, it seemed to Paul that he, too, entered. He seemed to feel himself go after her up the steps, into the warm, lighted building, into an exotic, a tropical world of shiny, glistening surfaces and basking ease. He reflected upon the mysterious dishes that were brought into the dining-room, the green bottles in buckets of ice, as he had seen them in the supper-party pictures of the Sunday supplement. A quick gust of wind brought the rain down with sudden vehemence, and Paul was startled to find that he was still outside in the slush of the gravel driveway; that his boots were letting in the water and his scanty overcoat was clinging wet about him; that the lights in front of the concert hall were out, and that the rain was driving in sheets between him and the orange glow of the windows above him. There it was, what he wanted—tangibly before him, like the fairy world of a Christmas pantomime; as the rain beat in his face, Paul wondered whether he were destined always to shiver in the black night outside, looking up at it.

He turned and walked reluctantly toward the car tracks. The end had to come sometime; his father in his night-clothes at the top of the stairs, explanations that did not explain, hastily improvised fictions that were forever tripping him up, his upstairs room and its horrible yellow wallpaper, the creaking bureau with the greasy plush collar-box, and over his painted wooden bed the pictures of George Washington and

John Calvin, and the framed motto, 'Feed my Lambs,' which had been worked in red worsted by his mother, whom Paul could not remember.

Half an hour later, Paul alighted from the Negley Avenue car and went slowly down one of the side streets off the main thoroughfare. It was a highly respectable street, where all the houses were exactly alike, and where business men of moderate means begot and reared large families of children, all of whom went to Sabbath School and learned the shorter catechism, and were interested in arithmetic; all of whom were as exactly alike as their homes, and of a piece with the monotony in which they lived. Paul never went up Cordelia Street without a shudder of loathing. His home was next the house of the Cumberland minister. He approached it to-night with the nerveless sense of defeat, the hopeless feeling of sinking back forever into ugliness and commonness that he had always had when he came home. The moment he turned into Cordelia Street he felt the waters close above his head. After each of these orgies of living, he experienced all the physical depression which follows a debauch; the loathing of respectable beds, of common food, of a house permeated by kitchen odours; a shuddering repulsion for the flavourless, colourless mass of every-day existence; a morbid desire for cool things and soft lights and fresh flowers.

The nearer he approached the house, the more absolutely unequal Paul felt to the sight of it all: his ugly sleeping chamber; the cold bathroom with the grimy zinc tub, the cracked mirror, the dripping spigots; his father, at the top of the stairs, his hairy legs sticking out from his nightshirt, his feet thrust into carpet slippers. He was so much later than usual that there would certainly be enquiries and reproaches. Paul stopped short before the door. He felt that he could not be accosted by his father to-night; that he could not toss again on that miserable bed. He would not go in. He would tell his father that he had no car-fare, and it was raining so hard he had gone home with one of the boys and stayed all night.

Meanwhile, he was wet and cold. He went around to the back of the house and tried one of the basement windows, found it open, raised it cautiously, and scrambled down the cellar wall to the floor. There he stood, holding his breath, terrified by the noise he had made; but the floor above him was silent, and there was no creak on the stairs. He found a soap-box, and carried it over to the soft ring of light that streamed from the furnace door, and sat down. He was horribly afraid of rats, so he did not try to sleep, but sat looking distrustfully at the dark, still terrified lest he might have awakened his father.

In such reactions, after one of the experiences which made days and nights out of the dreary blanks of the calendar, when his senses were deadened, Paul's head was always singularly clear. Suppose his father had heard him getting in at the window and had come down and shot him for a burglar? Then, again, suppose his father had come down, pistol in hand, and he had cried out in time to save himself, and his father had been horrified to think how nearly he had killed him? Then, again, suppose a day should come when his father would remember that night, and wish there had been no warning cry to stay his hand? With this last supposition Paul entertained himself until daybreak.

The following Sunday was fine; the sodden November chill was broken by the last flash of autumnal summer. In the morning Paul had to go to church and Sabbath School, as always. On seasonable Sunday afternoons the burghers of Cordelia Street usually sat out on their front "stoops," and talked to their neighbours on the next stoop, or called to those across the street in neighbourly fashion. The men sat placidly on gay cushions placed upon the steps that led down to the sidewalk, while the women, in the Sunday "waists," sat in rockers on the cramped porches, pretending to be greatly at their ease. The children played in the streets; there were so many of them that the place resembled the recreation grounds of a kindergarten. The men on the steps, all in their shirt-sleeves, their vests unbuttoned, sat with their legs well apart, their stomachs comfortably protruding, and talked of the prices of things, or told anecdotes of the sagacity of their various chiefs and overlords. They occasionally looked over the multitude of squabbling children, listened affectionately to their high-pitched, nasal voices, smiling to see their own proclivities reproduced in their offspring, and interspersed their legends of the iron kings with remarks about their sons' progress at school, their grades in arithmetic, and the amounts they had saved in their toy banks.

On this last Sunday of November, Paul sat all the afternoon on the lowest step of his "stoop," staring into the street, while his sisters, in their rockers, were talking to the minister's daughters next door about how many shirtwaists they had made in the last week, and how many waffles someone had eaten at the last church supper. When the weather was warm, and his father was in a particularly jovial frame of mind, the girls made lemonade, which was always brought out in a red-glass pitcher, ornamented with forget-me-nots in blue enamel. This the girls thought very fine, and the neighbours joked about the suspicious colour of the pitcher.

To-day Paul's father, on the top step, was talking to a young man who shifted a restless baby from knee to knee. He happened to be the young man who was daily held up to Paul as a model, and after whom it was his father's dearest hope that he would pattern. This young man was of a ruddy complexion, with a compressed, red mouth, and faded, nearsighted eyes, over which he wore thick spectacles, with gold bows that curved about his ears. He was clerk to one of the magnates of a great steel corporation, and was looked upon in Cordelia Street as a young man with a future. There was a story that, some five years ago—he was now barely twenty-six—he had been a trifle "dissipated," but in order to curb his appetites and save the loss of time and strength that a sowing of wild oats might have entailed, he had taken his chief's advice, oft reiterated to his employees, and at twenty-one had married the first woman whom he could persuade to share his fortunes. She happened to be an angular schoolmistress, much older than he, who also wore thick glasses, and who had now borne him four children, all nearsighted like herself.

The young man was relating how his chief, now cruising in the Mediterranean, kept in touch with all the details of the business, arranging his office hours on his yacht just as though he were at home, and "knocking off work enough to keep two stenographers busy." His father told, in turn, the plan his corporation was considering, of putting in an electric railway plant at Cairo. Paul snapped his teeth; he had an awful apprehension that they might spoil it all before he got there. Yet he rather liked to hear these legends of the iron kings, that were told and retold on Sundays and holidays; these stories of palaces in Venice, yachts on the Mediterranean, and high play at Monte Carlo appealed to his fancy, and he was interested in the triumphs of cash-boys who had become famous, though he had no mind for the cash-boy stage.

After supper was over, and he had helped to dry the dishes, Paul nervously asked his father whether he could go to George's to get some help in his geometry, and still more nervously asked for car-fare. This latter request he had to repeat, as his father, on principle, did not like to hear requests for money, whether much or little. He asked Paul whether he could not go to some boy who lived nearer, and told him that he ought not to leave his school work until Sunday; but he gave him the dime. He was not a poor man, but he had a worthy ambition to come up in the world. His only reason for allowing Paul to usher was that he thought a boy ought to be earning a little.

Paul bounded upstairs, scrubbed the greasy odour of the dishwater from his hands with the ill-smelling soap he hated, and then shook over his fingers a few drops of violet water from the bottle he kept hidden in his drawer. He left the house with his geometry conspicuously under his arm, and the moment he got out of Cordelia Street and boarded a downtown car, he shook off the lethargy of two deadening days, and began to live again.

The leading juvenile of the permanent stock company which played at one of the downtown theatres was an acquaintance of Paul's, and the boy had been invited to drop in at the Sunday-night rehearsals whenever he could. For more than a year Paul had spent every available moment loitering about Charley Edwards's dressing-room. He had won a place among Edwards's following not only because the young actor, who could not afford to employ a dresser, often found him useful, but because he recognized in Paul something akin to what churchmen term "vocation."

It was at the theatre and at Carnegie Hall that Paul really lived; the rest was but a sleep and a forgetting. This was Paul's fairy tale, and it had for him all the allurement of a secret love. The moment he inhaled the gassy, painty, dusty odour behind the scenes, he breathed like a prisoner set free, and felt within him the possibility of doing or saying splendid, brilliant things. The moment the cracked orchestra beat out the overture from "Martha," or jerked at the serenade from "Rigoletto," all stupid and ugly things slid from him, and his senses were deliciously, yet delicately fired.

Perhaps it was because, in Paul's world, the natural nearly always wore the guise of ugliness, that a certain element of artificiality seemed to him necessary in beauty. Perhaps it was because his experience of life elsewhere was so full of Sabbath-School picnics, petty economies, wholesome advice as to how to succeed in life, and the unescapable odours of cooking, that he found this existence so alluring, these smartly clad men and women so attractive, that he was so moved by these starry apple orchards that bloomed perennially under the limelight. It would be difficult to put it strongly enough how convincingly the stage entrance of that theatre was for Paul the actual portal of Romance. Certainly none of the company ever suspected it, least of all Charley Edwards. It was very like the old stories that used to float about London of fabulously rich Jews, who had subterranean halls, with palms, and fountains, and soft lamps and richly apparelled women who never saw the disenchanting light of London day. So, in the midst of that smoke-palled city, enamoured of figures and grimy toil, Paul had his secret temple, his wishing-carpet, his bit of blue-and-white Mediterranean shore bathed in perpetual sunshine.

Several of Paul's teachers had a theory that his imagination had been perverted by garish fiction; but the truth was he scarcely ever read at all. The books at home were not such as would either tempt or corrupt a youthful mind, and as for reading the novels that some of his friends urged upon him—well, he got what he wanted much more quickly from music; any sort of music, from an orchestra to a barrel-organ. He needed only the spark, the indescribable thrill that made his imagination master of his senses, and he could make plots and pictures enough of his own. It was equally true that he was not stage-struck—not, at any rate, in the usual acceptation of that expression. He had no desire to become an actor, any more than he had to become a musician. He felt no necessity to do any of these things; what he wanted was to see, to be in the atmosphere, float on the wave of it, to be carried out, blue league after league, away from everything.

After a night behind the scenes, Paul found the schoolroom more than ever repulsive; the bare floors and naked walls; the prosy men who never wore frock coats, or violets in their buttonholes; the women with their dull gowns, shrill voices, and pitiful seriousness about prepositions that govern the dative. He could not bear to have the other pupils think, for a moment, that he took these people seriously; he must convey to them that he considered it all trivial, and was there only by way of a joke, anyway. He had autographed pictures of all the members of the stock company which he showed his classmates, telling them the most incredible stories of his familiarity with these people, of his acquaintance with the soloists who came to Carnegie Hall, his suppers with them and the flowers he sent them. When these stories lost their effect, and his audience grew listless, he would bid all the boys goodbye, announcing that he was going to travel for a while; going to Naples, to California, to Egypt. Then, next Monday, he would slip back, conscious and nervously smiling; his sister was ill, and he would have to defer his voyage until spring.

Matters went steadily worse with Paul at school. In the itch to let his instructors know how heartily he despised them, and how thoroughly he was appreciated elsewhere, he mentioned once or twice that he had no time to fool with theorems; adding—with a twitch of the eyebrows and a touch of that nervous bravado which so perplexed them—that he was helping the people down at the stock company; they were old friends of his.

The upshot of the matter was that the Principal went to Paul's father, and Paul was taken out of school and put to work. The manager at Carnegie Hall was told to get another usher in his stead; the doorkeeper at the theatre was warned not to admit him to the house; and Charley Edwards remorsefully promised the boy's father not to see him again.

The members of the stock company were vastly amused when some of Paul's stories reached them—especially the women. They were hard-working women, most of them supporting indolent husbands or brothers, and they laughed rather bitterly at having stirred the boy to such fervid and florid inventions. They agreed with the faculty and with his father, that Paul's was a bad case.

The east-bound train was ploughing through a January snowstorm; the dull dawn was beginning to show grey when the engine whistled a mile out of Newark. Paul started up from the seat where he had lain curled in uneasy slumber, rubbed the breath-misted window-glass with his hand, and peered out. The snow was whirling in curling eddies above the white bottom lands, and the drifts lay already deep in the fields and along the fences, while here and there the tall dead grass and dried weed stalks protruded black above it. Lights shone from the scattered houses, and a gang of labourers who stood beside the track waved their lanterns.

Paul had slept very little, and he felt grimy and uncomfortable. He had made the all-night journey in a day coach because he was afraid if he took a Pullman he might be seen by some Pittsburgh business man who had noticed him in Denny and Carson's office. When the whistle woke him, he clutched quickly at his breast pocket, glancing about him with an uncertain smile. But the little, clay-bespattered Italians were still sleeping, the slatternly women across the aisle were in open-mouthed oblivion, and even the crumby, crying babies were for the time stilled. Paul settled back to struggle with his impatience as best he could.

When he arrived at the Jersey City station, he hurried through his breakfast, manifestly ill at ease and keeping a sharp eye about him. After he reached the Twenty-Third Street station, he consulted a cabman, and had himself driven to a men's furnishing establishment which was just opening for the day. He spent upward of two hours there, buying with endless reconsidering and great care. His new street suit he put on in the fitting-room; the frock coat and dress clothes he had bundled into the cab with his new shirts. Then he drove to a hatter's and a shoe house. His next errand was at Tiffany's, where he selected silver-mounted brushes and a scarf-pin. He would not wait to have his silver marked, he said. Lastly, he stopped at a trunk shop on Broadway, and had his purchases packed into various travelling-bags.

It was a little after one o'clock when he drove up to the Waldorf, and, after settling with the cabman, went into the office. He registered from Washington; said his mother and father had been abroad, and that he had come down to await the arrival of their steamer. He told his story plausibly and had no trouble, since he offered to pay for them in advance, in engaging his rooms; a sleeping-room, sitting-room, and bath.

Not once, but a hundred times Paul had planned this entry into New York. He had gone over every detail of it with Charley Edwards, and in his scrapbook at home there were pages of description about New York hotels, cut from the Sunday papers.

When he was shown to his sitting-room on the eighth floor, he saw at a glance that everything was as it should be; there was but one detail in his mental picture that the place did not realize, so he rang for the bell-boy and sent him down for flowers. He moved about nervously until the boy returned, putting away his new linen and fingering it delightedly as he did so. When the flowers came, he put them hastily into water, and then tumbled into a hot bath. Presently he came out of his white bathroom, resplendent in his new silk underwear, and playing with the tassels of his red robe. The snow was whirling so fiercely outside his windows that he could scarcely see across the street; but within, the air was deliciously soft and fragrant. He put the violets and jonquils on the tabouret beside the couch, and threw himself down with a long sigh, covering himself with a Roman blanket. He was thoroughly tired; he had been in such haste, he had stood up to such a strain, covered so much ground in the last twenty-four hours, that he wanted to think how it had all come about. Lulled by the sound of the wind, the warm air, and the cool fragrance of the flowers, he sank into deep, drowsy retrospection.

It had been wonderfully simple; when they had shut him out of the theatre and concert hall, when they had taken away his bone, the whole thing was virtually determined. The rest was a mere matter of opportunity. The only thing that at all surprised him was his own courage—for he realized well enough that he had always been tormented by fear, a sort of apprehensive dread which, of late years, as the meshes of the lies he had told closed about him, had been pulling the muscles of his body tighter and tighter. Until now, he could not remember a time when he had not been dreading something. Even when he was a little boy, it was always there—behind him, or before, or on either side. There had always been the shadowed corner, the dark place into which he dared not look, but from which something seemed always to be watching him—and Paul had done things that were not pretty to watch, he knew.

But now he had a curious sense of relief, as though he had at last thrown down the gauntlet to the thing in the corner.

Yet it was but a day since he had been sulking in the traces; but yesterday afternoon that he had been sent to the bank with Denny and Carson's deposit, as usual—but this time he was instructed to leave the book to be balanced. There was above two thousand dollars in cheques, and nearly a thousand in the banknotes which he had taken from the book and quietly transferred to his pocket. At the bank he had made out a new deposit slip. His nerves had been steady enough to permit of his returning to the office, where he had finished his work and asked for a full day's holiday to-morrow, Saturday, giving a perfectly reasonable pretext. The bank book, he knew, would not be returned before Monday or Tuesday, and his father would be out of town for the next week. From the time he slipped the banknotes into his pocket until he boarded the night train for New York, he had not known a moment's hesitation.

How astonishingly easy it had all been; here he was, the thing done; and this time there would be no awakening, no figure at the top of the stairs. He watched the snowflakes whirling by his window until he fell asleep.

When he awoke, it was four o'clock in the afternoon. He bounded up with a start; one of his precious days gone already! He spent nearly an hour in dressing, watching every stage of his toilet carefully in the mirror. Everything was quite perfect; he was exactly the kind of boy he had always wanted to be.

When he went downstairs, Paul took a carriage and drove up Fifth Avenue toward the Park. The snow had somewhat abated; carriages and tradesmen's wagons were hurrying soundlessly to and fro in the winter twilight; boys in woollen mufflers were shovelling off the doorsteps; the Avenue stages made fine spots of colour against the white street. Here and there on the corners whole flower gardens blooming behind glass windows, against which the snowflakes stuck and melted; violets, roses, carnations, lilies-of-the-valley—somehow vastly more lovely and alluring that they blossomed thus unnaturally in the snow. The Park itself was a wonderful stage winter-piece.

When he returned, the pause of the twilight had ceased, and the tune of the streets had changed. The snow was falling faster, lights streamed from the hotels that reared their many stories fearlessly up into the storm, defying the raging Atlantic winds. A long, black stream of carriages poured down the Avenue, intersected here and there by other streams, tending horizontally. There were a score of cabs about the entrance of his hotel, and his driver had to wait. Boys in livery were running in and out of the awning stretched across the sidewalk, up and down the red velvet carpet laid from the door to the street. Above, about, within it all, was the rumble and roar, the hurry and toss of thousands of human beings as hot for pleasure as himself, and on every side of him towered the glaring affirmation of the omnipotence of wealth.

The boy set his teeth and drew his shoulders together in a spasm of realization; the plot of all dramas, the text of all romances, the nerve-stuff of all sensations was whirling about him like the snowflakes. He burnt like a fagot in a tempest.

When Paul came down to dinner, the music of the orchestra floated up the elevator shaft to greet him. As he stepped into the thronged corridor, he sank back into one of the chairs against the wall to get his breath. The lights, the chatter, the perfumes, the bewildering medley of colour—he had, for a moment, the feeling of not being able to stand it. But only for a moment; these were his own people, he told himself. He went slowly about the corridors, through the writing-rooms, smoking-rooms, reception-rooms, as though he were exploring the chambers of an enchanted palace, built and peopled for him alone.

When he reached the dining-room he sat down at a table near a window. The flowers, the white linen, the many-coloured wine-glasses, the gay toilettes of the women, the low popping of corks, the undulating repetitions of the "Blue Danube" from the orchestra, all flooded Paul's dream with bewildering radiance. When the roseate tinge of his champagne was added—that cold, precious, bubbling stuff that creamed and foamed in his glass—Paul wondered that there were honest men in the world at all. This was what all the world was fighting for, he reflected; this was what all the struggle was about. He doubted the reality of his past. Had he ever known a place called Cordelia Street, a place where fagged-looking business men boarded the early car? Mere rivets in a machine they seemed to Paul—sickening men, with combings of children's hair always hanging to their coats, and the smell of cooking in their clothes. Cordelia Street—Ah, that belonged to another time and country! Had he not always been thus, had he not sat here night after night, from as far back as he could remember, looking pensively over just such shimmering textures, and slowly twirling the stem of a glass like this one between his thumb and middle finger? He rather thought he had.

He was not in the least abashed or lonely. He had no especial desire to meet or to know any of these people; all he demanded was the right to look on and conjecture, to watch the pageant. The mere stage properties were all he contended for. Nor was he lonely later in the evening, in his loge at the Opera. He was entirely rid of his nervous misgivings, of his forced aggressiveness, of the imperative desire to show himself different from his surroundings. He felt now that his surroundings explained him. Nobody questioned the purple; he had only to wear it passively. He had only to glance down at his dress coat to reassure himself that here it would be impossible for anyone to humiliate him.

He found it hard to leave his beautiful sitting-room to go to bed that night, and sat long watching the raging storm from his turret window. When he went to sleep, it was with the lights turned on in his bedroom; partly because of his old timidity, and partly so that, if he should wake in the night, there would be no wretched moment of doubt, no horrible suspicion of yellow wallpaper, or of Washington and Calvin above his bed.

On Sunday morning the city was practically snowbound. Paul breakfasted late, and in the afternoon he fell in with a wild San Francisco boy, a freshman at Yale, who said he had run down for a "little flyer" over Sunday. The young man offered to show Paul the night side of the town, and the two boys went off together after dinner, not returning to the hotel until seven o'clock the next morning. They had started out in the confiding warmth of a champagne friendship, but their parting in the elevator was singularly cool. The freshman pulled himself together to make his train, and Paul went to bed. He awoke at two o'clock in the afternoon, very thirsty and dizzy, and rang for ice-water, coffee, and the Pittsburgh papers.

On the part of the hotel management, Paul excited no suspicion. There was this to be said for him, that he wore his spoils with dignity and in no way made himself conspicuous. His chief greediness lay in his ears and eyes, and his excesses were not offensive ones. His dearest pleasures were the grey winter twilights in his sitting-room; his quiet enjoyment of his flowers, his clothes, his wide divan, his cigarette, and his sense of power. He could not remember a time when he had felt so at peace with himself. The mere release from the necessity of petty lying, lying every day and every day, restored his self-respect. He had never lied for pleasure, even at school; but to make himself noticed and admired, to assert his difference from other Cordelia Street boys; and he felt a good deal more manly, more honest, even, now that he had no need for boastful pretensions, now that he could, as his actor friends used to say, "dress the part." It was characteristic that remorse did not occur to him. His golden days went by without a shadow, and he made each as perfect as he could.

On the eighth day after his arrival in New York, he found the whole affair exploited in the Pittsburgh papers, exploited with a wealth of detail which indicated that local news of a sensational nature was at a low ebb. The firm of Denny and Carson announced that the boy's father had refunded the full amount of his theft, and that they had no intention of prosecuting. The Cumberland minister had been interviewed, and expressed his hope of yet reclaiming the motherless lad, and Paul's Sabbath-School teacher declared that she would spare no effort to that end. The rumour had reached Pittsburgh that the boy had been seen in a New York hotel, and his father had gone East to find him and bring him home.

Paul had just come in to dress for dinner; he sank into a chair, weak in the knees, and clasped his head in his hands. It was to be worse than jail, even; the tepid waters of Cordelia Street were to close over him finally and forever. The grey monotony stretched before him in hopeless, unrelieved years;—Sabbath-School, Young People's Meeting, the yellow-papered room, the damp dish-towels; it all rushed back upon him with sickening vividness. He had the old feeling that the orchestra had suddenly stopped, the sinking sensation that the play was over. The sweat broke out on his face, and he sprang to his feet, looked about him with his white, conscious smile, and winked at himself in the mirror. With something of the childish belief in miracles with which he had so often gone to class, all his lessons unlearned, Paul dressed and dashed whistling down the corridor to the elevator.

He had no sooner entered the dining-room and caught the measure of the music than his remembrance was lightened by his old elastic power of claiming the moment, mounting with it, and finding it all-sufficient. The glare and glitter about him, the mere scenic accessories had again, and for the last time, their old potency. He would show himself that he was game, he would finish the thing splendidly. He doubted, more than ever, the existence of Cordelia Street, and for the first time he drank his wine recklessly. Was he not, after all, one of these fortunate beings? Was he not still himself, and in his own place? He drummed a nervous accompaniment to the music and looked about him, telling himself over and over that it had paid.

He reflected drowsily, to the swell of the violin and the chill sweetness of his wine, that he might have done it more wisely. He might have caught an outbound steamer and been well out of their clutches before now. But the other side of the world had seemed too far away and too uncertain then; he could not have waited for it; his need had been too sharp. If he had to choose over again, he would do the same thing to-morrow. He looked affectionately about the dining-room, now gilded with a soft mist. Ah, it had paid indeed!

Paul was awakened next morning by a painful throbbing in his head and feet. He had thrown himself across the bed without undressing, and had slept with his shoes on. His limbs and hands were lead-heavy, and his tongue and throat were parched. There came upon him one of those fateful attacks of clear-headedness that never occurred except when he was physically exhausted and his nerves hung loose. He lay still and closed his eyes and let the tide of realities wash over him.

His father was in New York; "stopping at some joint or other," he told himself. The memory of successive summers on the front stoop fell upon him like a weight of black water. He had not a hundred dollars left; and he knew now, more than ever, that money was everything, the wall that stood between all he loathed and all he wanted. The thing was winding itself up; he had thought of that on his first glorious day in New York, and had even provided a way to snap the thread. It lay on his dressing-table now; he had got it out last night when he came blindly up from dinner—but the shiny metal hurt his eyes, and he disliked the look of it, anyway.

He rose and moved about with a painful effort, succumbing now and again to attacks of nausea. It was the old depression exaggerated; all the world had become Cordelia Street. Yet somehow he was not afraid of anything, was absolutely calm; perhaps because he had looked into the dark corner at last, and knew. It was bad enough, what he saw there; but somehow not so bad as his long fear of it had been. He saw everything clearly now. He had a feeling that he had made the best of it, that he had lived the sort of life he was meant to live, and for half an hour he sat staring at the revolver. But he told himself that was not the way, so he went downstairs and took a cab to the ferry.

When Paul arrived at Newark, he got off the train and took another cab, directing the driver to follow the Pennsylvania tracks out of the town. The snow lay heavy on the roadways and had drifted deep in the open fields. Only here and there the dead grass or dried weed stalks projected, singularly black, above it.

Once well into the country, Paul dismissed the carriage and walked, floundering along the tracks, his mind a medley of irrelevant things. He seemed to hold in his brain an actual picture of everything he had seen that morning. He remembered every feature of both his drivers, the toothless old woman from whom he had bought the red flowers in his coat, the agent from whom he had got his ticket, and all of his fellow-passengers on the ferry. His mind, unable to cope with vital matters near at hand, worked feverishly and deftly at sorting and grouping these images. They made for him a part of the ugliness of the world, of the ache in his head, and the bitter burning on his tongue. He stooped and put a handful of snow into his mouth as he walked, but that, too, seemed hot. When he reached a little hillside, where the tracks ran through a cut some twenty feet below him, he stopped and sat down.

The carnations in his coat were drooping with the cold, he noticed; their red glory over. It occurred to him that all the flowers he had seen in the show windows that first night must have gone the same way, long before this. It was only one splendid breath they had, in spite of their brave mockery at the winter outside the glass. It was a losing game in the end, it seemed, this revolt against the homilies by which the world is run. Paul took one of the blossoms carefully from his coat and scooped a little hole in the snow, where he covered it up. Then he dozed awhile, from his weak condition, seeming insensible to the cold.

The sound of an approaching train woke him and he started to his feet, remembering only his resolution, and afraid lest he should be too late. He stood watching the approaching locomotive, his teeth chattering, his lips drawn away from them in a frightened smile; once or twice he glanced nervously sidewise, as though he were being watched. When the right moment came, he jumped. As he fell, the folly of his haste occurred to him with merciless clearness, the vastness of what he had left undone. There flashed through his brain, clearer than ever before, the blue of Adriatic water, the yellow of Algerian sands.

He felt something strike his chest—his body was being thrown swiftly through the air, on and on, immeasurably far and fast, while his limbs gently relaxed. Then, because the picture-making mechanism was crushed, the disturbing visions flashed into black, and Paul dropped back into the immense design of things.

QUESTIONS

1. Technically we should classify the author's point of view as omniscient, for she enters into the minds of characters at will. Nevertheless, early in the story the focus changes rather abruptly. Locate the point where the change occurs. Through whose eyes do we see Paul prior to this point? Through whose eyes do we see him afterwards? What is the purpose of this shift? Does it offer any clue to the purpose of the story?

2. What details of Paul's appearance and behavior, as his teachers see him, indicate that he is abnormal?

3. Explain Paul's behavior. Why does he lie? What does he hate? What does he want? Contrast the world of Cordelia Street with the worlds that Paul finds at Carnegie Hall, at the Schenley, at the stock theater, and in New York.

4. Is Paul artistic? Describe his reactions to music, to painting, to literature, and to the theater. What value does he find in the arts?

5. Is Paul a static or a developing character? If the latter, at what points does he change? Why?

6. What do Paul's clandestine trips to the stock theater, his trip to New York, and his suicide have in common?

7. Compare Paul and the college boy he meets in New York. Are they two of a kind? If not, how do they differ?

8. What are the implications of the title? What does the last sentence of the story do to the reader's focus of vision?

9. Are there any clues to the causes of Paul's abnormality? How many? In what is the author chiefly interested?

10. In what two cities is the story set? Does this choice of settings have any symbolic value? Could the story have been set as validly in Cleveland and Detroit? in San Francisco and Los Angeles? in New Orleans and Atlanta?

James Thurber

THE CATBIRD SEAT

Mr. Martin bought the pack of Camels on Monday night in the most crowded cigar store on Broadway. It was theatre time and seven or eight men were buying cigarettes. The clerk didn't even glance at Mr. Martin, who put the pack in his overcoat pocket and went out. If any of the staff at F & S had seen him buy the cigarettes, they would have been astonished, for it was generally known that Mr. Martin did not smoke, and never had. No one saw him.

It was just a week to the day since Mr. Martin had decided to rub out Mrs. Ulgine Barrows. The term "rub out" pleased him because it

THE CATBIRD SEAT "The Catbird Seat" by James Thurber, copr. © 1957 by James Thurber, from *Alarms and Diversions*, published by Harper & Row. Reprinted by permission of Helen Thurber.

suggested nothing more than the correction of an error—in this case an error of Mr. Fitweiler. Mr. Martin had spent each night of the past week working out his plan and examining it. As he walked home now he went over it again. For the hundredth time he resented the element of imprecision, the margin of guesswork that entered into the business. The project as he had worked it out was casual and bold, the risks were considerable. Something might go wrong anywhere along the line. And therein lay the cunning of his scheme. No one would ever see in it the cautious, painstaking hand of Erwin Martin, head of the filing department at F & S, of whom Mr. Fitweiler had once said, "Man is fallible but Martin isn't." No one would see his hand, that is, unless it were caught in the act.

Sitting in his apartment, drinking a glass of milk, Mr. Martin reviewed his case against Mrs. Ulgine Barrows, as he had every night for seven nights. He began at the beginning. Her quacking voice and braying laugh had first profaned the halls of F & S on March 7, 1941 (Mr. Martin had a head for dates). Old Roberts, the personnel chief, had introduced her as the newly appointed special adviser to the president of the firm, Mr. Fitweiler. The woman had appalled Mr. Martin instantly, but he hadn't shown it. He had given her his dry hand, a look of studious concentration, and a faint smile. "Well," she had said, looking at the papers on his desk, "are you lifting the oxcart out of the ditch?" As Mr. Martin recalled that moment, over his milk, he squirmed slightly. He must keep his mind on her crimes as a special adviser, not on her peccadillos as a personality. This he found difficult to do, in spite of entering an objection and sustaining it. The faults of the woman as a woman kept chattering on in his mind like an unruly witness. She had, for almost two years now, baited him. In the halls, in the elevator, even in his own office, into which she romped now and then like a circus horse, she was constantly shouting these silly questions at him. "Are you lifting the oxcart out of the ditch? Are you tearing up the pea patch? Are you hollering down the rain barrel? Are you scraping around the bottom of the pickle barrel? Are you sitting in the catbird seat?"

It was Joey Hart, one of Mr. Martin's two assistants, who had explained what the gibberish meant. "She must be a Dodger fan," he had said. "Red Barber announces the Dodger games over the radio and he uses those expressions—picked 'em up down South." Joey had gone on to explain one or two. "Tearing up the pea patch" meant going on a rampage; "sitting in the catbird seat" meant sitting pretty, like a batter with three balls and no strikes on him. Mr. Martin dismissed all this with an effort. It had been annoying, it had driven him near to distraction, but he was too solid a man to be moved to murder by anything so childish. It was fortunate, he reflected as he passed on to the important charges against Mrs. Barrows, that he had stood up under it so well. He had maintained always an outward appearance of polite tolerance. "Why, I even believe you like the woman," Miss Paird, his other assistant, had once said to him. He had simply smiled.

A gavel rapped in Mr. Martin's mind and the case proper was resumed. Mrs. Ulgine Barrows stood charged with willful, blatant, and persistent attempts to destroy the efficiency and system of F & S. It was competent, material, and relevant to review her advent and rise to power. Mr. Martin had got the story from Miss Paird, who seemed always able to find things out. According to her, Mrs. Barrows had met Mr. Fitweiler at a party, where she had rescued him from the embraces of a powerfully built drunken man who had mistaken the president of F & S for a famous retired Middle Western football coach. She had led him to a sofa and somehow worked upon him a monstrous magic. The aging gentleman had jumped to the conclusion there and then that this was a woman of singular attainments, equipped to bring out the best in him and in the firm. A week later he had introduced her into F & S as his special adviser. On that day confusion got its foot in the door. After Miss Tyson, Mr. Brundage, and Mr. Bartlett had been fired and Mr. Munson had taken his hat and stalked out, mailing in his resignation later, old Roberts had been emboldened to speak to Mr. Fitweiler. He mentioned that Mr. Munson's department had been "a little disrupted" and hadn't they perhaps better resume the old system there? Mr. Fitweiler had said certainly not. He had the greatest faith in Mrs. Barrow's ideas. "They require a little seasoning, a little seasoning, is all," he had added. Mr. Roberts had given it up. Mr. Martin reviewed in detail all the changes wrought by Mrs. Barrows. She had begun chipping at the cornices of the firm's edifice and now she was swinging at the foundation stones with a pickaxe.

Mr. Martin came now, in his summing up, to the afternoon of Monday, November 2, 1942—just one week ago. On that day, at 3 P.M., Mrs. Barrows had bounced into his office. "Boo!" she had yelled. "Are you scraping around the bottom of the pickle barrel?" Mr. Martin had looked at her from under his green eyeshade, saying nothing. She had begun to wander about the office, taking it in with her great, popping eyes. "Do you really need *all* these filing cabinets?" she had demanded suddenly. Mr. Martin's heart had jumped. "Each of these files," he had said, keeping his voice even, "plays an indispensable part in the system of F & S." She had brayed at him, "Well, don't tear up the pea patch!" and gone to the door. From there she had bawled, "But you sure have got a lot of fine scrap in here!" Mr. Martin could no longer doubt that the finger was on his beloved department. Her pickaxe was on the upswing, poised for the first blow. It had not come yet; he had received no blue memo from the enchanted Mr. Fitweiler bearing nonsensical instructions deriving from the obscene woman. But there was no doubt in Mr. Martin's mind that one would be forthcoming. He must act quickly. Already a precious week had gone by. Mr. Martin stood up in his living room, still holding his milk glass. "Gentlemen of the jury," he said to himself, "I demand the death penalty for this horrible. person."

The next day Mr. Martin followed his routine, as usual. He polished his glasses more often and once sharpened an already sharp pencil, but not even Miss Paird noticed. Only once did he catch sight of his victim; she swept past him in the hall with a patronizing "Hi!" At five-thirty he walked home, as usual, and had a glass of milk, as usual. He had never drunk anything stronger in his life—unless you could count ginger ale. The late Sam Schlosser, the S of F & S, had praised Mr. Martin at a staff meeting several years before for his temperate habits. "Our most efficient worker neither drinks nor smokes," he had said. "The results speak for themselves." Mr. Fitweiler had sat by, nodding approval.

Mr. Martin was still thinking about that red-letter day as he walked over to the Schrafft's on Fifth Avenue near Forty-sixth Street. He got there, as he always did, at eight o'clock. He finished his dinner and the financial page of the *Sun* at a quarter to nine, as he always did. It was his custom after dinner to take a walk. This time he walked down Fifth Avenue at a casual pace. His gloved hands felt moist and warm, his forehead cold. He transferred the Camels from his overcoat to a jacket pocket. He wondered, as he did so, if they did not represent an unnecessary note of strain. Mrs. Barrows smoked only Luckies. It was his idea to puff a few puffs on a Camel (after the rubbing-out), stub it out in the ashtray holding her lipstick-stained Luckies, and thus drag a small red herring across the trail. Perhaps it was not a good idea. It would take time. He might even choke, too loudly.

Mr. Martin had never seen the house on West Twelfth Street where Mrs. Barrows lived, but he had a clear enough picture of it. Fortunately, she had bragged to everybody about her ducky first-floor apartment in the perfectly darling three-story red-brick. There would be no doorman or other attendants; just the tenants of the second and third floors. As he walked along, Mr. Martin realized that he would get there before nine-thirty. He had considered walking north on Fifth Avenue from Schrafft's to a point from which it would take him until ten o'clock to reach the house. At that hour people were less likely to be coming in or going out. But the procedure would have made an awkward loop in the straight thread of his casualness, and he had abandoned it. It was impossible to figure when people would be entering or leaving the house, anyway. There was a great risk at any hour. If he ran into anybody, he would simply have to place the rubbing-out of Ulgine Barrows in the inactive file forever. The same thing would hold true if there were someone in her apartment. In that case he would just say that he had been passing by, recognized her charming house, and thought to drop in.

It was eighteen minutes after nine when Mr. Martin turned into Twelfth Street. A man passed him, and a man and a woman, talking. There was no one within fifty paces when he came to the house, halfway down the block. He was up the steps and in the small vestibule in no time, pressing the bell under the card that said "Mrs. Ulgine Barrows." When the clicking in the lock started he jumped forward against the door. He got inside fast, closing the door behind him. A bulb in a lantern hung from the hall ceiling on a chain seemed to give a monstrously bright light. There was nobody on the stair, which went up ahead of him along the left wall. A door opened down the hall in the wall on the right. He went toward it swiftly, on tiptoe.

"Well, for God's sake, look who's here!" bawled Mrs. Barrows, and her braying laugh rang out like the report of a shotgun. He rushed past her like a football tackle, bumping her. "Hey, quit shoving!" she said, closing the door behind them. They were in her living room, which seemed to Mr. Martin to be lighted by a hundred lamps. "What's after you?" she said. "You're as jumpy as a goat." He found he was unable to speak. His heart was wheezing in his throat. "I—yes," he finally brought out. She was jabbering and laughing as she started to help him off with his coat. "No, no," he said. "I'll put it here." He took it off and put it on a chair near the door. "Your hat and gloves, too," she said. "You're in a lady's house." He put his hat on top of the coat. Mrs. Barrows seemed larger than he had thought. He kept his gloves on. "I was passing by," he said. "I recognized—is there anyone here?" She laughed louder than ever. "No," she said, "we're all alone. You're as white as a sheet, you funny man. Whatever *has* come over you? I'll mix you a toddy." She started toward a door across the room. "Scotch-and-soda be all right? But say, you don't drink, do you?" She turned and gave him her amused look. Mr. Martin pulled himself together. "Scotch-and-soda will be all right," he heard himself say. He could hear her laughing in the kitchen.

Mr. Martin looked quickly around the living room for the weapon. He had counted on finding one there. There were andirons and a poker and something in a corner that looked like an Indian club. None of them would do. It couldn't be that way. He began to pace around. He came to a desk. On it lay a metal paper knife with an ornate handle. Would it be sharp enough? He reached for it and knocked over a small brass jar. Stamps spilled out of it and it fell to the floor with a clatter. "Hey," Mrs. Barrows yelled from the kitchen, "are you tearing up the pea patch?" Mr. Martin gave a strange laugh. Picking up the knife, he tried its point against his left wrist. It was blunt. It wouldn't do.

When Mrs. Barrows reappeared, carrying two highballs, Mr. Martin, standing there with his gloves on, became acutely conscious of the fantasy he had wrought. Cigarettes in his pocket, a drink prepared for him—it was all too grossly improbable. It was more than that; it was impossible. Somewhere in the back of his mind a vague idea stirred, sprouted. "For heaven's sake, take off those gloves," said Mrs. Barrows. "I always wear them in the house," said Mr. Martin. The idea began to bloom, strange and wonderful. She put the glasses on a coffee table in front of a sofa and sat on the sofa. "Come over here, you odd little man," she said. Mr. Martin went over and sat beside her. It was difficult getting a cigarette out of the pack of Camels, but he managed it. She held a match for him, laughing. "Well," she said, handing him his drink, "this is perfectly marvellous. You with a drink and a cigarette."

Mr. Martin puffed, not too awkwardly, and took a gulp of the highball. "I drink and smoke all the time," he said. He clinked his glass against hers. "Here's nuts to that old windbag, Fitweiler," he said, and gulped again. The stuff tasted awful, but he made no grimace. "Really, Mr. Martin," she said, her voice and posture changing, "you are insulting our employer." Mrs. Barrows was now all special adviser to the president. "I am preparing a bomb," said Mr. Martin, "which will blow the old goat higher than hell." He had only had a little of the drink, which was not strong. It couldn't be that. "Do you take dope or something?" Mrs. Barrows asked coldly. "Heroin," said Mr. Martin. "I'll be coked to the gills when I bump that old buzzard off." "Mr. Martin!" she shouted, getting to her feet. "That will be all of that. You must go at once." Mr. Martin took another swallow of his drink. He tapped his cigarette out in the ashtray and put the pack of Camels on the coffee table. Then he got up. She stood glaring at him. He walked over and put on his hat and coat. "Not a word about this," he said, and laid an index finger against his lips. All Mrs. Barrows could bring out was "Really!" Mr. Martin put his hand on the doorknob. "I'm sitting in the catbird seat," he said. He stuck his tongue out at her and left. Nobody saw him go.

Mr. Martin got to his apartment, walking, well before eleven. No one saw him go in. He had two glasses of milk after brushing his teeth, and he felt elated. It wasn't tipsiness, because he hadn't been tipsy. Anyway, the walk had worn off all effects of the whiskey. He got in bed and read a magazine for a while. He was asleep before midnight.

Mr. Martin got to the office at eight-thirty the next morning, as usual. At a quarter to nine, Ulgine Barrows, who had never before arrived at work before ten, swept into his office. "I'm reporting to Mr. Fitweiler now!" she shouted. "If he turns you over to the police, it's no more than you deserve!" Mr. Martin gave her a look of shocked surprise. "I beg your pardon?" he said. Mrs. Barrows snorted and bounced out of the room, leaving Miss Paird and Joey Hart staring after her. "What's the matter with that old devil now?" asked Miss Paird. "I have no idea," said Mr. Martin, resuming his work. The other two looked at him and then at each other. Miss Paird got up and went out. She walked slowly past the closed door of Mr. Fitweiler's office. Mrs. Barrows was yelling inside, but she was not braying. Miss Paird could not hear what the woman was saying. She went back to her desk.

Forty-five minutes later, Mrs. Barrows left the president's office and went into her own, shutting the door. It wasn't until half an hour later that Mr. Fitweiler sent for Mr. Martin. The head of the filing department, neat, quiet, attentive, stood in front of the old man's desk. Mr. Fitweiler was pale and nervous. He took his glasses off and twiddled them. He made a small, bruffing sound in his throat. "Martin," he said, "you have been with us more than twenty years." "Twenty-two, sir," said Mr. Martin. "In that time," pursued the president, "your work and your—uh—manner have been exemplary." "I trust so, sir," said Mr. Martin. "I have understood, Martin," said Mr. Fitweiler, "that you have never taken a drink or smoked." "That is correct, sir," said Mr. Martin. "Ah, yes." Mr. Fitweiler polished his glasses. "You may describe what you did after leaving the office yesterday, Martin," he said. Mr. Martin allowed less than a second for his bewildered pause. "Certainly, sir," he said. "I walked home. Then I went to Schrafft's for dinner. Afterward I walked home again. I went to bed early, sir, and read a magazine for a while. I was asleep before eleven." "Ah, yes," said Mr. Fitweiler again. He was silent for a moment, searching for the proper words to say to the head of the filing department. "Mrs. Barrows," he said finally, "Mrs. Barrows has worked hard, Martin, very hard. It grieves me to report that she has suffered a severe breakdown. It has taken the form of a persecution complex accompanied by distressing hallucinations." "I am very sorry, sir," said Mr. Martin. "Mrs. Barrows is under the delusion," continued Mr. Fitweiler, "that you visited her last evening and behaved yourself in an—uh—unseemly manner." He raised his hand to silence Mr. Martin's little pained outcry. "It is the nature of these psychological diseases," Mr. Fitweiler said, "to fix upon the least likely and most innocent party as the—uh—source of persecution. These matters are not for the lay mind to grasp, Martin. I've just had my psychiatrist, Dr. Fitch, on the phone. He would not, of course, commit himself, but he made enough generalizations to substantiate my suspicions. I suggested to Mrs. Barrows, when she had completed her—uh—story to me this morning, that she visit Dr. Fitch, for I suspected a condition at once. She flew, I regret to say, into a rage, and demanded—uh—requested that I call you on the carpet. You may not know, Martin, but Mrs. Barrows had planned a reorganization of your department—

subject to my approval, of course, subject to my approval. This brought you, rather than anyone else, to her mind—but again that is a phenomenon for Dr. Fitch and not for us. So, Martin, I am afraid Mrs. Barrows' usefulness here is at an end." "I am dreadfully sorry, sir," said Mr. Martin.

It was at this point that the door to the office blew open with the suddenness of a gas-main explosion and Mrs. Barrows catapulted through it. "Is the little rat denying it?" she screamed. "He can't get away with that!" Mr. Martin got up and moved discreetly to a point beside Mr. Fitweiler's chair. "You drank and smoked at my apartment," she bawled at Mr. Martin, "and you know it! You called Mr. Fitweiler an old windbag and said you were going to blow him up when you got coked to the gills on your heroin!" She stopped yelling to catch her breath and a new glint came into her popping eyes. "If you weren't such a drab, ordinary little man," she said, "I'd think you'd planned it all. Sticking your tongue out, saying you were sitting in the catbird seat, because you thought no one would believe me when I told it! My God, it's really too perfect!" She brayed loudly and hysterically, and the fury was on her again. She glared at Mr. Fitweiler. "Can't you see how he has tricked us, you old fool? Can't you see his little game?" But Mr. Fitweiler had been surreptitiously pressing all the buttons under the top of his desk and employees of F & S began pouring into the room. "Stockton," said Mr. Fitweiler, "you and Fishbein will take Mrs. Barrows to her home. Mrs. Powell, you will go with them." Stockton, who had played a little football in high school, blocked Mrs. Barrows as she made for Mr. Martin. It took him and Fishbein together to force her out of the door into the hall, crowded with stenographers and office boys. She was still screaming imprecations at Mr. Martin, tangled and contradictory imprecations. The hubbub finally died out down the corridor.

"I regret that this has happened," said Mr. Fitweiler. "I shall ask you to dismiss it from your mind, Martin." "Yes, sir," said Mr. Martin, anticipating his chief's "That will be all" by moving to the door. "I will dismiss it." He went out and shut the door, and his step was light and quick in the hall. When he entered his department he had slowed down to his customary gait, and he walked quietly across the room to the W20 file, wearing a look of studious concentration.

QUESTIONS

1. How is suspense aroused and maintained in the story? What is the story's principal surprise?
2. Through whose consciousness are the events of the story chiefly seen? Are

there any departures from this strictly limited point of view? Where in the story are we taken most fully into Mr. Martin's mind? For what purpose?

3. At what point in the story do Mr. Martin's plans change? What happens to the point of view at this point? What does Thurber's handling of the point of view here tell us about the seriousness of the story's purpose?

4. Characterize Mr. Martin and Mrs. Barrows respectively. In what ways are they character foils?

5. Analyze the story in terms of its conflicts. What kinds of conflict are involved? Is there any internal conflict? What kind of conflict that *might* be expected in a murder story is missing?

6. Evaluate the surprise ending of the story by the criteria suggested on page 49.

7. What insights into the life of a business office does the story provide? What kind of insight does the story not provide? What is the story's greatest improbability?

8. What is the main purpose of the story?

9. Why does Thurber choose this particular expression of Mrs. Barrows' for his title rather than one of her others?

10. why is the title important to the story.

6

Symbol and
Irony

Most successful stories are characterized by compression. The writer's aim is to say as much as possible as briefly as possible. This does not mean that most good stories are brief. It means only that nothing is wasted and that each word and detail are chosen for maximum effectiveness. The force of an explosion is proportionate to the strength and amount of powder used and the smallness of the space it is confined in.

The writer achieves compression by exercising a rigid selectivity. He chooses those details and incidents which contribute most to the meaning he is after; he omits those whose usefulness is minimal. As far as possible he chooses details which are multi-valued—which serve a variety of purposes at once. A detail which expresses character at the same time that it advances the plot is more useful than a detail which does only one or the other.

This chapter will discuss two contributory resources of the writer for gaining compression: symbol and irony. Both of them may increase the explosive force of a story, but both demand awareness and maturity on the part of the reader.

A literary SYMBOL[1] is something which means *more* than what it is. It is an object, a person, a situation, an action, or some other item, which has a literal meaning in the story but suggests or represents other meanings as well. A very simple illustration is to be found in name-symbolism. Most names are simply labels. Seldom does a name tell anything about the person to whom it is attached—except possibly his nationality. In a story, however, the author may choose names for his characters which serve not only to label them but also to suggest

---

[1] *Literary* symbols are to be distinguished from *arbitrary* symbols, like letters of the alphabet, numbers, and algebraic signs, which have no meaning in and of themselves, and mean only something *else*, not some thing *more* than what they are.

something about them. In his fictional trilogy *The Forsyte Saga* John Galsworthy chooses Forsyte as the family name of his principal characters to indicate their practical foresightedness. The name Weatherall in "The Jilting of Granny Weatherall" and the name Laird in "Boys and Girls" have been referred to earlier as deliberately symbolic. In "The Destructors" the boys dub Mr. Thomas "Old Misery," an obvious reference to the lonely, miserable life he leads in the crippled house. In the same story, Blackie is the original leader of the gang while the usurper, Trevor, is called "T.", which could represent "Trouble." Is the name of the sadistic, task-oriented foreman, "McKillup," in "E Equals MC Squared" mere coincidence, or calculated characterization on the part of Hugh Garner?

More important than name-symbolism is the symbolic use of objects and actions. In some stories these symbols will fit so naturally into the literal context that their symbolic value will not at first be apparent except to the most perceptive reader. In other stories—usually stories with a less realistic surface—they will be so central and so obvious that they will demand symbolical interpretation if the story is to yield significant meaning. In the first kind of story the symbols *reinforce* and *add to* the meaning. In the second kind of story they *carry* the meaning.

In "Tears, Idle Tears" the calm white duck swimming in the lake becomes symbolically associated in Frederick's unconscious mind with the experience by which he gets over his "lonely shame" and is cured of his irrational fits of weeping. When his mother goes on ahead, she tells him to stay behind and "look at that duck" till he stops his noise. Looking at it, he begins to quiet down. "When it rolled one eye open over a curve, something unseeing in its expression calmed him." Clearly the duck is not mortified by his crying, as his mother is—does not notice it, in fact. When he tries to touch the duck, it slides away from him "without a blink, with automatic uncoyness," and gently propels itself around the curve of the bank. Years later, though Frederick has forgotten the girl on the park bench, and the boy she told him about, he can "still remember, with ease, pleasure and with a sense of lonely shame being gone, that calm white duck swimming off round the bank." For Frederick the duck has become an unconscious symbol of his release from shame and embarrassment. For the reader it has become a symbol of ease and calm, of unselfconscious independence. Bowen might equally well have used a squirrel or a rabbit to focus Frederick's memory of the event, but neither could have acquired such symbolical value for the reader.

In this context another creature also assumes representative significance. When Frederick's mother returns, a swan comes swimming "as though to greet her." Mrs. Dickinson touches "her fox fur lightly, sliding it up her shoulder. What a lovely mother to have." The swan symbolically reinforces Mrs. Dickinson's elegance and loveliness. A duck would have been less useful. And it would have been completely inappropriate had the author written, "as though to greet her, a goose came waddling."

The ability to recognize and identify symbols requires perception and tact. The great danger facing the student when he first becomes aware of symbolical values is a tendency to run wild—to find symbols everywhere and to read into the details of a story all sorts of fanciful meanings not legitimately supported by it. The beginning reader needs to remember that most stories operate almost wholly at the literal level, and that even in a story like "Tears, Idle Tears" the majority of the details are purely literal. A story should not be made the excuse for an exercise in ingenuity. It is better, indeed, to miss the symbolical meanings of a story than to pervert its meaning by discovering symbols which are nonexistent. Better to miss the boat than to jump wildly for it and drown.

The ability to interpret symbols is nevertheless essential for a full understanding of literature. The beginning reader should be alert for symbolical meanings, but should observe the following cautions:

1. The story must furnish a clue that a detail is to be taken symbolically. In "Horses of the Night" for instance, Chris becomes a symbol of sensitivity, loneliness, and alienation. The symbolical identification is established by the frequent references Chris makes to the riding horses, the house "made out of trees grown right there beside the lake" and the "inland sea" of Shallow Creek. The reader has already been informed of the actual and dire poverty of Chris's family. Vanessa's mother whispers to the grandmother when they first see Chris, "Heavens, look at the shirt and trousers—must've been his father's, poor kid." Later Grandfather Connor makes references to Chris's father: "Nobody but a simpleton would've taken up a homestead in a place like that. Anybody could've told him that land's no use for a thing except hay." It becomes very clear that Chris is taking refuge in a fantasy world, that he is unable to cope with the realities of his own existence and that he cannot relate to the people around him. This aspect of his character is reinforced later in the story when he becomes a traveling salesman, always confident that the line he is currently selling will make him successful. He consistently denies the economic depression of the time. The final tragic symbol of Chris's alienation is reflected in his insanity, his failure to face the realities of war. Symbols nearly always signal their existence by emphasis, repetition, or position. In the absence of such signals we should be reluctant to identify an item as symbolical.

2. The meaning of a literary symbol must be established and

supported by the entire context of the story. The symbol has its meaning *in* the story, not *outside* of it. Our meaning for the duck in "Tears, Idle Tears" is supported by the description Bowen gives of it and by its association with a turning point in the life of the story's protagonist. In another work of literature, in another context, the duck might have an entirely different symbolical meaning, or no symbolical meaning whatever. Certainly the duck in Ibsen's play *The Wild Duck* has a different meaning from the one in "Tears, Idle Tears," and Bowen's swan has a meaning different from that of the swans in Yeats's famous poem "The Wild Swans at Coole."

3. To be called a symbol, an item must suggest a meaning different *in kind* from its literal meaning; a symbol is something more than the representative of a class or type. Vanessa, in "Horses of the Night," is a deeply sensitive young girl, capable of great insight into the world around her. Throughout the story she agonizes over her supposed inability to understand other people and to communicate meaningfully with them. To some degree, she feels isolated and alone. In proportion as the story is successful, Vanessa comes to stand for people everywhere who feel an inadequacy in reaching out to others. The story acquaints us with a truth of human nature, not with just a biographical fact. But, to say this, is to say no more than that the story has a theme. Every interpretive story suggests a generalization about life, is more than a recounting of the specific fortunes of specific individuals. There is no point, therefore, in calling Vanessa a *symbol* of people who cannot, at times, interact meaningfully with their world. Vanessa *is* a girl with difficulty communicating. She is a member of the class of people who often feel isolated by their inability to communicate. We ought not to use the phrase *is a symbol of* when we can as easily use *is*, or *is an example of*, or *is an evidence of*. Chris, on the other hand, is something more than a quiet, thoughtful, sensitive young man who escapes into a fantasy world. He cannot communicate with people; he must escape into fantasy. In his desperation, Chris becomes insane. It is in this extreme that we see Chris as a symbol. He now symbolizes everyone's sense of isolation, everyone's feeling of being alone in a world, which for all of our sensitivity, we cannot understand. Chris is more than a sensitive young man, more than a type: he suggests a meaning of a different order from what he is.

4. A symbol may have more than one meaning. It may suggest a cluster of meanings. At its most effective a symbol is like a many-faceted jewel: it flashes different colors when turned in the light. This is not to say that it can mean anything we want it to: the area of possible meanings is always controlled by the context. Nevertheless, this possibility of complex meaning, plus concreteness and emotional power, gives the symbol its peculiar compressive value. The swan in

"Tears, Idle Tears" has an immediate emotional and imaginative force that an abstract description of Mrs. Dickinson would not have, and, though a relatively simple symbol, it suggests a cluster of qualities— elegance, loveliness, grace—that cannot be expressed in a single word. The foxes in Munro's story, "Boys and Girls," also symbolize a character, but they have a much wider range of meaning. For example, their captivity symbolizes the young narrator's knowledge that she too is caught by the word "girl." Killed at their prime, the foxes represent as well the girl's resentment that she must help her mother in the house, just as she develops competence in helping her father in his work. Many more comparisons can be drawn between the girl and the foxes, and indeed, "Boys and Girls" can be read on this symbolic level alone. Therein lies the symbol's value.

IRONY is a term with a range of meanings, all of them involving some sort of discrepancy or incongruity. It is a contrast in which one term of the contrast in some way mocks the other term. It is not to be confused with sarcasm, however, which is simply language designed to cause pain. The story writer uses irony to suggest the complexity of experience, to furnish indirectly an evaluation of his material, and at the same time to achieve compression.

Three kinds of irony may be distinguished here. VERBAL IRONY, the simplest and, for the story writer, the least important kind, is a figure of speech in which the opposite is said from what is intended. The discrepancy is between what is said and what is meant.

A plain example is offered by the implied author's remarks half-way through "E Equals MC Squared":

> "You having the bull-gang fix that press?" I asked him. "I know Colby reported to you that it was slipping."
> "That's no business of the inspectors. If you and that bohunk partner of yours had checked the gang press as you're supposed to, Colby mightn't have spoiled so many pieces."
> He was a real nice guy. I threw the long piece of T-stock back to him, and he had to grab it fast to keep it from dropping on his toes.

The irony lies in the sentence, "He was a real nice guy," because everything the reader learns about McKillup points to the opposite. There is irony also in the sentence, "That's no business of the inspectors." Surely the inspectors should be concerned with the precise and safe condition of the machines. Often, in the most effective uses of verbal irony, the literal meaning and its opposite are both implied at once.

In DRAMATIC IRONY the contrast is between what a character says or thinks and what the reader knows to be true. The value of this kind of irony lies in the comment it implies on the speaker or his expectations.

Thus, in "Tears, Idle Tears," when we are told that Frederick's mother "seldom openly punished him, but often revenged herself on him in small ways," and that Frederick "could feel how just this was," we know that his mother's behavior is actually *un*just. But Frederick's implicit faith in his mother's rightness reveals to us how young and trusting he is, how unversed he is in the ways of adult hypocrisy, and how ashamed he is of his own behavior though he cannot help it. Another effective example occurs in "I'm a Fool" when the swipe blames his lie at the race track on the whisky he had drunk and the man in the Windsor tie. The reader sees, as the swipe does not, that these are simply additional symptoms of his plight, not its cause. Perhaps the most thoroughgoing use of dramatic irony, however, is made by James Joyce in "A Little Cloud." Though the story is told from the point of view of Little Chandler, the reader sees that Chandler is badly mistaken in his appraisals of Gallaher, of himself, and of life in general. Whereas Chandler refers to Gallaher's exceptional talents, his unspoiled character, his "greatness," and his "triumphant life," the reader sees that Gallaher is a very ordinary person whose values are cheap and whose life has been tawdry. Chandler is equally deceived in his estimate of his own talents. When he dreams about himself as a poet, he thinks not in original images, but in reviewers' clichés. Also, the poem he so admires by Byron is seen by the reader to be sentimental and commonplace. But perhaps the chief irony comes when he thinks, "He was not so old—thirty-two. His temperament might be said to be just at the point of maturity." Joyce's whole account of this "little man" with "childish white teeth" who entertains "an infant hope" is one which emphasizes his childishness. Though he has been "to the Isle of Man" and has acquired a wife, he has never really grown up. In his final act of shouting at his child, he reveals his full immaturity.

In IRONY OF SITUATION, usually the most important kind for the story writer, the discrepancy is between appearance and reality, or between expectation and fulfillment, or between what is and what would seem appropriate. It is ironic in "The Destructors" that Old Misery's horoscope should read "Abstain from any dealings in first half of week. Danger of serious crash," for the horoscope is valid in a quite different sense from that which the words seem to indicate. In "Horses of the Night" Chris tells Vanessa that during the war ". . . a guy tended to concentrate on the horses because he didn't dare think what was happening to the men. Including himself." This statement is ironic because Chris has unknowingly told the story of his own life. In "E Equals MC Squared" it is ironical that the foreman, McKillup, is maimed when he refuses to accept the expert opinion of one of his subordinates, Ernie Colby, and operates the press himself during the lunch hour. This irony emphasizes McKillup's preoccupation with production regardless of the safety of the men. As a final example, the title of "Defender of the Faith" points to a complex irony, partly verbal, partly situational. The phrase "defender of the faith" ordinarily suggests a staunch religious champion and partisan, but insofar as Sergeant Marx fills this role, he does so against his will, even against his intention, for his motivation is to give fair and equal treatment to all his men—he does not want to be partial to Jews. Unwillingly, he is trapped into being a "defender of the faith" by Private Grossbart.

> The next morning, while chatting with Captain Barrett, I recounted the incident of the previous evening. Somehow, in the telling, it must have seemed to the Captain that I was not so much explaining Grossbart's position as defending it.

At the end of the story, however, when Marx has Grossbart's orders changed to the Pacific, the irony is that he becomes most truly a defender of his faith when he seems to be turning against it. "You call this watching out for me—what you did?" asks Grossbart. "No," answers Marx. "For all of us." The cause of the whole Jewish faith is set back when Jews like Grossbart get special favors for themselves, for other people will mistakenly attribute Grossbart's objectionable qualities to the Jewish people as a whole. Thus Marx is unwillingly a "defender of the faith" when he helps his co-religionist, and becomes truly a defender of the faith when he turns against him. These ironies underscore the difficulties involved in being at the same time a good Jew and a good man in a world where Jews are so often the objects of prejudice and persecution.

In all of these examples irony enables the author to gain power with economy. Like symbolism, irony makes it possible to suggest meanings without stating them. Simply by juxtaposing two discordant facts in the right solution, the writer can start a current of meaning flowing between them, as between the two poles in an electric battery. We don't need to be *told* that Frederick has implicit faith in his mother, we see it. We don't need to be told that the race-track swipe and Little Chandler are lacking in self-knowledge, we see it. We don't need to be told how difficult it is for a Jewish sergeant to balance justice and mercy in a position of command, we feel it. The ironic contrast generates meaning.

Rudy Wiebe

MILLSTONE FOR THE SUN'S DAY

Most of the people seemed to be already on the docks when the boy and his parents arrived, but the press parted swiftly for them. Without hesitation the boy passed down the long dock, the ladies smiling and the men reaching to pat his head, to where the boats lifted easily in the quick morning sunlight. Turning on the last quay, he saw the Yacht. Its white with imperial black piping burned under the solstice sun and, not quite able to believe it, he turned with a laugh to his mother just behind him.

"Mom, can I really ride on it?"

And his father's hand came down on his shoulder with his deep voice, the people all about them quiet and looking, "Joey, just go ahead— over there. We can't be late."

But the boy was looking at his mother still. Usually when he asked her a question his father did not answer. When the boy had come into the kitchen that morning to find the porridge steaming in his bowl but with the unexpected delight of brown sugar beside it, his father had been saying,

"Mary, it's better now than maybe later. You've never said anything against it until—"

But his mother, usually so gentle and quiet, her back stiffly turned and her hands slicing bananas—brown sugar and bananas both on porridge in one day, hey, this was really a holiday—interrupting fiercely, "We don't *have* to let them!"

His father stood rigid as at a blasphemy. "What—Mary—what in all the almighty world—not *have* to?" his voice hanging on incredible pitch, the sunlight in the big-windowed kitchen gleaming on the hair of his half-lifted, abruptly paralysed arm. Then he saw the boy in the doorway. "Joey! We didn't even hear you. And dressed already! Ready to go."

"Uh-huh—we better hurry, huh, for the ride?"

His father was smiling, bending to him, swinging him aloft so his head almost touched the ceiling, his father was so tall. The boy cried with delight as he swung up and over, and then he was plopped down facing the steaming porridge. He turned to his mother, laughing. "Mom, we can all ride the Yacht 'cause it was me drew the Lottery. At the meeting-house, eh Mom?"

MILLSTONE FOR THE SUN'S DAY From *Where is the Voice Coming From?* by Rudy Wiebe reprinted by permission of The Canadian Publishers. McClelland and Stewart Limited, Toronto.

But his mother did not turn or speak. When she moved at last, placing the tiny bowl of sliced bananas beside his porridge, she sat down beside him, her features tight and stiff, as now on the dock, but her eyes, now bunched against the direct sun, distorting even more her lovely face. The boy did not like her frown. She was always too happy for frowning; rather, singing in the kitchen, shaping towers and boats with his building blocks, walking in the Windy Woods and naming the birds flicking high on the tips of the ferns. Now, suddenly, the boy twisted from under his father's hand and tugged at her dress. "Mom, don't you *want* to ride in the Capitular's Yacht?"

She bent swiftly, her summer skirt flaring out like a dark blot and she was hugging him tight against her breast, silently. Over her shoulder he saw the dark lanes of the people up the lift of the dock, their pale faces turned stiff in their smiles against the dead-blue sky. His mother shivered, and he pushed back.

"Mom, shouldn't I of pulled the Lottery yesterday?" It was incomprehensible. He could remember the disappointment of his friend, Eric, behind him in the line and all the people in the meeting-house waving and clapping for him, the Capitular's hand holding his high to show the mark, the clapping hands flickering everywhere so that he could not see his parents though he knew exactly where they were from watching them as he inched forward in the long line. For an instant only he saw his father's black onyx ring flash in the sunlight from the great arched window in the rhythmic clapping at his winning draw. He was looking at his mother's face now, but her eyes avoided him. And then between the people beyond the sheen of her hair he caught a flash of white and he looked up. A slim white figure came down the dock, floating without sound or seeming motion, the gold-and-crimson ribbon across its breast merging with the crimson of the cantors he knew following.

"Mom!" the boy jogged her shoulder, "Look—look! It looks—just about all dressed up, like—" he stopped, his recognition shimmering away, then, "isn't it—like Miss Grierson? Look!"

His father's hand fell on his shoulder. "Joey, stand over here, where we belong," and he was hustled to the very edge of the quay where the Yacht waited, motionless as a castle in the water. Past his father's black trouser-leg the boy saw the long bent line of red figures and hats ebbing down between the people and heard the gentle sound that wavered, rising and falling, in the still air, a sound as he had never heard from them before though he had gone since before he could remember, as everyone once a week, and heard them chant in the rood-loft.

"Dad," the boy tugged at the trouser. "What're they singing?"

His father's hand slid over his mouth, the wide ring clicking against his teeth, and he could only look as the flaring baldachin of the

Capitular emerged at the head of the dock, flashing red-gold, and the procession stopped and parted, and at long last, in the rising sound, the Capitular at the head of the Lessor Capitulars moved down through the dividing ranks of the cantors to stand beside Miss Grierson in the middle of the dock before the boy and his parents.

The Capitular's benign smile broadened. "Joey." His voice was so deep in the motionless air. "Come forward please." The boy had no time to look to his mother. His father's hand was at his back and he was under the Capitular's raised palm. "Joey. You won the Lottery last evening. Therefore you are our special guest today. We will ride in the Yacht together to Sun Rock, and then perhaps around the island. Will you like that?"

Directly facing the Capitular, the question of what every child on the island dreamed of doing stirred a vague apprehension in the boy, for there was something—and then he forgot not only the correct words but also the bow for suddenly he knew and he spoke without thinking.

"Sir, your Highest—but—but there aren't my friends here."

From the low gasp of the people he knew his breach of whatever was correct and shrank back even as the laugh rumbled above him.

"Of course. But all your little friends *know* you are going with us. On the Yacht. They have all gone to the picnic at the Garden in the Valley, like you did on this day last year. But you are the special one, the only child," the hand was on his head now, the great form bending over him, "that can come on the Yacht. Because you drew the Lottery. Now, don't you like that?"

This time he remembered, and bowed. "Yes, Your Highest."

The hand lifted from his head and the sound of the cantors belled. The boy stood motionless, as they all, eyes on the gold slashing of the Capitular's robe, hearing,

The shepherd heard the sheep alway
  High hummocked humitry
The day of wrath to scath shall pass
  High seared in scarify

The diagonal gold and crimson on white of the other figure before him drew the boy's eye. So very close now, he could recognize Miss Grierson even less than from far away. Her face was immobile, as if caked in something not her own skin, and her eyes, which had laughed only days before with him and Eric building sandcastles in the schoolyard now stared away as through all the people and over the water and through the very sun itself. He stared at her in turn, the Capitular's long intoning above his head not moving him from his amazement. Then abruptly he was wheeled about and, as he twisted for one more look, his father's voice said, "Joey," and he had to turn.

Wonder of wonders to the boy, he walked up the short gangplank first, followed by his parents. And at the head of the gangplank, beard almost brushed into order, stood the old man who sunned himself day after day in the park across the street from the school. No child knew his name, or ever talked about him; no child had ever seen him do anything, but his standing there at rigid attention was merely a minor amazement as the boy and his parents, followed by the Capitular under his baldachin, stepped aboard. In a moment the deck was filled, the motors vibrated, and they were out on the water, smoothly, as if unmoving in their dignity.

No one said a word; motionless their faces sat upon their bodies like blocks. The boy squirmed, trying to look between, around them.

"Joey." The Capitular's voice stung him to stiffness. "You wish to explore the Yacht?" He had not and could not say it but the Capitular, seated in the circle of the Lesser Capitulars and the cantors, seemed to pluck out his thought. The gentle voice continued, "Yes. They always do. You are our guest—go."

The boy's mother, the only other person seated, was holding the boy's hand tightly. But when he looked at her, she nodded hastily. "Yes. I—I'll stay here—now." For an instant he was disappointed. But how often had he dreamed of exploring the largest, the most beautiful vessel on the island! He was gone, slipping between the people. The tall masts where the flags curled and stiffened in the breeze of their motion; the black-bronze railing; the polished wall of the wheelhouse where high above through the window glinted the skipper's glasses; the coiled ropes like barrels; the boy saw it all, and all was wonder. Finally he shouldered back, through the cluster of cantors and for a moment a press of skirts stopped him. And voices.

"—but I'm askin' yuh, why her? You'd think, of all the—" said a young feminine voice, but another interrupted.

"Look kiddo, don't bother. It never makes no difference. None. Just do what you're told."

"Well, it's a shame. And don't it make yuh think, huh?" the other insisted.

"I don't think. It never—" but the boy was pushing between them and the voice shifted, "Oh—it's Joey."

As the boy moved to avoid them the first girl stepped suddenly into his path. "Say, you're seeing the big Yacht. That's nice. Look at the view, over here," and her long bare arm was pulling him and he reluctantly ducked his head below the railing to look as she bent to him. "See the town. Looks nice, don't it, with all the nice tall buildings. And look, over there there's the boat factory." She was pointing in what he vaguely sensed was a kind of flurry, keeping his eyes away from the

Yacht. "And doesn't your father work—ain't he a director at the factory—see, over there—"

He had not followed her finger for the flotilla of small boats following had held him. All the boats of the island seemed spread behind the Yacht, bumped full of tiny people, cutting through the water in their wake, but he looked then at the tall chimneys of the factory. "Uh-huh," he said. "Sometimes he takes me along to his office or we look at the motors—" his voice trailed away. "Where's the smoke?"

"There's never no smoke today. See, everybody's here, coming with us." She was erect, gesturing vaguely, pushing him ahead between several girls, and then he was behind an air-funnel, momentarily alone. From deep within the ship rose a muffled throb and he could imagine the great motors running easily, motionless as rocks in their unseeing spinning. With a twist he pried himself between the people again.

And then he saw Miss Grierson. She was sitting, clustered about by girls all dressed, as he suddenly understood the girl talking to him had been, in white but without the band of gold and crimson over their breasts. He wanted to step forward, to tell her but he saw that she looked even more strange and rigid, sitting so motionless. His mother, now Miss Grierson. A pennant snapped high on the mast above him; he wished suddenly, overwhelmingly, that Eric was there.

He did not want to explore any more. But pushing to find his way back he came upon the old bearded man in a little gap away from everyone leaning over a great block of iron by the railing. The boy looked at it, for it seemed very familiar, but he could not quite decide what it was while the old man muttered to one of the Lesser Capitulars who was hunched down trying to work a rope through one of the innumerable holes in the iron.

"—ain't nothin' what it usta be. Naw sur. In the old days. Usta climb up there, before the sun come up, spend all night climbing, up the trail, through the dark with damn few torches. Just climb. And gettin' them up there was a job. Ha! But everything's gone soft, new stuff, and floating along in boats! Not like we usta climb, *before* sunrise."

The younger man looked up, face flushed. "Is that well tied, sir? This new rope . . ."

"It's gotta be new rope!" The old man bent over, not touching the knot. "Yeah," he said grudgingly. "I guess. And you take this platform contraption—" he struck the boards under the iron lightly with his scuffed boot. "One more o' the Cap's new ideas—" he snorted and the boy jumped a little "Useta be tough, man. None o' this soft psychology stuff. Carried it up right, right up there. We done it right then, but now—" the old man glared with a fierce brilliance at the other, his chin bristling over the mass of iron as the crest of Sun Rock emerged out of the mass of the island beyond the wide water. The boy turned frantically, slid between the stiff pillars of people; not stopping until he felt his mother's arm about his shoulder.

He stood, panting a little. He said nothing and she did not ask. The peak of Sun Rock grew above the people's heads and the boy understood that they were approaching much closer to the highest point of the island than they ever did in their family boat-picnics. He looked to his father, but his head was high, eyes distant as if he saw nothing. The Capitular's voice was saying, "We hope you had a nice exploration tour, Joey. We were just beginning to wonder where you might be." His Highest was not looking at him as he spoke, but rather at what seemed to the boy was a watch one of the Lesser Capitulars was holding before him. Everyone stood silent, grim as if they had never smiled. The Capitular's face was the only friendly one; and suddenly the boy stepped forward.

"Sir, Your Highest, I saw Miss Grierson. But she didn't—look at me. At school we always played in the sand, Eric and me, and she—is something—" The Capitular, still smiling, threw a swift glance at the sky and stood up. The cantors began, their sound lifting unintelligibly into the warm morning, united, plaintive, strangely harrowing. The boy turned sharply for his mother but the Capitular's soft hand was on his shoulder, his voice in his ear.

"Come, my boy. I want you to do one thing, something just for me. For this you were chosen yesterday when you drew the Lottery." The boy gazed wide-eyed at him. The Lottery was for the ride. He twisted, one glance finding his mother now standing. Her eyes were dilated and her face pulled out of shape, but she was nodding soundlessly to him. He could not but obey and he walked forward, the heavy hand now very tight on his shoulder, through the lane opening between the people, hearing the chant merge to words as the motors throbbed and died under his feet. And then over the cantors, the high voice of the Capitular lifting and they were standing before the riddled bulk of iron on its little platform, the people all about and sounding now also, the morning sun just visible over the high thrust of the Rock.

"—the-evergoodness-of-the-undying-and-golden—" but the boy did not hear, his eyes shifting from the water where there was now no bronze railing to interrupt his view of the wedge of boats sitting like gulls along the edge of the Rock's shadow on the blue-black water. In the hesitance of silence the Capitular bent to the boy, voice now almost sorrowful.

"Joey, do exactly as I say. This is the handle." The thick fingers pointed to a lever on a raised panel. "When I nod my head at you, pull it back. Just one little pull. It is very easy. But don't," the fingers closed on the boy's hand lifting, "don't touch it till I nod. Exactly then. That's my fine boy. Now, watch me. Exactly. When I nod."

The mesmerizing smile on the broad face, so close, held the boy watching the great arms lift as they did each week in the ambo, the sound of the cantors rising, rising to the top of comprehension and the world flaming with their incredible sound as the boy had never heard it in the rood-loft. He stood erect, swaying slightly to the sway of the people. Then the Capitular bowed to him, his hand found the handle and, standing all alone, facing the water now and the sun flush in his eyes over the peak of the Rock, he pulled.

The sound of the cantors was now the sound of all the people, swaying beyond the water's lift of the Yacht. The boy was the only one who saw the little platform stir and tilt at his feet and the iron slide from the deck like a living thing. Amazed, he stepped to the edge. The splattered circles of its falling led away from the very apex of the Rock's shadow on the water and he saw the mass of it waver down into blackness and the white rope snake along the waterline, his eyes following, and seeing suddenly, beyond the people tight to the rail, the rope ending in a white form falling from the Yacht in one smooth motion. The form hesitated, flat, spread-eagled on the water like a great head T crossed with a golden-and-crimson slash, before it smudged, then vanished in the black water. The boy stood, staring, remembering only the gaping hole in the mask-like face.

Under the sound of the people floating over the water, the old man was leaning over the railing, cursing softly. "—goddam motor block—so goddam many holes, gurgling to hear it above the chant! In the old days we used millstones. Clean, sure. Damn new-fangled stuff . . ."

The boy's fingers dug through his mother's thin black dress as she crouched down, clutching him to her.

"Mommie. Mommie—"

"Hush," said his mother. She shuddered in the sunlight. "Hush. Just hush."

QUESTIONS

1. What is a scapegoat? There are two scapegoats in this story. Who are they? Is it possible that both scapegoats were chosen by lot? Explain. Why would the adults choose a child to pull the handle?
2. What law of probability has the author suspended in writing this story? Granting this initial implausibility, does the story proceed naturally?
3. What is the fundamental irony in this story?

4. Most of the characters in the story speak in substandard language. What is the significance of this fact? Why do you think the author uses such long sentences?
5. The old man complains about "the damn new-fangled stuff." What is the significance of the modernization of the ritual?
6. What different attitudes towards the ritual are presented by (a) Joey's mother, (b) Joey's father, (c) the Capitular, (d) the old man, (e) the villagers in general and (f) Joey? Which would you suppose most nearly represents the attitude of the author? Why?
7. By transporting a primitive ritual into a modern setting, the author is able to say something about human nature and human society. What is it?
8. "Millstone for the Sun's Day" must obviously be interpreted symbolically or allegorically (as a pattern of symbols corresponding to some pattern in the outside world). To what extent is the meaning of its symbols fixed, to what extent open to various interpretations? What specific interpretations can you suggest?
9. Locate other examples of stories focusing on scapegoats. Sir James Frazer's *The Golden Bough* is an excellent source.

Albert Camus

THE GUEST

The schoolmaster was watching the two men climb toward him. One was on horseback, the other on foot. They had not yet tackled the abrupt rise leading to the schoolhouse built on the hillside. They were toiling onward, making slow progress in the snow, among the stones, on the vast expanse of the high, deserted plateau. From time to time the horse stumbled. He could not be heard yet but the breath issuing from his nostrils could be seen. The schoolmaster calculated that it would take them a half hour to get onto the hill. It was cold; he went back into the school to get a sweater.

He crossed the empty, frigid classroom. On the blackboard the four rivers of France, drawn with four different colored chalks, had been flowing toward their estuaries for the past three days. Snow had suddenly fallen in mid-October after eight months of drought without the transition of rain, and the twenty pupils, more or less, who lived in the villages scattered over the plateau had stopped coming. With fair weather they would return. Daru now heated only the single room that was his lodging, adjoining the classroom. One of the windows faced, like the classroom windows, the south. On that side the school was a few kilometers from the point where the plateau began to slope toward the south. In clear weather the purple mass of the mountain range where the gap opened onto the desert could be seen.

Somewhat warmed, Daru returned to the window from which he had first noticed the two men. They were no longer visible. Hence they must have tackled the rise. The sky was not so dark, for the snow had stopped falling during the night. The morning had dawned with a dirty light which had scarcely become brighter as the ceiling of clouds lifted. At two in the afternoon it seemed as if the day were merely beginning. But still this was better than those three days when the thick snow was falling amidst unbroken darkness with little gusts of wind that rattled the double door of the classroom. Then Daru had spent long hours in his room, leaving it only to go to the shed and feed the chickens or get some coal. Fortunately the delivery truck from Tadjid, the nearest village to the north, had brought his supplies two days before the blizzard. It would return in forty-eight hours.

Besides, he had enough to resist a siege, for the little room was cluttered with bags of wheat that the administration had left as a supply to distribute to those of his pupils whose families had suffered from the drought. Actually they had all been victims because they were all poor. Every day Daru would distribute a ration to the children. They had missed it, he knew, during these bad days. Possibly one of the fathers or big brothers would come this afternoon and he could supply them with grain. It was just a matter of carrying them over to the next harvest. Now shiploads of wheat were arriving from France and the worst was over. But it would be hard to forget that poverty, that army of ragged ghosts wandering in the sunlight, the plateaus burned to a cinder month after month, the earth shriveled up little by little, literally scorched, every stone bursting into dust under one's foot. The sheep had died then by thousands, and even a few men, here and there, sometimes without anyone's knowing.

In contrast with such poverty, he who lived almost like a monk, in his remote schoolhouse, had felt like a lord with his whitewashed walls, his narrow couch, his unpainted shelves, his well, and his weekly provisioning with water and food. And suddenly this snow, without warning, without the foretaste of rain. This is the way the region was, cruel to live in, even without men, who didn't help matters either. But Daru had been born here. Everywhere else, he felt exiled.

He went out and stepped forward on the terrace in front of the schoolhouse. The two men were now halfway up the slope. He recognized the horseman to be Balducci, the old gendarme he had known for a long time. Balducci was holding at the end of a rope an

Arab walking behind him with hands bound and head lowered. The gendarme waved a greeting to which Daru did not reply, lost as he was in contemplation of the Arab dressed in a faded blue *jellaba*, his feet in sandals but covered with socks of heavy raw wool, his head crowned with a narrow, short *chèche*. Balducci was holding back his horse in order not to hurt the Arab, and the group was advancing slowly.

Within earshot, Balducci shouted, "One hour to do the three kilometers from El Ameur!" Daru did not answer. Short and square in his thick sweater, he watched them climb. Not once had the Arab raised his head. "Hello," said Daru when they got up onto the terrace. "Come in and warm up." Balducci painfully got down from his horse without letting go of the rope. He smiled at the schoolmaster from under his bristling mustache. His little dark eyes, deepset under a tanned forehead, and his mouth surrounded with wrinkles made him look attentive and studious. Daru took the bridle, led the horse to the shed, and came back to the two men who were now waiting for him in the school. He led them into his room. "I am going to heat up the classroom," he said. "We'll be more comfortable there."

When he entered the room again, Balducci was on the couch. He had undone the rope tying him to the Arab, who had squatted near the stove. His hands still bound, the *chèche* pushed back on his head, the Arab was looking toward the window. At first Daru noticed only his huge lips, fat, smooth, almost Negroid; yet his nose was straight, his eyes dark and full of fever. The *chèche* uncovered an obstinate forehead and, under the weathered skin now rather discolored by the cold, the whole face had a restless and rebellious look. "Go into the other room," said the schoolmaster, "and I'll make you some mint tea." "Thanks," Balducci said. "What a chore! How I long for retirement." And addressing his prisoner in Arabic, he said, "Come on, you." The Arab got up and, slowly, holding his bound wrists in front of him, went into the classroom.

With the tea, Daru brought a chair. But Balducci was already sitting in state at the nearest pupil's desk, and the Arab had squatted against the teacher's platform facing the stove, which stood between the desk and the window. When he held out the glass of tea to the prisoner, Daru hesitated at the sight of his bound hands. "He might perhaps be untied." "Sure," said Balducci. "That was for the trip." He started to get to his feet. But Daru, setting the glass on the floor, had knelt beside the Arab. Without saying anything, the Arab watched him with his feverish eyes. Once his hands were free, he rubbed his swollen wrists against each other, took the glass of tea and sucked up the burning liquid in swift little sips.

"Good," said Daru. "And where are you headed?"

Balducci withdrew his mustache from the tea. "Here, son."

"Odd pupils! And you're spending the night?"

"No. I'm going back to El Ameur. And you will deliver this fellow to Tinguit. He is expected at police headquarters."

Balducci was looking at Daru with a friendly little smile.

"What's this story?" asked the schoolmaster. "Are you pulling my leg?"

"No, son. Those are the orders."

"The orders? I'm not . . ." Daru hesitated, not wanting to hurt the old Corsican. "I mean, that's not my job."

"What! What's the meaning of that? In wartime people do all kinds of jobs."

"Then I'll wait for the declaration of war!"

Balducci nodded. "O.K. But the orders exist and they concern you too. Things are bubbling, it appears. There is talk of a forth-coming revolt. We are mobilized, in a way."

Daru still had his obstinate look.

"Listen, son," Balducci said. "I like you and you've got to understand. There's only a dozen of us at El Ameur to patrol the whole territory of a small department and I must be back in a hurry. He couldn't be kept there. His village was beginning to stir; they wanted to take him back. You must take him to Tinguit tomorrow before the day is over. Twenty kilometers shouldn't faze a husky fellow like you. After that, all will be over. You'll come back to your pupils and your comfortable life."

Behind the wall the horse could be heard snorting and pawing the earth. Daru was looking out the window. Decidedly the weather was clearing and the light was increasing over the snowy plateau. When all the snow was melted, the sun would take over again and once more would burn the fields of stone. For days still, the unchanging sky would shed its dry light on the solitary expanse where nothing had any connection with man.

"After all," he said, turning around toward Balducci, "what did he do?" And, before the gendarme had opened his mouth, he asked, "Does he speak French?"

"No, not a word. We had been looking for him for a month, but they were hiding him. He killed his cousin."

"Is he against us?"

"I don't think so. But you can never be sure."

"Why did he kill?"

"A family squabble, I think. One owed grain to the other, it seems. It's not at all clear. In short, he killed his cousin with a billhook. You know, like a sheep, *kreezk!*"

Balducci made the gesture of drawing a blade across his throat, and the Arab, his attention attracted, watched him with a sort of anxiety. Daru felt a sudden wrath against the man, against all men with their rotten spite, their tireless hates, their blood lust.

But the kettle was singing on the stove. He served Balducci more tea, hesitated, then served the Arab again, who drank avidly a second time. His raised arms made the *jellaba* fall open, and the schoolmaster saw his thin, muscular chest.

"Thanks, son," Balducci said. "And now I'm off."

He got up and went toward the Arab, taking a small rope from his pocket.

"What are you doing?" Daru asked dryly.

Balducci, disconcerted, showed him the rope.

"Don't bother."

The old gendarme hesitated. "It's up to you. Of course, you are armed?"

"I have my shotgun."

"Where?"

"In the trunk."

"You ought to have it near your bed."

"Why? I have nothing to fear."

"You're crazy, son. If there's an uprising, no one is safe; we're all in the same boat."

"I'll defend myself. I'll have time to see them coming."

Balducci began to laugh, then suddenly the mustache covered the white teeth. "You'll have time? O.K. That's just what I was saying. You always have been a little cracked. That's why I like you; my son was like that."

"At the same time he took out his revolver and put it on the desk. "Keep it; I don't need two weapons from here to El Ameur."

The revolver shone against the black paint of the table. When the gendarme turned toward him, the schoolmaster caught his smell of leather and horseflesh.

"Listen, Balducci," Daru said suddenly, "all this disgusts me, beginning with your fellow here. But I won't hand him over. Fight, yes, if I have to. But not that."

The old gendarme stood in front of him and looked at him severely.

"You're being a fool," he said slowly. "I don't like it either. You don't get used to putting a rope on a man even after years of it, and you're even ashamed—yes, ashamed. But you can't let them have their way."

"I won't hand him over," Daru said again.

"It's an order, son, and I repeat it."

"That's right. Repeat to them what I've said to you: I won't hand him over."

Balducci made a visible effort to reflect. He looked at the Arab and at Daru. At last he decided.

"No, I won't tell them anything. If you want to drop us, go ahead; I'll not denounce you. I have an order to deliver the prisoner and I'm doing so. And now you'll just sign this paper for me."

"There's no need. I'll not deny that you left him with me."

"Don't be mean with me. I know you'll tell the truth. You're from around these parts and you are a man. But you must sign; that's the rule."

Daru opened his drawer, took out a little square bottle of purple ink, the red wooden penholder with the "sergeant-major" pen he used for models of handwriting, and signed. The gendarme carefully folded the paper and put it into his wallet. Then he moved toward the door.

"I'll see you off," Daru said.

"No," said Balducci. "There's no use being polite. You insulted me."

He looked at the Arab, motionless in the same spot, sniffed peevishly, and turned away toward the door. "Good-by, son," he said. The door slammed behind him. His footsteps were muffled by the snow. The horse stirred on the other side of the wall and several chickens fluttered in fright. A moment later Balducci reappeared outside the window leading the horse by the bridle. He walked toward the little rise without turning around and disappeared from sight with the horse following him.

Daru walked back toward the prisoner, who, without stirring, never took his eyes off him. "Wait," the schoolmaster said in Arabic and went toward the bedroom. As he was going through the door, he had a second thought, went to the desk, took the revolver, and stuck it in his pocket. Then, without looking back, he went into his room.

For some time he lay on his couch watching the sky gradually close over, listening to the silence. It was this silence that had seemed painful to him during the first days here, after the war. He had requested a post in the little town at the base of the foothills separating the upper plateaus from the desert. There rocky walls, green and black to the north, pink and lavender to the south, marked the frontier of eternal summer. He had been named to a post farther north, on the plateau itself. In the beginning, the solitude and the silence had been hard for him on these wastelands peopled only by stones. Occasionally, furrows suggested cultivation, but they had been dug to uncover a certain kind of stone good for building. The only plowing here was to harvest rocks. Elsewhere a thin layer of soil accumulated in the hollows would be scraped out to enrich paltry village gardens. This is the way it was: bare rock covered three quarters of the region. Towns sprang up, flourished, then disappeared; men came by, loved one another or fought bitterly, then died. No one in this desert, neither he nor his guest, mattered. And yet, outside this desert neither of them, Daru knew, could have really lived.

When he got up, no noise came from the classroom. He was amazed at the unmixed joy he derived from the mere thought that the Arab might have fled and that he would be alone with no decision to make. But the prisoner was there. He had merely stretched out between the stove and the desk and he was staring at the ceiling. In that position, his thick lips were particularly noticeable, giving him a pouting look. "Come," said Daru. The Arab got up and followed him. In the bedroom the schoolmaster pointed to a chair near the table under the window. The Arab sat down without ceasing to watch Daru.

"Are you hungry?"

"Yes," the prisoner said.

Daru set the table for two. He took flour and oil, shaped a cake in a frying pan, and lighted the little stove that functioned on bottled gas. While the cake was cooking, he went out to the shed to get cheese, eggs, dates, and condensed milk. When the cake was done he set it on the window sill to cool, heated some condensed milk diluted with water, and beat up the eggs into an omelette. In one of his motions he bumped into the revolver stuck in his right pocket. He set the bowl down, went into the classroom, and put the revolver in his desk drawer. When he came back to the room, night was falling. He put on the light and served the Arab. "Eat," he said. The Arab took a piece of the cake, lifted it eagerly to his mouth, and stopped short.

"And you?" he asked.

"After you. I'll eat too."

The thick lips opened slightly. The Arab hesitated, then bit into the cake determinedly.

The meal over, the Arab looked at the schoolmaster. "Are you the judge?"

"No, I'm simply keeping you until tomorrow."

"Why do you eat with me?"

"I'm hungry."

The Arab fell silent. Daru got up and went out. He brought back a camp cot from the shed and set it up between the table and the stove, at right angles to his own bed. From a large suitcase which, upright in a corner, served as a shelf for papers, he took two blankets and arranged them on the cot. Then he stopped, felt useless, and sat down on his bed. There was nothing more to do or to get ready. He had to look at this man. He looked at him therefore, trying to imagine his face bursting with rage. He couldn't do so. He could see nothing but the dark yet shining eyes and the animal mouth.

"Why did you kill him?" he asked in a voice whose hostile tone surprised him.

The Arab looked away. "He ran away. I ran after him."

He raised his eyes to Daru again and they were full of a sort of woeful interrogation. "Now what will they do to me?"

"Are you afraid?"

The Arab stiffened, turning his eyes away.

"Are you sorry?"

The Arab stared at him openmouthed. Obviously he did not understand. Daru's annoyance was growing. At the same time he felt awkward and self-conscious with his big body wedged between the two beds.

"Lie down there," he said impatiently. "That's your bed."

The Arab didn't move. He cried out, "Tell me!"

The schoolmaster looked at him.

"Is the gendarme coming back tomorrow?"

"I don't know."

"Are you coming with us?"

"I don't know. Why?"

The prisoner got up and stretched out on top of the blankets, his feet toward the window. The light from the electric bulb shone straight into his eyes and he closed them at once.

"Why?" Daru repeated, standing beside the bed.

The Arab opened his eyes under the blinding light and looked at him, trying not to blink. "Come with us," he said.

In the middle of the night, Daru was still not asleep. He had gone to bed after undressing completely; he generally slept naked. But when he suddenly realized that he had nothing on, he wondered. He felt vulnerable and the temptation came to him to put his clothes back on. Then he shrugged his shoulders; after all, he wasn't a child and, if it came to that, he could break his adversary in two. From his bed, he could observe him lying on his back, still motionless, his eyes closed under the harsh light. When Daru turned out the light, the darkness seemed to congeal all of a sudden. Little by little, the night came back to life in the window where the starless sky was stirring gently. The schoolmaster soon made out the body lying at his feet. The Arab was still motionless but his eyes seemed open. A faint wind was prowling about the schoolhouse. Perhaps it would drive away the clouds and the sun would reappear.

During the night the wind increased. The hens fluttered a little and then were silent. The Arab turned over on his side with his back to Daru, who thought he heard him moan. Then he listened for his guest's breathing, which had become heavier and more regular. He listened to that breathing so close to him and mused without being able to go to sleep. In the room where he had been sleeping alone for a year, this presence bothered him. But it bothered him also because it imposed on him a sort of brotherhood he refused to accept in the present circumstances; yet he was familiar with it. Men who share the same rooms, soldiers or prisoners, develop a strange alliance as if, having cast off their armor with their clothing, they fraternized every evening, over and above their differences, in the ancient community of dream and fatigue. But Daru shook himself; he didn't like such musings, and it was essential for him to sleep.

A little later, however, when the Arab stirred slightly, the schoolmaster was still not asleep. When the prisoner made a second move, he stiffened, on the alert. The Arab was lifting himself slowly on his arms with almost the motion of a sleepwalker. Seated upright in bed, he waited motionless without turning his head toward Daru, as if he were listening attentively. Daru did not stir; it had just occurred to him that the revolver was still in the drawer of his desk. It was better to act at once. Yet he continued to observe the prisoner, who, with the same slithery motion, put his feet on the ground, waited again, then stood up slowly. Daru was about to call out to him when the Arab began to walk, in a quite natural but extraordinarily silent way. He was heading toward the door at the end of the room that opened into the shed. He lifted the latch with precaution and went out, pushing the door behind him but without shutting it.

Daru had not stirred. "He is running away," he merely thought. "Good riddance!" Yet he listened attentively. The hens were not fluttering; the guest must be on the plateau. A faint sound of water reached him, and he didn't know what it was until the Arab again stood framed in the doorway, closed the door carefully, and came back to bed without a sound. Then Daru turned his back on him and fell asleep. Still later he seemed, from the depths of his sleep, to hear furtive steps around the schoolhouse. "I'm dreaming! I'm dreaming!" he repeated to himself. And he went on sleeping.

When he awoke, the sky was clear; the loose window let in a cold, pure air. The Arab was asleep, hunched up under the blankets now, his mouth open, utterly relaxed. But when Daru shook him he started dreadfully, staring at Daru with wild eyes as if he had never seen him and with such a frightened expression that the schoolmaster stepped back. "Don't be afraid. It is I. You must eat." The Arab nodded his head and said yes. Calm had returned to his face, but his expression was vacant and listless.

The coffee was ready. They drank it seated together on the cot as they munched their pieces of the cake. Then Daru led the Arab under the shed and showed him the faucet where he washed. He went back into the room, folded the blankets on the cot, made his own bed, and put the room in order. Then he went through the classroom and out onto the terrace. The sun was already rising in the blue sky; a soft, bright light enveloped the deserted plateau. On the ridge the snow was melting in spots. The stones were about to reappear. Crouched on the edge of the plateau, the schoolmaster looked at the deserted expanse. He thought of Balducci. He had hurt him, for he had sent him off as though he didn't want to be associated with him. He could still hear the gendarme's farewell and, without knowing why, he felt strangely empty and vulnerable.

At that moment, from the other side of the schoolhouse, the prisoner coughed. Daru listened to him almost despite himself and then, furious, threw a pebble that whistled through the air before sinking into the snow. That man's stupid crime revolted him, but to hand him over was contrary to honor; just thinking of it made him boil with humiliation. He simultaneously cursed his own people who had sent him this Arab and the Arab who had dared to kill and not managed to get away. Daru got up, walked in a circle on the terrace, waited motionless, and then went back into the schoolhouse.

The Arab, leaning over the cement floor of the shed, was washing his teeth with two fingers. Daru looked at him and said, "Come." He went back into the room ahead of the prisoner. He slipped a hunting jacket on over his sweater and put on walking shoes. Standing, he waited until the Arab had put on his *chèche* and sandals. They went into the classroom, and the schoolmaster pointed to the exit saying, "Go ahead." The fellow didn't budge. "I'm coming," said Daru. The Arab went out. Daru went back into the room and made a package with pieces of rusk, dates, and sugar in it. In the classroom, before going out, he hesitated a second in front of his desk, then crossed the threshold and locked the door. "That's the way," he said. He started toward the east, followed by the prisoner. But a short distance from the schoolhouse he thought he heard a slight sound behind him. He retraced his steps and examined the surroundings of the house; there was no one there. The Arab watched him without seeming to understand. "Come on," said Daru.

They walked for an hour and rested beside a sharp needle of limestone. The snow was melting faster and faster and the sun was drinking up the puddles just as quickly, rapidly cleaning the plateau, which gradually dried and vibrated like the air itself. When they resumed walking, the ground rang under their feet. From time to time a bird rent the space in front of them with a joyful cry. Daru felt a sort of rapture before the vast familiar expanse, now almost entirely yellow under its dome of blue sky. They walked an hour more, descending toward the south. They reached a sort of flattened elevation made up of crumbly rocks. From there on, the plateau sloped down—eastward toward a low plain on which could be made out a few spindly trees, and to the south toward outcroppings of rock that gave the landscape a chaotic look.

Daru surveyed the two directions. Not a man could be seen. He turned toward the Arab, who was looking at him blankly. Daru offered the package to him. "Take it," he said. "There are dates, bread, and sugar. You can hold out for two days. Here are a thousand francs too."

The Arab took the package and the money but kept his full hands at chest level as if he didn't know what to do with what was being given him.

"Now look," the schoolmaster said as he pointed in the direction of the east, "there's the way to Tinguit. You have a two-hour walk. At Tinguit are the administration and the police. They are expecting you."

The Arab looked toward the east, still holding the package and the money against his chest. Daru took his elbow and turned him rather roughly toward the south. At the foot of the elevation on which they stood could be seen a faint path. "That's the trail across the plateau. In a day's walk from here you'll find pasturelands and the first nomads. They'll take you in and shelter you according to their law."

The Arab had now turned toward Daru, and a sort of panic was visible in his expression. "Listen," he said.

Daru shook his head. "No, be quiet. Now I'm leaving you." He turned his back on him, took two long steps in the direction of the school, looked hesitantly at the motionless Arab, and started off again. For a few minutes he heard nothing but his own step resounding on the cold ground, and he did not turn his head. A moment later, however, he turned around. The Arab was still there on the edge of the hill, his arms hanging now, and he was looking at the schoolmaster. Daru felt something rise in his throat. But he swore with impatience, waved vaguely, and started off again. He had already gone a distance when he again stopped and looked. There was no longer anyone on the hill.

Daru hesitated. The sun was now rather high in the sky and beginning to beat down on his head. The schoolmaster retraced his steps, at first somewhat uncertainly, then with decision. When he reached the little hill, he was bathed in sweat. He climbed it as fast as he could and stopped, out of breath, on the top. The rock fields to the south stood out sharply against the blue sky, but on the plain to the east a steamy heat was rising. And in that light haze, Daru, with heavy heart, made out the Arab walking slowly on the road to prison.

A little later, standing before the window of the classroom, the schoolmaster was watching the clear light bathing the whole surface of the plateau. Behind him on the blackboard, among the winding French rivers, sprawled the clumsily chalked up words he had just read: "You handed over our brother. You will pay for this." Daru looked at the sky, the plateau, and, beyond, the invisible lands stretching all the way to the sea. In this vast landscape he had loved so much, he was alone.

QUESTIONS

1. What is the central conflict of the story? Is it external or internal? Can it be defined in terms of a dilemma?
2. Compare and contrast the attitudes of Daru and Balducci toward the prisoner and the situation. What is their attitude toward each other? Is either a bad or a cruel man? How does the conflict between Daru and Balducci intensify the central conflict?
3. Why did Daru give the prisoner his freedom? What reasons were there for not giving him his freedom?
4. In what respect is the title ironical? What kind of irony is this? Why does "The Guest" make a better title than "The Prisoner"?
5. This story contains the materials of explosive action—a revolver, a murderer, a state of undeclared war, an incipient uprising, a revenge note, etc.—but no violence occurs in the story. In what aspect of the situation is Camus principally interested?
6. This story has as its background a specific political situation—the French Algerian crisis in the years following World War II. How does Daru reflect France's plight? Is the story's meaning limited to this situation? What does the story tell us about good and evil and the nature of moral choice? How does the story differ in its treatment of these things from the typical Western story or the patriotic editorial?
7. In what respect is the ending of the story ironical? What kind of irony is this? What does it contribute to the meaning of the story?
8. Besides the ironies of the title and of the ending, there are other ironies in the story. Find and explain them. Daru uses verbal irony on page 213 when he exclaims, "Odd pupils!" Is verbal irony the same thing as sarcasm?
9. Comment on the following: (a) Daru's behavior toward firearms and how it helps reveal him; (b) Camus' reason for making the Arab a murderer; (c) the Arab's reason for taking the road to prison.

Ethel Wilson

HAPLY, THE SOUL OF MY GRANDMOTHER

CLOWN: *What is the opinion of Pythagoras concerning wild fowl?*

MALVOLIO: *That the soul of our grandam might haply inhabit a bird.*

—TWELFTH NIGHT, Act IV, Scene ii.

"It is airless," said Mrs. Forrester.

"Yes there is no air," said the woman half beside her half in front of her. The mouth of the tomb was no longer visible behind them, but there was light. They stepped carefully downwards. Mrs. Forrester looked behind her at her husband. She was inexcusably nervous and wanted a look or a gleam of reassurance from his face. But he did not appear to see her. He scrutinized the yellow walls which looked as if they were compounded of sandstone and clay. Marcus seemed to be looking for something, but there was nothing on the yellowish walls not even the marks of pick and shovel.

Mrs. Forrester had to watch her steps on the stairs of smoothed and worn pounded sandstone or clay, so she turned again, looking downwards. It did not matter whether she held her head up or down, there was no air. She breathed, of course, but what she breathed was not air but some kind of ancient vacuum. She supposed that this absence of air must affect the noses and mouths and lungs of Marcus and of the woman from Cincinnati and the guide and the soldier and that she need not consider herself to be special. So, although she suffered from the airlessness and a kind of blind something, very old, dead, she knew that she must not give way to her impulse to complain again, saying, "I can't breathe! There is no air!" and certainly she must not turn and stumble up the steps into the blazing heat as she wished to do; neither must she faint. She had never experienced panic before, but she recognized all this for near panic. She stiffened, controlled herself (she thought), then relaxed, breathed the vacuum as naturally as possible, and continued her way down into the earth from small light to light. They reached the first chamber which was partly boarded up.

Looking through the chinks of the planking they seemed to see a long and deep depression which because of its shape indicated that, once, a body had lain there, probably in a vast and ornate coffin constructed so as to magnify the size and great importance of its occupant. The empty depression spoke of a removal of some long object which, Mrs. Forrester knew, had lain there for thousands of years, hidden, sealed, alone, yet existing, in spite of the fact that generations of living men, know-alls, philosophers, scientists, slaves, ordinary people, kings, knew nothing about it. And then it had been suspected, and then discovered, and then taken away somewhere, and now there was only the depression which they saw. All that was mortal of a man or woman who had been all-powerful had lain there, accompanied by treasure hidden and sealed away by a generation from other generations (men do not trust their successors, and rightly), till only this great baked dried yellowish aridity of hills and valleys remained, which was called the Valley of the Kings. And somewhere in the valley were dead kings.

Peering between the boards and moving this way and that so as to obtain a better view, they saw that a frieze of figures ran round the walls above the level of the depression. The figures were all in profile, and although they were only two-dimensional, they had a look of intention and vigour which gave them life and great dignity. There was no corpulence; all were slim, wide of shoulder, narrow of hip. Mostly, Mrs. Forrester thought, they walked very erect. They did not seem to stand, or, if they stood, they stood as if springing already into motion. She thought, peering, that they seemed to walk, all in profile and procession, towards some seated Being, it might be a man, or it might be sexless, or it might be a cat, or even a large bird, no doubt an ibis. The moving figures proceeded either with hieratic gesture or bearing objects. The colours, in which an ochreous sepia predominated, were faintly clear. The airlessness of the chamber nearly overwhelmed her again and she put out her hand to touch her husband's arm. There was not much to see, was there? between these planks, so they proceeded on downwards. The guide, who was unintelligible, went first. The soldier followed them.

If ever I get out of this, thought Mrs. Forrester. The airlessness was only part of an ancientness, a strong persistence of the past into the now and beyond the now which terrified her. It was not the death of the place that so invaded her, although there was death; it was the long persistent life in which her bones and flesh and all the complex joys of her life and her machine-woven clothes and her lipstick that was so important to her were less than the bright armour of a beetle on which she could put her foot. Since all three of the visitors were silent in the tomb, it was impossible to know what the others felt. And anyway, one could not explain; and why explain (all this talk about "feelings"!).

The farther down the steps they went the more the air seemed to expire, until at the foot of the steps it really died. Here was the great chamber of the great king, and a sarcophagus had been left there, instructively, perhaps, so that the public, who came either for pleasure or instruction, should be able to see the sort of sight which the almost intoxicated excavators had seen as they removed the earth and allowed in the desecrating air—or what passed for air.

Since Mrs. Forrester was now occupied in avoiding falling down and thereby creating a small scene beside the sarcophagus which would annoy her and her husband very much indeed and would not help the lady from Cincinnati who had grown pale, none of the guide's talk was heard and no image of the sarcophagus or of the friezes or of the tomb itself remained in her mind. It was as a saved soul that she was aware of the general turning up towards the stairs, up towards the light, and she was not ashamed, now, to lay her hand upon her husband's arm, really for support, in going up the stairs.

They emerged into the sunlight which blinded them and the heat that beat up at them and bore down on them, and all but the two Egyptians fumbled for their dark glasses. The soldier rejoined his comrade at the mouth of the tomb, and the guide seemed to vanish round some cliff or crag. The two soldiers were unsoldierly in appearance although no doubt they would enjoy fighting anyone if it was necessary.

Marcus and Mrs. Forrester and the lady from Cincinnati whose name was Sampson or Samson looked around for a bit of shade. The lion-coloured crags on their left did of course cast a shade, but it was the kind of shade which did not seem to be of much use to them, for they would have to climb onto farther low crags to avail themselves of the shade, and the sun was so cruel in the Valley of the Kings that no European or North American could make shift to move one step unless it was necessary.

"Where's that guide?" said Marcus irritably, of no one, because no one knew. The guide had gone, probably to wave on the motor car which should have been waiting to pick them up. Mrs. Forrester could picture him walking, running, gesticulating, garments flowing, making all kinds of gratuitous movements in the heat. We're differently made, she thought, it's all those centuries.

"I think," said Mrs. Sampson timidly, "that this s-seems to be the best p-place."

"Yes," said Mrs. Forrester who was feeling better though still too hot and starved for air, "that's the best place. There's enough shade there for us all," and they moved to sit down on some yellow rocks which were too hot for comfort. Nobody talked of the tomb which was far below the ground on their right.

Mrs. Forrester spoke to her husband who did not answer. He looked morose. His dark brows were concentrated in a frown and it was obvious that he did not want to talk to her or to anybody else. Oh dear, she thought. It's the tomb—he's never like that unless it's really something. They sat in silence, waiting for whatever should turn up. The two soldiers smoked at some distance.

This is very uncomfortable, this heat, thought Mrs. Forrester, and the tomb has affected us unpleasantly. She reflected on Lord Carnarvon who had sought with diligence, worked ardently, superintended excavation, urged on discovery, was bitten by an insect—or so they said—and had died. She thought of a co-worker of his who lay ill with some fever in the small clay-built house past which they had driven that morning. Why do they do those things, these men? Why do they do it? They do it because they have to; they come here to be uncomfortable and unlucky and for the greatest fulfilment of their lives; just as men climb mountains; just as Arctic and Antarctic explorers go to the polar regions to be uncomfortable and unlucky and for the greatest fulfilment of their lives. They have to. The thought of the Arctic gave her a pleasant feeling and she determined to lift the pressure that seemed to have settled on all three of them which was partly tomb, no doubt, but chiefly the airlessness to which their lungs were not accustomed, and, of course, this heat.

She said with a sort of imbecile cheerfulness, "How about an ice-cream cone?"

Mrs. Sampson looked up at her with a pale smile and Marcus did not answer. No, she was not funny, and she subsided. Out of the rocks flew two great burnished-winged insects and attacked them like bombers. All three ducked and threw up their arms to protect their faces.

"Oh ..." and "oh ..." cried the women and forgot about the heat while the two vicious bright-winged insects charged them, one here, one there, with a clattering hiss. Mrs. Forrester did not know whether one of the insects had hit and bitten Marcus or Mrs. Sampson. She had driven them away, she thought, and as she looked around and her companions looked up and around, she saw that the insects, which had swiftly retired, now dived down upon them again.

The car came round a corner and stopped beside them. There was only the driver. The guide had departed and would no doubt greet them at the hotel with accusations and expostulations. They climbed into the car, the two women at the back and Marcus—still morose—in front with the driver. The car started. The visit to the tomb had not been a success, but at all events the two insects did not accompany them any farther.

They jolted along very fast in the dust which covered them and left a rolling column behind. At intervals the driver honked the horn because he liked doing it. In the empty desert he honked for pleasure. They had not yet reached the trail in the wide sown green belt that bordered the Nile.

The driver gave a last honk and drew up. As the dust settled, they saw, on their right, set back in the dead hills, a row of arches, not a colonnade but a row of similar arches separated laterally a little from each other and leading, evidently, into the hills. They must be tombs, or caves. These arches were black against the dusty yellow of the rock. Mrs. Forrester was forced to admit to herself that the row of arches into the hills was beautiful. There seemed to be about twenty or thirty arches, she estimated when she thought about it later.

There they sat.

"Well, what are we waiting for?" Marcus asked the driver.

The driver became voluble and then he turned to the women behind, as Marcus, who was impatient to get on, did not seem to co-operate.

"I think he has to w-wait a few minutes for someone who m-may be there. He has to pick someone up unless they've already gone," said Mrs. Sampson. "He has to w-wait."

The driver then signified that if they wished they could go up to the tombs within the arches. Without consultation together they all immediately said no. They sat back and waited. Can Marcus be ill? Mrs. Forrester wondered. He is too quiet.

Someone stood at the side of the car, at Mrs. Forrester's elbow. This was an aged bearded man clothed in a long ragged garment and a head-furnishing which was neither skull cap nor tarboosh. His face was mendicant but not crafty. He was too remote in being, Mrs. Forrester thought, but he was too close in space.

"Lady," he said, "I show you something" ("Go away," said Mrs. Forrester), and he produced a small object from the folds of his garment. He held it up, between finger and thumb, about a foot from Mrs. Forrester's face.

The object on which the two women looked was a small human hand, cut off below the wrist. The little hand was wrapped in grave-clothes, and the small fingers emerged from the wrapping, neat, gray, precise. The fingers were close together, with what appeared to be nails or the places for nails upon them. A tatter of grave-clothes curled and fluttered down from the chopped-off wrist.

"Nice hand. Buy a little hand, lady. Very good very old very cheap. Nice mummy hand."

"Oh g-go away!" cried Mrs. Sampson, and both women averted their faces because they did not like looking at the small mummy's hand.

The aged man gave up, and moving on with the persistence of the East he held the little hand in front of Marcus.

"Buy a mummy hand, gentleman sir. Very old very nice very cheap, sir. Buy a little hand."

Marcus did not even look at him.

"NIMSHI," he roared. Marcus had been in Egypt in the last war.

He roared so loud that the mendicant started back. He rearranged his features into an expression of terror. He shambled clumsily away with a gait which was neither running nor walking, but both. Before him he held in the air the neat little hand, the little raped hand, with the tatter of grave-clothes fluttering behind it. The driver, for whom the incident held no interest, honked his horn, threw his hands about to indicate that he would wait no longer, and then drove on.

When they had taken their places in the boat with large sails which carried them across the Nile to the Luxor side, Mrs. Forrester, completely aware of her husband's malaise but asking no questions, saw that this river and these banks and these tombs and temples and these strange agile people to whom she was alien and who were alien to her had not—at four o'clock in the afternoon—the charm that had surprised her in the lily green and pearly cool scene at six o'clock that morning. The sun was high and hot, the men were noisy, the Nile was just water, and she wished to get Marcus back to the hotel.

When they reached the hotel Marcus took off his outer clothes and lay on the bed.

"What is it, Marc?"

"Got a headache."

It was plain to see, now, that he was ill. Mrs. Forrester rang for cold bottled water for Marcus to drink and for ice for compresses. She rummaged in her toilet case and found that she had put in a thermometer as a sort of charm against disease. That was in Vancouver, and how brash, kind, happy, and desirable Vancouver seemed now. Marcus had a temperature of 104°.

There were windows on each side wall of the room. They were well screened and no flies could, one thought, get in; so, by having the windows open, the ghost of the breeze that blew off the Nile River entered and passed out of the room but did not touch Marcus. There was, however, one fly in the room, nearly as dangerous as a snake. Mrs. Forrester took the elegant little ivory-handled fly switch that she had used in Cairo and, sitting beside her husband, flicked gently when the fly buzzed near him.

"Don't."

"All right, dear," she said with the maddening indulgence of the well to the sick. She went downstairs.

"Is that compartment still available on the Cairo train tonight?" she asked.

"*Si*, madame."

"We will take it. My husband is not well."

"Not well! That is unfortunate, madame," said the official at the desk languidly. "I will arrange at once."

It was clear that the management did not sympathize with illness and would prefer to get rid of sick travellers immediately.

Mrs. Forrester went upstairs and changed the compress. She then went and sat by the window overlooking the Nile. She reflected again that this country, where insects carried curses in their wings, made her uneasy. It was too old and strange. She had said as much to Marcus who felt nothing of the kind. He liked the country. But then, she thought, I am far too susceptible to the power of Place, and Marcus is more sensible; these things do not affect him in this way, and, anyway, he knows Egypt. However high the trees and mountains of her native British Columbia, they were native to her. However wide the prairies, she was part of them. However fey the moors of Devon, however ancient Glastonbury or London, they were part of her. Greece was young and she was at home there. The Parthenon in ruins of glory was fresh and fair. And Socrates, drinking the hemlock among his friends as the evening sun smote Hymettus . . . was that last week . . . was he indeed dead? But now . . . let us go away from here.

Below the window, between a low wall and the river, knots of men stood, chattering loudly—Egyptians, Arabs, Abyssinians, and an old man with two donkeys. The air was full of shouting. They never ceased. They shouted, they laughed, they slapped their thighs, they quarrelled. No one could sleep. The sickest man could not sleep in that bright hot loud afternoon. This was their pleasure, cheaper than eating, drinking, or lust. But she could do nothing. The uproar went on. She changed the compress, bending over her husband's dark face and closed eyes and withdrawn look.

It's odd (and she returned to the thought of this country which in spite of its brightness and darkness and vigour was fearful to her), that I am Canadian and am fair, and have my roots in that part of England which was ravaged and settled by blond Norsemen; and Marcus is Canadian and is dark, and before generations of being Canadian he was Irish, and before generations of being Irish—did the dark Phoenicians come?—and he finds no strangeness here and I do.

In the late evening Marcus walked weakly onto the Cairo train. The compartment was close, small, and grimy. The compressed heat of the evening was intense. They breathed dust. Mrs. Forrester gently helped her husband on to the berth. He looked round.

"I can't sleep down here!" he said. "You mustn't go up above in all this heat!" But he could do no other.

"I shan't go up," she said consolingly. "See!" and she took bedclothes from the upper berth and laid them on the floor beside his berth. "I shall be cooler down here." There she lay all night long, breathing a little stale air and grit which entered by a small grid at the bottom of the door. "Oh . . . you sleeping on the floor . . .!" groaned Marcus.

And outside in the dark, she thought, as the train moved north, is that same country that in the early dawning looks so lovely. In the faint pearl of morning, peasants issue from huts far apart. The family—the father, the ox, the brother, the sons, the children, the women in trailing black, the dog, the asses—file to their work between the lines of pale green crops. There again is something hieratic, ageless, in their movements as they file singly one behind the other between the green crops, as the figures on the frieze had filed, one behind the other. Here and there in the morning stand the white ibis, sacred, unmolested, among the delicate green. How beguiling was the unawareness, and the innocency. Then, in that morning hour, and only then, had she felt no fear of Egypt. This scene was universal and unutterably lovely. She . . .
"A LITTLE HAND," said her husband loudly in the dark, and spoke strange words, and then was silent.

Yes, buy a little hand, sir, nice, cheap, very old. Buy a little hand. Whose hand?

When morning came Marcus woke and looked down in surprise.

"Whatever are you doing down there?" he asked in his ordinary voice.

"It was cooler," said his wife. "Did you sleep well?" and she scrambled up.

"Me? Sleep? Oh yes, I think I slept. But there was something . . . a hand . . . I seemed to dream about a hand . . . What hand? . . . Oh yes, that hand . . . I don't quite remember . . . in the tomb . . . you didn't seem to notice the lack of air in that tomb, did you . . . I felt something brushing us in there . . . brushing us all day . . . That was a heck of a day . . . Where's my tie?"

He stood up weakly. Without speaking, Mrs. Forrester handed her husband his tie.

Marcus, whose was that little hand, she thought and would think . . . whose was it? . . . Did it ever know you . . . did you ever know that hand? . . . Whose hand was it, Marcus? . . . oh let us go away from here!

QUESTIONS

1. Research some of the ancient and modern theories regarding reincarnation and karma.

2. The characters and events of the story are all seen as reflected through Mrs. Forrester's mind. How objective are her evaluations? To what extent are they reliable testimony, and how far only an index of her own mind?
3. In spite of her inner struggles, external appearances are very important to Mrs. Forrester. Find examples of this preoccupation.
4. Identify the various conflicts which Mrs. Forrester faces. How does she attempt to resolve them?
5. What is Mrs. Forrester's dominant emotion? How does the author create a build-up of this emotion?
6. Within the context of the entire story, what is the significance of the constant references to airlessness?
7. Is this story more about life or death? Justify your position.
8. What does the mummy's hand symbolize? How does it contribute to Mrs. Forrester's predominant emotion?
9. Explain the statement, ". . . I am far too susceptible to the power of Place, and Marcus is more sensible."
10. Why does the author say, "Greece was young and she was at home there. The Parthenon in ruins of glory was fresh and fair. And Socrates, drinking the hemlock among his friends as the evening sun smote Hymettus . . . was that last week . . . was he indeed dead?"
11. Mr. Forrester states that something was "brushing us all day" in the tomb. What does Mrs. Forrester believe was brushing against them? What do you think caused Mr. Forrester's illness?
12. Find examples of irony in the story. In what ways does Wilson's use of irony "suggest the complexity of experience"?
13. Wilson has chosen a very interesting title for her story. How would you explain both the title and the reference to *Twelfth Night*?

7

Emotion and Humor

Interpretive fiction presents the reader with significant and therefore durable insights into life. But these insights represent something more than mere intellectual comprehension; otherwise the story does nothing that cannot be done as well or better by psychology, history, or philosophy. Fiction derives its unique value from its power to give *felt* insights. Its truths take a deeper hold on our minds because they are conveyed through our feelings. Its effectiveness in awaking a sensuous and emotional apprehension of experience which enriches understanding is what distinguishes imaginative literature from other forms of discourse.

All successful stories arouse emotions in the reader. The adventure thriller causes fear, excitement, suspense, anxiety, exultation, surprise. Some stories make us laugh; some cause us to thrill with horror; some make us cry. We value all the arts precisely because they enrich and diversify our emotional life.

If a story is to be truly significant, however, it must pursue emotion indirectly, not directly. Emotion accompanying and producing insight, not emotion for itself, is the end of the interpretive writer. He writes in order to present a sample of experience truthfully; the emotions he arouses flow naturally from the experience presented.

Over a century ago, in a review of Hawthorne's *Tales*, Edgar Allan Poe made a famous but misleading pronouncement about the short story:

> A skilful literary artist has constructed a tale. If wise, he has not fashioned his thoughts to accommodate his incidents; but having conceived, with deliberate care, a certain unique or single *effect* to be brought out, he then invents such incidents—he then combines such events as may best aid him in establishing this preconceived effect. If his very initial sentence tend not to the outbringing of this effect, then he has failed in his first step. In the whole

composition there should be no word written, of which the tendency, direct or indirect, is not to the one pre-established design.

Poe's formulation has been enormously influential, for both good and bad. Historically it is important as being one of the first discussions of the short story as a unique form. Critically it is important because Poe so clearly here enunciates the basic critical principle of all art—the principle of artistic unity, requiring all details and elements of a piece to contribute harmoniously to the total design. Its influence has been deleterious because of the emphasis Poe put on a "unique" and "preconceived" *effect*.

The serious writer is an interpreter, not an inventor. Like a good actor, he is an intermediary between a segment of experience and an audience. The actor must pay some consideration to his audience: he must be careful, for instance, to face *toward* it, not away from it. But the great actor is the one who is wrapped up in the thoughts and feelings of the role he is playing, not the one who is continually stealing glances at the audience to determine the effect of his last gesture or bit of business. The actor who begins taking his cues from the audience rather than from the script soon becomes a "ham": he exaggerates and falsifies for the sake of effects. The writer, too, though he must pay some consideration to his reader, must focus his attention primarily on his subject. If he begins to think primarily of the effect of his tale on his reader, he begins to manipulate his material, to heighten reality, to contrive and falsify for the sake of effects. The serious writer selects and arranges his material in order to convey most effectively the feeling or truth of a human situation. The less serious writer selects and arranges his material so as to stimulate a response in the reader.

The discriminating reader, then, will distinguish between contrived emotion and that which springs naturally from a human story truly told. He will mark a difference between the story which attempts to "play upon" his feelings directly, as if he were a piano, and that which draws emotion forth as naturally as a plucked string draws forth sympathetic vibrations from another instrument in a room. The difference between the two types of story is the difference between escape and interpretation. In interpretive fiction emotion is the by-product, not the goal.

No doubt there is pleasure in having our emotions directly stimulated, and in some forms such pleasure is both delightful and innocent. We all enjoy the laugh that follows a good joke, and the story which attempts no more than to provoke laughter may be both pleasant and harmless. There is a difference, nevertheless, between the story written for humor's sake, and that in which the humor springs from a way of viewing experience. Humor may be as idle as the wisecrack, or as vicious as the practical joke; it becomes of significant value when it flows from a comic perception of life.

Most of us enjoy the gooseflesh and the tingle along the spine produced by the successful ghost story. There is something agreeable in letting our blood be chilled by bats in the moonlight, guttering candles, creaking doors, eerie shadows, piercing screams, inexplicable blood-stains, and weird noises. But the terror aroused by tricks and external "machinery" is a far cry from the terror evoked by some terrifying treatment of the human situation. The horror we experience in watching the Werewolf or Dracula or Frankenstein is far less signifi-cant than that we get from watching the bloody ambition of Macbeth or the jealousy of noble Othello. In the first, terror is the end-product; in the second, it is the natural accompaniment of a powerful revelation of life. In the first, we are always aware of a basic unreality; in the second, reality is terrifying.

The story designed merely to provoke laughter or to arouse terror may be an enjoyable and innocent pleasure. The story directed at stimulating tears belongs to a less innocent category. The difference is that the humor story and the terror story seldom ask to be taken for more than what they are: pleasant diversions to help us pass the time agreeably. We enjoy the custard pie in the face and the ghost in the moonlight without taking them seriously. The fiction which depends on such ingredients is pure escape. The tear-jerker, however, asks to be taken seriously. Like the street beggar who artfully disposes his rags, puts on dark glasses over perfectly good eyes, holds out a tin cup and wails about his seven starving children (there are really only two, and he doesn't know what has become of them), the tear-jerker cheats us. It is escape literature posing as its opposite; it is counterfeit interpretation. It cheats us by exaggerating and falsifying reality and by asking for compassion that isn't deserved.

The quality in a story which aims at drawing forth unmerited tender feeling is known as SENTIMENTALITY. Sentimentality is not the same as genuine emotion. Sentimentality is contrived or excessive or faked emotion. A story contains genuine emotion when it treats life faithfully and perceptively. The sentimentalized story oversimplifies and sweet ens life to get its feeling. It exaggerates, manipulates, and prettifies. It mixes tears with sugar.

Genuine emotion, like character, must be presented *indirectly*— must be *dramatized*. It cannot be produced by words that *name* emotions—like *angry, sad, pathetic, heart-breaking,* or *passionate*. If a writer is to draw forth genuine emotion, he must produce a character in a situation that deserves our sympathy, and must tell us enough about the character and the situation to make them real and convincing.

The sentimental writer is recognizable by a number of characteristics. First, he often tries to make words do what the situation faithfully presented by itself will not do. He *editorializes*—that is, comments on the story and, in a manner, instructs us how to feel. Or he overwrites and *poeticizes*—uses an immoderately heightened and distended language to accomplish his effect. Second, he makes an excessively selective use of detail. All artists, of course, must be selective in their use of detail, but the good writer uses representative details while the sentimentalist uses details that all point one way—toward producing emotion rather than conveying truth. The little child that dies will be shown as always uncomplaining and cheerful under adversity, never as naughty, querulous, or ungrateful. He will possibly be an orphan or the only child of a mother who loves him dearly; in addition he may be lame, hungry, ragged, and possessed of one toy, from which he cannot be parted. The villain will be all-villain, with a cruel laugh and a sharp whip, though he may reform at the end, for the sentimentalist is a profound believer in the heart of gold beneath the rough exterior. In short, reality will be unduly heightened and drastically oversimplified. Third, the sentimentalist will rely heavily on the stock response—an emotion that has its source outside the facts established by the story. In some readers certain situations and objects—babies, mothers, grandmothers, young love, patriotism, worship—produce an almost automatic response, whether the immediate situation warrants it or not. The sentimental writer, to affect such readers, has only to draw out certain stops, as on an organ, to produce an easily anticipated effect. He depends on stock materials to produce a stock response. He thus need not go to the trouble of picturing the situation in realistic and convincing detail. Finally, the sentimental writer presents, nearly always, a fundamentally "sweet" picture of life. He relies not only on stock characters and situations but also on stock themes. For him every cloud has its silver lining, every bad event its good side, every storm its rainbow following. If the little child dies, he goes to heaven or makes some life better by his death. Virtue is characteristically triumphant: the villain is defeated, the ne'er-do-well redeemed. True love is rewarded in some fashion; it is love—never hate—which makes the world go round. In short, the sentimental writer specializes in the sad but sweet. The tears called for are warm tears, never bitter. There is always sugar at the bottom of the cup.

For the mature reader emotion is a highly valued but not easily achieved component of a story. It is a by-product, not the end-product. It is gained by honestly portrayed characters in honestly drawn situations which reflect the complexity, the ambiguity, and the endless variety of life. It is produced by a carefully exercised restraint on the part of the writer rather than by his "pulling out all the stops." It is one of the chief rewards of art.

Dorothy Parker

THE WALTZ

Why, *thank you so much. I'd adore to.*

I don't want to dance with him. I don't want to dance with anybody. And even if I did, it wouldn't be him. He'd be well down among the last ten. I've seen the way he dances; it looks like something you do on Saint Walpurgis Night. Just think, not a quarter of an hour ago, here I was sitting, feeling so sorry for the poor girl he was dancing with. And now *I'm* going to be the poor girl. Well, well. Isn't it a small world?

And a peach of a world, too. A true little corker. Its events are so fascinatingly unpredictable, are not they? Here I was, minding my own business, not doing a stitch of harm to any living soul. And then he comes into my life, all smiles and city manners, to sue me for the favor of one memorable mazurka. Why, he scarcely knows my name, let alone what it stands for. It stands for Despair, Bewilderment, Futility, Degradation, and Premeditated Murder, but little does he wot. I don't wot his name, either; I haven't any idea what it is. Jukes, would be my guess from the look in his eyes. How do you do, Mr. Jukes? And how is that dear little brother of yours, with the two heads?

Ah, now why did he have to come around me, with his low requests? Why can't he let me lead my own life? I ask so little—just to be left alone in my quiet corner of the table, to do my evening brooding over all my sorrows. And he must come, with his bows and his scrapes and his may-I-have-this once. And I had to go and tell him that I'd adore to dance with him. I cannot understand why I wasn't struck right down dead. Yes, and being struck dead would look like a day in the country, compared to struggling out a dance with this boy. But what could I do? Everyone else at the table had got up to dance, except him and me. There was I, trapped. Trapped like a trap in a trap.

What can you say, when a man asks you to dance with him? I most certainly will *not* dance with you, I'll see you in hell first. Why, thank you, I'd like to awfully, but I'm having labor pains. Oh, yes, *do* let's dance together—it's so nice to meet a man who isn't a scaredy-cat about catching my beri-beri. No. There was nothing for me to do, but say I'd adore to. Well, we might as well get it over with. All right, Cannonball, let's run out on the field. You won the toss; you can lead.

Why, I think it's more of a waltz, really. Isn't it? We might just listen to the music a second. Shall we? Oh yes, it's a waltz. Mind? Why, I'm simply thrilled. I'd love to waltz with you.

I'd love to waltz with you. I'd love to waltz with you. I'd love to have my tonsils out, I'd love to be in a midnight fire at sea. Well, it's too late now. We're getting under way. *Oh.* Oh, dear. Oh, dear, dear, dear. Oh, this is even worse than I thought it would be. I suppose that's the one dependable law of life—everything is always worse than you thought it was going to be. Oh, if I had any real grasp of what this dance would be like, I'd have held out for sitting it out. Well, it will probably amount to the same thing in the end. We'll be sitting it out on the floor in a minute, if he keeps this up.

I'm so glad I brought it to his attention that this is a waltz they're playing. Heaven knows what might have happened, if he had thought it was something fast; we'd have blown the sides right out of the building. Why does he always want to be somewhere that he isn't? Why can't we stay in one place just long enough to get acclimated? It's this constant rush, rush, rush, that's the curse of American life. That's the reason that we're all of us so—*Ow!* For God's sake, don't *kick*, you idiot; this is only second down. Oh, my shin. My poor, poor shin, that I've had ever since I was a little girl!

Oh, no, no, no. Goodness, no. It didn't hurt the least little bit. And anyway it was my fault. Really it was. Truly. Well, you're just being sweet, to say that. It really was all my fault.

I wonder what I'd better do—kill him this instant, with my naked hands, or wait and let him drop in his traces. Maybe it's best not to make a scene. I guess I'll just lie low, and watch the pace get him. He can't keep this up indefinitely—he's only flesh and blood. Die he must, and die he shall, for what he did to me. I don't want to be of the over-sensitive type, but you can't tell me that kick was unpremeditated. Freud says there are no accidents. I've led no cloistered life, I've known dancing partners who have spoiled my slippers and torn my dress; but when it comes to kicking, I am Outraged Womanhood. When you kick me in the shin, *smile.*

Maybe he didn't do it maliciously. Maybe it's just his way of showing his high spirits. I suppose I ought to be glad that one of us is having such a good time. I suppose I ought to think myself lucky if he brings me back alive. Maybe it's captious to demand of a practically strange man that he leave your shins as he found them. After all, the poor boy's doing the best he can. Probably he grew up in the hill country, and never had no larnin'. I bet they had to throw him on his back to get shoes on him.

Yes, it's lovely, isn't it? It's simply lovely. It's the loveliest waltz. Isn't it? Oh, I think it's lovely, too.

Why, I'm getting positively drawn to the Triple Threat here. He's my hero. He has the heart of a lion, and the sinews of a buffalo. Look at him—never a thought of the consequences, never afraid of his face, hurling himself into every scrimmage, eyes shining, cheeks ablaze. And shall it be said that I hung back? No, a thousand times no. What's it to me if I have to spend the next couple of years in a plaster cast? Come on, Butch, right through them! Who wants to live forever?

Oh, Oh, dear. Oh, he's all right, thank goodness. For a while I thought they'd have to carry him off the field. Ah, I couldn't bear to have anything happen to him. I love him. I love him better than anybody in the world. Look at the spirit he gets into a dreary, commonplace waltz; how effete the other dancers seem, beside him. He is youth and vigor and courage, he is strength and gaiety and—*Ow!* Get off my instep, you hulking peasant! What do you think I am, anyway— a gangplank? *Ow!*

No, of course it didn't hurt. Why, it didn't a bit. Honestly. And it was all my fault. You see, that little step of yours—well, it's perfectly lovely, but it's just a tiny bit tricky to follow at first. Oh, did you work it up yourself? You really did? Well, aren't you amazing! Oh, now I think I've got it. Oh, I think it's lovely. I was watching you do it when you were dancing before. It's awfully effective when you look at it.

It's awfully effective when you look at it. I bet I'm awfully effective when you look at me. My hair is hanging along my cheeks, my skirt is swaddling about me, I can feel the cold damp of my brow. I must look like something out of "The Fall of the House of Usher." This sort of thing takes a fearful toll of a woman my age. And he worked up his little step himself, he with his degenerate cunning. And it was just a tiny bit tricky at first, but now I think I've got it. Two stumbles, slip, and a twenty yard dash; yes. I've got it. I've got several other things, too, including a split shin and a bitter heart. I hate this creature I'm chained to. I hated him the moment I saw his leering, bestial face. And here I've been locked in his noxious embrace for the thirty-five years this waltz has lasted. Is that orchestra never going to stop playing? Or must this obscene travesty of a dance go on until hell burns out?

Oh, they're going to play another encore. Oh, goody. Oh, that's lovely. Tired? I should say I'm not tired. I'd like to go on like this forever.

I should say I'm not tired. I'm dead, that's all I am. Dead, and in what a cause! And the music is never going to stop playing, and we're going on like this, Double-Time Charlie and I, throughout eternity. I suppose I won't care any more, after the first hundred thousand years. I suppose nothing will matter then, not heat nor pain nor broken heart nor cruel, aching weariness. Well. It can't come too soon for me.

I wonder why I didn't tell him I was tired. I wonder why I didn't suggest going back to the table. I could have said let's just listen to the music. Yes, and if he would, that would be the first bit of attention he has given it all evening. George Jean Nathan said that the lovely rhythms of the waltz should be listened to in stillness and not be accompanied by strange gyrations of the human body. I think that's what he said. I think it was George Jean Nathan. Anyhow, whatever he said and whoever he was and whatever he's doing now, he's better off than I am. That's safe. Anybody who isn't waltzing with this Mrs. O'Leary's cow I've got here is having a good time.

Still if we were back at the table, I'd probably have to talk to him. Look at him—what could you say to a thing like that! Did you go to the circus this year, what's your favorite kind of ice cream, how do you spell cat? I guess I'm as well off here. As well off as if I were in a cement mixer in full action.

I'm past all feeling now. The only way I can tell when he steps on me is that I can hear the splintering of bones. And all the events of my life are passing before my eyes. There was the time I was in a hurricane in the West Indies, there was the day I got my head cut open in the taxi smash, there was the night the drunken lady threw a bronze ash-tray at her own true love and got me instead, there was that summer that the sailboat kept capsizing. Ah, what an easy, peaceful time was mine, until I fell in with Swifty, here. I didn't know what trouble was, before I got drawn into this *danse macabre*. I think my mind is beginning to wander. It almost seems to me as if the orchestra were stopping. It couldn't be, of course; it could never, never be. And yet in my ears there is a silence like the sound of angel voices. . . .

Oh, they've stopped, the mean things. They're not going to play any more. Oh, darn. Oh, do you think they would? Do you really think so, if you gave them twenty dollars? Oh, that would be lovely. And look, do tell them to play this same thing. I'd simply adore to go on waltzing.

QUESTIONS

1. What is the author's purpose in using old-fashioned expressions such as "are not they?", "little does he wot"? Why does Porter begin with a line of dialog?
2. How old do you think the narrator is? Justify your opinion.
3. List the various names the narrator calls her dancing partner. Do they indicate a change of attitude? Explain.
4. How do you account for her apparent hypocrisy?
5. Two methods which writers use to achieve humor are (a) exaggeration, and (b) juxtaposition of the incongruous, the unrelated, the unexpected. Give several examples of each of these devices. Which do you consider most effective in this story? Why?
6. Does the humor in the story arise from observation or distortion of life? Document your answer. Why do you find this story funny? From your answer, can you draw any conclusions about humor in general?
7. Why do you think Parker wrote "The Waltz"?

Frank O'Connor

THE DRUNKARD

It was a terrible blow to Father when Mr. Dooley on the terrace died.
Mr. Dooley was a commercial traveller with two sons in the Domini-
cans and a car of his own, so socially he was miles ahead of us, but he
had no false pride. Mr. Dooley was an intellectual, and, like all
intellectuals the thing he loved best was conversation, and in his own
limited way Father was a well-read man and could appreciate an intelligent talker. Mr. Dooley was remarkably intelligent. Between
business acquaintances and clerical contacts, there was very little he
didn't know about what went on in town, and evening after evening he
crossed the road to our gate to explain to Father the news behind the
news. He had a low, palavering voice and a knowing smile, and Father
would listen in astonishment, giving him a conversational lead now
and again, and then stump triumphantly in to Mother with his face
aglow and ask: "Do you know what Mr. Dooley is after telling me?"
Ever since, when somebody has given me some bit of information off
the record I have found myself on the point of asking: "Was it Mr.
Dooley told you that?"

Till I actually saw him laid out in his brown shroud with the rosary
beads entwined between his waxy fingers I did not take the report of his
death seriously. Even then I felt there must be a catch and that some
summer evening Mr. Dooley must reappear at our gate to give us the
lowdown on the next world. But Father was very upset, partly because
Mr. Dooley was about one age with himself, a thing that always gives a
distinctly personal turn to another man's demise; partly because now he
would have no one to tell him what dirty work was behind the latest
scene at the Corporation. You could count on your fingers the number
of men in Blarney Lane who read the papers as Mr. Dooley did, and
none of these would have overlooked the fact that Father was only a
labouring man. Even Sullivan, the carpenter, a mere nobody, thought
he was a cut above Father. It was certainly a solemn event.

"Half past two to the Curragh," Father said meditatively, putting
down the paper.

"But you're not thinking of going to the funeral?" Mother asked in
alarm.

"'Twould be expected," Father said, scenting opposition. "I
wouldn't give it to say to them."

THE DRUNKARD From *The Stories of Frank O'Connor*. Copyright 1951 by Frank
O'Connor. Reprinted by permission of Joan Daves. Originally published in *The New
Yorker*.

"I think," said Mother with suppressed emotion, "it will be as much as anyone will expect if you go to the chapel with him."

("Going to the chapel," of course, was one thing, because the body was removed after work, but going to a funeral meant the loss of a half-day's pay.)

"The people hardly know us," she added.

"God between us and all harm," Father replied with dignity, "we'd be glad if it was our own turn."

To give Father his due, he was always ready to lose a half day for the sake of an old neighbour. It wasn't so much that he liked funerals as that he was a conscientious man who did as he would be done by; and nothing could have consoled him so much for the prospect of his own death as the assurance of a worthy funeral. And, to give Mother her due, it wasn't the half-day's pay she begrudged, badly as we could afford it.

Drink, you see, was Father's great weakness. He could keep steady for months, even for years, at a stretch, and while he did he was as good as gold. He was first up in the morning and brought the mother a cup of tea in bed, stayed at home in the evenings and read the paper; saved money and bought himself a new blue serge suit and bowler hat. He laughed at the folly of men who, week in, week out, left their hard-earned money with the publicans; and sometimes, to pass an idle hour, he took pencil and paper and calculated precisely how much he saved each week through being a teetotaller. Being a natural optimist he sometimes continued this calculation through the whole span of his prospective existence and the total was breathtaking. He would die worth hundreds.

If I had only known it, this was a bad sign; a sign he was becoming stuffed up with spiritual pride and imagining himself better than his neighbours. Sooner or later, the spiritual pride grew till it called for some form of celebration. Then he took a drink—not whisky, of course; nothing like that—just a glass of some harmless drink like lager beer. That was the end of Father. By the time he had taken the first he already realized that he had made a fool of himself, took a second to forget it and a third to forget that he couldn't forget, and at last came home reeling drunk. From this on it was "The Drunkard's Progress," as in the moral prints. Next day he stayed in from work with a sick head while Mother went off to make his excuses at the works, and inside a fortnight he was poor and savage and despondent again. Once he began he drank steadily through everything down to the kitchen clock. Mother and I knew all the phases and dreaded all the dangers. Funerals were one.

"I have to go to Dunphy's to do a half-day's work," said Mother in distress. "Who's to look after Larry?"

"I'll look after Larry," Father said graciously. "The little walk will do him good."

There was no more to be said, though we all knew I didn't need anyone to look after me, and that I could quite well have stayed at home and looked after Sonny, but I was being attached to the party to act as a brake on Father. As a brake I had never achieved anything, but Mother still had great faith in me.

Next day, when I got home from school, Father was there before me and made a cup of tea for both of us. He was very good at tea, but too heavy in the hand for anything else; the way he cut bread was shocking. Afterwards, we went down the hill to the church, Father wearing his best blue serge and a bowler cocked to one side of his head with the least suggestion of the masher. To his great joy he discovered Peter Crowley among the mourners. Peter was another danger signal, as I knew well from certain experiences after Mass on Sunday morning: a mean man, as Mother said, who only went to funerals for the free drinks he could get at them. It turned out that he hadn't even known Mr. Dooley! But Father had a sort of contemptuous regard for him as one of the foolish people who wasted their good money in public-houses when they could be saving it. Very little of his own money Peter Crowley wasted!

It was an excellent funeral from Father's point of view. He had it all well studied before we set off after the hearse in the afternoon sunlight.

"Five carriages!" he exclaimed. "Five carriages and sixteen covered cars. There's one alderman, two councillors and 'tis unknown how many priests. I didn't see a funeral like this from the road since Willie Mack, the publican, died."

"Ah, he was well liked," said Crowley in his husky voice.

"My goodness, don't I know that?" snapped Father. "Wasn't the man my best friend? Two nights before he died—only two nights—he was over telling me the goings-on about the housing contract. Them fellows in the Corporation are night and day robbers. But even I never imagined he was as well connected as that."

Father was stepping out like a boy, pleased with everything: the other mourners, and the fine houses along Sunday's Well. I knew the danger signals were there in full force: a sunny day, a fine funeral, and a distinguished company of clerics and public men were bringing out all the natural vanity and flightiness of Father's character. It was with something like genuine pleasure that he saw his old friend lowered into the grave; with the sense of having performed a duty and the pleasant awareness that however much he would miss poor Mr. Dooley in the long summer evenings, it was he and not poor Mr. Dooley who would do the missing.

"We'll be making tracks before they break up," he whispered to Crowley as the gravediggers tossed in the first shovelfuls of clay, and away he went, hopping like a goat from grassy hump to hump. The drivers, who were probably in the same state as himself, though without months of abstinence to put an edge on it, looked up hopefully.

"Are they nearly finished, Mick?" bawled one.

"All over now bar the last prayers," trumpeted Father in the tone of one who brings news of great rejoicing.

The carriages passed us in a lather of dust several hundred yards from the public-house, and Father, whose feet gave him trouble in hot weather, quickened his pace, looking nervously over his shoulder for any sign of the main body of mourners crossing the hill. In a crowd like that a man might be kept waiting.

When we did reach the pub the carriages were drawn up outside, and solemn men in black ties were cautiously bringing out consolation to mysterious females whose hands reached out modestly from behind the drawn blinds of the coaches. Inside the pub there were only the drivers and a couple of shawly women. I felt if I was to act as a brake at all, this was the time, so I pulled Father by the coattails.

"Dadda, can't we go home now?" I asked.

"Two minutes now," he said, beaming affectionately. "Just a bottle of lemonade and we'll go home."

This was a bribe, and I knew it, but I was always a child of weak character. Father ordered lemonade and two pints. I was thirsty and swallowed my drink at once. But that wasn't Father's way. He had long months of abstinence behind him and an eternity of pleasure before. He took out his pipe, blew through it, filled it, and then lit it with loud pops, his eyes bulging above it. After that he deliberately turned his back on the pint, leaned one elbow on the counter in the attitude of a man who did not know there was a pint behind him, and deliberately brushed the tobacco from his palms. He had settled down for the evening. He was steadily working through all the important funerals he had ever attended. The carriages departed and the minor mourners drifted in till the pub was half full.

"Dadda," I said, pulling his coat again, "can't we go home now?"

"Ah, your mother won't be in for a long time yet," he said benevolently enough. "Run out in the road and play, can't you?"

It struck me as very cool, the way grown-ups assumed that you could play all by yourself on a strange road. I began to get bored as I had so often been bored before. I knew Father was quite capable of lingering there till nightfall. I knew I might have to bring him home, blind drunk, down Blarney Lane, with all the old women at their doors, saying: "Mick Delaney is on it again." I knew that my mother would be half crazy with anxiety; that next day Father wouldn't go out to work; and before the end of the week she would be running down to the pawn with the clock under her shawl. I could never get over the lonesomeness of the kitchen without a clock.

I was still thirsty. I found if I stood on tiptoe I could just reach Father's glass, and the idea occurred to me that it would be interesting to know what the contents were like. He had his back to it and wouldn't notice. I took down the glass and sipped cautiously. It was a terrible disappointment. I was astonished that he could even drink such stuff. It looked as if he had never tried lemonade.

I should have advised him about lemonade but he was holding forth himself in great style. I heard him say that bands were a great addition to a funeral. He put his arms in the position of someone holding a rifle in reverse and hummed a few bars of Chopin's Funeral March. Crowley nodded reverently. I took a longer drink and began to see that porter might have its advantages. I felt pleasantly elevated and philosophic. Father hummed a few bars of the Dead March in *Saul*. It was a nice pub and a very fine funeral, and I felt sure that poor Mr. Dooley in Heaven must be highly gratified. At the same time I thought they might have given him a band. As Father said, bands were a great addition.

But the wonderful thing about porter was the way it made you stand aside, or rather float aloft like a cherub rolling on a cloud, and watch yourself with your legs crossed, leaning against a bar counter, not worrying about trifles but thinking deep, serious, grown-up thoughts about life and death. Looking at yourself like that, you couldn't help thinking after a while how funny you looked, and suddenly you got embarrassed and wanted to giggle. But by the time I had finished the pint, that phase too had passed; I found it hard to put back the glass, the counter seemed to have grown so high. Melancholia was supervening again.

"Well," Father said reverently, reaching behind him for his drink, "God rest the poor man's soul, wherever he is!" He stopped, looked first at the glass, and then at the people round him. "Hello," he said in a fairly good-humoured tone, as if he were just prepared to consider it a joke, even if it was in bad taste, "who was at this?"

There was silence for a moment while the publican and the old women looked first at Father and then at his glass.

"There was no one at it, my good man," one of the women said with an offended air. "Is it robbers you think we are?"

"Ah, there's no one here would do a thing like that, Mick," said the publican in a shocked tone.

"Well, someone did it," said Father, his smile beginning to wear off.

"If they did, they were them that were nearer it," said the woman darkly, giving me a dirty look; and at the same moment the truth began to dawn on Father. I suppose I must have looked a bit starry-eyed. He bent and shook me.

"Are you all right, Larry?" he asked in alarm.

Peter Crowley looked down at me and grinned.

"Could you beat that?" he exclaimed in a husky voice.

I could, and without difficulty. I started to get sick. Father jumped back in holy terror that I might spoil his good suit, and hastily opened the back door.

"Run! run! run!" he shouted.

I saw the sunlit wall outside with the ivy overhanging it, and ran. The intention was good but the performance was exaggerated, because I lurched right into the wall, hurting it badly, as it seemed to me. Being always very polite, I said "Pardon" before the second bout came on me. Father, still concerned for his suit, came up behind and cautiously held me while I got sick.

"That's a good boy!" he said encouragingly. "You'll be grand when you get that up."

Begor, I was not grand! Grand was the last thing I was. I gave one unmerciful wail out of me as he steered me back to the pub and put me sitting on the bench near the shawlies. They drew themselves up with an offended air, still sore at the suggestion that they had drunk his pint.

"God help us!" moaned one, looking pityingly at me. "Isn't it the likes of them would be fathers?"

"Mick," said the publican in alarm, spraying sawdust on my tracks, "that child isn't supposed to be in here at all. You'd better take him home quick in case a bobby would see him."

"Merciful God!" whimpered Father, raising his eyes to heaven and clapping his hands silently as he only did when distraught. "What misfortune was on me? Or what will his mother say? . . . If women might stop at home and look after their children themselves!" he added in a snarl for the benefit of the shawlies. "Are them carriages all gone, Bill?"

"The carriages are finished long ago, Mick," replied the publican.

"I'll take him home," Father said despairingly. . . . "I'll never bring you out again," he threatened me. "Here," he added, giving me the clean handkerchief from his breast pocket, "put that over your eye."

The blood on the handkerchief was the first indication that I got that I was cut, and instantly my temple began to throb and I set up another howl.

"Whisht, whisht, whisht!" Father said testily, steering me out the door. "One'd think you were killed. That's nothing. We'll wash it when we get home."

"Steady now, old scout!" Crowley said, taking the other side of me. "You'll be all right in a minute."

I never met two men who knew less about the effects of drink. The first breath of fresh air and the warmth of the sun made me groggier than ever and I pitched and rolled between wind and tide till Father started to whimper again.

"God Almighty, and the whole road out! What misfortune was on me didn't stop at my work! Can't you walk straight?"

I couldn't. I saw plain enough that, coaxed by the sunlight, every woman old and young in Blarney Lane was leaning over her half-door or sitting on her doorstep. They all stopped gabbling to gape at the strange spectacle of two sober, middle-aged men bringing home a drunken small boy with a cut over his eye. Father, torn between the shamefast desire to get me home as quick as he could, and the neighbourly need to explain that it wasn't his fault, finally halted outside Mrs. Roche's. There was a gang of old women outside a door at the opposite side of the road. I didn't like the look of them from the first. They seemed altogether too interested in me. I leaned against the wall of Mrs. Roche's cottage with my hands in my trousers pockets, thinking mournfully of poor Mr. Dooley in his cold grave on the Curragh, who would never walk down the road again, and, with great feeling, I began to sing a favourite song of Father's.

> Though lost to Monomia and cold in the grave
> He returns to Kincora no more.

"Wisha, the poor child!" Mrs. Roche said. "Haven't he a lovely voice, God bless him!"

That was what I thought myself, so I was the more surprised when Father said "Whisht!" and raised a threatening finger at me. He didn't seem to realize the appropriateness of the song, so I sang louder than ever.

"Whisht, I tell you!" he snapped, and then tried to work up a smile for Mrs. Roche's benefit. "We're nearly home now. I'll carry you the rest of the way."

But, drunk and all as I was, I knew better than to be carried home ignominiously like that.

"Now," I said severely, "can't you leave me alone? I can walk all right. 'Tis only my head. All I want is a rest."

"But you can rest at home in bed," he said viciously, trying to pick me up, and I knew by the flush on his face that he was very vexed.

"Ah, Jasus," I said crossly, "What do I want to go home for? Why the hell can't you leave me alone?"

For some reason the gang of old women at the other side of the road thought this very funny. They nearly split their sides over it. A gassy fury began to expand in me at the thought that a fellow couldn't have a drop taken without the whole neighbourhood coming out to make game of him.

"Who are ye laughing at?" I shouted, clenching my fists at them. "I'll make ye laugh at the other side of yeer faces if ye don't let me pass."

They seemed to think this funnier still; I had never seen such ill-mannered people.

"Go away, ye bloody bitches!" I said.

"Whisht, whisht, whisht, I tell you!" snarled Father, abandoning all pretence of amusement and dragging me along behind him by the hand. I was maddened by the women's shrieks of laughter. I was maddened by Father's bullying. I tried to dig in my heels but he was too powerful for me, and I could only see the women by looking back over my shoulder.

"Take care or I'll come back and show ye!" I shouted. "I'll teach ye to let decent people pass. Fitter for ye to stop at home and wash yeer dirty faces."

" 'Twill be all over the road," whimpered Father. "Never again, never again, not if I lived to be a thousand!"

To this day I don't know whether he was forswearing me or the drink. By way of a song suitable to my heroic mood I bawled "The Boys of Wexford," as he dragged me in home. Crowley, knowing he was not safe, made off and Father undressed me and put me to bed. I couldn't sleep because of the whirling in my head. It was very unpleasant, and I got sick again. Father came in with a wet cloth and mopped up after me. I lay in a fever, listening to him chopping sticks to start a fire. After that I heard him lay the table.

Suddenly the front door banged open and Mother stormed in with Sonny in her arms, not her usual gentle, timid self, but a wild, raging woman. It was clear that she had heard it all from the neighbours.

"Mick Delaney," she cried hysterically, "what did you do to my son?"

"Whisht, woman, whisht, whisht!" he hissed, dancing from one foot to the other. "Do you want the whole road to hear?"

"Ah," she said with a horrifying laugh, "the road knows all about it by this time. The road knows the way you filled your unfortunate innocent child with drink to make sport for you and that other rotten, filthy brute."

"But I gave him no drink," he shouted, aghast at the horrifying interpretation the neighbours had chosen to give his misfortune. "He took it while my back was turned. What the hell do you think I am?"

"Ah," she replied bitterly, "everyone knows what you are now. God forgive you, wasting our hard-earned few ha'pence on drink, and bringing up your child to be a drunken corner-boy like yourself."

Then she swept into the bedroom and threw herself on her knees by the bed. She moaned when she saw the gash over my eye. In the kitchen Sonny set up a loud bawl on his own, and a moment later Father appeared in the bedroom door with his cap over his eyes, wearing an expression of the most intense self-pity.

"That's a nice way to talk to me after all I went through," he whined.

"That's a nice accusation, that I was drinking. Not one drop of drink crossed my lips the whole day. How could it when he drank it all? I'm the one that ought to be pitied, with my day ruined on me, and I after being made a show for the whole road."

But next morning, when he got up and went out quietly to work with his dinner-basket, Mother threw herself on me in the bed and kissed me. It seemed it was all my doing, and I was being given a holiday till my eye got better.

"My brave little man!" she said with her eyes shining. "It was God did it you were there. You were his guardian angel."

QUESTIONS

1. What are the sources of humor in this story? Does the humor arise from observation of life or from distortion of life? What elements of the story seem to you funniest?
2. Is this a purely humorous story, or are there undertones of pathos in it? If the latter, from what does the pathos arise?
3. List what seem to you the chief insights into life and character presented by the story.
4. Is the title seriously meant? To whom does it refer?
5. The boy's drunkenness is seen from four points of view. What are they, and how do they differ?
6. What is the principal irony in the story?
7. The story is told in retrospect by a man recalling an incident from his boyhood. What does this removal in time do to the treatment of the material?
8. *Did* Larry's father forswear liquor? Support your answer with evidence from the story.

Anton Chekhov

THE DARLING

Olenka, the daughter of the retired collegiate assessor, Plemyan-nikov, was sitting on her back porch, lost in thought. It was hot, the flies were persistent and teasing, and it was pleasant to reflect that it would soon be evening. Dark rain-clouds were gathering from the east, and bringing from time to time a breath of moisture in the air.

THE DARLING From *The Darling and Other Stories* by Anton Chekhov, translated by Constance Garnett. Reprinted by permission of the Literary Estate of Constance Garnett and Chatto & Windus Ltd.

Kukin, who was the manager of an open-air theater called the Tivoli, and who lived in the lodge, was standing in the middle of the garden looking at the sky.

"Again!" he observed despairingly. "It's going to rain again! Rain every day, as though to spite me. I might as well hang myself! It's ruin! Fearful losses every day."

He flung up his hands, and went on, addressing Olenka:

"There! that's the life we lead, Olga Semyonovna. It's enough to make one cry. One works and does one's utmost; one wears oneself out, getting no sleep at night, and racks one's brain what to do for the best. And then what happens? To begin with, one's public is ignorant, boorish. I give them the very best operetta, a dainty masque, first rate music-hall artists. But do you suppose that's what they want! They don't understand anything of that sort. They want a clown; what they ask for is vulgarity. And then look at the weather! Almost every evening it rains. It started on the tenth of May, and it's kept it up all May and June. It's simply awful! The public doesn't come, but I've to pay the rent just the same, and pay the artists."

The next evening the clouds would gather again, and Kukin would say with an hysterical laugh:

"Well, rain away, then! Flood the garden, drown me! Damn my luck in this world and the next! Let the artists have me up! Send me to prison!—to Siberia!—the scaffold! Ha, ha, ha!"

The next day the same thing.

Olenka listened to Kukin with silent gravity, and sometimes tears came into her eyes. In the end his misfortunes touched her; she grew to love him. He was a small thin man, with a yellow face, and curls combed forward on his forehead. He spoke in a thin tenor; as he talked his mouth worked on one side, and there was always an expression of despair on his face; yet he aroused a deep and genuine affection in her. She was always fond of someone, and could not exist without loving. In earlier days she had loved her papa, who now sat in a darkened room, breathing with difficulty; she had loved her aunt who used to come every other year from Bryansk; and before that, when she was at school, she had loved her French master. She was a gentle, soft-hearted, compassionate girl, with mild, tender eyes and very good health. At the sight of her full rosy cheeks, her soft white neck with a little dark mole on it, and the kind, naïve smile, which came into her face when she listened to anything pleasant, men thought, "Yes, not half bad," and smiled too, while lady visitors could not refrain from seizing her hand in the middle of a conversation exclaiming in a gush of delight, "You darling!"

The house in which she had lived from her birth upwards, and which was left her in her father's will, was at the extreme end of the town, not far from the Tivoli. In the evenings and at night she could hear the band playing, and the crackling and banging of fireworks, and it seemed to her that it was Kukin struggling with his destiny, storming the entrenchments of his chief foe, the indifferent public; there was a sweet thrill at her heart, she had no desire to sleep, and when he returned home at daybreak, she tapped softly at her bedroom window, and showing him only her face and one shoulder through the curtain, she gave him a friendly smile. . . .

He proposed to her, and they were married. And when he had a closer view of her neck and her plump, fine shoulders, he threw up his hands, and said:

"You darling!"

He was happy, but as it rained on the day and night of his wedding, his face still retained an expression of despair.

They got on very well together. She used to sit in his office, to look after things in the Tivoli, to put down the accounts and pay the wages. And her rosy cheeks, her sweet, naïve, radiant smile, were to be seen now at the office window, now in the refreshment bar or behind the scenes of the theater. And already she used to say to her acquaintances that the theater was the chief and most important thing in life, and that it was only through the drama that one could derive true enjoyment and become cultivated and humane.

"But do you suppose the public understands that?" she used to say. "What they want is a clown. Yesterday we gave 'Faust Inside Out,' and almost all the boxes were empty; but if Vanichka and I had been producing some vulgar thing, I assure you the theater would have been packed. Tomorrow Vanichka and I are doing 'Orpheus in Hell.' Do come."

And what Kukin said about the theater and the actors she repeated. Like him she despised the public for their ignorance and their indifference to art; she took part in the rehearsals, she corrected the actors, she kept an eye on the behavior of the musicians, and when there was an unfavorable notice in the local paper, she shed tears, and then went to the editor's office to set things right.

The actors were fond of her and used to call her "Vanichka and I," and "the darling"; she was sorry for them and used to lend them small sums of money, and if they deceived her, she used to shed a few tears in private, but did not complain to her husband.

They got on well in the winter too. They took the theater in the town for the whole winter, and let it for short terms to a Little Russian company, or to a conjurer, or to a local dramatic society. Olenka grew stouter, and was always beaming with satisfaction, while Kukin grew thinner and yellower, and continually complained of their terrible losses, although he had not done badly all the winter. He used to cough at night, and she used to give him hot raspberry tea or lime-blossom water, to rub him with eau de Cologne and to wrap him in her warm shawls.

"You're such a sweet pet!" she used to say with perfect sincerity, stroking his hair. "You're such a pretty dear!"

Towards Lent he went to Moscow to collect a new troupe, and without him she could not sleep, but sat all night at her window, looking at the stars, and she compared herself with the hens, who are awake all night and uneasy when the cock is not in the henhouse. Kukin was detained in Moscow, and wrote that he would be back at Easter, adding some instructions about the Tivoli. But on the Sunday before Easter, late in the evening, came a sudden ominous knock at the gate; someone was hammering on the gate as though on a barrel—*boom, boom, boom!* The drowsy cook went flopping with her bare feet through the puddles, as she ran to open the gate.

"Please open," said someone outside in a thick bass. "There is a telegram for you."

Olenka had received telegrams from her husband before, but this time for some reason she felt numb with terror. With shaking hands she opened the telegram and read as follows:

IVAN PETROVICH DIED SUDDENLY TODAY. AWAITING
IMMATE INSTRUCTIONS FUFUNERAL TUESDAY.

That was how it was written in the telegram—"fufuneral," and the utterly incomprehensible word "immate." It was signed by the stage manager of the operatic company.

"My darling!" sobbed Olenka. "Vanichka, my precious, my darling! Why did I ever meet you! Why did I know you and love you! Your poor heartbroken Olenka is all alone without you!"

Kukin's funeral took place on Tuesday in Moscow, Olenka returned home on Wednesday, and as soon as she got indoors she threw herself on her bed and sobbed so loudly that it could be heard next door, and in the street.

"Poor darling!" the neighbors said, as they crossed themselves. "Olga Semyonovna, poor darling! How she does take on!"

Three months later Olenka was coming home from mass, melancholy and in deep mourning. It happened that one of her neighbors, Vasily Andreich Pustovalov, returning home from church, walked back beside her. He was the manager at Babakayev's, the timber merchant. He wore a straw hat, a white waistcoat, and a gold watchchain, and looked more like a country gentleman than a man in trade.

"Everything happens as it is ordained, Olga Semyonovna," he said gravely, with a sympathetic note in his voice; "and if any of our dear ones die, it must be because it is the will of God, so we ought to have fortitude and bear it submissively."

After seeing Olenka to her gate, he said goodbye and went on. All day afterwards she heard his sedately dignified voice, and whenever she shut her eyes she saw his dark beard. She liked him very much. And apparently she had made an impression on him too, for not long afterwards an elderly lady, with whom she was only slightly acquainted, came to drink coffee with her, and as soon as she was seated at table began to talk about Pustovalov, saying that he was an excellent man whom one could thoroughly depend upon, and that any girl would be glad to marry him. Three days later Pustovalov came himself. He did not stay long, only about ten minutes, and he did not say much, but when he left, Olenka loved him—loved him so much that she lay awake all night in a perfect fever, and in the morning she sent for the elderly lady. The match was quickly arranged, and then came the wedding.

Pustovalov and Olenka got on very well together when they were married.

Usually he sat in the office till dinnertime, then he went out on business, while Olenka took his place, and sat in the office till evening, making up accounts and booking orders.

"Timber gets dearer every year; the price rises 20 per cent," she would say to her customers and friends. "Only fancy we used to sell local timber, and now Vasichka always has to go for wood to the Mogilev district. And the freight!" she would add, covering her cheeks with her hands in horror. "The freight!"

It seemed to her that she had been in the timber trade for ages and ages, and that the most important and necessary thing in life was timber; and there was something intimate and touching to her in the very sound of words such as "balk," "post," "beam," "pole," "scantling," "batten," "lath," "plank," etc.

At night when she was asleep she dreamed of perfect mountains of planks and boards, and long strings of wagons, carting timber somewhere far away. She dreamed that a whole regiment of six-inch beams forty feet high, standing on end, was marching upon the timberyard; that logs, beams, and boards knocked together with the resounding crash of dry wood, kept falling and getting up again, piling themselves on each other. Olenka cried out in her sleep, and Pustovalov said to her tenderly: "Olenka, what's the matter, darling? Cross yourself!"

Her husband's ideas were hers. If he thought the room was too hot, or that business was slack, she thought the same. Her husband did not care for entertainment, and on holidays he stayed at home. She did likewise.

"You are always at home or in the office," her friends said to her.

"You should go to the theater, darling, or to the circus."

"Vasichka and I have no time to go to theaters," she would answer sedately. "We have no time for nonsense. What's the use of these theaters?"

On Saturdays Pustovalov and she used to go to the evening service; on holidays to early mass, and they walked side by side with softened faces as they came home from church. There was a pleasant fragrance about them both, and her silk dress rustled agreeably. At home they drank tea, with fancy bread and jams of various kinds, and afterwards they ate pie. Every day at twelve o'clock there was a savory smell of beetroot soup and of mutton or duck in their yard, and on fast-days of fish, and no one could pass the gate without feeling hungry. In the office the samovar was always boiling, and customers were regaled with tea and cracknels. Once a week the couple went to the baths and returned side by side, both red in the face.

"Yes, we have nothing to complain of, thank God," Olenka used to say to her acquaintances. "I wish everyone were as well off as Vasichka and I."

When Pustovalov went away to buy wood in the Mogilev district, she missed him dreadfully, lay awake and cried. A young veterinary surgeon in the army, called Smirnin, to whom they had let their lodge, used sometimes to come in in the evening. He used to talk to her and play cards with her, and this entertained her in her husband's absence. She was particularly interested in what he told her of his home life. He was married and had a little boy, but was separated from his wife because she had been unfaithful to him, and now he hated her and used to send her forty roubles a month for the maintenance of their son. And hearing of all this, Olenka sighed and shook her head. She was sorry for him.

"Well, God keep you," she used to say to him at parting, as she lighted him down the stairs with a candle. "Thank you for coming to cheer me up, and may the Mother of God give you health."

And she always expressed herself with the same sedateness and dignity, the same reasonableness, in imitation of her husband. As the veterinary surgeon was disappearing behind the door below, she would say:

"You know, Vladimir Platonych, you'd better make it up with your wife. You should forgive her for the sake of your son. You may be sure the little fellow understands."

And when Pustovalov came back, she told him in a low voice about the veterinary surgeon and his unhappy home life, and both sighed and shook their heads and talked about the boy, who, no doubt, missed his father, and by some strange connection of ideas, they went up to the holy icons, bowed to the ground before them and prayed that God would give them children.

And so the Pustovalovs lived for six years quietly and peaceably in love and complete harmony.

But behold! one winter day after drinking hot tea in the office, Vasily Andreich went out into the yard without his cap on to see about sending off some timber, caught cold and was taken ill. He had the best doctors, but he grew worse and died after four months' illness. And Olenka was a widow once more.

"I've nobody, now you've left me, my darling," she sobbed, after her husband's funeral. "How can I live without you, in wretchedness and misery! Pity me, good people, all alone in the world!"

She went about dressed in black with long "weepers," and gave up wearing hat and gloves for good. She hardly ever went out, except to church, or to her husband's grave, and led the life of a nun. It was not till six months later that she took off the weepers and opened the shutters of the windows. She was sometimes seen in the mornings, going with her cook to market her provisions, but what went on in her house and how she lived now could only be surmised. People guessed, from seeing her drinking tea in her garden with the veterinary surgeon, who read the newspaper aloud to her, and from the fact that, meeting a lady she knew at the post-office, she said to her:

"There is no proper veterinary inspection in our town, and that's the cause of all sorts of epidemics. One is always hearing of people's getting infection from the milk supply, or catching diseases from horses and cows. The health of domestic animals ought to be as well cared for as the health of human beings."

She repeated the veterinary surgeon's words, and was of the same opinion as he about everything. It was evident that she could not live a year without some attachment, and had found new happiness in the lodge. In anyone else this would have been censured, but no one could think ill of Olenka; everything she did was so natural. Neither she nor the veterinary surgeon said anything to other people of the change in their relations, and tried, indeed, to conceal it, but without success, for Olenka could not keep a secret. When he had visitors, men serving in his regiment, and she poured out tea or served the supper, she would begin talking of the cattle plague, of the foot and mouth disease, and of the municipal slaughterhouses. He was dreadfully embarrassed, and when the guests had gone, he would seize her by the hand and hiss angrily:

"I've asked you before not to talk about what you don't understand. When we veterinary surgeons are talking among ourselves, please don't put your word in. It's really annoying."

And she would look at him with astonishment and dismay, and ask him in alarm: "But, Volodichka, what *am* I to talk about?"

And with tears in her eyes she would embrace him, begging him not to be angry, and they were both happy.

But this happiness did not last long. The veterinary surgeon departed, departed forever with his regiment, when it was transferred to a distant place—to Siberia, it may be. And Olenka was left alone.

Now she was absolutely alone. Her father had long been dead, and his armchair lay in the attic, covered with dust and lame of one leg. She got thinner and plainer, and when people met her in the street they did not look at her as they used to, and did not smile to her; evidently her best years were over and left behind, and now a new sort of life had begun for her, which did not bear thinking about. In the evening Olenka sat in the porch, and heard the band playing and the fireworks popping in the Tivoli, but now the sound stirred no response. She looked into her yard without interest, thought of nothing, wished for nothing, and afterwards, when night came on she went to bed and dreamed of her empty yard. She ate and drank as it were unwillingly.

And what was worst of all, she had no opinions of any sort. She saw the objects about her and understood what she saw, but could not form any opinion about them, and did not know what to talk about. And how awful it is not to have any opinions! One sees a bottle, for instance, or the rain, or a peasant driving in his cart, but what the bottle is for, or the rain, or the peasant, and what is the meaning of it, one can't say, and could not even for a thousand roubles. When she had Kukin, or Pustovalov, or the veterinary surgeon, Olenka could explain everything, and give her opinion about anything you like, but now there was the same emptiness in her brain and in her heart as there was in her yard outside. And it was as harsh and as bitter as wormwood in the mouth.

Little by little the town grew in all directions. The road became a street, and where the Tivoli and the timber-yard had been, there were new turnings and houses. How rapidly time passes! Olenka's house grew dingy, the roof got rusty, the shed sank on one side, and the whole yard was overgrown with docks and stinging-nettles. Olenka herself had grown plain and elderly; in summer she sat in the porch, and her soul, as before, was empty and dreary and full of bitterness. In winter she sat at her window and looked at the snow. When she caught the scent of spring, or heard the chime of the church bells, a sudden rush of memories from the past came over her, there was a tender ache in her heart, and her eyes brimmed over with tears; but this was only for a minute, and then came emptiness again and the sense of the futility of life. The black kitten, Briska, rubbed against her and purred softly, but Olenka was not touched by these feline caresses. That was not what she needed. She wanted a love that would absorb her whole being, her whole soul and reason—that would give her ideas and an object in life, and would warm her old blood. And she would shake the kitten off her skirt and say with vexation:

"Get along; I don't want you!"

And so it was, day after day and year after year, and no joy, and no opinions. Whatever Mavra the cook said, she accepted.

One hot July day, towards evening, just as the cattle were being driven away, and the whole yard was full of dust, someone suddenly knocked at the gate. Olenka went to open it herself and was dumfounded when she looked out: she saw Smirnin, the veterinary surgeon, gray-headed, and dressed as a civilian. She suddenly remembered everything. She could not help crying and letting her head fall on his breast without uttering a word, and in the violence of her feeling she did not notice how they both walked into the house and sat down to tea.

"My dear Vladimir Platonych! What fate has brought you?" she muttered, trembling with joy.

"I want to settle here for good, Olga Semyonovna," he told her. "I have resigned my post, and have come to settle down and try my luck on my own account. Besides, it's time for my boy to go to school. He's a big boy. I am reconciled with my wife, you know."

"Where is she?" asked Olenka.

"She's at the hotel with the boy, and I'm looking for lodgings."

"Good gracious, my dear soul! Lodgings? Why not have my house? Why shouldn't that suit you? Why, my goodness, I wouldn't take any rent!" cried Olenka in a flutter, beginning to cry again. "You live here, and the lodge will do nicely for me. Oh, dear, how glad I am!"

Next day the roof was painted and the walls were whitewashed, and Olenka, with her arms akimbo, walked about the yard giving directions. Her face was beaming with her old smile, and she was brisk and alert as though she had waked from a long sleep. The veterinary's wife arrived—a thin, plain lady, with short hair and a peevish expression. With her was her little Sasha, a boy of ten, small for his age, blue-eyed, chubby, with dimples in his cheeks. And scarcely had the boy walked into the yard when he ran after the cat, and at once there was the sound of this gay, joyous laugh.

"Is that your puss, auntie?" he asked Olenka. "When she has little ones, do give us a kitten. Mamma is awfully afraid of mice."

Olenka talked to him, and gave him tea. Her heart warmed and there was a sweet ache in her bosom, as though the boy had been her own child. And when he sat at the table in the evening, going over his lessons, she looked at him with deep tenderness and pity as she murmured to herself:

"You pretty pet! . . . my precious! . . . Such a fair little thing, and so clever."

"'An island is a piece of land which is entirely surrounded by water,'" he read aloud.

"An island is a piece of land," she repeated, and this was the first opinion to which she gave utterance with positive conviction after so many years of silence and dearth of ideas.

Now she had opinions of her own, and at supper she talked to Sasha's parents, saying how difficult the lessons were at the high schools, but that yet the high school was better than a commercial one, since with a high school education all careers were open to one, such as being a doctor or an engineer.

Sasha began going to the high school. His mother departed to Kharkov to her sister's and did not return; his father used to go off every day to inspect cattle, and would often be away from home for three days together, and it seemed to Olenka as though Sasha was entirely abandoned, that he was not wanted at home, that he was being starved, and she carried him off to her lodge and gave him a little room there.

And for six months Sasha lived in the lodge with her. Every morning Olenka came into his bedroom and found him fast asleep, sleeping noiselessly with his hand under his cheek. She was sorry to wake him.

"Sashenka," she would say mournfully, "get up, darling. It's time for school."

He would get up, dress and say his prayers and then sit down to breakfast, drink three glasses of tea, and eat two large cracknels and half a buttered roll. All this time he was hardly awake and a little ill-humored in consequence.

"You don't quite know your fable, Sashenka," Olenka would say, looking at him as though he were about to set off on a long journey. "What a lot of trouble I have with you! You must work and do your best, darling, and obey your teachers."

"Oh, do leave me alone!" Sasha would say.

Then he would go down the street to school, a little figure, wearing a big cap and carrying a satchel on his shoulder. Olenka would follow him noiselessly.

"Sashenka!" she would call after him, and she would pop into his hand a date or a caramel. When he reached the street where the school was, he would feel ashamed of being followed by a tall, stout woman; he would turn round and say:

"You'd better go home, auntie. I can go the rest of the way alone."

She would stand still and look after him fixedly till he had disappeared at the school-gate.

Ah, how she loved him! Of her former attachments not one had been so deep; never had her soul surrendered to any feeling so spontaneously, so disinterestedly, and so joyously as now that her maternal instincts were aroused. For this little boy with the dimple in his cheek and the big school cap, she would have given her whole life, she would have given it with joy and tears of tenderness. Why? Who can tell why?

When she had seen the last of Sasha, she returned home, contented and serene, brimming over with love; her face, which had grown younger during the last six months, smiled and beamed; people meeting her looked at her with pleasure.

"Good morning, Olga Semyonovna, darling. How are you, darling?"

"The lessons at the high school are very difficult now," she would relate at the market. "It's too much; in the first class yesterday they gave him a fable to learn by heart, and a Latin translation and a problem. You know it's too much for a little chap."

And she would begin talking about the teachers, the lessons, and the schoolbooks, saying just what Sasha said.

At three o'clock they had dinner together: in the evening they learned their lessons together and cried. When she put him to bed, she would stay a long time making the cross over him and murmuring a prayer; then she would go to bed and dream of that far-away misty future when Sasha would finish his studies and become a doctor or an engineer, would have a big house of his own with horses and a carriage, would get married and have children. . . . She would fall asleep still thinking of the same thing, and tears would run down her cheeks from her closed eyes, while the black cat lay purring beside her, *Mrr, mrr, mrr*.

Suddenly there would come a loud knock at the gate.

Olenka would wake up breathless with alarm, her heart throbbing. Half a minute later would come another knock.

"It must be a telegram from Kharkov," she would think, beginning to tremble from head to foot. "Sasha's mother is sending for him from Kharkov. . . . Oh, mercy on us!"

She was in despair. Her head, her hands, and her feet would turn chill, and she would feel that she was the most unhappy woman in the world. But another minute would pass, voices would be heard: it would turn out to be the veterinary surgeon coming home from the club.

"Well, thank God!" she would think.

And gradually the load in her heart would pass off, and she would feel at ease. She would go back to bed thinking of Sasha, who lay sound asleep in the next room, sometimes crying out in his sleep:

"I'll give it you! Get away! Shut up!"

QUESTIONS

1. What is the chief characteristic of Olenka's emotional life? How deep are her emotions? How long do they last? Are they selfish or unselfish? How does she respond to affronts?

2. Is Olenka a conventional or an unconventional woman? What characteristics must a person have to evoke her love? Is sexuality an important part of her love?
3. What is the chief characteristic of Olenka's intellectual life? How strong is her individuality? Does she have any pride?
4. What is the effect on Olenka's health and happiness of having someone to love?
5. Examine individually each of the four persons to whom Olenka gives her love in the story. Are they presented favorably or unfavorably? Does Olenka have any effect on their characters and values?
6. What is the author's attitude toward Olenka? Does he ridicule her or admire her?
7. What does the story say about love?

Paul Gallico

THE ENCHANTED DOLL

Today is the anniversary of that afternoon in April a year ago that I first saw the strange and alluring doll in the window of Abe Sheftel's stationery, cigar, and toy shop on Third Avenue near Fifteenth Street, just around the corner from my office, where the white plate with the black lettering on my door reads: SAMUEL AMONY, M.D.

And I feel impelled to try to set down on paper some record of the things that resulted from that meeting, though I am afraid it will be a crudely told story, for I am not a writer, but a doctor.

I remember just how it was that day: the first hint of spring wafted across the East River, mingling with the soft-coal smoke from the factories and the street smells of the poor neighborhood. The wagon of an itinerant flower seller at the curb was all gay with tulips, hyacinths, and boxes of pansies, and near by a hurdy-gurdy was playing "Some Enchanted Evening."

As I turned the corner and came abreast of Sheftel's, I was made once more aware of the poor collection of toys in the dusty window, and I remembered the approaching birthday of a small niece of mine in Cleveland, to whom I was in the habit of despatching modest gifts.

Therefore, I stopped and examined the window to see if there might be anything appropriate and browsed through the bewildering array of unappealing objects—a red toy fire engine, crudely made lead soldiers, cheap baseballs, gloves and bats, all a-jumble with boxes of withered

THE ENCHANTED DOLL   From *Further Confessions of a Story Writer* by Paul Gallico. Copyright © 1961 by Paul Gallico. Reprinted by permission of Doubleday & Company, Inc.

cigars, cartons of cigarettes, bottles of ink, pens, pencils, gritty stationery, and garish cardboard cut-out advertisements for soft drinks.

And thus it was my eyes eventually came to rest upon the doll tucked away in one corner. She was overshadowed by the surrounding articles and barely visible through the grime of decades collected on Abe's window, but I could see that she was made all of rag, with a painted face, and represented a little girl with the strangest, tenderest, most alluring and winsome expression on her face.

I could not wholly make her out, due to the shadows and the film through which I was looking, but I was aware that a tremendous impression had been made upon me, that somehow a contact had been established between her and myself, almost as though she had called to me. It was exactly as though I had run into a person as one does sometimes with a stranger in a crowded room with whose personality one is indelibly impressed and which lingers on.

I went inside and replied to Abe's greeting of "Hello, Doc, what can I do for you? You out of tobacco again?" with: "Let me see that rag doll, the one in the corner by the roller skates. I've got to send something to a kid niece of mine. . . ."

Abe's eyebrows went up into his bald head and he came around the counter, the edges of his open vest flapping. "That doll?" he said. "That doll now could cost quite a bit of money, maybe more than you would want to pay. She's special made."

Nevertheless he took her from the window and placed her in my hands and here it was that I received my second shock, for she had the most amazing and wonderful quality. No more than a foot long, she was as supple and live to the touch as though there were flesh and bones beneath the clothes instead of rag stuffing.

It was indeed, as Abe had said, hand-made, and its creator had endowed it with such lifelike creatures and grace that it gave one the curious feeling of an alter presence. Yet there was even more than that to her. Could a doll be said to have sex appeal in the length and proportions of her legs, the shape of her head, the swirl of her skirt over her hips? Was it possible for an emotion to have been sewn into the seams marking the contours of the tiny figure? For though I am young, I have seen too much, both in peace and war, to be either sentimental or subject to hallucination. Yet to hold this doll was to feel a contact with something warm, mysterious, feminine, and wonderful. I felt that if I did not put her down I would become moved by her in some unbearable fashion.

I laid her on the counter. "What's the price, Abe?"

"Fifteen dollars."

It was my turn to look astonished. Abe said, "I told you, didn't I? I only make a dollar on it. I don't need to make no profit on you, Doc.

You can have it for fourteen. Uptown in some a them big stores she gets as much as twenny and twenny-fi dollars for 'em."

"Who is 'she'?"

"Some woman over on Thirteenth Street who makes 'em. She's been there about a couple of years. She buys her cigarettes and papers here. That's how I come to get one once in a while. They sell quick."

"What is she like? What is her name?"

Abe replied, "I dunno, exactly—something like 'Calamity.' She's a big, flashy, red-haired dame, but hard. Wears a lot of furs. Not your type, Doc."

I couldn't understand it, or make the connection between the woman Abe described and the exquisite little creature that lay on the counter. "I'll take her," I said. It was more than I could afford, for my practice is among the poor, where one goes really to learn medicine. Yet I could not leave her lying there on the counter amidst the boxes of chewing gum, matches, punchboards, and magazines, for she was a creation, and something, some part of a human soul, had gone into the making of her. I counted out $14 and felt like a fool.

I felt even more of one when I had got her home and was repacking her to send her off to Cleveland. Again I felt that powerful impact of the tiny figure and realized that I had the greatest reluctance to part with her. She filled the small bedroom I had behind my consulting room with her presence and brought an indescribable longing to my throat and a sadness to my heart. For the first time since I had come out of the Army and had taken up practice I realized that I was lonely and that sometimes the satisfaction to be derived through helping the sick is not enough.

I said to myself, "Okay, Sam, boy. That's all you need now, is to start playing with dolls. The guys with the butterfly net will be along any moment."

When I came back from posting it to my niece, I thought that would be the end of it, but it wasn't. I couldn't get it out of my head. I thought about it often and tried to reconcile the emotion it had aroused with what Abe had told me of the flashy red-haired woman who had created the object, but I could not. Once I was even tempted to pursue the matter, find out who she was and perhaps see her. But just at that time Virus X hit in our neighborhood and drove everything else out of my head.

It was three months or so later that my telephone rang and a woman's voice said, "Dr. Amony?"

"Yes?"

"I passed by your place once and saw your sign. Are you expensive? Do you cost a lot for a visit?"

I was repelled by the quality of the voice and the calculation in it.

Nevertheless I replied, "I charge a dollar. If you are really ill and cannot afford to pay, I charge nothing."

"Okay. I could pay a dollar. But no more. You can come over. Callamit is the name. Rose Callamit, 937 East Thirteenth Street, second floor."

I did not make the connection at the time.

When I pushed the button under the name plate at that address, the buzzer sounded, the latch gave way, and I mounted two narrow, musty flights of stairs, dimly lighted and creaking. A door was opened an inch or so and I felt I was being subjected to scrutiny. Then the unpleasant voice said, "Dr. Amony? You can come in. I'm Rose Callamit."

I was startled by her. She was almost six feet tall, with brick, henna-dyed hair and an overpowering smell of cheap perfume. She had dark eyes, almond-shaped and slanted slightly in an Oriental fashion, and her mouth was full, thick-lipped, and heavily made up. There was a horrible vitality and flashy beauty about her. I placed her age at somewhere between forty-five and fifty.

The deepest shock, however, I sustained when I entered the room, which was one of those front parlor-bedrooms of the old-fashioned brownstone houses, furnished femininely, but with utter vulgarity by means of cheap prints, cheap satin cushions, and cheap glass perfume bottles. But hanging from the wall, lying about on the bed, or tossed carelessly onto the top of an old trunk were a dozen or so rag dolls, all of them different, yet, even at first glance, filled with the same indescribable appeal and charm as that of the similar little creature that had made such a profound impression upon me. I realized that I was in the presence of the creator of those astonishing puppets.

Rose Callamit said, "Tall, dark, and handsome, eh? Ain't you kind of young to be around doctoring people?"

I answered her sharply, for I was angry, uncomfortable, and irritated. The rediscovery of these beautiful and touching creatures in this cheap, disgusting atmosphere and in connection with this horrible woman had upset me. "I'm older than you think, and my looks are none of your business. If you don't want me to treat you I'd just as soon go."

"Now now, Doctor. Can't you take a compliment?"

"I'm not interested in compliments. Are you the patient?"

"No. It's my cousin. She's sick in the back room. I'll take you to her."

Before we went in, I had to know. I asked, "Do you make these dolls?"

"Yup. Why?"

I was filled with a sense of desolation. I mumbled, "I bought one once, for a niece. . . ."

She laughed. "Bet you paid plenty for it. They're the rage. Okay, come on."

She led me through a connecting bath and washroom into the

smaller room at the back and opened the door partly, shouting, "Essie, it's the doctor!" Then, before she pushed it wide to admit me, she cried loudly and brutally, "Don't be surprised, Doctor, she's a cripple!"

The pale girl, clad in a flannel peignoir, in the chair over by the window had a look of utter despair on her countenance. I was disgusted and angry again. The way the woman had said it was in itself crippling. She was not alone telling me that Essie was a cripple; she was reminding Essie.

I tried to observe as much and as quickly as possible, for the doctor who comes into the sickroom must hear and feel and see with his skin as well as his eyes and ears.

She could not have been more than twenty-four or twenty-five. She seemed to be nothing but a pair of huge and misery-stricken eyes and what was shocking was how low the lamp of life appeared to be burning in them. She was very ill. From that first visit I remembered the underlying sweetness of her presence, the lovely brow and shapely head, now too big for her wasted frame, the translucent, blue-veined hands, flaxen hair but limp and lusterless. She had a mouth shaped to incredible pathos, soft, pale coral, and ready to tremble.

But I saw something else that astounded me and gave my heart a great lift. She was surrounded by small tables. On one of them were paints and brushes, on others, rag material, linen, stuffing threads and needles, the paraphernalia needed for the making of dolls.

Her present illness and her deformity were two separate things, yet it was the latter that caught my attention immediately even from the door, something about the way she sat, and made me wonder. The technical name for her condition would be unintelligible to you, but if it was what it looked to me at first glance, it was curable.

I asked, "Can you walk, Essie?"

She nodded listlessly.

"Please walk to me."

"Oh don't," Essie said. "Don't make me."

The pleading in her voice touched me, but I had to be sure. I said, "I'm sorry, Essie. Please do as I ask."

She rose unsteadily from her chair and limped toward me, dragging her left leg. I was certain I was right. "That's good," I said to her, smiled encouragingly, and held out my hands to her. Something strange happened. For a moment we seemed to be caught up in one another's eyes. I felt she was being swept away and drowning in the dark pool of her misery and despair while the air all about me was shaken with the force of her silent cry to me for help. Her hands lifted toward mine for an instant in imitation of my gesture, then fell back to her side. The spell was broken.

I asked, "How long have you been this way, Essie?"

Rose Callamit said, "Oh, Essie's been a cripple for years. I didn't call you for that. She's sick. I want to know what's the matter with her."

Oh yes, she was sick. Sick unto death perhaps. I had felt that as soon as I came into the room. With my glance I invited the big, vulgar woman to leave, but she only laughed. "Not on your life, Doc. I'm staying right here. You find out what's the matter with Essie and then you can tell me."

When I had finished my examination I accompanied Rose into the front room. "Well?" she said.

I asked, "Did you know that her deformity could be cured? That with the proper treatment she could be walking normally in—"

"Shut up, you!" Her cry of rage struck like a blow against my ears. "Don't you ever dare mention that to her. I've had her looked at by people who know. I won't have any young idiot raising false hopes. If you ever do, you're through here. I want to know what's ailing her. She don't eat or sleep or work good any more. What did you find out?"

"Nothing," I replied. "I don't know. There is nothing wrong organically. But there is something terribly wrong somewhere. I want to see her again. In the meantime I'm prescribing a tonic and a stimulant. I'd like to look in again after a few days."

"You'll keep your big mouth shut about curing her cripple, you understand? Otherwise I'll get another doctor."

"All right," I said. I had to be able to return to visit Essie again. Later, we would see. . . .

When I picked up my hat and bag to leave I said, "I thought you told me it was you who made those dolls."

She looked startled for a moment as though she had never expected the subject to come up again. "I do," she snapped. "I design 'em. I let the kid work at 'em sometimes to help take her mind off she's a cripple and won't ever have a man."

But when I walked out into the bright, hot July day with the kids playing hopscotch on the sidewalk and handball against the old brewery wall and traffic grinding by, my heart told me that Rose Callamit had lied and that I had found the sweet spirit behind the enchanted doll. But the cold, clammy messenger of doctor's instinct warned me also that unless I could determine the cause of her decline, that spirit would not be long for this earth.

Her name, I found out later, was Nolan, Essie Nolan, and she was slowly dying from no determinable cause. I was sure that Rose Callamit had something to do with it. Not that Rose was killing her consciously. The red-haired woman was actually frightened. She wanted Essie alive, not dead, for Essie was her source of revenue and meal ticket.

After I had made a number of visits, Rose did not even bother to keep up the pretense that it was she herself who made the dolls, and I was able to piece together something of the picture.

When Essie was fifteen, her parents had been killed in an accident which also resulted in her injury. A court had awarded her in guardianship to her only relative, the cousin, Rose Callamit. When Essie's inheritance proved meager, Rose vented her spite by harping on her deformity. Through the years of their association, the older woman had made her deeply sensitive to and ashamed of her lameness. Her theme was always, "You are a hopeless cripple. No man will ever look at you. You will never be married or have children."

When Essie came of age, her spirit apparently was broken and she was completely subjugated to the will of her cousin, for she continued to remain with her and under her sway, living a lonely and hopeless existence. It was about this time that Essie first began to make the rag dolls, and Rose, for all of her vulgarity, greed, and indolence, had the shrewdness to recognize their unique quality and irresistible appeal. After she had sold the first ones she kept Essie at it from morning until night. Some weeks she was able to clear as much as $300 or $400. None of this, as far as I was able to determine, went to Essie.

Essie was completely under the domination of Rose and was afraid of her, but it was not that which was killing her. It was something else, and I could not find out what. Nor was I ever allowed to see her alone. Rose was aways present. Never had I been so conscious of the difference between good and evil as in that room with the girl, whose poor suppressed nature fluttered so feebly in her wasted body, and that gross, thick-lipped woman with the greedy eyes and patchouli smell who exhaled the odor of wickedness.

I did not mention my belief in the possibility of cure for Essie's lameness. It was more important to discover immediately what it was that was killing her. Rose would not let her be moved to a hospital. She would not spare the money.

For ten days I thought I had arrested the process that was destroying Essie before my eyes. I stopped her work on the dolls. I brought her some books to read, some sweets, and a bottle of sherry. When I returned for my next visit, she smiled at me for the first time, and the tremulousness, longing, hunger, the womanliness and despair of the smile would have broken a heart of stone.

"That's better," I said. "Another ten days of no work. Rest, sleep, read. Then we'll see."

But Rose Callamit glowered and there was an unpleasant expression about her mouth. Her huge, overpowering bulk seemed to fill the room with hatred.

The next time I came to call she was waiting for me in her own room. She had seven one dollar bills in her hand. She said, "Okay, Doc. That's all. We don't need you any more."

"But Essie—"

"Essie's okay. Fit as a fiddle. So long, Doc . . ."

My eyes wandered to the old trunk in the corner. There were three new dolls lying on top of it. Was it only my imagination, or was there yet a new quality to these mute, bewitched figurines? Was each in its way a birth and a death in one, a greeting to the beauties, desires, and pleasures of life and at the same time a farewell?

I had the most powerful impulse to push the monstrous woman aside and crash through the doors to see my patient. But the habits of medical ethics are too hard to break. When a physician is dismissed, it is his duty to go unless he has reason to suspect that his patient is meeting with foul play. I had no such reason. I had failed to determine the cause of Essie's illness; Rose was undoubtedly calling in another doctor, for she needed Essie's work for an easy living and would unquestionably try to protect such a meal ticket.

Thus, with great heaviness of heart, I departed. But I thought about Essie night and day.

It was shortly after this that I became ill myself. Imperceptibly at first, then finally noticeably: loss of appetite, loss of weight, lethargy, irritability, at nightfall a half a degree to a degree of temperature, moments of weakness when I felt as though somehow I could not go on with my work. I let Dr. Saul up at the hospital go over me. He thumped and pounded and listened, the obvious routine, and reported, "Nothing wrong with you, Sam. Take it a little easier. You've probably been overworking. Nature's protest."

But I knew it wasn't that.

I began to look shocking; my skin was losing its tone, my cheekbones were beginning to show, and I was hollow-eyed from loss of sleep. I did not like the look in my eyes, or the expression about my mouth. Sometimes my nights and my dreams were filled with fever and in them I saw Essie struggling to reach me while Rose Callamit held her imprisoned in her ugly, shapeless arms. I had never been free from worry over failure to diagnose Essie's case.

My whole faith in myself as a doctor was badly shaken. A desperately stricken human being had called upon me for help and I had failed. I could not even help myself. What right had I to call myself a doctor? All through one awful night of remorse and reproach the phrase burned through my brain as though written in fire:

"Physician, heal thyself!"

Yes, heal myself before I was fit to heal others. But heal myself from what? If anything, my symptoms resembled those of Essie Nolan. Essie! Essie! Essie! Always Essie!

Was Essie my sickness? Had she always been from the first moment that I had encountered that extension of her enchanted spirit embodied in the rag doll in Abe Sheftel's shop?

And as morning grayed my back-yard window and the elevated train thundered by in increasing tempo, I knew my disease. I was in love with Essie Nolan. When I could couple the words "love" and "Essie," when I could look up and cry "I love Essie Nolan! I want her! I need her person and her soul, forever at my side!" it was as though I could feel the fire of healing medicine glowing through my veins.

It had always been Essie, the warmth and yearning need, the tenderness that she expressed with her presence, and the odd, offbeat beauty of her, too, a beauty that would only reach its full flower when I had cured and restored her in every way.

For now, as the scales fell from my eyes and my powers were released again through the acknowledging and freeing inside of me of the hunger, love, and compassion I had for her, I knew the sickness of Essie Nolan in full, to its last pitiful detail, and what I must do and why I must see her alone if only for a few minutes if she were not to be lost to me and to the world forever.

That morning I telephoned Abe Sheftel and said, "This is Dr. Amony, Abe. Will you do something for me?"

"Are you kiddin'? After what you done for my boy—you name it."

"Look here! You remember Rose Callamit? The doll woman? Yes. The next time she comes into the store, find some means of telephoning me. Then hold her there, somehow. Talk, or do something, anything to make her stay there a little. I need twenty minutes. Okay? Got it? I'll bless you the rest of my life."

I was in a sweat for fear it would happen while I was on an outside call, and each time I returned to the office that day I stopped by the store, but Abe would merely shake his head. Then, at five o'clock in the afternoon the phone rang. It was Abe. He said merely, "It could be now," and hung up.

It took me no more than a minute or two to run the few blocks to the brownstone house where Essie lived and press the buzzer under another name plate. When the door clicked open I went upstairs, two steps at a time. If the door was locked I would have to get the landlady. But I was in luck. Rose had expected to be gone only a few moments, apparently, and it was open. I hurried through the connecting bath and, entering the back room, found Essie.

There was so little of her left.

She was sitting up in bed, but now the absolute pallor had been replaced with two red fever spots that burned in the middle of her cheeks, a danger sign more deadly than the wastage of her hands and body. She was still surrounded by the paints and bits of colored cloth and threads, as though she did not wish to die before she had put together one more image, one more dream, one last reflection of the sweet self that life had apparently so cruelly doomed to wither.

She looked up when I came in, startled out of her lethargy. She had expected it to be Rose. Her hand went to her breast and she said my name. Not "Dr. Amony," but my given one—"Samuel!"

I cried, "Essie! Thank God I'm in time. I came to help you. I know what it is that has been . . . making you ill. . . ."

She was in that state where nothing escaped her. She felt my hesitation and knew I had avoided saying ". . . that is killing you," for she whispered, "Does it matter now?"

I said, "There's still time, Essie. I know your secret. I know how to make you well. But you must listen to me while I tell you. Your life depends on it."

A change came over her. She closed her eyes for an instant and murmured, "No. Don't, please. Let me go. I don't want to know. It will be over soon."

I had not thought that she might be unwilling or unable to face it. And yet I had to go on now. I sat down and took her hand.

"Essie. Please listen. Give me your mind. When a body is undernourished we give it food; when it is anemic, we supply blood; when it lacks iron or hormones we give it tonic. But you have had a different kind of leakage. You have been drained dry of something else without which the soul and body cannot be held together."

Her eyes opened and I saw that they were filled with horror and a glazing fear. She seemed about to lose consciousness as she begged, "No! Don't say it!"

I thought perhaps she might die then and there. But the only hope for her, for us both, was to go on.

"Essie! My brave, dear girl. It is nothing so terrible. You need not be afraid. It is only that you have been drained of love. Look at me, Essie!"

My eyes caught and held her. I willed her to remain alive, to stay with me, to hear me out. "See, Essie, a person has just so great a reservoir of love to expend. It is drawn upon through life and must ever be replenished with tenderness, affection, warmth, and hope. Thus the supply is always renewed. But yours has been emptied until there was nothing left."

I could not be sure that she still heard me. "It was Rose Callamit," I continued. "She took away your every hope of life, love, and fulfillment. But what she did later to you was a much blacker crime. For she took away *your children!*"

There, it was out! Had I killed her? Had it been I who loved her beyond words who had administered the death blow? And yet I thought I saw a flicker of life in those poor, stricken eyes, and even perhaps the faintest reflection of relief.

"Oh yes, they were your children, Essie, those enchanted creatures you created. When you were convinced that you had lost your chance to be a woman, you compensated for it by embodying your hopes, your dreams, and, like every creator, whether mother or artist, a piece of your heart went into each of the dolls you made. You created them with love; you loved them like your own children and then each one was taken from you at birth by that money-hungry monster and nothing was given to you to replace them. And so you continued to take them from your heart, your tissue, and your blood until your life was being drained away from you. Persons can die from lack of love."

Essie stirred. Her head beneath the flaxen hair moved ever so slightly. The glaze passed from her eyes. I thought I felt the response of faint pressure from the cold hand in mine.

I cried, "But you won't, Essie, because I am here to tell you that I love you, to refill you to overflowing with all that has been taken from you. Do you hear me, Essie? I am not your doctor. I am a man telling you that I love you and cannot live without you."

I caught her incredulous whisper. "Love me? But I am a cripple."

"If you were a thousand times a cripple, I would only love you a thousand times more. But it isn't true. Rose Callamit lied to you. You can be cured. In a year I will have you walking like any other girl."

For the first time since I had known her I saw tears in her eyes and a tinge of color to her lovely brow. Then she lifted her arms to me with an utter and loving simplicity.

I picked her up out of the bed, with the blanket wrapped around her. She had no weight at all: she was like a bird. And she clung to me with a kind of sweet desperation, so that I wondered where the strength in her arms came from and the glow of her cheek against mine; she who but a moment ago had seemed so close to death.

A door slammed. Another crashed open. Rose Callamit stormed into the room. I felt Essie shudder with the old fear and bury her face in my shoulder.

But Rose was too late. It was all over. There was nothing she could do any more, and she knew it. There was not even a word spoken as I walked past her then and there carrying my burden held closely to me and went out the door and down into the street.

August had come to New York. Heat was shimmering from the melting pavements; no air stirred; water from the hydrants was flushing the streets and kids were bathing in the flow, screaming and shouting, as I carried Essie home.

That was three years ago and I am writing this on an anniversary. Essie is busy with our son and is preparing to welcome our second-to-be-born. She does not make dolls now. There is no need.

We have many kinds of anniversaries, but this is the one I celebrate privately and give humble thanks for—the day when I first saw and fell in love with the message from Essie's soul imprisoned in the enchanted doll that cried out to me from the grimy window of Abe Sheftel's shop on Third Avenue.

QUESTIONS

1. In what ways does the opening setting (paragraphs 3, 5, 6) set the tone for the story? Describe its tone.
2. Though the title suggests a fairy tale, nothing supernatural happens in the story. Is the story a fairy tale or is it realistic? Consider both events and characters in your answer.
3. Characterize Samuel, Rose, and Essie. Are they round or flat characters?
4. Comment on the protagonist's declaration, "I have seen too much, both in peace and war, to be either sentimental or subject to hallucination." Are his actions and responses in the story those of a war veteran?
5. What function is served by Abe Sheftel's inaccurate memory of Rose Callamit's name?
6. Does the story contain any coincidences?
7. Both this story and "The Darling" make considerable use of direct characterization and direct presentation of emotion. Which relies more heavily on direct presentation with least accompanying dramatization? Does the time span of either story partially account for its use of direct presentation?
8. Both this story and "The Darling" have something to say about love. In what respect are they similar in what they say? In what respect different? Which says what it says more convincingly? Which story is sentimental?

William Faulkner

THAT EVENING SUN

1

Monday is no different from any other weekday in Jefferson now. The streets are paved now, and the telephone and electric companies are cutting down more and more of the shade trees—the water oaks, the maples and locusts and elms—to make room for iron poles bearing clusters of bloated and ghostly and bloodless grapes, and we have a city laundry which makes the rounds on Monday morning, gathering the bundles of clothes into bright-colored, specially made motorcars: the soiled wearing of a whole week now flees apparitionlike behind alert and irritable electric horns, with a long diminishing noise of rubber and asphalt like tearing silk, and even the Negro women who still take in white people's washing after the old custom, fetch and deliver it in automobiles.

But fifteen years ago, on Monday morning the quiet, dusty, shady streets would be full of Negro women with, balanced on their steady, turbaned heads, bundles of clothes tied up in sheets, almost as large as cotton bales, carried so without touch of hand between the kitchen door of the white house and the blackened washpot beside a cabin door in Negro Hollow.

Nancy would set her bundle on the top of her head, then upon the bundle in turn she would set the black straw sailor hat which she wore winter and summer. She was tall, with a high, sad face sunken a little where her teeth were missing. Sometimes we would go a part of the way down the lane and across the pasture with her, to watch the balanced bundle and the hat that never bobbed nor wavered, even when she walked down into the ditch and up the other side and stooped through the fence. She would go down on her hands and knees and crawl through the gap, her head rigid, uptilted, the bundle steady as a rock or a balloon, and rise to her feet again and go on.

Sometimes the husbands of the washing women would fetch and deliver the clothes, but Jesus never did that for Nancy, even before Father told him to stay away from our house, even when Dilsey was sick and Nancy would come to cook for us.

And then about half the time we'd have to go down the lane to Nancy's cabin and tell her to come on and cook breakfast. We would stop at the ditch, because Father told us to not have anything to do with Jesus—he was a short black man, with a razor scar down his face—and we would throw rocks at Nancy's house until she came to the door, leaning her head around it without any clothes on.

"What yawl mean, chunking my house?" Nancy said. "What you little devils mean?"

"Father says for you to come on and get breakfast," Caddy said. "Father says it's over a half an hour now, and you've got to come this minute."

"I ain't studying no breakfast," Nancy said. "I going to get my sleep out."

"I bet you're drunk," Jason said. "Father says you're drunk. Are you drunk, Nancy?"

"Who says I is?" Nancy said. "I got to get my sleep out. I ain't studying no breakfast."

So after a while we quit chunking the cabin and went back home. When she finally came, it was too late for me to go to school. So we thought it was whiskey until that day they arrested her again and they were taking her to jail and they passed Mr. Stovall. He was the cashier in the bank and a deacon in the Baptist church, and Nancy began to say:

"When you going to pay me, white man? When you going to pay me, white man? It's been three times now since you paid me a cent—" Mr. Stovall knocked her down, but she kept on saying, "When you going to pay me, white man? It's been three times now since—" until Mr. Stovall kicked her in the mouth with his heel and the marshal caught Mr. Stovall back, and Nancy lying in the street, laughing. She turned her head and spat out some blood and teeth and said, "It's been three times now since he paid me a cent."

That was how she lost her teeth, and all that day they told about Nancy and Mr. Stovall, and all that night the ones that passed the jail could hear Nancy singing and yelling. They could see her hands holding to the window bars, and a lot of them stopped along the fence, listening to her and the jailer trying to make her stop. She didn't shut up until almost daylight, when the jailer began to hear a bumping and scraping upstairs and he went up there and found Nancy hanging from the window bar. He said that it was cocaine and not whiskey, because no nigger would try to commit suicide unless he was full of cocaine, because a nigger full of cocaine wasn't a nigger any longer.

The jailer cut her down and revived her; then he beat her, whipped her. She had hung herself with her dress. She had fixed it all right, but when they arrested her she didn't have on anything except a dress and so she didn't have anything to tie her hands with and she couldn't make her hands let go of the window ledge. So the jailer heard the noise and ran up there and found Nancy hanging from the window, stark naked, her belly already swelling out a little, like a little balloon.

When Dilsey was sick in her cabin and Nancy was cooking for us, we could see her apron swelling out; that was before Father told Jesus to stay away from the house. Jesus was in the kitchen, sitting behind the stove, with his razor scar on his black face like a piece of dirty string. He said it was a watermelon that Nancy had under her dress.

"It never come off of your vine, though," Nancy said.

"Off of what vine?" Caddy said.

"I can cut down the vine it did come off of," Jesus said.

"What makes you want to talk like that before these chillen?" Nancy said. "Whyn't you go on to work? You done et. You want Mr. Jason to catch you hanging around his kitchen, talking that way before these chillen?"

"Talking what way?" Caddy said. "What vine?"

"I can't hang around white man's kitchen," Jesus said. "But white man can hang around mine. White man can come in my house, but I can't stop him. When white man want to come in my house, I ain't got no house. I can't stop him, but he can't kick me outen it. He can't do that."

Dilsey was still sick in her cabin. Father told Jesus to stay off our place. Dilsey was still sick. It was a long time. We were in the library after supper.

"Isn't Nancy through in the kitchen yet?" Mother said. "It seems to me that she has had plenty of time to have finished the dishes."

"Let Quentin go and see," Father said. "Go and see if Nancy is through, Quentin. Tell her she can go on home."

I went to the kitchen. Nancy was through. The dishes were put away and the fire was out. Nancy was sitting in a chair, close to the cold stove. She looked at me.

"Mother wants to know if you are through," I said.

"Yes," Nancy said. She looked at me. "I done finished." She looked at me.

"What is it?" I said. "What is it?"

"I ain't nothing but a nigger," Nancy said. "It ain't none of it my fault."

She looked at me, sitting in the chair before the cold stove, the sailor hat on her head. I went back to the library. It was the cold stove and all, when you think of a kitchen being warm and busy and cheerful. And with a cold stove and the dishes all put away, and nobody wanting to eat at that hour.

"Is she through?" Mother said.

"Yessum," I said.

"What is she doing?" Mother said.

"She's not doing anything. She's through."

"I'll go and see," Father said.

"Maybe she's waiting for Jesus to come and take her home," Caddy said.

"Jesus is gone," I said. Nancy told us how one morning she woke up and Jesus was gone.

"He quit me," Nancy said. "Done gone to Memphis, I reckon. Dodging them city *po*-lice for a while, I reckon."

"And a good riddance," Father said. "I hope he stays there."

"Nancy's scaired of the dark," Jason said.

"So are you," Caddy said.

"I'm not," Jason said.

"Scairy cat," Caddy said.

"I'm not," Jason said.

"You, Candace!" Mother said. Father came back.

"I am going to walk down the lane with Nancy," he said. "She says that Jesus is back."

"Has she seen him?" Mother said.

"No. Some Negro sent her word that he was back in town. I won't be long."

"You'll leave me alone, to take Nancy home?" Mother said. "Is her safety more precious to you than mine?"

"I won't be long," Father said.

"You'll leave these children unprotected, with that Negro about?"

"I'm going, too," Caddy said. "Let me go, Father."

"What would he do with them, if he were unfortunate enough to have them?" Father said.

"I want to go, too," Jason said.

"Jason!" Mother said. She was speaking to Father. You could tell that by the way she said the name. Like she believed that all day Father had been trying to think of doing the thing she wouldn't like the most, and that she knew all the time that after a while he would think of it. I stayed quiet, because Father and I both knew that Mother would want him to make me stay with her if she just thought of it in time. So Father didn't look at me. I was the oldest. I was nine and Caddy was seven and Jason was five.

"Nonsense," Father said. "We won't be long."

Nancy had her hat on. We came to the lane. "Jesus always been good to me," Nancy said. "Whenever he had two dollars, one of them was mine." We walked in the lane. "If I can just get through the lane," Nancy said, "I be all right then."

The lane was always dark. "This is where Jason got scaired on Halloween," Caddy said.

"I didn't," Jason said.

"Can't Aunt Rachel do anything with him?" Father said. Aunt Rachel was old. She lived in a cabin beyond Nancy's by herself. She had white hair and she smoked a pipe in the door, all day long; she didn't work any more. They said she was Jesus' mother. Sometimes she said she was and sometimes she said she wasn't any kin to Jesus.

"Yes you did," Caddy said. "You were scairder than Frony. You were scairder than T.P. even. Scairder than niggers."

"Can't nobody do nothing with him," Nancy said. "He say I done woke up the devil in him and ain't but one thing going to lay it down again."

"Well, he's gone now," Father said. "There's nothing for you to be afraid of now. And if you'd just let white men alone."

"Let what white men alone?" Caddy said. "How let them alone?"

"He ain't gone nowhere," Nancy said. "I can feel him. I can feel him now, in this lane. He hearing us talk, every word, hid somewhere, waiting. I ain't seen him, and I ain't going to see him again but once more, with that razor in his mouth. That razor on that string down his back, inside his shirt. And then I ain't going to be even surprised."

"I wasn't scaired," Jason said.

"If you'd behave yourself, you'd have kept out of this," Father said. "But it's all right now. He's probably in Saint Louis now. Probably got another wife by now and forgot all about you."

"If he has, I better not find out about it," Nancy said. "I'd stand there right over them, and every time he wropped her, I'd cut that arm off. I'd cut his head off and I'd slit her belly and I'd shove—"

"Hush," Father said.

"Slit whose belly, Nancy?" Caddy said.

"I wasn't scaired," Jason said. "I'd walk right down this lane by myself."

"Yah," Caddy said. "You wouldn't dare to put your foot down in it if we were not here too."

2

Dilsey was still sick, so we took Nancy home every night until Mother said, "How much longer is this going on? I to be left alone in this big house while you take home a frightened Negro?"

We fixed a pallet in the kitchen for Nancy. One night we waked up, hearing the sound. It was not singing and it was not crying, coming up the dark stairs. There was a light in Mother's room and we heard Father going down the hall, down the back stairs, and Caddy and I went into the hall. The floor was cold. Our toes curled away from it while we listened to the sound. It was like singing and it wasn't like singing, like the sound that Negroes make.

Then it stopped and we heard Father going down the back stairs, and we went to the head of the stairs. Then the sound began again, in the stairway, not loud, and we could see Nancy's eyes halfway up the stairs, against the wall. They looked like cat's eyes do, like a big cat against the wall, watching us. When we came down the steps to where she was, she quit making the sound again, and we stood there until Father came back up from the kitchen, with his pistol in his hand. He went back down with Nancy and they came back with Nancy's pallet.

We spread the pallet in our room. After the light in Mother's room went off, we could see Nancy's eyes again. "Nancy," Caddy whispered, "are you asleep, Nancy?"

Nancy whispered something. It was oh or no, I don't know which. Like nobody had made it, like it came from nowhere and went nowhere, until it was like Nancy was not there at all; that I had looked so hard at her eyes on the stairs that they had got printed on my eyeballs, like the sun does when you have closed your eyes and there is no sun. "Jesus," Nancy whispered. "Jesus."

"Was it Jesus?" Caddy said. "Did he try to come into the kitchen?"

"Jesus," Nancy said. Like this: Jeeeeeeeeeeeeeeesus, until the sound went out, like a match or a candle does.

"It's the other Jesus she means," I said.

"Can you see us, Nancy?" Caddy whispered. "Can you see our eyes too?"

"I ain't nothing but a nigger," Nancy said. "God knows. God knows."

"What did you see down there in the kitchen?" Caddy whispered. "What tried to get in?"

"God knows," Nancy said. We could see her eyes. "God knows."

Dilsey got well. She cooked dinner. "You'd better stay in bed a day or two longer," Father said.

"What for?" Dilsey said. "If I had been a day later, this place would be to rack and ruin. Get on out of here now, and let me get my kitchen straight again."

Dilsey cooked supper too. And that night, just before dark, Nancy came into the kitchen.

"How do you know he's back?" Dilsey said. "You ain't seen him."

"Jesus is a nigger," Jason said.

"I can feel him," Nancy said. "I can feel him laying yonder in the ditch."

"Tonight?" Dilsey said. "Is he there tonight?"

"Dilsey's a nigger too," Jason said.

"You try to eat something," Dilsey said.

"I don't want nothing," Nancy said.

"I ain't a nigger," Jason said.

"Drink some coffee," Dilsey said. She poured a cup of coffee for Nancy. "Do you know he's out there tonight? How come you know it's tonight?"

"I know," Nancy said. "He's there, waiting. I know. I done lived with him too long. I know what he is fixing to do fore he know it himself."

"Drink some coffee," Dilsey said. Nancy held the cup to her mouth and blew into the cup. Her mouth pursed out like a spreading adder's, like a rubber mouth, like she had blown all the color out of her lips with blowing the coffee.

"I ain't a nigger," Jason said. "Are you a nigger, Nancy?"

"I hellborn, child," Nancy said. "I won't be nothing soon. I going back where I come from soon."

3

She began to drink the coffee. While she was drinking, holding the cup in both hands, she began to make the sound again. She made the sound into the cup and the coffee sploshed out onto her hands and her dress. Her eyes looked at us and she sat there, her elbows on her knees, holding the cup in both hands, looking at us across the wet cup, making the sound.

"Look at Nancy," Jason said. "Nancy can't cook for us now. Dilsey's got well now."

"You hush up," Dilsey said. Nancy held the cup in both hands, looking at us, making the sound, like there were two of them: one looking at us and the other making the sound. "Whyn't you let Mr. Jason telefoam the marshal?" Dilsey said. Nancy stopped then, holding the cup in her long brown hands. She tried to drink some coffee again, but it sploshed out of the cup, onto her hands and her dress, and she put the cup down. Jason watched her.

"I can't swallow it," Nancy said. "I swallows but it won't go down me."

"You go down to the cabin," Dilsey said. "Frony will fix you a pallet and I'll be there soon."

"Won't no nigger stop him," Nancy said.

"I ain't a nigger," Jason said. "Am I, Dilsey?"

"I reckon not," Dilsey said. She looked at Nancy. "I don't reckon so. What you going to do, then?"

Nancy looked at us. Her eyes went fast, like she was afraid there wasn't time to look, without hardly moving at all. She looked at us, at all three of us at one time. "You member that night I stayed in yawls' room?" she said. She told about how we waked up early the next morning, and played. We had to play quiet, on her pallet, until Father woke up and it was time to get breakfast. "Go and ask your maw to let me stay here tonight," Nancy said. "I won't need no pallet. We can play some more."

Caddy asked Mother. Jason went too. "I can't have Negroes sleeping in the bedrooms," Mother said. Jason cried. He cried until Mother said he couldn't have any dessert for three days if he didn't stop. Then Jason said he would stop if Dilsey would make a chocolate cake. Father was there.

"Why don't you do something about it?" Mother said. "What do we have officers for?"

"Why is Nancy afraid of Jesus?" Caddy said. "Are you afraid of Father, Mother?"

"What could the officers do?" Father said. "If Nancy hasn't seen him, how could the officers find him?"

"Then why is she afraid?" Mother said.

"She says he is there. She says she knows he is there tonight."

"Yet we pay taxes," Mother said. "I must wait here alone in this big house while you take a Negro woman home."

"You know that I am not lying outside with a razor," Father said.

"I'll stop if Dilsey will make a chocolate cake," Jason said. Mother told us to go out and Father said he didn't know if Jason would get a chocolate cake or not, but he knew what Jason was going to get in about a minute. We went back to the kitchen and told Nancy.

"Father said for you to go home and lock the door, and you'll be all right," Caddy said. "All right from what, Nancy? Is Jesus mad at you?" Nancy was holding the coffee cup in her hands again, her elbows on her knees and her hands holding the cup between her knees. She was looking into the cup. "What have you done that made Jesus mad?" Caddy said. Nancy let the cup go. It didn't break on the floor, but the coffee spilled out, and Nancy sat there with her hands still making the shape of the cup. She began to make the sound again, not loud. Not singing and not unsinging. We watched her.

"Here," Dilsey said. "You quit that, now. You get aholt of yourself. You wait here. I going to get Versh to walk home with you." Dilsey went out.

We looked at Nancy. Her shoulders kept shaking, but she quit making the sound. We stood and watched her.

"What's Jesus going to do to you?" Caddy said. "He went away."

Nancy looked at us. "We had fun that night I stayed in yawls' room, didn't we?"

"I didn't," Jason said. "I didn't have any fun."

"You were asleep in Mother's room," Caddy said. "You were not there."

"Let's go down to my house and have some more fun," Nancy said.

"Mother won't let us," I said. "It's too late now."

"Don't bother her," Nancy said. "We can tell her in the morning. She won't mind."

"She wouldn't let us," I said.

"Don't ask her now," Nancy said. "Don't bother her now."

"She didn't say we couldn't go," Caddy said.

"We didn't ask," I said.

"If you go, I'll tell," Jason said.

"We'll have fun," Nancy said. "They won't mind, just to my house. I been working for yawl a long time. They won't mind."

"I'm not afraid to go," Caddy said. "Jason is the one that's afraid. He'll tell."

"I'm not," Jason said.

"Yes, you are," Caddy said. "You'll tell."

"I won't tell," Jason said. "I'm not afraid."

"Jason ain't afraid to go with me," Nancy said. "Is you, Jason?"

"Jason is going to tell," Caddy said. The lane was dark. We passed the pasture gate. "I bet if something was to jump out from behind that gate, Jason would holler."

"I wouldn't," Jason said. We walked down the lane. Nancy was talking loud.

"What are you talking so loud for, Nancy?" Caddy said.

"Who; me?" Nancy said. "Listen at Quentin and Caddy and Jason saying I'm talking loud."

"You talk like there was five of us here," Caddy said. "You talk like Father was here too."

"Who; me talking loud, Mr. Jason?" Nancy said.

"Nancy called Jason 'Mister,' " Caddy said.

"Listen how Caddy and Quentin and Jason talk," Nancy said.

"We're not talking loud," Caddy said. "You're the one that's talking like Father—"

"Hush," Nancy said; "hush, Mr. Jason."

"Nancy called Jason 'Mister' aguh—"

"Hush," Nancy said. She was talking loud when we crossed the ditch and stooped through the fence where she used to stoop through with the clothes on her head. Then we came to her house. We were going fast then. She opened the door. The smell of the house was like the lamp and the smell of Nancy was like the wick, like they were waiting for one another to begin to smell. She lit the lamp and closed the door and put the bar up. Then she quit talking loud, looking at us.

"What're we going to do?" Caddy said.

"What do yawl want to do?" Nancy said.

"You said we would have some fun," Caddy said.

There was something about Nancy's house; something you could smell besides Nancy and the house. Jason smelled it, even. "I don't want to stay here," he said. "I want to go home."

"Go home, then," Caddy said.

"I don't want to go by myself," Jason said.

"We're going to have some fun," Nancy said.

"How?" Caddy said.

Nancy stood by the door. She was looking at us, only it was like she had emptied her eyes, like she had quit using them. "What do you want to do?" she said.

"Tell us a story," Caddy said. "Can you tell a story?"

"Yes," Nancy said.

"Tell it," Caddy said. We looked at Nancy. "You don't know any stories."

"Yes," Nancy said. "Yes I do."

She came and sat in a chair before the hearth. There was a little fire there. Nancy built it up, when it was already hot inside. She built a good blaze. She told a story. She talked like her eyes looked, like her eyes watching us and her voice talking to us did not belong to her. Like she was living somewhere else, waiting somewhere else. She was outside the cabin. Her voice was inside and the shape of her, that Nancy that could stoop under a barbed wire fence with a bundle of clothes balanced on her head as though without weight, like a balloon, was there. But that was all. "And so this here queen come walking up to the ditch, where that bad man was hiding. She was walking up to the ditch, and she say, 'If I can just get past this here ditch,' was what she say . . ."

"What ditch?" Caddy said. "A ditch like that one out there? Why did a queen want to go into a ditch?"

"To get to her house," Nancy said. She looked at us. "She had to cross the ditch to get into her house quick and bar the door."

"Why did she want to go home and bar the door?" Caddy said.

4

Nancy looked at us. She quit talking. She looked at us. Jason's legs stuck straight out of his pants where he sat on Nancy's lap. "I don't think that's a good story," he said. "I want to go home."

"Maybe we had better," Caddy said. She got up from the floor. "I bet they are looking for us right now." She went toward the door.

"No," Nancy said. "Don't open it." She got up quick and passed Caddy. She didn't touch the door, the wooden bar.

"Why not?" Caddy said.

"Come back to the lamp," Nancy said. "We'll have fun. You don't have to go."

"We ought to go," Caddy said. "Unless we have a lot of fun." She and Nancy came back to the fire, the lamp.

"I want to go home," Jason said. "I'm going to tell."

"I know another story," Nancy said. She stood close to the lamp. She looked at Caddy, like when your eyes look up at a stick balanced on your nose. She had to look down to see Caddy, but her eyes looked like that, like when you are balancing a stick.

"I won't listen to it," Jason said. "I'll bang on the floor."

"It's a good one," Nancy said. "It's better than the other one."

"What's it about?" Caddy said. Nancy was standing by the lamp. Her hand was on the lamp, against the light, long and brown.

"Your hand is on that hot globe," Caddy said. "Don't it feel hot to your hand?"

Nancy looked at her hand on the lamp chimney. She took her hand away, slow. She stood there, looking at Caddy, wringing her long hand as though it were tied to her wrist with a string.

"Let's do something else," Caddy said.

"I want to go home," Jason said.

"I got some popcorn," Nancy said. She looked at Caddy and then at Jason and then at me and then at Caddy again. "I got some popcorn."

"I don't like popcorn," Jason said. "I'd rather have candy."

Nancy looked at Jason. "You can hold the popper." She was still wringing her hand; it was long and limp and brown.

"All right," Jason said. "I'll stay a while if I can do that. Caddy can't hold it. I'll want to go home again if Caddy holds the popper."

Nancy built up the fire. "Look at Nancy putting her hands in the fire," Caddy said. "What's the matter with you, Nancy?"

"I got popcorn," Nancy said. "I got some." She took the popper from under the bed. It was broken. Jason began to cry.

"Now we can't have any popcorn," he said.

"We ought to go home anyway," Caddy said. "Come on, Quentin."

"Wait," Nancy said; "wait. I can fix it. Don't you want to help me fix it?"

"I don't think I want any," Caddy said. "It's too late now."

"You help me, Jason," Nancy said. "Don't you want to help me?"

"No," Jason said. "I want to go home."

"Hush," Nancy said; "hush. Watch. Watch me. I can fix it so Jason can hold it and pop the corn." She got a piece of wire and fixed the popper.

"It won't hold good," Caddy said.

"Yes it will," Nancy said. "Yawl watch. Yawl help me shell some corn."

The popcorn was under the bed too. We shelled it into the popper and Nancy helped Jason hold the popper over the fire.

"It's not popping," Jason said. "I want to go home."

"You wait," Nancy said. "It'll begin to pop. We'll have fun then."

She was sitting close to the fire. The lamp was turned up so high it was beginning to smoke. "Why don't you turn it down some?" I said.

"It's all right," Nancy said. "I'll clean it. Yawl wait. The popcorn will start in a minute."

"I don't believe it's going to start," Caddy said. "We ought to start home, anyway. They'll be worried."

"No," Nancy said. "It's going to pop. Dilsey will tell um yawl with me. I been working for yawl long time. They won't mind if yawl at my house. You wait, now. It'll start popping any minute now."

Then Jason got some smoke in his eyes and he began to cry. He dropped the popper into the fire. Nancy got a wet rag and wiped Jason's face, but he didn't stop crying.

"Hush," she said. "Hush." He didn't hush. Caddy took the popper out of the fire.

"It's burned up," she said. "You'll have to get some more popcorn, Nancy."

"Did you put all of it in?" Nancy said.

"Yes," Caddy said. Nancy looked at Caddy. Then she took the

popper and opened it and poured the cinders into her apron and began to sort the grains, her hands long and brown, and we watched her.

"Haven't you got any more?" Caddy said.

"Yes," Nancy said; "yes. Look. This here ain't burnt. All we need to do is—"

"I want to go home," Jason said. "I'm going to tell."

"Hush," Caddy said. We all listened. Nancy's head was already turned toward the barred door, her eyes filled with red lamplight. "Somebody is coming," Caddy said.

Then Nancy began to make that sound again, not loud, sitting there above the fire, her long hands dangling between her knees; all of a sudden water began to come out on her face in big drops, running down her face, carrying in each one a little turning ball of firelight like a spark until it dropped off her chin. "She's not crying," I said.

"I ain't crying," Nancy said. Her eyes were closed. "I ain't crying. Who is it?"

"I don't know," Caddy said. She went to the door and looked out. "We've got to go now," she said. "Here comes Father."

"I'm going to tell," Jason said. "Yawl made me come."

The water still ran down Nancy's face. She turned in her chair. "Listen. Tell him. Tell him we going to have fun. Tell him I take good care of yawl until in the morning. Tell him to let me come home with yawl and sleep on the floor. Tell him I won't need no pallet. We'll have fun. You member last time how we had so much fun?"

"I didn't have fun," Jason said. "You hurt me. You put smoke in my eyes. I'm going to tell."

5

Father came in. He looked at us. Nancy did not get up.

"Tell him," she said.

"Caddy made us come down here," Jason said. "I didn't want to."

Father came to the fire. Nancy looked up at him. "Can't you go to Aunt Rachel's and stay?" he said. Nancy looked up at Father, her hands between her knees. "He's not here," Father said. "I would have seen him. There's not a soul in sight."

"He in the ditch," Nancy said. "He waiting in the ditch yonder."

"Nonsense," Father said. He looked at Nancy. "Do you know he's there?"

"I got the sign," Nancy said.

"What sign?"

"I got it. It was on the table when I come in. It was a hogbone, with blood meat still on it, laying by the lamp. He's out there. When yawl walk out that door, I gone."

"Gone where, Nancy?" Caddy said.

"I'm not a tattletale," Jason said.

"Nonsense," Father said.

"He out there," Nancy said. "He looking through that window this minute, waiting for yawl to go. Then I gone."

"Nonsense," Father said. "Lock up your house and we'll take you on to Aunt Rachel's."

"'Twon't do no good," Nancy said. She didn't look at Father now, but he looked down at her, at her long, limp, moving hands. "Putting it off won't do no good."

"Then what do you want to do?" Father said.

"I don't know," Nancy said. "I can't do nothing. Just put it off. And that don't do no good. I reckon it belong to me. I reckon what I going to get ain't no more than mine."

"Get what?" Caddy said. "What's yours?"

"Nothing," Father said. "You all must get to bed."

"Caddy made me come," Jason said.

"Go on to Aunt Rachel's," Father said.

"It won't do no good," Nancy said. She sat before the fire, her elbows on her knees, her long hands between her knees. "When even your own kitchen wouldn't do no good. When even if I was sleeping on the floor in the room with your chillen, and the next morning there I am, and blood—"

"Hush," Father said. "Lock the door and put out the lamp and go to bed."

"I scaired of the dark," Nancy said. "I scaired for it to happen in the dark."

"You mean you're going to sit right here with the lamp lighted?" Father said. Then Nancy began to make the sound again, sitting before the fire, her long hands between her knees. "Ah, damnation," Father said. "Come along, chillen. It's past bedtime."

"When yawl go home, I gone," Nancy said. She talked quieter now, and her face looked quiet, like her hands. "Anyway, I got my coffin money saved up with Mr. Lovelady." Mr. Lovelady was a short, dirty man who collected the Negro insurance, coming around to the cabins or the kitchens every Saturday morning, to collect fifteen cents. He and his wife lived at the hotel. One morning his wife committed suicide. They had a child, a little girl. He and the child went away. After a week or two he came back alone. We would see him going along the lanes and the back streets on Saturday mornings.

"Nonsense," Father said. "You'll be the first thing I'll see in the kitchen tomorrow morning."

"You'll see what you'll see, I reckon," Nancy said. "But it will take the Lord to say what that will be."

We left her sitting before the fire.

"Come and put the bar up," Father said. But she didn't move. She didn't look at us again, sitting quietly there between the lamp and the fire. From some distance down the lane we could look back and see her through the open door.

"What, Father?" Caddy said. "What's going to happen?"

"Nothing," Father said. Jason was on Father's back, so Jason was the tallest of all of us. We went down into the ditch. I looked at it, quiet. I couldn't see much where the moonlight and the shadows tangled.

"If Jesus *is* hid here, he can see us, can't he?" Caddy said.

"He's not there," Father said. "He went away a long time ago."

"You made me come," Jason said, high; against the sky it looked like Father had two heads, a little one and a big one. "I didn't want to."

We went up out of the ditch. We could still see Nancy's house and the open door, but we couldn't see Nancy now, sitting before the fire with the door open, because she was tired. "I just done got tired," she said. "I just a nigger. It ain't no fault of mine."

But we could hear her, because she began just after we came up out of the ditch, the sound that was not singing and not unsinging. "Who will do our washing now, Father?" I said.

"I'm not a nigger," Jason said, high and close above Father's head.

"You're worse," Caddy said, "you are a tattletale. If something was to jump out, you'd be scairder than a nigger."

"I wouldn't," Jason said.

"You'd cry," Caddy said.

"Caddy," Father said.

"I wouldn't!" Jason said.

"Scairy cat," Caddy said.

"Candace!" Father said.

QUESTIONS

1. Who is the protagonist of this story? Characterize her fully. Is she a round or flat character? How does she differ from the typical protagonist of a commercial story?

2. The central conflict in this story is man-vs.-man and is partly physical, the favorite kind of conflict of the writers of pulp fiction. But in this story the conflict is not resolved. The story ends without our knowing whether Jesus ever killed Nancy or not. Why? What is the real subject of the story?

3. Is Faulkner primarily interested in presenting Nancy's terror or in producing terror in the reader? Is he interested in terror for its own sake, or is he interested also in exploring the human causes of the terror?

4. Why is Jesus angry with Nancy? Is Jesus the villain of the story? Is Mr.

Stovall? Explore the causes of the central situation, taking into account:
   a. Jesus' speech about his house and white man's house.
   b. Nancy's attitude toward her sin.
   c. Father's advice to Nancy and his treatment of Jesus.
   d. The jailer's treatment of Nancy.
   e. Mother's attitude toward Blacks.
   f. The attitudes of Caddy and Jason toward Blacks.
5. The story explores the relationship which existed at that time between two worlds—the black and the white—and also the relationships within each. In reference to the latter, describe the following relationships: (a) Jesus and Nancy, (b) Father and Mother, (c) Caddy and Jason. Does each of these involve a conflict? Is fright confined to the first? How might those relationships differ in today's society?
6. How is Nancy's terror *dramatized?* How rational or irrational is it?
7. Explain the title. From what well-known song is it a quotation?
8. This story is given an unusual twist because an adult problem is seen through the eyes of children. How much do the three children understand of what is going on? What advantages does this point of view have?
9. Show how Nancy and Jason are parallel characters.
10. What is the irony in naming the antagonist "Jesus"?
11. Compare this story with "Haply, the Soul of My Grandmother" in plausibility and meaningfulness.

8

Fantasy

Truth in fiction is not the same as fidelity to fact. Fiction, after all, is the opposite of fact. It is a game of make-believe—though, at its best, a serious game—in which the author conceives characters and situations in his mind and sets them down on paper. And yet these characters and situations, if deeply imagined, may embody truths of human life and behavior more fully and significantly than any number of the miscellaneous facts reported on the front pages of our morning papers. The purpose of the interpretive artist is to communicate truths by means of imagined facts.

The story writer begins, then, by saying "Let's suppose . . ." "Let's suppose," for instance, "that a society exists where a ritual of human sacrifice is held once a year on a special day and a young child is chosen to be the executioner." From this initial supposition the author goes on to write a story ("Millstone for the Sun's Day") which, though entirely imaginary in the sense that it never happened, nevertheless reveals convincingly to us some truths of human behavior.

But now, what if the author goes a step further and supposes, not just something that might very well have happened though it didn't, but something highly improbable—something that could happen, say, only as the result of a very surprising coincidence? What if he begins, "Let's suppose that a woman-hater and an intelligent, attractive woman find themselves alone on a desert island"? This initial supposition causes us to stretch our imaginations a bit further, but is not this situation just as capable of revealing human truths as the former? The psychologist puts a rat in a maze (certainly an improbable situation for a rat), observes his reactions to the maze, and discovers some truth of rat-nature. The author may put his imagined characters on an imagined desert island, imaginatively study their reactions, and reveal some truth of human nature. The improbable initial situation may yield as much truth as the probable one.

From the improbable it is but one step further to the impossible (as we know it in this life). Why should not our author begin, "Let's suppose that a miser and his termagant wife find themselves in hell." Or, "Let's suppose that a timid but ambitious man discovers how to make himself invisible." Or, "Let's suppose that a primitive scapegoat ritual still survives in contemporary America." Could not these situations also be used to exhibit human truth?

The nonrealistic story, or FANTASY, is one which transcends the bounds of known reality. Commonly, it conjures up a strange and marvelous world, which one enters by falling down a rabbit-hole or climbing up a beanstalk or getting shipwrecked in an unfamiliar ocean or dreaming a dream; or else it introduces strange powers and occult forces into the world of ordinary reality, allowing one to foretell the future or communicate with the dead or separate his mind from his body or turn himself into a monster. It introduces human beings into a world where the ordinary laws of nature are suspended or superseded and where the landscape and its creatures are unfamiliar; or it introduces ghosts or fairies or dragons or werewolves or talking animals or invaders from Mars or miraculous occurrences into the normal world of human beings. Fables, ghost stories, science fiction— all are types of fantasy.

Fantasy may be escapist or interpretive, true or false. The space ship on its way to a distant planet may be filled with stock characters or with human beings. The author may be interested chiefly in exhibiting its mechanical marvels or providing thrills and adventures, or he may use it as a means of creating exacting circumstances in which human behavior may be sharply observed and studied. Fantasy, like other elements of fiction, may be employed sheerly for its own sake, or as a means of communicating an important insight. The appeal may be to our taste for the strange or to our need for the true. The important point to remember is that truth in fiction is not to be identified with realism in method. Stories which never depart from the three dimensions of actuality may distort and falsify life. Stories which fly on the wings of fantasy may be vehicles for truth. Fantasy may convey truth through symbolism or allegory, or simply by providing an unusual setting for the observation of human beings. Some of the world's greatest works of literature have been partly or wholly fantasy: *Odyssey, The Book of Job, The Divine Comedy, The Tempest, Pilgrim's Progress, Gulliver's Travels, Faust, Alice in Wonderland*. All of these have had important things to say about the human condition.

We must not judge a story, then, by whether or not it stays within the limits of the possible. Rather, we begin by granting every story a "Let's suppose"—an initial assumption. The initial assumption may be plausible or implausible. The writer may begin with an ordinary, everyday situation or with a far-fetched, improbable coincidence. Or he may be allowed to suspend a law of nature or to create a marvelous being or machine or place. But once we have granted him his impossibility, we have a right to demand probability in his treatment of it. The realm of fantasy is not a realm in which *all* laws of logic are suspended. We need to ask, too, for what reason the story employs the element of fantasy. Is it used simply for its own strangeness, or for thrills or surprises or laughs? Or is it used to illumine the more normal world of our experience? What is the purpose of the author's invention? Is it, like a roller coaster, simply a machine for producing thrills? Or does it, like an observation balloon, provide a vantage point from which we may view the world?

Ray Bradbury

APRIL 2000: THE THIRD EXPEDITION

The ship came down from space. It came from the stars and the black velocities, and the shining movements, and the silent gulfs of space. It was a new ship; it had fire in its body and men in its metal cells, and it moved with a clean silence, fiery and warm. In it were seventeen men, including a captain. The crowd at the Ohio field had shouted and waved their hands up into the sunlight, and the rocket had bloomed out great flowers of heat and color and run away into space on the *third* voyage to Mars!

Now it was decelerating with metal efficiency in the upper Martian atmospheres. It was still a thing of beauty and strength. It had moved in the midnight waters of space like a pale sea leviathan; it had passed the most ancient moon and thrown itself onward into one nothingness following another. The men within it had been battered, thrown about, sickened, made well again, each in his turn. One man had died, but now the remaining sixteen, with their eyes clear in their heads and their faces pressed to the thick glass ports, watched Mars swing up under them.

"Mars!" cried Navigator Lustig.

"Good old Mars!" said Samuel Hinkston, archaeologist.

"Well," said Captain John Black.

The rocket landed on a lawn of green grass. Outside, upon this lawn, stood an iron deer. Further up on the green stood a tall brown Victorian house, quiet in the sunlight, all covered with scrolls and rococo, its windows made of blue and pink and yellow and green colored glass.

Upon the porch were hairy geraniums and an old swing which was hooked into the porch ceiling and which now swung back and forth, back and forth, in a little breeze. At the summit of the house was a cupola with diamond leaded-glass windows and a dunce-cap roof! Through the front window you could see a piece of music titled "Beautiful Ohio" sitting on the music rest.

Around the rocket in four directions spread the little town, green and motionless in the Martian spring. There were white houses and red brick ones, and tall elm trees blowing in the wind, and tall maples and horse chestnuts. And church steeples with golden bells silent in them.

The rocket men looked out and saw this. Then they looked at one another and then they looked out again. They held to each other's elbows, suddenly unable to breathe, it seemed. Their faces grew pale.

"I'll be damned," whispered Lustig, rubbing his face with his numb fingers. "I'll be damned."

"It just can't be," said Samuel Hinkston.

"Lord," said Captain John Black.

There was a call from the chemist. "Sir, the atmosphere is thin for breathing. But there's enough oxygen. It's safe."

"Then we'll go out," said Lustig.

"Hold on," said Captain John Black. "How do we know what this is?"

"It's a small town with thin but breathable air in it, sir."

"And it's a small town the like of Earth towns," said Hinkston, the archaeologist. "Incredible. It can't be, but it *is*."

Captain John Black looked at him idly. "Do you think that the civilizations of two planets can progress at the same rate and evolve in the same way, Hinkston?"

"I wouldn't have thought so, sir."

Captain Black stood by the port. "Look out there. The geraniums. A specialized plant. That specific variety has only been known on Earth for fifty years. Think of the thousands of years it takes to evolve plants. Then tell me if it is logical that the Martians should have: one, leaded-glass windows; two, cupolas; three, porch swings; four, an instrument that looks like a piano and probably *is* a piano; and five, if you look closely through this telescopic lens here, is it logical that a Martian composer would have published a piece of music titled, strangely enough, 'Beautiful Ohio'? All of which means that we have an Ohio River on Mars!"

"Captain Williams, of course!" cried Hinkston.

"What?"

"Captain Williams and his crew of three men! Or Nathaniel York and his partner. That would explain it!"

"That would explain absolutely nothing. As far as we've been able to figure, the York expedition exploded the day it reached Mars, killing York and his partner. As for Williams and his three men, their ship exploded the second day after their arrival. At least the pulsations from their radios ceased at that time, so we figure that if the men were alive after that they'd have contacted us. And anyway, the York expedition was only a year ago, while Captain Williams and his men landed here some time during last August. Theorizing that they are still alive, could they, even with the help of a brilliant Martian race, have built such a town as this and *aged* it in so short a time? Look at that town out there; why, it's been standing here for the last seventy years. Look at the wood on the porch newel; look at the trees, a century old, all of them! No, this isn't York's work or Williams'. It's something else. I don't like it. And I'm not leaving the ship until I know what it is."

"For that matter," said Lustig, nodding, "Williams and his men, as well as York, landed on the *opposite* side of Mars. We were very careful to land on *this* side."

"An excellent point. Just in case a hostile local tribe of Martians killed off York and Williams, we have instructions to land in a further region, to forestall a recurrence of such a disaster. So here we are, as far as we know, in a land that Williams and York never saw."

"Damn it," said Hinkston, "I want to get out into this town, sir, with your permission. It may be there *are* similar thought patterns, civilization graphs on every planet in our sun system. We may be on the threshold of the greatest psychological and metaphysical discovery of our age!"

"I'm willing to wait a moment," said Captain John Black.

"It may be, sir, that we're looking upon a phenomenon that, for the first time, would absolutely prove the existence of God, sir."

"There are many people who are of good faith without such proof, Mr. Hinkston."

"I'm one myself, sir. But certainly a town like this could not occur without divine intervention. The *detail*. It fills me with such feelings that I don't know whether to laugh or cry."

"Do neither, then, until we know what we're up against."

"Up against?" Lustig broke in. "Against nothing, Captain. It's a good, quiet green town, a lot like the old-fashioned one I was born in. I like the looks of it."

"When were you born, Lustig?"

"Nineteen-fifty, sir."

"And you, Hinkston?"

"Nineteen fifty-five, sir. Grinnell, Iowa. And this looks like home to me."

"Hinkston, Lustig. I could be either of your fathers. I'm just eighty years old. Born in 1920 in Illinois, and through the grace of God and a science that, in the last fifty years, knows how to make *some* old men young again, here I am on Mars, not any more tired than the rest of you, but infinitely more suspicious. This town out here looks very peaceful and cool, and so much like Green Bluff, Illinois, that it frightens me. It's too *much* like Green Bluff." He turned to the radioman. "Radio Earth. Tell them we've landed. That's all. Tell them we'll radio a full report tomorrow."

"Yes, sir."

Captain Black looked out the rocket port with his face that should have been the face of a man eighty but seemed like the face of a man in his fortieth year. "Tell you what we'll do, Lustig; you and I and Hinkston'll look the town over. The other men'll stay aboard. If anything happens they can get the hell out. A loss of three men's better than a whole ship. If something bad happens, our crew can warn the next rocket. That's Captain Wilder's rocket, I think, due to be ready to take off next Christmas. If there's something hostile about Mars we certainly want the next rocket to be well armed."

"So are we. We've got a regular arsenal with us."

"Tell the men to stand by the guns then. Come on, Lustig, Hinkston."

The three men walked together down through the levels of the ship.

It was a beautiful spring day. A robin sat on a blossoming apple tree and sang continuously. Showers of petal snow sifted down when the wind touched the green branches, and the blossom scent drifted upon the air. Somewhere in the town someone was playing the piano and the music came and went, came and went, softly, drowsily. The song was "Beautiful Dreamer." Somewhere else a phonograph, scratchy and faded, was hissing out a record of "Roamin' in the Gloamin'," sung by Harry Lauder.

The three men stood outside the ship. They sucked and gasped at the thin, thin air and moved slowly so as not to tire themselves.

Now the phonograph record being played was:

> "Oh, give me a June night
> The moonlight and you . . ."

Lustig began to tremble. Samuel Hinkston did likewise.

The sky was serene and quiet, and somewhere a stream of water ran through the cool caverns and tree shadings of a ravine. Somewhere a horse and wagon trotted and rolled by, bumping.

"Sir," said Samuel Hinkston, "it must be, it *has* to be, that rocket travel to Mars began in the years before the first World War!"

"No."

"How else can you explain these houses, the iron deer, the pianos, the music?" Hinkston took the captain's elbow persuasively and looked into the captain's face. "Say that there were people in the year 1905 who hated war and got together with some scientists in secret and built a rocket and came out here to Mars————"

"No, no, Hinkston."

"Why not? The world was a different world in 1905; they could have kept it a secret much more easily."

"But a complex thing like a rocket, no, you couldn't keep it secret."

"And they came up here to live, and naturally the houses they built were similar to Earth houses because they brought the culture with them."

"And they've lived here all these years?" said the captain.

"In peace and quiet, yes. Maybe they made a few trips, enough to bring enough people here for one small town, and then stopped for fear of being discovered. That's why this town seems so old-fashioned. I don't see a thing, myself, older than the year 1927, do you? Or maybe, sir, rocket travel is older than we think. Perhaps it started in some part of the world centuries ago and was kept secret by the small number of men who came to Mars with only occasional visits to Earth over the centuries."

"You make it sound almost reasonable."

"It has to be. We've the proof here before us; all we have to do is find some people and verify it."

Their boots were deadened of all sound in the thick green grass. It smelled from a fresh mowing. In spite of himself, Captain John Black felt a great peace come over him. It had been thirty years since he had been in a small town, and the buzzing of spring bees on the air lulled and quieted him, and the fresh look of things was a balm to the soul.

They set foot upon the porch. Hollow echoes sounded from under the boards as they walked to the screen door. Inside they could see a bead curtain hung across the hall entry, and a crystal chandelier and a Maxfield Parrish painting framed on one wall over a comfortable Morris chair. The house smelled old, and of the attic, and infinitely comfortable. You could hear the tinkle of ice in a lemonade pitcher. In a distant kitchen, because of the heat of the day, someone was preparing a cold lunch. Someone was humming under her breath, high and sweet.

Captain John Black rang the bell.

Footsteps, dainty and thin, came along the hall, and a kind-faced lady of some forty years, dressed in a sort of dress you might expect in the year 1909, peered out at them.

"Can I help you?" she asked.

"Beg your pardon," said Captain Black uncertainly. "But we're looking for—that is, could you help us——" He stopped. She looked out at him with dark, wondering eyes.

"If you're selling something——" she began.

"No, wait!" he cried. "What town is this?"

She looked him up and down. "What do you mean, what town is it? How could you be in a town and not know the name?"

The captain looked as if he wanted to go sit under a shady apple tree. "We're strangers here. We want to know how this town got here and how you got here."

"Are you census takers?"

"No."

"Everyone knows," she said, "this town was built in 1868. Is this a game?"

"No, not a game!" cried the captain. "We're from Earth."

"Out of the *ground*, do you mean?" she wondered.

"No, we came from the third planet, Earth, in a ship. And we've landed here on the fourth planet, Mars——"

"This," explained the woman, as if she were addressing a child, "is Green Bluff, Illinois, on the continent of America, surrounded by the Atlantic and Pacific oceans, on a place called the world, or sometimes, the Earth. Go away now. Goodby."

She trotted down the hall, running her fingers through the beaded curtains.

The three men looked at one another.

"Let's knock the screen door in," said Lustig.

"We can't do that. This is private property. Good God!"

They went to sit down on the porch step.

"Did it ever strike you, Hinkston, that perhaps we got ourselves somehow, in some way, off track, and by accident came back and landed on Earth?"

"How could we have done that?"

"I don't know, I don't know. Oh God, let me think."

Hinkston said, "But we checked every mile of the way. Our chronometers said so many miles. We went past the Moon and out into space, and here we are. I'm *positive* we're on Mars."

Lustig said, "But suppose, by accident, in space, in time, we got lost in the dimensions and landed on an Earth that is thirty or forty years ago."

"Oh, go away, Lustig!"

Lustig went to the door, rang the bell, and called into the cool dim rooms: "What year is this?"

"Nineteen twenty-six, of course," said the lady, sitting in a rocking chair, taking a sip of her lemonade.

"Did you hear that?" Lustig turned wildly to the others. "Nineteen twenty-six. We *have* gone back in time! This *is* Earth!"

Lustig sat down, and the three men let the wonder and terror of the thought afflict them. Their hands stirred fitfully on their knees. The captain said, "I didn't ask for a thing like this. It scares the hell out of me. How can a thing like this happen? I wish we'd brought Einstein with us."

"Will anyone in this town believe us?" said Hinkston. "Are we playing with something dangerous? Time, I mean. Shouldn't we just take off and go home?"

"No. Not until we try another house."

They walked three houses down to a little white cottage under an oak tree. "I like to be as logical as I can be," said the captain. "And I don't believe we've put our finger on it yet. Suppose, Hinkston, as you originally suggested, that rocket travel occurred years ago? And when the Earth people lived here a number of years they began to get homesick for Earth. First a mild neurosis about it, then a full-fledged psychosis. Then threatened insanity. What would you do as a psychiatrist if faced with such a problem?"

Hinkston thought. "Well, I think I'd rearrange the civilization on Mars so it resembled Earth more and more each day. If there was any way of reproducing every plant, every road, and every lake, and even an ocean, I'd do so. Then by some vast crowd hypnosis I'd convince everyone in a town this size that this really *was* Earth, not Mars at all."

"Good enough, Hinkston. I think we're on the right track now. That woman in that house back there just *thinks* she's living on Earth. It protects her sanity. She and all the others in this town are the patients of the greatest experiment in migration and hypnosis you will ever lay eyes on in your life."

"That's it, sir!" cried Lustig.

"Right!" said Hinkston.

"Well." The captain sighed. "Now we've got somewhere. I feel better. It's all a bit more logical. That talk about time and going back and forth and traveling through time turns my stomach upside down. But *this* way——" The captain smiled. "Well, well, it looks as if we'll be fairly popular here."

"Or will we?" said Lustig. "After all, like the Pilgrims, these people came here to escape Earth. Maybe they won't be too happy to see us. Maybe they'll try to drive us out or kill us."

"We have superior weapons. This next house now. Up we go."

But they had hardly crossed the lawn when Lustig stopped and looked off across the town, down the quiet, dreaming afternoon street. "Sir," he said.

"What is it, Lustig?"

"Oh, sir, *sir*, what I *see*——" said Lustig, and he began to cry. His fingers came up, twisting and shaking, and his face was all wonder and joy and incredulity. He sounded as if at any moment he might go quite insane with happiness. He looked down the street and began to run, stumbling awkwardly, falling, picking himself up, and running on. "Look, look!"

"Don't let him get away!" The captain broke into a run.

Now Lustig was running swiftly, shouting. He turned into a yard halfway down the shady street and leaped up upon the porch of a large green house with an iron rooster on the roof.

He was beating at the door, hollering and crying, when Hinkston and the captain ran up behind him. They were all gasping and wheezing, exhausted from their run in the thin air. "Grandma! Grandpa!" cried Lustig.

Two old people stood in the doorway.

"David!" their voices piped, and they rushed out to embrace and pat him on the back and move around him. "David, oh, David, it's been so many years! How you've grown, boy; how big you are, boy. Oh, David boy, how are you?"

"Grandma, Grandpa!" sobbed David Lustig. "You look fine, fine!" He held them, turned them, kissed them, hugged them, cried on them, held them out again, blinking at the little old people. The sun was in the sky, the wind blew, the grass was green, the screen door stood wide.

"Come in, boy, come in. There's iced tea for you, fresh, lots of it!"

"I've got friends here." Lustig turned and waved at the captain and Hinkston frantically, laughing. "Captain, come on up."

"Howdy," said the old people. "Come in. Any friends of David's are our friends too. Don't stand there!"

In the living room of the old house it was cool, and a grandfather clock ticked high and long and bronzed in one corner. There were soft pillows on large couches and walls filled with books and a rug cut in a thick rose pattern, and iced tea in the hand, sweating, and cool on the thirsty tongue.

"Here's to our health." Grandma tipped her glass to her porcelain teeth.

"How long you been here, Grandma?" said Lustig.

"Ever since we died," she said tartly.

"Ever since you what?" Captain John Black set down his glass.

"Oh yes." Lustig nodded. "They've been dead thirty years."

"And you sit there calmly!" shouted the captain.

"Tush." The old woman winked glitteringly. "Who are you to question what happens? Here we are. What's life, anyway? Who does what for why and where? All we know is here we are, alive again, and no questions asked. A second chance." She toddled over and held out her thin wrist. "Feel." The captain felt. "Solid, ain't it?" she asked. He nodded. "Well, then," she said triumphantly, "why go around questioning?"

"Well," said the captain, "it's simply that we never thought we'd find a thing like this on Mars."

"And now you've found it. I dare say there's lots on every planet that'll show you God's infinite ways."

"Is this Heaven?" asked Hinkston.

"Nonsense, no. It's a world and we get a second chance. Nobody told us why. But then nobody told us why we were on Earth, either. That other Earth, I mean. The one you came from. How do we know there wasn't *another* before *that* one?"

"A good question," said the captain.

Lustig kept smiling at his grandparents. "Gosh, it's good to see you. Gosh, it's good."

The captain stood up and slapped his hand on his leg in a casual fashion. "We've got to be going. Thank you for the drinks."

"You'll be back, of course," said the old people. "For supper tonight?"

"We'll try to make it, thanks. There's so much to be done. My men are waiting for me back at the rocket and———"

He stopped. He looked toward the door, startled.

Far away in the sunlight there was a sound of voices, a shouting and a great hello.

"What's that?" asked Hinkston.

"We'll soon find out." And Captain John Black was out the front door abruptly, running across the green lawn into the street of the Martian town.

He stood looking at the rocket. The ports were open and his crew was streaming out, waving their hands. A crowd of people had gathered, and in and through and among these people the members of the crew were hurrying, talking, laughing, shaking hands. People did little dances. People swarmed. The rocket lay empty and abandoned.

A brass band exploded in the sunlight, flinging off a gay tune from upraised tubas and trumpets. There was a bang of drums and a shrill of fifes. Little girls with golden hair jumped up and down. Little boys shouted, "Hooray!" Fat men passed around ten-cent cigars. The town mayor made a speech. Then each member of the crew, with a mother on one arm, a father or sister on the other, was spirited off down the street into little cottages or big mansions.

"Stop!" cried Captain Black.

The doors slammed shut.

The heat rose in the clear spring sky, and all was silent. The brass band banged off around a corner, leaving the rocket to shine and dazzle alone in the sunlight.

"Abandoned!" said the captain. "They abandoned the ship, they did! I'll have their skins, by God! They had orders!"

"Sir," said Lustig, "don't be too hard on them. Those were all old relatives and friends."

"That's no excuse!"

"Think how they felt, Captain, seeing familiar faces outside the ship!"

"They had their orders, damn it!"

"But how would you have felt, Captain?"

"I would have obeyed orders——" The captain's mouth remained open.

Striding along the sidewalk under the Martian sun, tall, smiling, eyes amazingly clear and blue, came a young man of some twenty-six years. "John!" the man called out, and broke into a trot.

"What?" Captain John Black swayed.

"John, you old son of a bitch!"

The man ran up and gripped his hand and slapped him on the back.

"It's you," said Captain Black.

"Of course, who'd you *think* it was?"

"Edward!" The captain appealed now to Lustig and Hinkston, holding the stranger's hand. "This is my brother Edward. Ed, meet my men, Lustig, Hinkston! My brother!"

They tugged at each other's hands and arms and then finally embraced. "Ed!" "John, you bum, you!" "You're looking fine, Ed, but Ed, what *is* this? You haven't changed over the years. You died, I remember, when you were twenty-six and I was nineteen. Good God, so many years ago, and here you are and, Lord, what goes on?"

"Mom's waiting," said Edward Black, grinning.

"Mom?"

"And Dad too."

"Dad?" The captain almost fell as if he had been hit by a mighty weapon. He walked stiffly and without co-ordination. "Mom and Dad alive? Where?"

"At the old house on Oak Knoll Avenue."

"The old house." The captain stared in delighted amaze. "Did you hear that, Lustig, Hinkston?"

Hinkston was gone. He had seen his own house down the street and was running for it. Lustig was laughing. "You see, Captain, what happened to everyone on the rocket? They couldn't help themselves."

"Yes. Yes." The captain shut his eyes. "When I open my eyes you'll be gone." He blinked. "You're still there. God, Ed, but you look *fine*!"

"Come on, lunch's waiting. I told Mom."

Lustig said, "Sir, I'll be with my grandfolks if you need me."

"What? Oh, fine, Lustig. Later, then."

Edward seized his arm and marched him. "There's the house. Remember it?"

"Hell! Bet I can beat you to the front porch!"

They ran. The trees roared over Captain Black's head; the earth roared under his feet. He saw the golden figure of Edward Black pull ahead of him in the amazing dream of reality. He saw the house rush forward, the screen door swing wide. "Beat you!" cried Edward. "I'm an old man," panted the captain, "and you're still young. But then, you *always* beat me, I remember!"

In the doorway, Mom, pink, plump, and bright. Behind her, pepper-gray, Dad, his pipe in his hand.

"Mom, Dad!"

He ran up the steps like a child to meet them.

It was a fine long afternoon. They finished a late lunch and they sat in the parlor and he told them all about his rocket and they nodded and smiled upon him and Mother was just the same and Dad bit the end off a cigar and lighted it thoughtfully in his old fashion. There was a big turkey dinner at night and time flowing on. When the drumsticks were sucked clean and lay brittle upon the plates, the captain leaned back and exhaled his deep satisfaction. Night was in all the trees and coloring the sky, and the lamps were halos of pink light in the gentle house. From all the other houses down the street came sounds of music, pianos playing, doors slamming.

Mom put a record on the victrola, and she and Captain John Black had a dance. She was wearing the same perfume he remembered from the summer when she and Dad had been killed in the train accident. She was very real in his arms as they danced lightly to the music. "It's not every day," she said, "you get a second chance to live."

"I'll wake in the morning," said the captain. "And I'll be in my rocket, in space, and all this will be gone."

"No, don't think that," she cried softly. "Don't question. God's good to us. Let's be happy."

"Sorry, Mom."

The record ended in a circular hissing.

"You're tired, Son." Dad pointed with his pipe. "Your old bedroom's waiting for you, brass bed and all."

"But I should report my men in."

"Why?"

"Why? Well, I don't know. No reason, I guess. No, none at all. They're all eating or in bed. A good night's sleep won't hurt them."

"Good night, Son." Mom kissed his cheek. "It's good to have you home."

"It's good to *be* home."

He left the land of cigar smoke and perfume and books and gentle light and ascended the stairs, talking, talking with Edward. Edward pushed a door open, and there was the yellow brass bed and the old semaphore banners from college and a very musty raccoon coat which he stroked with muted affection. "It's too much," said the captain. "I'm numb and I'm tired. Too much has happened today. I feel as if I'd been out in a pounding rain for forty-eight hours without an umbrella or a coat. I'm soaked to the skin with emotion."

Edward slapped wide the snowy linens and flounced the pillows. He slid the window up and let the night-blooming jasmine float in. There was moonlight and the sound of distant dancing and whispering.

"So this is Mars," said the captain, undressing.

"This is it." Edward undressed in idle, leisurely moves, drawing his shirt off over his head, revealing golden shoulders and the good muscular neck.

The lights were out; they were in bed, side by side, as in the days how many decades ago? The captain lolled and was nourished by the scent of jasmine pushing the lace curtains out upon the dark air of the room. Among the trees, upon a lawn, someone had cranked up a portable phonograph and now it was playing softly, "Always."

The thought of Marilyn came to his mind.

"Is Marilyn here?"

His brother, lying straight out in the moonlight from the window, waited and then said, "Yes. She's out of town. But she'll be here in the morning."

The captain shut his eyes. "I want to see Marilyn very much."

The room was square and quiet except for their breathing.

"Good night, Ed."

A pause. "Good night, John."

He lay peacefully, letting his thoughts float. For the first time the stress of the day was moved aside; he could think logically now. It had all been emotion. The bands playing, the familiar faces. But now . . .

How? he wondered. How was all this made? And why? For what purpose? Out of the goodness of some divine intervention? Was God, then, really that thoughtful of his children? How and why and what for?

He considered the various theories advanced in the first heat of the afternoon by Hinkston and Lustig. He let all kinds of new theories drop in lazy pebbles down through his mind, turning, throwing out dull flashes of light. Mom. Dad. Edward. Mars. Earth. Mars. Martians.

Who had lived here a thousand years ago on Mars? Martians? Or had this always been the way it was today?

Martians. He repeated the word idly, inwardly.

He laughed out loud almost. He had the most ridiculous theory quite suddenly. It gave him a kind of chill. It was really nothing to consider, of course. Highly improbable. Silly. Forget it. Ridiculous.

But, he thought, just *suppose* . . . Just suppose, now, that there were Martians living on Mars and they saw our ship coming and saw us inside our ship and hated us. Suppose, now, just for the hell of it, that they wanted to destroy us, as invaders, as unwanted ones, and they wanted to do it in a very clever way, so that we would be taken off guard. Well, what would the best weapon be that a Martian could use against Earth Men with atomic weapons?

The answer was interesting. Telepathy, hypnosis, memory, and imagination.

Suppose all of these houses aren't real at all, this bed not real, but only figments of my own imagination, given substance by telepathy and hypnosis through the Martians, thought Captain John Black. Suppose these houses are really some *other* shape, a Martian shape, but, by playing on my desires and wants, these Martians have made this seem like my old home town, my old house, to lull me out of my suspicions. What better way to fool a man, using his own mother and father as bait?

And this town, so old, from the year 1926, long before *any* of my men were born. From a year when I was six years old and there *were* records of Harry Lauder, and Maxfield Parrish paintings *still* hanging, and bead curtains, and "Beautiful Ohio," and turn-of-the-century architecture. What if the Martians took the memories of a town *exclusively* from *my* mind? They say childhood memories are the clearest. And after they built the town from *my* mind, they populated it with the most-loved people from all the minds of the people on the rocket!

And suppose those two people in the next room, asleep, are not my mother and father at all. But two Martians, incredibly brilliant, with the ability to keep me under this dreaming hypnosis all of the time.

And that brass band today? What a startlingly wonderful plan it would be. First, fool Lustig, then Hinkston, then gather a crowd; and all the men in the rocket, seeing mothers, aunts, uncles, sweethearts, dead ten, twenty years ago, naturally, disregarding orders, rush out and abandon ship. What more natural? What more unsuspecting? What more simple? A man doesn't ask too many questions when his mother is suddenly brought back to life; he's much too happy. And here we all are tonight, in various houses, in various beds, with no weapons to protect us, and the rocket lies in the moonlight, empty. And wouldn't it be horrible and terrifying to discover that all of this was part of some great clever plan by the Martians to divide and conquer us, and kill us? Sometime during the night, perhaps, my brother here on this bed will change form, melt, shift, and become another thing, a terrible thing, a Martian. It would be very simple for him just to turn over in bed and put a knife into my heart. And in all those other houses down the street, a dozen other brothers or fathers suddenly melting away and taking knives and doing things to the unsuspecting, sleeping men of Earth. . . .

His hands were shaking under the covers. His body was cold. Suddenly it was not a theory. Suddenly he was very afraid.

He lifted himself in bed and listened. The night was very quiet. The music had stopped. The wind had died. His brother lay sleeping beside him.

Carefully he lifted the covers, rolled them back. He slipped from bed and was walking softly across the room when his brother's voice said, "Where are you going?"

"What?"

His brother's voice was quite cold. "I said, where do you think you're going?"

"For a drink of water."

"But you're not thirsty."

"Yes, yes, I am."

"No, you're not."

Captain John Black broke and ran across the room. He screamed. He screamed twice.

He never reached the door.

In the morning the brass band played a mournful dirge. From every house in the street came little solemn processions bearing long boxes, and along the sun-filled street, weeping, came the grandmas and mothers and sisters and brothers and uncles and fathers, walking to the churchyard, where there were new holes freshly dug and new tombstones installed. Sixteen holes in all, and sixteen tombstones.

The mayor made a little sad speech, his face sometimes looking like the mayor, sometimes looking like something else.

Mother and Father Black were there, with Brother Edward, and they cried, their faces melting now from a familiar face into something else.

Grandpa and Grandma Lustig were there, weeping, their faces shifting like wax, shimmering as all things shimmer on a hot day.

The coffins were lowered. Someone murmered about "the unexpected and sudden deaths of sixteen fine men during the night ———."

Earth pounded down on the coffin lids.

The brass band, playing "Columbia, the Gem of the Ocean," marched and slammed back into town, and everyone took the day off.

QUESTIONS

1. Science fiction is an obvious merging of scientific knowledge with imagination. Which facet dominates in this story? Justify your answer.
2. Ray Bradbury is usually meticulous in researching the background for his stories. What kind of research would he have undertaken for this story? Or do you consider it a complete figment of his imagination? Defend your answer.
3. Trace the use of metallic imagery. How does this contribute to the general tone of the story?
4. Science fiction stories demand a "suspension of disbelief" from the reader. Show how this story then becomes quite credible.
5. What is the ultimate explanation for the events in the story? Is this a rational explanation? Explain. In what ways does Bradbury try to keep his story as plausible as possible? Consider, for example, the characters: are they stock characters or human beings? Find and explain other devices that maintain a sense of reality.
6. Many stories focus on a time warp. Find the various time warps in this story.
7. What is the predominant irony in this story?
8. How does the point of view change in the story?
9. Several of Ray Bradbury's stories have been adapted for film. What features of "April 2000: The Third Expedition" render it suitable for dramatization?
10. Do you think that this story was devised purely for entertainment, or does it, "like an observation balloon, provide a vantage point from which we may view the world"?

John Collier

THUS I REFUTE BEELZY

"There goes the tea bell," said Mrs. Carter. "I hope Simon hears it."

They looked out from the window of the drawing-room. The long garden, agreeably neglected, ended in a waste plot. Here a little summer-house was passing close by beauty on its way to complete decay. This was Simon's retreat. It was almost completely screened by the tangled branches of the apple tree and the pear tree, planted too close together, as they always are in the suburbs. They caught a glimpse of him now and then, as he strutted up and down, mouthing and gesticulating, performing all the solemn mumbo-jumbo of small boys who spend long afternoons at the forgotten ends of long gardens.

"There he is, bless him!" said Betty.

THUS I REFUTE BEELZY   From *Presenting Moonshine* by John Collier. Copyright © 1940 by John Collier, © renewed 1967 by John Collier. Reprinted by permission of the Harold Matson Company, Inc.

"Playing his game," said Mrs. Carter. "He won't play with the other children any more. And if I go down there—the temper! And comes in tired out!"

"He doesn't have his sleep in the afternoons?" asked Betty.

"You know what Big Simon's ideas are," said Mrs. Carter. " 'Let him choose for himself,' he says. That's what he chooses, and he comes in as white as a sheet."

"Look! He's heard the bell," said Betty. The expression was justified, though the bell had ceased ringing a full minute ago. Small Simon stopped in his parade exactly as if its tinny dingle had at that moment reached his ear. They watched him perform certain ritual sweeps and scratchings with his little stick, and come lagging over the hot and flaggy grass toward the house.

Mrs. Carter led the way down to the play-room, or garden-room, which was also the tea-room for hot days. It had been the huge scullery of this tall Georgian house. Now the walls were cream-washed, there was coarse blue net in the windows, canvas-covered armchairs on the stone floor, and a reproduction of Van Gogh's *Sunflowers* over the mantelpiece.

Small Simon came drifting in, and accorded Betty a perfunctory greeting. His face was an almost perfect triangle, pointed at the chin, and he was paler than he should have been. "The little elf-child!" cried Betty.

Simon looked at her. "No," said he.

At that moment the door opened, and Mr. Carter came in, rubbing his hands. He was a dentist, and washed them before and after everything he did. "You!" said his wife. "Home already!"

"Not unwelcome, I hope," said Mr. Carter, nodding to Betty. "Two people cancelled their appointments: I decided to come home. I said, I hope I am not unwelcome."

"Silly!" said his wife. "Of course not."

"Small Simon seems doubtful," continued Mr. Carter. "Small Simon, are you sorry to see me at tea with you?"

"No, Daddy."

"No, what?"

"No, Big Simon."

"That's right. Big Simon and Small Simon. That sounds more like friends, doesn't it? At one time little boys had to call their father 'sir.' If they forgot—a good spanking. On the bottom, Small Simon! On the bottom!" said Mr. Carter, washing his hands once more with his invisible soap and water.

The little boy turned crimson with shame or rage.

"But now, you see," said Betty, to help, "you can call your father whatever you like."

"And what," asked Mr. Carter, "has Small Simon been doing this afternoon? While Big Simon has been at work."

"Nothing," muttered his son.

"Then you have been bored," said Mr. Carter. "Learn from experience, Small Simon. Tomorrow, do something amusing, and you will not be bored. I want him to learn from experience, Betty. That is my way, the new way."

"I have learned," said the boy, speaking like an old, tired man, as little boys so often do.

"It would hardly seem so," said Mr. Carter, "if you sit on your behind all the afternoon, doing nothing. Had *my* father caught me doing nothing, I should not have sat very comfortably."

"He played," said Mrs. Carter.

"A bit," said the boy, shifting on his chair.

"Too much," said Mrs. Carter. "He comes in all nervy and dazed. He ought to have his rest."

"He is six," said her husband. "He is a reasonable being. He must choose for himself. But what game is this, Small Simon, that is worth getting nervy and dazed over? There are very few games as good as all that."

"It's nothing," said the boy.

"Oh, come," said his father. "We are friends, are we not? You can tell me. I was a Small Simon once, just like you, and played the same games you play. Of course there were no aeroplanes in those days. With whom do you play this fine game? Come on, we must all answer civil questions, or the world would never go round. With whom do you play?"

"Mr. Beelzy," said the boy, unable to resist.

"Mr. Beelzy?" said his father, raising his eyebrows inquiringly at his wife.

"It's a game he makes up," said she.

"Not makes up!" cried the boy. "Fool!"

"That is telling stories," said his mother. "And rude as well. We had better talk of something different."

"No wonder he is rude," said Mr. Carter, "if you say he tells lies, and then insist on changing the subject. He tells you his fantasy: you implant a guilt feeling. What can you expect? A defence mechanism. Then you get a real lie."

"Like in *These Three*,"[1] said Betty. "Only different, of course. *She* was an unblushing little liar."

"I would have made her blush," said Mr. Carter, "in the proper part

---

[1] *These Three* is the movie version of Lillian Hellman's play *The Children's Hour*. Its protagonist is an apparently angelic little girl who is actually a psychopathic liar.

of her anatomy. But Small Simon is in the fantasy stage. Are you not, Small Simon? You just make things up."

"No, I don't," said the boy.

"You do," said his father. "And because you do, it is not too late to reason with you. There is no harm in a fantasy, old chap. There is no harm in a bit of make-believe. Only you have to know the difference between day dreams and real things, or your brain will never grow. It will never be the brain of a Big Simon. So come on. Let us hear about this Mr. Beelzy of yours. Come on. What is he like?"

"He isn't like anything," said the boy.

"Like nothing on earth?" said his father. "That's a terrible fellow."

"I'm not frightened of him," said the child, smiling. "Not a bit."

"I should hope not," said his father. "If you were, you would be frightening yourself. I am always telling people, older people than you are, that they are just frightening themselves. Is he a funny man? Is he a giant?"

"Sometimes he is," said the little boy.

"Sometimes one thing, sometimes another," said his father. "Sounds pretty vague. Why can't you tell us just what he's like?"

"I love him," said the small boy. "He loves me."

"That's a big word," said Mr. Carter. "That might be better kept for real things, like Big Simon and Small Simon."

"He is real," said the boy, passionately. "He's not a fool. He's real."

"Listen," said his father. "When you go down the garden there's nobody there. Is there?"

"No," said the boy.

"Then you think of him, inside your head, and he comes."

"No," said Small Simon. "I have to make marks. On the ground. With my stick."

"That doesn't matter."

"Yes, it does."

"Small Simon, you are being obstinate," said Mr. Carter. 'I am trying to explain something to you. I have been longer in the world than you have, so naturally I am older and wiser. I am explaining that Mr. Beelzy is a fantasy of yours. Do you hear? Do you understand?"

"Yes, Daddy."

"He is a game. He is a let's-pretend."

The little boy looked down at his plate, smiling resignedly.

"I hope you are listening to me," said his father. "All you have to do is to say, 'I have been playing a game of let's-pretend. With someone I make up, called Mr. Beelzy.' Then no one will say you tell lies, and you will know the difference between dreams and reality. Mr. Beelzy is a day dream."

The little boy still stared at his plate.

"He is sometimes there and sometimes not there," pursued Mr. Carter. "Sometimes he's like one thing, sometimes another. You can't really see him. Not as you see me. I am real. You can't touch him. You can touch me. I can touch you." Mr. Carter stretched out his big, white, dentist's hand, and took his little son by the nape of the neck. He stopped speaking for a moment and tightened his hand. The little boy sank his head still lower.

"Now you know the difference," said Mr. Carter, "between a pretend and a real thing. You and I are one thing; he is another. Which is the pretend? Come on. Answer me. What is the pretend?"

"Big Simon and Small Simon," said the little boy.

"Don't!" cried Betty, and at once put her hand over her mouth, for why should a visitor cry "Don't!" when a father is explaining things in a scientific and modern way? Besides, it annoys the father.

"Well, my boy," said Mr. Carter, "I have said you must be allowed to learn from experience. Go upstairs. Right up to your room. You shall learn whether it is better to reason, or to be perverse and obstinate. Go up. I shall follow you."

"You are not going to beat the child?" cried Mrs. Carter.

"No," said the little boy. "Mr. Beelzy won't let him."

"Go on up with you!" shouted his father.

Small Simon stopped at the door. "He said he wouldn't let anyone hurt me," he whimpered. "He said he'd come like a lion, with wings on, and eat them up."

"You'll learn how real he is!" shouted his father after him. "If you can't learn it at one end, you shall learn it at the other. I'll have your breeches down. I shall finish my cup of tea first, however," said he to the two women.

Neither of them spoke. Mr. Carter finished his tea, and unhurriedly left the room, washing his hands with his invisible soap and water.

Mrs. Carter said nothing. Betty could think of nothing to say. She wanted to be talking for she was afraid of what they might hear.

Suddenly it came. It seemed to tear the air apart. "Good God!" she cried. "What was that? He's hurt him." She sprang out of her chair, her silly eyes flashing behind her glasses. "I'm going up there!" she cried, trembling.

"Yes, let us go up," said Mrs. Carter. "Let us go up. That was not Small Simon."

It was on the second-floor landing that they found the shoe, with the man's foot still in it, like that last morsel of a mouse which sometimes falls unnoticed from the side of the jaws of the cat.

QUESTIONS

1. Explain the behavior of Little Simon. Why does he play by himself in the garden?

2. Characterize Big Simon fully, taking into account (a) his profession, (b) his ideas about child-raising, (c) his explanations of the older way of child-raising, (d) his habit of hand-washing, (e) his treatment of Mrs. Carter, (f) his treatment of the child. What are Mr. Carter's conceptions of the universe and of himself? Do you find any discrepancies between his avowals and his behavior? between his conception of himself and the actuality? What do these discrepancies suggest about the adequacy of his conception of the universe?

3. Explain the implications of Little Simon's answer to Big Simon's question "Which is the pretend?"

4. The unusual name Beelzy suggests, or may be a child's garbled version of, the name of a well-known supernatural being. What does this identification add to our understanding of the story? (If you do not recognize it, consult a dictionary.)

5. The title "Thus I Refute Beelzy" alludes to a well-known incident in the life of Dr. Samuel Johnson as reported by James Boswell:

> After we came out of the church, we stood talking for some time together of Bishop Berkeley's ingenious sophistry to prove the non-existence of matter, and that everything in the universe is merely ideal. I observed that though we are satisfied his doctrine is not true, it is impossible to refute it. I never shall forget the alacrity with which Johnson answered, striking his foot with mighty force against a large stone, till he rebounded from it, "I refute it *thus*."

How does Big Simon undertake to refute Beelzy? What judgment does the story make on the logic of his refutation?

6. The end of the story is a shocker. Is it only a shocker, or does it help the story make a thematic statement? Judge it by the criteria suggested in Chapter 2 (page 49) for evaluating surprise endings. Compare the ending of this story with that of "April 2000: The Third Expedition."

7. What is the theme of the story? Can it be so framed as to make a statement acceptable to a reader who disbelieves in Mr. Beelzy?

D.H. Lawrence

THE ROCKING-HORSE WINNER

There was a woman who was beautiful, who started with all the advantages, yet she had no luck. She married for love, and the love turned to dust. She had bonny children, yet she felt they had been thrust upon her, and she could not love them. They looked at her coldly, as if they were finding fault with her. And hurriedly she felt she must cover up some fault in herself. Yet what it was that she must cover up she never knew. Nevertheless, when her children were present, she always felt the centre of her heart go hard. This troubled her, and in her manner she was all the more gentle and anxious for her children, as if she loved them very much. Only she herself knew that at the centre of her heart was a hard little place that could not feel love, no, not for anybody. Everybody else said of her: "She is such a good mother. She adores her children." Only she herself, and her children themselves, knew it was not so. They read it in each other's eyes.

There were a boy and two little girls. They lived in a pleasant house, with a garden, and they had discreet servants, and felt themselves superior to anyone in the neighbourhood.

Although they lived in style, they felt always an anxiety in the house. There was never enough money. The mother had a small income, and the father had a small income, but not nearly enough for the social position which they had to keep up. The father went into town to some office. But though he had good prospects, these prospects never materialized. There was always the grinding sense of the shortage of money, though the style was always kept up.

At last the mother said: "I will see if I can't make something." But she did not know where to begin. She racked her brains, and tried this thing and the other, but could not find anything successful. The failure made deep lines come into her face. Her children were growing up, they would have to go to school. There must be more money, there must be more money. The father, who was always very handsome and expensive in his tastes, seemed as if he never would be able to do anything worth doing. And the mother, who had a great belief in herself, did not succeed any better, and her tastes were just as expensive.

And so the house came to be haunted by the unspoken phrase: There must be more money! There must be more money! The children could hear it all the time, though nobody said it aloud. They heard it at Christmas, when the expensive and splendid toys filled the nursery. Behind the shining modern rocking horse, behind the smart doll's-house, a voice would start whispering: "There must be more money! There must be more money!" And the children would stop playing, to listen for a moment. They would look into each other's eyes, to see if they had all heard. And each one saw in the eyes of the other two that they too had heard. "There must be more money! There must be more money!"

It came whispering from the springs of the still-swaying rocking horse, and even the horse, bending his wooden, champing head, heard it. The big doll, sitting so pink and smirking in her new pram, could hear it quite plainly, and seemed to be smirking all the more self-consciously because of it. The foolish puppy, too, that took the place of the Teddy bear, he was looking so extraordinarily foolish for no other reason but that he heard the secret whisper all over the house: "There must be more money!"

Yet nobody ever said it aloud. The whisper was everywhere, and therefore no one spoke it. Just as no one ever says: "We are breathing!" in spite of the fact that breath is coming and going all the time.

"Mother," said the boy Paul one day, "why don't we keep a car of our own? Why do we always use uncle's, or else a taxi?"

"Because we're the poor members of the family," said the mother.

"But why are we, mother?"

"Well—I suppose," she said slowly and bitterly, "it's because your father has no luck."

The boy was silent for some time.

"Is luck money, mother?" he asked, rather timidly.

"No, Paul. Not quite. It's what causes you to have money."

"Oh!" said Paul vaguely. "I thought when Uncle Oscar said filthy lucker, it meant money."

"Filthy lucre does mean money," said the mother. "But it's lucre, not luck."

"Oh!" said the boy. "Then what is luck, mother?"

"It's what causes you to have money. If you're lucky you have money. That's why it's better to be born lucky than rich. If you're rich, you may lose your money. But if you're lucky, you will always get more money."

"Oh! Will you? And is father not lucky?"

"Very unlucky, I should say," she said bitterly.

The boy watched her with unsure eyes.

"Why?" he asked.

"I don't know. Nobody ever knows why one person is lucky and another unlucky."

"Don't they? Nobody at all? Does nobody know?"

"Perhaps God. But He never tells."

"He ought to, then. And aren't you lucky, either, mother?"

"I can't be, if I married an unlucky husband."

"But by yourself, aren't you?"

"I used to think I was, before I married. Now I think I am very unlucky indeed."

"Why?"

"Well—never mind! Perhaps I'm not really," she said.

The child looked at her, to see if she meant it. But he saw, by the lines of her mouth, that she was only trying to hide something from him.

"Well, anyhow," he said stoutly, "I'm a lucky person."

"Why?" said his mother, with a sudden laugh.

He stared at her. He didn't even know why he had said it.

"God told me," he asserted, brazening it out.

"I hope He did, dear!" she said, again with a laugh, but rather bitter.

"He did mother!"

"Excellent!" said the mother, using one of her husband's exclamations.

The boy saw she did not believe him; or, rather, that she paid no attention to his assertion. This angered him somewhat, and made him want to compel her attention.

He went off by himself, vaguely, in a childish way, seeking for the clue to "luck." Absorbed, taking no heed of other people, he went about with a sort of stealth, seeking inwardly for luck. He wanted luck, he wanted it, he wanted it. When the two girls were playing dolls in the nursery, he would sit on his big rocking horse, charging madly into space, with a frenzy that made the little girls peer at him uneasily. Wildly the horse careered, the waving dark hair of the boy tossed, his eyes had a strange glare in them. The little girls dared not speak to him.

When he had ridden to the end of his mad little journey, he climbed down and stood in front of his rocking horse, staring fixedly into its lowered face. Its red mouth was slightly open, its big eye was wide and glassy-bright.

"Now!" he would silently command the snorting steed. "Now, take me to where there is luck! Now take me!"

And he would slash the horse on the neck with the little whip he had asked Uncle Oscar for. He knew the horse could take him to where there was luck, if only he forced it. So he would mount again, and start on his furious ride, hoping at last to get there. He knew he could get there.

"You'll break your horse, Paul!" said the nurse.

"He's always riding like that! I wish he'd leave off!" said his elder sister Joan.

But he only glared down on them in silence. Nurse gave him up. She could make nothing of him. Anyhow he was growing beyond her.

One day his mother and his Uncle Oscar came in when he was on one of his furious rides. He did not speak to them.

"Hallo, you young jockey! Riding a winner?" said his uncle.

"Aren't you growing too big for a rocking horse? You're not a very little boy any longer, you know," said his mother.

But Paul only gave a blue glare from his big, rather close-set eyes. He would speak to nobody when he was in full tilt. His mother watched him with an anxious expression on her face.

At last he suddenly stopped forcing his horse into the mechanical gallop, and slid down.

"Well, I got there!" he announced fiercely, his blue eyes still flaring, and his sturdy long legs straddling apart.

"Where did you get to?" asked his mother.

"Where I wanted to go," he flared back at her.

"That's right, son!" said Uncle Oscar. "Don't you stop till you get there. What's the horse's name?"

"He doesn't have a name," said the boy.

"Gets on without all right?" asked the uncle.

"Well, he has different names. He was called Sansovino last week."

"Sansovino, eh? Won the Ascot. How did you know his name?"

"He always talks about horse races with Bassett," said Joan.

The uncle was delighted to find that his small nephew was posted with all the racing news. Bassett, the young gardener, who had been wounded in the left foot in the war and had got his present job through Oscar Cresswell, whose batman he had been, was a perfect blade of the "turf." He lived in the racing events, and the small boy lived with him.

Oscar Cresswell got it all from Bassett.

"Master Paul comes and asks me, so I can't do more than tell him, sir," said Bassett, his face terribly serious, as if he were speaking of religious matters.

"And does he ever put anything on a horse he fancies?"

"Well—I don't want to give him away—he's a young sport, a fine sport, sir. Would you mind asking him yourself? He sort of takes a pleasure in it, and perhaps he'd feel I was giving him away, sir, if you don't mind."

Bassett was serious as a church.

The uncle went back to his nephew, and took him off for a ride in the car.

"Say, Paul, old man, do you ever put anything on a horse?" the uncle asked.

The boy watched the handsome man closely.

"Why, do you think I oughtn't to?" he parried.

"Not a bit of it! I thought perhaps you might give me a tip for the Lincoln."

The car sped on into the country, going down to Uncle Oscar's place in Hampshire.

"Honour bright?" said the nephew.

"Honour bright, son!" said the uncle.

"Well, then, Daffodil."

"Daffodil! I doubt it, sonny. What about Mirza?"

"I only know the winner," said the boy. "That's Daffodil."

"Daffodil, eh?"

There was a pause. Daffodil was an obscure horse comparatively.

"Uncle!"

"Yes, son?"

"You won't let it go any further, will you? I promised Bassett."

"Bassett be damned, old man! What's he got to do with it?"

"We're partners. We've been partners from the first. Uncle, he lent me my first five shillings, which I lost. I promised him, honour bright, it was only between me and him; only you gave me that ten-shilling note I started winning with, so I thought you were lucky. You won't let it go any further, will you?"

The boy gazed at his uncle from those big, hot, blue eyes, set rather close together. The uncle stirred and laughed uneasily.

"Right you are, son! I'll keep your tip private. Daffodil, eh? How much are you putting on him?"

"All except twenty pounds," said the boy. "I keep that in reserve."

The uncle thought it a good joke.

"You keep twenty pounds in reserve, do you, you young romancer? What are you betting, then?"

"I'm betting three hundred," said the boy gravely. "But it's between you and me, Uncle Oscar! Honour bright?"

The uncle burst into a roar of laughter.

"It's between you and me all right, you young Nat Gould," he said, laughing. "But where's your three hundred?"

"Bassett keeps it for me. We're partners."

"You are, are you! And what is Bassett putting on Daffodil?"

"He won't go quite as high as I do, I expect. Perhaps he'll go a hundred and fifty."

"What, pennies?" laughed the uncle.

"Pounds," said the child, with a surprised look at his uncle. "Bassett keeps a bigger reserve than I do."

Between wonder and amusement Uncle Oscar was silent. He pursued the matter no further, but he determined to take his nephew with him to the Lincoln races.

"Now, son," he said, "I'm putting twenty on Mirza, and I'll put five for you on any horse you fancy. What's your pick?"

"Daffodil, uncle."

"No, not the fiver on Daffodil!"

"I should if it was my own fiver," said the child.

"Good! Good! Right you are! A fiver for me and a fiver for you on Daffodil."

The child had never been to a race meeting before, and his eyes were blue fire. He pursed his mouth tight, and watched. A Frenchman just in front had put his money on Lancelot. Wild with excitement, he flayed his arms up and down, yelling "Lancelot! Lancelot!" in his French accent.

Daffodil came in first, Lancelot second, Mirza third. The child, flushed and with eyes blazing, was curiously serene. His uncle brought him four five-pound notes, four to one.

"What am I to do with these?" he cried, waving them before the boy's eyes.

"I suppose we'll talk to Bassett," said the boy. "I expect I have fifteen hundred now; and twenty in reserve; and this twenty."

His uncle studied him for some moments.

"Look here, son!" he said. "You're not serious about Bassett and that fifteen hundred, are you?"

"Yes, I am. But it's between you and me, uncle. Honour bright!"

"Honour bright all right, son! But I must talk to Bassett."

"If you'd like to be a partner, uncle, with Bassett and me, we could all be partners. Only, you'd have to promise, honour bright, uncle, not to let it go beyond us three. Bassett and I are lucky, and you must be lucky, because it was your ten shillings I started winning with. . . ."

Uncle Oscar took both Bassett and Paul into Richmond Park for an afternoon, and there they talked.

"It's like this, you see, sir," Bassett said. "Master Paul would get me talking about racing events, spinning yarns, you know, sir. And he was always keen on knowing if I'd made or if I'd lost. It's about a year since, now, that I put five shillings on Blush of Dawn for him—and we lost. Then the luck turned, with that ten shillings he had from you, that we put on Singhalese. And since that time, it's been pretty steady, all things considering. What do you say, Master Paul?"

"We're all right when we're sure," said Paul. "It's when we're not quite sure that we go down."

"Oh, but we're careful then," said Bassett.

"But when are you sure?" smiled Uncle Oscar.

"It's Master Paul, sir," said Bassett, in a secret, religious voice. "It's as if he had it from heaven. Like Daffodil, now, for the Lincoln. That was as sure as eggs."

"Did you put anything on Daffodil?" asked Oscar Cresswell.

"Yes, sir, I made my bit."

"And my nephew?"

Bassett was obstinately silent, looking at Paul.

"I made twelve hundred, didn't I, Bassett? I told uncle I was putting three hundred on Daffodil."

"That's right, said Bassett, nodding.

"But where's the money?" asked the uncle.

"I keep it safe locked up, sir. Master Paul he can have it any minute he likes to ask for it."

"What, fifteen hundred pounds?"

"And twenty! and forty, that is, with the twenty he made on the course."

"It's amazing!" said the uncle.

"If Master Paul offers you to be partners, sir, I would, if I were you; if you'll excuse me," said Bassett.

Oscar Cresswell thought about it.

"I'll see the money," he said.

They drove home again, and sure enough, Bassett came round to the garden-house with fifteen hundred pounds in notes. The twenty pounds reserve was left with Joe Glee, in the Turf Commission deposit.

"You see, it's all right, uncle, when I'm sure! Then we go strong, for all we're worth. Don't we, Bassett?"

"We do that, Master Paul."

"And when are you sure?" said the uncle, laughing.

"Oh, well, sometimes I'm absolutely sure, like about Daffodil," said the boy; "and sometimes I have an idea; and sometimes I haven't even an idea, have I, Bassett? Then we're careful, because we mostly go down."

"You do, do you! And when you're sure, like about Daffodil, what makes you sure, sonny?"

"Oh, well, I don't know," said the boy uneasily. "I'm sure, you know, uncle; that's all."

"It's as if he had it from heaven, sir," Bassett reiterated.

"I should say so!" said the uncle.

But he became a partner. And when the Leger was coming on, Paul was "sure" about Lively Spark, which was a quite inconsiderable horse. The boy insisted on putting a thousand on the horse, Bassett went for five hundred, and Oscar Cresswell two hundred. Lively Spark came in first, and the betting had been ten to one against him. Paul had made ten thousand.

"You see," he said, "I was absolutely sure of him."

Even Oscar Cresswell had cleared two thousand.

"Look here, son," he said, "this sort of thing makes me nervous."

"It needn't, uncle! Perhaps I shan't be sure again for a long time."

"But what are you going to do with your money?" asked the uncle.

"Of course," said the boy, "I started it for mother. She said she had no luck, because father is unlucky, so I thought if I was lucky, it might stop whispering."

"What might stop whispering?"

"Our house. I hate our house for whispering."

"What does it whisper?"

"Why—why"—the boy fidgeted—"why, I don't know. But it's always short of money, you know, uncle."

"I know it, son, I know it."

"You know people send mother writs, don't you, uncle?"

"I'm afraid I do," said the uncle.

"And then the house whispers, like people laughing at you behind your back. It's awful, that is! I thought if I was lucky . . ."

"You might stop it," added the uncle.

The boy watched him with big blue eyes that had an uncanny cold fire in them, and he said never a word.

"Well, then!" said the uncle. "What are we doing?"

"I shouldn't like mother to know I was lucky," said the boy.

"Why not, son?"

"She'd stop me."

"I don't think she would."

"Oh!"—and the boy writhed in an odd way—"I don't want her to know, uncle."

"All right, son! We'll manage it without her knowing."

They managed it very easily. Paul, at the other's suggestion, handed over five thousand pounds to his uncle, who deposited it with the family lawyer, who was then to inform Paul's mother that a relative had put five thousand pounds into his hands, which sum was to be paid out a thousand pounds at a time, on the mother's birthday, for the next five years.

"So she'll have a birthday present of a thousand pounds for five successive years," said Uncle Oscar. "I hope it won't make it all the harder for her later."

Paul's mother had her birthday in November. The house had been "whispering" worse than ever lately, and, even in spite of his luck, Paul could not bear up against it. He was very anxious to see the effect of the birthday letter, telling his mother about the thousand pounds.

When there were no visitors, Paul now took his meals with his parents, as he was beyond the nursery control. His mother went into town nearly every day. She had discovered that she had an odd knack of sketching furs and dress materials, so she worked secretly in the studio of a friend who was the chief "artist" for the leading drapers. She drew the figures of ladies in furs and ladies in silk and sequins for the newspaper advertisements. This young woman artist earned several thousand pounds a year, but Paul's mother only made several hundreds, and she was again dissatisfied. She so wanted to be first in something, and she did not succeed, even in making sketches for drapery advertisements.

She was down to breakfast on the morning of her birthday. Paul watched her face as she read her letters. He knew the lawyer's letter. As his mother read it, her face hardened and became more expressionless. Then a cold, determined look came on her mouth. She hid the letter under the pile of others, and said not a word about it.

"Didn't you have anything nice in the post for your birthday, mother?" said Paul.

"Quite moderately nice," she said, her voice cold and absent.

She went away to town without saying more.

But in the afternoon Uncle Oscar appeared. He said Paul's mother had had a long interview with the lawyer, asking if the whole five thousand could be advanced at once, as she was in debt.

"What do you think, uncle?" said the boy.

"I leave it to you, son."

"Oh, let her have it, then! We can get some more with the other," said the boy.

"A bird in the hand is worth two in the bush, laddie!" said Uncle Oscar.

"But I'm sure to know for the Grand National; or the Lincolnshire; or else the Derby. I'm sure to know for one of them," said Paul.

So Uncle Oscar signed the agreement, and Paul's mother touched the whole five thousand. Then something very curious happened. The voices in the house suddenly went mad, like a chorus of frogs on a spring evening. There were certain new furnishings, and Paul had a tutor. He was really going to Eton, his father's school, in the following autumn. There were flowers in the winter, and a blossoming of the luxury Paul's mother had been used to. And yet the voices in the house, behind the sprays of mimosa and almond blossom, and from under the piles of iridescent cushions, simply trilled and screamed in a sort of ecstasy: "There must be more money! Oh-h-h, there must be more money. Oh, now, now-w! Now-w-w—there must be more money!— more than ever! More than ever!"

It frightened Paul terribly. He studied away at his Latin and Greek with his tutors. But his intense hours were spent with Bassett. The Grand National had gone by: he had not "known," and had lost a hundred pounds. Summer was at hand. He was in agony for the Lincoln. But even for the Lincoln he didn't "know" and he lost fifty pounds. He became wild-eyed and strange, as if something were going to explode in him.

"Let it alone, son! Don't you bother about it!" urged Uncle Oscar. But it was as if the boy couldn't really hear what his uncle was saying.

"I've got to know for the Derby! I've got to know for the Derby!" the child reiterated, his big blue eyes blazing with a sort of madness.

His mother noticed how overwrought he was.

"You'd better go to the seaside. Wouldn't you like to go now to the seaside, instead of waiting? I think you'd better," she said, looking down at him anxiously, her heart curiously heavy because of him.

But the child lifted his uncanny blue eyes.

"I couldn't possibly go before the Derby, mother!" he said. "I couldn't possibly!"

"Why not?" she said, her voice becoming heavy when she was opposed. "Why not? You can still go from the seaside to see the Derby with your Uncle Oscar, if that's what you wish. No need for you to wait here. Besides, I think you care too much about these races. It's a bad sign. My family has been a gambling family, and you won't know till you grow up how much damage it has done. But it has done damage. I shall have to send Bassett away, and ask Uncle Oscar not to talk racing to you, unless you promise to be reasonable about it; go away to the seaside and forget it. You're all nerves!"

"I'll do what you like, mother, so long as you don't send me away till after the Derby," the boy said.

"Send you away from where? Just from this house?"

"Yes," he said, gazing at her.

"Why, you curious child, what makes you care about this house so much, suddenly? I never knew you loved it."

He gazed at her without speaking. He had a secret within a secret, something he had not divulged, even to Bassett or to his Uncle Oscar.

But his mother, after standing undecided and a little bit sullen for some moments, said:

"Very well, then! Don't go to the seaside till after the Derby, if you don't wish it. But promise me you won't let your nerves go to pieces. Promise you won't think so much about horse racing and events, as you call them!"

"Oh, no," said the boy casually. "I won't think much about them, mother. You needn't worry. I wouldn't worry, mother, if I were you."

"If you were me and I were you," said his mother, "I wonder what we should do!"

"But you know you needn't worry, mother, don't you?" the boy repeated.

"I should be awfully glad to know it," she said wearily.

"Oh, well, you can, you know. I mean, you ought to know you needn't worry," he insisted.

"Ought I? Then I'll see about it," she said.

Paul's secret of secrets was his wooden horse, that which had no name. Since he was emancipated from a nurse and a nursery-governess, he had had his rocking horse removed to his own bedroom at the top of the house.

"Surely, you're too big for a rocking horse!" his mother had remonstrated.

"Well, you see, mother, till I can have a real horse, I like to have some sort of animal about," had been his quaint answer.

"Do you feel he keeps you company?" she laughed.

"Oh, yes! He's very good, he always keeps me company, when I'm there," said Paul.

So the horse, rather shabby, stood in an arrested prance in the boy's bedroom.

The Derby was drawing near, and the boy grew more and more tense. He hardly heard what was spoken to him, he was very frail, and his eyes were really uncanny. His mother had sudden seizures of uneasiness about him. Sometimes, for half-an-hour, she would feel a sudden anxiety about him that was almost anguish. She wanted to rush to him at once, and know he was safe.

Two nights before the Derby, she was at a big party in town, when one of her rushes of anxiety about her boy, her first-born, gripped her heart till she could hardly speak. She fought with the feeling, might and main, for she believed in common sense. But it was too strong. She had to leave the dance and go downstairs to telephone to the country. The children's nursery-governess was terribly surprised and startled at being rung up in the night.

"Are the children all right, Miss Wilmot?"

"Oh, yes, they are quite all right."

"Master Paul? Is he all right?"

"He went to bed as right as a trivet. Shall I run up and look at him?"

"No," said Paul's mother reluctantly. "No! Don't trouble. It's all right. Don't sit up. We shall be home fairly soon." She did not want her son's privacy intruded upon.

"Very good," said the governess.

It was about one o'clock when Paul's mother and father drove up to their house. All was still. Paul's mother went to her room and slipped off her white fur coat. She had told her maid not to wait up for her. She heard her husband downstairs, mixing a whisky-and-soda.

And then, because of the strange anxiety at her heart, she stole upstairs to her son's room. Noiselessly she went along the upper corridor. Was there a faint noise? What was it?

She stood, with arrested muscles, outside his door, listening. There was a strange, heavy, and yet not loud noise. Her heart stood still. It was a soundless noise, yet rushing and powerful. Something huge, in violent, hushed motion. What was it? What in God's name was it? She ought to know. She felt that she knew the noise. She knew what it was.

Yet she could not place it. She couldn't say what it was. And on and on it went, like a madness.

Softly, frozen with anxiety and fear, she turned the door handle.

The room was dark. Yet in the space near the window, she heard and saw something plunging to and fro. She gazed in fear and amazement.

Then suddenly she switched on the light, and saw her son, in his green pyjamas, madly surging on the rocking horse. The blaze of light suddenly lit him up, as he urged the wooden horse, and lit her up, as she stood, blonde, in her dress of pale green and crystal, in the doorway.

"Paul!" she cried. "Whatever are you doing?"

"It's Malabar!" he screamed, in a powerful, strange voice. "It's Malabar."

His eyes blazed at her for one strange and senseless second, as he ceased urging his wooden horse. Then he fell with a crash to the ground, and she, all her tormented motherhood flooding upon her, rushed to gather him up.

But he was unconscious, and unconscious he remained, with some brain-fever. He talked and tossed, and his mother sat stonily by his side.

"Malabar! It's Malabar! Bassett, Bassett, I know! It's Malabar!"

So the child cried, trying to get up and urge the rocking horse that gave him his inspiration.

"What does he mean by Malabar?" asked the heart-frozen mother.

"I don't know," said the father stonily.

"What does he mean by Malabar?" she asked her brother Oscar.

"It's one of the horses running for the Derby," was the answer.

And, in spite of himself, Oscar Cresswell spoke to Bassett, and himself put a thousand on Malabar: at fourteen to one.

The third day of the illness was critical: they were waiting for a change. The boy, with his rather long, curly hair, was tossing ceaselessly on the pillow. He neither slept nor regained consciousness, and his eyes were like blue stones. His mother sat, feeling her heart had gone, turned actually into a stone.

In the evening, Oscar Cresswell did not come, but Bassett sent a message, saying could he come up for one moment, just one moment? Paul's mother was very angry at the intrusion, but on second thought she agreed. The boy was the same. Perhaps Bassett might bring him to consciousness.

The gardener, a shortish fellow with a little brown moustache, and sharp little brown eyes, tiptoed into the room, touched his imaginary cap to Paul's mother, and stole to the bedside, staring with glittering, smallish eyes, at the tossing, dying child.

"Master Paul!" he whispered. "Master Paul! Malabar come in first all right, a clean win. I did as you told me. You've made over seventy thousand pounds, you have; you've got over eighty thousand. Malabar came in all right, Master Paul."

"Malabar! Malabar! Did I say Malabar, mother? Did I say Malabar? Do you think I'm lucky, mother? I knew Malabar, didn't I? Over eighty thousand pounds! I call that lucky, don't you, mother? Over eighty thousand pounds! I knew, didn't I know I knew? Malabar came in all right. If I ride my horse till I'm sure, then I tell you, Bassett, you can go as high as you like. Did you go for all you were worth, Bassett?"

"I went a thousand on it, Master Paul."

"I never told you, mother, that if I can ride my horse, and get there, then I'm absolutely sure—oh, absolutely! Mother, did I ever tell you? I am lucky."

"No, you never did," said the mother.

But the boy died in the night.

And even as he lay dead, his mother heard her brother's voice saying to her: "My God, Hester, you're eighty-odd thousand to the good and a poor devil of a son to the bad. But, poor devil, poor devil, he's best gone out of a life where he rides his rocking horse to find a winner."

symbols

QUESTIONS

1. In the phraseology of its beginning ("There was a woman . . ."), its simple style, its direct characterization, and its use of the wish-motif—especially that of the wish which is granted only on conditions that nullify its desirability (cf. the story of King Midas)—this story has the qualities of a fairy tale. Its differences, however—in characterization, setting, and ending—are especially significant. What do they tell us about the purpose of the story?
2. Characterize the mother fully. How does she differ from the stepmothers in fairy tales like "Cinderella" and "Hansel and Gretel"? How does the boy's mistake about *filthy lucker* clarify her thinking and her motivations? Why had her love for her husband turned to dust? Why is she "unlucky"?
3. What kind of child is Paul? What are his motivations?
4. The initial assumptions of the story are that (a) a boy might get divinatory powers by riding a rocking horse, (b) a house can whisper. Could the second of these be accepted as little more than a metaphor? Once we have granted these initial assumptions, does the story develop plausibly?
5. It is ironical that the boy's attempt to stop the whispers should only increase them. Is this a plausible irony? Why? What does it tell us about the theme of the story? Why is it ironical that the whispers should be especially audible at Christmas time? What irony is contained in the boy's last speech?
6. In what way is the boy's furious riding on the rocking horse an appropriate symbol for materialistic pursuits?
7. How might a sentimental writer have ended the story?
8. How many persons in the story are affected (or infected) by materialism?
9. What is the theme of the story?

9

The Scale of Value

Our purpose in *Story and Structure* has been to develop, not literary critics, but proficient readers—readers who choose wisely and read well. Yet good reading involves criticism, for choice necessitates judgment. Though we need not, to read well, be able to settle the relative claims of Munro and Callaghan, or of Hemingway and Faulkner, we do need to discriminate between the genuine and the spurious, the consequential and the trivial, the significant and the merely entertaining. Our first object, naturally, is enjoyment; but full development as human beings requires that we enjoy most what is most worth enjoying.

There are no easy rules for literary judgment. Such judgment depends ultimately on our perceptivity, intelligence, and experience; it is a product of how much and how alertly we have lived and how much and how well we have read. Yet at least two basic principles may be set up. *First, every story is to be initially judged by how fully it achieves its central purpose.* Each element in the story is to be judged by the effectiveness of its contribution to the central purpose. In a good story every element works with every other element for the accomplishment of this central purpose. It follows that no element in the story may be judged in isolation.

Perhaps the most frequent mistake made by poor readers when called upon for a judgment is to judge the elements of the story in isolation, independently of each other. For example, a student once wrote of "I'm a Fool" that it is not a very good story "because it is not written in good English." And certainly the style of the story, if judged by itself, is very poor indeed: the language is slangy and ungrammatical; the sentences are often disjointed and broken-backed; the narrator constantly digresses and is at times so incapable of expressing himself that he can only say "etc., etc., you know." But no high level of discrimination is needed to see that just such a style is essential to the purpose of the story. The uneducated race-track swipe, whose failure in school life has made him feel both scornful and envious of boys who "go to high schools and college," can hardly speak otherwise than as he does here; the digressions, moreover, are not truly digressions, for each of them supplies additional insight into the character of the swipe, which is the true subject of the story. In "The Enchanted Doll," on the other hand, which is also told from the first-person point of view, the style fails to support the intelligence and sensitivity of the narrator. Here the protagonist is represented as an educated man more than ordinarily perceptive and open to fresh experience. He responds to a doll in a window as though the doll had actually called to him, and he tells us that "the doctor who comes into the sickroom must hear and see with his skin as well as his eyes and ears." Yet this discriminating narrator (who, like Sergeant Marx in "Defender of the Faith," is a war veteran) continually uses sentimental clichés in telling his story. The felt presence of the doll in his room, he says, "brought an indescribable longing to my throat and a sadness to my heart." When he visits Essie, "Something strange happened. For a moment we seemed to be caught up in one another's eyes." Unless he can determine the cause of her sickness, "that spirit would not be long for this earth." Departing "with great heaviness of heart," he thinks about her "night and day." Then, "the scales" fall from his eyes, and he cries out, "I love Essie Nolan! . . . I need her person and her soul forever at my side." And so on. The other characters—Rose Callamit and Abe Sheftel—also speak in clichés, but we expect it of them. We do not expect it of the doctor.

The principle of judgment just applied to style may be applied to every other element in a story. We cannot say that "First Born Son" is a poor story because it does not have an exciting, fast-moving plot: plot can be judged only in relation to the other elements in the story and to its central purpose, and in this relationship the plot of "First Born Son" is a good one. We cannot say that "Millstone for the Sun's Day" is a poor story because it contains no such complex characterization as is to be found in "I'm a Fool." The purpose of "Millstone for the Sun's Day" is to make a generalization about the persistence of dark communal impulses in human life and for this purpose its characterization is adequate: a more complete characterization might obscure this central purpose. Similarly, we cannot call "The Enchanted Doll" a good story just because it has a true and deeply significant theme. A theme is successful insofar as it is supported and justified by the other elements in the story, and in this story the characterizations are so flat, the contrasts between good and evil so exaggerated, the plot so obviously derived from formula, and the appeals to stock response so blatant (flower-sellers, hurdy-gurdies, children playing hopscotch, young lovers fond of children, an idealistic doctor living in poverty and ministering to the poor, innocence oppressed, a quotation from Jesus, and, finally, motherhood) that the theme (itself designed to appeal to stock response) is robbed of reality and significance.

Every first-rate story is an organic whole. All of its parts are related, and all are necessary to the central purpose of the story. One of the most frequent characteristics of commercial fiction, on the other hand, is the introduction of an irrelevant "love interest" to add additional reader appeal. One can be sure that if a Hollywood movie were made of "Horses of the Night," the relationship between Chris and Vanessa would have evolved into much more than the genuine understanding and respect we find in the story. Their camping out under the stars would no doubt have resulted in Chris breaking down and confessing his love for Vanessa, despite the disparity in age. Vanessa would have constantly grieved for Chris while he was at war instead of forgetting about him for long periods of time. As told by Margaret Laurence, the story has a unity and singleness of purpose which testify to the superb tale-spinning artistry of its author and which a typical Hollywood treatment would shatter.

Once a story has been judged successful in achieving its central purpose, we may apply a second principle of judgment. *A story, if successful, may be judged by the significance of its purpose.* If every story is to be judged by how successfully it integrates its materials into an organic unity, it is also to be judged by the extent and the range and the value of the materials integrated. This principle returns us to our distinction between escape and interpretation. If a story's only aim is to entertain, whether by mystifying, surprising, thrilling, provoking to laughter or tears, or furnishing a substitute dream life, we may judge it of less value than a story whose aim is to *reveal.* "E Equals MC Squared," "The Waltz," "Horses of the Night," and "A Secret Lost in the Water" are all successful stories if we judge them by the degree to which they fulfill their central purpose. But "E Equals MC Squared" has a more significant purpose than "The Waltz," and "Horses of the Night" a more significant one than "A Secret Lost in the Water." When a story does provide some revelation—does make some serious statement about life—we may measure it by the breadth and depth of that revelation. "Horses of the Night" and "E Equals MC Squared" are both fine stories, but "Horses of the Night" attempts a deeper probing than does "E Equals MC Squared." The situation with which it is concerned is more crucial, cuts deeper. The story reveals a more significant range and depth of life.

Some stories, then, like "The Waltz" provide good fun and innocent merriment. Others, like "Horses of the Night" and "E Equals MC Squared" afford the good reader a deeper enjoyment through the insights they give into life. A third type, like many of the soap operas of television and radio, offer a cheaper and less innocent pleasure by providing escape under the guise of interpretation. Such stories, while professing to present real-life situations and every-day people and happenings, actually, by their shallowness of characterization, their falsifications of plot, their use of stock themes and stock emotions, present us with dangerous oversimplifications and distortions. They seriously misrepresent life, and are harmful to the extent that they keep us from a more sensitive, more discriminating response to experience.

The above types of stories do not fall into sharp, distinct categories. There are no fortified barriers running between them to inform us when we are passing from one realm into another. There are no appointed officials to whom we can apply for certain information. Our only passports are our own good judgments, based on our accumulated experience both with literature and life. Nevertheless, certain questions, if asked wisely and with consideration for the two principles developed in this chapter, may help us both to understand the stories we read and to place them with rough accuracy on a scale of value that rises through many gradations from "Poor" to "Good" to "Great." These questions, most of them explored in the previous chapters of this book, are for convenience summarized here.

GENERAL QUESTIONS FOR ANALYSIS AND EVALUATION

Plot

1. Who is the protagonist of the story? What are the conflicts? Are they physical, intellectual, moral, or emotional? Is the main conflict between sharply differentiated good and evil, or is it more subtle and complex?
2. Does the plot have unity? Are all of the episodes relevant to the total meaning or effect of the story? Does each incident grow logically out of the preceding incident and lead naturally to the next? Is the ending happy, unhappy, or indeterminate? Is it fairly achieved?
3. What use does the story make of chance and coincidence? Are these occurrences used to initiate, to complicate, or to resolve the story? How improbable are they?
4. How is suspense created in the story? Is the interest confined to "What happens next?" or are larger concerns involved? Can you find examples of mystery? Of dilemma?
5. What use does the story make of surprise? Are the surprises achieved fairly? Do they serve a significant purpose? Do they divert the reader's attention from weaknesses in the story?
6. To what extent is this a "formula" story?

Characters

7. What means does the author use to reveal character? Are the characters sufficiently dramatized? What use is made of character contrasts?

8. Are the characters consistent in their actions? Adequately motivated? Plausible? Does the author successfully avoid stock characters?
9. Is each character fully enough developed to justify his role in the story? Are the main characters round or flat?
10. Is any of the characters a developing character? If so, is his change a large or a small one? Is it a plausible change for him? Is it sufficiently motivated? Is it given sufficient time?

Theme
11. Does the story have a theme? What is it? Is it implicit or explicit?
12. Does the theme reinforce or oppose popular notions of life? Does it furnish a new insight or refresh or deepen an old one?

Point of View
13. What point of view does the story use? Is it consistent in its use of this point of view? If shifts are made, are they justified?
14. What advantages has the chosen point of view? Does it furnish any clues as to the purpose of the story?
15. If the point of view is that of one of the characters, does this character have any limitations which affect his interpretation of events or persons?
16. Does the author use point of view primarily to reveal or conceal? Does he ever unfairly withhold important information known to the focal character?

Symbol and Irony
17. Does the story make use of symbols? If so, do the symbols carry or merely reinforce the meaning of the story?
18. Does the story anywhere utilize irony of situation? Dramatic irony? Verbal irony? What functions do the ironies serve?

Emotion and Humor
19. Does the story aim directly at an emotional *effect*, or is emotion merely its natural by-product?
20. Is the emotion sufficiently dramatized? Is the author anywhere guilty of sentimentality?

Fantasy
21. Does the story employ fantasy? If so, what is the initial assumption? Does the story operate logically from this assumption?
22. Is the fantasy employed for its own sake or to express some human truth? If the latter, what truth?

General
23. Is the primary interest of the story in plot, character, theme, or some other element?
24. What contribution to the story is made by its setting? Is the particular setting essential, or could the story have happened anywhere?

25. What are the characteristics of the author's style? Are they appropriate to the nature of his story?
26. What light is thrown on the story by its title?
27. Do all elements of the story work together to support a central purpose? Is any part irrelevant or inappropriate?
28. What do you conceive to be the story's central purpose? How fully has it achieved that purpose?
29. Does the story offer chiefly escape or interpretation? How significant is the story's purpose?
30. Does the story gain or lose on a second reading?

Exercise A

The following three stories have two points of comparison: they are all very brief, and their plots hinge on an overheard conversation. In intention and literary quality, however, they differ sharply. One is a skillfully written story meant purely for entertainment. Another gives the surface appearance of saying something serious about life, but is so false in its treatment of its materials that the statement is robbed of any real significance. Another conveys a genuine and moving insight for the qualified reader. Match the stories with the above descriptions, and support your decision with a thorough analysis.

Lord Dunsany

THE GUEST

A young man came into an ornate restaurant at eight o'clock in London.

He was alone, but two places had been laid at the table which was reserved for him. He had chosen the dinner very carefully, by letter a week before.

A waiter asked him about the other guest.

"You probably won't see him till the coffee comes," the young man told him; so he was served alone.

Those at adjacent tables might have noticed the young man continually addressing the empty chair and carrying on a monologue with it throughout his elaborate dinner.

THE GUEST From *Fifty-one Tales* by Lord Dunsany. Reprinted by permission of the author's estate. First published in 1915.

"I think you knew my father," he said to it over the soup.

"I sent for you this evening," he continued, "because I want you to do me a good turn; in fact I must insist on it."

There was nothing eccentric about the man except for this habit of addressing an empty chair, certainly he was eating as good a dinner as any sane man could wish for.

After the Burgundy had been served he became more voluble in his monologue, not that he spoiled his wine by drinking excessively.

"We have several acquaintances in common," he said. "I met King Seti a year ago in Thebes. I should think he has altered very little since you knew him. I thought his forehead a little low for a king's. Cheops has left the house that he built for your reception, he must have prepared for you for years and years. I suppose you have seldom been entertained like that. I ordered this dinner over a week ago. I thought then that a lady might have come with me, but as she wouldn't I've asked you. She may not after all be as lovely as Helen of Troy. Was Helen very lovely? Not when you knew her, perhaps. You were lucky in Cleopatra, you must have known her when she was in her prime.

"You never knew the mermaids nor the fairies nor the lovely goddesses of long ago, that's where we have the best of you."

He was silent when the waiters came to his table, but rambled merrily on as soon as they left, still turned to the empty chair.

"You know I saw you here in London only the other day. You were on a motor bus going down Ludgate Hill. It was going much too fast. London is a good place. But I shall be glad enough to leave it. It was in London I met the lady that I was speaking about. If it hadn't been for London I probably shouldn't have met her, and if it hadn't been for London she probably wouldn't have had so much besides me to amuse her. It cuts both ways."

He paused once to order coffee, gazing earnestly at the waiter and putting a sovereign into his hand. "Don't let it be chicory," said he.

The waiter brought the coffee, and the young man dropped a tabloid of some sort into his cup.

"I don't suppose you come here very often," he went on. "Well, you probably want to be going. I haven't taken you much out of your way, there is plenty for you to do in London."

Then having drunk his coffee he fell on to the floor by a foot of the empty chair, and a doctor who was dining in the room bent over him and announced to the anxious manager the visible presence of the young man's guest.

Katherine Mansfield

MISS BRILL

Although it was so brilliantly fine—the blue sky powdered with gold and great spots of light like white wine splashed over the Jardins Publiques—Miss Brill was glad that she had decided on her fur. The air was motionless, but when you opened your mouth there was just a faint chill, like a chill from a glass of iced water before you sip, and now and again a leaf came drifting—from nowhere, from the sky. Miss Brill put up her hand and touched her fur. Dear little thing! It was nice to feel it again. She had taken it out of its box that afternoon, shaken out the moth powder, given it a good brush, and rubbed the life back into the dim little eyes. "What has been happening to me?" said the sad little eyes. Oh, how sweet it was to see them snap at her again from the red eiderdown! ... But the nose, which was of some black composition, wasn't at all firm. It must have had a knock, somehow. Never mind—a little dab of black sealing-wax when the time came—when it was absolutely necessary. . . . Little rogue! Yes, she really felt like that about it. Little rogue biting its tail just by her left ear. She could have taken it off and laid it on her lap and stroked it. She felt a tingling in her hands and arms, but that came from walking, she supposed. And when she breathed, something light and sad—no, not sad, exactly—something gentle seemed to move in her bosom.

There were a number of people out this afternoon, far more than last Sunday. And the band sounded louder and gayer. That was because the Season had begun. For although the band played all the year round on Sundays, out of season it was never the same. It was like some one playing with only the family to listen; it didn't care how it played if there weren't any strangers present. Wasn't the conductor wearing a new coat, too? She was sure it was new. He scraped with his foot and flapped his arms like a rooster about to crow, and the bandsmen sitting in the green rotunda blew out their cheeks and glared at the music. Now there came a little "flutey" bit—very pretty!—a little chain of bright drops. She was sure it would be repeated. It was; she lifted her head and smiled.

Only two people shared her "special" seat: a fine old man in a velvet coat, his hands clasped over a huge carved walking-stick, and a big old woman, sitting upright, with a roll of knitting on her embroidered apron. They did not speak. This was disappointing, for Miss Brill

MISS BRILL   "Miss Brill" by Katherine Mansfield from *The Short Stories of Katherine Mansfield*, published by Alfred A. Knopf, Inc.

always looked forward to the conversation. She had become really quite expert, she thought, at listening as though she didn't listen, at sitting in other people's lives just for a minute while they talked round her.

She glanced, sideways, at the old couple. Perhaps they would go soon. Last Sunday, too, hadn't been as interesting as usual. An Englishman and his wife, he wearing a dreadful Panama hat and she button boots. And she'd gone on the whole time about how she ought to wear spectacles; she knew she needed them; but that it was no good getting any; they'd be sure to break and they'd never keep on. And he'd been so patient. He'd suggested everything—gold rims, the kind that curved round your ears, little pads inside the bridge. No, nothing would please her. "They'll always be sliding down my nose!" Miss Brill had wanted to shake her.

The old people sat on the bench, still as statues. Never mind, there was always the crowd to watch. To and fro, in front of the flower beds and the band rotunda, the couples and groups paraded, stopped to talk, to greet, to buy a handful of flowers from the old beggar who had his tray fixed to the railings. Little children ran among them, swooping and laughing; little boys with big white silk bows under their chins, little girls, little French dolls, dressed up in velvet and lace. And sometimes a tiny staggerer came suddenly rocking into the open from under the trees, stopped, stared, as suddenly sat down "flop," until its small high-stepping mother, like a young hen, rushed scolding to its rescue. Other people sat on the benches and green chairs, but they were nearly always the same, Sunday after Sunday, and—Miss Brill had often noticed—there was something funny about nearly all of them. They were odd, silent, nearly all old, and from the way they stared they looked as though they'd just come from dark little rooms or even—even cupboards!

Behind the rotunda the slender trees with yellow leaves down drooping, and through them just a line of sea, and beyond the blue sky with gold-veined clouds.

Tum-tum-tum tiddle-um! tiddle-um! tum tiddley-um tum ta! blew the band.

Two young girls in red came by and two young soldiers in blue met them, and they laughed and paired and went off arm-in-arm. Two peasant women with funny straw hats passed, gravely, leading beautiful smoke-colored donkeys. A cold, pale nun hurried by. A beautiful woman came along and dropped her bunch of violets, and a little boy ran after to hand them to her, and she took them and threw them away as if they'd been poisoned. Dear me! Miss Brill didn't know whether to admire that or not! And now an ermine toque and a gentleman in gray met just in front of her. He was tall, stiff, dignified, and she was wearing the ermine toque she'd bought when her hair was yellow. Now everything, her hair, her face, even her eyes, was the same color as the shabby ermine, and her hand, in its cleaned glove, lifted to dab her lips, was a tiny yellowish paw. Oh, she was so pleased to see him—delighted! She rather thought they were going to meet that afternoon. She described where she'd been—everywhere, here, there, along by the sea. The day was so charming—didn't he agree? And wouldn't he, perhaps? . . . But he shook his head, lighted a cigarette, slowly breathed a great deep puff into her face, and, even while she was still talking and laughing, flicked the match away and walked on. The ermine toque was alone; she smiled more brightly than ever. But even the band seemed to know what she was feeling and played more softly, played tenderly, and the drum beat, "The Brute! The Brute!" over and over. What would she do? What was going to happen now? But as Miss Brill wondered, the ermine toque turned, raised her hand as though she'd seen some one else, much nicer, just over there, and pattered away. And the band changed again and played more quickly, more gayly than ever, and the old couple on Miss Brill's seat got up and marched away, and such a funny old man with long whiskers hobbled along in time to the music and was nearly knocked over by four girls walking abreast.

Oh, how fascinating it was! How she enjoyed it! How she loved sitting here, watching it all! It was like a play. It was exactly like a play. Who could believe the sky at the back wasn't painted? But it wasn't till a little brown dog trotted on solemn and then slowly trotted off, like a little "theater" dog, a little dog that had been drugged, that Miss Brill discovered what it was that made it so exciting. They were all on the stage. They weren't only the audience, not only looking on; they were acting. Even she had a part and came every Sunday. No doubt somebody would have noticed if she hadn't been there; she was part of the performance after all. How strange she'd never thought of it like that before! And yet it explained why she made such a point of starting from home at just the same time each week—so as not to be late for the performance—and it also explained why she had quite a queer, shy feeling at telling her English pupils how she spent her Sunday afternoons. No wonder! Miss Brill nearly laughed out loud. She was on the stage. She thought of the old invalid gentleman to whom she read the newspaper four afternoons a week while he slept in the garden. She had got quite used to the frail head on the cotton pillow, the hollowed eyes, the open mouth and the high pinched nose. If he'd been dead she mightn't have noticed for weeks; she wouldn't have minded. But suddenly he knew he was having the paper read to him by an actress! "An actress!" The old head lifted; two points of light quivered in the old eyes. "An actress—are ye?" And Miss Brill smoothed the newspaper as though it were the manuscript of her part and said gently: "Yes, I have been an actress for a long time."

The band had been having a rest. Now they started again. And what they played was warm, sunny, yet there was just a faint chill—a something, what was it?—not sadness—no, not sadness—a something that made you want to sing. The tune lifted, lifted, the light shone; and it seemed to Miss Brill that in another moment all of them, all the whole company, would begin singing. The young ones, the laughing ones who were moving together, they would begin, and the men's voices, very resolute and brave, would join them. And then she too, she too, and the others on the benches—they would come in with a kind of accompaniment—something low, that scarcely rose or fell, something so beautiful—moving. . . . And Miss Brill's eyes filled with tears and she looked smiling at all the other members of the company. Yes, we understand, we understand, she thought—though what they understood she didn't know.

Just at that moment a boy and a girl came and sat down where the old couple had been. They were beautifully dressed; they were in love. The hero and heroine, of course, just arrived from his father's yacht. And still soundlessly singing, still with that trembling smile, Miss Brill prepared to listen.

"No, not now," said the girl. "Not here, I can't."

"But why? Because of that stupid old thing at the end there?" asked the boy. "Why does she come here at all—who wants her? Why doesn't she keep her silly old mug at home?"

"It's her fu-fur which is so funny," giggled the girl. "It's exactly like a fried whiting."

"Ah, be off with you!" said the boy in an angry whisper. Then: "Tell me, ma petite chère—"

"No, not here," said the girl. "Not yet."

On her way home she usually bought a slice of honeycake at the baker's. It was her Sunday treat. Sometimes there was an almond in her slice, sometimes not. It made a great difference. If there was an almond it was like carrying home a tiny present—a surprise—something that might very well not have been there. She hurried on the almond Sundays and struck the match for the kettle in quite a dashing way.

But today she passed the baker's by, climbed the stairs, went into the little dark room—her room like a cupboard—and sat down on the red eiderdown. She sat there for a long time. The box that the fur came out of was on the bed. She unclasped the necklet quickly; quickly, without looking, laid it inside. But when she put the lid on she thought she heard something crying.

F. R. Buckley

GOLD-MOUNTED GUNS

Evening had fallen on Longhorn City, and already, to the south, an eager star was twinkling in the velvet sky, when a spare, hard-faced man slouched down the main street and selected a pony from the dozen hitched beside Tim Geogehan's general store. The town, which in the daytime suffered from an excess of eye-searing light in its open spaces, confined its efforts at artificial lighting to the one store, the one saloon, and its neighbor, the Temple of Chance; so it was from a dusky void that the hard-faced man heard himself called by name.

"Tommy!" a subdued voice accosted him.

The hard-faced man made, it seemed, a very slight movement—a mere flick of the hand at his low-slung belt; but it was a movement perfectly appraised by the man in the shadows.

"Wait a minute!" the voice pleaded.

A moment later, his hands upraised, his pony's bridle-reins caught in the crook of one arm, a young man moved into the zone of light that shone bravely out through Tim Geogehan's back window.

"Don't shoot," he said, trying to control his nervousness before the weapon unwaveringly trained upon him. "I'm—a friend."

For perhaps fifteen seconds the newcomer and the hard-faced man examined each other with the unwinking scrutiny of those who take chances of life and death. The younger, with that lightning draw fresh in his mind, noted the sinister droop of a gray moustache over a hidden mouth, and shivered a little as his gaze met that of a pair of steel-blue eyes. The man with the gun saw before him a rather handsome face, marred, even in this moment of submission, by a certain desperation.

"What do you want?" he asked, tersely.

"Can I put my hands down?" countered the other.

The lean man considered.

"All things bein' equal," he said, "I think I'd rather you'd first tell me how you got round to callin' me Tommy. Been askin' people in the street?"

"No," said the boy. "I only got into town this afternoon, an' I ain't a fool anyway. I seen you ride in this afternoon, and the way folks backed away from you made me wonder who you was. Then I seen them gold-mounted guns of yourn, an' of course I knew. Nobody ever had guns like them but Pecos Tommy. I could ha' shot you while you was gettin' your horse, if I'd been that way inclined."

GOLD-MOUNTED GUNS By F. R. Buckley, from *Redbook Magazine*, March 1922. Reprinted by permission of Willis Kingsley Wing. Copyright © 1922 by F. R. Buckley; renewed 1950. First published in 1922.

The lean man bit his moustache.

"Put 'em down. What do you want?"

"I want to join you."

"You want to *what?*"

"Yeah, I know it sounds foolish to you, mebbe," said the young man. "But, listen—your side-kicker's in jail down in Rosewell. I figured I could take his place—anyway, till he got out. I know I ain't got any record, but I can ride, an' I can shoot the pips out of a ten-spot at ten paces, an'—I got a little job to bring into the firm, to start with."

The lean man's gaze narrowed.

"Have, eh?" he asked, softly.

"It ain't anythin' like you go in for as a rule," said the boy, apologetically, "but it's a roll of cash an'—I guess it'll show you I'm straight. I only got on to it this afternoon. Kind of providential I should meet you right now."

The lean man chewed his moustache. His eyes did not shift.

"Yeah," he said, slowly. "What you quittin' punchin' for?"

"Sick of it."

"Figurin' robbin' trains is easier money?"

"No," said the young man, "I ain't. But I like a little spice in life. They ain't none in punchin'."

"Got a girl?" asked the lean man.

The boy shook his head. The hard faced man nodded reflectively.

"Well, what's the job?" he asked.

The light from Geogehan's window was cut off by the body of a man who, cupping his hands about his eyes, stared out into the night, as if to locate the buzz of voices at the back of the store.

"If you're goin' to take me on," said the young man, "I can tell you while we're riding toward it. If you ain't—why, there's no need to go no further."

The elder slipped back into its holster the gold-mounted gun he had drawn, glanced once at the obscured window and again, piercingly, at the boy whose face now showed white in the light of the rising moon. Then he turned his pony and mounted.

"Come on," he commanded.

Five minutes later the two had passed the limits of the town, heading for the low range of hills which encircled it to the south—and Will Arblaster had given the details of his job to the unemotional man at his side.

"How do you know the old guy's got the money?" came a level question.

"I saw him come out of the bank this afternoon, grinnin' all over his face an' stuffin' it into his pants pocket," said the boy. "An' when he was gone, I kind of inquired who he was. His name's Sanderson, an' he lives in this yer cabin right ahead a mile. Looked kind of a soft old geezer—kind that'd give up without any trouble. Must ha' been quite some cash there, judgin' by the size of the roll. But I guess when *you* ask him for it, he won't mind lettin' it go."

"I ain't goin' to ask him," said the lean man. "This is your job."

The boy hesitated.

"Well, if I do it right," he asked, with a trace of tremor in his voice, "will you take me along with you sure?"

"Yeah—I'll take you along."

The two ponies rounded a shoulder of the hill: before the riders there loomed, in the moonlight, the dark shape of a cabin, its windows unlighted. The lean man chuckled.

"He's out."

Will Arblaster swung off his horse.

"Maybe," he said, "but likely the money ain't. He started off home, an' if he's had to go out again, likely he's hid the money some place. Folks know *you're* about. I'm goin' to see."

Stealthily he crept toward the house. The moon went behind a cloud bank, and the darkness swallowed him. The lean man, sitting his horse, motionless, heard the rap of knuckles on the door—then a pause, and the rattle of the latch. A moment later came the heavy thud of a shoulder against wood—a cracking sound, and a crash as the door went down. The lean man's lips tightened. From within the cabin came the noise of one stumbling over furniture, then the fitful fire of a match illumined the windows. In the quiet, out there in the night, the man on the horse, twenty yards away, could hear the clumping of the other's boots on the rough board floor, and every rustle of the papers that he fumbled in his search. Another match scratched and sputtered, and then, with a hoarse cry of triumph, was flung down. Running feet padded across the short grass and Will Arblaster drew up, panting.

"Got it!" he gasped. "The old fool! Put it in a tea canister right on the mantelshelf. Enough to choke a horse! Feel it!"

The lean man, unemotional as ever, reached down and took the roll of money.

"Got another match?" he asked.

Willie struck one, and, panting, watched while his companion, moistening a thumb, ruffled through the bills.

"Fifty tens," said the lean man. "Five hundred dollars. Guess I'll carry it."

His cold blue eyes turned downward, and focused again with piercing attention on the younger man's upturned face. The bills were stowed in a pocket of the belt right next one of those gold-mounted guns which, earlier in the evening, had covered Willie Arblaster's heart. For a moment, the lean man's hand seemed to hesitate over its butt;

then, as Willie smiled and nodded, it moved away. The match burned out.

"Let's get out of here," the younger urged; whereupon the hand which had hovered over the gun butt grasped Will Arblaster's shoulder.

"No, not yet," he said quietly, "not just yet. Get on your hawss, an' set still awhile."

The young man mounted. "What's the idea?"

"Why!" said the level voice at his right. "This is a kind of novelty to me. Robbin' trains, you ain't got any chance to see results, like: this here's different. Figure this old guy'll be back pretty soon. I'd like to see what he does when he finds his wad's gone. Ought to be amusin'!"

Arblaster chuckled uncertainly.

"Ain't he liable to—"

"He can't see us," said the lean man with a certain new cheerfulness in his tone. "An' besides, he'll think we'd naturally be miles away; an' besides that, we're mounted, all ready."

"What's that?" whispered the young man, laying a hand on his companion's arm.

The other listened.

"Probably him," he said. "Now stay still."

There were two riders—by their voices, a man and a girl: they were laughing as they approached the rear of the house, where, roughly made of old boards, stood Pa Sanderson's substitute for a stable. They put up the horses; then their words came clearer to the ears of the listeners, as they turned the corner of the building, walking toward the front door.

"I feel mean about it, anyhow," said the girl's voice. "You going on living here, Daddy, while—"

"Tut-tut-tut!" said the old man. "What's five hundred to me? I ain't never had that much in a lump, an' shouldn't know what to do with it if I had. 'Sides, your Aunt Elviry didn't give it you for nothin'. 'If she wants to go to college,' says she, 'let her prove it by workin'. I'll pay half, but she's got to pay t'other half.' Well, you worked, an'—Where on earth did I put that key?"

There was a silence, broken by the grunts of the old man as he contorted himself in the search of his pockets: and then the girl spoke: the tone of her voice was the more terrible for the restraint she was putting on it.

"Daddy—the—the—did you leave the money in the house?"

"Yes. What is it?" cried the old man.

"Daddy—the door's broken down, and—"

There was a hoarse cry: boot heels stumbled across the boards, and again a match flared. Its pale light showed a girl standing in the doorway of the cabin, her hands clasped on her bosom—while beyond the wreckage of the door a bent figure with silver hair tottered away from the mantelshelf. In one hand Pa Sanderson held the flickering match, in the other a tin box.

"Gone!" he cried in his cracked voice. "Gone!"

Willie Arblaster drew a breath through his teeth and moved uneasily in his saddle. Instantly a lean, strong hand, with a grip like steel, fell on his wrist and grasped it. The man behind the hand chuckled.

"Listen!" he said.

"Daddy—Daddy—don't take on so—please don't," came the girl's voice, itself trembling with repressed tears. There was a scrape of chair legs on the floor as she forced the old man into his seat by the fireplace. He hunched there, his face in his hands, while she struck a match and laid the flame to the wick of the lamp on the table. As it burned up she went back to her father, knelt by him, and threw her arms about his neck.

"Now, now, now!" she pleaded. "Now, Daddy, it's all right. Don't take on so. It's all right."

But he would not be comforted.

"I can't replace it!" cried Pa Sanderson, dropping trembling hands from his face. "It's gone! Two years you've been away from me; two years you've slaved in a store; and now I've—"

"Hush, hush!" the girl begged. "Now, Daddy—it's all right. I can go on working, and—"

With a convulsive effort, the old man got to his feet. "Two years more slavery, while some skunk drinks your money, gambles it—throws it away!" he cried. "Curse him! Whoever it is, curse him! Where's God's justice? What's a man goin' to believe when years of scrapin' like your aunt done, an' years of slavin' like yours in Laredo there, an' all our happiness today can be wiped out by a damned thief in a minute?"

The girl put her little hand over her father's mouth.

"Don't, Daddy," she choked. "It only makes it worse. Come and lie down on your bed, and I'll make you some coffee. Don't cry, Daddy darling. Please."

Gently, like a mother with a little child, she led the heartbroken old man out of the watchers' line of vision, out of the circle of lamplight. More faintly, but still with heartrending distinctness, the listeners could hear the sounds of weeping.

The lean man sniffed, chuckled, and pulled his bridle.

"Some circus!" he said appreciatively. "C'mon, boy."

His horse moved a few paces, but Will Arblaster's did not. The lean man turned in his saddle.

"Ain't you comin'?" he asked.

For ten seconds, perhaps, the boy made no answer. Then he urged his pony forward until it stood side by side with his companion's.

"No," he said. "An'—an' I ain't goin' to take that money, neither."

"Huh?"

The voice was slow and meditative.

"Don't know as ever I figured what this game meant," he said. "Always seemed to me that all the hardships was on the stick-up man's side—gettin' shot at an' chased and so on. Kind of fun, at that. Never thought 'bout—old men cryin'."

"That ain't my fault," said the lean man.

"No," said Will Arblaster, still very slowly. "But I'm goin' to take that money back. You didn't have no trouble gettin' it, so you don't lose nothin'."

"Suppose I say I won't let go of it?" suggested the lean man with a sneer.

"Then," snarled Arblaster, "I'll blow your damned head off an' take it! Don't you move, you! I've got you covered. I'll take the money out myself."

His revolver muzzle under his companion's nose, he snapped open the pocket of the belt and extracted the roll of bills. Then, regardless of a possible shot in the back, he swung off his horse and shambled, with the mincing gait of the born horseman, into the lighted doorway of the cabin. The lean man, unemotional as ever, sat perfectly still, looking alternately at the cloud-dappled sky and at the cabin, from which now came a murmur of voices harmonizing with a strange effect of joy, to the half-heard bass of the night-wind.

It was a full ten minutes before Will Arblaster reappeared in the doorway alone, and made, while silhouetted against the light, a quick movement of his hand across his eyes, then stumbled forward through the darkness toward his horse. Still the lean man did not move.

"I'm—sorry," said the boy as he mounted. "But—"

"I ain't," said the lean man quietly. "What do you think I made you stay an' watch for, you young fool?"

The boy made no reply. Suddenly the hair prickled on the back of his neck and his jaw fell.

"Say," he demanded hoarsely at last, "ain't you Pecos Tommy?"

The lean man's answer was a short laugh.

"But you got his guns, an' the people in Longhorn all kind of fell back!" the boy cried. "If you ain't him, who are you?"

The moon had drifted from behind a cloud and flung a ray of light across the face of the lean man as he turned it, narrow-eyed, toward Arblaster. The pallid light picked out with terrible distinctness the grim lines of that face—emphasized the cluster of sun wrinkles about the corners of the piercing eyes and marked as if with underscoring black lines the long sweep of the fighting jaw.

"Why," said the lean man dryly, "I'm the sheriff that killed him yesterday. Let's be ridin' back."

Exercise B

The three stories which follow all deal with prisoners sentenced to execution. Though each is by a world-famous author, they differ markedly in quality. One of them would have to be set down as an escape story in which terror, horror, and suspense are exploited principally for their own sakes. The other two are serious in intention and make significant statements about life. One of them, however, is probably more successful as a story and certainly richer and more complex in the meanings it suggests. Match the stories with the above descriptions. Support your decision with a reasoned analysis, using the study questions for whatever help they may provide.

Jean-Paul Sartre

THE WALL

They pushed us into a large white room and my eyes began to blink because the light hurt them. Then I saw a table and four fellows seated at the table, civilians, looking at some papers. The other prisoners were herded together at one end and we were obliged to cross the entire room to join them. There were several I knew, and others who must have been foreigners. The two in front of me were blond with round heads. They looked alike. I imagine they were French. The smaller one kept pulling at his trousers, out of nervousness.

This lasted about three hours. I was dog-tired and my head was empty. But the room was well-heated, which struck me as rather agreeable; we had not stopped shivering for twenty-four hours. The guards led the prisoners in one after the other in front of the table. Then the four fellows asked them their names and what they did. Most of the time that was all—or perhaps from time to time they would ask such questions as: "Did you help sabotage the munitions?" or, "Where were you on the morning of the ninth and what were you doing?" They didn't even listen to the replies, or at least they didn't seem to. They just remained silent for a moment and looked straight ahead, then they began to write. They asked Tom if it was true he had served in the International Brigade. Tom couldn't say he hadn't because of the papers they had found in his jacket. They didn't ask Juan anything, but after he told them his name, they wrote for a long while.

"It's my brother José who's the anarchist," Juan said. "You know perfectly well he's not here now. I don't belong to any party. I never did take part in politics." They didn't answer.

Then Juan said, "I didn't do anything. And I'm not going to pay for what the others did."

His lips were trembling. A guard told him to stop talking and led him away. It was my turn.

"Your name is Pablo Ibbieta?"

I said yes.

The fellow looked at his papers and said, "Where is Ramon Gris?"

"I don't know."

"You hid him in your house from the sixth to the nineteenth."

"I did not."

They continued to write for a moment and the guards led me away. In the hall, Tom and Juan were waiting between two guards. We started walking. Tom asked one of the guards, "What's the idea?" "How do you mean?" the guard asked. "Was that just the preliminary questioning, or was that the trial?" "That was the trial," the guard said. "So now what? What are they going to do with us?" The guard answered drily, "The verdict will be told you in your cell."

In reality, our cell was one of the cellars of the hospital. It was terribly cold there because it was very drafty. We had been shivering all night long and it had hardly been any better during the day. I had spent the preceding five days in a cellar in the archbishop's palace, a sort of dungeon that must have dated back to the Middle Ages. There were lots of prisoners and not much room, so they housed them just anywhere. But I was not homesick for my dungeon. I hadn't been cold there, but I had been alone, and that gets to be irritating. In the cellar I had company. Juan didn't say a word; he was afraid, and besides, he was too young to have anything to say. But Tom was a good talker and knew Spanish well.

In the cellar there were a bench and four straw mattresses. When they led us back we sat down and waited in silence. After a while Tom said, "Our goose is cooked."

"I think so too," I said. "But I don't believe they'll do anything to the kid."

Tom said, "They haven't got anything on him. He's the brother of a fellow who's fighting, and that's all."

I looked at Juan. He didn't seem to have heard.

Tom continued, "You know what they do in Saragossa? They lay the guys across the road and then they drive over them with trucks. It was a Moroccan deserter who told us that. They say it's just to save ammunition."

I said, "Well, it doesn't save gasoline."

I was irritated with Tom; he shouldn't have said that.

He went on, "There are officers walking up and down the roads with their hands in their pockets, smoking, and they see that it's done right. Do you think they'd put 'em out of their misery? Like hell they do. They just let 'em holler. Sometimes as long as an hour. The Moroccan said the first time he almost puked."

"I don't believe they do that here," I said, "unless they really are short of ammunition."

The daylight came in through four air vents and a round opening that had been cut in the ceiling, to the left, and which opened directly onto the sky. It was through this hole, which was ordinarily closed by means of a trapdoor, that they unloaded coal into the cellar. Directly under the hole, there was a big pile of coal dust; it had been intended for heating the hospital, but at the beginning of the war they had evacuated the patients and the coal had stayed there unused; it even got rained on from time to time, when they forgot to close the trapdoor.

Tom started to shiver. "God damn it," he said, "I'm shivering. There, it is starting again."

He rose and began to do gymnastic exercises. At each movement, his shirt opened and showed his white, hairy chest. He lay down on his back, lifted his legs in the air and began to do the scissors movement. I watched his big buttocks tremble. Tom was tough, but he had too much fat on him. I kept thinking that soon bullets and bayonet points would sink into that mass of tender flesh as though it were a pat of butter.

I wasn't exactly cold, but I couldn't feel my shoulders or my arms. From time to time, I had the impression that something was missing and I began to look around for my jacket. Then I would suddenly remember they hadn't given me a jacket. It was rather awkward. They had taken our clothes to give them to their own soldiers and had left us only our shirts and these cotton trousers the hospital patients wore in mid-summer. After a moment, Tom got up and sat down beside me, breathless.

"Did you get warmed up?"

"Damn it, no. But I'm all out of breath."

Around eight o'clock in the evening, a Major came in with two falangists.

"What are the names of those three over there?" he asked the guard.

"Steinbock, Ibbieta and Mirbal," said the guard.

The Major put on his glasses and examined his list.

"Steinbock—Steinbock . . . Here it is. You are condemned to death. You'll be shot tomorrow morning."

He looked at his list again.

"The other two, also," he said.

"That's not possible," said Juan. "Not me."

The Major looked at him with surprise. "What's your name?"

"Juan Mirbal."

"Well, your name is here," said the Major, "and you're condemned to death."

"I didn't do anything," said Juan.

The Major shrugged his shoulders and turned toward Tom and me.

"You are both Basque?"

"No, nobody's Basque."

He appeared exasperated.

"I was told there were three Basques. I'm not going to waste my time running after them. I suppose you don't want a priest?"

We didn't even answer.

Then he said, "A Belgian doctor will be around in a little while. He has permission to stay with you all night."

He gave a military salute and left.

"What did I tell you?" Tom said. "We're in for something swell."

"Yes," I said. "It's a damned shame for the kid."

I said that to be fair, but I really didn't like the kid. His face was too refined and it was disfigured by fear and suffering, which had twisted all his features. Three days ago, he was just a kid with a kind of affected manner some people like. But now he looked like an aging fairy, and I thought to myself he would never be young again, even if they let him go. It wouldn't have been a bad thing to show him a little pity, but pity makes me sick, and besides, I couldn't stand him. He hadn't said anything more, but he had turned gray. His face and hands were gray. He sat down again and stared, round-eyed, at the ground. Tom was goodhearted and tried to take him by the arm, but the kid drew himself away violently and made an ugly face. "Leave him alone," I said quietly. "Can't you see he's going to start to bawl?" Tom obeyed regretfully. He would have liked to console the kid; that would have kept him occupied and he wouldn't have been tempted to think about himself. But it got on my nerves. I had never thought about death, for the reason that the question had never come up. But now it had come up, and there was nothing else to do but think about it.

Tom started talking. "Say, did you ever bump anybody off?" he asked me. I didn't answer. He started to explain to me that he had bumped off six fellows since August. He hadn't yet realized what we were in for, and I saw clearly he didn't *want* to realize it. I myself hadn't quite taken it in. I wondered if it hurt very much. I thought about the bullets; I imagined their fiery hail going through my body. All that was beside the real question; but I was calm, we had all night in which to realize it. After a while Tom stopped talking and I looked at him out of the corner of my eye. I saw that he, too, had turned gray and that he looked pretty miserable. I said to myself, "It's starting." It was almost dark, a dull light filtered through the air vents across the coal pile and made a big spot under the sky. Through the hole in the ceiling I could already see a star. The night was going to be clear and cold.

The door opened and two guards entered. They were followed by a blond man in a tan uniform. He greeted us.

"I'm the doctor," he said. "I've been authorized to give you any assistance you may require in these painful circumstances."

He had an agreeable, cultivated voice.

I said to him, "What are you going to do here?"

"Whatever you want me to do. I shall do everything in my power to lighten these few hours."

"Why did you come to us? There are lots of others: the hospital's full of them."

"I was sent here," he answered vaguely. "You'd probably like to smoke, wouldn't you?" he added suddenly. "I've got some cigarettes and even some cigars."

He passed around some English cigarettes and some *puros*, but we refused them. I looked him straight in the eye and he appeared uncomfortable.

"You didn't come here out of compassion," I said to him. "In fact, I know who you are. I saw you with some fascists in the barracks yard the day I was arrested."

I was about to continue, when all at once something happened to me which surprised me: the presence of this doctor had suddenly ceased to interest me. Usually, when I've got hold of a man I don't let go. But somehow the desire to speak had left me. I shrugged my shoulders and turned away. A little later, I looked up and saw he was watching me with an air of curiosity. The guards had sat down on one of the mattresses. Pedro, the tall thin one, was twiddling his thumbs, while the other one shook his head occasionally to keep from falling asleep.

"Do you want some light?" Pedro suddenly asked the doctor. The other fellow nodded, "Yes." I think he was not over-intelligent, but doubtless he was not malicious. As I looked at his big, cold, blue eyes, it seemed to me the worst thing about him was his lack of imagination. Pedro went out and came back with an oil lamp which he set on the corner of the bench. It gave a poor light, but it was better than nothing; the night before we had been left in the dark. For a long while I stared at the circle of light the lamp threw on the ceiling. I was fascinated. Then, suddenly, I came to, the light circle paled, and I felt as if I were being crushed under an enormous weight. It wasn't the thought of death, and it wasn't fear; it was something anonymous. My cheeks were burning hot and my head ached.

I roused myself and looked at my two companions. Tom had his head in his hands and only the fat, white nape of his neck was visible. Juan was by far the worst off; his mouth was wide open and his nostrils were trembling. The doctor came over to him and touched him on the shoulder, as though to comfort him; but his eyes remained cold. Then I saw the Belgian slide his hand furtively down Juan's arm to his wrist. Indifferent, Juan let himself be handled. Then, as though absent-mindedly, the Belgian laid three fingers over his wrist; at the same time, he drew away somewhat and managed to turn his back to me. But I leaned over backward and saw him take out his watch and look at it a moment before relinquishing the boy's wrist. After a moment, he let the inert hand fall and went and leaned against the wall. Then, as if he had suddenly remembered something very important that had to be noted down immediately, he took a notebook from his pocket and wrote a few lines in it. "The son-of-a-bitch," I thought angrily. "He better not come and feel my pulse; I'll give him a punch in his dirty jaw."

He didn't come near me, but I felt he was looking at me. I raised my head and looked back at him. In an impersonal voice, he said, "Don't you think it's frightfully cold here?"

He looked purple with cold.

"I'm not cold," I answered him.

He kept looking at me with a hard expression. Suddenly I understood, and I lifted my hands to my face. I was covered with sweat. Here, in this cellar, in mid-winter, right in a draft, I was sweating. I ran my fingers through my hair, which was stiff with sweat; at the same time, I realized my shirt was damp and sticking to my skin. I had been streaming with perspiration for an hour, at least, and had felt nothing. But this fact hadn't escaped that Belgian swine. He had seen the drops rolling down my face and had said to himself that it showed an almost pathological terror; and he himself had felt normal and proud of it because he was cold. I wanted to get up and go punch his face in, but I had hardly started to make a move before my shame and anger had disappeared. I dropped back onto the bench with indifference.

I was content to rub my neck with my handkerchief because now I felt the sweat dripping from my hair onto the nape of my neck and that was disagreeable. I soon gave up rubbing myself, however, for it didn't do any good; my handkerchief was already wringing wet and I was still sweating. My buttocks, too, were sweating, and my damp trousers stuck to the bench.

Suddenly, Juan said, "You're a doctor, aren't you?"

"Yes," said the Belgian.

"Do people suffer—very long?"

"Oh! When . . . ? No, no," said the Belgian, in a paternal voice, "it's quickly over."

His manner was as reassuring as if he had been answering a paying patient.

"But I . . . Somebody told me—they often have to fire two volleys."

"Sometimes," said the Belgian, raising his head, "it just happens that the first volley doesn't hit any of the vital organs."

"So then they have to reload their guns and aim all over again?" Juan thought for a moment, then added hoarsely, "But that takes time!"

He was terribly afraid of suffering. He couldn't think about anything else, but that went with his age. As for me, I hardly thought about it any more and it certainly was not fear of suffering that made me perspire.

I rose and walked toward the pile of coal dust. Tom gave a start and looked at me with a look of hate. I irritated him because my shoes squeaked. I wondered if my face was as putty-colored as his. Then I noticed that he, too, was sweating. The sky was magnificent; no light at all came into our dark corner and I had only to lift my head to see the Big Bear. But it didn't look the way it had looked before. Two days ago, from my cell in the archbishop's palace, I could see a big patch of sky and each time of day brought back a different memory. In the morning, when the sky was a deep blue, and light, I thought of beaches along the Atlantic; at noon, I could see the sun, and I remembered a bar in Seville where I used to drink manzanilla and eat anchovies and olives; in the afternoon, I was in the shade, and I thought of the deep shadow which covers half of the arena while the other half gleams in the sunlight: it really gave me a pang to see the whole earth reflected in the sky like that. Now, however, no matter how much I looked up in the air, the sky no longer recalled anything. I liked it better that way. I came back and sat down next to Tom. There was a long silence.

Then Tom began to talk in a low voice. He had to keep talking, otherwise he lost his way in his own thoughts. I believe he was talking to me, but he didn't look at me. No doubt he was afraid to look at me, because I was gray and sweating. We were both alike and worse than mirrors for each other. He looked at the Belgian, the only one who was alive.

"Say, do you understand? I don't."

Then I, too, began to talk in a low voice. I was watching the Belgian. "Understand what? What's the matter?"

"Something's going to happen to us that I don't understand."

There was a strange odor about Tom. It seemed to me that I was more sensitive to odors than ordinarily. With a sneer, I said, "You'll understand, later."

"That's not so sure," he said stubbornly. "I'm willing to be courageous, but at least I ought to know . . . Listen, they're going to take us out into the courtyard. All right. The fellows will be standing in line in front of us. How many of them will there be?"

"Oh, I don't know. Five, or eight. Not more."

"That's enough. Let's say there'll be eight of them. Somebody will shout 'Shoulder arms!' and I'll see all eight rifles aimed at me. I'm sure I'm going to feel like going through the wall. I'll push against the wall as hard as I can with my back, and the wall won't give in. The way it is in a nightmare. . . . I can imagine all that. Ah, if you only knew how well I can imagine it!"

"Skip it!" I said. "I can imagine it too."

"It must hurt like the devil. You know they aim at your eyes and mouth so as to disfigure you," he added maliciously. "I can feel the wounds already. For the last hour I've been having pains in my head and neck. Not real pains—it's worse still. They're the pains I'll feel tomorrow morning. And after that, then what?"

I understood perfectly well what he meant, but I didn't want to seem to understand. As for the pains, I, too, felt them all through my body, like a lot of little gashes. I couldn't get used to them, but I was like him, I didn't think they were very important.

"After that," I said roughly, "you'll be eating daisies."

He started talking to himself, not taking his eyes off the Belgian, who didn't seem to be listening to him. I knew what he had come for, and that what we were thinking didn't interest him. He had come to look at our bodies, our bodies which were dying alive.

"It's like in a nightmare," said Tom. "You want to think of something, you keep having the impression you've got it, that you're going to understand, and then it slips away from you, it eludes you and it's gone again. I say to myself, afterwards, there won't be anything. But I don't really understand what that means. There are moments when I almost do—and then it's gone again. I start to think of the pains, the bullets, the noise of the shooting. I am a materialist, I swear it; and I'm not going crazy, either. But there's something wrong. I see my own corpse. That's not hard, but it's *I* who see it, with *my* eyes. I'll have to get to the point where I think—where I think I won't see anything more. I won't hear anything more, and the world will go on for the others. We're not made to think that way, Pablo. Believe me, I've already stayed awake all night waiting for something. But this is not the same thing. This will grab us from behind, Pablo, and we won't be ready for it."

"Shut up," I said. "Do you want me to call a father confessor?"

He didn't answer. I had already noticed that he had a tendency to prophesy and call me "Pablo" in a kind of pale voice. I didn't like that very much, but it seems all the Irish are like that. I had a vague impression that he smelled of urine. Actually, I didn't like Tom very much, and I didn't see why, just because we were going to die together, I should like him any better. There are certain fellows with whom it would be different—with Ramon Gris, for instance. But between Tom and Juan, I felt alone. In fact, I liked it better that way. With Ramon I might have grown soft. But I felt terribly hard at that moment, and I wanted to stay hard.

Tom kept on muttering, in a kind of absent-minded way. He was certainly talking to keep from thinking. Naturally, I agreed with him, and I could have said everything he was saying. It's not *natural* to die. And since I was going to die, nothing seemed natural any more: neither the coal pile, nor the bench, nor Pedro's dirty old face. Only it was disagreeable for me to think the same things Tom thought. And I knew perfectly well that all night long, within five minutes of each other, we would keep on thinking things at the same time, sweating or shivering at the same time. I looked at him sideways and, for the first time, he seemed strange to me. He had death written on his face. My pride was wounded. For twenty-four hours I had lived side by side with Tom, I had listened to him, I had talked to him, and I knew we had nothing in common. And now we were as alike as twin brothers, simply because we were going to die together. Tom took my hand without looking at me.

"Pablo, I wonder . . . I wonder if it's true that we just cease to exist."

I drew my hand away.

"Look between your feet, your dirty dog."

There was a puddle between his feet and water was dripping from his trousers.

"What's the matter?" he said, frightened.

"You're wetting your pants," I said to him.

"It's not true," he said furiously. "I can't be . . . I don't feel anything."

The Belgian had come closer to him. With an air of false concern, he asked, "Aren't you feeling well?"

Tom didn't answer. The Belgian looked at the puddle without comment.

"I don't know what that is," Tom said savagely, "but I'm not afraid. I swear to you, I'm not afraid."

The Belgian made no answer. Tom rose and went to the corner. He came back, buttoning his fly, and sat down, without a word. The Belgian was taking notes.

We were watching the doctor. Juan was watching him too. All three of us were watching him because he was alive. He had the gestures of a living person, the interests of a living person; he was shivering in this cellar the way living people shiver; he had an obedient, well-fed body. We, on the other hand, didn't feel our bodies any more—not the same way, in any case. I felt like touching my trousers, but I didn't dare to. I looked at the Belgian, well-planted on his two legs, master of his muscles—and able to plan for tomorrow. We were like three shadows deprived of blood; we were watching him and sucking his life like vampires.

Finally he came over to Juan. Was he going to lay his hand on the nape of Juan's neck for some professional reason, or had he obeyed a charitable impulse? If he had acted out of charity, it was the one and only time during the whole night. He fondled Juan's head and the nape of his neck. The kid let him do it, without taking his eyes off him. Then, suddenly, he took hold of the doctor's hand and looked at it in a funny way. He held the Belgian's hand between his own two hands and there was nothing pleasing about them, those two gray paws squeezing that fat red hand. I sensed what was going to happen and Tom must have sensed it, too. But all the Belgian saw was emotion, and he smiled paternally. After a moment, the kid lifted the big red paw to his mouth and started to bite it. The Belgian drew back quickly and stumbled toward the wall. For a second, he looked at us with horror. He must have suddenly understood that we were not men like himself. I began to laugh, and one of the guards started up. The other had fallen asleep with his eyes wide open, showing only the whites.

I felt tired and over-excited at the same time. I didn't want to think any more about what was going to happen at dawn—about death. It didn't make sense, and I never got beyond just words, or emptiness. But whenever I tried to think about something else I saw the barrels of rifles aimed at me. I must have lived through my execution twenty times in succession; one time I thought it was the real thing; I must have dozed off for a moment. They were dragging me toward the wall and I was resisting; I was imploring their pardon. I woke with a start and looked at the Belgian. I was afraid I had cried out in my sleep. But he was smoothing his mustache; he hadn't noticed anything. If I had wanted to, I believe I could have slept for a while. I had been awake for the last forty-eight hours, and I was worn out. But I didn't want to lose two hours of life. They would have had to come and wake me at dawn. I would have followed them, drunk with sleep, and I would have gone off without so much as "Gosh!" I didn't want it that way, I didn't want to die like an animal. I wanted to understand. Besides, I was afraid of having nightmares. I got up and began to walk up and down and, so as to think about something else, I began to think about my past life. Memories crowded in on me, helter-skelter. Some were good and some were bad—at least that was how I had thought of them *before*. There were faces and happenings. I saw the face of a little *novilero* who had gotten himself horned during the *Feria*, in Valencia. I saw the face of one of my uncles, of Ramon Gris. I remembered all kinds of things that had happened: how I had been on strike for three months in 1926, and had almost died of hunger. I recalled a night I had spent on a bench in Granada; I hadn't eaten for three days, I was nearly wild, I didn't want to give up the sponge. I had to smile. With what eagerness I had run after happiness, and women, and liberty! And to what end? I wanted to liberate Spain, I admired Py Margall, I had belonged to the anarchist movement, I had spoken at public meetings. I took everything as seriously as if I had been immortal.

At that time I had the impression that I had my whole life before me, and I thought to myself, "It's all a god-damned lie." Now it wasn't worth anything because it was finished. I wondered how I had ever been able to go out and have a good time with girls. I wouldn't have lifted my little finger if I had ever imagined that I would die like this. I saw my life before me, finished, closed, like a bag, and yet what was inside was not finished. For a moment I tried to appraise it. I would have liked to say to myself, "It's been a good life." But it couldn't be appraised, it was only an outline. I had spent my time writing checks on eternity, and had understood nothing. Now, I didn't miss anything. There were a lot of things I might have missed: the taste of manzanilla, for instance, or the swims I used to take in summer in a little creek near Cadiz. But death had taken the charm out of everything.

Suddenly the Belgian had a wonderful idea.

"My friends," he said to us, "if you want me to—and providing the military authorities give their consent—I could undertake to deliver a word or some token from you to your loved ones. . . ."

Tom growled, "I haven't got anybody."

I didn't answer. Tom waited for a moment, then he looked at me with curiosity. "Aren't you going to send any message to Concha?"

"No."

I hated that sort of sentimental conspiracy. Of course, it was my fault, since I had mentioned Concha the night before, and I should have kept my mouth shut. I had been with her for a year. Even as late as last night, I would have cut my arm off with a hatchet just to see her again for five minutes. That was why I had mentioned her. I couldn't help it. Now I didn't care any more about seeing her. I hadn't anything more to say to her. I didn't even want to hold her in my arms. I loathed my body because it had turned gray and was sweating—and I wasn't even sure that I didn't loathe hers too. Concha would cry when she heard about my death; for months she would have no more interest in life. But still it was I who was going to die. I thought of her beautiful, loving eyes. When she looked at me something went from her to me. But I thought to myself that it was all over; if she looked at me *now* her gaze would not leave her eyes, it would not reach out to me. I was alone.

Tom too was alone, but not the same way. He was seated astride his chair and had begun to look at the bench with a sort of smile, with surprise, even. He reached out his hand and touched the wood cautiously, as though he were afraid of breaking something, then he drew his hand back hurriedly, and shivered. I wouldn't have amused myself touching that bench, if I had been Tom, that was just some more Irish play-acting. But somehow it seemed to me too that the different objects had something funny about them. They seemed to have grown paler, less massive than before. I had only to look at the bench, the lamp or the pile of coal dust to feel I was going to die. Naturally, I couldn't think clearly about my death, but I saw it everywhere, even on the different objects, the way they had withdrawn and kept their distance, tactfully, like people talking at the bedside of a dying person. It was *his own death* Tom had just touched on the bench.

In the state I was in, if they had come and told me I could go home quietly, that my life would be saved, it would have left me cold. A few hours, or a few years of waiting are all the same, when you've lost the illusion of being eternal. Nothing mattered to me any more. In a way, I was calm. But it was a horrible kind of calm—because of my body. My body—I saw with its eyes and I heard with its ears, but it was no longer I. It sweat and trembled independently, and I didn't recognize it any longer. I was obliged to touch it and look at it to know what was happening to it, just as if it had been someone else's body. At times I still felt it, I felt a slipping, a sort of headlong plunging, as in a falling airplane, or else I heard my heart beating. But this didn't give me confidence. In fact, everything that came from my body had something damned dubious about it. Most of the time it was silent, it stayed put and I didn't feel anything other than a sort of heaviness, a loathsome presence against me. I had the impression of being bound to an enormous vermin.

The Belgian took out his watch and looked at it.

"It's half-past three," he said.

The son-of-a-bitch! He must have done it on purpose. Tom jumped up. We hadn't yet realized the time was passing. The night surrounded us like a formless, dark mass; I didn't even remember it had started.

Juan started to shout. Wringing his hands, he implored, "I don't want to die! I don't want to die!"

He ran the whole length of the cellar with his arms in the air, then he dropped down onto one of the mattresses, sobbing. Tom looked at him with dismal eyes and didn't even try to console him any more. The fact was, it was no use; the kid made more noise than we did, but he was less affected, really. He was like a sick person who defends himself against his malady with a high fever. When there's not even any fever left, it's much more serious.

He was crying. I could tell he felt sorry for himself; he was thinking about death. For one second, one single second, I too felt like crying, crying out of pity for myself. But just the contrary happened. I took one look at the kid, saw his thin, sobbing shoulders, and I felt I was inhuman. I couldn't feel pity either for these others or for myself. I said to myself, "I want to die decently."

Tom had gotten up and was standing just under the round opening looking out for the first signs of daylight. I was determined, I wanted to die decently, and I only thought about that. But underneath, ever since the doctor had told us the time, I felt time slipping, flowing by, one drop at a time.

It was still dark when I heard Tom's voice.

"Do you hear them?"

"Yes."

People were walking in the courtyard.

"What the hell are they doing? After all, they can't shoot in the dark."

After a moment, we didn't hear anything more. I said to Tom, "There's the daylight."

Pedro got up yawning, and came and blew out the lamp. He turned to the man beside him. "It's hellish cold."

The cellar had grown gray. We could hear shots at a distance.

"It's about to start," I said to Tom. "That must be in the back courtyard."

Tom asked the doctor to give him a cigarette. I didn't want any; I didn't want either cigarettes or alcohol. From that moment on, the shooting didn't stop.

"Can you take it in?" Tom said.

He started to add something, then he stopped and began to watch the door. The door opened and a lieutenant came in with four soldiers. Tom dropped his cigarette.

"Steinbock?"

Tom didn't answer. Pedro pointed him out.

"Juan Mirbal?"

"He's the one on the mattress."

"Stand up," said the Lieutenant.

Juan didn't move. Two soldiers took hold of him by the armpits and stood him up on his feet. But as soon as they let go of him he fell down.

The soldiers hesitated a moment.

"He's not the first one to get sick," said the Lieutenant. "You'll have to carry him, the two of you. We'll arrange things when we get there." He turned to Tom. "All right, come along."

Tom left between two soldiers. Two other soldiers followed, carrying the kid by his arms and legs. He was not unconscious; his eyes were wide open and tears were rolling down his cheeks. When I started to go out, the Lieutenant stopped me.

"Are you Ibbieta?"

"Yes."

"You wait here. They'll come and get you later on."

They left. The Belgian and the two jailers left too, and I was alone. I didn't understand what had happened to me, but I would have liked it better if they had ended it all right away. I heard the volleys at almost regular intervals; at each one, I shuddered. I felt like howling and tearing my hair. But instead, I gritted my teeth and pushed my hands deep into my pockets, because I wanted to stay decent.

An hour later, they came to fetch me and took me up to the first floor in a little room which smelt of cigar smoke and was so hot it seemed to me suffocating. Here there were two officers sitting in comfortable chairs, smoking, with papers spread out on their knees.

"Your name is Ibbieta?"

"Yes."

"Where is Ramon Gris?"

"I don't know."

The man who questioned me was small and stocky. He had hard eyes behind his glasses.

"Come nearer," he said to me.

I went nearer. He rose and took me by the arms, looking at me in a way calculated to make me go through the floor. At the same time he pinched my arms with all his might. He didn't mean to hurt me; it was quite a game; he wanted to dominate me. He also seemed to think it was necessary to blow his fetid breath right into my face. We stood like that for a moment, only I felt more like laughing than anything else. It takes a lot more than that to intimidate a man who's about to die: it didn't work. He pushed me away violently and sat down again.

"It's your life or his," he said. "You'll be allowed to go free if you tell us where he is."

After all, these two bedizened fellows with their riding crops and boots were just men who were going to die one day. A little later than I, perhaps, but not a great deal. And there they were, looking for names among their papers, running after other men in order to put them in prison or do away with them entirely. They had their opinions on the future of Spain and on other subjects. Their petty activities seemed to me to be offensive and ludicrous. I could no longer put myself in their place. I had the impression they were crazy.

The little fat fellow kept looking at me, tapping his boots with his riding crop. All his gestures were calculated to make him appear like a spirited, ferocious animal.

"Well? Do you understand?"

"I don't know where Gris is," I said. "I thought he was in Madrid."

The other officer lifted his pale hand indolently. This indolence was also calculated. I saw through all their little tricks, and I was dumbfounded that men should still exist who took pleasure in that kind of thing.

"You have fifteen minutes to think it over," he said slowly. "Take him to the linen-room, and bring him back here in fifteen minutes. If he continues to refuse, he'll be executed at once."

They knew what they were doing. I had spent the night waiting. After that, they had made me wait another hour in the cellar, while they shot Tom and Juan, and now they locked me in the linen-room. They must have arranged the whole thing the night before. They figured that sooner or later people's nerves wear out and they hoped to get me that way.

They made a big mistake. In the linen-room I sat down on a ladder because I felt very weak, and I began to think things over. Not their proposition, however. Naturally I knew where Gris was. He was hiding in his cousins' house, about two miles outside of the city. I knew, too, that I would not reveal his hiding place, unless they tortured me (but they didn't seem to be considering that). All that was definitely settled and didn't interest me in the least. Only I would have liked to understand the reasons for my own conduct. I would rather die than betray Gris. Why? I no longer liked Ramon Gris. My friendship for him had died shortly before dawn along with my love for Concha, along with my own desire to live. Of course I still admired him—he was hard. But it was not for that reason that I was willing to die in his place; his life was no more valuable than mine. No life was of any value. A man was going to be stood up against a wall and fired at till he dropped dead. It didn't make any difference whether it was I or Gris or somebody else. I knew perfectly well he was more useful to the Spanish cause than I was, but I didn't give a God damn about Spain or anarchy, either; nothing had any importance now. And yet, there I was. I could save my skin by betraying Gris and I refused to do it. It seemed more ludicrous to me than anything else; it was stubbornness.

I thought to myself, "Am I hard-headed!" And I was seized with a strange sort of cheerfulness.

They came to fetch me and took me back to the two officers. A rat darted out under our feet and that amused me. I turned to one of the falangists and said to him, "Did you see that rat?"

He made no reply. He was gloomy, and took himself very seriously. As for me, I felt like laughing, but I restrained myself because I was afraid that if I started, I wouldn't be able to stop. The falangist wore mustaches. I kept after him, "You ought to cut off those mustaches, you fool."

I was amused by the fact that he let hair grow all over his face while he was still alive. He gave me a kind of half-hearted kick, and I shut up.

"Well," said the fat officer, "have you thought things over?"

I looked at them with curiosity, like insects of a very rare species.

"I know where he is," I said. "He's hiding in the cemetery. Either in one of the vaults, or in the gravediggers' shack."

I said that just to make fools of them. I wanted to see them get up and fasten their belts and bustle about giving orders.

They jumped to their feet.

"Fine. Moles, go ask Lieutenant Lopez for fifteen men. And as for you," the little fat fellow said to me, "if you've told the truth, I don't go back on my word. But you'll pay for this, if you're pulling our leg."

They left noisily and I waited in peace, still guarded by the falangists. From time to time I smiled at the thought of the face they were going to make. I felt dull and malicious. I could see them lifting up the gravestones, or opening the doors of the vaults one by one. I saw the whole situation as though I were another person: the prisoner determined to play the hero, the solemn falangists with their mustaches and the men in uniform running around among the graves. It was irresistibly funny.

After half an hour, the little fat fellow came back alone. I thought he had come to give the order to execute me. The others must have stayed in the cemetery.

The officer looked at me. He didn't look at all foolish.

"Take him out in the big courtyard with the others," he said. "When military operations are over, a regular tribunal will decide his case."

I thought I must have misunderstood.

"So they're not—they're not going to shoot me?" I asked.

"Not now, in any case. Afterwards, that doesn't concern me."

I still didn't understand.

"But why?" I said to him.

He shrugged his shoulders without replying, and the soldiers led me away. In the big courtyard there were a hundred or so prisoners, women, children and a few old men. I started to walk around the grass plot in the middle. I felt absolutely idiotic. At noon we were fed in the dining hall. Two or three fellows spoke to me. I must have known them, but I didn't answer. I didn't even know where I was.

Toward evening, about ten new prisoners were pushed into the courtyard. I recognized Garcia, the baker.

He said to me, "Lucky dog! I didn't expect to find you alive."

"They condemned me to death," I said, "and then they changed their minds. I don't know why."

"I was arrested at two o'clock," Garcia said.

"What for?"

Garcia took no part in politics.

"I don't know," he said. "They arrest everybody who doesn't think the way they do."

He lowered his voice.

"They got Gris."

I began to tremble.

"When?"

"This morning. He acted like a damned fool. He left his cousins' house Tuesday because of a disagreement. There were any number of fellows who would have hidden him, but he didn't want to be indebted to anybody any more. He said, 'I would have hidden at Ibbieta's, but since they've got him, I'll go hide in the cemetery.'"

"In the cemetery?"

"Yes. It was the god-damnedest thing. Naturally they passed by there this morning; that had to happen. They found him in the gravediggers' shack. They opened fire at him and they finished him off."

"In the cemetery!"

Everything went around in circles, and when I came to I was sitting on the ground. I laughed so hard the tears came to my eyes.

QUESTIONS

1. The country in which the story takes place, the historical event which forms its background, and even the nationalities of the main characters can all be identified. What are they, and what are the clues?
2. What is the wall referred to in the title? What symbolical value does it acquire in the story?
3. The substance of the story concerns the physiological and psychological reactions of three men sentenced to imminent death. Trace the reactions of each. How are they similar? Are there significant differences?
4. What are the motivations of the Belgian doctor? Why does he make Pablo so angry? What does he represent for all three of the condemned men?
5. Pablo's anticipation of death results for him in a changed understanding of the significance of life. Describe this change. How does it express itself in his motivations, his interests, his relationships, his attitudes toward his captors? What, finally, is his principal motivation?
6. Jean-Paul Sartre, French novelist and philosopher, is closely associated with the modern philosophical movement known as existentialism. According to this philosophy, the universe is irrational, meaningless, and absurd. It has no supernatural sanctions, it supports no transcendental values. Yet man, in this universe, has freedom to choose and to act, and by

the quality of his choices and actions he defines himself as a man. It is thus the part of wisdom for man to acknowledge the meaninglessness of life, and the part of courage to accept it; by his own actions he can create value in a universe otherwise without it. Though his heroism will not be rewarded, he can be heroic. How is this philosophy reflected in the story?

7. What contributions to the story are made by (a) the fact that the fascists have the upper hand, (b) Juan's being executed despite his noninvolvement in political or military activities, (c) Pablo's refusal to betray Ramon Gris even though he no longer cares about him, and (d) the ironic coincidence by which Gris is killed and Pablo spared?

Edgar Allan Poe

THE PIT AND THE PENDULUM   wrote the Raven

> Impie tortorum longos hic turba furores
> Sanguinis innocui, non satiata, aluit.
> Sospite nunc patriâ, fracto nunc funeris antro,
> Mors ubi dira fuit vita salusque patent.[1]

> [*Quatrain composed for the gates of a market to be erected upon the site of the Jacobin Club House at Paris.*]

I was sick—sick unto death with that long agony; and when they at length unbound me, and I was permitted to sit, I felt that my senses were leaving me. The sentence—the dread sentence of death—was the last of distinct accentuation which reached my ears. After that, the sound of the inquisitorial voices seemed merged in one dreamy indeterminate hum. It conveyed to my soul the idea of *revolution*—perhaps from its association in fancy with the burr of a mill-wheel. This only for a brief period; for presently I heard no more. Yet, for a while, I saw; but with how terrible an exaggeration! I saw the lips of the black-robed judges. They appeared to me white—whiter than the sheet upon which I trace these words—and thin even to grotesqueness; thin with the intensity of their expression of firmness—of immovable resolution—of stern contempt of human torture. I saw that the decrees of what to me was Fate were still issuing from those lips. I saw them writhe with a deadly locution. I saw them fashion the syllables of my name; and I shuddered

---

[1] The Latin inscription may be translated as follows: "Here, impiously, a mob of torturers maintained, unsatisfied, their long rage for innocent blood. Now, the country delivered and the dungeon of death destroyed, life and safety are manifest where death was fearful."

THE PIT AND THE PENDULUM   First published in 1842.

because no sound succeeded. I saw, too, for a few moments of delirious horror, the soft and nearly imperceptible waving of the sable draperies which enwrapped the walls of the apartment. And then my vision fell upon the seven tall candles upon the table. At first they wore the aspect of charity, and seemed white slender angels who would save me; but then, all at once, there came a most deadly nausea over my spirit, and I felt every fibre in my frame thrill as if I had touched the wire of a galvanic battery, while the angel forms became meaningless spectres, with heads of flame, and I saw that from them there would be no help. And then there stole into my fancy, like a rich musical note, the thought of what sweet rest there must be in the grave. The thought came gently and stealthily, and it seemed long before it attained full appreciation; but just as my spirit came at length properly to feel and entertain it, the figures of the judges vanished, as if magically, from before me; the tall candles sank into nothingness; their flames went out utterly; the blackness of darkness supervened; all sensations appeared swallowed up in a mad rushing descent as of the soul into Hades. Then silence, and stillness, and night were the universe.

I had swooned; but still will not say that all of consciousness was lost. What of it there remained I will not attempt to define, or even to describe; yet all was not lost. In the deepest slumber—no! In delirium—no! In a swoon—no! In death—no! even in the grave all *is not* lost. Else there is no immortality for man. Arousing from the most profound of slumbers, we break the gossamer web of *some* dream. Yet in a second afterward (so frail may that web have been) we remember not that we have dreamed. In the return to life from the swoon there are two stages; first, that of the sense of mental or spiritual; secondly, that of the sense of physical, existence. It seems probable that if, upon reaching the second stage, we could recall the impressions of the first, we should find these impressions eloquent in memories of the gulf beyond. And that gulf is—what? How at least shall we distinguish its shadows from those of the tomb? But if the impressions of what I have termed the first stage, are not, at will, recalled, yet, after long interval, do they not come unbidden, while we marvel whence they come? He who has never swooned, is not he who finds strange palaces and wildly familiar faces in coals that glow; is not he who beholds floating in mid-air the sad visions that the many may not view; is not he who ponders over the perfume of some novel flower; is not he whose brain grows bewildered with the meaning of some musical cadence which has never before arrested his attention.

Amid frequent and thoughtful endeavors to remember, amid earnest struggles to regather some token of the state of seeming nothingness into which my soul had lapsed, there have been moments when I have dreamed of success; there have been brief, very brief periods when I have conjured up remembrances which the lucid reason of a later epoch assures me could have had reference only to that condition of seeming unconsciousness. These shadows of memory tell, indistinctly, of tall figures that lifted and bore me in silence down—down—still down—till a hideous dizziness oppressed me at the mere idea of the interminableness of the descent. They tell also of a vague horror at my heart, on account of that heart's unnatural stillness. Then comes a sense of sudden motionlessness throughout all things; as if those who bore me (a ghastly train!) had outrun, in their descent, the limits of the limitless, and paused from the wearisomeness of their toil. After this I call to mind flatness and dampness; and then all is *madness*—the madness of a memory which busies itself among forbidden things.

Very suddenly there came back to my soul motion and sound—the tumultuous motion of the heart, and, in my ears, the sound of its beating. Then a pause in which all is blank. Then again sound, and motion, and touch—a tingling sensation pervading my frame. Then the mere consciousness of existence, without thought—a condition which lasted long. Then, very suddenly, *thought*, and shuddering terror, and earnest endeavor to comprehend my true state. Then a strong desire to lapse into insensibility. Then a rushing revival of soul and a successful effort to move. And now a full memory of the trial, of the judges, of the sable draperies, of the sentence, of the sickness, of the swoon. Then entire forgetfulness of all that followed, of all that a later day and much earnestness of endeavor have enabled me vaguely to recall.

So far, I had not opened my eyes. I felt that I lay upon my back, unbound. I reached out my hand, and it fell heavily upon something damp and hard. There I suffered it to remain for many minutes, while I strove to imagine where and *what* I could be. I longed, yet dared not, to employ my vision. I dreaded the first glance at objects around me. It was not that I feared to look upon things horrible, but that I grew aghast lest there should be *nothing* to see. At length, with a wild desperation at heart, I quickly unclosed my eyes. My worst thoughts, then, were confirmed. The blackness of eternal night encompassed me. I struggled for breath. The intensity of the darkness seemed to oppress and stifle me. The atmosphere was intolerably close. I still lay quietly, and made effort to exercise my reason. I brought to mind the inquisitorial proceedings, and attempted from that point to deduce my real condition. The sentence had passed; and it appeared to me that a very long interval of time had since elapsed. Yet not for a moment did I suppose myself actually dead. Such a supposition, notwithstanding what we read in fiction, is altogether inconsistent with real existence;—but where and in what state was I? The condemned to death, I knew, perished usually at the *autos-da-fé*, and one of these had been held on the very night of the day of my trial. Had I been remanded to my dungeon, to await the next sacrifice, which would not take place for many months? This I at once saw could not be. Victims had been in immediate demand. Moreover, my dungeon, as well as all the condemned cells at Toledo, had stone floors, and light was not altogether excluded.

A fearful idea now suddenly drove the blood in torrents upon my heart, and for a brief period I once more relapsed into insensibility. Upon recovering, I at once started to my feet, trembling convulsively in every fibre. I thrust my arms wildly above and around me in all directions. I felt nothing; yet dreaded to move a step, lest I should be impeded by the walls of a *tomb*. Perspiration burst from every pore, and stood in cold big beads upon my forehead. The agony of suspense grew at length intolerable, and I cautiously moved forward, with my arms extended, and my eyes straining from their sockets in the hope of catching some faint ray of light. I proceeded for many paces; but still all was blackness and vacancy. I breathed more freely. It seemed evident that mine was not, at least, the most hideous of fates.

And now, as I still continued to step cautiously onward, there came thronging upon my recollection a thousand vague rumors of the horrors of Toledo. Of the dungeons there had been strange things narrated—fables I had always deemed them—but yet strange, and too ghastly to repeat, save in a whisper. Was I left to perish of starvation in this subterranean world of darkness; or what fate, perhaps even more fearful, awaited me? That the result would be death, and a death of more than customary bitterness, I knew too well the character of my judges to doubt. The mode and the hour were all that occupied or distracted me.

My outstretched hands at length encountered some solid obstruction. It was a wall, seemingly of stone masonry—very smooth, slimy, and cold. I followed it up; stepping with all the careful distrust with which certain antique narratives had inspired me. This process, however, afforded me no means of ascertaining the dimensions of my dungeon, as I might make its circuit and return to the point whence I set out without being aware of the fact, so perfectly uniform seemed the wall. I therefore sought the knife which had been in my pocket, when led into the inquisitorial chamber; but it was gone; my clothes had been exchanged for a wrapper of coarse serge. I had thought of forcing the blade in some minute crevice of the masonry, as as to identify my point of departure. The difficulty, nevertheless, was but trivial; although, in the disorder of my fancy, it seemed at first insuperable. I tore a part of the hem from the robe and placed the fragment at full length, and at right angles to the wall. In groping my way around the prison, I could not fail to encounter this rag upon completing the circuit. So, at least, I thought; but I had not counted upon the extent of the dungeon, or upon my own weakness. The ground was moist and slippery. I staggered onward for some time, when I stumbled and fell. My excessive fatigue induced me to remain prostrate; and sleep soon overtook me as I lay.

Upon awaking, and stretching forth an arm, I found beside me a loaf and a pitcher with water. I was too much exhausted to reflect upon this circumstance, but ate and drank with avidity. Shortly afterward, I resumed my tour around the prison, and with much toil, came at last upon the fragment of the serge. Up to the period when I fell, I had counted fifty-two paces, and, upon resuming my walk, I had counted forty-eight more—when I arrived at the rag. There were in all, then, a hundred paces; and, admitting two paces to the yard, I presumed the dungeon to be fifty yards in circuit. I had met, however, with many angles in the wall, and thus I could form no guess at the shape of the vault, for vault I could not help supposing it to be.

I had little object—certainly no hope—in these researches; but a vague curiosity prompted me to continue them. Quitting the wall, I resolved to cross the area of the enclosure. At first, I proceeded with extreme caution, for the floor, although seemingly of solid material, was treacherous with slime. At length, however, I took courage, and did not hesitate to step firmly; endeavoring to cross in as direct a line as possible. I had advanced some ten or twelve paces in this manner, when the remnant of the torn hem of my robe became entangled between my legs. I stepped on it, and fell violently on my face.

In the confusion attending my fall, I did not immediately apprehend a somewhat startling circumstance, which yet, in a few seconds afterward, and while I still lay prostrate, arrested my attention. It was this—my chin rested upon the floor of the prison, but my lips, and the upper portion of my head, although seemingly at a less elevation than the chin, touched nothing. At the same time, my forehead seemed bathed in a clammy vapor, and the peculiar smell of decayed fungus arose to my nostrils. I put forward my arm, and shuddered to find that I had fallen at the very brink of a circular pit, whose extent, of course, I had no means of ascertaining at the moment. Groping about the masonry just below the margin, I succeeded in dislodging a small fragment, and let it fall into the abyss. For many seconds I hearkened to its reverberations as it dashed against the sides of the chasm in its descent; at length there was a sullen plunge into water, succeeded by loud echoes. At the same moment, there came a sound resembling the quick opening and as rapid closing of a door overhead, while a faint gleam of light flashed suddenly through the gloom, and as suddenly faded away.

I saw clearly the doom which had been prepared for me, and

congratulated myself upon the timely accident by which I had escaped. Another step before my fall, and the world had seen me no more. And the death just avoided was of that very character which I had regarded as fabulous and frivolous in the tales respecting the Inquisition. To the victims of its tyranny, there was the choice of death with its direct physical agonies, or death with its most hideous moral horrors. I had been reserved for the latter. By long suffering my nerves had been unstrung, until I trembled at the sound of my own voice, and had become in every respect a fitting subject for the species of torture which awaited me.

Shaking in every limb, I groped my way back to the wall—resolving there to perish rather than risk the terrors of the wells, of which my imagination now pictured many in various positions about the dungeon. In other conditions of mind, I might have had courage to end my misery at once, by a plunge into one of these abysses; but I was the veriest of cowards. Neither could I forget what I had read of these pits— that the *sudden* extinction of life formed no part of their most horrible plan.

Agitation of spirit kept me awake for many long hours, but at length I again slumbered. Upon arousing, I found by my side, as before, a loaf and a pitcher of water. A burning thirst consumed me, and I emptied the vessel at a draught. It must have been drugged—for scarcely had I drunk, before I became irresistibly drowsy. A deep sleep fell upon me— a sleep like that of death. How long it lasted of course, I know not; but when, once again, I unclosed my eyes, the objects around me were visible. By a wild, sulphurous lustre, the origin of which I could not at first determine, I was enabled to see the extent and aspect of the prison.

In its size I had been greatly mistaken. The whole circuit of its walls did not exceed twenty-five yards. For some minutes this fact occasioned me a world of vain trouble; vain indeed—for what could be of less importance, under the terrible circumstances which environed me, than the mere dimensions of my dungeon? But my soul took a wild interest in trifles, and I busied myself in endeavors to account for the error I had committed in my measurement. The truth at length flashed upon me. In my first attempt at exploration I had counted fifty-two paces, up to the period when I fell: I must then have been within a pace or two of the fragment of serge; in fact, I had nearly performed the circuit of the vault. I then slept—and, upon awakening, I must have returned upon my steps—thus supposing the circuit nearly double what it actually was. My confusion of mind prevented me from observing that I began my tour with the wall to the left, and ended it with the wall to the right.

I had been deceived too, in respect to the shape of the enclosure. In feeling my way I had found many angles, and thus deduced an idea of great irregularity; so potent is the effect of total darkness upon one arousing from lethargy or sleep! The angles were simply those of a few slight depressions, or niches, at odd intervals. The general shape of the prison was square. What I had taken for masonry seemed now to be iron, or some other metal, in huge plates, whose sutures or joints occasioned the depression. The entire surface of this metallic enclosure was rudely daubed in all the hideous and repulsive devices to which the charnel superstition of the monks has given rise. The figures of fiends in aspects of menace, with skeleton forms, and other more really fearful images, overspread and disfigured the walls. I observed that the outlines of these monstrosities were sufficiently distinct, but that the colors seemed faded and blurred, as if from the effects of a damp atmosphere. I now noticed the floor, too, which was of stone. In the centre yawned the circular pit from whose jaws I had escaped; but it was the only one in the dungeon.

All this I saw indistinctly and by much effort: for my personal condition had been greatly changed during slumber. I now lay upon my back, and at full length, on a species of low framework of wood. To this I was securely bound by a long step resembling a surcingle. It passed in many convolutions about my limbs and body, leaving at liberty only my head, and my left arm to such extent that I could, by dint of much exertion, supply myself with food from an earthen dish which lay by my side on the floor. I saw, to my horror, that the pitcher had been removed. I say to my horror—for I was consumed with intolerable thirst. This thirst it appeared to be the design of my persecutors to stimulate: for the food in the dish was meat pungently seasoned.

Looking upward, I surveyed the ceiling of my prison. It was some thirty or forty feet overhead, and constructed much as the side walls. In one of its panels a very singular figure riveted my whole attention. It was the painted figure of Time as he is commonly represented, save that, in lieu of a scythe, he held what, at a casual glance, I supposed to be the pictured image of a huge pendulum, such as we see on antique clocks. There was something, however, in the appearance of this machine which caused me to regard it more attentively. While I gazed directly upward at it (for its position was immediately over my own) I fancied that I saw it in motion. In an instant afterward the fancy was confirmed. Its sweep was brief, and of course slow. I watched it for some minutes, somewhat in fear, but more in wonder. Wearied at length with observing its dull movement, I turned my eyes upon the other objects in the cell.

A slight noise attracted my notice, and, looking to the floor, I saw several enormous rats traversing it. They had issued from the well which lay just within view to my right. Even then, while I gazed, they came up in troops, hurriedly, with ravenous eyes, allured by the scent of the meat. From this it required much effort and attention to scare them away.

It might have been half an hour, perhaps even an hour (for I could take but imperfect note of time), before I again cast my eyes upward. What I then saw confounded and amazed me. The sweep of the pendulum had increased in extent by nearly a yard. As a natural consequence its velocity was also much greater. But what mainly disturbed me was the idea that it had perceptibly *descended*. I now observed—with what horror it is needless to say—that its nether extremity was formed of a crescent of glittering steel, about a foot in length from horn to horn; the horns upward, and the under edge evidently as keen as that of a razor. Like a razor also, it seemed massy and heavy, tapering from the edge into a solid and broad structure above. It was appended to a weighty rod of brass, and the whole *hissed* as it swung through the air.

I could no longer doubt the doom prepared for me by monkish ingenuity in torture. My cognizance of the pit had become known to the inquisitorial agents—*the pit*, whose horrors had been destined for so bold a recusant as myself—*the pit*, typical of hell, and regarded by rumor as the Ultima Thule of all their punishments. The plunge into this pit I had avoided by the merest of accidents, and I knew that surprise, or entrapment into torment, formed an important portion of all the grotesquerie of these dungeon deaths. Having failed to fall, it was no part of the demon plan to hurl me into the abyss; and thus (there being no alternative) a different and a milder destruction awaited me. Milder! I half smiled in my agony as I thought of such application of such a term.

What boots it to tell of the long, long hours of horror more than mortal, during which I counted the rushing oscillations of the steel! Inch by inch—line by line—with a descent only appreciable at intervals that seemed ages—down and still down it came! Days passed—it might have been that many days passed—ere it swept so closely over me as to fan me with its acrid breath. The odor of the sharp steel forced itself into my nostrils. I prayed—I wearied heaven with my prayer for its more speedy descent. I grew frantically mad, and struggled to force myself upward against the sweep of the fearful scimitar. And then I fell suddenly calm, and lay smiling at the glittering death, as a child at some rare bauble.

There was another interval of utter insensibility; it was brief; for, upon again lapsing into life, there had been no perceptible descent in the pendulum. But it might have been long—for I knew there were demons who took note of my swoon, and who could have arrested the vibration at pleasure. Upon my recovery, too, I felt very—oh, inexpressibly sick and weak, as if through long inanition. Even amid the agonies of that period, the human nature craved food. With painful effort I outstretched my left arm as far as my bonds permitted, and took possession of the small remnant which had been spared me by the rats. As I put a portion of it within my lips, there rushed to my mind a half formed thought of joy—of hope. Yet what business had *I* with hope? It was, as I say, a half formed thought—man has many such which are never completed. I felt that it was of joy—of hope; but I felt also that it had perished in its formation. In vain I struggled to perfect—to regain it. Long suffering had nearly annihilated all my ordinary powers of mind. I was an imbecile—an idiot.

The vibration of the pendulum was at right angles to my length. I saw that the crescent was designed to cross the region of the heart. It would fray the serge of my robe—it would return and repeat its operations—again—and again. Notwithstanding its terrifically wide sweep (some thirty feet or more) and the hissing vigor of its descent, sufficient to sunder these very walls of iron, still the fraying of my robe would be all that, for several minutes, it would accomplish. And at this thought I paused. I dared not go further than this reflection. I dwelt upon it with a pertinacity of attention—as if, in so dwelling, I could arrest *here* the descent of the steel. I forced myself to ponder upon the sound of the crescent as it should pass across the garment—upon the peculiar thrilling sensation which the friction of cloth produces on the nerves. I pondered upon all this frivolity until my teeth were on edge.

Down—steadily down it crept. I took a frenzied pleasure in contrasting its downward with its lateral velocity. To the right—to the left—far and wide—with the shriek of a damned spirit; to my heart with the stealthy pace of the tiger! I alternately laughed and howled, as the one or the other idea grew predominant.

Down—certainly, relentlessly down! It vibrated within three inches of my bosom! I struggled violently—furiously—to free my left arm. This was free only from the elbow to the hand. I could reach the latter, from the platter beside me, to my mouth, with great effort, but no farther. Could I have broken the fastenings above the elbow, I would have seized and attempted to arrest the pendulum. I might as well have attempted to arrest an avalanche!

Down—still unceasingly—still inevitably down! I gasped and struggled at each vibration. I shrunk convulsively at its every sweep. My eyes followed its outward or upward whirls with the eagerness of the most unmeaning despair; they closed themselves spasmodically at the descent, although death would have been a relief, oh! how unspeakable! Still I quivered in every nerve to think how slight a sinking of the machinery would precipitate that keen, glistening axe upon my bosom.

It was *hope* that prompted the nerve to quiver—the frame to shrink. It was *hope*—the hope that triumphs on the rack—that whispers to the death-condemned even in the dungeons of the Inquisition.

I saw that some ten or twelve vibrations would bring the steel in actual contact with my robe—and with this observation there suddenly came over my spirit all the keen, collected calmness of despair. For the first time during many hours—or perhaps days—I *thought*. It now occurred to me, that the bandage, or surcingle, which enveloped me, was *unique*. I was tied by no separate cord. The first stroke of the razor-like crescent athwart any portion of the band would so detach it that it might be unwound from my person by means of my left hand. But how fearful, in that case, the proximity of the steel! The result of the slightest struggle, how deadly! Was it likely, moreover, that the minions of the torturer had not foreseen and provided for this possibility! Was it probable that the bandage crossed my bosom in the track of the pendulum? Dreading to find my faint, and, as it seemed, my last hope frustrated, I so far elevated my head as to obtain a distinct view of my breast. The surcingle enveloped my limbs and body close in all directions—*save in the path of the destroying crescent.*

Scarcely had I dropped my head back into its original position, when there flashed upon my mind what I cannot better describe than as the unformed half of that idea of deliverance to which I have previously alluded, and which a moiety only floated indeterminately through my brain when I raised food to my burning lips. The whole thought was now present—feeble, scarcely sane, scarcely definite—but still entire. I proceded at once, with the nervous energy of despair, to attempt its execution.

For many hours the immediate vicinity of the low framework upon which I lay had been literally swarming with rats. They were wild, bold, ravenous; their red eyes glaring upon me as if they waited but for motionlessness on my part to make me their prey. "To what food," I thought, "have they been accustomed in the well?"

They had devoured, in spite of all my efforts to prevent them, all but a small remnant of the contents of the dish. I had fallen into an habitual see-saw or wave of the hand about the platter, and, at length, the unconscious uniformity of the movement deprived it of effect. In their voracity, the vermin frequently fastened their sharp fangs in my fingers. With the particles of the oily and spicy viand which now remained, I thoroughly rubbed the bandage wherever I could reach it; then, raising my hand from the floor, I lay breathlessly still.

At first, the ravenous animals were startled and terrified at the change—at the cessation of movement. They shrank alarmedly back; many sought the well. But this was only for a moment. I had not counted in vain upon their voracity. Observing that I remained without motion, one or two of the boldest leaped upon the framework, and smelt at the surcingle. This seemed the signal for a general rush. Forth from the well they hurried in fresh troops. They clung to the wood—they overran it, and leaped in hundreds upon my person. The measured movement of the pendulum disturbed them not at all. Avoiding its strokes, they busied themselves with the anointed bandage. They pressed—they swarmed upon me in ever accumulating heaps. They writhed upon my throat; their cold lips sought my own; I was half stifled by their thronging pressure; disgust, for which the world has no name, swelled my bosom, and chilled, with a heavy clamminess, my heart. Yet one minute, and I felt that the struggle would be over. Plainly I perceived the loosening of the bandage. I knew that in more than one place it must be already severed. With a more than human resolution I lay *still*.

Nor had I erred in my calculations—nor had I endured in vain. I at length felt that I was *free*. The surcingle hung in ribands from my body. But the stroke of the pendulum already pressed upon my bosom. It had divided the serge of the robe. It had cut through the linen beneath. Twice again it swung, and a sharp sense of pain shot through every nerve. But the moment of escape had arrived. At a wave of my hand my deliverers hurried tumultuously away. With a steady movement—cautious, sidelong, shrinking, and slow—I slid from the embrace of the bandage and beyond the reach of the scimitar. For the moment, at least, *I was free*.

Free!—and in the grasp of the Inquisition! I had scarcely stepped from my wooden bed of horror upon the stone floor of the prison, when the motion of the hellish machine ceased, and I beheld it drawn up, by some invisible force, through the ceiling. This was a lesson which I took desperately to heart. My every motion was undoubtedly watched. Free!—I had but escaped death in one form of agony, to be delivered unto worse than death in some other. With that thought I rolled my eyes nervously around on the barriers of iron that hemmed me in. Something unusual—some change which, at first, I could not appreciate distinctly—it was obvious, had taken place in the apartment. For many minutes of a dreamy and trembling abstraction, I busied myself in vain, unconnected conjecture. During this period, I became aware, for the first time, of the origin of the sulphurous light which illumined the cell. It proceeded from a fissure, about half an inch in width, extending entirely around the prison at the base of the walls, which thus appeared, and were, completely separated from the floor. I endeavored, but of course in vain, to look through the aperture.

As I arose from the attempt, the mystery of the alteration in the chamber broke at once upon my understanding. I have observed that, although the outlines of the figures upon the walls were sufficiently distinct, yet the colors seemed blurred and indefinite. These colors had now assumed, and were momentarily assuming, a startling and most intense brilliancy, that gave to the spectral and fiendish portraitures an aspect that might have thrilled even firmer nerves than my own. Demon eyes, of a wild and ghastly vivacity, glared upon me in a thousand directions, where none had been visible before, and gleamed with the lurid lustre of a fire that I could not force my imagination to regard as unreal.

Unreal!—Even while I breathed there came to my nostrils the breath of the vapor of heated iron! A suffocating odour pervaded the prison! A deeper glow settled each moment in the eyes that glared at my agonies! A richer tint of crimson diffused itself over the pictured horrors of blood. I panted! I gasped for breath! There could be no doubt of the design of my tormentors—oh! most unrelenting! oh! most demoniac of men! I shrank from the glowing metal to the centre of the cell. Amid the thought of the fiery destruction that impended, the idea of the coolness of the well came over my soul like balm. I rushed to its deadly brink. I threw my straining vision below. The glare from the enkindled roof illumined its inmost recesses. Yet, for a wild moment, did my spirit refuse to comprehend the meaning of what I saw. At length it forced—it wrestled its way into my soul—it burned itself in upon my shuddering reason. Oh! for a voice to speak!—oh! horror—oh! any horror but this! With a shriek, I rushed from the margin, and buried my face in my hands—weeping bitterly.

The heat rapidly increased, and once again I looked up, shuddering as with a fit of the ague. There had been a second change in the cell—and now the change was obviously in the *form*. As before, it was in vain that I at first endeavoured to appreciate or understand what was taking place. But not long was I left in doubt. The Inquisitorial vengeance had been hurried by my twofold escape, and there was to be no more dallying with the King of Terrors. The room had been square. I saw that two of its iron angles were now acute—two, consequently, obtuse. The fearful difference quickly increased with a low rumbling or moaning sound. In an instant the apartment had shifted its form into that of a lozenge. But the alteration stopped not here—I neither hoped nor desired it to stop. I could have clasped the red walls to my bosom as a garment of eternal peace. "Death," I said, "any death but that of the pit!" Fool! might I not have known that *into the pit* it was the object of the burning iron to urge me? Could I resist its glow? or, if even that, could I withstand its pressure? And now, flatter and flatter grew the lozenge, with a rapidity that left me no time for contemplation. Its centre, and of course, its greatest width, came just over the yawning gulf. I shrank back—but the closing walls pressed me resistlessly onward. At length for my seared and writhing body there was no longer an inch of foothold on the firm floor of the prison. I struggled no more, but the agony of my soul found vent in one loud, long, and final scream of despair. I felt that I tottered upon the brink—I averted my eyes—

There was a discordant hum of human voices! There was a loud blast as of many trumpets! There was a harsh grating as of a thousand thunders! The fiery walls rushed back! An outstretched arm caught my own as I fell, fainting, into the abyss. It was that of General Lasalle. The French army had entered Toledo. The Inquisition was in the hands of its enemies.

QUESTIONS

1. The Spanish Inquisition was suppressed in 1808 when Napoleon's army, of which General Lasalle was a divisional commander, invaded Spain. How relevant is historical background to this story, would you guess, as compared with "The Wall"?

2. As in "The Wall," the psychological reactions of the narrator to his experience are stressed throughout the story. Compare the nature and quality of these reactions in the two stories. Does the narrator in this story undergo any significant change? What are the respective motivations of the authors in stressing this material?

3. How much do we know about the narrator and his past life? Why has he been singled out for torture instead of being put to death in an *auto da fé*? Why are we not told more?

4. Compare the behavior of the torturers in this story with that of the captors in "The Wall." Which are respectively more ingenious? vigilant? patient? brutal? terrifying? plausible? Compare also the various devices used in the two stories for death or torture. How do they differ?

5. Comment on the symbolism of the paintings on the walls and ceiling of the torture chamber.

6. The narrator escapes from destruction three times. How narrow are these escapes? Comment on the manner by which each is achieved.

7. What function other than a plot function is served by the rats?

8. What is the main coincidence of the story? How does it compare in plausibility with the coincidence in "The Wall"? Comment on the purposes for which these coincidences are respectively used.

9. Why does not Poe reveal what was in the Pit?

Franz Kafka

IN THE PENAL COLONY

"It's a remarkable piece of apparatus," said the officer to the explorer and surveyed with a certain air of admiration the apparatus which was after all quite familiar to him. The explorer seemed to have accepted merely out of politeness the Commandant's invitation to witness the execution of a soldier condemned to death for disobedience and insulting behavior to a superior. Nor did the colony itself betray much interest in this execution. At least, in the small sandy valley, a deep hollow surrounded on all sides by naked crags, there was no one present save the officer, the explorer, the condemned man, who was a stupid-looking wide-mouthed creature with bewildered hair and face, and the soldier who held the heavy chain controlling the small chains locked on the prisoner's ankles, wrists and neck, chains which were themselves attached to each other by communicating links. In any case, the condemned man looked so like a submissive dog that one might have thought he could be left to run free on the surrounding hills and would only need to be whistled for when the execution was due to begin.

The explorer did not much care about the apparatus and walked up and down behind the prisoner with almost visible indifference while the officer made the last adjustments, now creeping beneath the structure, which was bedded deep in the earth, now climbing a ladder to inspect its upper parts. These were tasks that might well have been left to a mechanic, but the officer performed them with great zeal, whether because he was a devoted admirer of the apparatus or because of other reasons the work could be entrusted to no one else. "Ready now!" he called at last and climbed down from the ladder. He looked uncommonly limp, breathed with his mouth wide open and had tucked two fine ladies' handkerchiefs under the collar of his uniform. "These uniforms are too heavy for the tropics, surely," said the explorer, instead of making some inquiry about the apparatus, as the officer had expected. "Of course," said the officer, washing his oily and greasy hands in a bucket of water that stood ready, "but they mean home to us; we don't want to forget about home. Now just have a look at this machine," he added at once, simultaneously drying his hands on a towel and indicating the apparatus. "Up till now a few things still had to be set by hand, but from this moment it works all by itself." The explorer nodded and followed him. The officer, anxious to secure himself against all contingencies, said: "Things sometimes go wrong, of course; I hope that nothing goes wrong today, but we have to allow for the possibility. The machinery should go on working continuously for twelve hours. But if anything does go wrong it will only be some small matter that can be set right at once."

"Won't you take a seat?" he asked finally, drawing a cane chair out from among a heap of them and offering it to the explorer, who could not refuse it. He was now sitting at the edge of a pit, into which he glanced for a fleeting moment. It was not very deep. On one side of the pit the excavated soil had been piled up in a rampart, on the other side of it stood the apparatus. "I don't know," said the officer, "if the Commandant has already explained this apparatus to you." The explorer waved one hand vaguely; the officer asked for nothing better, since now he could explain the apparatus himself. "This apparatus," he said, taking hold of a crank handle and leaning against it, "was invented by our former Commandant. I assisted at the very earliest experiments and had a share in all the work until its completion. But the credit of inventing it belongs to him alone. Have you ever heard of our former Commandant? No? Well, it isn't saying too much if I tell you that the organization of the whole penal colony is his work. We who were his friends knew even before he died that the organization of the colony was so perfect that his successor, even with a thousand new schemes in his head, would find it impossible to alter anything, at least for many years to come. And our prophecy has come true; the new Commandant has had to acknowledge its truth. A pity you never met the old Commandant!—But," the officer interrupted himself, "I am rambling on, and here stands his apparatus before us. It consists, as you see, of three parts. In the course of time each of these parts has acquired a kind of popular nickname. The lower one is called the 'Bed,' the upper one the 'Designer,' and this one here in the middle that moves up and down is called the 'Harrow.'" "The Harrow?" asked the explorer. He had not been listening very attentively, the glare of the sun in the shadeless valley was altogether too strong, it was difficult to collect one's thoughts. All the more did he admire the officer, who in spite of his tight-fitting full-dress uniform coat, amply befrogged and weighed down by epaulettes, was pursuing his subject with such enthusiasm and, besides talking, was still tightening a screw here and there with a spanner. As for the soldier, he seemed to be in much the same condition as the explorer. He had wound the prisoner's chain round both his wrists, propped himself on his rifle, let his head hang and was paying no attention to anything. That did not surprise the explorer, for the officer was speaking French, and certainly neither the soldier nor the prisoner understood a word of French. It was all the more remarkable, therefore, that the prisoner was none the less making an effort to follow the officer's explanations. With a kind of drowsy persistence he directed his gaze wherever the officer pointed a finger, and at the interruption of the explorer's question he, too, as well as the officer, looked round.

"Yes, the Harrow," said the officer, "a good name for it. The needles are set in like the teeth of a harrow and the whole thing works something like a harrow, although its action is limited to one place and contrived with much more artistic skill. Anyhow, you'll soon understand it. On the Bed here the condemned man is laid—I'm going to describe the apparatus first before I set it in motion. Then you'll be able to follow the proceedings better. Besides, one of the cog wheels in the Designer is badly worn; it creaks a lot when it's working; you can hardly hear yourself speak; spare parts, unfortunately, are difficult to get here.—Well, here is the Bed, as I told you. It is completely covered with a layer of cotton wool; you'll find out why later. On this cotton wool the condemned man is laid, face down, quite naked, of course; here are straps for the hands, here for the feet, and here for the neck, to bind him fast. Here at the head of the bed, where the man, as I said, first lays down his face, is this little gag of felt, which can be easily regulated to go straight into his mouth. It is meant to keep him from screaming and biting his tongue. Of course the man is forced to take the felt into his mouth, for otherwise his neck would be broken by the strap." "Is that cotton wool?" asked the explorer, bending forward. "Yes, certainly," said the officer, with a smile, "feel it for yourself." He took the explorer's hand and guided it over the bed. "It's specially prepared cotton wool, that's why it looks so different; I'll tell you presently what it's for." The explorer already felt a dawning interest in the apparatus; he sheltered his eyes from the sun with one hand and gazed up at the structure. It was a huge affair. The Bed and the Designer were of the same size and looked like two dark wooden chests. The Designer hung about two meters above the Bed; each of them was bound at the corners with four rods of brass that almost flashed out rays in the sunlight. Between the chests shuttled the Harrow on a ribbon of steel.

The officer had scarcely noticed the explorer's previous indifference, but he was now well aware of his dawning interest; so he stopped explaining in order to leave a space of time for quiet observation. The condemned man imitated the explorer; since he could not use a hand to shelter his eyes he gazed upwards without shade.

"Well, the man lies down," said the explorer, leaning back in his chair and crossing his legs.

"Yes," said the officer, pushing his cap back a little and passing one hand over his heated face, "now listen! Both the Bed and the Designer have an electric battery each; the Bed needs one for itself, the Designer for the Harrow. As soon as the man is strapped down, the Bed is set in motion. It quivers in minute, very rapid vibrations, both from side to side and up and down. You will have seen similar apparatus in hospitals; but in our Bed the movements are all precisely calculated; you see, they have to correspond very exactly to the movements of the Harrow. And the Harrow is the instrument for the actual execution of the sentence."

"And how does the sentence run?" said the explorer.

"You don't know that either?" said the officer in amazement, and bit his lips. "Forgive me if my explanations seem rather incoherent. I do beg your pardon. You see, the Commandant always used to do the explaining; but the new Commandant shirks this duty; yet that such an important visitor"—the explorer tried to deprecate the honor with both hands; the officer, however, insisted—"that such an important visitor should not even be told about the kind of sentence we pass is a new development, which—" He was just on the point of using strong language but checked himself and said only: "I was not informed, it is not my fault. In any case, I am certainly the best person to explain our procedure, since I have here"—he patted his breast pocket—"the relevant drawings made by our former Commandant."

"The Commandant's own drawings?" asked the explorer. "Did he combine everything in himself, then? Was he soldier, judge, mechanic, chemist and draughtsman?"

"Indeed he was," said the officer, nodding assent, with a remote, glassy look. Then he inspected his hands critically; they did not seem clean enough to him for touching the drawings; so he went over to the bucket and washed them again. Then he drew out a small leather wallet and said: "Our sentence does not sound severe. Whatever commandment the prisoner has disobeyed is written upon his body by the Harrow. This prisoner, for instance"—the officer indicated the man—"will have written on his body: HONOR THY SUPERIORS!"

The explorer glanced at the man; he stood, as the officer pointed him out, with bent head, apparently listening with all his ears in an effort to catch what was being said. Yet the movement of his blubber lips, closely pressed together, showed clearly that he could not understand a word. Many questions were troubling the explorer, but at the sight of the prisoner he asked only: "Does he know his sentence?" "No," said the officer, eager to go on with his exposition, but the explorer interrupted him: "He doesn't know the sentence that has been passed on him?" "No," said the officer again, pausing a moment as if to let the explorer elaborate his question, and then said: "There would be no point in telling him. He'll learn it on his body." The explorer intended to make no answer, but he felt the prisoner's gaze turned on him; it seemed to ask if he approved such ongoings. So he bent forward again, having already leaned back in his chair, and put another question: "But surely he knows that he has been sentenced?" "Nor that either," said the officer, smiling at the explorer as if expecting him to make further surprising remarks. "No," said the explorer, wiping his forehead, "then he can't know either whether his defense was effective?" "He has had no chance of putting up a defense," said the officer, turning his eyes away as if speaking to himself and so sparing the explorer the shame of hearing self-evident matters explained. "But he must have had some chance of defending himself," said the explorer, and rose from his seat.

The officer realized that he was in danger of having his exposition of the apparatus held up for a long time; so he went up to the explorer, took him by the arm, waved a hand towards the condemned man, who was standing very straight now that he had so obviously become the center of attention—the soldier had also given the chain a jerk—and said: "This is how the matter stands. I have been appointed judge in this penal colony. Despite my youth. For I was the former Commandant's assistant in all penal matters and know more about the apparatus than anyone. My guiding principle is this: Guilt is never to be doubted. Other courts cannot follow that principle, for they consist of several opinions and have higher courts to scrutinize them. That is not the case here, or at least, it was not the case in the former Commandant's time. The new man has certainly shown some inclination to interfere with my judgments, but so far I have succeeded in fending him off and will go on succeeding. You wanted to have the case explained; it is quite simple, like all of them. A captain reported to me this morning that this man, who had been assigned to him as a servant and sleeps before his door, had been asleep on duty. It is his duty, you see, to get up every time the hour strikes and salute the captain's door. Not an exacting duty, and very necessary, since he has to be a sentry as well as a servant, and must be alert in both functions. Last night the captain wanted to see if the man was doing his duty. He opened the door as the clock struck two and there was his man curled up asleep. He took his riding whip and lashed him across the face. Instead of getting up and begging pardon, the man caught hold of his master's legs, shook him and cried: 'Throw that whip away or I'll eat you alive.'—That's the evidence. The captain came to me an hour ago, I wrote down his statement and appended the sentence to it. Then I had the man put in chains. That was all quite simple. If I had first called the man before me and interrogated him, things would have got into a confused tangle. He would have told lies, and had I exposed these lies he would have backed them up with more lies, and so on and so forth. As it is, I've got him and I won't let him go.—Is that quite clear now? But we're wasting time, the execution should be beginning and I haven't finished explaining the apparatus yet." He pressed the explorer back into his chair, went up again to the apparatus and began: "As you see, the shape of the Harrow corresponds to the human form; here is the harrow for the torso, here are the harrows for the legs. For the head there is only this one small spike. Is that quite clear?" He bent amiably forward towards the explorer, eager to provide the most comprehensive explanations.

The explorer considered the Harrow with a frown. The explanation of the judicial procedure had not satisfied him. He had to remind himself that this was in any case a penal colony where extraordinary measures were needed and that military discipline must be enforced to the last. He also felt that some hope might be set on the new Commandant, who was apparently of a mind to bring in, although gradually, a new kind of procedure which the officer's narrow mind was incapable of understanding. This train of thought prompted his next question: "Will the Commandant attend the execution?" "It is not certain," said the officer, wincing at the direct question, and his friendly expression darkened. "That is just why we have to lose no time. Much as I dislike it, I shall have to cut my explanations short. But of course tomorrow, when the apparatus has been cleaned—its one drawback is that it gets so messy—I can recapitulate all the details. For the present, then, only the essentials.—When the man lies down on the Bed and it begins to vibrate, the Harrow is lowered onto his body. It regulates itself automatically so that the needles barely touch his skin; once contact is made the steel ribbon stiffens immediately into a rigid band. And then the performance begins. An ignorant onlooker would see no difference between one punishment and another. The Harrow appears to do its work with uniform regularity. As it quivers, its points pierce the skin of the body which is itself quivering from the vibration of the Bed. So that the actual progress of the sentence can be watched, the Harrow is made of glass. Getting the needles fixed in the glass was a technical problem, but after many experiments we overcame the difficulty. No trouble was too great for us to take, you see. And now anyone can look through the glass and watch the inscription taking form on the body. Wouldn't you care to come a little nearer and have a look at the needles?"

The explorer got up slowly, walked across and bent over the Harrow. "You see," said the officer, "there are two kinds of needles arranged in multiple patterns. Each long needle has a short one beside it. The long needle does the writing, and the short needle sprays a jet of water to wash away the blood and keep the inscription clear. Blood and water together are then conducted here through small runnels into this main runnel and down a waste pipe into the pit." With his finger the officer traced the exact course taken by the blood and water. To make the picture as vivid as possible he held both hands below the outlet of the waste pipe as if to catch the outflow, and when he did this the explorer drew back his head and feeling behind him with one hand sought to return to his chair. To his horror he found that the condemned man too had obeyed the officer's invitation to examine the Harrow at close quarters and had followed him. He had pulled forward the sleepy soldier with the chain and was bending over the glass. One could see that his uncertain eyes were trying to perceive what the two gentlemen had been looking at, but since he had not understood the explanation he could not make head or tail of it. He was peering this way and that way. He kept running his eyes along the glass. The explorer wanted to drive him away, since what he was doing was probably culpable. But the officer firmly restrained the explorer with one hand and with the other took a clod of earth from the rampart and threw it at the soldier. He opened his eyes with a jerk, saw what the condemned man had dared to do, let his rifle fall, dug his heels into the ground, dragged his prisoner back so that he stumbled and fell immediately, and then stood looking down at him, watching him struggling and rattling in his chains. "Set him on his feet!" yelled the officer, for he noticed that the explorer's attention was being too much distracted by the prisoner. In fact he was even leaning right across the Harrow, without taking any notice of it, intent only on finding out what was happening to the prisoner. "Be careful with him!" cried the officer again. He ran round the apparatus, himself caught the condemned man under the shoulders and with the soldier's help got him up on his feet, which kept slithering from under him.

"Now I know all about it," said the explorer as the officer came back to him. "All except the most important thing," he answered, seizing the explorer's arm and pointing upwards: "In the Designer are all the cogwheels that control the movements of the Harrow, and this machinery is regulated according to the inscription demanded by the sentence. I am still using the guiding plans drawn by the former Commandant. Here they are"—he extracted some sheets from the leather wallet—"but I'm sorry I can't let you handle them, they are my most precious possessions. Just take a seat and I'll hold them in front of you like this, then you'll be able to see everything quite well." He spread out the first sheet of paper. The explorer would have liked to say something appreciative, but all he could see was a labyrinth of lines crossing and re-crossing each other, which covered the paper so thickly that it was difficult to discern the blank spaces between them. "Read it," said the officer. "I can't," said the explorer. "Yet it's clear enough," said the officer. "It's very ingenious," said the explorer evasively, "but I can't make it out." "Yes," said the officer with a laugh, putting the paper away again, "it's no calligraphy for school children. It needs to be studied closely. I'm quite sure that in the end you would understand it too. Of course the script can't be a simple one; it's not supposed to kill a man straight off, but only after an interval of, on an average, twelve hours; the turning point is reckoned to come at the sixth hour. So there have to be lots and lots of flourishes around the actual script; the script itself runs round the body only in a narrow girdle; the rest of the body is reserved for the embellishments. Can you appreciate now the work accomplished by the Harrow and the whole apparatus?—Just watch it!" He ran up the ladder, turned a wheel, called down: "Look out, keep to one side!" and everything started working. If the wheel had not creaked, it would have been marvelous. The officer, as if surprised by the noise of the wheel, shook his fist at it, then spread out his arms in excuse to the explorer and climbed down rapidly to peer at the working of the machine from below. Something perceptible to no one save himself was still not in order; he clambered up again, did something with both hands in the interior of the Designer, then slid down one of the rods, instead of using the ladder, so as to get down quicker, and with the full force of his lungs, to make himself heard at all in the noise, yelled in the explorer's ear: "Can you follow it? The Harrow is beginning to write; when it finishes the first draft of the inscription on the man's back, the layer of cotton wool begins to roll and slowly turns the body over, to give the Harrow fresh space for writing. Meanwhile the raw part that has been written on lies on the cotton wool, which is specially prepared to staunch the bleeding and so makes all ready for a new deepening of the script. Then these teeth at the edge of the Harrow, as the body turns further round, tear the cotton wool away from the wounds, throw it into the pit, and there is more work for the Harrow. So it keeps on writing deeper and deeper for the whole twelve hours. The first six hours the condemned man stays alive almost as before, he suffers only pain. After two hours the felt gag is taken away, for he has no longer strength to scream. Here, into this electrically heated basin at the head of the bed, some warm rice pap is poured, from which the man, if he feels like it, can take as much as his tongue can lap. Not one of them ever misses the chance. I can remember none, and my experience is extensive. Only about the sixth hour does the man lose all desire to eat. I usually kneel down here at that moment and observe what happens. The man rarely swallows his last mouthful, he only rolls it round his mouth and spits it out into the pit. I have to duck just then or he would spit it in my face. But how quiet he grows at just about the sixth hour! Enlightenment comes to the most dull-witted. It begins around the eyes. From there it radiates. A moment that might tempt one to get under the Harrow oneself. Nothing more happens than that the man begins to understand the inscription, he purses his mouth as if he were listening. You have seen how difficult it is to decipher the script with one's eyes; but our man deciphers it with his wounds. To be sure, that is a hard task; he needs six hours to accomplish it. By that time the Harrow has pierced him quite through and casts him into the pit, where he pitches down upon the blood and water and the cotton wool. Then the judgment has been fulfilled, and we, the soldier and I, bury him."

The explorer had inclined his ear to the officer and with his hands in his jacket pockets watched the machine at work. The condemned man watched it too, but uncomprehendingly. He bent forward a little and was intent on the moving needles when the soldier, at a sign from the officer, slashed through his shirt and trousers from behind with a knife, so that they fell off; he tried to catch at his falling clothes to cover his nakedness, but the soldier lifted him into the air and shook the last remnants from him. The officer stopped the machine, and in the sudden silence the condemned man was laid under the Harrow. The chains were loosened and the straps fastened on instead; in the first moment that seemed almost a relief to the prisoner. And now the Harrow was adjusted a little lower, since he was a thin man. When the needle points touched him a shudder ran over his skin; while the soldier was busy strapping his right hand, he flung out his left hand blindly; but it happened to be in the direction towards where the explorer was standing. The officer kept watching the explorer sideways, as if seeking to read from his face the impression made on him by the execution, which had been at least cursorily explained to him.

The wrist strap broke; probably the soldier had drawn it too tight. The officer had to intervene, the soldier held up the broken piece of strap to show him. So the officer went over to him and said, his face still turned towards the explorer: "This is a very complex machine, it can't be helped that things are breaking or giving way here and there; but one must not thereby allow oneself to be diverted in one's general judgment. In any case, this strap is easily made good; I shall simply use a chain; the delicacy of the vibrations for the right arm will of course be a little impaired." And while he fastened the chains, he added: "The resources for maintaining the machine are now very much reduced. Under the former Commandant I had free access to a sum of money set aside entirely for this purpose. There was a store, too, in which spare parts were kept for repairs of all kinds. I confess I have been almost prodigal with them, I mean in the past, not now as the new Commandant pretends, always looking for an excuse to attack our old way of doing things. Now he has taken charge of the machine money himself, and if I send for a new strap they ask for the broken old strap as evidence, and the new strap takes ten days to appear and then is of shoddy material and not much good. But how I am supposed to work the machine without a strap, that's something nobody bothers about."

The explorer thought to himself: It's always a ticklish matter to intervene decisively in other people's affairs. He was neither a member of the penal colony nor a citizen of the state to which it belonged. Were he to denounce this execution or actually try to stop it, they could say to him: You are a foreigner, mind your own business. He could make no answer to that, unless he were to add that he was amazed at himself in this connection, for he traveled only as an observer, with no intention at all of altering other people's methods of administering justice. Yet here he found himself strongly tempted. The injustice of the procedure and the inhumanity of the execution were undeniable. No one could suppose that he had any selfish interest in the matter, for the condemned man was a complete stranger, not a fellow countryman or even at all sympathetic to him. The explorer himself had recommendations from high quarters, had been received here with great courtesy, and the very fact that he had been invited to attend the execution seemed to suggest that his views would be welcome. And this was all the more likely since the Commandant, as he had heard only too plainly, was no upholder of the procedure and maintained an attitude almost of hostility to the officer.

At that moment the explorer heard the officer cry out in rage. He had just, with considerable difficulty, forced the felt gag into the condemned man's mouth when the man in an irresistible access of nausea shut his eyes and vomited. Hastily the officer snatched him away from the gag and tried to hold his head over the pit; but it was too late, the vomit was running all over the machine. "It's all the fault of that Commandant!" cried the officer, senselessly shaking the brass rods in front, "the machine is befouled like a pigsty." With trembling hands he indicated to the explorer what had happened. "Have I not tried for hours at a time to get the Commandant to understand that the prisoner must fast for a whole day before the execution. But our new, mild doctrine thinks otherwise. The Commandant's ladies stuff the man with sugar candy before he's led off. He has lived on stinking fish his whole life long and now he has to eat sugar candy! But it could still be possible, I should have nothing to say against it, but why won't they get me a new felt gag, which I have been begging for the last three months. How should a man not feel sick when he takes a felt gag into his mouth which more than a hundred men have already slobbered and gnawed in their dying moments?"

The condemned man had laid his head down and looked peaceful, the soldier was busy trying to clean the machine with the prisoner's shirt. The officer advanced towards the explorer, who in some vague presentiment fell back a pace, but the officer seized him by the hand, and drew him to one side. "I should like to exchange a few words with you in confidence," he said, "may I?" "Of course," said the explorer, and listened with downcast eyes.

"This procedure and method of execution, which you are now having the opportunity to admire, has at the moment no longer any open adherents in our colony. I am its sole advocate, and at the same time the sole advocate of the old Commandant's tradition. I can no longer reckon on any further extension of the method, it takes all my energy to maintain it as it is. During the old Commandant's lifetime the colony was full of his adherents; his strength of conviction I still have in some measure, but not an atom of his power; consequently the adherents have skulked out of sight, there are still many of them but none of them will admit it. If you were to go into the teahouse today, on execution day, and listen to what is being said, you would perhaps hear only ambiguous remarks. These would all be made by adherents, but under the present Commandant and his present doctrines they are of no use to me. And now I ask you: because of this Commandant and the women who influence him, is such a piece of work, the work of a lifetime"—he pointed to the machine—"to perish? Ought one to let that happen? Even if one has only come as a stranger to our island for a few days? But there's no time to lose, an attack of some kind is impending on my function as judge; conferences are already being held in the Commandant's office from which I am excluded; even your coming here today seems to me a significant move; they are cowards and use you as a screen, you, a stranger.—How different an execution was in the old days! A whole day before the ceremony the valley was packed with people; they all came only to look on; early in the morning the Commandant appeared with his ladies; fanfares roused the whole camp; I reported that everything was in readiness; the assembled company—no high official dared to absent himself—arranged itself round the machine; this pile of cane chairs is a miserable survival from that epoch. The machine was freshly cleaned and glittering, I got new spare parts for almost every execution. Before hundreds of spectators— all of them standing on tiptoe as far as the heights there—the condemned man was laid under the Harrow by the Commandant himself. What is left today for a common soldier to do was then my task, the task of the presiding judge, and was an honor for me. And then the execution began! No discordant noise spoilt the working of the machine. Many did not care to watch it but lay with closed eyes in the sand; they all knew: Now Justice is being done. In the silence one heard nothing but the condemned man's sighs, half muffled by the felt gag. Nowadays the machine can no longer wring from anyone a sigh louder than the felt gag can stifle; but in those days the writing needles let drop an acid fluid, which we're no longer permitted to use. Well, and then came the sixth hour! It was impossible to grant all the requests to be allowed to watch it from near by. The Commandant in his wisdom ordained that the children should have the preference; I, of course, because of my office had the privilege of always being at hand; often enough I would be squatting there with a small child in either arm. How we all absorbed the look of transfiguration on the face of the sufferer, how we bathed our cheeks in the radiance of that justice, achieved at last and fading so quickly! What times these were, my comrade!" The officer had obviously forgotten whom he was addressing; he had embraced the explorer and laid his head on his shoulder. The explorer was deeply embarrassed, impatiently he stared over the officer's head. The soldier had finished his cleaning job and was now pouring rice pap from a pot into the basin. As soon as the condemned man, who seemed to have recovered entirely, noticed this action he began to reach for the rice with his tongue. The soldier kept pushing him away, since the rice pap was certainly meant for a later hour, yet it was just as unfitting that the soldier himself should thrust his dirty hands into the basin and eat out of it before the other's avid face.

The officer quickly pulled himself together. "I didn't want to upset you," he said, "I know it is impossible to make those days credible now. Anyhow, the machine is still working and it is still effective in itself. It is effective in itself even though it stands alone in this valley. And the corpse still falls at the last into the pit with an incomprehensibly gentle wafting motion, even though there are no hundreds of people swarming around like flies as formerly. In those days we had to put a strong fence round the pit, it has long since been torn down."

The explorer wanted to withdraw his face from the officer and looked round him at random. The officer thought he was surveying the valley's desolation; so he seized him by the hands, turned him round to meet his eyes, and asked: "Do you realize the shame of it?"

But the explorer said nothing. The officer left him alone for a little; with legs apart, hands on hips, he stood very still, gazing at the ground. Then he smiled encouragingly at the explorer and said: "I was quite near you yesterday when the Commandant gave you the invitation. I heard him giving it. I know the Commandant. I divined at once what he was after. Although he is powerful enough to take measures against me, he doesn't dare to do it yet, but he certainly means to use your verdict against me, the verdict of an illustrious foreigner. He has calculated it carefully: this is your second day on the island, you did not know the old Commandant and his ways, you are conditioned by European ways of thought, perhaps you object on principle to capital punishment in general and to such mechanical instruments of death in particular, besides you will see that the execution has no support from the public, a shabby ceremony—carried out with a machine already somewhat old and worn—now, taking all that into consideration, would it not be likely (so thinks the Commandant) that you might disapprove of my methods? And if you disapprove, you wouldn't conceal the fact (I'm still speaking from the Commandant's point of view), for you are a man to feel confidence in your own well-tried conclusions. True, you have seen and learned to appreciate the peculiarities of many peoples, and so you would not be likely to take a strong line against our proceedings, as you might do in your own country. But the Commandant has no need of that. A casual, even an unguarded remark will be enough. It doesn't even need to represent what you really think, so long as it can be used speciously to serve his purpose. He will try to prompt you with sly questions, of that I am certain. And his ladies will sit around you and prick up their ears; you might be saying something like this: 'In our country we have a different criminal procedure,' or 'In our country the prisoner is interrogated before he is sentenced,' or 'We haven't used torture since the Middle Ages.' All these statements are as true as they seem natural to you, harmless remarks that pass no judgment on my methods. But how would the Commandant react to them? I can see him, our good Commandant, pushing his chair away immediately and rushing on to the balcony, I can see his ladies streaming out after him, I can hear his voice—the ladies call it a voice of thunder—well, and this is what he says: 'A famous Western investigator, sent out to study criminal procedure in all the countries of the world, has just said that our old tradition of administering justice is inhumane. Such a verdict from such a personality makes it impossible for me to countenance these methods any longer. Therefore from this very day I ordain . . .' and so on. You may want to interpose that you never said any such thing, that you never called my methods inhumane, on the contrary your profound experience leads you to believe they are most humane and most in consonance with human dignity, and you admire the machine greatly—but it will be too late; you won't even get onto the balcony, crowded as it will be with ladies; you may try to draw attention to yourself; you may want to scream out; but a lady's hand will close your lips—and I and the work of the old Commandant will be done for."

The explorer had to suppress a smile; so easy, then, was the task he had felt to be so difficult. He said evasively: "You overestimate my influence; the Commandant has read my letters of recommendation, he knows that I am no expert in criminal procedure. If I were to give an opinion, it would be as a private individual, an opinion no more influential than that of any ordinary person, and in any case much less influential than that of the Commandant, who, I am given to understand, has very extensive powers in this penal colony. If his attitude to your procedure is as definitely hostile as you believe, then I fear the end of your tradition is at hand, even without any humble assistance from me."

Had it dawned on the officer at last? No, he still did not understand. He shook his head emphatically, glanced briefly round at the condemned man and the soldier, who both flinched away from the rice, came close up to the explorer and without looking at his face but fixing his eye on some spot on his coat said in a lower voice than before: "You don't know the Commandant; you feel yourself—forgive the expression—a kind of outsider so far as all of us are concerned; yet, believe me, your influence cannot be rated too highly. I was simply delighted when I heard that you were to attend the execution all by yourself. The Commandant arranged it to aim a blow at me, but I shall turn it to my advantage. Without being distracted by lying whispers and contemptuous glances—which could not have been avoided had a crowd of people attended the execution—you have heard my explanations, seen the machine and are now in course of watching the execution. You have doubtless already formed your own judgment; if you still have some small uncertainties the sight of the execution will resolve them. And now I make this request to you: help me against the Commandant!"

The explorer would not let him go on. "How could I do that," he cried, "it's quite impossible. I can neither help nor hinder you."

"Yes, you can," the officer said. The explorer saw with a certain apprehension that the officer had clenched his fists. "Yes, you can," repeated the officer, still more insistently. "I have a plan that is bound to succeed. You believe your influence is insufficient. I know that it is sufficient. But even granted that you are right, is it not necessary, for the sake of preserving this tradition, to try even what might prove insufficient? Listen to my plan, then. The first thing necessary for you to carry it out is to be as reticent as possible today regarding your verdict on these proceedings. Unless you are asked a direct question you must say nothing at all; but what you do say must be brief and general; let it be remarked that you would prefer not to discuss the matter, that you are out of patience with it, that if you are to let yourself go you would use strong language. I don't ask you to tell any lies; by no means; you should only give curt answers, such as: 'Yes, I saw the execution,' or 'Yes, I had it explained to me.' Just that, nothing more. There are grounds enough for any impatience you betray, although not such as will occur to the Commandant. Of course, he will mistake your meaning and interpret it to please himself. That's what my plan depends on. Tomorrow in the Commandant's office there is to be a large conference of all the high administrative officials, the Commandant presiding. Of course the Commandant is the kind of man to have turned these conferences into public spectacles. He has had a gallery built that is always packed with spectators. I am compelled to take part in the conferences, but they make me sick with disgust. Now, whatever happens you will certainly be invited to this conference; if you behave today as I suggest the invitation will become an urgent request. But if for some mysterious reason you're not invited, you'll have to ask for an invitation; there's no doubt of your getting it then. So tomorrow you're sitting in the Commandant's box with the ladies. He keeps looking up to make sure you're there. After various trivial and ridiculous matters, brought in merely to impress the audience—mostly harbor works, nothing but harbor works!—our judicial procedure comes up for discussion too. If the Commandant doesn't introduce it, or not soon enough, I'll see that it's mentioned. I'll stand up and report that today's execution has taken place. Quite briefly, only a statement. Such a statement is not usual, but I shall make it. The Commandant thanks me, as always, with an amiable smile, and then he can't restrain himself, he seizes the excellent opportunity. 'It has just been reported,' he will say, or words to that effect, 'that an execution has taken place. I should like merely to add that this execution was witnessed by the famous explorer who has, as you all know, honored our colony so greatly by his visit to us. His presence at today's session of our conference also contributes to the importance of this occasion. Should we not now ask the famous explorer to give us his verdict on our traditional mode of execution and the procedure that leads up to it?' Of course there is loud applause, general agreement, I am more insistent than anyone. The Commandant bows to you and says: 'Then in the name of the assembled company, I put the question to you.' And now you advance to the front of the box. Lay your hands where everyone can see them, or the ladies will catch them and press your fingers.—And then at last you can speak out. I don't know how I'm going to endure the tension of waiting for that moment. Don't put any restraint on yourself when you make your speech, publish the truth aloud, lean over the front of the box, shout, yes indeed, shout your verdict, your unshakable conviction, at the Commandant. Yet perhaps you wouldn't care to do that, it's not in keeping with your character, in your country perhaps people do these things differently, well, that's all right too, that will be quite as effective, don't even stand up, just say a few words, even in a whisper, so that only the officials beneath you will hear them, that will be quite enough, you don't even need to mention the lack of public support for the execution, the creaking wheel, the broken strap, the filthy gag of felt, no, I'll take all that upon me, and, believe me, if my indictment doesn't drive him out of the conference hall, it will force him to his knees to make the acknowledgment: Old Commandant, I humble myself before you.—That is my plan; will you help me to carry it out? But of course you are willing, what is more, you must." And the officer seized the explorer by both arms and gazed, breathing heavily, into his face. He had shouted the last sentence so loudly that even the soldier and the condemned man were startled into attending; they had not understood a word but they stopped eating and looked over at the explorer, chewing their previous mouthfuls.

From the very beginning the explorer had no doubt about what answer he must give; in his lifetime he had experienced too much to have any uncertainty here; he was fundamentally honorable and unafraid. And yet now, facing the soldier and the condemned man, he did hesitate, for as long as it took to draw one breath. At last, however, he said, as he had to: "No." The officer blinked several times but did not turn his eyes away. "Would you like me to explain?" asked the explorer. The officer nodded wordlessly. "I do not approve of your procedure," said the explorer then, "even before you took me into your confidence— of course I shall never in any circumstances betray your confidence—I was already wondering whether it would be my duty to intervene and whether my intervention would have the slightest chance of success. I realized to whom I ought to turn: to the Commandant, of course. You have made that fact even clearer, but without having strengthened my resolution, on the contrary, your sincere conviction has touched me, even though it cannot influence my judgment."

The officer remained mute, turned to the machine, caught hold of a brass rod, and then, leaning back a little, gazed at the Designer as if to assure himself that all was in order. The soldier and the condemned man seemed to have come to some understanding; the condemned man was making signs to the soldier, difficult though his movements were because of the tight straps; the soldier was bending down to him; the condemned man whispered something and the soldier nodded.

The explorer followed the officer and said: "You don't know yet what I mean to do. I shall tell the Commandant what I think of the procedure, certainly, but not at a public conference, only in private; nor shall I stay here long enough to attend any conference; I am going away early tomorrow morning, or at least embarking on my ship."

It did not look as if the officer had been listening. "So you did not find the procedure convincing," he said to himself and smiled, as an old man smiles at childish nonsense and yet pursues his own meditations behind the smile.

"Then the time has come," he said at last, and suddenly looked at the explorer with bright eyes that held some challenge, some appeal for co-operation. "The time for what?" asked the explorer uneasily, but got no answer.

"You are free," said the officer to the condemned man in the native tongue. The man did not believe it at first. "Yes, you are set free," said the officer. For the first time the condemned man's face woke to real animation. Was it true? Was it only a caprice of the officer's, that might change again? Had the foreign explorer begged him off? What was it? One could read these questions on his face. But not for long. Whatever it might be, he wanted to be really free if he might, and he began to struggle so far as the Harrow permitted him.

"You'll burst my straps," cried the officer, "lie still! We'll soon loosen them." And signing the soldier to help him, he set about doing so. The condemned man laughed wordlessly to himself, now he turned his face left towards the officer, now right towards the soldier, nor did he forget the explorer.

"Draw him out," ordered the officer. Because of the Harrow this had to be done with some care. The condemned man had already torn himself a little in the back through his impatience.

From now on, however, the officer paid hardly any attention to him. He went up to the explorer, pulled out the small leather wallet again, turned over the papers in it, found the one he wanted and showed it to the explorer. "Read it," he said. "I can't," said the explorer, "I told you before that I can't make out these scripts." "Try taking a close look at it," said the officer and came quite near to the explorer so that they might read it together. But when even that proved useless, he outlined the script with his little finger, holding it high above the paper as if the surface dared not be sullied by touch, in order to help the explorer to follow the script in that way. The explorer did make an effort, meaning to please the officer in this respect at least, but he was quite unable to follow. Now the officer began to spell it, letter by letter, and then read out the words. " 'BE JUST!' is what is written there," he said, "surely you can read it now." The explorer bent so close to the paper that the officer feared he might touch it and drew it farther away; the explorer made no remark, yet it was clear that he still could not decipher it. " 'BE JUST!' is what is written there," said the officer once more. "Maybe," said the explorer, "I am prepared to believe you." "Well, then," said the officer, at least partly satisfied, and climbed up the ladder with the paper; very carefully he laid it inside the Designer and seemed to be changing the disposition of all the cogwheels; it was a troublesome piece of work and must have involved wheels that were extremely small, for sometimes the officer's head vanished altogether from sight inside the Designer, so precisely did he have to regulate the machinery.

The explorer, down below, watched the labor uninterruptedly, his neck grew stiff and his eyes smarted from the glare of sunshine over the sky. The soldier and the condemned man were now busy together. The man's shirt and trousers, which were already lying in the pit, were fished out by the point of the soldier's bayonet. The shirt was abominably dirty and its owner washed it in the bucket of water. When he put on the shirt and trousers both he and the soldier could not help guffawing, for the garments were of course slit up behind. Perhaps the condemned man felt it incumbent on him to amuse the soldier, he turned round and round in his slashed garments before the soldier, who squatted on the ground beating his knees with mirth. All the same, they presently controlled their mirth out of respect for the gentlemen.

When the officer had at length finished his task aloft, he surveyed the machinery in all its details once more, with a smile, but this time shut the lid of the Designer, which had stayed open till now, climbed down, looked into the pit and then at the condemned man, noting with satisfaction that the clothing had been taken out, then went over to wash his hands in the water bucket, perceived too late that it was disgustingly dirty, was unhappy because he could not wash his hands, in the end thrust them into the sand—this alternative did not please him, but he had to put up with it—then stood upright and began to unbutton his uniform jacket. As he did this, the two ladies' handkerchiefs he had tucked under his collar fell into his hands. "Here are your handkerchiefs," he said, and threw them to the condemned man. And to the explorer he said in explanation: "A gift from the ladies."

In spite of the obvious haste with which he was discarding first his uniform jacket and then all his clothing, he handled each garment with loving care, he even ran his fingers caressingly over the silver lace on the jacket and shook a tassel into place. This loving care was certainly out of keeping with the fact that as soon as he had a garment off he flung it at once with a kind of unwilling jerk into the pit. The last thing left to him was his short sword with the sword belt. He drew it out of the scabbard, broke it, then gathered all together, the bits of the sword, the scabbard and the belt, and flung them so violently down that they clattered into the pit.

Now he stood naked there. The explorer bit his lips and said nothing. He knew very well what was going to happen, but he had no right to obstruct the officer in anything. If the judicial procedure which the officer cherished were really so near its end—possibly as a result of his own intervention, as to which he felt himself pledged—then the officer was doing the right thing; in his place the explorer would not have acted otherwise.

The soldier and the condemned man did not understand at first what was happening, at first they were not even looking on. The condemned man was gleeful at having got the handkerchiefs back, but he was not allowed to enjoy them for long, since the soldier snatched them with a sudden, unexpected grab. Now the condemned man in turn was trying to twitch them from under the belt where the soldier had tucked them, but the soldier was on his guard. So they were wrestling, half in jest. Only when the officer stood quite naked was their attention caught. The condemned man especially seemed struck with the notion that some great change was impending. What had happened to him was now going to happen to the officer. Perhaps even to the very end. Apparently the foreign explorer had given the order for it. So this was revenge. Although he himself had not suffered to the end, he was to be revenged to the end. A broad, silent grin now appeared on his face and stayed there all the rest of the time.

The officer, however, had turned to the machine. It had been clear enough previously that he understood the machine well, but now it was almost staggering to see how he managed it and how it obeyed him. His hand had only to approach the Harrow for it to rise and sink several times till it was adjusted to the right position for receiving him; he touched only the edge of the Bed and already it was vibrating; the felt gag came to meet his mouth, one could see that the officer was really reluctant to take it but he shrank from it only a moment, soon he submitted and received it. Everything was ready, only the straps hung down at the sides, yet they were obviously unnecessary, the officer did not need to be fastened down. Then the condemned man noticed the loose straps, in his opinion the execution was incomplete unless the straps were buckled, he gestured eagerly to the soldier and they ran together to strap the officer down. The latter had already stretched out one foot to push the lever that started the Designer; he saw the two men coming up; so he drew his foot back and let himself be buckled in. But now he could not reach the lever; neither the soldier nor the condemned man would be able to find it, and the explorer was determined not to lift a finger. It was not necessary; as soon as the straps were fastened the machine began to work; the Bed vibrated, the needles flickered above the skin, the Harrow rose and fell. The explorer had been staring at it quite a while before he remembered that a wheel in the Designer should have been creaking, but everything was quiet, not even the slightest hum could be heard.

Because it was working so silently the machine simply escaped one's attention. The explorer observed the soldier and the condemned man. The latter was the more animated of the two, everything in the machine interested him, now he was bending down and now stretching up on tiptoe, his forefinger was extended all the time pointing out details to the soldier. This annoyed the explorer. He was resolved to stay till the end, but he could not bear the sight of these two. "Go back home," he said. The soldier would have been willing enough, but the condemned man took the order as a punishment. With clasped hands he implored to be allowed to stay, and when the explorer shook his head and would not relent, he even went down on his knees. The explorer saw that it was no use merely giving orders, he was on the point of going over and driving them away. At that moment he heard a noise above him in the Designer. He looked up. Was that cogwheel going to make trouble after all? But it was something quite different. Slowly the lid of the Designer rose up and then clicked wide open. The teeth of a cogwheel showed themselves and rose higher, soon the whole wheel was visible, it was as if some enormous force were squeezing the Designer so that there was no longer room for the wheel, the wheel moved up till it came to the very edge of the Designer, fell down, rolled along the sand a little on its rim and then lay flat. But a second wheel was already rising after it, followed by many others, large and small and indistinguishably minute, the same thing happened to all of them, at every moment one imagined the Designer must now really be empty, but another complex of numerous wheels was already rising into sight, falling down, trundling along the sand and lying flat. This phenomenon made the condemned man completely forget the explorer's command, the cogwheels fascinated him, he was always trying to catch one and at the same time urging the soldier to help, but always drew back his hand in alarm, for another wheel always came hopping along which, at least on its first advance, scared him off.

The explorer, on the other hand, felt greatly troubled; the machine was obviously going to pieces; its silent working was a delusion; he had a feeling that he must now stand by the officer, since the officer was no longer able to look after himself. But while the tumbling cogwheels absorbed his whole attention he had forgotten to keep an eye on the rest of the machine; now that the last cogwheel had left the Designer, however, he bent over the Harrow and had a new and still more unpleasant surprise. The Harrow was not writing, it was only jabbing, and the Bed was not turning the body over but only bringing it up quivering against the needles. The explorer wanted to do something, if possible, to bring the whole machine to a standstill, for this was no exquisite torture such as the officer desired, this was plain murder. He stretched out his hands. But at that moment the Harrow rose with the body spitted on it and moved to the side, as it usually did only when the twelfth hour had come. Blood was flowing in a hundred streams, not mingled with water, the water jets too had failed to function. And now the last action failed to fulfil itself, the body did not drop off the long needles, streaming with blood it went on hanging over the pit without falling into it. The Harrow tried to move back to its old position, but as if it had itself noticed that it had not yet got rid of its burden it stuck after all where it was, over the pit. "Come and help!" cried the explorer to the other two, and himself seized the officer's feet. He wanted to push against the feet while the others seized the head from the opposite side and so the officer might be slowly eased off the needles. But the other two could not make up their minds to come; the condemned man actually turned away; the explorer had to go over to them and force them into position at the officer's head. And here, almost against his will, he had to look at the face of the corpse. It was as it had been in life; no sign was visible of the promised redemption; what the others had found in the machine the officer had not found; the lips were firmly pressed together, the eyes were open, with the same expression as in life, the look was calm and convinced, through the forehead went the point of the great iron spike.

As the explorer, with the soldier and the condemned man behind him, reached the first houses of the colony, the soldier pointed to one of them and said: "There is the teahouse."

In the ground floor of the house was a deep, low, cavernous space, its walls and ceiling blackened with smoke. It was open to the road all along its length. Although this teahouse was very little different from the other houses of the colony, which were all very dilapidated, even up to the Commandant's palatial headquarters, it made on the explorer the impression of a historic tradition of some kind, and he felt the power of past days. He went near to it, followed by his companions, right up between the empty tables which stood in the street before it, and breathed the cool, heavy air that came from the interior. "The old man's buried here," said the soldier, "the priest wouldn't let him lie in the churchyard. Nobody knew where to bury him for a while, but in the end they buried him here. The officer never told you about that, for sure, because of course that's what he was most ashamed of. He even tried several times to dig the old man up by night, but he was always chased away." "Where is the grave?" asked the explorer, who found it impossible to believe the soldier. At once both of them, the soldier and the condemned man, ran before him pointing with outstretched hands in the direction where the grave should be. They led the explorer right up to the back wall, where guests were sitting at a few tables. They were apparently dock laborers, strong men with short, glistening, full black beards. None had a jacket, their shirts were torn, they were poor, humble creatures. As the explorer drew near, some of them got up, pressed close to the wall, and stared at him. "It's a foreigner," ran the whisper around him, "he wants to see the grave." They pushed one of the tables aside, and under it there was really a gravestone. It was a simple stone, low enough to be covered by a table. There was an inscription on it in very small letters, the explorer had to kneel down to read it. This was what it said: "Here rests the old Commandant. His adherents, who now must be nameless, have dug this grave and set up this stone. There is a prophecy that after a certain number of years the Commandant will rise again and lead his adherents from this house to recover the colony. Have faith and wait!" When the explorer had read this and risen to his feet he saw all the bystanders around him smiling, as if they too had read the inscription, had found it ridiculous and were expecting him to agree with them. The explorer ignored this, distributed a few coins among them, waiting till the table was pushed over the grave again, quitted the teahouse and made for the harbor.

The soldier and the condemned man had found some acquaintances in the teahouse, who detained them. But they must have soon shaken them off, for the explorer was only halfway down the long flight of steps leading to the boats when they came rushing after him. Probably they wanted to force him at the last minute to take them with him.

While he was bargaining below with a ferryman to row him to the steamer, the two of them came headlong down the steps, in silence, for they did not dare to shout. But by the time they reached the foot of the steps the explorer was already in the boat, and the ferryman was just casting off from the shore. They could have jumped into the boat, but the explorer lifted a heavy knotted rope from the floor boards, threatened them with it and so kept them from attempting the leap.

QUESTIONS

1. How does this story compare in reality with "The Wall" and "The Pit and the Pendulum"? To what extent should each of these stories be judged as a realistic story or a fantasy?
2. How does this story differ from "The Wall" and "The Pit and the Pendulum" as to (a) its protagonist, (b) the point of view from which it is told, (c) its focus of interest?
3. What kind of person is the officer? What are his principal motivations? Is he a sadist? What motivates his behavior toward the explorer? Why does he think the explorer will help him?
4. Does the officer regard the machine as inhumane? Why not? What feature of the judgment is he most enthusiastic over? Why, at the end, does he commit suicide? What is signified by his breaking his sword?
5. Compare the treatment, in this story and "The Pit and the Pendulum," of ingenious torture machines. How do the interests of the two authors differ?
6. Are there any similarities between this story and "Millstone for the Sun's Day"?
7. The old Commandant and the new Commandant obviously represent different human attitudes and different systems of belief. Formulate in abstract terms the differences between these attitudes and beliefs. Can they be expressed in social terms? in political terms? in religious terms? All three?
8. What symbolical meaning or meanings may be assigned to (a) the old Commandant, (b) the new Commandant, (c) the machine, (d) the penal colony?
9. Where do the sympathies of the explorer lie? Do his attitudes towards the officer and toward the machine change at all during the story?
10. On which side—that of the old Commandant or of the new Commandant—do the sympathies of the author lie? (Do not answer this crucial question hastily. Reputable critics have disagreed on it.) Could the author have been divided in his own allegiance, or not definitely committed to either side?
11. How do the following details fit within the framework of a general interpretation of the story?
    a. the former popularity of executions as compared with present public indifference toward them,

b. the fact that children were given favored positions at executions in the old days,
c. the sixth-hour Enlightenment,
d. the difficulty of getting spare parts for the machine,
e. the machine's final falling apart,
f. the fact that the old Commandant combined everything in himself—"soldier, judge, mechanic, chemist and draughtsman" (page 371),
g. the grave of the old Commandant and the prophecy of his return,
h. the guiding plans drawn out by the old Commandant (page 371),
i. the fact that the new Commandant is surrounded by ladies and that he is interested in "harbor works,"
j. the nature of the sentence decreed for the prisoner,
k. the fact that the prisoner does not know his sentence, and has had no chance of putting up a defence,
l. the guiding principle that "Guilt is never to be doubted" (page 372),
m. the nature of the sentence the officer prescribes for himself,
n. the failure of the machine to do its job properly on the officer,
o. the explorer's driving off the soldier and the condemned man as he makes his escape.

Part Two

STORIES FOR FURTHER READING

This story may be used as additional reading material for the chapter Symbol and Irony.

Andreas Schroeder

THE ROLLER RINK

I will admit at the very outset of the following history that parts of it may be untrue. Unfortunately, I can no longer tell which parts—I have been reworking these notes for such a long time now that my own fabricated sections have become indistinguishably blended with the original facts. I am not even certain precisely how I first stumbled into the environs of the story, though I seem to recall it was while I was stranded in a small village in southern Germany many years ago. I remember nursing a particularly vicious headache at the time and attending to several impressive bruises (unfortunately I have no idea where I might have sustained these knocks) when, for some reason, I noticed a long, oval building standing fairly far back from the street. There was a jagged hole broken through one of its walls.

Normally I wouldn't have paid much attention, but directly below the hole I saw the imprint of a body which presumably had fallen through the hole and lain for some time on the grass below. From the hole itself I could hear the smooth rush of countless ball-bearinged wheels against a background of lilting electric-organ music.

The oval building was a Roller Rink, and a very popular one it appeared, for when I approached the front booth for my ticket I was given a card indicating my application had been noted and instructing me to take a room in one of the nearby hotels until my turn came up. I took a room as directed and settled in for a wait which lasted many months and often threatened to drive me quite mad with boredom, had I not had the company of others who were also waiting to take their turn. I soon discovered that virtually the entire village was comprised of hotels and boarding houses, all of which were constantly filled to capacity with persons waiting to be admitted into the Rink.

After almost three seasons had passed, an errand boy brought the message that I was to present myself the following morning at the front ticket booth to complete certain formalities prerequisite to my entry into the hall. I spent that night with my waiting companions celebrating the good news, accepting the tearful goodbyes and good wishes accorded those about to take their turn. In the morning, after a hurried breakfast, I paid my bill and headed for the Rink.

THE ROLLER RINK   From *The Late Man,* a collection of modern parables by Andreas Schroeder (Sono Nis Press, 1972. Copyright Andreas Schroeder.)

My excitement was such by this time that I paid scant attention to the "formalities" and am consequently unable to reproduce them here, but I do remember being ushered assiduously into the Dressing-Room, a large, high-ceilinged almost clinical looking chamber with white walls and a bevy of brisk girls in white smocks always available to help newcomers into their skates.

My enquiries about the hole in the wall—my initial reason for seeking entry into the Rink—were politely but firmly ignored, and I was entreated to hurry with the putting on of my skates to make room for others who had waited as long as I and were understandably impatient. I realized there was little I could do for the present and decided therefore to have a closer look at the hole once I was mobile and able to inspect this mystery on my own.

To maintain one's balance in this Rink implied learning to skate from scratch, regardless of any former skating experience, and irrespective of the skater's age or native abilities.

At first, people landed on their knees, slid about on their backsides or completely disappeared; others, though not immediately recognizable as themselves, suddenly flickered into view and bounced heavily across my vision. At times, then more and more often, they struggled by, eventually streaked by, pieces of wall stood firmly for a moment, then glanced away hesitantly, soon casually, and I began to lose sight of the individual boards and sections of rail. Later, possibly much later, people receded swiftly in perspective, about-faced, dipped and rolled smoothly away, and the business of maintaining my balance became a matter of personal, not public survival.

By the time I was secure enough on my feet to think about destinations, many more months had passed, and I had almost forgotten what I had entered the Rink to find. Almost as an afterthought, one day, I set course for the far wall where I had seen the hole.

The hole was not there. The hole was no longer there. There was no hole. There had never been a hole broken through the wall of this Roller Rink.

Standing against the railing alongside the wall, I couldn't decide which statement was the true explanation for what I couldn't find. A long, smoothly dove-tailed, highly varnished barrier receded unbroken into the distance, where it curved slightly and disappeared. Wherever it might have been, the hole was no longer anywhere in evidence.

Though I was badly disappointed with this conclusion, there seemed to be little I could do to change it. Standing as I was on the edge of the main stream of traffic, I suffered several near-accidents as the skaters, unaccustomed to stopping or circumnavigating others who had stopped, collided with me from behind and nearly pulled me down. I soon realized that stopping virtually anywhere on the course was extremely dangerous, and that the safest thing was to keep moving at a steady, moderate rate, regardless of any irregularities which aroused my curiosity. This way, at least, there tended to be no surprises.

Of the following dozen years there is little to tell. I skated incessantly, round and round the enormous oval hall, gradually losing all sense of time before my entry into the Rink. From the continual circling I developed a mild but perpetual dizziness which dulled the senses in a peculiarly pleasant sort of way, so that I stopped even my formerly habitual jotting down of notes. There seemed little point to it after all; what minor changes occurred in the daily routine were hardly sufficient to warrant mention.

Not that my subsequent life became completely uneventful; there were enough clashes and quarrels with other skaters to provide an often disagreeable overtone to my life in the Rink. Most of the squabbles occurred when I began to tire of the persistently monotonous pace and attempted to skate in reverse or engage in a little racing. Invariably, the ripples of indignation and even fear which passed through the crowd soon forced me to realign myself in the proper manner and subside. The skaters clung to each other timidly, carefully balancing their proprieties before themselves in sober ritual. Confrontations for any reason whatsoever were considered entirely unacceptable. Instead, the singing of hymns and patriotic songs was encouraged, effectively masking the sounds of argument or dispute.

In retrospect, now, I doubt that I would have lasted many more years in that Rink had I not been offered, by the Rink directors, a course in roller rink management. I was informed that, though my rebellious-ness had compromised my position to some extent, the directors were willing to consider the past a period of adjustment, and that I would be given this unusual chance to redeem myself.

My studies would encompass the entire area of skate mechanics, the styles and techniques of the skill, the different types of music and their effects on the skating masses, also designs of rinks, the various kinds of flooring, different brands of varnish, paint, leather padding and the variety of layouts available for lobby and rest areas. I was to study the arts of timing and pacing, the various rhythms, the tension of centrifugal and gravitational forces played off against one another for balance; in short, the entire problem of the man on wheels.

Though I balked somewhat at the tone of the offer I decided to accept, realizing that I had been in the Rink too long to remember how to survive elsewhere, and hoping this would make my life in the Rink a little more interesting or at least endurable. Under diligent direction I began to spend hours every day repairing torn buckles and straps, replacing lost bearings, exchanging worn wheels and tightening loose or damaged screws. With my manual in one pocket and a small set of portable tools in the other, I spent whole weeks cruising the skating floor, helping hapless skaters who had run into difficulties. As time passed I worked with increasing desperation, feeling always on the edge of disillusionment, always on the verge of betrayal, hoping somehow that a deeper involvement would result in a more secure commitment to the idea of the Rink itself. For when I stopped to think about it, I could feel it slipping from my grasp like a smooth round elusive stone, the belief in the skaters, the Rink, the skating round and round the interminable oval, the never-ending repairs to equipment which stumbled along for a short while, then collapsed again. It began to make less and less sense to me how I could have abandoned all that I had been before (though I had to admit I could no longer remember with any certainty just what I had been) with little more than a shrug of the shoulders and a vague curiosity about a hole in the wall which I couldn't even locate anymore.

The more I realized this, the more I tried to smother my uneasiness in additional work, driving myself with a fiercely clenched mind, deeper and deeper into the tendrils of a vocation leading to Supervisor of Those Who Skate.

When, ten years later, I had chased myself through the entire course, I took up my post as administrator of the large, well-worn Rink and settled in for a term of helping the skaters through their paces.

The Rink, by this time, had been growing too small for my taste and I made immediate application for permission to undertake major renovations throughout the hall. There was bickering, grumbling and much frustrating pedantry, but the permission eventually materialized and the work was launched. By spring of the following year the renovations were almost complete, with work going on solely in the main rink of the skating complex. This area was, as you might imagine, my special concern.

Through my studies I had begun to realize that the secret to a happy congregation and a long-lasting Rink was to position its walls in such a way as to make the skater believe he is moving constantly in a straight line. With this in mind I laboured long hours over the walls and floor to ensure absolute smoothness and continuity. As I sanded and polished each board again and again, it seemed to me that I was not only smoothing the way for others, but straightening the compromising curvature out of my own life.

When the renovations were entirely completed several weeks later, a great inauguration celebration was proposed.

It was decided we would begin the ceremony by all skating once over the entire area of the Rink. At the signal of the jukebox operator (who had recorded a new piece of music designed especially with the new walls in mind) we would begin, with myself in front and the whole skating pack following in neat, orderly rows behind.

The planned celebration was to last throughout an entire week and drew much attention and excitement among the masses which gathered in the Rink lobby on the first day of the feast. It took much effort to prod the entire crowd into its correct position for the beginning of the journey; confused skaters stumbled about everywhere, falling against railings, losing their balance to crash into already assembled lines which promptly lost their cohesion; there was much quibbling over which rows were the most desirable and who should warrant skating where. When everyone was finally in his place, I raised my hand and waved for silence.

The jukebox operator gave the sign. Smoothly, as if driven by electricity, I glided off, pulling my assistant supervisor after me. Row after row set off, until soon the entire herd was in motion, swaying leisurely, easily, from foot to foot. Old women smiled at old men who grinned and nudged each other playfully; the atmosphere was high-spirited, contented and free.

A little time passed. I began to increase the pace bit by bit; the floor was so smooth and the wall so continuous, there was nothing by which anyone could gauge their speed—so there were no complaints. I tried to count the boards in the wall to keep track of our progress but we were soon skating so fast that the boards blurred as we rolled by and I found it difficult to decide where one board ended and the next began. Someone behind me had begun a hymn; I remember being annoyed for an instant that someone should have started the singing without my prior consent, but there was no sense in making a scene on such a special occasion and, besides, we were now speeding along at such a rate that my turning around would have meant placing the balance of the entire skating assemblage in jeopardy.

Suddenly, I thought I felt myself beginning to edge very slowly toward the right, toward the wall. Surprised, uneasy, I looked down at my skates; everything seemed in order, the wheels were spinning along quietly, the leather straps were tight and the metal clamps for the toes seemed secure. It was when I pushed a little harder with my right leg in an attempt to reposition myself into my former place, that I heard the click. It sounded as if a bearing had chipped.

Puzzled, I looked up to see that I was still moving very slowly toward the wall. Trying to ignore the noise in the bearings (which was becoming more and more pronounced) I strained once again toward the left. My skates resolutely refused to shift—and suddenly it dawned on me that we had reached that section of the wall at which the curve began.

I turned my head, glanced back—nothing but elation, singing, horseplay—no-one noticed the drift of the curve.

A flood of anger, exasperation and resentment poured through my mind as I began to realize the implications of this trap, but there was no longer time for thought; I struggled bitterly now, closer and closer to the speeding wall; my skates making a terrific racket but everyone singing so loudly that no-one could hear. My eyes began to hurt; I saw nothing but smooth continuous boards streaking past my pupils back into my skull—stooped down in a grasping effort to undo my straps, thinking possibly to leap out of them, more image than idea—a split-second later I felt my shoulder brush the wall, my right skate screamed along the varnish, dug in, my body swung around and slammed into the wall, I saw an enormous blackness and then there was nothing. . . .

Total silence. Or a gentle hissing sound around the edges of a hole which may not even be an exit, which possibly exists in outline only, in the imagination of a skater just escaped into the confines of a larger surrounding rink. There is room for argument of course, and some evidence that there was, in fact, an actual hole. But it may perhaps be appropriate to point out that it is not as uncommon a thing as it might appear, for a man to construct his past in ramp-like fashion to launch himself into a future he might not otherwise be able to afford. It is possible, for instance, that this gaping story is itself the hole through which the man in question fell, or that it is a substitute for the hole he never found. Another possibility may be arrived at by superimposing the identities of the man at the beginning and the man at the end, placing them on opposite poles of the story's own oval configuration.

Of course it may be that none of these possibilities apply, being suggested, as they are, by the author himself who has admitted from the beginning that an undeterminable part of this fiction may have been fabricated and therefore be untrue. For one thing, it must be pointed out that such feinting is characteristic by persons attempting to make good an escape by confusing their pursuers with false leads and half-true information. But of course this warning, too, is suspect, having been made by the presumed escapee himself. . . .

This story may be used as additional reading material for the chapter Theme.

Clark Blaise

HOW I BECAME A JEW

Cincinnati, September 1950

"I don't suppose you've attended classes with the colored before, have you, Gerald?" the principal inquired. He was a jockey-sized man whose dark face collapsed around a graying mustache. His name was DiCiccio.

"No, sir."

"You'll find quite a number in your classes here—" he gestured to the kids on the playground, and the Negroes among them seemed to multiply before my eyes. "My advice is not to expect any trouble and they won't give you any."

"We don't expect none from them," my mother said with great reserve, the emphasis falling slightly on the last word.

DiCiccio's eyes wandered over us, calculating but discreet. He was taking in my porkiness, my brushed blond hair, white shirt and new gabardines. And my Georgia accent.

"My boy is no troublemaker."

"I can see that, Mrs. Gordon."

"But I'm here to tell you—just let me hear of any trouble and I'm going straight off to the po-lice."

And now DiCiccio's smile assessed her, as though to say *are you finished?* "That wouldn't be in Gerald's best interest, Mrs. Gordon. We have no serious discipline problems in the elementary school but even if we did, Mrs. Gordon, outside authorities are never the answer. Your boy has to live with them. Police are never a solution." He pronounced the word "pleece" and I wanted to laugh. "Even in the Junior High," he said, jerking his thumb in the direction of the black, prisonlike structure beyond the playground. "There are problems there." His voice was still far-off and I was smiling.

DiCiccio's elementary school was new: bright, low and long, with greenboards and yellow chalk, aluminum frames and blond, unblemished desks. My old school in Georgia, near Moultrie, had had a room for each grade up through the sixth. Here in Cincinnati the sixth grade itself had ten sections.

"And Gerald, *please* don't call me 'sir.' Don't call anyone that," the

HOW I BECAME A JEW   Excerpt from *Tribal Justice* by Clark Blaise. Copyright © 1974 by Clark Blaise. Reprinted by permission of Doubleday & Company, Inc.

principal said with sudden urgency. "That's just asking for it. The kids might think you're trying to flatter the teacher or something."

"Well, I swan—" my mother began. "He learned respect for his elders and nobody is taking that respect away. Never."

"Look—" and now the principal leaned forward, growing smaller as he approached the desk, "I know how Southern schools work. I know 'sir' and 'ma'm.' I know they must have beaten it into you. But I'm trying to be honest, Mrs. Gordon. Your son has a lot of things going against him and I'm trying to help. This intelligence of his can only hurt him unless he learns how to use it. He's white—enough said. And I assume Gordon isn't a Jewish name, is it? Which brings up another thing, Mrs. Gordon. Take a look at those kids out there, the white ones. They look like little old men, don't they? Those are *Jews*, Gerald, and they're as different from the others as you are from the colored. They were born in Europe and they're living here with their grandparents— don't ask me why, it's a long story. Let's just say they're a little hard to play with. A little hard to like, O.K.?" Then he settled back and caught his breath.

"They're the Israelites!" I whispered, as though the Bible had come to life. Then I was led to class.

But the sixth grade was not a home for long; not for the spelling champ and fastest reader in Colquitt County, Georgia. They gave me tests, sent me to a university psychologist who tested my memory and gave me some codes to crack. Then I was advanced.

Seventh grade was in the old building: Leonard Sachs Junior High. A greenish statue of Abraham Lincoln stood behind black iron bars, pointing a finger to the drugstore across the street. The outside steps were pitted and sagging. The hallways were tawny above the khaki lockers, and clusters of dull yellow globes were bracketed to the walls, like torches in the catacombs. By instinct I preferred the used to the new, sticky wood to cold steel, and I would have felt comfortable on that first walk down the hall to my new class, but for the stench of furtive, unventilated cigarette smoke. The secretary led me past rooms with open doors; all the techers were men. Many were shouting while the classes turned to whistle at the ringing *tap-tap* of the secretary's heels. Then she stopped in front of a closed door and rapped. The noise inside partially abated and finally a tall bald man with furry ears opened the door.

"This is Gerald Gordon, Mr. Terleski. He's a transfer from Georgia and they've skipped him up from sixth."

"They have, eh?" A few students near the door laughed. They were already pointing at me. "George, you said?"

"Gerald Gordon *from* Georgia," said the secretary.

"Georgia Gordon!" a Negro boy shouted. "Georgia Gordon. Sweet Georgia Gordon."

Terleski didn't turn. He took the folder from the girl and told me to find a seat. But the front boys in each row linked arms and wouldn't let me through. I walked to the window row and laid my books on the ledge. The door closed. Terleski sat at his desk and opened my file but didn't look up.

"Sweet Georgia," crooned the smallish, fair-skinned Negro nearest me. He brushed my notebook to the floor. I bent over and got a judo chop on the inside of my knees.

"Sweet Georgia, you get off the floor, hear?" A very fat, coal-black girl in a pink sweater was helping herself to paper from my three-ring binder. "Mr. Tee, Sweet Georgia taking a nap," she called.

He grumbled. I stood up. My white shirt and baggy gabardines were brown with dust.

"This boy is *not* named Sweet Georgia. He *is* named Gerald Gordon," said Terleski with welcome authority. "And I guess he's some kind of genius. They figured out he was too smart for the sixth grade. They gave him tests at the university and—listen to this—Gerald Gordon is a borderline genius."

A few whistled. Terleski looked up. "Isn't that *nice* for Gerald Gordon? What can we do to make you happy, Mr. Gordon?"

"Nothing, sir," I answered.

"Not a thing? Not an itsy-bitsy thing, sir?"

I shook my head, lowered it.

"Might we expect you to at least look at the rest of us? We wouldn't want to presume, but—"

"Sweet Georgia crying, Mr. Tee," giggled Pink Sweater.

"And he all dirty," added the frontseater. "How come you all dirty, Sweet Georgia-man?" Pink Sweater was awarding my paper to all her friends.

"Come to the desk, Mr. Gordon."

I shuffled forward, holding my books over the dust smears.

"Face your classmates, sir. Look at them. Do you see any borderline types out there? Any friends?"

I sniffled loudly. My throat ached. There were some whites, half a dozen or so grinning in the middle of the room. I looked for girls and saw two white ones. Deep in the rear sat some enormous Negroes, their boots looming in the aisle. They looked at the ceiling and didn't even bother to whisper as they talked. They wore pastel T-shirts with cigarette packs twisted in the shoulder. And—God!—I thought, they had mustaches. Terleski repeated his question, and for the first time in my life I knew that whatever answer I gave would be wrong.

"Mr. Gordon's reading comprehension is equal to the average college freshman. Oh, Mr. Gordon, just average? Surely there must be some mistake."

I started crying, tried to hold it back, couldn't, and bawled. I remembered the rows of gold stars beside my name back in Colquitt County, Georgia, and the times I had helped the teacher by grading my fellow students.

A few others picked up my crying: high-pitched blubbering from all corners. Terleski stood, scratched his ear, then screamed: "Shut up!" A rumbling monotone persisted from the Negro rear. Terleski handed me his handkerchief and said, "Wipe your face." Then he said to the class: "I'm going to let our borderline genius himself continue. Read this, sir, just like an average college freshman." He passed me my file.

I put it down and knuckled my eyes violently. They watched me hungrily, laughing at everything. Terleski poked my ribs with the corner of the file. "Read!"

I caught my breath with a long, loud shudder.

"Gerald Gordon certainly possesses the necessary intellectual equipment to handle work on a seventh grade level, and long consultations with the boy indicate a commensurate emotional maturity. No problem anticipated in adjusting to a new environment."

"Beautiful," Terleski announced. "Beautiful. He's in the room five minutes and he's crying like a baby. Spends his first three minutes on the floor getting dirty, needs a hanky from the teacher to wipe his nose, and he has the whole class laughing at him and calling him names. Beautiful. That's what I call real maturity. Is that all the report says, sir?"

"Yes, sir."

"You're lying, Mr. Gordon. That's not very mature. Tell the class what else it says."

"I don't want to, sir."

"You don't want to. *I* want you to. *Read!*"

"It says: *'I doubt only the ability of the Cincinnati Public Schools to supply a worthy teacher.'*"

"Well— that's what we wanted to hear, Mr. Gordon. Do you doubt it?"

"No, sir."

"Am I worthy enough to teach you?"

"Yes, sir."

"What do I teach?"

"I don't know, sir."

"What have you learned already?"

"Nothing yet, sir."

"What's the capital of the Virgin Islands?"

"Charlotte Amalie," I said.

That surprised him, but he didn't show it for long. "Then I can't teach you a thing, can I, Mr. Gordon? You must know everything there is to know. You must have all your merit badges. So it looks like we're going to waste each other's time, doesn't it? Tell the class where Van Diemen's Land is."

"That's the old name for Tasmania, Sir. Australia, capital is Hobart."

"If it's Australia that would make the capital Canberra, wouldn't it, Mr. Gordon?"

"For the whole country, yes, sir."

"So there's still something for you to learn, isn't there, Mr. Gordon?"

The kids in the front started to boo. "Make room for him back there," the teacher said, pointing to the middle. "And *now*, maybe the rest of you can tell me the states that border on Ohio. Does *anything* border on Ohio?"

No one answered while I waved my hand. I cared desperately that my classmates learn where Ohio was. And finally, ignoring me, Mr. Terleski told them.

Recess: on the sticky pavement in sight of Lincoln's statue. The windows of the first two floors were screened and softball was the sport. The white kids in the gym class wore institutional shorts; the other half—the Negroes—kept their jeans and T-shirts since they weren't allowed in the dressing room. I was still in my dusty new clothes. We all clustered around the gym teacher, who wore a Cincinnati Redlegs cap. He appointed two captains, both white. "Keep track of the score, fellas. And tell me after how you do at the plate individually." He blew his whistle and scampered off to supervise a basketball game around the corner.

The captains were Arno Kolko and Wilfrid Skurow, both fat and pale, with heavy eyebrows and thick hair climbing down their necks and up from their shirts. Hair like that—I couldn't believe it. I was twelve, and had been too ashamed to undress in the locker room. These must be Jews, I told myself. The other whites were shorter than the captains. They wore glasses and had bristly hair. Many of them shaved. Their arms were pale and veined. I moved towards them.

"Where *you* going, boy?" came a high-pitched but adult voice behind me. I turned and faced a six-foot Negro who was biting an unlit cigarette. He had a mustache and, up high on his yellow biceps, a flag tattoo. "Ain't nobody picked you?"

"No," I hesitated, not knowing if I were agreeing or answering.

"Then stay where you're at. Hey—y'all want him?"

Skurow snickered. I had been accustomed to being a low-priority pick back in ball-playing Colquitt County, Georgia. I started to walk away.

"Come back here, boy. Squirrel picking you."

"But you're not a captain."

"Somebody *say* I ain't a captain?" The other Negroes had fanned out under small clouds of blue smoke and started basketball games on the painted courts. "That leaves me and you," said Squirrel. "We standing them."

"I want to be with them," I protested.

"We don't want you," said one of the Jews.

The kid who said it was holding the bat cross-handed as he took some practice swings. I had at least played a bit of softball back in Colquitt County, Georgia. The kids in my old neighborhood had built a diamond near a housing development after a bulldozer operator had cleared the lot for us during his lunch hour. Some of the carpenters had given us timber scrap for a fence and *twice*—I remember the feeling precisely to this day—I had lofted fly balls tightly down the line and over the fence. No question, my superiority to the Arno Kolkos of this world.

"We get first ups," said Squirrel. "All *you* gotta do, boy, is get yourself on base and then move your ass fast enough to get home on anything I hit. And if I don't hit a home run, you gotta bring me home next."

"Easy," said I.

First three times up, it worked. I got on and Squirrel blasted on one hop to the farthest corner of the playground. But he ran the bases in a flash, five or six strides between the bases, and I was getting numb in the knees from staying ahead even with a two-base lead. Finally, I popped up for an out. Then Squirrel laid down a bunt and made it to third on some loose play. I popped out again and had to take his place on third, anticipating a stroll home on his next home run. But he bunted again, directly at Skurow the pitcher, who beat me home for a force-out to end the inning.

"Oh, you're a great one, Sweet Georgia," Squirrel snarled from a position at deep short. He was still biting his unlit cigarette. "You're a plenty heavy hitter, man. Where you learn to hit like that?"

"Georgia," I said, slightly embarrassed for my state.

"Georgia? *Joe-ja?*" He lit his cigarette and tossed me the ball. "Then I guess you're the worst baseball player in the whole state, Sweet Georgia. I *thought* you was different."

"From what?"

"From them." He pointed to our opponents. They were talking to themselves in a different language. I felt the power of a home-run swing lighten my arms, but it was too late.

"I play here," said Squirrel. "Pitch them slow then run to first. Ain't none of them can beat my peg or get it by me."

A kid named Izzie, first up, bounced to me and I tagged him. Then a scrawny kid lifted a goodly fly to left—the kind I had hit for doubles—but Squirrel was waiting for it. Then Wilfred Skurow lumbered up: the most menacing kid I'd ever seen. Hair in swirls on his neck and throat, sprouting wildly from his chest and shoulders. Sideburns, but getting bald. Glasses so thick his eyeballs looked screwed in. But no form. He lunged a chopper to Squirrel, who scooped it and waited for me to cover first. Skurow was halfway down the line, then quit. Squirrel stood straight, tossed his cigarette away, reared back, and fired the ball with everything he had. I heard it leave his hand, then didn't move till it struck my hand and deflected to my skull, over the left eye. I was knocked backwards, and couldn't get up. Skurow circled the bases; Squirrel sat at third and laughed. Then the Jews walked off together and I could feel my forehead tightening into a lump. I tried to stand, but instead grew dizzy and suddenly remembered Colquitt County. I sat alone until the bells rang and the grounds were empty.

Every Saturday near Moultrie, I had gone to the movies. In the balcony they let the colored kids in just for Saturday. Old ones came Wednesday night for Jim Crow melodramas with colored actors. But we came especially equipped for those Saturday mornings when the colored kids sat in the dark up in the balcony, making noise whenever we did. We waited for too much noise, or a popcorn box that might be dropped on us. Then we reached into our pockets and pulled out our broken yo-yos. We always kept our broken ones around. Half a yo-yo is great for sailing since it curves and doesn't lose speed. And it's very hard. So we stood, aimed for the projection beam, and fired the yo-yos upstairs. They loomed on the screen like bats, filled the air like bombs. Some hit metal, others the floor, but some struck home judging from the yelps of the colored kids and their howling. Minutes later the lights went on upstairs and we heard the ushers ordering them out.

A second bell rang.

"That burr-head nigger son-of-a-bitch," I cried. "That goddam nigger." I picked myself up and ran inside.

I was late for geometry but my transfer card excused me. When I opened the door two Negro girls dashed out pursued by two boys about twice my size. One of the girls was Pink Sweater, who ducked inside a girls' room. The boys waited outside. The windows in the geometry room were open, and a few boys were sailing paper planes over the street and sidewalk. The teacher was addressing himself to a small group of students who sat in a semicircle around his desk. He was thin and red-cheeked with a stiff pelt of curly hair.

"I say, do come in, won't you? That's a nasty lump you've got there. Has it been seen to?"

"Sir?"

"Over your eye. Surely you're aware of it. It's really quite unsightly."

"I'm supposed to give you this—" I presented the slip for his signing.

"Gerald Gordon is it? Spiro here."

"Where?"

"Here—I'm Spiro. Geoffrey Spiro, on exchange. And you?"

"Me what?"

"Where are you from?"

"Colquitt County, Georgia."

He smiled as though he knew the place well and liked it. "That's South, aye? Ex-cellent. Let us say for tomorrow you'll prepare a talk on Georgia—brief topical remarks, race, standard of living, labor unrest and what not. Hit the high points, won't you, old man? Now then, class"—he raised his voice only slightly, not enough to disturb the colored boys making *ack-ack* sounds at pedestrians below—"I should like to introduce to you Mr. Gerald Gordon. You have your choice, sir, of joining these students in the front and earning an 'A' grade, or going back there and getting a 'B,' provided of course you don't leave the room."

"I guess I'll stay up here, sir," I said.

"Ex-cellent. Your fellow students, then, from left to right are: Mr. Lefkowitz, Miss Annaliese Graff, Miss Marlene Leopold, Mr. Willie Goldberg, Mr. Irwin Roth, and Mr. Harry Frazier. In the back, Mr. Morris Gordon (no relative, I trust), Miss Etta Bluestone, Mr. Orville Goldberg (he's Willie's twin), and Mr. Henry Moore. Please be seated."

Henry Moore was colored, as were the Goldberg twins, Orville and Wilbur. The girls, Annaliese, Marlene, and Etta, were pretty and astonishingly mature, as ripe in their way as Wilfrid Skurow in his. Harry Frazier was a straw-haired athletic sort, eating a sandwich. The lone chair was next to Henry Moore, who was fat and smiled and had no mustache or tattoo. I took the geometry book from my scuffed, zippered notebook.

"The truth is," Mr. Spiro began, "that both Neville Chamberlain and Mr. Roosevelt were fascist, and quite in sympathy with Hitler's anticommunist ends, if they quibbled on his means. His evil was mere overzealousness. Public opinion in the so-called democracies could never have mustered against *any* anticommunist, whatever his program—short of invasion, of course. *Klar?*" He stopped in order to fish out a book of matches for Annaliese, who was tapping a cigarette on her desk.

"*Stimmt?*" he asked, and the class nodded. Harry Frazier wadded his waxed paper and threw it back to one of his classmates by the window, shouting, "Russian MIG!" I paged through the text, looking for diagrams. No one else had a book out and my activity seemed to annoy them.

"So in conclusion, Hitler was merely the tool of a larger fascist conspiracy, encouraged by England and the United States. What *is* it, Gerald?"

"Sir—what are we talking about?" I was getting a headache, and the egg on my brow seemed ready to burst. The inner semi-circle stared back at me, except for Harry Frazier.

"Sh!" whispered Morris Gordon.

"At *shul* they don't teach it like that," said Irwin Roth, who had a bald spot from where I sat. "In *shul* they say it happened because God was punishing us for falling away. He was testing us. They don't say nothing from the English and the Americans. They don't even say nothing from the Germans."

"Because we didn't learn our letters good," said Morris Gordon. The matches were passed from the girls to all the boys who needed them.

"*What* happened?" I whispered to Henry Moore, who was smiling and nodding as though he knew.

"Them *Jews*, man. Ain't it great?"

"Then the rabbi is handing you the same bloody bullshit they've been handing out since I went to *shul*—ever since the bloody Diaspora," Spiro said. "God, how I detest it."

"What's *shul*, Henry? What's the Diaspora?"

"Look," Spiro continued, now a little more calmly, "there's only one place in the world where they're building socialism, really honestly *building* it"—his hands formed a rigid rectangle over the desk—"and that's Israel. I've seen children your age who've never handled money. I've played football on turf that was desert a year before. The desert blooms, and the children sing and dance and shoot—yes, shoot—superbly. They're all brothers and sisters, and they belong equally to every parent in the *kibbutz*. They'd die for one another. No fighting, no name-calling, no sickness. They're big, straight and strong and tall, and handsome, like the Israelites. I've seen it for myself. Why any Jew would come to America is beyond me, unless he wants to be spat on and corrupted."

"*Gott*, if the rabbi knew what goes on here," said Roth, slapping his forehead.

"What's a rabbi, Henry? *Tell me what a rabbi is!*"

"Whatever is your problem, Gerald?" Spiro cut in.

"Sir—I've lost the place. I just skipped the sixth grade and maybe that's where we learned it all. I don't understand what you-all are saying."

"I must say I speak a rather good English," said Spiro. The class laughed. "Perhaps you'd be happier with the others by the window. All that *rat-tat-tat* seems like jolly good fun, quite a lift, I imagine. It's all perfectly straightforward here. It's *your* country we're talking about, after all. Not mine. Not theirs."

"It's not the same thing up North," I said.

"No, I daresay ... look, why don't you toddle down to the nurse's office and get something for your head? That's a good lad, and you show up tomorrow if you're feeling better and tell us all about Georgia. Then I'll explain the things you don't know. You just think over what I've said, O.K.?"

I was feeling dizzy—the bump, the smoke—my head throbbed, and my new school clothes were filthy. I brushed myself hard and went into the boys' room to comb my hair, but two large Negroes sitting on the window ledge, stripped to their shorts and smoking cigars, chased me out.

Downstairs, the nurse bawled me out for coming in dirty, then put an ice pack over my eye.

"Can I go home?" I asked.

The nurse was old and fat, and wore hexagonal Ben Franklin glasses. After half an hour she put an adhesive patch on and since only twenty minutes were left, she let me go.

I stopped for a coke at the drugstore across from Lincoln's statue. Surprising, I thought, the number of school kids already out, smoking and having cokes. I waited in the drugstore until the sidewalk was jammed with the legitimately dismissed, afraid that some truant officer might question my early release. I panicked as I passed the cigar counter on my way out, for Mr. Terleski was buying cigarettes and a paper. I was embarrassed for him, catching him smoking, but he saw me, smiled, and walked over.

"Hello, son," he said, "what happened to the head?"

"Nothing," I said, "sir."

"About this morning—I want you to know there was nothing personal in anything I said. Do you believe me?"

"Yes, sir."

"If I didn't do it in *my* way first, they'd do it in their way and it wouldn't be pretty. And Gerald—don't raise your hand again, O.K.?"

"All right," I said. "Good-by."

"*Very* good," said Mr. Terleski. "Nothing else? No *sir?*"

"I don't think so," I said.

The street to our apartment was lined with shops: tailors with dirty windows, cigar stores piled with magazines, some reading rooms where bearded old men were talking, and a tiny branch of a supermarket chain. Everywhere there were school kids: Jews, I could tell from their heads. Two blocks away, just a few feet before our apartment block, about a dozen kids turned into the dingy yard of the synagogue. An old man shut the gates in a hurry just as I stopped to look in, and another old man opened the main door to let them inside. The tall spiked fence was painted a glossy black. I could see the kids grabbing black silk caps from a cardboard box, then going downstairs. The old gatekeeper, a man with bad breath and puffy skin, ordered me to go.

At home, my mother was preparing dinner for a guest and she was in no mood to question how I got the bump on the head. The guest was Grady, also from Moultrie, a whip-thin red-faced man in his forties who had been the first of my father's friends to go North. He had convinced my father. His wife and kids were back in Georgia selling their house, so he was eating Georgia food with us till she came back. Grady was the man we had to thank, my father always said.

"Me and the missus is moving again soon's she gets back," he announced at dinner. "Had enough of it here."

"Back to Georgia?" my father asked.

"Naw, Billy, out of Cincinnati. Gonna find me a place somewheres in Kentucky. Come in to work every day and go back at night and live like a white man. A man can forget he's white in Cincinnati."

"Ain't that the truth," said my mother.

"How many niggers you got in your room at school, Jerry?" Grady asked me.

"That depends on the class," I said. "In geometry there aren't any hardly."

"See?" said Grady. "You know five years ago there wasn't hardly no more than ten per cent in that school? Now it's sixty and still going up. By the time your'n gets through he's gonna be the onliest white boy in the school."

"He'll be gone before *that*," my father promised. "I been thinking of moving to Kentucky myself."

"Really?" said my mother.

"I ain't even been to a baseball game since they got that nigger," Grady boasted, "and I ain't ever going. I used to love it."

"You're telling me," said my father.

"If they just paid me half in Georgia what they paid me here, I'd be on the first train back," said Grady. "Sometimes I reckon it's the devil himself just tempting me."

"I heard of kids today that live real good and don't even see any money," I said. "Learned it in school."

"That where you learned to stand in front of a softball bat?" my mother retorted, and my parents laughed. Grady coughed.

"And let me tell you," he began, "them kids that goes to them mixed schools gets plenty loony ideas. That thing he just said sounded comminist to me. Yes, sir, that was a Comminist Party member told him that. I don't think no kid of mine could get away with a lie like that in my house. No, sir, they got to learn the truth sometime, and after they do, the rest is lies."

Then Father slapped the fork from my hands. "Get back to your room," he shouted. "You don't get no more dinner till I see your homework done!" He stood behind me, with his hand digging into my shoulder. "Now say good night to Grady."

"Good night," I mumbled.

"Good night *what?*" my mother demanded. "Good night *what?*"

"Sir," I cried, "sir, sir, sir! Good night, sir!" the last word almost screamed from the hall in front of my bedroom. I slammed the door and fell on the bed in the darkened room. Outside, I could hear the threats and my mother's apologies. "Don't hit him too hard, Billy, he done got that knot on the head already." But no one came.

They started talking of Georgia, and they forgot the hours. I thought of my first school day up North—then planned the second, the third—and I thought of Leonard Sachs Junior High, Squirrel, and the Jews. The Moultrie my parents and Grady were talking about seemed less real, then finally, terrifying. I pictured myself in the darkened balcony under a rain of yo-yos, thrown by a crowd of Squirrels.

I concentrated on the place I wanted to live. There was an enormous baseball stadium where I could hit home runs down the line; Annaliese Graff was in the stands and Mr. Terleski was a coach. We wore little black caps, even Squirrel, and there were black bars outside the park where old men were turning people away. Grady was refused, and Spiro and millions of others, even my parents—though I begged their admission. *No, stimmt?* We were building socialism and we had no parents and we did a lot of singing and dancing (even Henry Moore, even the chocolatey Goldberg twins, Orville and Wilbur) and Annaliese Graff without her cigarettes asked me the capitals of obscure countries. "Israel," I said aloud, letting it buzz; "Israel," and it replaced Mozambique as my favorite word; *Israel, Israel, Israel,* and the dread of the days to come lifted, the days I would learn once and for all if Israel could be really real.

Eudora Welty

A VISIT OF CHARITY

It was mid-morning—a very cold, bright day. Holding a potted plant before her, a girl of fourteen jumped off the bus in front of the Old Ladies' Home, on the outskirts of town. She wore a red coat, and her straight yellow hair was hanging down loose from the pointed white cap all the little girls were wearing that year. She stopped for a moment beside one of the prickly dark shrubs with which the city had beautified the Home, and then proceeded slowly toward the building, which was of whitewashed brick and reflected the winter sunlight like a block of ice. As she walked vaguely up the steps she shifted the small pot from hand to hand; then she had to set it down and remove her mittens before she could open the heavy door.

"I'm a Campfire Girl. . . . I have to pay a visit to some old lady," she told the nurse at the desk. This was a woman in a white uniform who looked as if she were cold; she had close-cut hair which stood up on the very top of her head exactly like a sea wave. Marian, the little girl, did not tell her that this visit would give her a minimum of only three points in her score.

"Acquainted with any of our residents?" asked the nurse. She lifted one eyebrow and spoke like a man.

"With any old ladies? No—but—that is, any of them will do," Marian stammered. With her free hand she pushed her hair behind her ears, as she did when it was time to study Science.

The nurse shrugged and rose. "You have a nice *multifloria cineraria* there," she remarked as she walked ahead down the hall of closed doors to pick out an old lady.

There was loose, bulging linoleum on the floor. Marian felt as if she were walking on the waves, but the nurse paid no attention to it. There was a smell in the hall like the interior of a clock. Everything was silent until, behind one of the doors, an old lady of some kind cleared her throat like a sheep bleating. This decided the nurse. Stopping in her tracks, she first extended her arm, bent her elbow, and leaned forward from the hips—all to examine the watch strapped to her wrist; then she gave a loud double-rap on the door.

"There are two in each room," the nurse remarked over her shoulder.

"Two what?" asked Marian without thinking. The sound like a sheep's bleating almost made her turn around and run back.

One old woman was pulling the door open in short, gradual jerks, and when she saw the nurse a strange smile forced her old face dangerously awry. Marian, suddenly propelled by the strong, impatient arm of the nurse, saw next the side-face of another old woman, even older, who was lying flat in bed with a cap on and a counterpane drawn up to her chin.

"Visitor," said the nurse, and after one more shove she was off up the hall.

Marian stood tongue-tied; both hands held the potted plant. The old woman, still with that terrible, square smile (which was a smile of welcome) stamped on her bony face, was waiting. . . . Perhaps she said something. The old woman in bed said nothing at all, and she did not look around.

Suddenly Marian saw a hand, quick as a bird claw, reach up in the air and pluck the white cap off her head. At the same time, another claw to match drew her all the way into the room, and the next moment the door closed behind her.

"My, my, my," said the old lady at her side.

Marian stood enclosed by a bed, a washstand, and a chair; the tiny room had altogether too much furniture. Everything smelled wet—even the bare floor. She held onto the back of the chair, which was wicker and felt soft and damp. Her heart beat more and more slowly, her hands got colder and colder, and she could not hear whether the old women were saying anything or not. She could not see them very clearly. How dark it was! The window shade was down, and the only door was shut. Marian looked at the ceiling. . . . It was like being caught in a robber's cave, just before one was murdered.

"Did you come to be our little girl for a while?" the first robber asked.

Then something was snatched from Marian's hand—the little potted plant.

"Flowers!" screamed the old woman. She stood holding the pot in an undecided way. "Pretty flowers," she added.

Then the old woman in bed cleared her throat and spoke. "They are not pretty," she said, still without looking around, but very distinctly.

Marian suddenly pitched against the chair and sat down in it.

"Pretty flowers," the first old woman insisted. "Pretty—pretty. . . ."

Marian wished she had the little pot back for just a moment—she had forgotten to look at the plant herself before giving it away. What did it look like?

"Stinkweeds," said the other old woman sharply. She had a bunchy white forehead and red eyes like a sheep. Now she turned them toward Marian. The fogginess seemed to rise in her throat again, and she bleated, "Who—are—you?"

To her surprise, Marian could not remember her name. "I'm a Campfire Girl," she said finally.

"Watch out for the germs," said the old woman like a sheep, not addressing anyone.

"One came out last month to see us," said the first old woman.

A sheep or a germ? wondered Marian dreamily, holding onto the chair.

"Did not!" cried the other old woman.

"Did so! Read to us out of the Bible, and we enjoyed it!" screamed the first.

"Who enjoyed it!" said the woman in bed. Her mouth was unexpectedly small and sorrowful, like a pet's.

"We enjoyed it," insisted the other. "You enjoyed it—I enjoyed it."

"We all enjoyed it," said Marian, without realizing that she had said a word.

The first old woman had just finished putting the potted plant high, high on the top of the wardrobe, where it could hardly be seen from below. Marian wondered how she had ever succeeded in placing it there, how she could ever have reached so high.

"You mustn't pay any attention to old Addie," she now said to the little girl. "She's ailing today."

"Will you shut your mouth?" said the woman in bed. "I am not."

"You're a story."

"I can't stay but a minute—really, I can't," said Marian suddenly. She looked down at the wet floor and thought that if she were sick in here they would have to let her go.

With much to-do the first old woman sat down in a rocking chair—still another piece of furniture!—and began to rock. With the fingers of one hand she touched a very dirty cameo pin on her chest. "What do you do at school?" she asked.

"I don't know . . ." said Marian. She tried to think but she could not.

"Oh, but the flowers are beautiful," the old woman whispered. She seemed to rock faster and faster; Marian did not see how anyone could rock so fast.

"Ugly," said the woman in bed.

"If we bring flowers—" Marian began, and then fell silent. She had almost said that if Campfire Girls brought flowers to the Old Ladies' Home, the visit would count one extra point, and if they took a Bible with them on the bus and read it to the old ladies, it counted double. But the old woman had not listened, anyway; she was rocking and watching the other one, who watched back from the bed.

"Poor Addie is ailing. She has to take medicine—see?" she said, pointing a horny finger at a row of bottles on the table, and rocking so high that her black comfort shoes lifted off the floor like a little child's.

"I am no more sick than you are," said the woman in bed.

"Oh yes you are!"

"I just got more sense than you have, that's all," said the other old woman, nodding her head.

"That's only the contrary way she talks when *you all* come," said the first old lady with sudden intimacy. She stopped the rocker with a neat pat of her feet and leaned toward Marian. Her hand reached over—it felt like a petunia leaf, clinging and just a little sticky.

"Will you hush! Will you hush!" cried the other one.

Marian leaned back rigidly in her chair.

"When I was a little girl like you, I went to school and all," said the old woman in the same intimate, menacing voice. "Not here—another town. . . ."

"Hush!" said the sick woman. "You never went to school. You never came and you never went. You never were anywhere—only here. You never were born! You don't know anything. Your head is empty, your heart and hands and your old black purse are all empty, even that little old box that you brought with you, you brought empty—you showed it to me. And yet you talk, talk, talk, talk, talk all the time until I think I'm losing my mind. Who are you? You're a stranger—a perfect stranger! Don't you know you're a stranger? Is it possible that they have actually done a thing like this to anyone—sent them in a stranger to talk, and rock, and tell away her whole long rigmarole? Do they seriously suppose that I'll be able to keep it up, day in, day out, night in, night out, living in the same room with a terrible old woman—forever?"

Marian saw the old woman's eyes grow bright and turn toward her. This old woman was looking at her with despair and calculation in her face. Her small lips suddenly dropped apart, and exposed a half circle of false teeth with tan gums.

"Come here, I want to tell you something," she whispered. "Come here!"

Marian was trembling, and her heart nearly stopped beating altogether for a moment.

"Now, now, Addie," said the first old woman. "That's not polite. Do you know what's really the matter with old Addie today?" She, too, looked at Marian; one of her eyelids drooped low.

"The matter?" the child repeated stupidly. "What's the matter with her?"

"Why, she's mad because it's her birthday!" said the first old woman, beginning to rock again and giving a little crow as though she had answered her own riddle.

"It is not, it is not!" screamed the old woman in bed. "It is not my birthday, no one knows when that is but myself, and will you please be quiet and say nothing more, or I'll go straight out of my mind!" She turned her eyes toward Marian again, and presently she said in the soft, foggy voice, "When the worst comes to the worst, I ring this bell, and the nurse comes." One of her hands was drawn out from under the patched counterpane—a thin little hand with enormous black freckles. With a finger which would not hold still she pointed to a little bell on the table among the bottles.

"How old are you?" Marian breathed. Now she could see the old woman in bed very closely and plainly, and very abruptly, from all sides, as in dreams. She wondered about her—she wondered for a moment as though there was nothing else in the world to wonder about. It was the first time such a thing had happened to Marian.

"I won't tell!"

The old face on the pillow, where Marian was bending over it, slowly gathered and collapsed. Soft whimpers came out of the small open mouth. It was a sheep that she sounded like—a little lamb. Marian's face drew very close, the yellow hair hung forward.

"She's crying!" She turned a bright, burning face up to the first old woman.

"That's Addie for you," the old woman said spitefully.

Marian jumped up and moved toward the door. For the second time, the claw almost touched her hair, but it was not quick enough. The little girl put her cap on.

"Well, it was a real visit," said the old woman, following Marian through the doorway and all the way out into the hall. Then from behind she suddenly clutched the child with her sharp little fingers. In an affected, high-pitched whine she cried, "Oh, little girl, have you a penny to spare for a poor old woman that's not got anything of her own? We don't have a thing in the world—not a penny for candy—not a thing! Little girl, just a nickel—a penny—"

Marian pulled violently against the old hands for a moment before she was free. Then she ran down the hall, without looking behind her and without looking at the nurse, who was reading *Field & Stream* at her desk. The nurse, after another triple motion to consult her wrist watch, asked automatically the question put to visitors in all institutions: "Won't you stay and have dinner with *us*?"

Marian never replied. She pushed the heavy door open into the cold air and ran down the steps.

Under the prickly shrub she stopped and quickly, without being seen, retrieved a red apple she had hidden there.

Her yellow hair under the white cap, her scarlet coat, her bare knees all flashed in the sunlight as she ran to meet the big bus rocketing through the street.

"Wait for me!" she shouted. As though at an imperial command, the bus ground to a stop.

She jumped on and took a big bite out of the apple.

This story may be used as additional reading material for the chapter Emotion and Humor.

Carson McCullers

A DOMESTIC DILEMMA

On Thursday Martin Meadows left the office early enough to make the first express bus home. It was the hour when the evening lilac glow was fading in the slushy streets, but by the time the bus had left the Midtown terminal the bright city night had come. On Thursdays the maid had a half-day off and Martin liked to get home as soon as possible, since for the past year his wife had not been—well. This Thursday he was very tired and, hoping that no regular commuter would single him out for conversation, he fastened his attention to the newspaper until the bus had crossed the George Washington Bridge. Once on 9-W Highway Martin always felt that the trip was halfway done, he breathed deeply, even in cold weather when only ribbons of draught cut through the smoky air of the bus, confident that he was breathing country air. It used to be that at this point he would relax and begin to think with pleasure of his home. But in this last year nearness brought only a sense of tension and he did not anticipate the journey's end. This evening Martin kept his face close to the window and watched the barren fields and lonely lights of passing townships. There was a moon, pale on the dark earth and areas of late, porous snow; to Martin the countryside seemed vast and somehow desolate that evening. He took his hat from the rack and put his folded newspaper in the pocket of his overcoat a few minutes before time to pull the cord.

The cottage was a block from the bus stop, near the river but not directly on the shore; from the living-room window you could look across the street and opposite yard and see the Hudson. The cottage was modern, almost too white and new on the narrow plot of yard. In summer the grass was soft and bright and Martin carefully tended a flower border and a rose trellis. But during the cold, fallow months the yard was bleak and the cottage seemed naked. Lights were on that evening in all the rooms in the little house and Martin hurried up the front walk. Before the steps he stopped to move a wagon out of the way.

The children were in the living room, so intent on play that the opening of the front door was at first unnoticed. Martin stood looking at his safe, lovely children. They had opened the bottom drawer of the secretary and taken out the Christmas decorations. Andy had managed to plug in the Christmas tree lights and the green and red bulbs glowed with out-of-season festivity on the rug of the living room. At the moment he was trying to trail the bright cord over Marianne's rocking horse. Marianne sat on the floor pulling off an angel's wings. The children wailed a startling welcome. Martin swung the fat little baby girl up to his shoulder and Andy threw himself against his father's legs.

"Daddy, Daddy, Daddy!"

Martin sat down the little girl carefully and swung Andy a few times like a pendulum. Then he picked up the Christmas tree cord.

"What's all this stuff doing out? Help me put it back in the drawer. You're not to fool with the light socket. Remember I told you that before. I mean it, Andy."

The six-year-old child nodded and shut the secretary drawer. Martin stroked his fair soft hair and his hand lingered tenderly on the nape of the child's frail neck.

"Had supper yet, Bumpkin?"

"It hurt. The toast was hot."

The baby girl stumbled on the rug and, after the first surprise of the fall, began to cry; Martin picked her up and carried her in his arms back to the kitchen.

"See, Daddy," said Andy. "The toast—"

Emily had laid the children's supper on the uncovered porcelain table. There were two plates with the remains of cream-of-wheat and eggs and silver mugs that had held milk. There was also a platter of cinnamon toast, untouched, except for one tooth-marked bite. Martin sniffed the bitten piece and nibbled gingerly. Then he put the toast into the garbage pail.

"Hoo—phui—What on earth!"

Emily had mistaken the tin of cayenne for the cinnamon.

"I like to have burnt up," Andy said. "Drank water and ran outdoors and opened my mouth. Marianne didn't eat none."

"Any," corrected Martin. He stood helpless, looking around the walls of the kitchen. "Well, that's that, I guess," he said finally. "Where is your mother now?"

"She's up in you alls' room."

Martin left the children in the kitchen and went up to his wife. Outside the door he waited for a moment to still his anger. He did not knock and once inside the room he closed the door behind him.

Emily sat in the rocking chair by the window of the pleasant room. She had been drinking something from a tumbler and as he entered she put the glass hurriedly on the floor behind the chair. In her attitude there was confusion and guilt which she tried to hide by a show of spurious vivacity.

"Oh, Marty! You home already? The time slipped up on me. I was just going down—" She lurched to him and her kiss was strong with sherry. When he stood unresponsive she stepped back a pace and giggled nervously.

"What's the matter with you? Standing there like a barber pole. Is anything wrong with you?"

"Wrong with *me*?" Martin bent over the rocking chair and picked up the tumbler from the floor. "If you could only realize how sick I am— how bad it is for all of us."

Emily spoke in a false, airy voice that had become too familiar to him. Often at such times she affected a slight English accent copying perhaps some actress she admired. "I haven't the vaguest idea what you mean. Unless you are referring to the glass I used for a spot of sherry. I had a finger of sherry—maybe two. But what is the crime in that, pray tell me? I'm quite all right. Quite all right."

"So anyone can see."

As she went into the bathroom Emily walked with careful gravity. She turned on the cold water and dashed some on her face with her cupped hands, then patted herself dry with the corner of a bath towel. Her face was delicately featured and young, unblemished.

"I was just going down to make dinner." She tottered and balanced herself by holding to the door frame.

"I'll take care of dinner. You stay up here. I'll bring it up."

"I'll do nothing of the sort. Why, whoever heard of such a thing?"

"Please," Martin said.

"Leave me alone. I'm quite all right. I was just on the way down—"

"Mind what I say."

"Mind your grandmother."

She lurched toward the door, but Martin caught her by the arm. "I don't want the children to see you in this condition. Be reasonable."

"Condition!" Emily jerked her arm. Her voice rose angrily. "Why, because I drink a couple of sherries in the afternoon you're trying to make me out a drunkard. Condition! Why, I don't even touch whiskey. As well you know. *I* don't swill liquor at bars. And that's more than you can say. I don't even have a cocktail at dinnertime. I only sometimes have a glass of sherry. What, I ask you, is the disgrace of that? Condition!"

Martin sought words to calm his wife. "We'll have a quiet supper by ourselves up here. That's a good girl." Emily sat on the side of the bed and he opened the door for a quick departure.

"I'll be back in a jiffy."

As he busied himself with the dinner downstairs he was lost in the familiar question as to how this problem had come upon his home. He himself had always enjoyed a good drink. When they were still living in Alabama they had served long drinks or cocktails as a matter of course.

For years they had drunk one or two—possibly three drinks before dinner, and at bedtime a long nightcap. Evenings before holidays they might get a buzz on, might even become a little tight. But alcohol had never seemed a problem to him, only a bothersome expense that with the increase in the family they could scarcely afford. It was only after his company had transferred him to New York that Martin was aware that certainly his wife was drinking too much. She was tippling, he noticed, during the day.

The problem acknowledged, he tried to analyze the source. The change from Alabama to New York had somehow disturbed her; accustomed to the idle warmth of a small Southern town, the matrix of the family and cousinship and childhood friends, she had failed to accommodate herself to the stricter, lonelier mores of the North. The duties of motherhood and housekeeping were onerous to her. Homesick for Paris City, she had made no friends in the suburban town. She read only magazines and murder books. Her interior life was insufficient without the artifice of alcohol.

The revelations of incontinence insidiously undermined his previous conceptions of his wife. There were times of unexplainable malevolence, times when the alcoholic fuse caused an explosion of unseemly anger. He encountered a latent coarseness in Emily, inconsistent with her natural simplicity. She lied about drinking and deceived him with unsuspected stratagems.

Then there was an accident. Coming home from work one evening about a year ago, he was greeted with screams from the children's room. He found Emily holding the baby, wet and naked from her bath. The baby had been dropped, her frail, frail skull striking the table edge, so that a thread of blood was soaking into the gossamer hair. Emily was sobbing and intoxicated. As Martin cradled the hurt child, so infinitely precious at that moment, he had an affrighted vision of the future.

The next day Marianne was all right. Emily vowed that never again would she touch liquor, and for a few weeks she was sober, cold and downcast. Then gradually she began—not whiskey or gin—but quantities of beer, or sherry, or outlandish liqueurs; once he had come across a hatbox of empty crème de menthe bottles. Martin found a dependable maid who managed the household competently. Virgie was also from Alabama and Martin had never dared tell Emily the wage scale customary in New York. Emily's drinking was entirely secret now, done before he reached the house. Usually the effects were almost imperceptible—a looseness of movement or the heavy-lidded eyes. The times of irresponsibilities, such as the cayenne-pepper toast were rare, and Martin could dismiss his worries when Virgie was at the house. But, nevertheless, anxiety was always latent, a threat of undefined disaster that underlaid his days.

"Marianne!" Martin called, for even the recollection of that time brought the need for reassurance. The baby girl, no longer hurt, but no less precious to her father, came into the kitchen with her brother. Martin went on with the preparations for the meal. He opened a can of soup and put two chops in the frying pan. Then he sat down by the table and took Marianne on his knees for a pony ride. Andy watched them, his fingers wobbling the tooth that had been loose all that week.

"Andy-the-candyman!" Martin said. "Is that old critter still in your mouth? Come closer, let Daddy have a look."

"I got a string to pull it with." The child brought from his pocket a tangled thread. "Virgie said to tie it to the tooth and tie the other end to the doorknob and shut the door real suddenly."

Martin took out a clean handkerchief and felt the loose tooth carefully. "That tooth is coming out of my Andy's mouth tonight. Otherwise I'm awfully afraid we'll have a tooth tree in the family."

"A what?"

"A tooth tree," Martin said. "You'll bite into something and swallow that tooth. And the tooth will take root in poor Andy's stomach and grow into a tooth tree with sharp little teeth instead of leaves."

"Shoo, Daddy," Andy said. But he held the tooth firmly between his grimy little thumb and forefinger. "There ain't any tree like that. I never seen one."

"There *isn't* any tree like that and I never *saw* one."

Martin tensed suddenly. Emily was coming down the stairs. He listened to her fumbling footsteps, his arm embracing the little boy with dread. When Emily came into the room he saw from her movements and her sullen face that she had again been at the sherry bottle. She began to yank open drawers and set the table.

"Condition!" she said in a furry voice. "You talk to me like that. Don't think I'll forget. I remember every dirty lie you say to me. Don't you think for a minute that I forget."

"Emily!" he begged. "The children—"

"The children—yes! Don't think I don't see through your dirty plots and schemes. Down here trying to turn my own children against me. Don't think I don't see and understand."

"Emily! I beg you—please go upstairs."

"So you can turn my children—my very own children—" Two large tears coursed rapidly down her cheeks. "Trying to turn my little boy, my Andy, against his own mother."

With drunken impulsiveness Emily knelt on the floor before the startled child. Her hands on his shoulders balanced her. "Listen, my Andy—you wouldn't listen to any lies your father tells you? You wouldn't believe what he says? Listen, Andy, what was your father telling you before I came downstairs?" Uncertain, the child sought his father's face. "Tell me. Mama wants to know."

"About the tooth tree."

"What?"

The child repeated the words and she echoed them with unbelieving terror. "The tooth tree!" she swayed and renewed her grasp on the child's shoulder. "I don't know what you're talking about. But listen, Andy, Mama is all right, isn't she?" The tears were spilling down her face and Andy drew back from her, for he was afraid. Grasping the table edge, Emily stood up.

"See! You have turned my child against me."

Marianne began to cry, and Martin took her in his arms.

"That's all right, you can take *your* child. You have always shown partiality from the very first. I don't mind, but at least you can leave me my little boy."

Andy edged close to his father and touched his leg. "Daddy," he wailed.

Martin took the children to the foot of the stairs. "Andy, you take up Marianne and Daddy will follow you in a minute."

"But Mama?" the child asked, whispering.

"Mama will be all right. Don't worry."

Emily was sobbing at the kitchen table, her face buried in the crook of her arm. Martin poured a cup of soup and set it before her. Her rasping sobs unnerved him; the vehemence of her emotion, irrespective of the source, touched in him a strain of tenderness. Unwillingly he laid his hand on her dark hair. "Sit up and drink the soup." Her face as she looked up at him was chastened and imploring. The boy's withdrawal or the touch of Martin's hand had turned the tenor of her mood.

"Ma-Martin," she sobbed. "I'm so ashamed."

"Drink the soup."

Obeying him, she drank between gasping breaths. After a second cup she allowed him to lead her up to their room. She was docile now and more restrained. He laid her nightgown on the bed and was about to leave the room when a fresh round of grief, the alcoholic tumult, came again.

"He turned away. My Andy looked at me and turned away."

Impatience and fatigue hardened his voice, but he spoke warily. "You forget that Andy is still a little child—he can't comprehend the meaning of such scenes."

"Did I make a scene? Oh Martin, did I make a scene before the children?"

Her horrified face touched and amused him against his will. "Forget it. Put on your nightgown and go to sleep."

"My child turned away from me. Andy looked at his mother and turned away. The children—"

She was caught in the rhythmic sorrow of alcohol. Martin withdrew from the room, saying: "For God's sake go to sleep. The children will forget by tomorrow."

As he said this he wondered if it was true. Would the scene glide so easily from memory—or would it root in the unconscious to fester in the after-years? Martin did not know, and the last alternative sickened him. He thought of Emily, foresaw the morning-after humiliation: the shards of memory, the lucidities that glared from the obliterating darkness of shame. She would call the New York office twice—possibly three or four times. Martin anticipated his own embarrassment, wondering if the others at the office could possibly suspect. He felt that his secretary had divined the trouble long ago and that she pitied him. He suffered a moment of rebellion against his fate, he hated his wife.

Once in the children's room he closed the door and felt secure for the first time that evening. Marianne fell down on the floor, picked herself up and calling: "Daddy, watch me," fell again, got up, and continued the falling-calling routine. Andy sat in the child's low chair, wobbling the tooth. Martin ran the water in the tub, washed his own hands in the lavatory, and called the boy into the bathroom.

"Let's have another look at that tooth." Martin sat on the toilet, holding Andy between his knees. The child's mouth gaped and Martin grasped the tooth. A wobble, a quick twist and the nacreous milk tooth was free. Andy's face was for the first moment split between terror, astonishment, and delight. He mouthed a swallow of water, and spat into the lavatory.

"Look, Daddy! It's blood. Marianne!"

Martin loved to bathe his children, loved inexpressibly the tender, naked bodies as they stood in the water so exposed. It was not fair of Emily to say that he showed partiality. As Martin soaped the delicate boy-body of his son he felt that further love would be impossible. Yet he admitted the difference in the quality of his emotions for the two children. His love for his daughter was graver, touched with a strain of melancholy, a gentleness that was akin to pain. His pet names for the little boy were the absurdities of daily inspiration—he called the little girl always Marianne, and his voice as he spoke it was a caress. Martin patted dry the fat baby stomach and the sweet little genital fold. The washed child faces were radiant as flower petals, equally loved.

"I'm putting the tooth under my pillow. I'm supposed to get a quarter."

"What for?"

"*You* know, Daddy. Johnny got a quarter for his tooth."

"Who puts the quarter there?" asked Martin. "I used to think the fairies left it in the night. It was a dime in my day, though."

"That's what they say in kindergarten."

"Who does put it there?"

"Your parents," Andy said. "You!"

Martin was pinning the cover on Marianne's bed. His daughter was already asleep. Scarcely breathing, Martin bent over and kissed her forehead, kissed again the tiny hand that lay palm-upward, flung in slumber beside her head.

"Good night, Andy-man."

The answer was only a drowsy murmur. After a minute Martin took out his change and slid a quarter underneath the pillow. He left a night light in the room.

As Martin prowled about the kitchen making a late meal, it occurred to him that the children had not once mentioned their mother or the scene that must have seemed to them incomprehensible. Absorbed in the instant—the tooth, the bath, the quarter—the fluid passage of child-time had borne these weightless episodes like leaves in the swift current of a shallow stream while the adult enigma was beached and forgotten on the shore. Martin thanked the Lord for that.

But his own anger, repressed and lurking, rose again. His youth was being frittered by a drunkard's waste, his very manhood subtly undermined. And the children, once the immunity of incomprehension passed—what would it be like in a year or so? With his elbows on the table he ate his food brutishly, untasting. There was no hiding the truth—soon there would be gossip in the office and in the town; his wife was a dissolute woman. Dissolute. And he and his children were bound to a future of degradation and slow ruin.

Martin pushed away from the table and stalked into the living room. He followed the lines of a book with his eyes but his mind conjured miserable images: he saw his children drowned in the river, his wife a disgrace on the public street. By bedtime the dull, hard anger was like a weight upon his chest and his feet dragged as he climbed the stairs.

The room was dark except for the shafting light from the half-opened bathroom door. Martin undressed quietly. Little by little, mysteriously, there came in him a change. His wife was asleep, her peaceful respiration sounding gently in the room. Her high-heeled shoes with the carelessly dropped stockings made to him a mute appeal. Her underclothes were flung in disorder on the chair. Martin picked up the girdle and the soft, silk brassière and stood for a moment with them in his hands. For the first time that evening he looked at his wife. His eyes rested on the sweet forehead, the arch of the fine brow. The brow had descended to Marianne, and the tilt at the end of the delicate nose. In his son he could trace the high cheekbones and pointed chin. Her body was full-bosomed, slender and undulant. As Martin watched the tranquil slumber of his wife the ghost of the old anger vanished. All thoughts of blame or blemish were distant from him now. Martin put out the bathroom light and raised the window. Careful not to awaken Emily he slid into the bed. By moonlight he watched his wife for the last time. His hand sought the adjacent flesh and sorrow paralleled desire in the immense complexity of love.

This story may be used as additional reading material for the chapter Character.

Alden Nowlan

THE GLASS ROSES

Every night for six weeks the wind had risen to gale force as soon as the sun went down. Lying on his straw-filled bunk, Stephen heard it howl under the eaves of the bunkhouse, batter the tarpapered walls and make despondent, blowing sounds in the snow-weighted boughs of the spruces. He drew the dirty army blankets tighter under his chin. The sound alone was enough to make him shiver.

In the sooty obscurity of a gas lantern, four men played cards beside the pot-bellied wood stove. They were burly, red-faced men in wool work pants and checkered jackshirts. Each night since Stephen had joined the pulp-cutting crew, and through each of the days when snow kept them from work, they had played Auction 45's. Like everything else they did, their card playing was serious and purposeful. They spoke only when they made their bids. To Stephen, watching them from his upper bunk, it seemed they sat frozen for hours, moving only their hands. Enviously he studied their faintly humped backs and ox-like shoulders. He thought despairingly of his own willowy fifteen-year-old body. The more he observed the easy strength of these men, the oftener he worked himself into aching exhaustion at the end of a pulpsaw, the more certain he was that he could never become a man.

The huskiest and most solemn of the card players was the foreman of the crew of six who occupied the bunkhouse. This man was Stephen's father. "You got to start actin' like a man if you want to hold down a

THE GLASS ROSES   From *Miracle at Indian River* by Alden Nowlan © 1968 by Clarke, Irwin & Company Limited. Used by permission.

man's job," he had warned. "There ain't no room for kids in the pulp woods." The boy winced, remembering the too-familiar squint of doubt, the hard knots of disappointment above the cold grey eyes.

A gust shook the camp and made the white flame of the lantern flicker. Beside him in the bunk, the Polack stirred, moaning, in his sleep. Stephen raised himself on an elbow and shook his shoulder. With a muffled groan he jerked awake.

"I guess you was havin' a nightmare," Stephen whispered.

The Polack ran his fingers through his dishevelled hair.

"Yes."

His eyes, which seemed to focus on the other side of the room, were so bleak with fear that Stephen swung around and looked in the same direction. He saw only the greasy, unbarked slabs of the wall.

The Polack chuckled. He had such nightmares almost every night, but the fear seemed to leave him as soon as he was wholly awake. "It is strange, the things one remembers," he murmured.

As they always did, Stephen and the Polack spoke too low for the others to hear. In talking with the others, the Polack garbled his sentences as though his mouth were full of cotton wool. Stephen had stood speechless with astonishment when, on their second day as partners at the edge of the northwest clearing, he had first heard him speak English coherently.

"Yeah?" Stephen invited. His fascination with tales of far places had attracted him to the Polack. But he felt that his interest in such stories was childish: an aspect of the boyish daydreaming that he was expected to scorn now that he was becoming a man. Apprehensively he glanced over the edge of his bunk to assure himself that none of the others overheard.

The Polack lay back on the sour-smelling pillows and gazed at the newspaper-lined ceiling.

His voice made Stephen's flesh tingle as at the approach of sleep.

"In our house in Tarnopol, there were glass roses. Pretty little flowers made of red glass. My mother was very proud of them. She would let no one touch them. . . . When the first bombs fell, farther down the street, the glass roses were shaken from the mantel and they fell on the floor and broke in a million pieces." He raised himself on his elbows to roll a cigarette. "That is a very silly thing for one to remember."

Stephen thought for a long moment. "I don't think it's silly," he said.

"There is not much room in the world for glass roses," the Polack said gently, blowing purple tobacco smoke toward the ceiling.

The card players rose from their benches. One by one they went outdoors to urinate. Each time the door opened, Stephen's flesh goose-pimpled in the clutch of the cold. His father and the others grunted and spat in the stove, then pulled off their boots and pants and climbed into their bunks. The last man extinguished the lantern. In the darkness Stephen thought of glass roses and listened to the wail of the ten-below-zero wind.

The cook, whose quarters were separated from the bunkhouse by a partition of rough boards, woke the men at five-thirty. After eating their breakfast of pork and pancakes by lanternlight, they gathered up their saws and axes and started in pairs for their various stations in the woods. The first mustard-coloured streaks of daylight were appearing on the black-forested, snow-shrouded horizon.

The wind had fallen somewhat, but it was still raw enough to lacerate Stephen's temples. The cold gnawed at his legs and forced watery mucus from his nostrils. Head down, he walked beside the Polack in the deep-rutted logging road.

"Sometimes I think this country does not like people," the Polack shouted above the wind.

Stephen laughed, almost in embarrassment. The Polack was the only foreigner he had ever known, and he often said things no ordinary pulp-cutter would have dreamt of saying.

"Or perhaps it is only that God made this country to teach man humility," the Polack yelled, his voice a flapping wisp in the wind.

Stephen laughed again. As they went deeper into the woods, great spruce and fir trees broke the force of the wind. In a way, Stephen reflected, it was fun to be with the Polack. When he worked with the other men, they spoke only when it was necessary to give commands or criticism. But he knew his father despised the Polack and he suspected that they had been consigned together as the crew's clumsiest and weakest members.

The day's work began. Stephen chopped a notch in a spruce. Each time his axe struck the tree, showers of snow poured from the branches and sifted down his neck. Twice he misjudged his stroke and hit the trunk with the handle, the shock of it burning his wrists. The axe made him feel stupid and ridiculous. It did not belong to him. He could not think of himself as a woodsman. In using the axe, he was pretending to be something he was not, something he might never be. When his father worked an axe, it was as though the blade grew out of his arm.

He and the Polack took hold of opposite ends of the saw and knelt by the tree. On the first stroke Stephen exerted too much pressure and the blade buckled.

"You try too hard, kid," the Polack murmured. "You act as if the saw were the most important thing in the world."

"Maybe."

"The world would not come to an end if it took us all day to cut this one tree down."

"I guess not."

Stephen decided glumly that foreigners did not know when to keep their mouths shut. The Polack grinned. Purring, the saw sank slowly into the frozen wood.

As they cut deeper, the weight of the tree lay heavy on the blade. Stephen closed his eyes, the better to concentrate on the effort of bringing the saw back each time the Polack pulled it away from him. He thought of the dozens of trees they would have to fell before the end of the day, the millions of trees he would have to fell before he died. For as long as he lived, he would kneel beside a tree, a slave to the monotonous rhythm of the pulpsaw.

"Gently, now, gently," the Polack admonished.

"Look, I don't need no advice," Stephen gritted. "You take care of your end of the saw and I'll look after mine. Okay?"

The Polack grinned again. After ten minutes of sawing, the tree creaked like a dry hinge and gave away. Snow rose like the smoke of an explosion when it struck the ground.

They chopped off limbs and sawed the tree into four-foot lengths. "I'm sorry I made you angry," the Polack said.

Stephen blinked and looked away. In his world, men did not tender apologies.

"It don't matter," he mumbled.

"Today when we eat lunch I will tell you about Cracow."

"Cracow," Stephen said, liking the sound of the word.

"Cracow," the Polack repeated.

He paused for a moment before completing his saw stroke.

"Once I was there and saw the cathedral."

Stephen let go of the saw and beat his mittened hands together. "What was it like—the cathedral?"

"Very beautiful. You would like to hear about it, eh?"

"Yes," Stephen said, feeling a little twinge of guilt. He was a man now. Men did not tell one another fairy tales about cathedrals. But his father and the men at the bunkhouse need never know—

"I was only eight years old when I saw Cracow. My oldest brother was in the cavalry. He had red things on his shoulders—epaulettes—and he wore a sabre. That day there was a parade for the president." The Polack sighed. "He was killed on the first day of the war, my brother. They were very pretty, but not much good against tanks, those cavalrymen."

"Sabres," Stephen said, "Jesus." He was thinking of the yelling, sabre-wielding horsemen he had seen in movies. The Polack ran his hand through thick black hair.

"Now we must get back to work," he said. "At noon I will tell you about the cathedral."

For a few minutes they sawed in silence.

"Look," Stephen stammered suddenly.

"Yes, what should I look at, eh?"

"Oh, I don't mean, look. I mean, well, I'm sorry I got mad at you."

He flushed, feeling childish and ludicrous, wishing he had kept his mouth shut.

"We are friends then?"

"Yeah."

Convinced that he had been guilty of a babyish weakness, Stephen began sawing furiously.

By noon their sandwiches were frozen as hard as cedar shingles. Squatting behind a windbreak of logs, they speared them on slivers of pine and held them over a small fire until they were fried in the fat of margarine and bologna. They drank boiled tea out of tin mugs without removing their mittens.

As they ate, the Polack talked of an ancient city and of a cathedral with spires and domes. He told of bearded, black-robed priests and of chanting monks and of altar boys who carried burning incense through the streets during holy-day processions. Stephen sat enthralled, scarcely noticing the Canada Jays, white and mouse-grey like the colour of winter, though they flew almost close enough to snatch the food from his hands.

"I was very small then," the Polack said. "I was nine when the Russians came to Tarnopol. When the Germans came, I was twelve."

Stephen chewed sizzling bologna. "I'd like to see Poland," he said. "I'd like to see Poland and France and Italy. I'd like—" He left the sentence unfinished. He was not certain what he felt.

The Polack moved closer to the fire. The evergreens bowed, as though in resignation, before the wind. "I am not Polish," he said. "I am Ukrainian."

"You ain't a Polack then?" Stephen asked in bewilderment.

The Polack shrugged. "Yesterday the Ukrainians were called Poles. Today they are called Russians. Me, I am either a Polack or a Canadian."

For a few minutes they ate in silence.

"My name is Leka," the Polack said abruptly.

"Leka," Stephen repeated.

"Now I think we had better forget about the cathedrals and begin to think of the pulpwood. Your father, the foreman, says we cut the least of any pair of choppers in the woods."

"Yeah, I know," Stephen said bitterly.

Suddenly the Polack reached out and pinched the boy's cold-reddened cheek.

"Don't be so sad, little one," he smiled.

Stephen stood up and kicked snow over the fire.

"Tomorrow perhaps I will tell you about Wiesbaden."

"Wiesbaden, is that in Poland?"

"Wiesbaden is in Germany. During the war I worked there: making hand grenades for the Germans. Every April we were given a holiday in honour of Hitler's birthday." The Polack laughed. "When the planes came, the British and Americans, we used to hope some of their bombs would hit the factory. But they never did."

The Polack smiled at Stephen as though in some mysterious way he were pitying him, rather than himself.

"No, I don't think I want to talk about Wiesbaden. I will tell you more about Tarnopol and my mother's glass roses. It is better to talk about things like that." The Polack rolled a cigarette and scratched a match on the zipper of his windbreaker.

"The roses that got smashed," Stephen said.

"Eh? Yes, the roses that got smashed." He picked up his axe and selected a tree. "They were very pretty, those little glass roses, I need only close my eyes and I can see them."

"But they got smashed," Stephen insisted.

The Polack's axe thudded home. "In the morning, when the sun came up, the first little shafts of light would strike those roses. You see, the mantel was opposite the window. Yes, they were very beautiful. . . ."

The tree notched, Stephen fetched the pulpsaw. The Polack spat out his cigarette and knelt opposite him. Stephen shut his eyes and forced the blade into the obdurate wood.

"Gently, now, gently," the Polack counselled.

Now there was neither time nor energy for talk. By midafternoon Stephen slumped and staggered with weariness. Dull pains nagged his shoulders, hips and calves. But more crushing than the weariness was the conviction that he was a weakling. He could not believe that his father, or any of the other choppers, knew tiredness such as his. Sometimes he wondered if he suffered from a wasting disease. He almost hoped that this was so, for then his weakness would be thought less shameful.

With darkness settling around them, they trudged back to the camp. Only pride kept Stephen from throwing himself down as soon as he entered the bunkhouse. Noticing his father's sharp, searching look, he clenched his teeth and straightened.

The men washed their hands and faces in cold water, then filed into the cookhouse. As always the room smelled of fat and boiled tea. The choppers winked at one another as the Polack crossed himself before beginning on his hard-boiled eggs and fried potatoes.

"Guess the Polack don't trust you," one of the men said to the cook.

The cook did not smile. Like most woods cooks, he frowned on conversation at the table. The Polack gave no sign that he heard. Meeting his father's eyes, Stephen grinned guiltily.

When the choppers had finished their dessert of stewed prunes and drained their coffee mugs, they shuffled back to the bunkhouse. They sat on benches beside the stove and rolled their after-supper cigarettes. Stephen's father pulled on his mackinaw. "Come out here a minute will you, Stephen?" he growled. "I want you to give me a hand with something."

"Yeah, sure." He leapt to his feet, then looked around in embarrassment: he did not want the men to notice the nervous alacrity with which he responded to his father's commands. After all, he was no little boy to be cowed into obedience. Putting on his windbreaker and cap, he followed his father into the night.

The man stood in the shelter of the tool shed. The world was a maelstrom of darkness and wind.

"I wanted to talk to you alone for a minute."

"Sure."

"You seem to be gettin' awful chummy with that Polack," his father declared abruptly.

"Huh?" Stephen gaped in astonishment. The wind striped his back like an alder switch. "He ain't no special friend of mine," he said, not sure whether or not he lied.

"Some of the men's laughin' about him pattin' and pokin' you. I don't like to hear anybody laughin' at my son."

It wasn't true. The Polack did not "pat and poke" him. Then, uneasily, he recalled that the Polack often *did* pinch his cheek or throw an arm across his shoulder. Usually he was only half-aware of these gestures. His father fidgeted when he had to shake hands. But little casual caresses were part of the Polack's speech.

"Them Wops and Bohunks and Polacks has gotta lotta funny ideas. They ain't our kinda people. You gotta watch them."

"Yeah." The wind hurled pellets of frozen snow against his face.

"If he bothers you, let me know and I'll kick the guts outta him."

"Yeah."

"This work ain't too hard for you, is it?"

He wants me to quit, Stephen thought. He wants to shame me into quitting.

"No, it ain't too hard for me. Not by a God damn sight."

"Don't be afraid of hard work. Work never killed nobody."

"No, I guess it never did," Stephen said, shivering.

"Just make that Polack keep his hands off you."

"Yeah."

"I've seen fellers like him before."

"Yeah."

"Well, we better go in. It's cold enough to break the stones."

Inside, Stephen climbed into his bunk. In a little while the Polack climbed in beside him. Eying him dubiously, Stephen edged away until his back pressed against the cold, splintery beams where the wall joined the ceiling. The card players went to their seats by the stove. Before the first game was finished, the Polack fell asleep. The wind howled until Stephen expected it to wrench the roof from the camp. When the Polack began to tremble and moan, Stephen hesitated for a long time before he reached out to wake him.

This story may be used as additional reading material for the chapter Character.

Ernest Hemingway

THE CAPITAL OF THE WORLD

Madrid is full of boys named Paco, which is the diminutive of the name Francisco, and there is a Madrid joke about a father who came to Madrid and inserted an advertisement in the personal columns of *El Liberal* which said: PACO MEET ME AT HOTEL MONTANA NOON TUESDAY ALL IS FORGIVEN PAPA, and how a squadron of Guardia Civil had to be called out to disperse the eight hundred young men who answered the advertisement. But this Paco, who waited on table at the Pension Luarca, had no father to forgive him, nor anything for the father to forgive. He had two older sisters who were chambermaids at the Luarca, who had gotten their place through coming from the same village as a former Luarca chambermaid who had proven hardworking and honest and hence given her village and its products a good name; and these sisters had paid his way on the autobus to Madrid and gotten him his job as an apprentice waiter. He came from a village in a part of Extremadura where conditions were incredibly primitive, food scarce, and comforts unknown, and he had worked hard ever since he could remember.

He was a well built boy with very black, rather curly hair, good teeth and a skin that his sisters envied, and he had a ready and unpuzzled smile. He was fast on his feet and did his work well and he loved his sisters, who seemed beautiful and unsophisticated; he loved Madrid, which was still an unbelievable place, and he loved his work which, done under bright lights, with clean linen, the wearing of evening clothes, and abundant food in the kitchen, seemed romantically beautiful.

There were from eight to a dozen other people who lived at the Luarca and ate in the dining-room, but for Paco, the youngest of the three waiters who served at table, the only ones who really existed were the bull-fighters.

Second-rate matadors lived at that pension because the address in the Calle San Jeronimo was good, the food was excellent and the room and board was cheap. It is necessary for a bull-fighter to give the appearance, if not of prosperity, at least of respectability, since decorum and dignity rank above courage as the virtues most highly prized in Spain, and bull-fighters stayed at the Luarca until their last pesetas were gone. There is no record of any bull-fighter having left the Luarca for a better or more expensive hotel; second-rate bull-fighters never became first rate; but the descent from the Luarca was swift since anyone could stay there who was making anything at all and a bill was never presented to a guest unasked until the woman who ran the place knew that the case was hopeless.

At this time there were three full matadors living at the Luarca as well as two very good picadors, and one excellent banderillero. The Luarca was luxury for the picadors and the banderilleros who, with their families in Seville, required lodging in Madrid during the spring season; but they were well paid and in the fixed employ of fighters who were heavily contracted during the coming season and the three of these subalterns would probably make much more apiece than any of the three matadors. Of the three matadors one was ill and trying to conceal it; one had passed his short vogue as a novelty; and the third was a coward.

The coward had at one time, until he had received a peculiar atrocious horn wound in the lower abdomen at the start of his first season as a full matador, been exceptionally brave and remarkably skilful and he still had many of the hearty mannerisms of his days of success. He was jovial to excess and laughed constantly with and without provocation. He had, when successful, been very addicted to practical jokes, but he had given them up now. They took an assurance that he did not feel. This matador had an intelligent, very open face and he carried himself with much style.

The matador who was ill was careful never to show it and was meticulous about eating a little of all the dishes that were presented at the table. He had a great many handkerchiefs which he laundered himself in his room and, lately, he had been selling his fighting suits. He had sold one, cheaply, before Christmas and another in the first week of April. They had been very expensive suits, had always been well kept and he had one more. Before he had become ill he had been a very promising, even a sensational, fighter and, while he himself could not read, he had clippings which said that in his debut in Madrid he had been better than Belmonte. He ate alone at a small table and looked up very little.

The matador who had once been a novelty was very short and brown and very dignified. He also ate alone at a separate table and he smiled very rarely and never laughed. He came from Valladolid, where the people are extremely serious, and he was a capable matador; but his style had become old-fashioned before he had ever succeeded in endearing himself to the public through his virtues, which were courage and a calm capability, and his name on a poster would draw no one to a bull ring. His novelty had been that he was so short that he could barely see over the bull's withers, but there were other short fighters, and he had never succeeded in imposing himself on the public's fancy.

Of the picadors one was a thin, hawk-faced, grey-haired man, lightly built but with legs and arms like iron, who always wore cattleman's boots under his trousers, drank too much every evening and gazed amorously at any woman in the pension. The other was huge, dark, brown-faced, good-looking, with black hair like an Indian and enormous hands. Both were great picadors although the first was reputed to have lost much of his ability through drink and dissipation, and the second was said to be too headstrong and quarrelsome to stay with any matador more than a single season.

The banderillero was middle-aged, grey, cat-quick in spite of his years and, sitting at the table, he looked a moderately prosperous business man. His legs were still good for this season, and when they should go he was intelligent and experienced enough to keep regularly employed for a long time. The difference would be that when his speed of foot would be gone he would always be frightened where now he was assured and calm in the ring and out of it.

On this evening every one had left the dining-room except the hawk-faced picador who drank too much, the birthmarked-faced auctioneer of watches at the fairs and festivals of Spain, who also drank too much, and two priests from Galicia who were sitting at a corner table and drinking if not too much certainly enough. At that time wine was included in the price of the room and board at the Luarca, and the waiters had just brought fresh bottles of Valdepeñas to the tables of the auctioneer, then to the picador and, finally, to the two priests.

The three waiters stood at the end of the room. It was the rule of the house that they should remain on duty until the diners whose tables they were responsible for should all have left, but the one who served the table of the two priests had an appointment to go to an Anarcho-Syndicalist meeting and Paco had agreed to take over his table for him.

Upstairs the matador who was ill was lying face down on his bed alone. The matador who was no longer a novelty was sitting looking out of his window preparatory to walking out to the café. The matador who was a coward had the older sister of Paco in his room with him and was trying to get her to do something which she was laughingly refusing to do. This matador was saying "Come on, little savage."

"No," said the sister. "Why should I?"

"For a favour."

"You've eaten and now you want me for dessert."

"Just once. What harm can it do?"

"Leave me alone. Leave me alone, I tell you."

"It is a very little thing to do."

"Leave me alone, I tell you."

Down in the dining-room the tallest of the waiters, who was overdue at the meeting, said, "Look at those black pigs drink."

"That's no way to speak," said the second waiter. "They are decent clients. They do not drink too much."

"For me it is a good way to speak," said the tall one. "There are the two curses of Spain, the bulls and the priests."

"Certainly not the individual bull and the individual priest," said the second waiter.

"Yes," said the tall waiter. "Only through the individual can you attack the class. It is necessary to kill the individual bull and the individual priest. All of them. Then there are no more."

"Save it for the meeting," said the other waiter.

"Look at the barbarity of Madrid," said the tall waiter. "It is now half-past eleven o'clock and these are still guzzling."

"They only started to eat at ten," said the other waiter. "As you know there are many dishes. That wine is cheap and these have paid for it. It is not a strong wine."

"How can there be solidarity of workers with fools like you?" asked the tall waiter.

"Look," said the second waiter who was a man of fifty. "I have worked all my life. In all that remains of my life I must work. I have no complaints against work. To work is normal."

"Yes, but the lack of work kills."

"I have always worked," said the older waiter. "Go on to the meeting. There is no necessity to stay."

"You are a good comrade," said the tall waiter. "But you lack all ideology."

"Mejor si me falta eso que el otro," said the older waiter (meaning it is better to lack that than work). "Go on to the *mitin.*"

Paco had said nothing. He did not yet understand politics but it always gave him a thrill to hear the tall waiter speak of the necessity for killing the priests and the Guardia Civil. The tall waiter represented to him revolution and revolution also was romantic. He himself would like to be a good catholic, a revolutionary, and have a steady job like this, while, at the same time, being a bull-fighter.

"Go on to the meeting, Ignacio," he said. "I will respond for your work."

"The two of us," said the older waiter.

"There isn't enough for one," said Paco. "Go on to the meeting."

"Pues, me voy," said the tall waiter. "And thanks."

In the meantime, upstairs, the sister of Paco had gotten out of the embrace of the matador as skilfully as a wrestler breaking a hold and said, now angry, "These are the hungry people. A failed bullfighter. With your ton-load of fear. If you have so much of that, use it in the ring."

"That is the way a whore talks."

"A whore is also a woman, but I am not a whore."

"You'll be one."

"Not through you."

"Leave me," said the matador who, now, repulsed and refused, felt the nakedness of his cowardice returning.

"Leave you? What hasn't left you?" said the sister. "Don't you want me to make up the bed? I'm paid to do that."

"Leave me," said the matador, his broad good-looking face wrinkled into a contortion that was like crying. "You whore. You dirty little whore."

"Matador," she said, shutting the door. "My matador."

Inside the room the matador sat on the bed. His face still had the contortion which, in the ring, he made into a constant smile which frightened those people in the first row of seats who knew what they were watching. "And this," he was saying aloud. "And this. And this."

He could remember when he had been good and it had only been three years before. He could remember the weight of the heavy gold-brocaded fighting jacket on his shoulders on that hot afternoon in May when his voice had still been the same in the ring as in the café, and how he sighted along the point-dipping blade at the place in the top of the shoulders where it was dusty in the short-haired black hump of muscle above the wide, wood-knocking, splintered-tipped horns that lowered as he went in to kill, and how the sword pushed in as easy as into a mound of stiff butter with the palm of his hand pushing the pommel, his left arm crossed low, his left shoulder forward, his weight on his left leg, and then his weight wasn't on his leg. His weight was on his lower belly and as the bull raised his head the horn was out of sight in him and he swung over on it twice before they pulled him off it. So now when he went in to kill, and it was seldom, he could not look at the horns and what did any whore know about what he went through before he fought? And what had they been through that laughed at him? They were all whores and they knew what they could do with it.

Down in the dining-room the picador sat looking at the priests. If there were women in the room he stared at them. If there were no women he would stare with enjoyment at a foreigner, *un inglés*, but lacking women or strangers, he now stared with enjoyment and insolence at the two priests. While he stared the birth-marked auctioneer rose and folding his napkin went out, leaving over half the wine in the last bottle he had ordered. If his accounts had been paid up at Luarca he would have finished the bottle.

The two priests did not stare back at the picador. One of them was saying, "It is ten days since I have been waiting here to see him and all day I sit in the ante-chamber and he will not receive me."

"What is there to do?"

"Nothing. What can one do? One cannot go against authority."

"I have been here for two weeks for nothing. I wait and they will not see me."

"We are from the abandoned country. When the money runs out we can return."

"To the abandoned country. What does Madrid care about Galicia? We are a poor province."

"One understands the action of our brother Basilio."

"Still I have no real confidence in the integrity of Basilio Alvarez."

"Madrid is where one learns to understand. Madrid kills Spain."

"If they would simply see one and refuse."

"No. You must be broken and worn out by waiting."

"Well, we shall see. I can wait as well as another."

At this moment the picador got to his feet, walked over to the priests' table and stood, grey-headed and hawk-faced, staring at them and smiling.

"A torero," said one priest to the other.

"And a good one," said the picador and walked out of the dining-room, grey-jacketed, trim-waisted, bow-legged, in tight breeches over his high-heeled cattleman's boots that clicked on the floor as he swaggered quite steadily, smiling to himself. He lived in a small, tight, professional world of personal efficiency, nightly alcoholic triumph, and insolence. Now he lit a cigar and tilting his hat at an angle in the hallway went out to the café.

The priests left immediately after the picador, hurriedly conscious of being the last people in the dining-room, and there was no one in the room now but Paco and the middle-aged waiter. They cleared the tables and carried the bottles into the kitchen.

In the kitchen was the boy who washed the dishes. He was three years older than Paco and was very cynical and bitter.

"Take this," the middle-aged waiter said, and poured out a glass of the Valdepeñas and handed it to him.

"Why not?" the boy took the glass.

"Tu, Paco?" the waiter asked.

"Thank you," said Paco. The three of them drank.

"I will be going," said the middle-aged waiter.

"Good night," they told him.

He went out and they were alone. Paco took a napkin one of the priests had used and standing straight, his heels planted, lowered the napkin and with head following the movement, swung his arms in the motion of a slow sweeping veronica. He turned and advancing his right foot slightly, made the second pass, gained a little terrain on the imaginary bull and made a third pass, slow, perfectly timed and suave, then gathered the napkin to his waist and swung his hips away from the bull in a media-veronica.

The dishwasher, whose name was Enrique, watched him critically and sneeringly.

"How is the bull?" he said.

"Very brave," said Paco. "Look."

Standing slim and straight he made four more perfect passes, smooth, elegant and graceful.

"And the bull?" asked Enrique standing against the sink, holding his wine glass and wearing his apron.

"Still has lots of gas," said Paco.

"You make me sick," said Enrique.

"Why?"

"Look."

Enrique removed his apron and citing the imaginary bull he sculptured four perfect, languid gypsy veronicas and ended up with a rebolera that made the apron swing in a stiff arc past the bull's nose as he walked away from him.

"Look at that," he said. "And I wash dishes."

"Why?"

"Fear," said Enrique. *"Miedo.* The same fear you would have in a ring with a bull."

"No," said Paco. "I wouldn't be afraid."

"Leche!" said Enrique. "Everyone is afraid. But a torero can control his fear so that he can work the bull. I went in an amateur fight and I was so afraid I couldn't keep from running. Every one thought it was very funny. So would you be afraid. If it wasn't for fear every bootblack in Spain would be a bull-fighter. You, a country boy, would be frightened worse than I was."

"No," said Paco.

He had done it too many times in his imagination. Too many times he had seen the horns, seen the bull's wet muzzle, the ear twitching, then the head go down and the charge, the hoofs thudding and the hot bull pass him as he swung the cape, to re-charge as he swung the cape again, then again, and again, and again, to end winding the bull around him in his great media-veronica, and walk swingingly away, with bull hairs caught in the gold ornaments of his jacket from the close passes; the bull standing hypnotized and the crowd applauding. No, he would not be afraid. Others, yes. Not he. He knew he would not be afraid. Even if he ever was afraid he knew that he could do it anyway. He had confidence. "I wouldn't be afraid," he said.

Enrique said, *'Leche,'* again.

Then he said, "If we should try it?"

"How?"

"Look," said Enrique. "You think of the bull but you do not think of the horns. The bull has such force that the horns rip like a knife, they stab like a bayonet, and they kill like a club. Look," he opened a table drawer and took out two meat knives. "I will bind these to the legs of a chair. Then I will play bull for you with the chair held before my head. The knives are the horns. If you make those passes then they mean something."

"Lend me your apron," said Paco. "We'll do it in the dining-room."

"No," said Enrique, suddenly not bitter. "Don't do it, Paco."

"Yes," said Paco. "I'm not afraid."

"You will be when you see the knives come."

"We'll see," said Paco. "Give me the apron."

At this time, while Enrique was binding the two heavy-bladed razor-sharp meat knives fast to the legs of the chair with two soiled napkins holding the half of each knife, wrapping them tight and then knotting them, the two chambermaids, Paco's sisters, were on their way to the cinema to see Greta Garbo in 'Anna Christie'. Of the two priests, one was sitting in his underwear reading his breviary and the other was wearing a nightshirt and saying the rosary. All the bull-fighters except the one who was ill had made their evening appearance at the Café Fornos, where the big, dark-haired picador was playing billiards, the short, serious matador was sitting at a crowded table before a coffee and milk, along with the middle-aged banderillero and other serious workmen.

The drinking, grey-headed picador was sitting with a glass of cazalas brandy before him staring with pleasure at a table where the matador whose courage was gone sat with another matador who had renounced the sword to become a banderillero again, and two very houseworn-looking prostitutes.

The auctioneer stood on the street corner talking with friends. The tall waiter was at the Anarcho-Syndicalist meeting waiting for an opportunity to speak. The middle-aged waiter was seated on the terrace of the Café Alvarez drinking a small beer. The woman who owned the Luarca was already asleep in her bed, where she lay on her back with the bolster between her legs; big, fat, honest, clean, easy-going, very religious and never having ceased to miss or pray daily for her husband, dead, now, twenty years. In his room, alone, the matador who was ill lay face down on his bed with his mouth against a handkerchief.

Now, in the deserted dining-room, Enrique tied the last knot in the napkins that bound the knives to the chair legs and lifted the chair. He pointed the legs with the knives on them forward and held the chair over his head with the two knives pointing straight ahead, one on each side of his head.

"It's heavy," he said. "Look, Paco. It is very dangerous. Don't do it." He was sweating.

Paco stood facing him, holding the apron spread, holding a fold of it bunched in each hand, thumbs up, first finger down, spread to catch the eye of the bull.

"Charge straight," he said. "Turn like a bull. Charge as many times as you want."

"How will you know when to cut the pass?" asked Enrique. It's better to do three and then a media."

"All right," said Paco. "But come straight. Huh, torito! Come on, little bull!"

Running with head down Enrique came toward him and Paco swung the apron just ahead of the knife blade as it passed close in front of his belly and as it went by it was, to him, the real horn, white-tipped, black, smooth, and as Enrique passed him and turned to rush again it was the hot, blood-flanked mass of the bull that thudded by, then turned like a cat and came again as he swung the cape slowly. Then the bull turned and came again and, as he watched the onrushing point, he stepped his left foot two inches too far forward and the knife did not pass, but had slipped in as easily as into a wineskin and there was a hot scalding rush above and around the sudden inner rigidity of steel and Enrique shouting, "Ay! Ay! Let me get it out! Let me get it out!" and Paco slipped forward on the chair the apron cape still held, Enrique pulling on the chair as the knife turned in him, in him, Paco.

The knife was out now and he sat on the floor in the widening warm pool.

"Put the napkin over it. Hold it!" said Enrique. "Hold it tight. I will run for the doctor. You must hold in the haemorrhage."

"There should be a rubber cup," said Paco. He had seen that used in the ring.

"I came straight," said Enrique, crying. "All I wanted was to show the danger."

"Don't worry," said Paco, his voice sounding far away. "But bring the doctor."

In the ring they lifted you and carried you, running with you, to the operating room. If the femoral artery emptied itself before you reached there they called the priest.

"Advise one of the priests," said Paco, holding the napkin tight against his lower abdomen. He could not believe that this had happened to him.

But Enrique was running down the Carrera San Jeronimo to the all-night first-aid station and Paco was alone, first sitting up, then huddled over, then slumped on the floor, until it was over, feeling his life go out of him as dirty water empties from a bathtub when the plug is drawn. He was frightened and he felt faint and he tried to say an act of contrition and he remembered how it started but before he had said, as fast as he could, 'Oh, my God, I am heartily sorry for having offended Thee who are worthy of all my love and I firmly resolve . . .' he felt too faint and he was lying face down on the floor and it was over very quickly. A severed femoral artery empties itself faster than you can believe.

As the doctor from the first-aid station came up the stairs accompanied by a policeman who held on to Enrique by the arm, the two sisters of Paco were still in the moving-picture palace of the Gran Via, where they were intensely disappointed in the Garbo film, which showed the great star in miserable low surroundings when they had been accustomed to see her surrounded by great luxury and brilliance. The audience disliked the film thoroughly and were protesting by whistling and stamping their feet. All the other people from the hotel were doing almost what they had been doing when the accident happened, except that the two priests had finished their devotions and were preparing for sleep, and the grey-haired picador had moved his drink over to the table with the two houseworn prostitutes. A little later he went out of the café with one of them. It was the one for whom the matador who had lost his nerve had been buying drinks.

The boy Paco had never known about any of this nor about what all these people would be doing on the next day and on other days to come. He had no idea how they really lived nor how they ended. He did not even realize they ended. He died, as the Spanish phrase has it, full of illusions. He had not had time in his life to lose any of them, nor even, at the end, to complete an act of contrition.

He had not even had time to be disappointed in the Garbo picture which disappointed all Madrid for a week.

This story may be used as additional reading material for the chapter Theme.

Hernando Téllez

JUST LATHER, THAT'S ALL

He said nothing when he entered. I was passing the best of my razors back and forth on a strop. When I recognized him I started to tremble. But he didn't notice. Hoping to conceal my emotion, I continued sharpening the razor. I tested it on the meat of my thumb, and then held it up to the light. At that moment he took off the bullet-studded belt that his gun holster dangled from. He hung it up on a wall hook and placed his military cap over it. Then he turned to me, loosening the knot of his tie, and said, "It's hot as hell. Give me a shave." He sat in the chair.

I estimated he had a four-day beard. The four days taken up by the latest expedition in search of our troops. His face seemed reddened, burned by the sun. Carefully, I began to prepare the soap. I cut off a few slices, dropped them into the cup, mixed in a bit of warm water, and began to stir with the brush. Immediately the foam began to rise. "The other boys in the group should have this much beard, too." I continued stirring the lather.

"But we did all right, you know. We got the main ones. We brought back some dead, and we've got some others still alive. But pretty soon they'll all be dead."

"How many did you catch?" I asked.

"Fourteen. We had to go pretty deep into the woods to find them. But we'll get even. Not one of them comes out of this alive, not one."

He leaned back on the chair when he saw me with the lather-covered brush in my hand. I still had to put the sheet on him. No doubt about it, I was upset. I took a sheet out of a drawer and knotted it around my customer's neck. He wouldn't stop talking. He probably thought I was in sympathy with his party.

JUST LATHER, THAT'S ALL   By Hernando Téllez, translated by Donald A. Yates, from *Great Spanish Short Stories*, selected and introduced by Angel Flores, copyright 1962. Dell Publishing Co., Inc. Reprinted by permission of Angel Flores.

"The town must have learned a lesson from what we did the other day," he said.

"Yes," I replied, securing the knot at the base of his dark, sweaty neck.

"That was a fine show, eh?"

"Very good," I answered, turning back for the brush. The man closed his eyes with a gesture of fatigue and sat waiting for the cool caress of the soap. I had never had him so close to me. The day he ordered the whole town to file into the patio of the school to see the four rebels hanging there, I came face to face with him for an instant. But the sight of the mutilated bodies kept me from noticing the face of the man who had directed it all, the face I was now about to take into my hands. It was not an unpleasant face, certainly. And the beard, which made him seem a bit older than he was, didn't suit him badly at all. His name was Torres. Captain Torres. A man of imagination, because who else would have thought of hanging the naked rebels and then holding target practice on certain parts of their bodies? I began to apply the first layer of soap. With his eyes closed, he continued. "Without any effort I could go straight to sleep," he said, "but there's plenty to do this afternoon." I stopped the lathering and asked with a feigned lack of interest: "A firing squad?" "Something like that, but a little slower." I got on with the job of lathering his beard. My hands started trembling again. The man could not possibly realize it, and this was in my favor. But I would have preferred that he hadn't come. It was likely that many of our faction had seen him enter. And an enemy under one's roof imposes certain conditions. I would be obliged to shave that beard like any other one, carefully, gently, like that of any customer, taking pains to see that no single pore emitted a drop of blood. Being careful to see that the little tufts of hair did not lead the blade astray. Seeing that his skin ended up clean, soft, and healthy, so that passing the back of my hand over it I couldn't feel a hair. Yes, I was secretly a rebel, but I was also a conscientious barber, and proud of the preciseness of my profession. And this four-days' growth of beard was a fitting challenge.

I took the razor, opened up the two protective arms, exposed the blade and began the job, from one of the sideburns downward. The razor responded beautifully. His beard was inflexible and hard, not too long, but thick. Bit by bit the skin emerged. The razor rasped along, making its customary sound as fluffs of lather mixed with bits of hair gathered along the blade. I paused a moment to clean it, then took up the strop again to sharpen the razor, because I'm a barber who does things properly. The man, who had kept his eyes closed, opened them now, removed one of his hands from under the sheer, felt the spot on his face where the soap had been cleared off, and said, "Come to the school today at six o'clock." "The same thing as the other day?" I asked horrified. "It could be better," he replied. "What do you plan to do?" "I don't know yet. But we'll amuse ourselves." Once more he leaned back and closed his eyes. I approached him with the razor poised. "Do you plan to punish them all?" I ventured timidly. "All." The soap was drying on his face. I had to hurry. In the mirror I looked toward the street. It was the same as ever: the grocery store with two or three customers in it. Then I glanced at the clock: two-twenty in the afternoon. The razor continued on its downward stroke. Now from the other sideburn down. A thick, blue beard. He should have let it grow like some poets or priests do. It would suit him well. A lot of people wouldn't recognize him. Much to his benefit, I thought, as I attempted to cover the neck area smoothly. There, for sure, the razor had to be handled masterfully, since the hair, although softer, grew into little swirls. A curly beard. One of the tiny pores could be opened up and issue forth its pearl of blood. A good barber such as I prides himself on never allowing this to happen to a client. And this was a first-class client. How many of us had he ordered shot? How many of us had he ordered mutilated? It was better not to think about it. Torres did not know that I was his enemy. He did not know it nor did the rest. It was a secret shared by very few, precisely so that I could inform the revolutionaries of what Torres was doing in the town and of what he was planning each time he undertook a rebel-hunting excursion. So it was going to be very difficult to explain that I had him right in my hands and let him go peacefully—alive and shaved.

The beard was now almost completely gone. He seemed younger, less burdened by years than when he had arrived. I suppose this always happens with men who visit barber shops. Under the stroke of my razor Torres was being rejuvenated—rejuvenated because I am a good barber, the best in the town, if I may so. A little more lather here, under his chin, on his Adam's apple, on this big vein. How hot it is getting! Torres must be sweating as much as I. But he is not afraid. He is a calm man, who is not even thinking about what he is going to do with the prisoners this afternoon. On the other hand I, with this razor in my hands, stroking and re-stroking this skin, trying to keep blood from oozing from these pores, can't even think clearly. Damn him for coming, because I'm a revolutionary and not a murderer. And how easy it would be to kill him. And he deserves it. Does he? No! What the devil! No one deserves to have someone else make the sacrifice of becoming a murderer. What do you gain by it? Nothing. Others come along and still others, and the first ones kill the second ones and they the next ones and it goes on like this until everything is a sea of blood. I could cut this throat just so, zip! zip! I wouldn't give him time to complain and since he has his eyes closed he wouldn't see the glistening knife blade or my glistening eyes. But I'm trembling like a real murderer. Out of his neck a gush of blood would spout onto the sheet, on the chair, on my hands, on the floor. I would have to close the door. And the blood would keep inching along the floor, warm, ineradicable, uncontainable, until it reached the street, like a little scarlet stream. I'm sure that one solid stroke, one deep incision, would prevent any pain. He wouldn't suffer. But what would I do with the body? Where would I hide it? I would have to flee, leaving all I have behind, and take refuge far away, far, far away. But they would follow until they found me. "Captain Torres' murderer. He slit his throat while he was shaving him—a coward." And then on the other side. "The avenger of us all. A name to remember. (And here they would mention my name.) He was the town barber. No one knew he was defending our cause."

And what of all this? Murderer or hero? My destiny depends on the edge of this blade. I can turn my hand a bit more, press a little harder on the razor, and sink it in. The skin would give way like silk, like rubber, like the strop. There is nothing more tender than human skin and the blood is always there, ready to pour forth. A blade like this doesn't fail. It is my best. But I don't want to be a murderer, no sir. You came to me for a shave. And I perform my work honorably. . . . I don't want blood on my hands. Just lather, that's all. You are an executioner and I am only a barber. Each person has his own place in the scheme of things. That's right. His own place.

Now his chin had been stroked clean and smooth. The man sat up and looked into the mirror. He rubbed his hands over his skin and felt it fresh, like new.

"Thanks," he said. He went to the hanger for his belt, pistol and cap. I must have been very pale; my shirt felt soaked. Torres finished adjusting the buckle, straightened his pistol in the holster and after automatically smoothing down his hair, he put on the cap. From his pants pocket he took out several coins to pay me for my services. And he began to head toward the door. In the doorway he paused for a moment, and turning to me he said:

"They told me that you'd kill me. I came to find out. But killing isn't easy. You can take my word for it." And he headed on down the street.

This story may be used as additional reading material for the chapter Symbol and Irony, and the Chapter Fantasy.

Nathaniel Hawthorne

YOUNG GOODMAN BROWN

Young Goodman Brown came forth at sunset, into the street of Salem village, but put his head back, after crossing the threshold, to exchange a parting kiss with his young wife. And Faith, as the wife was aptly named, thrust her own pretty head into the street, letting the wind play with the pink ribbons of her cap, while she called to Goodman Brown.

"Dearest heart," whispered she, softly and rather sadly, when her lips were close to his ear, "prithee, put off your journey until sunrise, and sleep in your own bed to-night. A lone woman is troubled with such dreams and such thoughts, that she's afeard of herself, sometimes. Pray, tarry with me this night, dear husband, of all nights in the year!"

"My love and my Faith," replied young Goodman Brown, "of all nights in the year, this one night must I tarry away from thee. My journey, as thou callest it, forth and back again, must needs be done 'twixt now and sunrise. What, my sweet, pretty wife, does thou doubt me already, and we but three months married!"

"Then God bless you!" said Faith with the pink ribbons, "and may you find all well, when you come back."

"Amen!" cried Goodman Brown. "Say thy prayers, dear Faith, and go to bed at dusk, and no harm will come to thee."

So they parted; and the young man pursued his way, until, being about to turn the corner by the meeting-house, he looked back and saw the head of Faith still peeping after him, with a melancholy air, in spite of her pink ribbons.

"Poor little Faith!" thought he, for his heart smote him. "What a wretch am I, to leave her on such an errand! She talks of dreams, too. Methought, as she spoke, there was trouble in her face, as if a dream had warned her what work is to be done to-night. But no, no! 't would kill her to think it. Well; she's a blessed angel on earth; and after this one night, I'll cling to her skirts and follow her to Heaven."

With this excellent resolve for the future, Goodman Brown felt himself justified in making more haste on his present evil purpose. He had taken a dreary road, darkened by all the gloomiest trees of the forest, which barely stood aside to let the narrow path creep through, and closed immediately behind. It was all as lonely as could be; and there is this peculiarity in such a solitude, that the traveller knows not who may

YOUNG GOODMAN BROWN First published in 1846.

be concealed by the innumerable trunks and the thick boughs overhead; so that, with lonely footsteps, he may yet be passing through an unseen multitude.

"There may be a devilish Indian behind every tree," said Goodman Brown to himself; and he glanced fearfully behind him, as he added, "What if the devil himself should be at my very elbow!"

His head being turned back, he passed a crook of the road, and looking forward again, beheld the figure of a man, in grave and decent attire, seated at the foot of an old tree. He arose at Goodman Brown's approach, and walked onward, side by side with him.

"You are late, Goodman Brown," said he. "The clock of the Old South was striking, as I came through Boston; and that is full fifteen minutes agone."

"Faith kept me back awhile," replied the young man, with a tremor in his voice, caused by the sudden appearance of his companion, though not wholly unexpected.

It was now deep dusk in the forest, and deepest in that part of it where these two were journeying. As nearly as could be discerned, the second traveller was about fifty years old, apparently in the same rank of life as Goodman Brown, and bearing a considerable resemblance to him, though perhaps more in expression than features. Still, they might have been taken for father and son. And yet, though the elder person was as simply clad as the younger, and as simple in manner too, he had an indescribable air of one who knew the world, and would not have felt abashed at the governor's dinner-table, or in King William's court, were it possible that his affairs should call him thither. But the only thing about him that could be fixed upon as remarkable, was his staff, which bore the likeness of a great black snake, so curiously wrought, that it might almost be seen to twist and wriggle itself like a living serpent. This, of course, must have been an ocular deception, assisted by the uncertain light.

"Come, Goodman Brown!" cried his fellow-traveller, "this is a dull pace for the beginning of a journey. Take my staff, if you are so soon weary."

"Friend," said the other, exchanging his slow pace for a full stop, "having kept covenant by meeting thee here, it is my purpose now to return whence I came. I have scruples, touching the matter thou wot'st of."

"Sayest thou so?" replied he of the serpent, smiling apart. "Let us walk on, nevertheless, reasoning as we go, and if I convince thee not, thou shalt turn back. We are but a little way in the forest, yet."

"Too far, too far!" exclaimed the goodman, unconsciously resuming his walk. "My father never went into the woods on such an errand, nor his father before him. We have been a race of honest men and good

Christians, since the days of the martyrs. And shall I be the first of the name of Brown that ever took this path and kept—"

"Such company, thou wouldst say," observed the elder person, interrupting his pause. "Well said, Goodman Brown! I have been as well acquainted with your family as with ever a one among the Puritans; and that's no trifle to say. I helped your grandfather, the constable, when he lashed the Quaker woman so smartly through the streets of Salem. And it was I that brought your father a pitch-pine knot, kindled at my own hearth, to set fire to an Indian village, in King Philip's war. They were my good friends, both; and many a pleasant walk have we had along this path, and returned merrily after midnight. I would fain be friends with you, for their sake."

"If it be as thou sayest," replied Goodman Brown, "I marvel they never spoke of these matters. Or, verily, I marvel not, seeing that the least rumor of the sort would have driven them from New England. We are a people of prayer, and good works to boot, and abide no such wickedness."

"Wickedness or not," said the traveller with the twisted staff, "I have a very general acquaintance here in New England. The deacons of many a church have drunk the communion wine with me; the selectmen, of divers towns, make me their chairman; and a majority of the Great and General Court are firm supporters of my interest. The governor and I, too—but these are state secrets."

"Can this be so!" cried Goodman Brown, with a stare of amazement at his undisturbed companion. "Howbeit, I have nothing to do with the governor and council; they have their own ways, and are no rule for a simple husbandman like me. But, were I to go on with thee, how should I meet the eye of that good old man, our minister, at Salem village? Oh, his voice would make me tremble, both Sabbath-day and lecture-day!"

Thus far, the elder traveller had listened with due gravity, but now burst into a fit of irrepressible mirth, shaking himself so violently, that his snakelike staff actually seemed to wriggle in sympathy.

"Ha! ha! ha!" shouted he, again and again; then composing himself, "Well, go on, Goodman Brown, go on; but, prithee, don't kill me with laughing!"

"Well, then, to end the matter at once," said Goodman Brown, considerably nettled, "there is my wife, Faith. It would break her dear little heart; and I'd rather break my own!"

"Nay, if that be the case," answered the other, "e'en go thy ways, Goodman Brown. I would not, for twenty old women like the one hobbling before us, that Faith should come to any harm."

As he spoke, he pointed his staff at a female figure on the path, in whom Goodman Brown recognized a very pious and exemplary dame, who had taught him his catechism in youth, and was still his moral and spiritual adviser, jointly with the minister and Deacon Gookin.

"A marvel, truly, that Goody Cloyse should be so far in the wilderness, at nightfall!" said he. "But, with your leave, friend, I shall take a cut through the woods, until we have left this Christian woman behind. Being a stranger to you, she might ask whom I was consorting with, and whither I was going."

"Be it so," said his fellow-traveller. "Betake you to the woods, and let me keep the path."

Accordingly, the young man turned aside, but took care to watch his companion, who advanced softly along the road, until he had come within a staff's length of the old dame. She, meanwhile, was making the best of her way, with singular speed for so aged a woman, and mumbling some indistinct words, a prayer, doubtless, as she went. The traveller put forth his staff, and touched her withered neck with what seemed the serpent's tail.

"The devil!" screamed the pious old lady.

"Then Goody Cloyse knows her old friend?" observed the traveller, confronting her, and leaning on his writhing stick.

"Ah, forsooth, and is it your worship, indeed?" cried the good dame. "Yea, truly is it, and in the very image of my old gossip, Goodman Brown, the grandfather of the silly fellow that now is. But, would your worship believe it? my broomstick hath strangely disappeared, stolen, as I suspect, by that unhanged witch, Goody Cory, and that, too, when I was all anointed with the juice of smallage and cinque-foil and wolf's-bane—"

"Mingled with fine wheat and the fat of a new-born babe," said the shape of old Goodman Brown.

"Ah, your worship knows the recipe," cried the old lady, cackling aloud. "So, as I was saying, being all ready for the meeting, and no horse to ride on, I made up my mind to foot it; for they tell me there is a nice young man to be taken into communion to-night. But now your good worship will lend me your arm, and we shall be there in a twinkling."

"That can hardly be," answered her friend. "I may not spare you my arm, Goody Cloyse, but here is my staff, if you will."

So saying, he threw it down at her feet, where, perhaps, it assumed life, being one of the rods which its owner had formerly lent to the Egyptian Magi. Of this fact, however, Goodman Brown could not take cognizance. He had cast up his eyes in astonishment, and looking down again, beheld neither Goody Cloyse nor the serpentine staff, but his fellow-traveller alone, who waited for him as calmly as if nothing had happened.

"That old woman taught me my catechism!" said the young man; and there was a world of meaning in this simple comment.

They continued to walk onward, while the elder traveller exhorted his companion to make good speed and persevere in the path, discoursing so aptly, that his arguments seemed rather to spring up in the bosom of his auditor, than to be suggested by himself. As they went he plucked a branch of maple, to serve for a walking-stick, and began to strip it of the twigs and little boughs, which were wet with evening dew. The moment his fingers touched them, they became strangely withered and dried up, as with a week's sunshine. Thus the pair proceeded, at a good free pace, until suddenly, in a gloomy hollow of the road, Goodman Brown sat himself down on the stump of a tree, and refused to go any farther.

"Friend," said he, stubbornly, "my mind is made up. Not another step will I budge on this errand. What if a wretched old woman do choose to go to the devil, when I thought she was going to Heaven! Is that any reason why I should quit my dear Faith, and go after her?"

"You will think better of this by and by," said his acquaintance, composedly. "Sit here and rest yourself awhile; and when you feel like moving again, there is my staff to help you along."

Without more words, he threw his companion the maple stick, and was as speedily out of sight as if he had vanished into the deepening gloom. The young man sat a few moments by the roadside, applauding himself greatly, and thinking with how clear a conscience he should meet the minister, in his morning walk, nor shrink from the eye of good old Deacon Gookin. And what calm sleep would be his, that very night, which was to have been spent so wickedly, but purely and sweetly now, in the arms of Faith! Amidst these pleasant and praiseworthy meditations, Goodman Brown heard the tramp of horses along the road, and deemed it advisable to conceal himself within the verge of the forest, conscious of the guilty purpose that had brought him thither, though now so happily turned from it.

On came the hoof-tramps and the voices of the riders, two grave old voices, conversing soberly as they drew near. These mingled sounds appeared to pass along the road, within a few yards of the young man's hiding-place; but owing, doubtless, to the depth of the gloom, at that particular spot, neither the travellers nor their steeds were visible. Though their figures brushed the small boughs by the wayside, it could not be seen that they intercepted, even for a moment, the faint gleam from the strip of bright sky, athwart which they must have passed. Goodman Brown alternately crouched and stood on tiptoe, pulling aside the branches, and thrusting forth his head as far as he durst, without discerning so much as a shadow. It vexed him the more, because he could have sworn, were such a thing possible, that he recognized the voices of the minister and Deacon Gookin, jogging along quietly, as they were wont to do, when bound to some ordination or ecclesiastical council. While yet within hearing, one of the riders stopped to pluck a switch.

"Of the two, reverend Sir," said the voice like the deacon's, "I had rather miss an ordination dinner than to-night's meeting. They tell me that some of our community are to be here from Falmouth and beyond, and others from Connecticut and Rhode Island; besides several of the Indian powwows, who, after their fashion, know almost as much deviltry as the best of us. Moreover, there is a goodly young woman to be taken into communion."

"Mighty well, Deacon Gookin!" replied the solemn old tones of the minister. "Spur up, or we shall be late. Nothing can be done, you know, until I get on the ground."

The hoofs clattered again, and the voices, talking so strangely in the empty air, passed on through the forest, where no church had ever been gathered, nor solitary Christian prayed. Whither, then, could these holy men be journeying, so deep into the heathen wilderness? Young Goodman Brown caught hold of a tree, for support, being ready to sink down on the ground, faint and over-burthened with the heavy sickness of his heart. He looked up to the sky, doubting whether there really was a Heaven above him. Yet, there was the blue arch, and the stars brightening in it.

"With Heaven above, and Faith below, I will yet stand firm against the devil!" cried Goodman Brown.

While he still gazed upward, into the deep arch of the firmament, and had lifted his hands to pray, a cloud, though no wind was stirring, hurried across the zenith, and hid the brightening stars. The blue sky was still visible, except directly overhead, where this black mass of cloud was sweeping swiftly northward. Aloft in the air, as if from the depths of the cloud, came a confused and doubtful sound of voices. Once, the listener fancied that he could distinguish the accents of town's-people of his own, men and women, both pious and ungodly, many of whom he had met at the communion-table, and had seen others rioting at the tavern. The next moment, so indistinct were the sounds, he doubted whether he had heard aught but the murmur of the old forest, whispering without a wind. Then came a stronger swell of those familiar tones, heard daily in the sunshine, at Salem village, but never, until now, from a cloud at night. There was one voice, of a young woman, uttering lamentations, yet with an uncertain sorrow, and entreating for some favor, which, perhaps, it would grieve her to obtain. And all the unseen multitude, both saints and sinners, seemed to encourage her onward.

"Faith!" shouted Goodman Brown, in a voice of agony and desperation; and the echoes of the forest mocked him, crying—"Faith! Faith!" as if bewildered wretches were seeking her, all through the wilderness.

The cry of grief, rage, and terror was yet piercing the night, when the unhappy husband held his breath for a response. There was a scream, drowned immediately in a louder murmur of voices fading into far-off laughter, as the dark cloud swept away, leaving the clear and silent sky above Goodman Brown. But something fluttered lightly down through the air, and caught on the branch of a tree. The young man seized it and beheld a pink ribbon.

"My Faith is gone!" cried he, after one stupefied moment. "There is no good on earth, and sin is but a name. Come, devil! for to thee is this world given."

And maddened with despair, so that he laughed loud and long, did Goodman Brown grasp his staff and set forth again, at such a rate, that he seemed to fly along the forest path, rather than to walk or run. The road grew wilder and drearier, and more faintly traced, and vanished at length, leaving him in the heart of the dark wilderness, still rushing onward, with the instinct that guides mortal man to evil. The whole forest was peopled with frightful sounds; the creaking of the trees, the howling of wild beasts, and the yell of Indians; while, sometimes, the wind tolled like a distant church bell, and sometimes gave a broad roar around the traveller, as if all Nature were laughing him to scorn. But he was himself the chief horror of the scene, and shrank not from its other horrors.

"Ha! ha! ha!" roared Goodman Brown, when the wind laughed at him. "Let us hear which will laugh loudest! Think not to frighten me with your deviltry! Come witch, come wizard, come Indian powwow, come devil himself! and here comes Goodman Brown. You may as well fear him as he fear you!"

In truth, all through the haunted forest, there could be nothing more frightful than the figure of Goodman Brown. On he flew, among the black pines, brandishing his staff with frenzied gestures, now giving vent to an inspiration of horrid blasphemy, and now shouting forth such laughter, as set all the echoes of the forest laughing like demons around him. The fiend in his own shape is less hideous, than when he rages in the breast of man. Thus sped the demoniac on his course, until, quivering among the trees, he saw a red light before him, as when the felled trunks and branches of a clearing have been set on fire, and throw up their lurid blaze against the sky, at the hour of midnight. He paused, in a lull of the tempest that had driven him onward, and heard the swell of what seemed a hymn, rolling solemnly from a distance, with the weight of many voices. He knew the tune. It was a familiar one in the choir of the village meeting-house The verse died heavily away, and was lengthened by a chorus, not of human voices, but of all the sounds of the benighted wilderness, pealing in awful harmony together. Goodman Brown cried out; and his cry was lost to his own ear, by its unison with the cry of the desert.

In the interval of silence, he stole forward, until the light glared full upon his eyes. At one extremity of an open space, hemmed in by the dark wall of the forest, arose a rock, bearing some rude, natural resemblance either to an altar or a pulpit, and surrounded by four blazing pines, their tops aflame, their stems untouched, like candles at an evening meeting. The mass of foliage, that had overgrown the summit of the rock, was all on fire, blazing high into the night, and fitfully illuminating the whole field. Each pendent twig and leafy festoon was in a blaze. As the red light arose and fell, a numerous congregation alternately shone forth, then disappeared in shadow, and again grew, as it were, out of the darkness, peopling the heart of the solitary woods at once.

"A grave and dark-clad company!" quoth Goodman Brown.

In truth, they were such. Among them, quivering to-and-fro, between gloom and splendor, appeared faces that would be seen, next day, at the council-board of the province, and others which, Sabbath after Sabbath, looked devoutly heavenward, and benignantly over the crowded pews, from the holiest pulpits in the land. Some affirm that the lady of the governor was there. At least, there were high dames well known to her, and wives of honored husbands, and widows a great multitude, and ancient maidens, all of excellent repute, and fair young girls, who trembled lest their mothers should espy them. Either the sudden gleams of light, flashing over the obscure field, bedazzled Goodman Brown, or he recognized a score of the church members of Salem village, famous for their especial sanctity. Good old Deacon Gookin had arrived, and waited at the skirts of that venerable saint, his reverend pastor. But, irreverently consorting with these grave, reputable, and pious people, these elders of the church, these chaste dames and dewy virgins, there were men of dissolute lives and women of spotted fame, wretches given over to all mean and filthy vice, and suspected even of horrid crimes. It was strange to see, that the good shrank not from the wicked, nor were the sinners abashed by the saints. Scattered, also, among their pale-faced enemies, were the Indian priests, or powwows, who had often scared their native forest with more hideous incantations than any known to English witchcraft.

"But, where is Faith?" thought Goodman Brown; and, as hope came into his heart, he trembled.

Another verse of the hymn arose, a slow and mournful strain, such as the pious love, but joined to words which expressed all that our nature can conceive of sin, and darkly hinted at far more. Unfathomable to mere mortals is the lore of fiends. Verse after verse was sung, and still the chorus of the desert swelled between, like the deepest tone of a mighty organ. And, with the final peal of that dreadful anthem, there came a sound, as if the roaring wind, the rushing streams, the howling beasts, and every other voice of the unconverted wilderness were mingling and according with the voice of guilty man, in homage to the prince of all. The four blazing pines threw up a loftier flame, and obscurely discovered shapes and visages of horror on the smoke-wreaths, above the impious assembly. At the same moment, the fire on the rock shot redly forth, and formed a glowing arch above its base, where now appeared a figure. With reverence be it spoken, the apparition bore no slight similitude, both in garb and manner, to some grave devine of the New England churches.

"Bring forth the converts!" cried a voice, that echoed through the field and rolled into the forest.

At the word, Goodman Brown stepped forth from the shadow of the trees, and approached the congregation, with whom he felt a loathful brotherhood, by the sympathy of all that was wicked in his heart. He could have well-nigh sworn, that the shape of his own dead father beckoned him to advance, looking downward from a smoke-wreath, while a woman, with dim features of despair, threw out her hand to warn him back. Was it his mother? But he had no power to retreat one step, nor to resist, even in thought, when the minister and good old Deacon Gookin seized his arms, and led him to the blazing rock. Thither came also the slender form of a veiled female, led between Goody Cloyse, that pious teacher of the catechism, and Martha Carrier, who had received the devil's promise to be queen of hell. A rampant hag was she! And there stood the proselytes, beneath the canopy of fire.

"Welcome, my children," said the dark figure, "to the communion of your race! Ye have found, thus young, your nature and your destiny. My children, look behind you!"

They turned; and flashing forth, as it were, in a sheet of flame, the fiend-worshippers were seen; the smile of welcome gleamed darkly on every visage.

"There," resumed the sable form, "are all whom ye have reverenced from youth. Ye deemed them holier than yourselves, and shrank from your own sin, contrasting it with their lives of righteousness and prayerful aspirations heavenward. Yet, here are they all, in my worshipping assembly! This night it shall be granted you to know their secret deeds; how hoary-bearded elders of the church have whispered wanton words to the young maids of their households; how many a woman, eager for widow's weeds, has given her husband a drink at bedtime, and let him sleep his last sleep in her bosom; how beardless youths have made haste to inherit their father's wealth; and how fair damsels—blush not, sweet ones!—have dug little graves in the garden, and bidden me, the sole guest, to an infant's funeral. By the sympathy of your human hearts for sin, ye shall scent out all the places—whether in church, bed-chamber, street, field, or forest—where crime has been committed, and shall exult to behold the whole earth one stain of guilt, one mighty blood-spot. Far more than this! It shall be yours to penetrate, in every bosom, the deep mystery of sin, the fountain of all wicked arts, and which inexhaustibly supplies more evil impulses than human power—than my power, at its utmost!—can make manifest in deeds. And now, my children, look upon each other."

They did so; and, by the blaze of the hell-kindled torches, the wretched man beheld his Faith, and the wife her husband, trembling before that unhallowed altar.

"Lo! there ye stand, my children," said the figure, in a deep and solemn tone, almost sad, with its despairing awfulness, as if his once angelic nature could yet mourn for our miserable race. "Depending upon one another's hearts, ye had still hoped that virture were not all a dream! Now are ye undeceived!—Evil is the nature of mankind. Evil must be your only happiness. Welcome, again, my children, to the communion of your race!"

"Welcome!" repeated the fiend-worshippers, in one cry of despair and triumph.

And there they stood, the only pair, as it seemed, who were yet hesitating on the verge of wickedness, in this dark world. A basin was hollowed, naturally, in the rock. Did it contain water, reddened by the lurid light? or was it blood? or, perchance, a liquid flame? Herein did the Shape of Evil dip his hand, and prepare to lay the mark of baptism upon their foreheads, that they might be partakers of the mystery of sin, more conscious of the secret guilt of others, both in deed and thought, than they could now be of their own. The husband cast one look at his pale wife, and Faith at him. What polluted wretches would the next glance show them to each other, shuddering alike at what they disclosed and what they saw!

"Faith! Faith!" cried the husband. "Look up to Heaven, and resist the Wicked One!"

Whether Faith obeyed, he knew not. Hardly had he spoken, when he found himself amid calm night and solitude, listening to a roar of the wind, which died heavily away through the forest. He staggered against the rock, and felt it chill and damp, while a hanging twig, that had been all on fire, besprinkled his cheek with the coldest dew.

The next morning, young Goodman Brown came slowly into the street of Salem village staring around him like a bewildered man. The good old minister was taking a walk along the grave-yard, to get an appetite for breakfast and meditate his sermon, and bestowed a blessing, as he passed, on Goodman Brown. He shrank from the venerable saint, as if to avoid an anathema. Old Deacon Gookin was at domestic worship, and the holy words of his prayer were heard through the open window. "What God doth the wizard pray to?" quoth Goodman Brown. Goody Cloyse, that excellent old Christian, stood in the early sunshine, at her own lattice, catechising a little girl, who had brought her a pint of morning's milk. Goodman Brown snatched away the child, as from the grasp of the fiend himself. Turning the corner by the meeting-house, he spied the head of Faith, with the pink ribbons, gazing anxiously forth, and bursting into such joy at sight of him that she skipt along the street, and almost kissed her husband before the whole village. But Goodman Brown looked sternly and sadly into her face, and passed on without a greeting.

Had Goodman Brown fallen asleep in the forest, and only dreamed a wild dream of a witch-meeting?

Be it so, if you will. But alas! it was a dream of evil omen for young Goodman Brown. A stern, a sad, a darkly meditative, a distrustful, if not a desperate man did he become, from the night of that fearful dream. On the Sabbath day, when the congregation were singing a holy psalm, he could not listen, because an anthem of sin rushed loudly upon his ear, and drowned all the blessed strain. When the minister spoke from the pulpit, with power and fervid eloquence, and with his hand on the open Bible, of the sacred truths of our religion, and of saint-like lives, and triumphant deaths, and of future bliss or misery unutterable, then did Goodman Brown turn pale, dreading lest the roof should thunder down upon the gray blasphemer and his hearers. Often, awaking suddenly at midnight, he shrank from the bosom of Faith, and at morning or eventide, when the family knelt down at prayer, he scowled, and muttered to himself, and gazed sternly at his wife, and turned away. And when he had lived long, and was borne to his grave, a hoary corpse, followed by Faith, an aged woman, and children and grand-children, a goodly procession, besides neighbors not a few, they carved no hopeful verse upon his tombstone; for his dying hour was gloom.

This story may be used as additional reading material for the chapter Escape and Interpretation.

Joseph Conrad

YOUTH

This could have occurred nowhere but in England, where men and sea interpenetrate, so to speak—the sea entering into the life of most men, and the men knowing something or everything about the sea, in the way of amusement, of travel, or of bread-winning.

We were sitting round a mahogany table that reflected the bottle, the claret glasses, and our faces as we leaned on our elbows. There was a director of companies, an accountant, a lawyer, Marlow, and myself. The director had been a *Conway* boy, the accountant had served four years at sea, the lawyer—a fine crusted Tory, High Churchman, the best of old fellows, the soul of honor—had been chief officer in the P. & O. service in the good old days when mail-boats were square-rigged at least on two masts, and used to come down the China Sea before a fair monsoon with stun'-sails set alow and aloft. We all began life in the merchant service. Between the five of us there was the strong bond of the sea, and also the fellowship of the craft, which no amount of enthusiasm for yachting, cruising, and so on can give, since one is only the amusement of life and the other is life itself.

Marlow (at least I think that is how he spelt his name) told the story, or rather the chronicle, of a voyage:

"Yes, I have seen a little of the Eastern seas; but what I remember best is my first voyage there. You fellows know there are those voyages that seem ordered for the illustration of life, that might stand for a symbol of existence. You fight, work, sweat, nearly kill yourself, sometimes do kill yourself, trying to accomplish something—and you can't. Not from any fault of yours. You simply can do nothing, neither great nor little—not a thing in the world—not even marry an old maid, or get a wretched 600-ton cargo of coal to its port of destination.

"It was altogether a memorable affair. It was my first voyage to the East, and my first voyage as second mate; it was also my skipper's first command. You'll admit it was time. He was sixty if a day; a little man, with a broad, not very straight back, with bowed shoulders and one leg more bandy than the other, he had that queer twisted-about appearance you see so often in men who work in the fields. He had a nutcracker

YOUTH   Reprinted from *Youth: A Narrative and Two Other Stories* by Joseph Conrad. Reprinted by permission of J. M. Dent and Sons Ltd., London, and the Trustees of the Joseph Conrad Estate. Written in 1898.

face—chin and nose trying to come together over a sunken mouth—and it was framed in iron-gray fluffy hair, that looked like a chin strap of cotton-wool sprinkled with coal dust. And he had blue eyes in that old face of his, which were amazingly like a boy's, with that candid expression some quite common men preserve to the end of their days by a rare internal gift of simplicity of heart and rectitude of soul. What induced him to accept me was a wonder. I had come out of a crack Australian clipper, where I had been third officer, and he seemed to have a prejudice against crack clippers as aristocratic and high-toned. He said to me, 'You know, in this ship you will have to work.' I said I had to work in every ship I had ever been in. 'Ah, but this is different, and you gentlemen out of them big ships; . . . but there! I dare say you will do. Join tomorrow.'

"I joined tomorrow. It was twenty-two years ago; and I was just twenty. How time passes! It was one of the happiest days of my life. Fancy! Second mate for the first time—a really responsible officer! I wouldn't have thrown up my new billet for a fortune. The mate looked me over carefully. He was also an old chap, but of another stamp. He had a Roman nose, a snow-white, long beard, and his name was Mahon, but he insisted that it should be pronounced Mann. He was well connected; yet there was something wrong with his luck, and he had never got on.

"As to the captain, he had been for years in coasters, then in the Mediterranean, and last in the West Indian trade. He had never been round the Capes. He could just write a kind of sketchy hand, and didn't care for writing at all. Both were thorough good seamen of course, and between those two old chaps I felt like a small boy between two grandfathers.

"The ship also was old. Her name was the *Judea*. Queer name, isn't it? She belonged to a man Wilmer, Wilcox—some name like that; but he has been bankrupt and dead these twenty years or more, and his name don't matter. She had been laid up in Shadwell basin for ever so long. You can imagine her state. She was all rust, dust, grime—soot aloft, dirt on deck. To me it was like coming out of a palace into a ruined cottage. She was about 400 tons, had a primitive windlass, wooden latches on the doors, not a bit of brass about her, and a big square stern. There was on it, below her name in big letters, a lot of scroll work, with the gilt off, and some sort of a coat of arms, with the motto 'Do or Die' underneath. I remember it took my fancy immensely. There was a touch of romance in it, something that made me love the old thing—something that appealed to my youth!

"We left London in ballast—sand ballast—to load a cargo of coal in a northern port for Bankok. Bankok! I thrilled. I had been six years at sea, but had only seen Melbourne and Sydney, very good places, charming places in their way—but Bankok!

"We worked out of the Thames under canvas, with a North Sea pilot on board. His name was Jermyn, and he dodged all day long about the galley drying his handkerchief before the stove. Apparently he never slept. He was a dismal man, with a perpetual tear sparkling at the end of his nose, who either had been in trouble, or was in trouble, or expected to be in trouble—couldn't be happy unless something went wrong. He mistrusted my youth, my common sense, and my seamanship, and made a point of showing it in a hundred little ways. I dare say he was right. It seems to me I knew very little then, and I know not much more now; but I cherish a hate for that Jermyn to this day.

"We were a week working up as far as Yarmouth Roads, and then we got into a gale—the famous October gale of twenty-two years ago. It was wind, lightning, sleet, snow, and a terrific sea. We were flying light, and you may imagine how bad it was when I tell you we had smashed bulwarks and a flooded deck. On the second night she shifted her ballast into the lee bow, and by that time we had been blown off somewhere on the Dogger Bank. There was nothing for it but go below with shovels and try to right her, and there we were in that vast hold, gloomy like a cavern, the tallow dips stuck and flickering on the beams, the gale howling above, the ship tossing about like mad on her side; there we all were, Jermyn, the captain, everyone, hardly able to keep our feet, engaged on that gravedigger's work, and trying to toss shovelfuls of wet sand up to windward. At every tumble of the ship you could see vaguely in the dim light men falling down with a great flourish of shovels. One of the ship's boys (we had two), impressed by the weirdness of the scene, wept as if his heart would break. We could hear him blubbering somewhere in the shadows.

"On the third day the gale died out, and by-and-by a north-country tug picked us up. We took sixteen days in all to get from London to the Tyne! When we got into dock we had lost our turn for loading, and they hauled us off to a pier where we remained for a month. Mrs. Beard (the captain's name was Beard) came from Colchester to see the old man. She lived on board. The crew of runners had left, and there remained only the officers, one boy, and the steward, a mulatto who answered to the name of Abraham. Mrs. Beard was an old woman, with a face all wrinkled and ruddy like a winter apple, and the figure of a young girl. She caught sight of me once, sewing on a button, and insisted on having my shirts to repair. This was something different from the captains' wives I had known on board crack clippers. When I brought her the shirts, she said: 'And the socks? They want mending, I am sure, and John's—Captain Beard's—things are all in order now. I would be glad of something to do.' Bless the old woman. She overhauled my outfit for me, and meantime I read for the first time 'Sartor Resartus' and Burnaby's 'Ride to Khiva.' I didn't understand much of the first then; but I remember I preferred the soldier to the philosopher at the time; a preference which life has only confirmed. One was a man, and the other was either more—or less. However, they are both dead, and Mrs. Beard is dead, and youth, strength, genius, thoughts, achievements, simple hearts—all die. . . . No matter.

"They loaded us at last. We shipped a crew. Eight able seamen and two boys. We hauled off one evening to the buoys at the dock-gates, ready to go out, and with a fair prospect of beginning the voyage next day. Mrs. Beard was to start for home by a late train. When the ship was fast we went to tea. We sat rather silent through the meal—Mahon, the old couple, and I. I finished first, and slipped away for a smoke, my cabin being in a deckhouse just against the poop. It was high water, blowing fresh with a drizzle; the double dock-gates were opened, and the steam colliers were going in and out in the darkness with their lights burning bright, a great plashing of propellers, rattling of winches, and a lot of hailing on the pier-heads. I watched the procession of headlights gliding high and of green lights gliding low in the night, when suddenly a red gleam flashed at me, vanished, came into view again, and remained. The fore-end of a steamer loomed up close. I shouted down the cabin, 'Come up, quick!' and then heard a startled voice saying afar in the dark, 'Stop her, sir.' A bell jingled. Another voice cried warningly, 'We are going right into that bark, sir.' The answer to this was a gruff 'All right,' and the next thing was a heavy crash as the steamer struck a glancing blow with the bluff of her bow about our fore-rigging. There was a moment of confusion, yelling, and running about. Steam roared. Then somebody was heard saying, 'All clear, sir.' . . . 'Are you all right?' asked the gruff voice. I had jumped forward to see the damage, and hailed back, 'I think so.' 'Easy astern,' said the gruff voice. A bell jingled. 'What steamer is that?' screamed Mahon. By that time she was no more to us than a bulky shadow maneuvering a little way off. They shouted at us some name—a woman's name, Miranda or Melissa—or some such thing. 'This means another month in this beastly hole,' said Mahon to me, as we peered with lamps about the splintered bulwarks and broken braces. 'But where's the captain?'

"We had not heard or seen anything of him all that time. We went aft to look. A doleful voice arose hailing somewhere in the middle of the dock, '*Judea* ahoy!' . . . How the devil did he get there? . . . 'Hallo!' we shouted. 'I am adrift in our boat without oars,' he cried. A belated waterman offered his services, and Mahon struck a bargain with him for half-a-crown to tow our skipper alongside; but it was Mrs. Beard that came up the ladder first. They had been floating about the dock in that mizzly cold rain for nearly an hour. I was never so surprised in my life.

"It appears that when he heard my shout 'Come up,' he understood at once what was the matter, caught up his wife, ran on deck, and across, and down into our boat, which was fast to the ladder. Not bad for a sixty-year-old. Just imagine that old fellow saving heroically in his arms that old woman—the woman of his life. He set her down on a thwart, and was ready to climb back on board when the painter came adrift somehow, and away they went together. Of course in the confusion we did not hear him shouting. He looked abashed. She said cheerfully, 'I suppose it does not matter my losing the train now?' 'No, Jenny—you go below and get warm,' he growled. Then to us: 'A sailor has no business with a wife—I say. There I was, out of the ship. Well, no harm done this time. Let's go and look at what that fool of a steamer smashed.'

"It wasn't much, but it delayed us three weeks. At the end of that time, the captain being engaged with his agents, I carried Mrs. Beard's bag to the railway station and put her all comfy into a third-class carriage. She lowered the window to say, 'You are a good young man. If you see John—Captain Beard—without his muffler at night, just remind him from me to keep his throat well wrapped up.' 'Certainly, Mrs. Beard,' I said. 'You are a good young man; I noticed how attentive you are to John—to Captain—' The train pulled out suddenly; I took my cap off to the old woman: I never saw her again. . . . Pass the bottle.

"We went to sea next day. When we made that start for Bankok we had been already three months out of London. We had expected to be a fortnight or so—at the outside.

"It was January, and the weather was beautiful—the beautiful sunny winter weather that has more charm than in the summertime, because it is unexpected, and crisp, and you know it won't, it can't, last long. It's like a windfall, like a godsend, like an unexpected piece of luck.

"It lasted all down the North Sea, all down Channel; and it lasted till we were three hundred miles or so to the westward of the Lizards: then the wind went round to the sou'west and began to pipe up. In two days it blew a gale. The *Judea*, hove to, wallowed on the Atlantic like an old candlebox. It blew day after day: it blew with spite, without interval, without mercy, without rest. The world was nothing but an immensity of great foaming waves rushing at us, under a sky low enough to touch with the hand and dirty like a smoked ceiling. In the stormy space surrounding us there was as much flying spray as air. Day after day and night after night there was nothing round the ship but the howl of the wind, the tumult of the sea, the noise of water pouring over her deck. There was no rest for her and no rest for us. She tossed, she pitched, she stood on her head, she sat on her tail, she rolled, she groaned, and we had to hold on while on deck and cling to our bunks when below, in a constant effort of body and worry of mind.

"One night Mahon spoke through the small window of my berth. It opened right into my very bed, and I was lying there sleepless, in my boots, feeling as though I had not slept for years, and could not if I tried. He said excitedly—

"'You got the sounding-rod in here, Marlow? I can't get the pumps to suck. By God! it's no child's play.'

"I gave him the sounding-rod and lay down again, trying to think of various things—but I thought only of the pumps. When I came on deck they were still at it, and my watch relieved at the pumps. By the light of the lantern brought on deck to examine the sounding-rod I caught a glimpse of their weary, serious faces. We pumped all the four hours. We pumped all night, all day, all the week—watch and watch. She was working herself loose, and leaked badly—not enough to drown us at once, but enough to kill us with the work at the pumps. And while we pumped the ship was going from us piecemeal: the bulwarks went, the stanchions were torn out, the ventilators smashed, the cabin door burst in. There was not a dry spot in the ship. She was being gutted bit by bit. The longboat changed, as if by magic, into matchwood where she stood in her gripes. I had lashed her myself, and was rather proud of my handiwork, which had withstood so long the malice of the sea. And we pumped. And there was no break in the weather. The sea was white like a sheet of foam, like a caldron of boiling milk; there was not a break in the clouds, no—not the size of a man's hand—no, not for so much as ten seconds. There was for us no sky, there were for us no stars, no sun, no universe—nothing but angry clouds and an infuriated sea. We pumped watch and watch, for dear life; and it seemed to last for months, for years, for all eternity, as though we had been dead and gone to a hell for sailors. We forgot the day of the week, the name of the month, what year it was, and whether we had ever been ashore. The sails blew away, she lay broadside on under a weather-cloth, the ocean poured over her, and we did not care. We turned those handles, and had the eyes of idiots. As soon as we had crawled on deck I used to take a round turn with a rope about the men, the pumps, and the mainmast, and we turned, we turned incessantly, with the water to our waists, to our necks, over our heads. It was all one. We had forgotten how it felt to be dry.

"And there was somewhere in me the thought: By Jove! this is the deuce of an adventure—something you read about; and it is my first voyage as second mate—and I am only twenty—and here I am lasting it out as well as any of these men, and keeping my chaps up to the mark. I was pleased. I would not have given up the experience for worlds. I had moments of exultation. Whenever the old dismantled craft pitched heavily with her counter high in the air, she seemed to me to throw up, like an appeal, like a defiance, like a cry to the clouds without mercy, the words written on her stern: '*Judea*, London. Do or Die.'

"O youth! The strength of it, the faith of it, the imagination of it! To me she was not an old rattletrap carting about the world a lot of coal for a freight—to me she was the endeavor, the test, the trial of life. I think of her with pleasure, with affection, with regret—as you would think of someone dead you have loved. I shall never forget her. . . . Pass the bottle.

"One night when, tied to the mast, as I explained, we were pumping on, deafened with the wind, and without spirit enough in us to wish ourselves dead, a heavy sea crashed aboard and swept clean over us. As soon as I got my breath I shouted, as in duty bound, 'Keep on, boys!' when suddenly I felt something hard floating on deck strike the calf of my leg. I made a grab at it and missed. It was so dark we could not see each other's faces within a foot—you understand.

"After that thump the ship kept quiet for a while, and the thing, whatever it was, struck my leg again. This time I caught it—and it was a saucepan. At first, being stupid with fatigue and thinking of nothing but the pumps, I did not understand what I had in my hand. Suddenly it dawned upon me, and I shouted, 'Boys, the house on deck is gone. Leave this, and let's look for the cook.'

"There was a deckhouse forward, which contained the galley, the cook's berth, and the quarters of the crew. As we had expected for days to see it swept away, the hands had been ordered to sleep in the cabin—the only safe place in the ship. The steward, Abraham, however, persisted in clinging to his berth, stupidly, like a mule—from sheer fright I believe, like an animal that won't leave a stable falling in an earthquake. So we went to look for him. It was chancing death, since once out of our lashings we were as exposed as if on a raft. But we went. The house was shattered as if a shell had exploded inside. Most of it had gone overboard—stove, men's quarters, and their property, all was gone; but two posts, holding a portion of the bulkhead to which Abraham's bunk was attached, remained as if by a miracle. We groped in the ruins and came upon this, and there he was, sitting in his bunk, surrounded by foam and wreckage, jabbering cheerfully to himself. He was out of his mind; completely and for ever mad, with this sudden shock coming upon the fag-end of his endurance. We snatched him up, lugged him aft, and pitched him head-first down the cabin companion. You understand there was no time to carry him down with infinite precautions and wait to see how he got on. Those below would pick him up at the bottom of the stairs all right. We were in a hurry to go back to the pumps. That business could not wait. A bad leak is an inhuman thing.

"One would think that the sole purpose of that fiendish gale had been to make a lunatic of that poor devil of a mulatto. It eased before morning, and next day the sky cleared, and as the sea went down the leak took up. When it came to bending a fresh set of sails the crew demanded to put back—and really there was nothing else to do. Boats gone, decks swept clean, cabin gutted, men without a stitch but what they stood in, stores spoiled, ship strained. We put her head for home, and—would you believe it? The wind came east right in our teeth. It blew fresh, it blew continuously. We had to beat up every inch of the way, but she did not leak so badly, the water keeping comparatively smooth. Two hours' pumping in every four is no joke—but it kept her afloat as far as Falmouth.

"The good people there live on casualties of the sea, and no doubt were glad to see us. A hungry crowd of shipwrights sharpened their chisels at the sight of that carcass of a ship. And, by Jove! they had pretty pickings off us before they were done. I fancy the owner was already in a tight place. There were delays. Then it was decided to take part of the cargo out and calk her topsides. This was done, the repairs finished, cargo reshipped; a new crew came on board, and we went out—for Bankok. At the end of a week we were back again. The crew said they weren't going to Bankok—a hundred and fifty days' passage—in a something hooker that wanted pumping eight hours out of the twenty-four; and the nautical papers inserted again the little paragraph: 'Judea. Bark. Tyne to Bankok; coals; put back to Falmouth leaky and with crew refusing duty.'

"There were more delays—more tinkering. The owner came down for a day, and said she was as right as a little fiddle. Poor old Captain Beard looked like the ghost of a Geordie skipper—through the worry and humiliation of it. Remember he was sixty, and it was his first command. Mahon said it was a foolish business, and would end badly. I loved the ship more than ever, and wanted awfully to get to Bankok. To Bankok! Magic name, blessed name. Mesopotamia wasn't a patch on it. Remember I was twenty, and it was my first second mate's billet, and the East was waiting for me.

"We went out and anchored in the outer roads with a fresh crew—the third. She leaked worse than ever. It was as if those confounded shipwrights had actually made a hole in her. This time we did not even go outside. The crew simply refused to man the windlass.

"They towed us back to the inner harbor, and we became a fixture, a feature, an institution of the place. People pointed us out to visitors as 'That 'ere bark that's going to Bankok—has been here six months—put back three times.' On holidays the small boys pulling about in boats would hail, 'Judea, ahoy!' and if a head showed above the rail shouted, 'Where you bound to?—Bankok?' and jeered. We were only three on board. The poor old skipper mooned in the cabin. Mahon undertook the cooking, and unexpectedly developed all a Frenchman's genius for preparing nice little messes. I looked languidly after the rigging. We became citizens of Falmouth. Every shopkeeper knew us. At the barber's or tobacconist's they asked familiarly, 'Do you think you will ever get to Bankok?' Meantime the owner, the underwriters, and the charterers squabbled amongst themselves in London, and our pay went on. . . . Pass the bottle.

"It was horrid. Morally it was worse than pumping for life. It seemed as though we had been forgotten by the world, belonged to nobody, would get nowhere; it seemed that, as if bewitched, we would have to live for ever and ever in that inner harbor, a derision and a byword to generations of longshore loafers and dishonest boatmen. I obtained three months' pay and a five days' leave, and made a rush for London. It took me a day to get there and pretty well another to come back—but three months' pay went all the same. I don't know what I did with it. I went to a music hall, I believe, lunched, dined, and supped in a swell place in Regent Street, and was back on time, with nothing but a complete set of Byron's works and a new railway rug to show for three months' work. The boatman who pulled me off to the ship said: 'Hallo! I thought you had left the old thing. *She* will never get to Bankok.' 'That's all *you* know about it,' I said scornfully—but I didn't like that prophecy at all.

"Suddenly a man, some kind of agent to somebody, appeared with full powers. He had grog blossoms all over his face, an indomitable energy, and was a jolly soul. We leaped into life again. A hulk came alongside, took our cargo, and then we went into dry dock to get our copper stripped. No wonder she leaked. The poor thing, strained beyond endurance by the gale, had, as if in disgust, spat out all the oakum of her lower seams. She was recalked, new coppered, and made as tight as a bottle. We went back to the hulk and reshipped our cargo.

"Then on a fine moonlight night, all the rats left the ship.

"We had been infested with them. They had destroyed our sails, consumed more stores than the crew, affably shared our beds and our dangers, and now, when the ship was made seaworthy, concluded to clear out. I called Mahon to enjoy the spectacle. Rat after rat appeared on our rail, took a last look over his shoulder, and leaped with a hollow thud into the empty hulk. We tried to count them, but soon lost the tale. Mahon said: 'Well, well! don't talk to me about the intelligence of rats. They ought to have left before, when we had that narrow squeak from foundering. There you have the proof how silly is the superstition about them. They leave a good ship for an old rotten hulk, where there is nothing to eat, too, the fools! . . . I don't believe they know what is safe or what is good for them, any more than you or I.'

"And after some more talk we agreed that the wisdom of rats had been grossly overrated, being in fact no greater than that of men.

"The story of the ship was known, by this, all up the Channel from Land's End to the Forelands, and we could get no crew on the south coast. They sent us one all complete from Liverpool, and we left once more—for Bankok.

"We had fair breezes, smooth water right into the tropics, and the old *Judea* lumbered along in the sunshine. When she went eight knots everything cracked aloft, and we tied our caps to our heads; but mostly she strolled on at the rate of three miles an hour. What could you expect? She was tired—that old ship. Her youth was where mine is— where yours is—you fellows who listen to this yarn; and what friend would throw your years and your weariness in your face? We didn't grumble at her. To us aft, at least, it seemed as though we had been born in her, reared in her, had lived in her for ages, had never known any other ship. I would just as soon have abused the old village church at home for not being a cathedral.

"And for me there was also my youth to make me patient. There was all the East before me, and all life, and the thought that I had been tried in that ship and had come out pretty well. And I thought of men of old who, centuries ago, went that road in ships that sailed no better, to the land of palms, and spices, and yellow sands, and of brown nations ruled by kings more cruel than Nero the Roman and more splendid than Solomon the Jew. The old bark lumbered on, heavy with her age and the burden of her cargo, while I lived the life of youth in ignorance and hope. She lumbered on through an interminable procession of days; and the fresh gilding flashed back at the setting sun, seemed to cry out over the darkening sea the words painted on her stern, '*Judea*, London. Do or Die.'

"Then we entered the Indian Ocean and steered northerly for Java Head. The winds were light. Weeks slipped by. She crawled on, do or die, and people at home began to think of posting us as overdue.

"One Saturday evening, I being off duty, the men asked me to give them an extra bucket of water or so—for washing clothes. As I did not wish to screw on the fresh-water pump so late, I went forward whistling, and with a key in my hand to unlock the forepeak scuttle, intending to serve the water out of a spare tank we kept there.

"The smell down below was as unexpected as it was frightful. One would have thought hundreds of paraffin lamps had been flaring and smoking in that hole for days. I was glad to get out. The man with me coughed and said, 'Funny smell, sir.' I answered negligently, 'It's good for the health, they say,' and walked aft.

"The first thing I did was to put my head down the square of the midship ventilator. As I lifted the lid a visible breath, something like a thin fog, a puff of faint haze, rose from the opening. The ascending air was hot, and had a heavy, sooty, paraffiny smell. I gave one sniff, and put down the lid gently. It was no use choking myself. The cargo was on fire.

"Next day she began to smoke in earnest. You see it was to be expected, for though the coal was of a safe kind, that cargo had been so handled, so broken up with handling, that it looked more like smithy coal than anything else. Then it had been wetted—more than once. It rained all the time we were taking it back from the hulk, and now with this long passage it got heated, and there was another case of spontaneous combustion.

"The captain called us into the cabin. He had a chart spread on the table, and looked unhappy. He said, 'The coast of West Australia is near, but I mean to proceed to our destination. It is the hurricane month too; but we will just keep her head for Bankok, and fight the fire. No more putting back anywhere, if we all get roasted. We will try first to stifle this 'ere damned combustion by want of air.'

"We tried. We battened down everything, and still she smoked. The smoke kept coming out through imperceptible crevices; it forced itself through bulkheads and covers; it oozed here and there and everywhere in slender threads, in an invisible film, in an incomprehensible manner. It made its way into the cabin, into the forecastle; it poisoned the sheltered places on the deck; it could be sniffed as high as the mainyard. It was clear that if the smoke came out the air came in. This was disheartening. This combustion refused to be stifled.

"We resolved to try water, and took the hatches off. Enormous volumes of smoke, whitish, yellowish, thick, greasy, misty, choking, ascended as high as the trucks. All hands cleared out aft. Then the poisonous cloud blew away, and we went back to work in a smoke that was no thicker now than that of an ordinary factory chimney.

"We rigged the force pump, got the hose along, and by-and-by it burst. Well, it was as old as the ship—a prehistoric hose, and past repair. Then we pumped with the feeble head-pump, drew water with buckets, and in this way managed in time to pour lots of Indian Ocean into the main hatch. The bright stream flashed in sunshine, fell into a layer of white crawling smoke, and vanished on the black surface of coal. Steam ascended mingling with the smoke. We poured salt water as into a barrel without a bottom. It was our fate to pump in that ship, to pump out of her, to pump into her; and after keeping water out of her to save ourselves from being drowned, we frantically poured water into her to save ourselves from being burnt.

"And she crawled on, do or die, in the serene weather. The sky was a miracle of purity, a miracle of azure. The sea was polished, was blue, was pellucid, was sparkling like a precious stone, extending on all sides, all round to the horizon—as if the whole terrestrial globe had been one jewel, one colossal sapphire, a single gem fashioned into a planet. And on the luster of the great calm waters the *Judea* glided imperceptibly, enveloped in languid and unclean vapors, in a lazy cloud that drifted to leeward, light and slow: a pestiferous cloud defiling the splendor of sea and sky.

"All this time of course we saw no fire. The cargo smoldered at the bottom somewhere. Once Mahon, as we were working side by side, said to me with a queer smile: 'Now, if she only would spring a tidy leak— like that time when we first left the Channel—it would put a stopper on this fire. Wouldn't it?' I remarked irrelevantly, 'Do you remember the rats?'

"We fought the fire and sailed the ship too as carefully as though nothing had been the matter. The steward cooked and attended on us. Of the other twelve men, eight worked while four rested. Everyone took his turn, captain included. There was equality, and if not exactly fraternity, then a deal of good feeling. Sometimes a man, as he dashed a bucketful of water down the hatchway, would yell out, 'Hurrah for Bankok!' and the rest laughed. But generally we were taciturn and serious—and thirsty. Oh! how thirsty! And we had to be careful with the water. Strict allowance. The ship smoked, the sun blazed. . . . Pass the bottle

"We tried everything. We even made an attempt to dig down to the fire. No good, of course. No man could remain more than a minute below. Mahon, who went first, fainted there, and the man who went to fetch him out did likewise. We lugged them out on deck. Then I leaped down to show how easily it could be done. They had learned wisdom by that time, and contented themselves by fishing for me with a chain-hook tied to a broom handle, I believe. I did not offer to go and fetch up my shovel, which was left down below.

"Things began to look bad. We put the longboat into the water. The second boat was ready to swing out. We had also another, a fourteen-foot thing, on davits aft, where it was quite safe.

"Then behold, the smoke suddenly decreased. We redoubled our efforts to flood the bottom of the ship. In two days there was no smoke at all. Everybody was on the broad grin. This was on a Friday. On Saturday no work, but sailing the ship of course was done. The men washed their clothes and their faces for the first time in a fortnight, and had a special dinner given them. They spoke of spontaneous combustion with contempt, and implied *they* were the boys to put out combustions. Somehow we all felt as though we each had inherited a large fortune. But a beastly smell of burning hung about the ship. Captain Beard had hollow eyes and sunken cheeks. I had never noticed so much before how twisted and bowed he was. He and Mahon prowled soberly about hatches and ventilators, sniffing. It struck me suddenly poor Mahon was a very, very old chap. As to me, I was as pleased and proud as though I had helped to win a great naval battle. O Youth!

"The night was fine. In the morning a homeward-bound ship passed us hull down—the first we had seen for months; but we were nearing the land at last, Java Head being about 190 miles off, and nearly due north.

"Next day it was my watch on deck from eight to twelve. At breakfast the captain observed, 'It's wonderful how that smell hangs about the cabin.' About ten, the mate being on the poop, I stepped down on the main deck for a moment. The carpenter's bench stood abaft the mainmast: I leaned against it sucking at my pipe, and the carpenter, a young chap, came to talk to me. He remarked, 'I think we have done very well, haven't we?' and then I perceived with annoyance the fool was trying to tilt the bench. I said curtly, 'Don't, Chips,' and immediately became aware of a queer sensation, of an absurd delusion—I seemed somehow to be in the air. I heard all round me like a pent-up breath released—as if a thousand giants simultaneously had said Phoo!—and felt a dull concussion which made my ribs ache suddenly. No doubt about it—I was in the air, and my body was describing a short parabola. But short as it was, I had the time to think several thoughts in, as far as I can remember, the following order: 'This can't be the carpenter—What is it?—Some accident—Submarine volcano?—Coals, gas!—By Jove! we are being blown up—Everybody's dead—I am falling into the afterhatch—I see fire in it.'

"The coal dust suspended in the air of the hold had glowed dull red at the moment of the explosion. In the twinkling of an eye, in an infinitesimal fraction of a second since the first tilt of the bench, I was sprawling full length on the cargo. I picked myself up and scrambled out. It was quick like a rebound. The deck was a wilderness of smashed timber, lying crosswise like trees in a wood after a hurricane; an immense curtain of soiled rags waved gently before me—it was the mainsail blown to strips. I thought, The masts will be toppling over directly; and to get out of the way bolted on all fours toward the poop-ladder. The first person I saw was Mahon, with eyes like saucers, his mouth open, and the long white hair standing straight on end round his head like a silver halo. He was just about to go down when the sight of the main deck stirring, heaving up, and changing into splinters before his eyes, petrified him on the top step. I stared at him in unbelief, and he stared at me with a queer kind of shocked curiosity. I did not know that I had no hair, no eyebrows, no eyelashes, that my young mustache was burnt off, that my face was black, one cheek laid open, my nose cut, and my chin bleeding. I had lost my cap, one of my slippers, and my shirt was torn to rags. Of all this I was not aware. I was amazed to see the ship still afloat, the poop-deck whole—and, most of all, to see anybody alive. Also the peace of the sky and the serenity of the sea were distinctly surprising. I suppose I expected to see them convulsed with horror. . . . Pass the bottle.

"There was a voice hailing the ship from somewhere—in the air, in the sky—I couldn't tell. Presently I saw the captain—and he was mad. He asked me eagerly, 'Where's the cabin-table?' and to hear such a question was a frightful shock. I had just been blown up, you understand, and vibrated with that experience—I wasn't quite sure whether I was alive. Mahon began to stamp with both feet and yelled at him, 'Good God! don't you see the deck's blown out of her?' I found my voice, and stammered out as if conscious of some gross neglect of duty, 'I don't know where the cabin-table is.' It was like an absurd dream.

"Do you know what he wanted next? Well, he wanted to trim the yards. Very placidly, and as if lost in thought, he insisted on having the foreyard squared. 'I don't know if there's anybody alive,' said Mahon, almost tearfully. 'Surely,' he said, gently, 'there will be enough left to square the foreyard.'

"The old chap, it seems, was in his own berth, winding up the chronometers, when the shock sent him spinning. Immediately it occurred to him—as he said afterwards—that the ship had struck something, and he ran out into the cabin. There, he saw, the cabin-table had vanished somewhere. The deck being blown up, it had fallen down into the lazarette of course. Where we had our breakfast that morning he saw only a great hole in the floor. This appeared to him so awfully mysterious, and impressed him so immensely, that what he saw and heard after he got on deck were mere trifles in comparison. And, mark, he noticed directly the wheel deserted and his bark off her course—and his only thought was to get that miserable, stripped, undecked, smoldering shell of a ship back again with her head pointing at her port of destination. Bankok! That's what he was after. I tell you this quiet, bowed, bandy-legged, almost deformed little man was immense in the singleness of his idea and in his placid ignorance of our agitation. He motioned us forward with a commanding gesture, and went to take the wheel himself.

"Yes; that was the first thing we did—trim the yards of that wreck! No one was killed, or even disabled, but everyone was more or less hurt. You should have seen them! Some were in rags, with black faces, like coal-heavers, like sweeps, and had bullet heads that seemed closely cropped, but were in fact singed to the skin. Others, of the watch below, awakened by being shot out from their collapsing bunks, shivered incessantly, and kept on groaning even as we went about our work. But they all worked. That crew of Liverpool hard cases had in them the right stuff. It's my experience they always have. It is the sea that gives it—the vastness, the loneliness surrounding their dark stolid souls. Ah! well! we stumbled, we crept, we fell, we barked our shins on the wreckage, we hauled. The masts stood, but we did not know how much they might be charred down below. It was nearly calm, but a long swell ran from the west and made her roll. They might go at any moment. We looked at them with apprehension. One could not foresee which way they would fall.

"Then we retreated aft and looked about us. The deck was a tangle of planks on edge, of planks on end, of splinters, of ruined woodwork. The masts rose from that chaos like big trees above a matted undergrowth. The interstices of that mass of wreckage were full of something whitish, sluggish, stirring—of something that was like a greasy fog. The smoke of the invisible fire was coming up again, was trailing, like a poisonous thick mist in some valley choked with dead wood. Already lazy wisps were beginning to curl upwards amongst the mass of splinters. Here and there a piece of timber, stuck upright, resembled a post. Half of a fife-rail had been shot through the foresail, and the sky made a patch of glorious blue in the ignobly soiled canvas. A portion of several boards holding together had fallen across the rail, and one end protruded overboard, like a gangway leading upon nothing, like a gangway leading over the deep sea, leading to death—as if inviting us to walk the plank at once and be done with our ridiculous troubles. And still the air, the sky—a ghost, something invisible was hailing the ship.

"Someone had the sense to look over, and there was the helmsman, who had impulsively jumped overboard, anxious to come back. He yelled and swam lustily like a merman, keeping up with the ship. We threw him a rope, and presently he stood amongst us streaming with water and very crestfallen. The captain had surrendered the wheel, and apart, elbow on rail and chin in hand, gazed at the sea wistfully. We asked ourselves, What next? I thought, Now, this is something like. This is great. I wonder what will happen. O youth!

"Suddenly Mahon sighted a steamer far astern. Captain Beard said, 'We may do something with her yet.' We hoisted two flags, which said in the international language of the sea, 'On fire. Want immediate assistance.' The steamer grew bigger rapidly, and by-and-by spoke with two flags on her foremast, 'I am coming to your assistance.'

"In half an hour she was abreast, to windward, within hail, and rolling slightly, with her engines stopped. We lost our composure, and yelled all together with excitement, 'We've been blown up.' A man in a white helmet, on the bridge, cried, 'Yes! All right! all right!' and he nodded his head, and smiled, and made soothing motions with his hand as though at a lot of frightened children. One of the boats dropped in the water, and walked towards us upon the sea with her long oars. Four Calashes pulled a swinging stroke. This was my first sight of Malay seamen. I've known them since, but what struck me then was their unconcern: they came alongside, and even the bowman standing up and holding to our main-chains with the boat-hook did not deign to lift his head for a glance. I thought people who had been blown up deserved more attention.

"A little man, dry like a chip and agile like a monkey, clambered up. It was the mate of the steamer. He gave one look, and cried, 'O boys— you had better quit.'

"We were silent. He talked apart with the captain for a time—seemed to argue with him. Then they went away together to the steamer.

"When our skipper came back we learned that the steamer was the *Sommerville*, Captain Nash, from West Australia to Singapore via Batavia with mails, and that the agreement was she should tow us to Anjer or Batavia, if possible, where we could extinguish the fire by scuttling, and then proceed on our voyage—to Bankok! The old man seemed excited. 'We will do it yet,' he said to Mahon, fiercely. He shook his fist at the sky. Nobody else said a word.

"At noon the steamer began to tow. She went ahead slim and high, and what was left of the *Judea* followed at the end of seventy fathom of tow-rope—followed her swiftly like a cloud of smoke with mastheads protruding above. We went aloft to furl the sails. We coughed on the yards, and were careful about the bunts. Do you see the lot of us there, putting a neat furl on the sails of that ship doomed to arrive nowhere? There was not a man who didn't think that at any moment the masts would topple over. From aloft we could not see the ship for smoke, and they worked carefully, passing the gaskets with even turns. 'Harbor furl—aloft there!' cried Mahon from below.

"You understand this? I don't think one of those chaps expected to get down in the usual way. When we did I heard them saying to each other, 'Well, I thought we would come down overboard, in a lump— sticks and all—blame me if I didn't.' 'That's what I was thinking to myself,' would answer wearily another battered and bandaged scare-crow. And, mind, these were men without the drilled-in habit of obedience. To an onlooker they would be a lot of profane scallywags without a redeeming point. What made them do it—what made them obey me when I, thinking consciously how fine it was, made them drop the bunt of the foresail twice to try and do it better? What? They had no professional reputation—no examples, no praise. It wasn't a sense of duty; they all knew well enough how to shirk, and laze, and dodge— when they had a mind to it—and mostly they had. Was it the two pounds ten a month that sent them there? They didn't think their pay half good enough. No; it was something in them, something inborn and subtle and everlasting. I don't say positively that the crew of a French or German merchantman wouldn't have done it, but I doubt whether it would have been done in the same way. There was a completeness in it, something solid like a principle, and masterful like an instinct—a disclosure of something secret—of that hidden something, that gift of good or evil that makes racial difference, that shapes the fate of nations.

"It was that night at ten that, for the first time since we had been fighting it, we saw the fire. The speed of the towing had fanned the smoldering destruction. A blue gleam appeared forward, shining below the wreck of the deck. It wavered in patches, it seemed to stir and creep like the light of a glowworm. I saw it first, and told Mahon. 'Then the game's up,' he said. 'We had better stop this towing, or she will burst out suddenly fore and aft before we can clear out.' We set up a yell; rang bells to attract their attention; they towed on. At last Mahon and I had to crawl forward and cut the rope with an ax. There was no time to cast off the lashings. Red tongues could be seen licking the wilderness of splinters under our feet as we made our way back to the poop.

"Of course they very soon found out in the steamer that the rope was gone. She gave a loud blast of her whistle, her lights were seen sweeping in a wide circle, she came up ranging close alongside, and stopped. We were all in a tight group on the poop looking at her. Every man had saved a little bundle or a bag. Suddenly a conical flame with a twisted top shot up forward and threw upon the black sea a circle of light, with the two vessels side by side and heaving gently in its center. Captain Beard had been sitting on the gratings still and mute for hours, but now he rose slowly and advanced in front of us, to the mizzen-shrouds. Captain Nash hailed: 'Come along! Look sharp. I have mail bags on board. I will take you and your boats to Singapore.'

"'Thank you! No!' said our skipper. 'We must see the last of the ship.'

"'I can't stand by any longer,' shouted the other. 'Mails—you know.'

"'Ay! ay! We are all right.'

"'Very well! I'll report you in Singapore. . . . Good-by!'

"He waved his hand. Our men dropped their bundles quietly. The steamer moved ahead, and passing out of the circle of light, vanished at once from our sight, dazzled by the fire which burned fiercely. And then I knew that I would see the East first as commander of a small boat. I thought it fine; and the fidelity to the old ship was fine. We should see the last of her. Oh the glamour of youth! Oh the fire of it, more dazzling than the flames of the burning ship, throwing a magic light on the wide earth, leaping audaciously to the sky, presently to be quenched by time, more cruel, more pitiless, more bitter than the sea—and like the flames of the burning ship surrounded by an impenetrable night.

"The old man warned us in his gentle and inflexible way that it was part of our duty to save for the underwriters as much as we could of the ship's gear. Accordingly we went to work aft, while she blazed forward to give us plenty of light. We lugged out a lot of rubbish. What didn't we save? An old barometer fixed with an absurd quantity of screws nearly cost me my life: a sudden rush of smoke came upon me, and I just got away in time. There were various stores, bolts of canvas, coils of rope; the poop looked like a marine bazaar, and the boats were lumbered to the gunwales. One would have thought the old man wanted to take as much as he could of his first command with him. He was very, very quiet, but off his balance evidently. Would you believe it? He wanted to take a length of old stream-cable and a kedge-anchor with him in the longboat. We said, 'Ay, ay, sir,' deferentially, and on the quiet let the thing slip overboard. The heavy medicine chest went that way, two bags of green coffee, tins of paint—fancy, paint!—a whole lot of things. Then I was ordered with two hands into the boats to make a stowage and get them ready against the time it would be proper for us to leave the ship.

"We put everything straight, stepped the longboat's mast for our skipper, who was to take charge of her, and I was not sorry to sit down for a moment. My face felt raw, every limb ached as if broken, I was aware of all my ribs, and would have sworn to a twist in the backbone. The boats, fast astern, lay in a deep shadow, and all around I could see the circle of the sea lighted by the fire. A gigantic flame arose forward straight and clear. It flared fierce, with noises like the whir of wings, with rumbles as of thunder. There were cracks, detonations, and from the cone of flame the sparks flew upwards, as man is born to trouble, to leaky ships, and to ships that burn.

"What bothered me was that the ship, lying broadside to the swell and to such wind as there was—a mere breath—the boats would not keep astern where they were safe, but persisted, in a pig-headed way boats have, in getting under the counter and then swinging alongside. They were knocking about dangerously and coming near the flame, while the ship rolled on them, and, of course, there was always the danger of the masts going over the side at any moment. I and my two boat-keepers kept them off as best we could with oars and boat-hooks; but to be constantly at it became exasperating, since there was no reason why we should not leave at once. We could not see those on board, nor could we imagine what caused the delay. The boat-keepers were swearing feebly, and I had not only my share of the work, but also had to keep at it two men who showed a constant inclination to lay themselves down and let things slide.

"At last I hailed 'On deck there,' and someone looked over. 'We're ready here,' I said. The head disappeared, and very soon popped up again. 'The captain says, All right, sir, and to keep the boats well clear of the ship.'

"Half an hour passed. Suddenly there was a frightful racket, rattle, clanking of chain, hiss of water, and millions of sparks flew up into the shivering column of smoke that stood leaning slightly above the ship. The catheads had burned away, and the two red-hot anchors had gone to the bottom, tearing out after them two hundred fathom of red-hot chain. The ship trembled, the mass of flame swayed as if ready to collapse, and the fore top-gallant-mast fell. It darted down like an arrow of fire, shot under, and instantly leaping up within an oar's-length of the boats, floated quietly, very black on the luminous sea. I hailed the deck again. After some time a man in an unexpectedly cheerful but also muffled tone, as though he had been trying to speak with his mouth shut, informed me, 'Coming directly, sir,' and vanished. For a long time I heard nothing but the whir and roar of the fire. There were also whistling sounds. The boats jumped, tugged at the painters, ran at each other playfully, knocked their sides together, or, do what we would, swung in a bunch against the ship's side. I couldn't stand it any longer, and swarming up a rope, clambered aboard over the stern.

"It was as bright as day. Coming up like this, the sheet of fire facing me was a terrifying sight, and the heat seemed hardly bearable at first. On a settee cushion dragged out of the cabin, Captain Beard, with his legs drawn up and one arm under his head, slept with the light playing on him. Do you know what the rest were busy about? They were sitting on deck right aft, round an open case, eating bread and cheese and drinking bottled stout.

"On the background of flames twisting in fierce tongues above their heads they seemed at home like salamanders, and looked like a band of desperate pirates. The fire sparkled in the whites of their eyes, gleamed on patches of white skin seen through the torn shirts. Each had the marks as of a battle about him—bandaged heads, tied-up arms, a strip of dirty rag round a knee—and each man had a bottle between his legs and a chunk of cheese in his hand. Mahon got up. With his handsome and disreputable head, his hooked profile, his long white beard, and with an uncorked bottle in his hand, he resembled one of those reckless sea-robbers of old making merry amidst violence and disaster. 'The last meal on board,' he explained solemnly. 'We had nothing to eat all day, and it was no use leaving all this.' He flourished the bottle and indicated the sleeping skipper. 'He said he couldn't swallow anything, so I got him to lie down,' he went on; and as I stared, 'I don't know whether you are aware, young fellow, the man had no sleep to speak of for days—and there will be dam' little sleep in the boats.' 'There will be no boats by-and-by if you fool about much longer,' I said, indignantly. I walked up to the skipper and shook him by the shoulder. At last he opened his eyes, but did not move. 'Time to leave her, sir,' I said, quietly.

"He got up painfully, looked at the flames, at the sea sparkling round the ship, and black, black as ink farther away; he looked at the stars shining dim through a thin veil of smoke in a sky black, black as Erebus.

"'Youngest first,' he said.

"And the ordinary seaman, wiping his mouth with the back of his hand, got up, clambered over the taffrail, and vanished. Others followed. One, on the point of going over, stopped short to drain his bottle, and with a great swing of his arm flung it at the fire. 'Take this!' he cried.

"The skipper lingered disconsolately, and we left him to commune alone for awhile with his first command. Then I went up again and brought him away at last. It was time. The ironwork on the poop was hot to the touch.

"Then the painter of the longboat was cut, and the three boats, tied together, drifted clear of the ship. It was just sixteen hours after the explosion when we abandoned her. Mahon had charge of the second boat, and I had the smallest—the 14-foot thing. The longboat would have taken the lot of us; but the skipper said we must save as much property as we could—for the underwriters—and so I got my first command. I had two men with me, a bag of biscuits, a few tins of meat, and a breaker of water. I was ordered to keep close to the longboat, that in case of bad weather we might be taken into her.

"And do you know what I thought? I thought I would part company as soon as I could. I wanted to have my first command all to myself. I wasn't going to sail in a squadron if there were a chance for independent cruising. I would make land by myself. I would beat the other boats. Youth! All youth! The silly, charming, beautiful youth.

"But we did not make a start at once. We must see the last of the ship. And so the boats drifted about that night, heaving and setting on the swell. The men dozed, waked, sighed, groaned. I looked at the burning ship.

"Between the darkness of earth and heaven she was burning fiercely upon a disc of purple sea shot by the blood-red play of gleams; upon a disc of water glittering and sinister. A high, clear flame, an immense and lonely flame, ascended from the ocean, and from its summit the black smoke poured continuously at the sky. She burned furiously, mournful and imposing like a funeral pile kindled in the night, surrounded by the sea, watched over by the stars. A magnificent death had come like a grace, like a gift, like a reward to that old ship at the end of her laborious days. The surrender of her weary ghost to the keeping of stars and sea was stirring like the sight of a glorious triumph. The masts fell just before daybreak, and for a moment there was a burst and turmoil of sparks that seemed to fill with flying fire the night patient and watchful, the vast night lying silent upon the sea. At daylight she was only a charred shell, floating still under a cloud of smoke and bearing a glowing mass of coal within.

"Then the oars were got out, and the boats forming in a line moved round her remains as if in procession—the longboat leading. As we pulled across her stern a slim dart of fire shot out viciously at us, and suddenly she went down, head first, in a great hiss of steam. The unconsumed stern was the last to sink; but the paint had gone, had cracked, had peeled off, and there were no letters, there was no word, no stubborn device that was like her soul, to flash at the rising sun her creed and her name.

"We made our way north. A breeze sprang up, and about noon all the boats came together for the last time. I had no mast or sail in mine, but I made a mast out of a spare oar and hoisted a boat-awning for a sail, with a boat-hook for a yard. She was certainly overmasted, but I had the satisfaction of knowing that with the wind aft I could beat the other two. I had to wait for them. Then we all had a look at the captain's chart, and, after a sociable meal of hard bread and water, got our last instructions. These were simple: steer north, and keep together as much as possible. 'Be careful with that jury rig, Marlow,' said the captain; and Mahon, as I sailed proudly past his boat, wrinkled his curved nose and hailed, 'You will sail that ship of yours under water if you don't look out, young fellow.' He was a malicious old man—and may the deep sea where he sleeps now rock him gently, rock him tenderly to the end of time!

"Before sunset a thick rain-squall passed over the two boats, which were far astern, and that was the last I saw of them for a time. Next day I sat steering my cockle-shell—my first command—with nothing but water and sky around me. I did sight in the afternoon the upper sails of a ship far away, but said nothing, and my men did not notice her. You see I was afraid she might be homeward bound, and I had no mind to turn back from the portals of the East. I was steering for Java—another blessed name—like Bankok, you know. I steered many days.

"I need not tell you what it is to be knocking about in an open boat. I remember nights and days of calm when we pulled, we pulled, and the boat seemed to stand still, as if bewitched within the circle of the sea horizon. I remember the heat, the deluge of rain-squalls that kept us bailing for dear life (but filled our water cask), and I remember sixteen hours on end with a mouth dry as a cinder and a steering-oar over the stern to keep my first command head on to a breaking sea. I did not know how good a man I was till then. I remember the drawn faces, the dejected figures of my two men, and I remember my youth and the feeling that will never come back any more—the feeling that I could last for ever, outlast the sea, the earth, and all men; the deceitful feeling that lures us on to joys, to perils, to love, to vain effort—to death; the triumphant conviction of strength, the heat of life in the handful of dust, the glow in the heart that with every year grows dim, grows cold, grows small, and expires—and expires, too soon, too soon—before life itself.

"And this is how I see the East. I have seen its secret places and have looked into its very soul; but now I see it always from a small boat, a high outline of mountains, blue and afar in the morning; like faint mist at noon; a jagged wall of purple at sunset. I have the feel of the oar in my hand, the vision of a scorching blue sea in my eyes. And I see a bay, a wide bay, smooth as glass and polished like ice, shimmering in the dark. A red light burns far off upon the gloom of the land, and the night is soft and warm. We drag at the oars with aching arms, and suddenly a puff of wind, a puff faint and tepid and laden with strange odors of blossoms, of aromatic wood, comes out of the still night—the first sigh of the East on my face. That I can never forget. It was impalpable and enslaving, like a charm, like a whispered promise of mysterious delight.

"We had been pulling this finishing spell for eleven hours. Two pulled, and he whose turn it was to rest sat at the tiller. We had made out the red light in that bay and steered for it, guessing it must mark some small coasting port. We passed two vessels, outlandish and high-sterned, sleeping at anchor, and, approaching the light, now very dim, ran the boat's nose against the end of a jutting wharf. We were blind with fatigue. My men dropped the oars and fell off the thwarts as if dead. I made fast to a pile. A current rippled softly. The scented obscurity of the shore was grouped into vast masses, a density of colossal clumps of vegetation, probably—mute and fantastic shapes. And at their foot the semicircle of a beach gleamed faintly, like an illusion. There was not a light, not a stir, not a sound. The mysterious East faced me, perfumed like a flower, silent like death, dark like a grave.

"And I sat weary beyond expression, exulting like a conqueror, sleepless and entranced as if before a profound, a fateful enigma.

"A splashing of oars, a measured dip reverberating on the level of water, intensified by the silence of the shore into loud claps, made me jump up. A boat, a European boat, was coming in. I invoked the name of the dead; I hailed: *Judea* ahoy! A thin shout answered.

"It was the captain. I had beaten the flagship by three hours, and I was glad to hear the old man's voice again, tremulous and tired. 'Is it you, Marlow?' 'Mind the end of that jetty, sir,' I cried.

"He approached cautiously, and brought up with the deep-sea

leadline which we had saved—for the underwriters. I eased my painter and fell alongside. He sat, a broken figure at the stern, wet with dew, his hands clasped in his lap. His men were asleep already. 'I had a terrible time of it,' he murmured. 'Mahon is behind—not very far.' We conversed in whispers, in low whispers, as if afraid to wake up the land. Guns, thunder, earthquakes would not have awakened the men just then.

"Looking around as we talked, I saw away at sea a bright light traveling in the night. 'There's a steamer passing the bay,' I said. She was not passing, she was entering, and she even came close and anchored. 'I wish,' said the old man, 'you would find out whether she is English. Perhaps they could give us a passage somewhere.' He seemed nervously anxious. So by dint of punching and kicking I started one of my men into a state of somnambulism, and giving him an oar, took another and pulled towards the lights of the steamer.

"There was a murmur of voices in her, metallic hollow clangs of the engine room, footsteps on the deck. Her ports shone, round like dilated eyes. Shapes moved about, and there was a shadowy man high up on the bridge. He heard my oars.

"And then, before I could open my lips, the East spoke to me, but it was in a Western voice. A torrent of words was poured into the enigmatical, the fateful silence; outlandish, angry words, mixed with words and even whole sentences of good English, less strange but even more surprising. The voice swore and cursed violently; it riddled the solemn peace of the bay by a volley of abuse. It began by calling me Pig, and from that went crescendo into unmentionable adjectives—in English. The man up there raged aloud in two languages, and with a sincerity in his fury that almost convinced me I had, in some way, sinned against the harmony of the universe. I could hardly see him, but began to think he would work himself into a fit.

"Suddenly he ceased, and I could hear him snorting and blowing like a porpoise. I said—

" 'What steamer is this, pray?'

" 'Eh? What's this? And who are you?'

" 'Castaway crew of an English bark burnt at sea. We came here tonight. I am the second mate. The captain is in the long-boat, and wishes to know if you would give us a passage somewhere.'

" 'Oh, my goodness! I say. . . . This is the *Celestial* from Singapore on her return trip. I'll arrange with your captain in the morning . . . and . . . I say . . . did you hear me just now?'

" 'I should think the whole bay heard you.'

" 'I thought you were a shore boat. Now, look here—this infernal lazy scoundrel of a caretaker has gone to sleep again—curse him. The light is out, and I nearly ran foul of the end of this damned jetty. This is the third time he plays me this trick. Now, I ask you, can anybody stand this kind of thing? It's enough to drive a man out of his mind. I'll report him. . . . I'll get the Assistant Resident to give him the sack, by . . . See—there's no light. It's out, isn't it? I take you to witness the light's out. There should be a light, you know. A red light on the—'

" 'There was a light,' I said, mildly.

" 'But it's out, man! What's the use of talking like this? You can see for yourself it's out—don't you? If you had to take a valuable steamer along this God-forsaken coast you would want a light too. I'll kick him from end to end of his miserable wharf. You'll see if I don't. I will—'

" 'So I may tell my captain you'll take us?' I broke in.

" 'Yes, I'll take you. Good night,' he said, brusquely.

"I pulled back, made fast again to the jetty, and then went to sleep at last. I had faced the silence of the East. I had heard some of its languages. But when I opened my eyes again the silence was as complete as though it had never been broken. I was lying in a flood of light, and the sky had never looked so far, so high, before. I opened my eyes and lay without moving.

"And then I saw the men of the East—they were looking at me. The whole length of the jetty was full of people. I saw brown, bronze, yellow faces, the black eyes, the glitter, the color of an Eastern crowd. And all these beings stared without a murmur, without a sigh, without a movement. They stared down at the boats, at the sleeping men who at night had come to them from the sea. Nothing moved. The fronds of palms stood still against the sky. Not a branch stirred along the shore, and the brown roofs of hidden houses peeped through the green foliage, through the big leaves that hung shining and still like leaves forged of heavy metal. This was the East of the ancient navigators, so old, so mysterious, resplendent and somber, living and unchanged, full of danger and promise. And these were the men. I sat up suddenly. A wave of movement passed through the crowd from end to end, passed along the heads, swayed the bodies, ran along the jetty like a ripple on the water, like a breath of wind on a field—and all was still again. I see it now—the wide sweep of the bay, the glittering sands, the wealth of green infinite and varied, the sea blue like the sea of a dream, the crowd of attentive faces, the blaze of vivid color—the water reflecting it all, the curve of the shore, the jetty, the high-sterned outlandish craft floating still, and the three boats with tired men from the West sleeping unconscious of the land and the people and of the violence of sunshine. They slept thrown across the thwarts, curled on bottomboards, in the careless attitudes of death. The head of the old skipper, leaning back in the stern of the longboat, had fallen on his breast, and he looked as though he would never wake. Farther out old Mahon's face was upturned to the sky, with the long white beard spread out on his breast, as though he had been shot where he sat at the tiller; and a man, all in a heap in the bow of the boat, slept with both arms embracing the stem-head and with his cheek laid on the gunwale. The East looked at them without a sound.

"I have known its fascinations since: I have seen the mysterious shores, the still water, the lands of brown nations, where a stealthy Nemesis lies in wait, pursues, overtakes so many of the conquering race, who are proud of their wisdom, of their knowledge, of their strength. But for me all the East is contained in that vision of my youth. It is all in that moment when I opened my young eyes on it. I came upon it from a tussle with the sea—and I was young—and I saw it looking at me. And this is all that is left of it! Only a moment; a moment of strength, of romance, of glamour—of youth! . . . A flick of sunshine upon a strange shore, the time to remember, the time for a sigh, and—good-by—Night—Good-by . . . !"

He drank.

"Ah! The good old time—the good old time. Youth and the sea. Glamour and the sea! The good, strong sea, the salt, bitter sea, that could whisper to you and roar at you and knock your breath out of you."

He drank again.

"By all that's wonderful, it is the sea, I believe, the sea itself—or is it youth alone? Who can tell? But you here—you all had something out of life: money, love—whatever one gets on shore—and, tell me, wasn't that the best time, that time when we were young at sea; young and had nothing, on the sea that gives nothing, except hard knocks—and sometimes a chance to feel your strength—that only—that you all regret?"

And we all nodded at him: the man of finance, the man of accounts, the man of law, we all nodded at him over the polished table that like a still sheet of brown water reflected our faces, lined, wrinkled; our faces marked by toil, by deceptions, by success, by love; our weary eyes looking still, looking always, looking anxiously for something out of life, that while it is expected is already gone—has passed unseen, in a sigh, in a flash—together with the youth, with the strength, with the romance of illusions.

This story may be used as additional reading material for the chapter Plot.

Thomas H. Raddall

WINTER'S TALE

The air in the classroom was warm and rather stuffy, because it had snowed a little the night before, and Stevens the janitor had stoked up his great furnace fiercely. Grade Nine, coming in rosy-cheeked from the snow outside, found it oppressive, but nobody dared to open a window. Old Mr. Burtle, who conducted the educational fortunes of Grade Nine, was Principal of the school and a martyr to asthma.

The rest of the big brick school was empty and silent. The lower grades were not required to answer roll-call until half-past nine. It was just one minute past nine by the clock on the classroom wall when James hung his school-bag on the back of his seat and flung an arithmetic manual on the desk. He also produced two pencils and sharpened them with his jack-knife, dropping the shavings on the floor and keeping a wary eye on Old Gander Burtle, who disapproved of that procedure. All about him was a bustle of preparation. Fifty boys and girls were busy with books, pencils, and erasers.

"Attention!" demanded Old Gander, with his asthmatic cough. Everybody sat up very straight. "We shall sing the morning hymn." The class arose with a clatter, shuffled a little, and then burst raucously into "Awake my soul and with the sun" as Old Gander raised his bony forefinger. James had a point of vantage when they stood up to sing; for his desk was near the windows and he could look down into the street, two storeys below. It was certainly too nice a morning to spend indoors. The sky was blue, without a speck of cloud anywhere, sun very bright on the snow, and wisps of smoke rising straight into the air from a forest of chimneys that stretched away southward. The snow was not deep enough for sleighing. There were a few wheel-tracks in the street, and the sidewalks were a mess of brown slush already, and when the several hundred kids of the lower grades had scampered in, there would be nothing but thin black puddles. Grade Nine intoned a long "Ahhh-men!" and sat down. It was five minutes past nine by the clock on the wall.

The act of sitting down in unison always produced a clatter, but this morning the effect was astounding. The hardwood floor began to move up and down very rapidly, like a gigantic piston of some sort; the walls

WINTER'S TALE   From *The Pied Piper of Dipper Creek and Other Tales* by Thomas H. Raddall, reprinted by permission of the Canadian Publishers, McClelland and Stewart Limited, Toronto.

swayed drunkenly to and fro, so that the blackboards came down and were followed by plaster, crumbling away from the walls in lumps and whole sheets. The great clock dropped from its fastening high on the wall, missed Old Gander's head by an inch, and spewed a tangle of springs and cogs over the heaving floor. The opaque glass in the door of the boys' coat-room sprang across the classroom, sailing over James' head, and went to pieces in a mighty splatter on the wall in front of him. The windows vanished, sashes and all. Not only the inner everyday windows, but the big storm-windows that were screwed on outside every Fall and taken off in the spring. The room, the big echoing school, the whole world, were filled with tremendous sound that came in waves, each visible in breakers of plaster dust.

Then the sound was gone, as suddenly as it had come, and in its place there was a strange and awful hush that was emphasized, somehow, by distant noises of falling plaster and tinkling glass. Grade Nine was on its feet, staring at Old Gander through a fog of plaster dust, and Old Gander stared back at them, with his scanty grey hair all on end, and his long seamed face the colour of snow when rain is turning it to slush. A waft of cold air came in from the street, where the windows should have been, and the fog cleared before it. A girl broke the silence, screaming shrilly. James perceived that her cheek was laid open from ear to mouth, with a great red river pouring down her chin, and that others were putting fingers to cut faces and heads, and staring strangely at the stains. Grade Nine was covered with plaster dust, and looked like a company of startled ghosts, and when James saw the thin red trickles running out of those white masks he knew he was dreaming, because things like that did not really happen. The girl with the red mask screamed again, and there was a chorus of screams, and then with one impulse the class turned and fled, as if it were Friday afternoon fire practice. James heard them clattering down the stairs into the street, with glass grinding and tinkling under their shoes. For a moment James was poised for similar flight, but in that moment he remembered the time he was frightened by a signboard groaning in the wind at night, and Dad's deep steady voice saying, "Never run from anything, son, till you've had a good look at it. Most times it's not worth running from."

Old Gander was standing beside his desk like a statue, staring at the lone survivor of his class. His watery blue eyes seemed awfully large. They looked like Mum's breakfast saucers. James moved jerkily towards him, licking plaster-dust from his lips. "What is it, Mister Burtle?" His own voice seemed queer and very far away, the way it sounded when you talked in your sleep and woke yourself up. Old Gander gazed at James in enormous surprise, as though he had never seen James before, as if James were speaking some foreign language not authorized by the School Board. Then he said in his old asthmatic voice, "James! Is that you, James?" and without waiting for a reply he added, as though it were the most ordinary thing in the world, "Some of the little boys have been playing with dynamite in the basement." James nodded slowly. Old Gander knew everything. The kids in the lower grades said he had eyes in the back of his head. He was a very wise old man.

They stood, silent, in the wrecked classroom for a space of minutes. Another gust of chill air stirred the thin hairs that stood out like a halo from the schoolmaster's head.

"You are a good boy, James," murmured Old Gander in a dazed voice. James squared his shoulders instinctively. After all, he was a sergeant in the school cadet corps. It was all right for the others to go if they wanted to. Old Gander passed a shaking hand back over his head, smoothing down the straggled hairs. Bits of plaster fell upon his dusty shoulders in a small shower, like a brittle sort of dandruff. "I think," he said vaguely, "we'd better see if there is any fire."

"Yes, sir," James said. It occurred to him that Mr. Burtle ought to look in the basement where the little boys had played with the dynamite. "I'll go through the upstairs classrooms, sir."

"Very good," murmured Old Gander, as if James were a superior officer. "I will search the lower floor and then the basement." And he added, "Don't stay up here very long, James." They separated.

James passed from room to room on the second floor. Each was like the one he had left, with blackboards tumbled off walls, heaps of plaster, doors hanging splintered in the jambs. Along the south side of the school the windows had disappeared into the street, but on the north side the shattered sashes were festooned over desks, and shards of glass in the tumbled plaster gave it the glitter of snow. The big assembly hall occupied most of the north side. Miraculously, the doors were still in place, but they refused to open. One was split badly in the panel, and James peeped through at a tangle of wood, piled against the doors on the inside. He thrust an arm through the hole and pushed some of the rubbish aside. The hall was a strange sight. The tall windows which occupied almost the entire north wall had come inwards, had swept across the hall, carrying chairs with them, and the shattered sashes had wedged against the south wall and the side doors in a complete barricade. There was no trace of fire.

James walked down the stairs, along the lower hall, and out through the main entrance into the snow. The stained glass that formerly cast a prism of colours from the transom over the great main door had gone outwards, and was littered over the snow in a jig-saw puzzle of many hues. Old Gander stood there in the snow amid the coloured fragments, staring up at the mute ruins of his school. James gave him a glance, no more. Something else had caught his eye. To the north-east, over the roofs of silent houses, a mighty mushroom was growing in the sky. The stalk of the mushroom was pure white, and it extended an enormous distance upward from invisible roots in the harbour; and at the top it was unfolding, spreading out rapidly in greasy curls, brown and black, that caught the December sun and gleamed with a strange effect of varnish. An evil mushroom that writhed slightly on its stalk, and spread its eddying top until it overshadowed the whole North End, strange and terrible and beautiful. James could not take his eyes from it.

Behind him a voice was speaking, a woman's voice that penetrated the mighty singing in his ears from a great distance. Miss M'Clintock, the Grade Seven teacher, arriving early for the day's work. She was a tall woman, masterful to the point of severity. There was a wild look on her face that astonished James; for he had spent a term under her much-libelled rule and had never seen her anything but calm and dignified. "... all along the street. I can't tell you what I've seen this morning. Are you listening to me, Mr. Burtle?" Old Gander removed his wide gaze from the ravaged building. "My first really modern school," he murmured in that quaint asthmatic falsetto. "Dear, dear. What will the School Board say?"

James was watching that poisonous fungus in the sky again, but something Miss M'Clintock was saying made him look towards the houses about the school. They were like the school, void of window-glass, and in some cases of doors as well. There was a great silence everywhere, a dead quiet in which nothing moved except Old Gander and Miss M'Clintock and James and the mysterious mushroom that grew in the sky. But now over the whole city there came a great sigh, an odd breathless sound that was like a gasp and like a moan, and yet was neither. James saluted Old Gander awkwardly. "I—I guess I'd better go home now, sir." If Mr. Burtle heard him, he gave no sign. Miss M'Clintock said, "What a blessing the lower grades don't go in till half-past nine. All those big windows. Your hand is bleeding, James." James nodded and left them, walking out through the school gate and into the street.

Now there was a flurry of movement and a chorus of wild human sounds about the shattered houses. An oil wagon stood at the kerb, with a pair of great Percheron horses lying inert under the broken shaft. The teamster squatted beside them in the slush with his hands on their heads, addressing blood-stained people who scurried past without attention. "Dead!" he said to James in a queer surprised voice. "An' not a mark on 'em. Would you think a man could stand a Thing that killed a horse?" James began to run.

Home was not far up the street. The old brown house stood two hundred yards from the school. (Dad had said, "It'll be handy for the kids going to school. When I get back we'll look for something better.") Just now it was silent, without doors or windows. Ragged wisps of curtain dangled in the gaping window-frames fluttering with every stir of the December breeze like signals of distress. James went up the front steps shouting, "Mum! Mum!" The house was cold and still. Like a tomb. James ran, frantic, through that ominous quiet. Margery's room was empty, the bed littered with broken glass. Mum's room. His own room. Broken glass, crumbled plaster, shattered doors. Slivers of glass thrust like arrows through the panels of Margery's door. Bare laths where the plaster should have been, like the naked ribs of a skeleton. In the lower hall the long stove-pipe from the big anthracite heater lay in crumpled lengths, with soot mingled in the littered plaster, and the painting of Fujiyama that Dad brought home from a trip to the East was half-buried in the rubble, broken and forlorn. Confusion reigned, too, in the living room; a window-sash, void of glass, was wedged against the piano, and the dusty mahogany was scored deep by invisible claws. In the wrecked kitchen he heard voices at last. Mum's voice, outside, in the garden. The rear door and the storm porch were lying, splintered, in the tiny scullery, amid a welter of broken chinaware and tumbled pots.

Mum's voice again, "James! Is that you, James?" James scrambled through the wreckage of the back door and ran into her arms, and they stood in the snow for several minutes, Mum and Margery and James, holding each other in silence. There was a bloody handkerchief about Mum's forehead, and little rivulets of blackish-red drying on her cheeks. Margery wore a coat over her nightdress.

Mum said, "I was looking out of the kitchen window, and suddenly across the way all the windows glowed red, as if they'd caught a gleam of sunset. Then our windows seemed to jump inwards." James said quickly, "Are you hurt, Mum?" but she shook her head. "Just cut a little about the forehead, I think, James. The window in Margery's room came right in on her bed, and she walked downstairs in her bare feet without a scratch. Over all that broken glass! It's a miracle, really."

"Why are you standing out here?" James demanded. It was cold, there in the snow without a coat. Mum waved her hand vaguely towards the street. "Somebody shouted, 'They're shelling the city—get behind your house!' So we came out here."

"I don't see how that could be," James considered gravely. "All the houses along the street are just like ours—doors and windows blown to pieces, and all the plaster down. The school, too. They couldn't do that. Not all at once, I mean."

There were sounds from next door. Old Mrs. Cameron appeared, embracing her husband in a strange hysterical way. He was breathing very heavily, for he was a fleshy man. Sweat made little clean streaks in the grime of his face. Mr. Cameron was something in the railway.

"Station roof came down!" he shouted across to them. "All that steel and glass! Crawled out somehow! Ran all the way!" They came slowly to the garden fence, arms about each other, and Mum walked to meet them flanked by Margery and James.

"You hurt, Mrs. Gordon?" Mum shook her bandaged head again. "Nothing serious. Mr. Cameron, what does it all mean?" Mr. Cameron took an arm from his wife's waist and wiped his streaming face with a sleeve. "There was a terrible explosion in the harbour, down by the Richmond wharves. A munitions boat, they say. A French boat with two thousand tons of T.N.T. on board. She came up the harbour flying the red flag—the powder flag—and ran into another ship in the Narrows. She caught fire and blew up. It was like an earthquake. The whole North End of the city is smashed flat. Houses like bundles of toothpicks. And the boat went to pieces about the size of a plum—that big ship! When I ran up North Street the sky was raining bits of iron. I don't think many got out of the station alive."

Mum shivered. "No use standing here," James said. They went into the house and tramped silently through the shattered rooms. A motor-truck went past, soldiers leaning from the cab, shouting something urgent and incoherent. The street emerged from its dream-like silence for a second time that morning. Feet were suddenly splattering in the slush along the sidewalks, voices calling, shouting, screaming. Another truck went by, one of the olive-green army ambulances, going slowly. Soldiers hung from the doors, from the rear step, shouting up at the yawning windows. "What are they saying?" Mum said.

James said, "Sounds like, 'Get out of your houses.'" Mr. Cameron appeared on the sidewalk outside, shouting in to them through cupped hands. ". . . out! Magazine's on fire. Big magazine at the Dockyard! On fire!"

"Put on your coats and overshoes first," Mum said, her mouth in a thin white line. "Where's your coat, James?"

"In school," he mumbled, embarrassed. It was hanging in the coat-room, covered with plaster dust, like all the others, and he had run away forgetting everything, like the other kids after all. "Put on your old one," Mum said. Margery went upstairs, and after a few minutes came down again, dressed in a woollen suit. They went down the street steps together, and beheld a strange and tragic procession approaching from the direction of the city. Men, women, and children in all sorts of attire, pouring along the sidewalks, choking the street itself. Some carried suit-cases and bundles. Others trundled hand-carts and perambulators laden with household treasures. Two out of three were bandaged and bloody, and all were daubed with soot and plaster. Their eyes glistened with an odd quality of fear and excitement, and they cried out to Mum as they stumbled past, "Get out! Out in the fields! There's another one coming! Dockyard's afire!"

Margery said, awed, "It's like pictures of the Belgian refugees." James looked at Mum's firm mouth and held his own chin high. They joined the exodus without words or cries. The human stream flowed westward. Every sidestreet was a tributary pouring its quota into the sad river. Open spaces began to appear between the houses, with little signboards offering "Lots for Sale." Then the open fields. The nearest fields were black with people already, standing in the snow with rapt white faces turned to the north-east, as in some exotic worship. The vanguard of the rabble halted uncertainly, like sheep confronted by a fence, and under the increasing pressure of those behind a great confusion arose. Their backs were to the stricken city. Before them lay the little valley of the Dutch Village Road, and beyond it the timbered ridges that cupped the city's water supply. Cries arose. "Here! Stop here!" And counter cries, "Too near! Move on!" At last someone shouted, "The woods! Take to the woods!" It was taken up, passed back from lip to lip. The stream moved on with a new pace, but Mum turned off the road into a field. They halted in a group of those strange expectant faces.

At the roadside was a pile of lumber. James went to the pile and pulled down some boards, made a small platform for Mum and Margery. Some of the people turned from their fearful gazing and said, "That's good. Better than standing in the snow." The lumber pile disappeared in a space of minutes. The great retreat poured past the field towards the Dutch Village Road for half an hour. Then it thinned, disintegrated into scattered groups, and was gone. The street was empty. The field was a human mass. Many of the women were in flimsy house-dresses, hatless and coatless. Two were clutching brooms in blue fingers. A blond girl, with rouge-spots flaming like red lamps in her white cheeks, said, "Standing room only," with a catch in her voice. Nobody laughed. Most of the men were old. North-eastward rose fountains of smoke, black, white, and brown, merging in a great pall over the North End. The weird mushroom of those first tremendous minutes had shrivelled and disappeared in the new cloud. People watched the biggest of the black fountains. "That's the Dockyard," they said.

Two hours went by; long hours, cold hours. Still the people faced that black pillar of doom, braced for a mighty upheaval that did not come. There were more smoke fountains now, gaining in volume, creeping to right and left. A tall old man joined the crowd breathlessly, cried in a cracked voice, "The fire engines are smashed. The city is doomed." A murmur arose over the field, a long bitter sigh, like the stir of wind among trees. Someone said, "Nineteen days to Christmas," and laughed harshly. Three hours, and no blast from the burning Dockyard. Only the smoke poured up into the December sky. Old Mrs. Cameron came to them. She had become separated from her husband in the crowd and was weeping. "Joey! Joey!" she moaned, very softly. James thought this very strange. Joe Cameron had been killed at the Somme last year, and her other son's name was George. He was in France, too, in another regiment. But Mrs. Cameron kept moaning "Joey! Joey!" and wiping her eyes. She had no coat.

James said, "Looks as if we might be here a long time. I'll go back to the house and get some blankets, and something to eat." Mum caught him to her swiftly. "No," she said, through her teeth. Surprisingly, old Mrs. Cameron said, "That's right, James. I'll go with you. Mrs. Gordon, you stay here with Margery." Margery was not well. James looked at Mum. "Anywhere outdoors we'll be just as safe as here. I won't be in the house very long." Mum stared at him queerly. "You sound like your father, James." They set off at a brisk pace, old Mrs. Cameron clutching his arm. The snow in the field had been packed to a hard crust under a thousand feet. Farther on, where the houses stood in silent rows, it was like a city of the dead. Blinds and curtains flapped lazily in gaping window-frames. Clothing, silverware, all sorts of odds and ends were littered over hallways and doorsteps, dropped in the sudden flight. There were bloody hand-prints on splintered doors, red splashes on floors and entries. The slush on the sidewalks was tinged a dirty pink in many places, where the hegira had passed.

Home at last. Smoke curled, a thin wisp, from the kitchen chimney. It was absurd, that faithful flicker in the stove, when all the doors and windows were gone and the winter breeze wandered at will through the empty rooms. They paused outside for a moment. Old Mrs. Cameron said, "We must rush in and snatch up what we want. Don't stay longer than it takes to count a hundred. Remember, James." She moved towards her doorstep, drawing a deep breath. James nodded dumbly. He clattered up the steps, making a noise that seemed tremendous in the stark silence, then along the lower hall and upstairs, where his steps were muffled in fallen plaster. All the way he counted aloud. Numbers had a sudden and enormous significance. Margery's bed was full of broken glass, cumbered with wreckage of the window-sash. He stripped a blanket from his own bed and passed into Mum's room. Mum's big eiderdown was there on the bed. Her room faced south, and the window-glass had all blown out into the street. A gust of chill air came through the empty frame, and the bedroom door slammed shockingly. The interior doors had been open at the time of the great blast, and had suffered little injury. The slam gave James a sudden feeling of suffocation and made his heart beat terribly. He went to the door quickly and twisted the handle. It came away in his hand, and the handle on the other side fell with a sharp thud, taking the shaft with it. "Hundred-'n-ten, hundred-'n-'leven." James dropped his burden and tried to force back the catch with bits of wood. They splintered and broke, without accomplishment. Outside, old Mrs. Cameron was calling, "James! James!" her voice very loud in the awful silence. Fear came to James in a rush. He fancied that sidelong earthquake again, and the big brown house tumbling into the street, a bundle of toothpicks, as Mr. Cameron had said about the houses up Richmond way. He went to the window, and debated throwing the blankets into the street and jumping after them. It looked a terrible distance down there. Mrs. Cameron caught sight of him staring down at her, and waved her arms awkwardly and shouted. She had a blanket under each arm, a loaf of bread in one hand and a pot of jam in the other. Inspiration came to James at last. Dad's rifle kit. In the bottom drawer in Mum's big chiffonier. He snatched out the drawer, brought forth a tiny screwdriver, prised back the catch with it. Freedom! He came down the stairs in four leaps, dragging blanket and eiderdown, and was out in the street, sucking in an enormous breath. Old Mrs. Cameron scolded. "I thought you were never coming, James. You should have counted."

"I couldn't get out," James said. The breeze felt very cold on his brow. He put up a hand and wiped big drops of perspiration. As they approached the field again James stopped suddenly. "I forgot to get something to eat." He was very close to tears. Old Mrs. Cameron pulled at his arm. "I have bread and jam," she said. Mum and Margery were standing on the little wooden raft in the snow. Mum clutched James against her, and held him there a long time. It was two o'clock in the afternoon.

At half-past three an olive-green truck appeared from the city, stopped in the road by the field. Soldiers came. "Any badly injured here?" There were none. All the people in the field had walked there unaided. Most of them were bandaged roughly, but nobody wanted to go to the hospital. The hospital was in the city, too near that ominous pillar of smoke. Somebody said so. A soldier said, "It's all right now. You'd better go back to your homes. You'll freeze here. The magazine's all right. Some sailors went in and turned the cocks and flooded it." The truck roared away towards the city again. People stood looking at each other, with many side-glances at the smoke over burning Richmond. The old white-haired man wandered among them, shaking his bony fists at the smoke, a fierce exultation in his long face. "Woe unto ye, Sodom and Gomorrah! Alas, alas for Babylon, that mighty city! she shall be a heap." Old Mrs. Cameron muttered, "God have mercy." The girl with the rouge spots said, "You're getting your cities mixed, old man." A man cried, "Better to burn than freeze," and shouldering his bundle, walked off in the direction of the city, whistling "Tipperary." A few bold ones followed him. Then people began to move out of the field into the road in groups, walking slowly, cautiously, towards the city. The old man went with them, crying out in his wild voice. Nobody paid any attention.

Mum, James, and Margery got home at half-past four in the afternoon. Mr. Cameron was standing outside his house, staring up at the sky. The sunshine had vanished. The sky had turned grey, like steel. "It's going to snow," he said.

Mum said, "We'll have to spend the night in the kitchen." James looked at the kitchen stove-pipe. It was all right. He put coal on the faithful fire, and got the coal shovel out of the cellar and began to scoop plaster and broken glass from the kitchen floor, throwing it out into the snow. He counted the shovelfuls. There were seventy-five. "There's an awful lot of plaster in a room," Margery observed. Mum took a broom and swept up the fine stuff that escaped James' big shovel. They looked at the yawning window-frames. "That old storm-window," James said suddenly. "It's still in the cellar." They carried it up to the kitchen, and Mum and Margery steadied it while James mounted a table and drove nails to hold it in place of the vanished west window. It was meant to go on outside, of course, but there was no ladder, and it was terribly heavy. "We must have something to cover the other window," Mum said. They stared at each other. The people in the field had said you could not get glass or tarpaper in the city for love or money. James said, "The lumber—back in the field." Mum thought for a moment. "That lumber's gone by now, James. Besides, you couldn't carry a board all that way." They gathered up the living-room carpet, tugging it from under the tumbled furniture and shaking it clean of plaster. They folded it double and nailed it over the north window-frame on the inside, and James stuffed the gaps between nails with dish-cloths and towels. There were two doors to the kitchen. The one opening into the lower hall had been open at the time of the explosion, and was unhurt. The other, opening into the shattered scullery, had been blown bodily off its lock and hinges. Mum and James pushed it back into place and wedged it there tightly with pieces of wood. "The snow will drift into the house everywhere," Mum said. "But we can't help that." James nodded soberly. "The water-pipes are going to freeze and burst." They debated nailing a carpet over the bathroom window. Finally Mum said, "The hall stove is out and the stove-pipe is down. The pipes will freeze whether we cover the windows or not. We must let the taps run and hope for the best. We can get help in the morning, I hope. To-night it's everyone for himself."

Through the makeshift storm-window they could see snow falling rapidly in the winter dusk. Mum made tea, and they ate bread and butter hungrily by the light of a candle. The stove created a halo of warmth about itself, but the rising wind began to whistle through the impromptu window coverings. Margery said, "Couldn't we go somewhere for the night?" Mum shook her head. "Everybody's in the same mess," James said. "Lots of the houses looked worse than ours." Mum looked at the fingers of fine snow that were growing along the kitchen floor under the windows. "We must keep the stove going, James." James carried chairs from the living-room, grouped them close about the stove, and stuffed a towel into the crack under the hall door. The candle on the kitchen table guttered blue in the cross draught from the windows. "Thirteen hours before we see daylight again," Mum whispered, as if to herself.

There was a knocking. James opened the hall door carefully, and saw the dim figure of a soldier framed in the front doorway, rapping knuckles against the splintered jamb. "Does James Gordon live here?" Mum stepped into the hall, shielding the candle with her hand. "Colonel James Gordon lives here. But he's—away, just now." The dim figure lifted a hand in a perfunctory salute. "I mean young James Gordon that goes to the big brick school down the street." James stepped forward, but Mum caught his shoulder firmly. "What do you want with James?" The soldier made as if to salute again, but took off his fur hat and ducked his head instead. He was a young man with a uniform far too big for him, and a long solemn face, rather sheep-like in the candle-light. "We—the sergeant, I mean—has been sent up to this here school for a—well, a special kinda job, ma'am. The awf'cer telephoned to the head schoolmaster's house. He lives 'way down in the city somewheres, but he said there was a boy named James Gordon lived handy the school an' would show us how to get in the basement, an' all like that."

James moved quickly, and Mum's hand slipped from his shoulder and fell to her side. "I won't be long, Mum." The soldier mumbled, "It's only a coupla hundred yards." Mum said, "Put on your coat and overshoes, James."

It was pitch dark, and the night was thick with snow. James led the way. The soldier plodded silently behind him. It was strange to be going to school at night, and the great silent building seemed very grim and awful with its long rows of black window-holes. A dark blur in the main doorway disintegrated, came towards them. Four men in fur hats and long flapping overcoats. Soldiers. "You find the kid, Mac?" James' soldier said, "Yeah. This is him. Where's the sergeant?" One man waved a vague arm at the dim bulk of the school. "Scoutin' around in

there somewheres, lightin' matches. Tryin' to find the basement door."
James said, "Which door do you want? You can get in the basement
from the street if you like."

"Ah," grunted the second soldier; "that's the ticket, son."

A tiny point of light appeared within the school, flickered down the
stairs. James wondered why the sergeant looked upstairs for a basement
door. A stout figure, muffled in a khaki greatcoat, was revealed behind
the feeble flame of the match. The sergeant came out into the snow
swearing into a turned-up collar. With the shapeless fur hat on his head
he looked strangely like a bear roused out of a winter den. "Here's the
kid, Sarge." The sergeant regarded him. "Hello, son." James pointed.
"The basement door is around there." He showed them. The door had
been blown off its hinges and wedged, a bundle of twisted wood, in the
frame. They pulled at the splintered wood stoutly, and the doorway was
clear. On the basement steps the sergeant lit another match. Their
voices echoed strangely in that murky cavern.

James knew them now for soldiers of the Composite Battalion, made
up of detachments from various home-guard units. They wore the
clumsy brown fur hats and hideous red rubber galoshes that were issued
to the home guard for winter wear. Some people called them 'The
Safety Firsts'; and it was common for cheeky boys to hurl snowballs
after their patrols from the shadow of alleyways, chanting—

"Com-Po-Zite!
They won't fight!"

Mum had cautioned James against such pleasantry. Somebody had to
stay at home, and these men were mostly physical unfits, rejected by the
overseas regiments.

"Big as all Hell," declared the sergeant, after a tour of the echoing
basement. "Hold a thousand, easy." The soldiers said, "Yeah." The
sergeant fumbled in the big pocket of his greatcoat and brought forth a
dark bottle. He took a long swig, wiped his moustache with a sweep of
mittened hand, and passed the bottle around. "Gonna be a cold job," he
rumbled. "All the windows gone, an' snow blowin' in everywheres.
Concrete floor, too." The sheep-faced soldier said, "What-say we tear
up some floorboards upstairs an' cover some of these cellar winders?"
The sergeant spat, with noise. "They gotta send up a workin' party
from the Engineers if they want that done. We got dirty work enough."
The soldiers nodded their hats again, and said "Yeah" and "Betcha
life."

Wind swirled through the gloomy basement in icy gusts. The men
leaned against the wall, huddled in their greatcoats, cigarettes glowing
in the darkness. James walked up the concrete steps to street level and
stood inside the doorway, staring into the snowy dark. He wondered

how long he was supposed to stay. A glow-worm appeared down the street, a feeble thing that swam slowly through the whirl of snow towards the school. James experienced a sudden twinge of fright. There was a great white shape behind it. Then a voice from the darkness above that ghostly shape: "Hulloa!" James cleared his throat. "Hulloa!" A man rode up to the doorway on a white horse. A lantern dangled from the horse's neck, like a luminous bell. The rider leaned over, and a face became visible in the pale glow. He was a detective of the city police, and James recognized his mount as one of the pair that used to pull the Black Maria in the days before the war. He was riding bare-back, feet hanging down, and the big policeman looked very odd, perched up there. "Anyone else around, son?" James jerked his head towards the black hole of the basement entrance. "Some soldiers. Down there, sir. Do you want them?" The policeman turned his horse awkwardly. "Just tell 'em the first wagon will be right along." He kicked the glistening side of his mount and disappeared as silently as he had come, lantern a-swing. James shouted the message down into the darkness. "Okay!" There was a lull in the wind, and the bottle gurgled in the sudden stillness.

Another glow-worm came, as silent as the first. But as it turned in towards the school James caught a faint rattle of wheels, and a hoarse voice bellowed, "Whoa hoa!" The soldiers came stumbling up the steps in the darkness, and James went with them towards the light. It was a wagon, one of the low drays that clattered along Water Street from morn to night. A man climbed stiffly from the seat. He was crusted with snow, even to his moustache and eyebrows. "Let's have the lantern, fella," demanded the sergeant. They walked to the back of the wagon, and the sheep-faced soldier held the lantern high while the sergeant whipped a long tarpaulin from the mysterious freight.

"Niggers!" rumbled the sergeant loudly. James, peering between the soldiers in astonishment, beheld six figures lying side by side on the dray: three men, two women, and a young girl. They were stiff and impassive, like the dummies you saw in shop windows. The women had dirty rags of cotton dress. One of the men wore a pair of trousers. The rest were naked. Ebony flesh gleamed in the lantern light. The snowflakes drifted lightly on the calm up-turned faces. Their eyes were closed, hands lay easily at their sides, as if they were content to sleep there, naked to the storm. "Looka!" called the sheep-faced soldier. "They bin hit, Sarge. But there's no blood!" The sergeant stooped over for a better look. Two of the dark faces were scored deeply, as if some vandal had gouged wax from the dummies with a chisel. "Concussion," announced the sergeant with immense assurance. "That's what. Drives the blood inwards. They was dead before they got hit. That boat went to pieces like shrapnel." He called it "sharpnel."

The teamster was complaining. ". . . get a move on, you guys. This snow gets much deeper I gotta go back to the barn an' shift to sleds. There's work to do." Two of the soldiers picked up a dummy by head and feet, carried it awkwardly down the basement steps, and dropped it. There was a dull 'flap' when it struck the concrete. They came up the steps quickly. "Froze?" asked Sarge. "Stiff as a board," they said. The wagon was cleared of its silent passengers and went away into the night. The sergeant struck matches while the men arranged the bodies in a neat row. "Once," a soldier said, "I worked in a meat packin' plant. In T'ronta, that was."

"Well," Sarge rumbled, "you're keeping your hand in."

Another lantern swam up the street. Another dray. More silent figures under the tarpaulin. White people this time. A man and four young women, nude, flesh gleaming like marble in the lantern light. There was blood, a lot of it, dried black like old paint. "Musta bin farther away," observed the sergeant. "Them niggers was from Africville, right by the place she went off." T'ronta said curiously. "Funny, them bein' stripped this way. Was their clo'es blowed off, would you say?" The teamster shook his head. "Nuh. These was all pulled outa the wreckage by the troops this afternoon. Clo'es caught an' tore off, I guess. Besides, lotsa people sleeps late winter mornin's. Prob'ly didn't have much on, anyway." More wagons. The intervals diminished. The sheep-faced soldier said, "The awf'cer's forgot us. We oughta bin relieved by now." "Quit beefin'," said Sarge. "All the troops is up Richmond way, pullin' stiffs outa the wreckage, huntin' for livin' ones. If it's okay for them it's okay for us." A teamster gave them a spare lantern which they stood on the basement floor, and in the fitful glow of that lonely thing the dummies lay in orderly rows, toes up, faces towards the dim ceiling. The shadows of the soldiers performed a grotesque dance on the walls as they went about their work. Sarge pulled something from his greatcoat pocket, and James gave it a sidewise glance, expecting to see the bottle. Sarge thrust it back into the pocket again, but James had seen the silver figure of a baseball pitcher, and knew it had been wrenched from the big cup his school had won last summer. He said nothing. Sarge said, "You still here, son? We don't need you no more. Better go home."

Mum greeted James anxiously in the candle-lit kitchen. "How pale you are, James! What did they want? You've been gone three hours." James looked at the stove. "Nothing. Nothing much, Mum. I guess they—just wanted to fix up the school a bit." They sat in the cushioned chairs, huddling over the stove. Margery had her feet in the oven. James went upstairs and brought down blankets, and they muffled themselves up in the chairs. Mum said, "Don't you want something to eat, James?

There's tea on the stove, and there's bread and butter." "Not hungry," James said in a low voice.

It was a long night. James had never known a night could be so long. Sometimes you would doze a little, and you would see the faces of the dead people on the drays as plain as anything. Then you would wake up with a start and find yourself sliding off the chair, and feeling terribly cold. Several times he took the hod and the candle down into the cellar and brought up more coal. When the candles burned down to the table he lit new ones and stuck them in the hot grease. After a while there was a pool of grease on the table, hard and wrinkled and dirty-white, like frozen slush in the street. Draughts came through the window-covers and under both doors, like invisible fingers of ice, and you had to keep your feet hooked in the rung of your chair, off the floor. The candles gave a thin blue light and made a continual fluttering sound, like the wings of a caged bird. Sometimes the house shook in the gusts, and twice James had to climb on the table and hammer more nails to keep the carpet in place. Snow drifted in between the carpet and the window-frame, and formed thin white dunes along the floor next the wall. The heat thrown off by the kitchen stove was lost between the bare laths of the walls and ceiling.

"There must be a lot of dead, poor souls," Mum said.

"Yes," James said.

"In the morning, James, you must go to the telegraph office and send a cable to your father. He'll be frantic."

"Yes," James said.

Mum had washed the blood from her face and tied a clean rag of bedsheet over the cuts on her forehead. James thought she looked very white and hollow, somehow. But when he looked in her eyes there was something warm and strong in them that made him feel better. When you looked in Mum's eyes you felt that everything was all right. Margery had drawn a blanket over her head, like a hood, and her head was bent, hidden in the shadow. Mum said, "Are you awake, Margery?"

"Yes," Margery said quickly.

"Are you all right?"

"Yes."

"It will be morning soon," Mum said.

But it was a long time. They sat, stiff and cramped, over the stove, and listened to the snow sweeping into the rooms upstairs, and the flap-flap of broken laths, and blinds blowing to rags in the empty window-frames; and the night seemed to go on for ever, as though the world had come to a dark end and the sun would never come back again. James thought of Sarge, and the sheep-faced man, and T'ronta, carrying frozen dummies into the school basement, and wondered if the awf'cer had remembered them. Daylight crept through the storm-window at last, a poor grey thing that gave a bleak look to everything in the kitchen. Stove, blankets—nothing could ward off the cold then. The grey light seemed to freeze everything it touched. Outside, the snow still swept fiercely against the carpet and the glass. James found potatoes in the cellar, and rescued bacon and eggs from the wreck of the pantry. Mum brushed the snow and bits of plaster from the bacon and put it in a frying-pan. It smelt good.

The telegraph office was full of people waving bits of scribbled paper. The ruins of plate-glass windows had been shovelled out into the street, and the frames boarded up. Outside, a newsboy was selling papers turned out by some miracle on battered presses in the night. They consisted of a single sheet, with "HALIFAX IN RUINS" in four-inch letters at the top. Within the telegraph office, lamps cast a yellow glow. There was a great buzz of voices and the busy clack-clack of instruments. James had to wait a long time in the line that shuffled past the counter. A broad cheerful face greeted him at last.

"What's yours, son?"

"I want to send a cable to Colonel James Gordon, in France."

The man leaned over the counter and took a better look at him. "Hello! Are you Jim Gordon's son? So you are. I'd know that chin anywhere. How old are you, son?"

"Four—going on fifteen," James said.

"Soon be old enough to fight, eh? What's your Dad's regiment?"

James paused. "That'll cost extra, won't it?" he suggested shrewdly. "Everybody in the army knows my father."

The man smiled. "Sure," he agreed reasonably. "But France is a big place, son. It's their misfortune, of course, but there's probably a lot of people in France don't know your Dad."

James said, "It's the Ninetieth."

"Ah, of course. Jim Gordon of the Ninetieth. There's an outfit will keep old Hindenburg awake nights, son, and don't you forget it. What d'you want to say?"

James placed both hands on the counter. "Just this: 'All's well. James Gordon.' That's all."

The man wrote it down, and looked up quickly. "All's well? That counts three words, son, at twenty-five cents a word. Why not just, 'All well'?"

James put his chin up. "No. 'All's well.' Send it like that."

INDEX OF PRINCIPAL TOPICS AND OF STORIES DISCUSSED